Strategic Management for Transport and Logistics

Richard Skiba

AFTER MIDNIGHT
PUBLISHING

Copyright © 2024 by Richard Skiba

All rights reserved.

No portion of this book may be reproduced in any form without written permission from the publisher or author, except as permitted by copyright law.

This publication is designed to provide accurate and authoritative information in regard to the subject matter covered. While the publisher and author have used their best efforts in preparing this book, they make no representations or warranties with respect to the accuracy or completeness of the contents of this book and specifically disclaim any implied warranties of merchantability or fitness for a particular purpose. No warranty may be created or extended by sales representatives or written sales materials. The advice and strategies contained herein may not be suitable for your situation. You should consult with a professional when appropriate. Neither the publisher nor the author shall be liable for any loss of profit or any other commercial damages, including but not limited to special, incidental, consequential, personal, or other damages.

Skiba, Richard (author)

Strategic Management for Transport and Logistics

ISBN 978-1-7636112-4-5 (paperback) 978-1-7636112-5-2 (eBook)

Non-fiction

Contents

1. Introduction — 1
2. Sectors within Transport and Logistics — 14
3. Jobs within the Transport and Logistics Industry — 39
4. Logistics Defined — 62
5. Maintaining Operational Procedures for Transport and Logistics Enterprises — 91
6. Monitoring the Safety of Transport Activities — 157
7. Managing International Freight Transfer — 211
8. Managing a Supply Chain — 282
9. Manage Facility and Inventory Requirements — 337
10. Implementing and Monitoring Transport Logistics — 369
11. Managing Export Logistics — 390
12. Establishing International Distribution Networks — 410
13. Developing, Implementing and Reviewing Purchasing Strategies — 442
14. Implementing and Monitoring Environmental Protection Policies and Procedures — 469
15. Managing Work Area Safety — 493
16. Managing People Performance — 512

References — 547

Index — 559

Chapter 1
Introduction

Transport and logistics encompass a complex array of processes crucial for the seamless flow of goods or services from their point of origin to their destination. This multifaceted system involves various stages such as production, storage, inventory management, delivery, and distribution. Often interchangeably referred to as transportation and logistics, it constitutes a vital component of the broader supply chain ecosystem. At its core, transport and logistics entail proactive measures aimed at safely and efficiently facilitating the movement of products from manufacturers to sellers and ultimately to end-users or consumers [1].

The overarching objective of managing transport and logistics, particularly for businesses and entities engaged in cargo consolidation, revolves around the meticulous oversight of supply flow. This entails ensuring that goods traverse from point A to point B seamlessly and in adherence to predefined schedules. Timeliness is of paramount importance, with a focus on delivering products to customers within stipulated timeframes. Moreover, the integrity of the goods must be preserved throughout the transportation process, minimizing the risk of damage or deterioration.

Effective transport and logistics management demand a strategic approach encompassing various elements. It necessitates meticulous planning to optimize routes and modes of transportation, taking into account factors such as distance, cost, and environmental considerations [1]. Leveraging advanced technologies such as GPS tracking systems and logistics software enables real-time monitoring of shipments, facilitating proactive decision-making and intervention when necessary. Additionally, maintaining robust inventory management practices ensures adequate stock levels to meet demand fluctuations while minimizing excess inventory and associated costs.

Collaboration and coordination among stakeholders play a pivotal role in the success of transport and logistics operations. Seamless communication and information sharing between manufacturers, carriers, distributors, and retailers are essential for streamlining processes and resolving any unforeseen challenges promptly [1]. Moreover, fostering strong partnerships with reliable transportation providers and logistics partners enhances operational efficiency and fosters a resilient supply chain ecosystem.

In essence, effective management of transport and logistics is indispensable for businesses seeking to optimize their supply chain operations and meet the evolving demands of the market. By prioritizing timely delivery, product integrity, and operational efficiency, organizations can gain a competitive edge and enhance customer satisfaction, thereby solidifying their position in the marketplace.

Transportation and logistics serve as vital components within the operations of companies across various industries, offering a multitude of benefits that extend beyond individual organizations to the broader supply chain network. The reasons for utilizing transportation and logistics are diverse, ranging from facilitating the movement of goods to ensuring timely delivery and optimizing resource utilization. By optimizing transportation and logistics processes, businesses stand to gain significant advantages, both in terms of operational efficiency and cost-effectiveness.

The logistics industry serves as a crucial facilitator of trade and entrepreneurial activities, connecting multiple parties involved in the exchange of goods through diverse supply chain networks. Whether it's business-to-business (B2B), business-to-consumer (B2C), or consumer-to-consumer (C2C) transactions, logistics companies play a pivotal role in transporting, storing, and delivering goods across various modes of transportation [2]. In today's rapidly evolving landscape, these companies are continuously adapting to the changing economic patterns and the increasing digitization of commerce to meet the demands of a global marketplace.

The significance of the logistics industry on a global scale is underscored by its substantial economic value. In 2021, the industry was valued at over 8.4 trillion euros, a figure projected to surpass 13.7 trillion euros by 2027 [2]. Correspondingly, global total logistics costs amounted to a staggering nine trillion U.S. dollars in 2020, accounting for approximately 10.7 percent of the world's Gross Domestic Product (GDP) of 85.24 trillion U.S. dollars that year. These figures highlight the critical role that logistics plays in driving economic activity and facilitating international trade [2].

Among the regions, the Asia-Pacific logistics market stands out as the largest in the world, with a market size estimated at around 3.9 trillion U.S. dollars in 2020 alone

[2]. This dominance can be attributed to several factors, including the expansion of trade routes, the emergence of Asia as a manufacturing hub, and the rapid growth of e-commerce in the region. Notably, the container trade flow within Asia surpassed that of any other trade lane in the world, reaching a volume of 41.5 million twenty-foot equivalent units (TEUs) in 2021 [2]. This illustrates the immense scale of trade activities within the Asia-Pacific region and underscores its pivotal role in shaping global logistics trends and dynamics.

The onset of the COVID-19 pandemic in 2020 had a profound and immediate impact on the global transportation and logistics industry, disrupting supply chains and causing a significant decline in international trade activity [2]. As countries imposed lockdowns and travel restrictions to contain the spread of the virus, demand for goods plummeted, leading to widespread disruptions across various sectors. The transportation sector, particularly air and maritime shipping, bore the brunt of these disruptions, with a sharp decline in passenger and cargo volumes observed throughout the year.

Despite the initial downturn, the transportation and logistics industry demonstrated resilience and adaptability in the face of adversity. With the gradual easing of restrictions and the rollout of vaccination campaigns, consumer demand rebounded in 2021, driving a swift recovery in trade activity. Worldwide air freight logistics traffic, for instance, surged to 65.6 million metric tons in 2021, with further growth projected to reach 68.4 million metric tons in 2022 [2]. Leading air freight carriers such as FedEx, UPS, and Qatar Airways played a pivotal role in facilitating the movement of goods and restoring supply chain connectivity on both international and domestic fronts.

In contrast, global maritime shipping faced significant challenges due to supply chain disruptions and port congestion exacerbated by the pandemic. Seaborne trade transport volumes declined sharply in 2020, reflecting the broader economic impact of the pandemic on global trade flows. However, the international maritime trade carried by container ships remained relatively stable compared to the pre-pandemic period, with 1.85 billion metric tons loaded in 2020 [2]. This resilience underscores the critical role of maritime shipping in sustaining global trade and ensuring the uninterrupted flow of essential goods and commodities.

Rail freight traffic, meanwhile, experienced a notable decrease in activity worldwide in 2020, reflecting the broader contraction in economic activity and trade volumes. However, certain regions, such as Africa, witnessed a more modest decline in freight activity, highlighting regional variations in the impact of the pandemic on transportation and logistics. Despite these challenges, the transportation and logistics industry demonstrated remarkable resilience and adaptability, leveraging technology and innovation to navigate the complexities of the pandemic and sustain operations in an uncertain environment. As the world gradually emerges from the grips of the pandemic, the industry remains poised for recovery and growth, albeit with continued vigilance and adaptation to evolving market dynamics and challenges [2].

The global freight forwarding sector, with a market size of 192.5 billion euros in 2021, plays a pivotal role in streamlining and expediting the transportation process within the logistics industry. Companies such as DHL, Kuehne + Nagel, DSV, and DB Schenker stand out as leaders in this market, providing comprehensive freight forwarding solutions to businesses worldwide [2]. These industry giants leverage their extensive networks and expertise to facilitate the movement of goods across borders and continents, offering customers quicker and more efficient transportation options to meet their logistical needs.

Among the top players in the global freight forwarding market, Kuehne + Nagel, Sinotrans, and DHL emerge as the world's top ocean freight forwarders by ocean freight volume, measured in twenty-foot equivalent units (TEUs) [2]. Their extensive fleets and logistical capabilities enable them to handle a vast array of cargo, from raw materials to finished products, with precision and efficiency. This underscores the critical role of ocean freight forwarding in facilitating global trade and supply chain connectivity, particularly in an era of increasing globalization and interconnectivity.

In the realm of e-commerce, logistics assumes heightened significance as it shoulders the responsibility of planning, controlling, and executing the movement of goods from suppliers to end-users. The exponential growth of the global e-commerce industry, fuelled by changing consumer preferences and technological advancements, has propelled the e-commerce logistics market to new heights, reaching 441 billion euros in 2021 [2]. The COVID-19 pandemic further accelerated this trend, as lockdowns and social distancing measures drove a surge in online shopping activity, creating unprecedented demand for e-commerce logistics services.

The pandemic-induced e-commerce boom has had a profound impact on the global freight industry, with shipping giants UPS Inc. and FedEx Corp. emerging as dominant players in the freight carrier market in 2021. With freight revenues exceeding 70 billion U.S. dollars each, these industry leaders capitalized on the surge in e-commerce sales, leveraging their robust logistics networks to meet the growing demand for fast and reliable shipping services. However, the outlook for the e-commerce logistics market in 2022 is clouded by a host of macroeconomic uncertainties, including geopolitical tensions, inflationary pressures, and supply chain shocks.

The ongoing Russia-Ukraine war, coupled with broader economic challenges, has raised concerns about a potential global recession, prompting a slowdown in the performance of major e-commerce companies and the associated logistics market. As businesses navigate these turbulent waters, agility, resilience, and strategic foresight will be essential for adapting to evolving market conditions and seizing opportunities for growth and innovation in the ever-evolving landscape of global logistics and freight forwarding.

One of the primary benefits of optimizing transportation and logistics is the increase in operational efficiency. By actively monitoring the movement of products throughout the supply chain, businesses can identify inefficiencies, errors, and discrepancies in real-time. This proactive approach enables prompt intervention and resolution of issues, thereby streamlining processes and improving overall operational efficiency. By addressing bottlenecks and optimizing workflows, companies can enhance productivity and reduce the time required to fulfill customer orders [1].

Furthermore, effective management of transportation and logistics contributes to cost reduction initiatives within the supply chain. Greater visibility into transportation routes, inventory levels, and distribution channels allows businesses to identify cost-saving opportunities and eliminate wasteful expenditure. By avoiding unnecessary purchases, minimizing downtime, and optimizing resource allocation, companies can achieve significant cost savings over time. Additionally, by implementing recognized areas for improvement and leveraging data-driven insights, organizations can make informed decisions to manage costs more effectively and enhance profitability.

An optimized transportation and logistics process also has a positive impact on production output and business performance. By streamlining operations, reducing downtime, and minimizing delays in transportation, companies can improve production turnaround times and meet customer demand more efficiently. This, in turn, enhances customer satisfaction and strengthens the competitive position of the organization in the market. Moreover, by ensuring timely delivery of raw materials and finished products, businesses can minimize inventory holding costs and optimize inventory management practices.

Enhanced inventory management is another key benefit of optimizing transportation and logistics. By increasing supply chain visibility and implementing robust inventory tracking systems, businesses can prevent stockouts, reduce excess inventory, and minimize the risk of product damages [1]. This enables companies to maintain optimal inventory levels, improve order fulfillment rates, and enhance customer service levels. Additionally, by synchronizing inventory levels with demand forecasts and production schedules, organizations can optimize working capital utilization and reduce carrying costs associated with excess inventory.

Moreover, an organized transportation and logistics system plays a crucial role in preventing disruptions within the supply chain. By identifying potential bottlenecks, inefficiencies, and risks in advance, businesses can implement contingency plans and mitigation strategies to mitigate the impact of disruptions. This proactive approach helps minimize downtime, avoid stockouts, and ensure continuity of operations, even in the face of unforeseen events or disruptions. By fostering resilience and agility within the supply chain, companies can enhance their ability to adapt to changing market conditions and maintain a competitive edge in the long run [1].

Transportation and logistics are integral components of supply chain management, encompassing a spectrum of activities aimed at ensuring the smooth movement of goods and services from production to consumption. While the terms "transportation" and "logistics" are often used interchangeably, they represent distinct aspects of the broader supply chain process [1].

Transportation primarily focuses on the physical movement of products from one location to another. It involves the actual execution of delivery processes, including considerations such as packaging, route planning, and mode of transport selection. Within transportation operations, several key functions are crucial for effective logistics management. These include operations management, which involves organizing and optimizing processes related to manufacturing and service delivery; vehicle and fleet management, which entails coordinating delivery vehicles to maximize efficiency and resource utilization; and infrastructure administration, which involves securing and maintaining transportation infrastructure such as roads, ports, airports, railways, and pipelines [1].

In contrast, logistics encompasses a broader scope of activities beyond transportation, encompassing the entire supply chain process from sourcing raw materials to delivering finished products to consumers. While transportation is a critical component of logistics, it is just one aspect of a larger system designed to ensure the timely and efficient flow of goods and services. Within the realm of logistics, various processes contribute to the seamless functioning of the supply chain. These include material sourcing, warehouse receiving, product storage, inventory management, order fulfillment, packaging, shipping, delivery, and distribution [1].

The distinction between transportation and logistics lies in their respective focuses and scopes. Transportation primarily deals with the physical movement of goods, emphasizing aspects such as route optimization and vehicle management. On the other hand, logistics encompasses a broader range of activities aimed at managing the entire supply chain process, from procurement to distribution, with a focus on optimizing efficiency, timeliness, and customer satisfaction.

The transport and logistics sector, like many others, faces a myriad of challenges that can significantly impact its operations and effectiveness. The outbreak of the Covid-19 pandemic proved to be a formidable obstacle for companies across the globe, regardless of their size. According to a report from the International Finance Corporation (IFC), both small-to-medium and large logistics companies encountered setbacks as a result of disruptions caused by the pandemic [1]. Lockdowns, travel restrictions, and supply chain disruptions created logistical hurdles that forced companies to adapt rapidly to changing circumstances.

Among the challenges faced by the transport and logistics industry, rising fuel prices loom large as a persistent concern. The escalation of fuel prices can stem from various factors, with geopolitical tensions and conflicts among major oil-producing nations being significant contributors. These price fluctuations have immediate and far-reaching implications for the transportation sector, impacting operating costs and profit margins. The industry must navigate this volatile landscape, adjusting pricing models and optimizing fuel efficiency to mitigate the financial strain.

Another pressing issue confronting the industry is the shortage of qualified truck drivers. In the United States, the American Trucking Association reported a historic increase of 80,000 truck driver shortages in 2021 [1]. Factors such as the demanding nature of the profession, the aging workforce, and the toll of stress and loneliness on drivers contribute to this shortfall. To address this challenge, policymakers have introduced initiatives such as the "Strengthening Supply Chains Through Truck Driver Incentives Act," which aims to attract and retain new drivers through targeted incentives and support measures.

Meeting evolving customer expectations poses yet another challenge for the transport and logistics sector. With the rise of e-commerce and on-demand services, consumers expect fast, reliable, and transparent delivery experiences. Retail giants have set high standards for customer satisfaction, prompting logistics companies to innovate and streamline their operations to meet these demands. Failure to adapt to changing consumer preferences can lead to diminished competitiveness and loss of market share in an increasingly competitive landscape.

Sustainability concerns have also emerged as a significant challenge for the transport and logistics industry. With a growing emphasis on environmental stewardship and corporate social responsibility, consumers are increasingly favouring companies that prioritize sustainability practices. Reducing greenhouse gas emissions, minimizing carbon footprints, and embracing alternative fuels are key objectives for businesses seeking to align with sustainability goals. While these initiatives may entail initial financial investments, they offer long-term benefits in terms of operational efficiency, brand reputation, and market differentiation.

The transport and logistics sector play a crucial role in the global economy, serving as the backbone of various industries and facilitating the movement of goods and services [3]. However, this sector is also a significant contributor to carbon dioxide emissions, with road-based transport logistics alone responsible for 38% of total emissions in the European Union's transport sector in 2019 [3]. Despite its essential function, the transport and logistics industry faces sustainability challenges, with issues related to corporate social responsibility and sustainability reporting lagging behind in implementation [4]. The sector is urged to adopt more environmentally friendly practices to mitigate its impact on the environment [4].

Efficiency is a key concern in the transport and logistics sector, with a focus on optimizing delivery routes, enhancing transport systems, and streamlining the warehouse-transport process [5]. Innovations, especially during challenging times like the COVID-19 pandemic, have been instrumental in driving progress within the industry [6]. The pandemic has also highlighted the importance of automation, technology integration, and the need for a sustainable and flexible transportation system in the logistics and transportation sector [7]. These advancements have aimed to improve operational efficiency and meet evolving consumer demands [6].

Carbon management is another critical aspect that has garnered attention within the logistics and transportation sector, given its significant contribution to global carbon emissions [8]. Despite logistics accounting for 5.5% of global carbon emissions, there has been a lack of specific focus on carbon management within the industry [8]. Addressing carbon emissions and implementing sustainable practices are essential for the sector to align with global environmental goals and reduce its carbon footprint [8].

The impact of the COVID-19 pandemic on the transportation and logistics industry has been substantial, leading to disruptions in supply chains, changes in consumer behaviour, and the need for strategic adaptations [7]. Strategies such as the introduction of new technologies, collaboration within the industry, and a focus on resilience have been highlighted as crucial for the sector's recovery and future growth [7]. The pandemic has underscored the importance of preparedness and adaptability in ensuring the continuity of operations within the transport and logistics sector [7].

Logistics infrastructure plays a pivotal role in supporting economic growth and international trade, with well-developed infrastructure contributing to the efficient movement of goods and services [9]. The relationship between logistics infrastructure development and real sector productivity is crucial, as it influences the ease of goods transmission mechanisms and overall sector-wise growth [9]. Enhancing logistics infrastructure can lead to improved efficiency, reduced costs, and increased competitiveness within the transport and logistics sector [9].

Incorporating sustainability practices, such as green logistics strategies, is essential for the long-term viability of the transport and logistics sector [10]. Establishing green transport corridors and promoting intermodality can help reduce the environmental impact of transportation activities and enhance overall sustainability [10]. Embracing green logistics not only benefits the environment but also aligns with changing consumer preferences for eco-friendly and socially responsible practices [10].

The transport and logistics sector's response to emerging technologies, such as Intelligent Transportation Systems (ITS) and digital twins, has been instrumental in enhancing operational efficiency and improving decision-making processes [11]. ITS applications in traffic management, public transport, safety management, and logistics have enabled the sector to leverage data-driven insights for better resource utilization and enhanced service delivery [12]. Embracing digital innovations is crucial for staying competitive and meeting the evolving demands of the modern logistics landscape [11].

Logistics, projected to be the fastest-growing industry between 2023–2030 according to Precedence Research, is witnessing a substantial surge in growth, largely propelled by the exponential rise of e-commerce [13]. With customers' evolving expectations driving shifts in logistics practices, the industry is undergoing a significant transformation. In the UK alone, the logistics industry employs approximately 1.25 million people and is anticipated to become the country's fastest-growing sector, as indicated by the Office for National Statistics (ONS) [13]. Similarly, in the US and Europe, the freight and logistics markets are expected to witness remarkable growth, with projections reaching 1.62 trillion US dollars and 1.26 trillion euros, respectively [13]. This growth is particularly evident in the sea and inland waterway segments, driven by infrastructure investments from key European countries such as Germany, France, and Italy.

The importance of logistics transformation lies in its ability to manage increasingly complex networks and streamline data and document management processes to enhance efficiency and productivity. As businesses scale up, the need for seamless data management and talent management becomes paramount. Enterprise Content Management (ECM) systems play a crucial role in this regard, providing a centralized platform for accessing real-time information across global operations. DHL exemplifies the significance of ECM platforms, utilizing modern technologies to manage a diverse range of documents across various operational domains. By leveraging ECM systems, organizations can enhance scalability, data management, and talent retention, thereby driving innovation and competitiveness in the logistics landscape [13].

Despite the growing emphasis on digital transformation, a significant portion of shipping and logistics firms have yet to formulate digital strategies. According to S&P Global, 34% of firms do not have a digital transformation strategy in place, although they are considering one [13]. This highlights the urgent need for industry-wide adoption of digital-enabling technologies to overcome barriers such as skill shortages and enhance operational efficiency. Cloud computing emerges as a pivotal technology for driving digital transformation in the logistics sector, offering unparalleled scalability, accessibility, and security. By migrating to cloud-based ECM platforms, organizations can streamline collaboration, facilitate real-time decision-making, and ensure compliance with evolving regulatory standards.

Supply chain optimization is another critical focus area for logistics organizations, with Gartner reporting that 38% of enterprises are prioritizing the optimization of end-to-end processes. In an era characterized by growing complexity and volatility, fine-tuning operations across warehouses, inventory management, and delivery processes is essential for enhancing business performance and resilience. Automation and intelligent content management solutions play a central role in this endeavour, enabling organizations to automate workflows, streamline document management, and drive cost savings. For instance, global leader SEW-EURODRIVE achieved significant cost and time savings by harnessing the power of an Intelligent Content Automation platform, underscoring the transformative potential of advanced technologies in logistics optimization [13].

Looking ahead, artificial intelligence (AI) is poised to revolutionize the logistics industry, with 50% of supply chain organizations expected to invest in AI-powered applications and advanced analytics through 2024, according to Gartner [13]. As the COVID-19 pandemic underscores the need for agile decision-making and operational resilience, AI-powered solutions offer unprecedented capabilities for extracting actionable insights from vast amounts of data. By harnessing AI for process automation, predictive analytics, and intelligent decision-making, logistics organizations can drive innovation, enhance efficiency, and stay ahead of the curve in an increasingly competitive market landscape.

Real-time supply chain visibility emerges as a strategic imperative for logistics organizations, with 70% of companies prioritizing it as one of their top three strategic goals, according to Geodis [13]. Despite the growing demand for visibility, only a fraction of companies have achieved full supply chain visibility, highlighting the need for improved communication and collaboration among supply chain partners. ECM systems play a crucial role in enhancing visibility by serving as centralized repositories for critical documents and data, enabling stakeholders to access up-to-date information and respond quickly to changing market dynamics.

In light of these trends, warehouse automation is poised to emerge as a key priority for logistics organizations, with more than 80% of warehouses currently lacking automation. However, as businesses recognize the imperative of automating and optimizing processes to meet customer demands and scale operations, investments in warehouse automation are expected to increase significantly in the coming years. By embracing automation and optimization technologies, organizations can enhance operational efficiency, minimize human error, and drive cost savings, thereby positioning themselves for success in an increasingly digital and competitive marketplace [13].

Transport and logistics managers play a crucial role in overseeing the movement of goods and ensuring efficient operations within the supply chain. To effectively manage transportation and logistics processes, these professionals need to possess a diverse skill set and knowledge base. Here are some key areas of expertise that transport and logistics managers need to know:

- Supply Chain Management: Understanding the entire supply chain process, from sourcing raw materials to delivering finished products to customers, is essential for transport and logistics managers. They should be familiar with supply chain concepts such as inventory management, demand forecasting, and supplier relationship management.

- Transportation Modes and Regulations: Transport and logistics managers need to have in-depth knowledge of various transportation modes, including road, rail, air, and sea. They should be well-versed in transportation regulations and compliance requirements, both domestically and internationally, to ensure the safe and legal movement of goods.

- Route Optimization and Planning: Efficient route planning is critical for minimizing transportation costs and maximizing delivery efficiency. Transport and logistics managers should be proficient in route optimization techniques and use advanced software tools to plan and manage transportation routes effectively.

- Warehouse Management: Warehouse operations are an integral part of the logistics process. Transport and logistics managers need to understand warehouse layout and design, inventory management principles, and warehouse technologies to optimize storage space and streamline operations.

- Risk Management: Transport and logistics managers must be able to identify and mitigate potential risks within the supply chain, such as disruptions due to natural disasters, geopolitical events, or labour strikes. They should have contingency plans in place to minimize the impact of disruptions on operations.

- Technology and Data Analytics: Embracing technology and data analytics is essential for modern transport and logistics managers. They should be familiar with transportation management systems (TMS), warehouse management systems (WMS), and other digital tools to track shipments, analyse data, and make informed decisions.

- Customer Service and Communication: Providing excellent customer service is paramount in the transportation and logistics industry. Transport and logistics managers should have strong communication skills to liaise with customers, suppliers, and internal teams effectively. They should be responsive to customer needs and capable of resolving any issues that may arise during the transportation process.

- Environmental Sustainability With increasing awareness of environmental issues, transport and logistics managers need to prioritize sustainability initiatives within their operations. They should explore ways to reduce carbon emissions, minimize waste, and adopt eco-friendly transportation practices to contribute to a greener supply chain.

At its essence, logistics management serves as a critical component of supply chain management, orchestrating the seamless flow of goods, services, and information from the point of origin to the point of consumption to meet customer demands. This multifaceted domain is indispensable for maintaining operational efficiency across various stages, encompassing order processing, inventory management, transportation, and more. To navigate this complex landscape effectively, strategic planning and data-driven decision-making are paramount, ensuring that resources are optimized to meet customer requirements while minimizing unnecessary expenses [14].

The foundation of logistics management rests on seven essential functions, each integral to the smooth operation of any logistics operation. These functions encompass a broad spectrum of activities, from order processing to product packaging, all aimed at ensuring the timely and efficient delivery of products to end customers. Industries spanning e-commerce to manufacturing rely on these core functions to uphold payment and delivery terms, foster customer satisfaction, and sustain a competitive edge in the market.

Order processing stands as a fundamental logistics function, bridging inventory management with customer requirements by receiving, fulfilling, and verifying customer orders. Effective order processing not only improves customer experience but also ensures future customer commitments can be met through adequate inventory levels and replenishment capacity. Likewise, product and material handling logistics involve the movement, protection, and storage of goods throughout the supply chain, ensuring safe transit and maintaining product quality while optimizing labour efficiency.

Inventory control management serves as a cornerstone of logistics operations, balancing stock levels to meet customer orders without excess that ties up resources. Beyond cost reduction, inventory control contributes to just-in-time inventory systems, enhancing responsiveness to market changes and streamlining supply chain strategy. Storage and warehouse logistics play a crucial role in optimizing space and accessibility, directly influencing order fulfillment and customer satisfaction by ensuring products are readily available for packing and shipping.

Transportation and delivery management logistics are pivotal in orchestrating logistics operations, involving decisions related to transport modes, routes, and costs. Integration with other logistics functions reduces costs while maintaining delivery effectiveness, navigating complex transportation networks with regulatory compliance and cost optimization. Packaging also holds significance, protecting products during transit, complying with customs regulations, and influencing customer experience and satisfaction.

Leveraging inventory management software and advanced analytics tools revolutionizes supply chain management, providing insights into logistics operations and enabling data-driven decisions. Real-time data optimization extends into transportation management and customer order tracking, offering a holistic approach to logistics management driven by actionable insights and enhanced efficiency.

Chapter 2

Sectors within Transport and Logistics

The transport and logistics industry is a vital sector comprising companies that offer services for the movement of people or goods from one location to another. Within the framework of the Global Industry Classification Standard (GICS), transport is categorized under the industrials sector, reflecting its fundamental role in supporting economic activities and facilitating trade [15]. This sector encompasses a diverse range of industries, each specializing in different modes of transportation and related infrastructures. Among these are logistics, air freight or airlines, marine transport, road transport, and rail transport, each playing a crucial role in the global movement of goods and people.

Logistics, as a significant component of the transport and logistics industry, focuses on the planning, coordination, and management of the flow of goods, information, and resources throughout the supply chain. It involves activities such as warehousing, inventory management, transportation optimization, and distribution. Logistics companies play a pivotal role in ensuring the efficient and timely delivery of products to their destinations, contributing to the smooth functioning of supply chains across various industries.

Air freight or airlines represent another integral aspect of the transport and logistics industry, providing rapid transportation services for both passengers and cargo. Air transport offers unparalleled speed and connectivity, making it ideal for time-sensitive shipments, perishable goods, and long-distance travel. Airlines operate extensive networks of routes and destinations, connecting cities and countries worldwide and facilitating global trade and tourism.

Marine transport, encompassing shipping and maritime logistics, is essential for the movement of goods across oceans and waterways. Ships and vessels transport vast quantities of cargo, including raw materials, commodities, and manufactured goods, between ports and terminals worldwide. Maritime transport is crucial for international trade, as the majority of global trade by volume is conducted through seaborne shipping, making ports and shipping lanes vital nodes in the global supply chain.

Road transport and rail transport play indispensable roles in the transport and logistics industry, providing essential links between production centres, distribution hubs, and end consumers. Road transport, including trucks and vans, is responsible for the majority of inland freight transportation, delivering goods to businesses, retailers, and households. Rail transport, on the other hand, offers an efficient and environmentally friendly mode of transportation for bulk cargo, raw materials, and intermodal freight, connecting industrial centres and supporting economic development along rail corridors.

The transport and logistics industry encompasses a wide range of sectors that work together to facilitate the movement of goods, services, and people from one location to another. These sectors include:

- Road Transport: This sector involves the transportation of goods and passengers by road, including trucks, vans, buses, and other vehicles. Road transport is crucial for the movement of goods within cities, regions, and countries, and includes both freight and passenger transportation services.

- Rail Transport: Rail transport involves the movement of goods and passengers by trains on railway tracks. It plays a vital role in long-distance freight transportation, as well as commuter and intercity passenger travel. Rail transport is known for its efficiency, capacity, and environmental sustainability.

- Maritime Transport: Maritime transport involves the transportation of goods and passengers by sea using ships, vessels, and boats. This sector includes container shipping, bulk cargo transportation, ferry services, cruise lines, and offshore operations. Maritime transport is essential for international trade, connecting ports and facilitating global supply chains.

- Air Transport: Air transport involves the transportation of goods and passengers by airplanes and helicopters. It is known for its speed, efficiency, and ability to connect distant locations. Air transport is crucial for express delivery services, perishable goods, time-sensitive cargo, and international passenger travel.

- Logistics Services: Logistics services encompass a wide range of activities related to the management and coordination of transportation, warehousing, inventory, and distribution. This sector includes freight forwarding, third-party logistics (3PL) providers, supply chain management firms, customs brokerage, warehousing, and distribution centres.

- Supply Chain Management: Supply chain management (SCM) involves the planning, coordination, and optimization of activities related to the procurement, production, storage, and distribution of goods and services. It includes functions such as demand forecasting, inventory management, order fulfillment, and supplier relationship management.

- Freight Forwarding: Freight forwarding involves the organization and coordination of shipments on behalf of shippers, including arranging transportation, customs clearance documentation, and insurance. Freight forwarders act as intermediaries between shippers and carriers to ensure the smooth movement of goods from origin to destination.

- Warehousing and Distribution: Warehousing and distribution involve the storage, handling, and distribution of goods within facilities such as warehouses, distribution centres, and fulfillment centres. This sector includes activities such as inventory management, order picking, packing, and shipping to fulfill customer orders.

- Courier and Express Delivery Services: Courier and express delivery services provide fast, door-to-door delivery of parcels, documents, and small packages. This sector includes companies such as FedEx, UPS, DHL, and other courier companies that specialize in time-sensitive deliveries.

- Public Transport: Public transport includes services such as buses, trains, subways, trams, and ferries that provide transportation to the general public. Public transport plays a crucial role in urban mobility, commuter travel, and reducing traffic congestion and pollution in cities.

Road transport stands as a cornerstone within the broader spectrum of the transportation and logistics industry, playing a pivotal role in the movement of goods and passengers across cities, regions, and countries. This sector encompasses a diverse array of vehicles, including trucks, vans, buses, and other motorized vehicles, which form the backbone of road-based transportation networks worldwide. Road transport is indispensable for facilitating commerce, trade, and mobility, serving as a primary mode of transportation for both freight and passengers.

Figure 1: Road transport (freight). Public domain, via Wikimedia Commons.

In the realm of freight transportation, road transport serves as a vital link in the supply chain, enabling the seamless movement of goods from production facilities to distribution centres, retailers, and ultimately, consumers. Trucks and vans, in particular, are instrumental in transporting a wide range of commodities, including raw materials, finished products, perishable goods, and consumer goods, among others. With their flexibility, accessibility, and door-to-door delivery capabilities, road transport vehicles provide a crucial last-mile connection, ensuring that goods reach their intended destinations efficiently and on time.

Figure 2: Road transport (freight) - Typical Road Train, Australia. B-train with two dolly/semi units.. Thomas Schoch, CC BY-SA 3.0, via Wikimedia Commons.

Moreover, road transport plays a significant role in supporting the functioning of urban and interurban passenger transportation systems, catering to the mobility needs of individuals and communities. Buses, coaches, and other forms of public transportation provide essential services for commuters, students, tourists, and other travellers, offering a cost-effective and accessible mode of transit within cities and across long distances. Additionally, private vehicles, including cars and motorcycles, contribute to the mobility of individuals, families, and businesses, facilitating personal travel, commuting, and leisure activities.

Figure 3: Road transport (passenger) - BYD electric bus on line 1 in Eslöv. Barcaviktor25, CC BY-SA 4.0, via Wikimedia Commons.

The importance of road transport extends beyond its role in facilitating economic activities and mobility to encompass broader societal benefits. Efficient road transportation networks contribute to social integration, enabling access to education, healthcare, employment opportunities, and recreational facilities. Moreover, road transport plays a critical role in emergency response and disaster relief efforts, facilitating the rapid movement of aid supplies, medical personnel, and equipment to affected areas during crises and natural disasters.

However, road transport also presents various challenges and considerations, including congestion, traffic accidents, environmental impact, and infrastructure maintenance. Addressing these challenges requires a holistic approach that integrates technological innovations, policy interventions, and sustainable practices to enhance the efficiency, safety, and sustainability of road transportation systems. Despite these challenges, road transport remains an indispensable component of the transportation and logistics industry, serving as a vital artery that connects communities, businesses, and economies, driving growth, development, and prosperity.

Rail transport stands as a fundamental pillar within the realm of transportation and logistics, representing a mode of transportation that involves the movement of goods and passengers by trains along dedicated railway tracks. This mode of transport serves as a critical component of both freight logistics and passenger travel, offering a range of benefits including efficiency, capacity, and environmental sustainability. Rail transport networks span vast distances, connecting cities, regions, and countries, and play a pivotal role in facilitating long-distance freight transportation and commuter and intercity passenger travel.

Figure 4: Rail (freight) - Canada National EMD SD70M-2 8015, EMD SD75I 5690 and EMD SD60F 5517 with a freight train between Hinton and Jasper, Canada. Kabelleger / David Gubler, CC BY-SA 4.0, via Wikimedia Commons.

One of the primary functions of rail transport is the movement of freight over long distances, making it an indispensable mode for the transportation of goods such as raw materials, commodities, manufactured products, and bulk cargo. Rail freight services are renowned for their efficiency and capacity to transport large volumes of goods economically, particularly over long distances. Rail transport networks form an integral part of global supply chains, serving industries ranging from agriculture, mining, and manufacturing to retail and logistics, and contributing to the efficient movement of goods across domestic and international markets.

In addition to its role in freight transportation, rail transport serves as a vital mode of passenger travel, providing essential commuter and intercity transportation services. Rail passenger services offer numerous advantages, including speed, reliability, and convenience, making them an attractive option for travellers seeking efficient and sustainable alternatives to road and air travel. Commuter rail systems serve urban and suburban areas, facilitating daily travel for workers, students, and residents, while intercity passenger rail services connect major cities and regions, offering a comfortable and environmentally friendly mode of long-distance travel.

Figure 5: Rail (passenger) - SNCB Desiro ML (Class AM08 08197) at Antwerp Central Station level -2 platform 22 looking towards the main hall. Trougnouf, CC BY 4.0, via Wikimedia Commons.

Rail transport is renowned for its environmental sustainability, offering significant advantages over other modes of transportation in terms of energy efficiency and emissions reduction. Trains are inherently more fuel-efficient than trucks and cars, consuming less energy per ton-mile of freight or passenger-mile travelled. Additionally, rail transport produces fewer greenhouse gas emissions and air pollutants compared to road and air transport, making it an environmentally friendly mode of transportation that contributes to efforts to mitigate climate change and reduce air pollution.

Despite its numerous benefits, rail transport also presents various challenges and considerations, including infrastructure maintenance, capacity constraints, and competition from other modes of transportation. Addressing these challenges requires ongoing investment in rail infrastructure, technology, and regulatory frameworks to enhance the efficiency, safety, and sustainability of rail transport networks. Overall, rail transport remains a vital component of the transportation and logistics industry, offering efficient, sustainable, and reliable solutions for the movement of goods and passengers over long distances.

Maritime transport stands as a cornerstone of global commerce, encompassing the transportation of goods and passengers by sea using a diverse array of vessels, including ships, boats, and other maritime craft. This sector encompasses a wide range of activities, including container shipping, bulk cargo transportation, ferry services, cruise lines, and offshore operations, each playing a distinct role in facilitating maritime transport and supporting various industries and economic activities. Maritime transport is indispensable for international trade, serving as a vital link in global supply chains and connecting ports worldwide, thereby facilitating the exchange of goods, raw materials, and commodities between countries and regions.

One of the primary functions of maritime transport is the movement of goods across vast distances, making it an essential mode for international trade and commerce. Container shipping, in particular, has revolutionized global trade by enabling the efficient and cost-effective transportation of goods in standardized containers, facilitating the movement of manufactured products, raw materials, and consumer goods between production centres, ports, and markets worldwide. Bulk cargo transportation, including the shipment of commodities such as coal, grain, oil, and minerals, also forms a significant part of maritime transport, supporting industries ranging from agriculture, mining, and energy to manufacturing and construction.

Figure 6: Cargo ship Corona J I saw during my vacations at Puerto Cortes, the main Port of Honduras. Luis Alfredo Romero, CC BY-SA 4.0, via Wikimedia Commons.

In addition to its role in freight transportation, maritime transport serves as a vital mode of passenger travel and leisure, encompassing ferry services, cruise lines, and maritime tourism. Ferry services provide essential transportation links between islands, coastal communities, and ports, offering a convenient and reliable mode of transit for commuters, travellers, and vehicles. Cruise lines cater to leisure travellers seeking immersive maritime experiences, offering luxury accommodations, amenities, and entertainment aboard cruise ships that traverse the world's oceans, rivers, and seas, providing passengers with unique travel experiences and opportunities for exploration and adventure.

Figure 7: Cruise ship, CARNIVAL VISTA - IMO 9692569, in Willemstad, Curaçao. Photo: Gordon Leggett/Wikimedia Commons.

Maritime transport plays a critical role in supporting offshore operations, including offshore exploration and production activities in the oil and gas industry, offshore wind energy projects, and marine research and exploration endeavours. Specialized vessels and platforms are deployed to offshore locations to conduct drilling, extraction, and construction activities. contributing to the development of offshore resources and renewable energy sources, as well as scientific research and exploration of marine ecosystems and resources.

Despite its numerous benefits, maritime transport also presents various challenges and considerations, including navigational safety, environmental impact, and regulatory compliance. Addressing these challenges requires the implementation of stringent safety standards, environmental protection measures, and international regulations governing maritime operations, as well as investments in technology, infrastructure, and workforce training to enhance the efficiency, safety, and sustainability of maritime transport networks. Overall, maritime transport remains a vital component of the transportation and logistics industry, serving as a lifeline for global trade, economic development, and connectivity, while also offering unique opportunities for travel, exploration, and leisure activities on the high seas.

Renowned for its unparalleled speed, efficiency, and ability to traverse vast distances, air transport serves as a critical link in global supply chains and facilitates connectivity between distant locations worldwide. This mode of transport plays an indispensable role in various industries and economic activities, particularly in the transportation of time-sensitive cargo, perishable goods, and express delivery services, as well as international passenger travel.

One of the primary functions of air transport is the rapid movement of goods and cargo, making it an essential mode for express delivery services and time-sensitive shipments. Air freight services enable the swift transportation of goods between airports, facilitating just-in-time delivery, inventory management, and supply chain optimization for businesses across industries. High-value and perishable goods, including pharmaceuticals, electronics, fresh produce, and seafood, rely on air transport for expedited delivery to global markets, ensuring product freshness, quality, and shelf life while minimizing transit times and inventory holding costs.

Figure 8: Air transport - Emirates Airbus A380-861 (reg. A6-EER, msn 139) at Munich Airport (IATA: MUC; ICAO: EDDM) departing 26L. Julian Herzog, CC BY 4.0, via Wikimedia Commons.

In addition to its role in freight transportation, air transport serves as a vital mode of passenger travel, offering fast, convenient, and efficient air travel options for domestic and international journeys. Commercial airlines operate a vast network of routes connecting cities, regions, and countries worldwide, providing travellers with seamless access to destinations and facilitating business travel, tourism, and leisure activities. Air transport offers numerous advantages for passengers, including time savings, comfort, and accessibility, making it a preferred mode of travel for both business and leisure travellers seeking expedited and hassle-free transportation options.

Air transport plays a critical role in supporting international trade and economic development by facilitating the movement of goods and people across borders and continents. Cargo airlines operate global networks of air cargo hubs and freighter aircraft, transporting goods between production centres, distribution centres, and markets worldwide, thereby enabling businesses to access global markets and meet customer demands efficiently. Commercial airlines operate scheduled passenger services connecting major cities and destinations worldwide, contributing to the growth of tourism, business travel, and cultural exchange, while also fostering economic growth and prosperity.

Despite its numerous benefits, air transport also presents various challenges and considerations, including safety, security, environmental impact, and regulatory compliance. Addressing these challenges requires the implementation of stringent safety and security measures, environmental protection initiatives, and international regulations governing air transport operations. Investments in technology, infrastructure, and workforce training are essential to enhance the efficiency, safety, and sustainability of air transport networks, ensuring the continued viability and growth of this critical mode of transportation within the broader transportation and logistics industry.

Logistics services represent a crucial facet of the transportation and logistics industry, encompassing a diverse array of activities aimed at managing and coordinating the movement and storage of goods throughout the supply chain. This sector plays a pivotal role in ensuring the efficient flow of products from manufacturers to end customers, encompassing various services such as freight forwarding, third-party logistics (3PL) providers, supply chain management firms, customs brokerage, warehousing, and distribution centres Logistics services are essential for businesses seeking to streamline their operations, optimize inventory management, and enhance the overall efficiency and effectiveness of their supply chain processes.

Freight forwarding stands as a fundamental component of logistics services, involving the transportation of goods from one location to another via various modes of transport, including air, sea, rail, and road. Freight forwarders act as intermediaries between shippers and carriers, managing the logistics of cargo transportation, arranging for transportation services, and handling documentation, customs clearance, and other logistics-related tasks on behalf of their clients. These services enable businesses to navigate the complexities of international trade and transportation, ensuring the timely and cost-effective delivery of goods to their intended destinations.

Third-party logistics (3PL) providers offer comprehensive logistics solutions to businesses seeking to outsource their logistics operations and supply chain management functions. These providers offer a range of services, including transportation, warehousing, inventory management, order fulfillment, and distribution, allowing businesses to focus on their core competencies while leveraging the expertise and resources of third-party logistics experts. 3PL providers play a vital role in optimizing supply chain performance, reducing logistics costs, and enhancing overall operational efficiency for their clients, making them indispensable partners for businesses across industries.

Supply chain management firms specialize in the strategic planning, coordination, and optimization of supply chain activities, encompassing procurement, production, inventory management, logistics, and distribution. These firms work closely with businesses to design and implement customized supply chain solutions tailored to their specific needs and objectives, helping them achieve greater visibility, agility, and responsiveness in their supply chain operations. Supply chain management firms leverage advanced technologies, data analytics, and industry best practices to optimize supply chain performance, minimize risks, and drive continuous improvement across the supply chain.

Customs brokerage services play a crucial role in facilitating international trade by managing customs clearance processes, import and export documentation, and compliance with customs regulations and requirements. These services help businesses navigate the complexities of international trade regulations, tariffs, and duties, ensuring the smooth and efficient movement of goods across borders while minimizing delays, costs, and compliance risks. Customs brokers act as intermediaries between importers/exporters and customs authorities, representing their clients' interests and facilitating the timely clearance of goods through customs checkpoints.

Warehousing and distribution centres serve as vital nodes within the logistics network, providing storage, handling, and distribution services for goods at various stages of the supply chain. These facilities play a critical role in inventory management, order fulfillment, and customer service, enabling businesses to store, consolidate, and distribute goods efficiently and effectively. Warehousing and distribution centres utilize advanced technologies and automation systems to optimize storage space, enhance inventory accuracy, and improve order processing and fulfillment capabilities, supporting the seamless flow of goods through the supply chain and ensuring timely delivery to customers.

Supply chain management (SCM) stands at the core of the modern business landscape, encompassing a broad spectrum of activities aimed at optimizing the flow of goods and services from suppliers to end customers. At its essence, SCM involves the strategic planning, coordination, and integration of various supply chain processes to ensure the efficient and cost-effective movement of products throughout the supply chain. This multifaceted discipline encompasses a range of functions, including demand forecasting, inventory management, order fulfillment, and supplier relationship management, all of which are critical for maintaining smooth and efficient supply chain operations.

One of the key components of supply chain management is demand forecasting, which involves predicting future demand for products or services based on historical data, market trends, and other relevant factors. Accurate demand forecasting enables businesses to anticipate customer needs, plan production and inventory levels accordingly, and minimize the risk of stockouts or excess inventory. By leveraging advanced forecasting techniques and data analytics tools, companies can optimize their demand forecasting processes, enhance inventory management practices, and improve overall supply chain efficiency.

Inventory management is another vital aspect of supply chain management, focusing on the efficient control and optimization of inventory levels throughout the supply chain. Effective inventory management involves balancing the costs associated with holding inventory against the risks of stockouts and lost sales. By implementing inventory control measures such as just-in-time (JIT) inventory systems, safety stock policies, and inventory optimization techniques, businesses can minimize carrying costs, reduce inventory holding times, and improve cash flow while ensuring adequate stock availability to meet customer demand.

Order fulfillment is a critical function within the supply chain management process, encompassing the entire process of receiving, processing, picking, packing, and shipping customer orders. Efficient order fulfillment requires seamless coordination between various supply chain activities, including inventory management, warehouse operations, transportation logistics, and customer service. By optimizing order fulfillment processes and leveraging technologies such as warehouse management systems (WMS) and transportation management systems (TMS), businesses can improve order accuracy, reduce order cycle times, and enhance customer satisfaction levels.

Supplier relationship management (SRM) is an integral part of supply chain management, focusing on the strategic management of relationships with suppliers and other external partners. Effective SRM involves identifying and selecting reliable suppliers, negotiating favourable terms and contracts, monitoring supplier performance, and fostering collaborative partnerships aimed at driving mutual value and innovation. By cultivating strong and collaborative relationships with suppliers, businesses can mitigate supply chain risks, improve supply chain resilience, and gain competitive advantages in terms of cost, quality, and flexibility.

Freight forwarding entails the intricate orchestration and coordination of shipments on behalf of shippers, encompassing a myriad of logistical tasks ranging from arranging transportation to managing customs clearance, documentation, and insurance requirements. Acting as intermediaries between shippers and carriers, freight forwarders play a pivotal role in navigating the complexities of international trade and logistics, ensuring the efficient and timely delivery of goods from origin to destination.

One of the primary responsibilities of freight forwarders is to arrange transportation for shipments, selecting the most suitable modes of transport based on factors such as shipment size, weight, destination, and urgency. Whether by air, sea, road, or rail, freight forwarders leverage their expertise and industry connections to secure reliable and cost-effective transportation options that meet the specific needs and requirements of shippers. By coordinating the movement of goods across various transportation networks, freight forwarders help optimize transit times, minimize transportation costs, and mitigate logistical risks associated with shipping.

In addition to transportation logistics, freight forwarders play a crucial role in managing customs clearance processes, ensuring compliance with regulatory requirements, and facilitating the smooth flow of goods across international borders. This involves preparing and submitting the necessary documentation, such as commercial invoices, packing lists, and certificates of origin, to customs authorities, as well as coordinating inspections and audits as required. By navigating the complexities of customs procedures and regulations, freight forwarders help streamline cross-border trade and minimize the risk of delays or disruptions in the supply chain.

Furthermore, freight forwarders provide invaluable support to shippers by handling the complexities of cargo documentation and insurance arrangements. From preparing shipping documents and bills of lading to securing cargo insurance coverage, freight forwarders ensure that all necessary paperwork is in order and that shipments are adequately protected against loss or damage during transit. By offering comprehensive documentation and insurance services, freight forwarders provide shippers with peace of mind and confidence in the integrity and security of their shipments throughout the transportation process.

Warehousing and distribution are pivotal components of the logistics and supply chain landscape, playing a critical role in the efficient storage, handling, and movement of goods within the global trade ecosystem. At its essence, warehousing encompasses the physical infrastructure and facilities designed to store and manage inventories of goods, ranging from raw materials to finished products. These facilities, which include warehouses, distribution centres, fulfillment centres, and cross-docking facilities, serve as strategic nodes within the supply chain network, facilitating the timely and seamless flow of goods from production to consumption.

Figure 9: Modern warehouse with pallet rack storage system. Axisadman, CC BY-SA 3.0, via Wikimedia Commons.

Within these warehousing facilities, a myriad of activities takes place to ensure the smooth operation of the supply chain. Inventory management stands as a fundamental function, involving the systematic control and tracking of stock levels to meet customer demand while minimizing excess inventory carrying costs. By employing advanced inventory management systems and techniques, such as just-in-time (JIT) inventory and lean inventory practices, warehouses can optimize inventory levels, reduce storage costs, and improve overall operational efficiency.

Moreover, warehousing and distribution encompass a range of order fulfillment activities aimed at processing and dispatching customer orders in a timely and accurate manner. This includes order picking, packing, and shipping, where goods are retrieved from inventory, packaged securely, and dispatched for delivery to end customers. The efficiency and accuracy of these fulfillment processes are critical to ensuring customer satisfaction and loyalty, as timely order fulfillment is essential in meeting customer expectations and maintaining competitiveness in the marketplace.

In addition to storage and order fulfillment, warehousing and distribution also involve value-added services aimed at enhancing the quality and value of goods throughout the supply chain. This may include product labelling, kitting, assembly, customization, and packaging services tailored to meet specific customer requirements. By offering these value-added services, warehouses can differentiate themselves in the market and provide additional value to customers, thereby strengthening customer relationships and driving business growth.

Furthermore, warehousing and distribution play a vital role in facilitating the efficient movement of goods across various transportation modes and distribution channels. By strategically locating warehouses and distribution centres near key transportation hubs and consumer markets, companies can minimize transportation costs, reduce lead times, and improve overall supply chain responsiveness. This strategic positioning enables companies to optimize their distribution networks, streamline logistics operations, and meet the dynamic demands of today's global marketplace.

Courier and express delivery services represent a vital segment within the broader transport and logistics industry, offering rapid and efficient door-to-door delivery solutions for parcels, documents, and small packages. These services cater to the growing demand for swift and reliable delivery options in today's fast-paced global marketplace, where businesses and consumers alike expect timely and convenient shipping solutions. Companies operating in this sector, such as FedEx, UPS, DHL, and various regional and local courier firms, play a pivotal role in facilitating the seamless movement of goods and documents across local, national, and international boundaries.

Figure 10: DHL Van in Ottawa. MB-one, CC BY-SA 4.0 <https://creativecommons.org/licenses/by-sa/4.0>, via Wikimedia Commons.

One of the defining characteristics of courier and express delivery services is their emphasis on speed and responsiveness, allowing customers to send and receive shipments within tight timeframes. Whether it's delivering urgent documents to meet critical deadlines or shipping time-sensitive goods to satisfy customer demands, courier companies specialize in expediting deliveries through expedited transit times and specialized handling processes. This focus on speed and efficiency has made courier and express delivery services indispensable partners for businesses operating in industries where time-critical deliveries are paramount, such as e-commerce, healthcare, manufacturing, and professional services.

In addition to their speed and reliability, courier and express delivery services offer a range of value-added features and capabilities designed to enhance the customer experience and meet diverse shipping requirements. These include real-time tracking and visibility tools that enable senders and recipients to monitor the status and location of their shipments throughout the delivery process. By providing transparency and accountability, these tracking systems empower customers with greater control over their shipments and help build trust and confidence in the delivery service provider.

Furthermore, courier and express delivery services leverage advanced technology and logistics infrastructure to optimize delivery routes, maximize efficiency, and minimize transit times. From sophisticated route optimization algorithms to automated sorting and handling systems, these companies invest heavily in technology-driven solutions to streamline operations, reduce costs, and improve service levels. By harnessing the power of automation, data analytics, and digital platforms, courier firms can achieve greater operational agility, scalability, and competitiveness in today's rapidly evolving logistics landscape.

Moreover, courier and express delivery services play a critical role in facilitating global trade and commerce by connecting businesses and consumers with suppliers, vendors, and markets worldwide. With their extensive network of distribution hubs, transportation assets, and international partnerships, courier companies enable seamless cross-border shipping and logistics, facilitating the flow of goods and information across diverse geographies and regulatory environments. This global reach and connectivity empower businesses of all sizes to expand their reach, enter new markets, and compete effectively on a global scale, driving economic growth and prosperity.

Public transport is a fundamental component of urban infrastructure, encompassing a diverse range of services such as buses, trains, subways, trams, and ferries that cater to the transportation needs of the general public. In urban centres around the world, public transport systems form the backbone of sustainable mobility solutions, offering affordable, accessible, and efficient transportation options for residents and visitors alike. By providing mass transit services that connect key destinations within cities and metropolitan areas, public transport plays a vital role in facilitating daily commuting, leisure travel, and access to essential services, education, and employment opportunities.

One of the primary functions of public transport is to alleviate traffic congestion and reduce reliance on private vehicles, thereby mitigating the negative impacts of urban sprawl, air pollution, and greenhouse gas emissions. By offering viable alternatives to car travel, public transport systems help alleviate traffic congestion on roads and highways, improve air quality, and promote sustainable modes of transportation that prioritize collective mobility over individual vehicle ownership. Through strategic route planning, efficient scheduling, and integrated multi-modal networks, public transport authorities strive to optimize service coverage, frequency, and reliability to meet the diverse travel needs of urban populations while minimizing environmental impacts.

Figure 11: Alicante Tram FGV's 4200 series arriving to Holanda stop (Playa de San Juan). kallerna, CC BY-SA 4.0, via Wikimedia Commons.

Moreover, public transport plays a crucial role in fostering social inclusion and equitable access to transportation services for all segments of society, including low-income individuals, seniors, persons with disabilities, and marginalized communities. By providing affordable and accessible transportation options that connect residential neighbourhoods with employment centres, educational institutions, healthcare facilities, and recreational amenities, public transport helps bridge spatial inequalities and improve mobility outcomes for underserved populations. Additionally, public transport services contribute to social cohesion by fostering interactions and connections between diverse communities, promoting cultural exchange, and enhancing urban liveability and quality of life for residents.

Furthermore, public transport systems serve as catalysts for economic development and urban growth by supporting vibrant, dynamic urban centres that attract investment, tourism, and talent. By enhancing connectivity and accessibility, public transport infrastructure stimulates economic activity, job creation, and business development along transit corridors and within transit-oriented developments. Moreover, public transport investments contribute to land value appreciation, property development, and urban regeneration initiatives, driving sustainable urban growth and revitalization. Through collaborative planning, investment, and governance, public transport stakeholders seek to harness the transformative potential of transit-oriented development to create more inclusive, resilient, and liveable cities for present and future generations.

In conclusion, public transport is an indispensable component of urban mobility systems, providing essential transportation services that connect people, places, and opportunities within cities and metropolitan regions. By promoting sustainable travel behaviours, reducing traffic congestion, and enhancing accessibility, public transport plays a vital role in advancing environmental sustainability, social equity, and economic prosperity in urban areas. As cities continue to grow and evolve, the importance of investing in modern, efficient, and integrated public transport systems will become increasingly evident, paving the way for more inclusive, resilient, and liveable urban environments for all.

As such, the various sectors within transport and logistics are interconnected components of a complex system that collaboratively facilitate the movement of goods, services, and people across different modes of transportation, storage facilities, and distribution networks. These sectors work together in a coordinated manner to ensure the efficient, reliable, and timely delivery of products and services from point of origin to point of consumption, thereby supporting economic activity, trade, and commerce on both local and global scales.

At the heart of the transport and logistics ecosystem lies the coordination and integration of different modes of transportation, including road, rail, maritime, and air transport. Each mode of transportation serves distinct purposes and caters to specific types of cargo, distances, and delivery requirements. For instance, road transport is well-suited for short-haul and last-mile delivery operations within urban areas, while rail transport is more efficient for long-distance freight movements and bulk cargo transportation. Maritime transport, on the other hand, is essential for international trade and shipping of goods across oceans and seas, while air transport provides rapid and expedited delivery options for time-sensitive cargo and perishable goods.

Furthermore, the seamless functioning of transport and logistics sectors relies on the integration of supporting infrastructure such as ports, airports, rail terminals, and distribution centres. These infrastructure assets serve as critical nodes within the supply chain network, facilitating the transfer, handling, and storage of goods between different modes of transportation and enabling the smooth flow of cargo across various logistical touchpoints. By strategically locating infrastructure facilities along key transportation corridors and trade routes, logistics stakeholders optimize operational efficiencies, reduce transit times, and minimize transportation costs associated with cargo handling and storage.

Moreover, the success of transport and logistics operations hinges on effective coordination and collaboration between different stakeholders, including shippers, carriers, freight forwarders, logistics service providers, customs authorities, and regulatory agencies. These stakeholders work together to plan, execute, and monitor transportation activities, ensuring compliance with regulatory requirements, industry standards, and customer expectations. By fostering strong partnerships and leveraging advanced technologies such as transportation management systems (TMS), warehouse management systems (WMS), and supply chain visibility platforms, logistics stakeholders streamline communication, enhance visibility, and improve decision-making across the entire supply chain ecosystem.

Additionally, the integration of supply chain management practices and logistics services is crucial for optimizing end-to-end processes and delivering value-added solutions to customers. Supply chain management encompasses a range of activities, including demand forecasting, inventory optimization, order fulfillment, and supplier relationship management, which are essential for synchronizing supply and demand, minimizing stockouts, and maximizing inventory turnover. By partnering with third-party logistics (3PL) providers, supply chain managers can outsource non-core logistics functions such as warehousing, transportation, and distribution, allowing them to focus on strategic activities that drive business growth and competitiveness.

Overall, the collaboration and synergy among the various sectors within transport and logistics are essential for ensuring the smooth operation of supply chain networks, optimizing resource utilization, and meeting customer requirements in an increasingly dynamic and interconnected global economy. By embracing innovation, digitalization, and best practices in logistics management, stakeholders can unlock new opportunities for efficiency gains, cost savings, and sustainable growth, thereby enhancing the resilience and agility of transport and logistics systems to navigate future challenges and disruptions.

Furthermore, the various sectors within transport and logistics are closely intertwined with virtually every industry, playing a pivotal role in facilitating the movement of goods, services, and people across supply chains and value networks. These sectors serve as the backbone of global trade and commerce, providing essential infrastructure, transportation services, and logistical support to industries ranging from manufacturing and retail to healthcare, agriculture, and e-commerce.

One of the key ways in which transport and logistics sectors interact with other industries is through the transportation of raw materials, components, and finished goods. Manufacturing industries rely on efficient transportation networks to procure raw materials from suppliers, transport them to production facilities, and distribute finished products to customers. Whether it's the delivery of steel for automotive manufacturing or the shipment of electronics components for assembly, transport and logistics sectors play a critical role in ensuring the timely and cost-effective movement of goods within manufacturing supply chains.

Similarly, retail and consumer goods industries heavily depend on transport and logistics services to maintain seamless supply chain operations and meet consumer demand. From warehousing and inventory management to order fulfillment and last-mile delivery, logistics providers collaborate with retailers and e-commerce platforms to ensure that products are stocked on shelves or delivered to doorsteps in a timely manner. The rise of e-commerce has further amplified the importance of efficient logistics networks, with consumers expecting fast, reliable, and convenient delivery options for online purchases.

In the agricultural sector, transport and logistics play a vital role in the distribution of perishable goods such as fruits, vegetables, and dairy products from farms to markets and grocery stores. Refrigerated transportation and cold chain logistics are essential for preserving the quality and freshness of agricultural products during transit, ensuring that they reach consumers in optimal condition. Moreover, logistics services are critical for managing seasonal fluctuations in supply and demand, optimizing transportation routes, and minimizing food waste throughout the supply chain.

Healthcare is another industry where transport and logistics are indispensable, particularly for the distribution of pharmaceuticals, medical supplies, and equipment. Timely and reliable transportation of medical products is crucial for maintaining healthcare supply chains, supporting patient care, and responding to emergencies such as pandemics or natural disasters. Transport and logistics providers work closely with healthcare institutions, pharmaceutical companies, and regulatory agencies to ensure compliance with strict quality standards, temperature-sensitive requirements, and safety protocols for medical shipments.

Furthermore, the energy and natural resources sectors rely on transport and logistics for the transportation of commodities such as oil, gas, minerals, and renewable energy sources. Whether it's the shipping of crude oil via tankers, the transportation of coal by rail, or the delivery of wind turbine components by specialized cargo vessels, logistics services are essential for supporting energy production, infrastructure development, and environmental sustainability initiatives.

In essence, the transport and logistics sectors serve as enablers of economic activity and trade across a diverse range of industries, providing essential services and infrastructure that underpin global supply chains and value creation. By fostering collaboration, innovation, and efficiency within and across industries, transport and logistics sectors contribute to economic growth, job creation, and societal well-being, driving prosperity and progress in both developed and emerging markets around the world.

Chapter 3

Jobs within the Transport and Logistics Industry

The transport and logistics sector offers a broad spectrum of career opportunities spanning various disciplines and specialties, each playing a crucial role in ensuring the efficient movement of goods and services within supply chains. Professionals in this sector include data analysts who harness data to derive insights into operational efficiency and consumer behaviour, consultants who advise on optimizing logistics strategies, supply chain managers who oversee the entire process from procurement to distribution, procurement officers responsible for sourcing goods and services, and logistics managers who coordinate transportation and warehousing operations.

These roles are integral to different types of businesses within the transport and logistics sector. Freight companies, for instance, manage the transportation of goods across various modes such as road, rail, air, and sea, ensuring timely delivery and cost efficiency. Distribution companies specialize in the movement of goods from manufacturing facilities to retail outlets or directly to consumers, optimizing routes and logistics networks to minimize transit times and costs. Supply chain and logistics companies take a holistic approach, integrating procurement, production, inventory management, and distribution to enhance overall supply chain efficiency and profitability.

Specialized areas within the transport and logistics sector include distribution logistics, focusing on the efficient and timely delivery of goods to end customers, which is crucial in meeting consumer expectations in today's fast-paced markets. Disposal logistics involves managing the transportation and disposal of waste materials, adhering to environmental regulations and sustainability principles. The advent of digital logistics represents a growing area that leverages technology, such as computer software, artificial intelligence, and automation, to streamline operations, optimize routing, and improve decision-making processes across the supply chain.

Australia, in particular, relies heavily on the transport and logistics sector due to its geographic isolation from major international markets. Efficient domestic supply chains are essential for Australian businesses to compete globally, ensuring that goods are transported swiftly and cost-effectively from production sites to consumers across vast distances. The sector's ability to innovate and adopt advanced technologies plays a critical role in maintaining Australia's competitiveness in international trade, driving economic growth, and supporting industries ranging from mining and agriculture to retail and manufacturing.

In the USA, the transport and logistics sector offers a wide array of job opportunities across various roles and specialties, reflecting the sector's critical role in facilitating commerce and supply chain operations. Here are some key aspects of transport and logistics jobs in the USA:

- Types of Jobs: The sector encompasses diverse roles, including logistics managers, supply chain analysts, transportation coordinators, warehouse supervisors, freight brokers, customs brokers, fleet managers, and logistics engineers. Each role contributes uniquely to the efficient movement of goods and services across the country.

- Employment Sectors: Transport and logistics jobs are found in a range of industries and organizations. These include transportation companies (such as trucking, rail, air cargo, and maritime), logistics and supply chain management firms, distribution centres, e-commerce companies, manufacturing facilities, retail chains, government agencies (like the Department of Transportation), and consulting firms specializing in logistics and supply chain optimization.

- Job Functions: Job functions within the transport and logistics sector vary widely. Logistics managers oversee the entire supply chain process, ensuring smooth coordination from procurement to distribution. Supply chain analysts use data analytics to optimize logistics operations, predict demand, and enhance efficiency. Transportation coordinators manage the movement of goods via various modes of transport, negotiating rates and ensuring compliance with regulations. Warehouse supervisors oversee inventory management, order fulfillment, and logistics within distribution centres.

- Skills and Qualifications: Common skills sought in transport and logistics jobs include supply chain management, logistics planning, inventory control, transportation management, route optimization, procurement, warehousing, and distribution. Analytical skills are crucial for roles involving data analysis and forecasting. Many positions also require knowledge of logistics software and systems (such as ERP and WMS) and familiarity with regulatory requirements related to transportation and customs.

- Industry Growth and Demand: The demand for transport and logistics professionals in the USA remains strong due to the country's large and diverse economy, extensive infrastructure, and global trade relationships. E-commerce growth has particularly fuelled demand for logistics services and professionals capable of managing complex supply chains and last-mile delivery logistics.

- Career Development: Careers in transport and logistics offer opportunities for career growth and advancement. Professionals can advance from entry-level roles to managerial and executive positions with experience and further education. Industry certifications (such as Certified Supply Chain Professional - CSCP, Certified in Transportation and Logistics - CTL, or Certified Logistics Professional - CLP) can enhance career prospects and demonstrate expertise in specialized areas of logistics.

- Salary and Compensation: Salaries in transport and logistics vary depending on the specific role, level of responsibility, industry sector, and geographical location.

Overall, transport and logistics jobs in the USA offer rewarding career opportunities for individuals interested in operations, supply chain management, and ensuring the efficient movement of goods and services across local, national, and international markets. The sector continues to evolve with advancements in technology and logistics practices, making it an exciting field for professionals seeking dynamic and impactful careers.

Likewise, transport and logistics jobs in Europe encompass a broad range of roles vital to the efficient movement of goods and people across the continent and beyond. Here's an overview of key aspects of transport and logistics jobs in Europe:

- Types of Jobs: Similar to the USA, the transport and logistics sector in Europe offers diverse career opportunities. Common roles include logistics coordinators, supply chain managers, freight forwarders, customs specialists, transportation planners, warehouse managers, and logistics analysts. These roles span various sectors, including transportation companies, logistics service providers, manufacturing firms, retail chains, and government agencies.

- Employment Sectors: The transport and logistics sector in Europe is extensive and interconnected. It includes national and international transportation companies (road transport, rail, air cargo, maritime), logistics providers offering warehousing and distribution services, e-commerce platforms, supply chain management firms, and public transportation agencies. The sector also plays a crucial role in supporting Europe's robust export-import activities and intra-European trade.

- Job Functions: Job functions in European transport and logistics jobs are multifaceted. Logistics managers oversee the end-to-end supply chain process, from procurement and inventory management to distribution and customer delivery. Supply chain analysts utilize data analytics to optimize logistics operations, improve efficiency, and forecast demand. Transportation planners coordinate the movement of goods and passengers using various modes of transport, ensuring timely and cost-effective delivery.

- Skills and Qualifications: Skills required for transport and logistics jobs in Europe include supply chain management, logistics planning, inventory control, transportation management, customs regulations, and international trade compliance. Proficiency in logistics software (such as ERP systems and WMS) and strong analytical abilities are increasingly important. Multilingual skills can be advantageous, given Europe's diverse linguistic landscape and cross-border trade dynamics.

- Industry Growth and Demand: The demand for transport and logistics professionals in Europe remains robust due to the continent's extensive infrastructure network, high volume of trade, and geographic proximity to major global markets. E-commerce growth, accelerated by digital transformation and changing consumer behaviours, has further fuelled demand for logistics services and skilled professionals capable of managing complex supply chains.

- Career Development: European transport and logistics careers offer opportunities for advancement and specialization. Professionals can progress from entry-level positions to managerial roles and senior leadership positions with experience and additional qualifications. Industry certifications such as Certified Supply Chain Professional (CSCP), Certified Logistics Professional (CLP), and International Air Transport Association (IATA) certifications can enhance career prospects.

- Salary and Compensation: Salaries in European transport and logistics jobs vary depending on factors such as job role, experience level, industry sector, and geographical location. According to Eurostat and national statistics offices across European countries, wages in the transport and logistics sector generally reflect the region's economic conditions, labour market trends, and cost of living.

Overall, transport and logistics jobs in Europe offer dynamic career opportunities for individuals interested in operations, supply chain management, and ensuring efficient logistics operations across the continent and globally. The sector continues to evolve with technological advancements and regulatory changes, making it an attractive field for professionals seeking impactful and rewarding careers in a pivotal industry.

In logistics management, critical thinking is an indispensable skill due to the inherent complexity and unpredictability of the industry. Logistics professionals frequently encounter various challenges, such as supply chain disruptions, transportation delays, or inventory issues, which demand quick and effective solutions. The ability to analyse situations critically allows them to assess problems, identify root causes, and devise strategic responses to minimize disruptions and maintain operations.

Moreover, the logistics sector operates under strict time constraints and deadlines. Timeliness is crucial as the movement of goods and resources relies heavily on adhering to schedules and delivery timelines. Professionals must be adept at prioritizing tasks, managing resources efficiently, and implementing strategies that ensure prompt delivery and customer satisfaction.

Employers in the logistics field highly value individuals with strong analytical skills. These skills enable professionals to interpret data, forecast demand, optimize routes, and streamline processes to enhance efficiency and reduce costs. Proficiency in logistics technology and software is equally essential. Familiarity with systems for inventory management, supply chain visibility, and transportation tracking not only facilitates smooth operations but also supports data-driven decision-making.

Critical thinking in logistics management extends beyond technical competencies. Soft skills such as interpersonal communication, collaboration, and customer service are equally crucial. Logistics professionals often interact with various stakeholders, including suppliers, carriers, customers, and team members. Effective communication and people management skills enable them to build strong relationships, negotiate effectively, and resolve conflicts, thereby ensuring seamless collaboration across the supply chain.

Traits like decisiveness, problem-solving abilities, and logical reasoning are invaluable in handling the pressures of logistics operations. When faced with unexpected challenges or high-stress situations, professionals must remain calm, think rationally, and make informed decisions promptly. The ability to maintain composure under pressure ensures that logistics operations continue smoothly and efficiently, even during crises or peak demand periods.

Continuous improvement is another trait highly valued in logistics professionals. The industry is dynamic, with evolving technologies and market trends influencing operations. Professionals who actively seek opportunities to enhance their skills, stay updated on industry developments, and implement innovative solutions contribute to the continuous improvement of logistics processes and organizational performance.

Various Job Roles in the Industry

Jobs in the transport and logistics industry encompass a diverse range of roles, sometimes categorized into both blue-collar and white-collar positions, each playing a crucial part in the smooth operation and management of supply chains and transportation networks.

Blue-collar roles form the backbone of the operational workforce within the industry. Forklift operators, for instance, are responsible for manoeuvring heavy loads within warehouses and distribution centres, ensuring efficient movement of goods. Store persons manage inventory within storage facilities, while container unloaders specialize in unloading cargo from shipping containers upon arrival. Receipt and dispatch clerks oversee the inbound and outbound flow of goods, ensuring accurate documentation and compliance with shipping protocols. Pickers/packers assemble customer orders and prepare them for shipment, while offsiders and dock hands assist in various manual tasks required in logistics operations. All trades and labourers, including machine operators and mechanical fitters, contribute to the maintenance and operation of equipment essential to logistics activities. Inventory controllers manage stock levels, ensuring optimal inventory management practices are maintained, while managers and supervisors provide leadership and oversight to ensure operational efficiency and adherence to safety standards.

Figure 12: Worker cleaning windshield of a locomotive waiting at a platform of Dessau train station, Germany. Roy Zuo, CC BY-SA 4.0, via Wikimedia Commons.

On the other hand, white-collar roles in transport and logistics are centred around strategic planning, management, and coordination of supply chain activities. At the top level, roles such as Supply Chain Director and General Manager of Logistics & Supply Chain involve high-level strategic decision-making and leadership, overseeing the entire supply chain operations of an organization. Supply Chain Managers and Inventory & Materials Managers are responsible for managing inventory levels, optimizing warehouse operations, and coordinating logistics activities to meet customer demand efficiently. Supply Chain & Logistics Coordinators play a pivotal role in liaising between different departments and external stakeholders to ensure seamless logistics operations. Supply Planners/Managers and Demand Planners/Managers focus on forecasting and planning inventory requirements based on market demand and sales projections, respectively. Supply Chain Planners/Analysts analyse data and trends to improve supply chain efficiency and optimize logistics networks. Strategic Sourcing Managers and Procurement Managers handle sourcing strategies, vendor relationships, and contract negotiations to secure cost-effective and high-quality materials and services for the organization. Purchasing Managers oversee purchasing activities and vendor management, ensuring timely procurement of goods and services at competitive prices. Contracts Managers and Sourcing Program/Project Managers manage contractual agreements and sourcing projects, ensuring compliance with legal and regulatory requirements. Strategic Sourcing Specialists and General Managers of Strategic Sourcing focus on developing and implementing strategic sourcing initiatives to drive cost savings and improve supplier performance. Head of Procurement oversees the entire procurement function, setting procurement policies, strategies, and goals to align with organizational objectives.

Overall, the diverse array of roles in transport and logistics cater to both the operational and strategic needs of the industry, contributing collectively to the efficient movement of goods, effective supply chain management, and overall business success in a dynamic and competitive global marketplace.

Logistics coordinator

A logistics coordinator plays a pivotal role in the smooth and efficient operation of supply chains within various industries. This job entails overseeing and optimizing the movement of products from the point of origin to the final destination. With a primary focus on logistics management, these professionals are instrumental in analysing and improving workflows and processes across all stages of the supply chain.

One of the key responsibilities of a logistics coordinator is to monitor order fulfillment. This involves tracking orders from the moment they are placed until they reach the customer, ensuring that deliveries are timely and meet customer expectations. By closely monitoring order status and inventory levels, logistics coordinators can identify potential delays or issues and take proactive measures to resolve them, thus maintaining high levels of customer satisfaction.

In addition to overseeing order fulfillment, logistics coordinators are tasked with checking the status of production. They collaborate closely with production teams to ensure that manufacturing schedules align with demand forecasts and order requirements. This coordination ensures that production timelines are adhered to, minimizing bottlenecks and optimizing production efficiency.

Correspondence management is another critical aspect of the logistics coordinator's role. They act as a liaison between suppliers, manufacturers, and shipping companies, facilitating effective communication and information flow. This involves negotiating contracts, resolving disputes, and addressing any logistical challenges that may arise during the transportation and distribution of goods.

Beyond day-to-day operations, logistics coordinators also play a strategic role in optimizing supply chain performance. They analyse data related to transportation costs, inventory levels, and lead times to identify areas for improvement. By leveraging analytical skills and logistics software, they develop strategies to streamline processes, reduce costs, and enhance overall efficiency in supply chain operations.

The skills required for success in this role include strong organizational abilities, attention to detail, and proficiency in logistics management systems. Effective time management and the ability to work under pressure are also crucial, as logistics coordinators often juggle multiple tasks and deadlines simultaneously. Excellent communication skills are essential for building relationships with internal teams, external suppliers, and customers, ensuring seamless coordination throughout the supply chain.

Supply Manager

A Supply Manager, sometimes referred to as a Global Supply Manager, holds a critical position within organizations responsible for overseeing the procurement and management of supplies needed for production. Their primary objective is to ensure that the supply chain efficiently meets consumer demand while maintaining high standards of quality and cost-effectiveness. This role involves strategic planning, collaboration with various stakeholders, and integrating advanced technologies to streamline procurement processes.

One of the core responsibilities of a Supply Manager is to manage the supply chain to ensure that all necessary materials and resources are available to meet production schedules. This includes forecasting demand, assessing inventory levels, and working closely with suppliers to negotiate contracts and maintain consistent supply. By analysing market trends and demand forecasts, Supply Managers can anticipate fluctuations in consumer needs and adjust procurement strategies accordingly.

Collaboration with logistics managers is another crucial aspect of the role. Supply Managers work closely with logistics professionals to optimize sourcing timelines and strategies. This collaboration ensures that materials are sourced and delivered in a timely manner to support production schedules and minimize disruptions. By aligning procurement with logistics, they can enhance efficiency throughout the supply chain, from supplier selection to delivery to manufacturing facilities.

Integrating automation and advanced technologies into supply chain processes is becoming increasingly important for Supply Managers. They leverage tools such as supply chain management software, predictive analytics, and inventory optimization systems to streamline operations and improve decision-making. Automation helps in reducing manual tasks, improving accuracy in forecasting demand, and optimizing inventory levels, ultimately leading to cost savings and operational efficiency.

In addition to operational tasks, Supply Managers play a strategic role in supplier relationship management. They establish and maintain relationships with key suppliers, negotiate contracts, and monitor supplier performance to ensure adherence to quality standards and delivery schedules. Effective supplier management contributes to the overall reliability and resilience of the supply chain, mitigating risks and optimizing supply chain continuity.

The skills required for success in this role include strong analytical abilities, strategic thinking, and negotiation skills. Supply Managers must possess a deep understanding of supply chain dynamics, market trends, and regulatory requirements. Excellent communication and interpersonal skills are essential for building and maintaining effective relationships with suppliers and internal stakeholders. Overall, Supply Managers play a crucial role in driving operational excellence, ensuring supply chain efficiency, and contributing to the overall success and profitability of the organization.

Buyer

The role of a Buyer, also known as a Purchasing Agent, is integral to the supply chain management process, focused on acquiring materials, products, or equipment essential for a specific segment of the supply chain. Buyers are responsible for ensuring that their organization procures necessary goods at optimal prices, quality, and within designated timelines to meet operational demands. This role involves a combination of strategic planning, supplier relationship management, and meticulous attention to detail in procurement processes.

Buyers start their responsibilities by conducting thorough research into consumer needs, market trends, and competitor activities. This analysis helps them identify the types and quantities of goods needed to support business operations effectively. By understanding market dynamics, Buyers can anticipate changes in demand and adjust their purchasing strategies accordingly to maintain supply continuity.

A significant aspect of the Buyer's role is identifying and qualifying suppliers capable of meeting quality and delivery standards. They evaluate potential suppliers based on criteria such as reliability, product quality, pricing, and compliance with regulatory requirements. Negotiating favourable terms and conditions, including pricing, payment terms, and delivery schedules, is crucial to achieving cost-effective procurement outcomes while maintaining supplier relationships.

Once contracts are established, Buyers monitor inventory levels and consumption patterns to initiate timely reorders. They maintain communication with suppliers to ensure consistent availability of goods, minimize stockouts, and prevent disruptions in production or sales activities. Documenting all purchasing transactions accurately and maintaining records of supplier performance are essential for tracking expenses, analysing procurement efficiency, and complying with audit requirements.

In addition to operational tasks, Buyers play a strategic role in cost management and budgeting within their organization. They collaborate closely with internal stakeholders, such as production managers and inventory controllers, to align procurement activities with business objectives and financial targets. By optimizing purchasing decisions and controlling costs, Buyers contribute directly to enhancing profitability and maintaining competitive advantage in the market.

Key skills for success in this role include strong analytical skills, negotiation prowess, attention to detail, and proficiency in procurement software and tools. Effective communication and relationship-building abilities are also critical for fostering productive partnerships with suppliers and internal teams. Overall, Buyers play a vital role in ensuring the smooth flow of goods through the supply chain, supporting operational efficiency, and driving sustainable growth for their organizations.

Logistics Manager

As a pivotal figure in supply chain management, the Logistics Manager plays a critical role in overseeing the procurement, distribution, and transportation of products and materials within a business or organization. Their primary responsibility is to optimize the efficiency and cost-effectiveness of logistics operations while ensuring seamless workflows across the supply chain.

One of the key duties of a Logistics Manager is to manage the purchasing and distribution of products and materials. They collaborate closely with suppliers and vendors to negotiate favourable terms, including pricing, delivery schedules, and quality standards. By maintaining strong relationships with suppliers, Logistics Managers ensure a reliable and consistent flow of materials necessary for production and operations.

Inventory management is another crucial aspect of the Logistics Manager's role. They oversee inventory levels across manufacturing facilities, warehouses, and distribution centres to prevent stockouts or excess inventory. This involves forecasting demand, monitoring consumption patterns, and implementing inventory control strategies to optimize stock levels and minimize carrying costs.

Budgeting and cost management are integral to the responsibilities of a Logistics Manager. They set and manage budgets for various segments of the supply chain, including transportation, warehousing, and procurement. By analysing logistics costs and identifying opportunities for cost savings, Logistics Managers contribute to improving profitability and operational efficiency.

Logistics Managers also play a strategic role in optimizing distribution channels and workflows. They establish and implement standards and procedures to streamline logistics operations, improve productivity, and ensure compliance with regulatory requirements. This may include optimizing transportation routes, selecting appropriate shipping methods, and implementing logistics technologies to enhance tracking and efficiency.

Effective communication and leadership skills are essential for Logistics Managers to coordinate activities among different departments, suppliers, and external logistics partners. They provide guidance and support to logistics teams, monitor performance metrics, and implement continuous improvement initiatives to enhance operational processes and meet customer service expectations.

Logistics Analyst

As a crucial player in the realm of logistics and supply chain management, a Logistics Analyst is tasked with analysing and optimizing various aspects of the supply chain to enhance efficiency and effectiveness. This role involves a blend of analytical prowess, strategic thinking, and collaboration with cross-functional teams to achieve operational improvements.

One of the primary responsibilities of a Logistics Analyst is to study and evaluate the entire supply chain of an organization. This involves scrutinizing processes from procurement through to distribution, identifying inefficiencies, bottlenecks, and areas for improvement. By conducting detailed analyses of production workflows, inventory levels, transportation routes, and supplier performance, Logistics Analysts gain insights into where enhancements can be made to streamline operations.

Collaboration is key for Logistics Analysts, who frequently work alongside logistics managers, coordinators, and other stakeholders within the organization. They provide data-driven recommendations and insights to support decision-making processes aimed at optimizing supply chain activities. This collaboration extends to implementing changes, such as adjusting inventory levels, refining transportation strategies, or negotiating better terms with suppliers, all aimed at improving overall efficiency and cost-effectiveness.

Monitoring spending and cost analysis are integral components of the Logistics Analyst's role. They track expenditures related to logistics operations, compare actual costs against budgets, and identify opportunities for cost savings. By analysing spending patterns and identifying cost drivers, Logistics Analysts contribute to financial stewardship within the organization, ensuring that logistics activities align with budgetary constraints and financial goals.

Optimizing inventory management is another critical duty of Logistics Analysts. They evaluate inventory levels, turnover rates, and storage practices to ensure that sufficient stock is maintained to meet demand without excess. By employing techniques such as demand forecasting and inventory modelling, Logistics Analysts help minimize carrying costs while ensuring product availability and preventing stockouts.

Furthermore, Logistics Analysts focus on enhancing transportation logistics to improve delivery speed and reliability. They analyse transportation routes, modes of transport, and carrier performance to optimize delivery times and reduce transportation costs. By leveraging data analytics and logistics software, they identify opportunities for route optimization, consolidation of shipments, and selection of efficient transportation methods tailored to meet customer delivery expectations.

Fleet Manager

As a pivotal role in transportation logistics, a Fleet Manager is responsible for overseeing and managing the transportation operations within an organization, ensuring efficiency, safety, and compliance with regulations. This role involves a diverse set of responsibilities that encompass both strategic planning and hands-on management of the fleet of vehicles.

One of the primary duties of a Fleet Manager is to ensure the effective management of the transportation department. This includes hiring and supervising drivers and mechanics, who are essential for the day-to-day operations of the fleet. Fleet Managers need to recruit skilled drivers and mechanics, oversee their training and development, and manage their performance to ensure optimal productivity and safety standards.

Optimizing delivery routes is another critical aspect of a Fleet Manager's role. They analyse transportation logistics to determine the most efficient routes for deliveries, considering factors such as traffic patterns, fuel efficiency, and delivery schedules. By optimizing routes, Fleet Managers can reduce transportation costs, improve delivery times, and enhance overall operational efficiency.

Safety is paramount in fleet management, and Fleet Managers are responsible for establishing and enforcing safety standards for drivers and vehicles. They implement policies and procedures to promote safe driving practices, conduct regular safety inspections of vehicles, and ensure compliance with federal and state transportation regulations. This proactive approach helps mitigate risks and ensures the safety of drivers, passengers, and other road users.

Maintenance of the fleet is another critical responsibility of Fleet Managers. They oversee regular maintenance schedules for vehicles, coordinate repairs and inspections, and ensure that all vehicles are in optimal condition for safe and efficient operation. Fleet Managers also manage vehicle acquisitions, making decisions about purchasing new vehicles or replacing outdated ones to maintain a reliable and modern fleet.

Documentation and reporting are essential components of the Fleet Manager's role. They maintain accurate records of fleet operations, including vehicle maintenance logs, fuel usage, driver performance, and incident reports. By documenting these aspects, Fleet Managers can track efficiency metrics, identify areas for improvement, and comply with reporting requirements mandated by regulatory agencies and company policies.

Lastly, Fleet Managers establish training protocols to ensure that employees adhere to federal and state transportation regulations and company policies. They conduct training sessions on safe driving practices, regulatory compliance, and fleet management procedures to enhance employee skills and knowledge. This training helps maintain compliance with transportation laws and regulations while promoting a culture of safety and professionalism within the transportation department.

Facilities Manager

As a Facilities Manager, this role is pivotal in overseeing the smooth and efficient operation of physical facilities within an organization, which can include office spaces, manufacturing plants, or distribution centres. The primary responsibility of a Facilities Manager is to ensure that these facilities are well-maintained, safe, and compliant with all relevant regulations.

One of the core duties of a Facilities Manager is to oversee building maintenance and repairs. They are responsible for coordinating and scheduling maintenance tasks such as HVAC systems, plumbing, electrical systems, and general upkeep of the building infrastructure. This ensures that the facilities remain in optimal condition and that any issues are promptly addressed to minimize disruptions to operations.

Regular inspections are a critical aspect of the Facilities Manager's role. They conduct routine inspections of facilities to assess their condition, identify maintenance needs, and ensure compliance with safety standards and regulations. These inspections help in proactive maintenance planning and ensure that facilities meet safety and operational requirements.

Safety and security are paramount concerns for a Facilities Manager. They collaborate with security professionals to implement and maintain security measures that protect the building, its occupants, and assets. This includes establishing security protocols, monitoring access control systems, and responding to security incidents to maintain a safe working environment.

Establishing safety protocols and contingency plans is another key responsibility. Facilities Managers develop and implement safety procedures to prevent accidents and ensure compliance with local, state, and federal safety regulations. They also create contingency plans to address emergencies such as fire, natural disasters, or workplace incidents, ensuring that employees are trained and prepared to respond effectively.

Compliance with regulations is a fundamental aspect of the Facilities Manager's role. They stay updated on workplace safety regulations, environmental standards, and industry-specific requirements to ensure that facilities adhere to all legal and regulatory obligations. This involves maintaining accurate records, conducting audits, and implementing necessary changes to achieve and maintain compliance.

Communication and coordination are essential skills for Facilities Managers. They liaise with contractors, vendors, and internal stakeholders to coordinate maintenance activities, renovations, or facility upgrades. Effective communication ensures that projects are completed on time, within budget, and meet the organization's operational needs.

Distribution Centre Manager

As a Distribution Center Manager, this role is pivotal in overseeing the operations of a distribution centre where goods are received, stored, processed for orders, and shipped to customers or other locations. These professionals are responsible for ensuring the efficient and effective functioning of all aspects of the distribution process.

One of the primary duties of a Distribution Center Manager is to oversee the receiving and storage operations. They manage the intake of goods from suppliers, ensuring accuracy in quantities and quality checks. They also oversee the allocation of storage space within the distribution centre, optimizing layouts to maximize efficiency in storing and retrieving goods.

Order fulfillment is another critical responsibility. Distribution Center Managers ensure that customer orders are processed accurately and timely. They coordinate with warehouse staff to pick, pack, and prepare orders for shipment according to specified requirements and delivery schedules. This involves implementing efficient workflows and using technology to streamline order processing.

Efficiency and safety are paramount concerns in distribution centres. Distribution Center Managers work to improve storage practices and layout designs to enhance operational efficiency. They implement safety standards and regulations to create a safe working environment for employees and ensure compliance with occupational health and safety requirements.

Financial oversight is also part of the role. Distribution Center Managers monitor financial transactions related to inventory management, order fulfillment, and operational expenses. They track budgets, analyse costs, and optimize resources to achieve financial objectives while maintaining operational efficiency.

Communication and leadership skills are essential for Distribution Center Managers. They collaborate with internal teams, such as logistics, procurement, and customer service, to coordinate activities and resolve issues related to inventory management and order fulfillment. They also manage relationships with external stakeholders, such as suppliers and transportation providers, to ensure seamless operations.

Production Manager

As a Production Manager, this role is pivotal in overseeing and optimizing the manufacturing processes within an organization. These professionals are responsible for managing the entire production process, ensuring efficiency, quality, and productivity across all manufacturing operations.

One of the primary duties of a Production Manager is to analyse and optimize production processes. They assess the speed and efficiency of manufacturing equipment and personnel to identify areas for improvement. This involves monitoring production metrics, such as cycle times, downtime, and throughput, to streamline workflows and enhance productivity.

Production Managers play a crucial role in providing projections and productivity reports to senior management. They compile and analyse production data to forecast future manufacturing needs, including resource requirements, production schedules, and workforce allocation. By providing accurate projections, they assist in strategic decision-making and resource planning.

Implementing new strategies and technologies is another key responsibility. Production Managers introduce innovative solutions, such as automation and advanced manufacturing techniques, to improve efficiency and reduce costs. They collaborate with engineering and technology teams to implement new systems and equipment that enhance manufacturing capabilities.

Ensuring production quality standards is a critical aspect of the role. Production Managers enforce strict quality control measures to maintain high standards of product quality and consistency. They establish and monitor quality assurance processes, conduct regular inspections, and implement corrective actions to address any deviations from quality standards.

Communication and leadership skills are essential for Production Managers. They coordinate with cross-functional teams, including engineering, procurement, and logistics, to coordinate production activities and resolve operational challenges. They also provide leadership to production teams, fostering a culture of continuous improvement and accountability.

Contract Administrator

As a Contract Administrator, this role revolves around managing and overseeing the contractual agreements between an organization and its suppliers, buyers, or third-party service providers. The primary responsibility is to handle all aspects of contract negotiations, drafting, monitoring, and ensuring compliance to facilitate smooth and legally sound business transactions.

One of the core duties of a Contract Administrator is to negotiate and draft contractual agreements. They engage in discussions with suppliers, buyers, or service providers to define terms and conditions that align with the organization's interests. This includes specifying deliverables, pricing structures, payment terms, warranties, and other critical provisions essential for the smooth execution of contracts.

Monitoring the progress of contracts is another key responsibility. Contract Administrators track timelines, milestones, and deliverables outlined in contracts to ensure all parties meet their obligations. They maintain detailed records of contract terms and conditions, amendments, and correspondence to facilitate transparency and accountability throughout the contract lifecycle.

Ensuring contract fulfillment is crucial to the role. Contract Administrators oversee the implementation of contracts to verify that all parties adhere to agreed-upon terms. This involves coordinating with internal stakeholders and external partners to resolve any issues that may arise and prevent potential contract disputes.

Financial oversight is also a significant aspect of the role. Contract Administrators ensure that contracts are financially advantageous for the organization by negotiating favourable terms and conditions. They may analyse contract costs, pricing structures, and financial implications to optimize profitability and mitigate financial risks associated with contracts.

Compliance with state and federal laws is paramount in contract administration. Contract Administrators stay informed about relevant regulations and legal requirements to ensure that contracts comply with applicable laws. They ensure that contractual agreements protect the organization's legal interests and mitigate potential legal liabilities.

Effective communication and negotiation skills are essential for Contract Administrators. They collaborate with various stakeholders, including legal counsel, procurement teams, finance departments, and external parties, to facilitate contract negotiations and resolve contractual issues promptly and efficiently.

Purchasing Manager

As a Purchasing Manager, this role entails overseeing and managing the procurement activities within an organization to ensure efficient and cost-effective sourcing of goods and services. The primary responsibility of a Purchasing Manager is to lead a team of buyers or procurement professionals, guiding them in the strategic procurement process to meet the organization's operational needs and financial objectives.

One of the key duties of a Purchasing Manager is to hire, train, and supervise a team of buyers. They are responsible for recruiting skilled professionals who can effectively negotiate with suppliers, analyse market trends, and make informed purchasing decisions. Training and development programs are also essential to ensure that buyers stay updated with industry best practices and procurement strategies.

Setting purchasing standards and budgets is crucial for a Purchasing Manager. They establish guidelines and policies for procurement processes, including vendor selection criteria, pricing structures, quality standards, and delivery schedules. Budgetary considerations play a significant role in their decisions to optimize spending while maintaining quality and operational efficiency.

Evaluating potential vendors and suppliers is another vital responsibility. Purchasing Managers assess supplier capabilities, reliability, and financial stability to build a robust supplier base. They conduct supplier evaluations, negotiate contracts, and establish long-term relationships that align with the organization's strategic goals and procurement needs.

Monitoring and approving contract negotiations are pivotal in the role. Purchasing Managers oversee contract terms and conditions to ensure compliance with legal and regulatory requirements. They review contract proposals, negotiate pricing and terms, and finalize agreements that provide the best value and mitigate risks for the organization.

Holding vendors accountable to contract terms is essential for ensuring transparency and performance. Purchasing Managers monitor supplier performance metrics, such as delivery times, quality standards, and customer service responsiveness.

They address any issues or discrepancies promptly to maintain smooth operations and uphold contractual obligations.

Providing financial reports and analysis to senior management is a critical aspect of the role. Purchasing Managers prepare budget forecasts, cost analyses, and expenditure reports to demonstrate cost savings, procurement efficiencies, and return on investment. They collaborate with finance departments to align procurement strategies with overall financial goals and objectives.

Effective communication and leadership skills are fundamental for Purchasing Managers. They collaborate with internal stakeholders, including finance, operations, and legal teams, to streamline procurement processes and resolve procurement-related challenges. Their ability to negotiate effectively, manage vendor relationships, and optimize purchasing strategies contributes to the organization's success in achieving operational excellence and cost savings.

Operations Analyst

As an Operations Analyst, the primary focus is on optimizing business operations by evaluating existing processes, identifying inefficiencies, and proposing improvements. These professionals play a crucial role in enhancing operational efficiency across various departments within an organization, including supply chain management, manufacturing, finance, and customer service.

One of the key responsibilities of an Operations Analyst is to conduct thorough analyses of current processes and workflows. They review financial and production reports from different stages of the supply chain to assess performance metrics such as cost-effectiveness, production output, and resource utilization. By examining these reports, Operations Analysts can pinpoint areas where inefficiencies exist and where improvements are needed.

Identifying issues that impact efficiency is central to the role. Operations Analysts use data-driven insights to identify bottlenecks, delays, or other obstacles that hinder operational performance. This involves conducting root cause analysis and understanding the underlying factors contributing to operational challenges, whether they stem from technology limitations, process gaps, or resource constraints.

Recommendation of solutions is a critical aspect of the job. Based on their analyses, Operations Analysts develop and propose solutions to enhance efficiency and productivity. They may suggest process reengineering, automation initiatives, or technology upgrades to streamline operations and achieve cost savings. These recommendations are often presented to senior management or cross-functional teams for implementation.

Applying projection models and forecasting techniques is another essential duty. Operations Analysts utilize statistical methods and modelling tools to forecast future trends, demand patterns, and operational needs. By predicting scenarios and outcomes, they help organizations make informed decisions regarding resource allocation, inventory management, production planning, and customer service strategies.

Researching competitors and industry trends is integral to staying competitive. Operations Analysts continuously monitor market dynamics, competitor strategies, and industry best practices to benchmark performance and identify opportunities for improvement. This market intelligence informs strategic planning and decision-making, ensuring that the organization remains agile and responsive to market changes.

Collaboration with cross-functional teams is key to implementing operational improvements. Operations Analysts work closely with departments such as IT, finance, logistics, and production to align strategies and initiatives. Effective communication and teamwork are essential to successfully implement recommended changes and monitor their impact on business operations.

Procurement Manager

As a Procurement Manager, the primary responsibility revolves around overseeing the acquisition of goods and services necessary for a company's operations. This role is pivotal in ensuring that an organization obtains high-quality materials at competitive prices and in a timely manner to support production and other business activities.

One of the core duties of a Procurement Manager is to manage the procurement team effectively. This involves hiring, training, and mentoring procurement staff members to ensure they have the skills and knowledge needed to execute their roles efficiently. Establishing departmental policies and procedures is also crucial for maintaining consistency and compliance within the procurement process.

Facilitating negotiations with vendors and suppliers is a key aspect of the role. Procurement Managers engage in supplier relationship management, working to secure favourable terms, pricing, and contracts. They analyse market trends, conduct supplier evaluations, and leverage purchasing power to negotiate cost-effective agreements that meet quality standards and delivery schedules.

Collaboration with various department managers is essential. Procurement Managers work closely with divisions such as purchasing, inventory management, and fleet management to align procurement strategies with broader organizational goals. They coordinate efforts to monitor stock levels, optimize inventory turnover, and establish efficient delivery routes to minimize lead times and logistics costs.

Addressing issues related to product quality is another critical responsibility. Procurement Managers ensure that purchased goods meet specified quality standards and regulatory requirements. They implement quality assurance processes, conduct supplier audits, and resolve any disputes or discrepancies related to product specifications, performance, or delivery timelines.

Strategic planning and forecasting play a significant role in procurement management. Procurement Managers analyse demand forecasts, economic indicators, and industry trends to anticipate future supply needs and mitigate supply chain risks. They develop sourcing strategies that balance cost considerations with supply chain resilience and sustainability objectives.

Maintaining compliance with relevant regulations and ethical standards is paramount. Procurement Managers adhere to legal requirements, industry regulations, and company policies governing procurement practices. They uphold ethical sourcing practices, promote supplier diversity initiatives, and ensure transparency and accountability in all procurement transactions.

Commodity Manager

A Commodity Manager holds a critical role within organizations, tasked with overseeing the procurement and management of specific commodities essential for business operations. These professionals are strategic in their approach, analysing market trends and economic conditions to identify opportunities for securing the best deals on goods, materials, and equipment necessary for the organization's supply chain. By monitoring market dynamics and supplier landscapes, they aim to minimize procurement risks and maximize profitability.

Central to the role of a Commodity Manager is the responsibility to optimize spending across various segments of the supply chain. This involves conducting thorough cost analyses, negotiating favourable pricing agreements, and identifying cost-effective alternatives to mitigate financial risks. They utilize their market insights to strategically source commodities, ensuring the organization maintains a competitive edge in terms of cost efficiency and profitability.

Building and maintaining strong relationships with vendors and suppliers are fundamental aspects of the job. Commodity Managers establish partnerships based on trust and mutual benefit, fostering long-term collaborations that contribute to reliable supply chains. They negotiate contracts, terms, and conditions, and resolve any disputes that may arise, ensuring smooth and productive supplier relationships that align with the organization's strategic goals.

Collaboration with other managers across different functional areas is crucial for optimizing inventory management and preventing shrinkage or waste. Commodity

Managers work closely with inventory managers, logistics professionals, and production teams to synchronize procurement activities with demand forecasts and production schedules. By aligning procurement strategies with operational needs, they enhance supply chain efficiency and responsiveness to market fluctuations.

Risk management is another key responsibility of Commodity Managers. They proactively assess and mitigate risks associated with commodity price fluctuations, supply shortages, geopolitical issues, and regulatory changes. Through effective risk mitigation strategies and contingency planning, they safeguard the organization's supply chain continuity and resilience against external disruptions.

Supply Chain Manager

A Supply Chain Manager holds a pivotal role within organizations, responsible for overseeing and optimizing all aspects of the supply chain from procurement and production to distribution and delivery. Their primary objective is to ensure the efficient flow of goods and services through the entire supply chain process, ultimately contributing to the organization's operational efficiency and profitability.

One of the core responsibilities of a Supply Chain Manager is to evaluate and refine existing procedures and workflows for maximum efficiency. They continuously assess supply chain operations, identify bottlenecks, and implement strategic improvements to streamline processes. By leveraging their expertise in supply chain dynamics, they introduce cost-effective solutions and innovative technologies to enhance productivity and reduce operational costs.

Budget management is another critical aspect of the role. Supply Chain Managers collaborate closely with financial stakeholders to set and monitor budgets related to procurement, inventory management, transportation, and logistics. They analyse cost structures, negotiate favourable pricing with suppliers, and implement strategies to optimize spending while maintaining high-quality standards and operational effectiveness.

Ensuring compliance with safety protocols, industry regulations, and ethical standards is paramount for Supply Chain Managers. They oversee adherence to health, safety, and environmental guidelines throughout the supply chain network. This includes implementing robust quality control measures, conducting audits, and ensuring that suppliers and vendors meet contractual obligations and regulatory requirements.

Building and nurturing strong relationships with suppliers, vendors, and other external partners is crucial for effective supply chain management. Supply Chain Managers cultivate partnerships based on trust, reliability, and mutual benefit, fostering collaborative environments that support the organization's supply chain goals. They negotiate contracts, manage supplier performance, resolve conflicts, and drive continuous improvement initiatives across the supply chain network.

Director of Operations

The role of a Director of Operations is integral to the strategic management and efficiency of an organization, encompassing a broad array of responsibilities that contribute directly to its overall success. As a senior leader, the Director of Operations oversees the operational aspects of the business, focusing on optimizing processes, enhancing productivity, and driving profitability across various departments.

One of the primary duties of a Director of Operations is to provide strategic guidance to lower-level managers and departments. They collaborate with these managers to establish hiring criteria, develop comprehensive training programs, and ensure that operational teams are well-equipped to meet organizational objectives. By setting clear guidelines and expectations, the Director of Operations plays a critical role in fostering a cohesive and high-performing workforce.

Assessing productivity and workflows is another key responsibility. Directors of Operations analyse operational metrics, performance indicators, and workflow efficiencies to identify areas for improvement. They implement strategic changes and initiatives aimed at enhancing operational efficiency, reducing costs, and optimizing resource allocation to achieve maximum productivity across the organization.

Budget management is a fundamental aspect of the role. Directors of Operations are responsible for budgeting departmental expenses, monitoring spending, and controlling costs within allocated budgets. They work closely with finance teams to develop financial forecasts, analyse budget variances, and make data-driven decisions to ensure financial sustainability and profitability.

Reporting and providing insights to C-level executives are critical functions of the Director of Operations. They compile and present comprehensive reports on key performance metrics such as sales, revenue, productivity, and waste management. These reports include strategic analyses, actionable insights, and projections that inform executive decision-making and support long-term business planning and growth initiatives.

Furthermore, the Director of Operations plays a pivotal role in driving organizational change and continuous improvement. They lead cross-functional initiatives to streamline processes, enhance operational effectiveness, and adapt to evolving market conditions and industry trends. By fostering a culture of innovation and efficiency, Directors of Operations position their organizations for sustainable growth and competitive advantage in the marketplace.

Chapter 4

Logistics Defined

In the realm of business operations, logistics is the backbone that ensures the seamless flow of materials and products throughout the supply chain, from their point of origin to their final destination. At its core, logistics encompasses a comprehensive set of activities and processes aimed at efficiently managing the movement, storage, and distribution of goods and resources. These components collectively support the operational efficiency and competitiveness of businesses across various industries [16].

Customer service stands as a fundamental component of logistics, focusing on meeting customer expectations regarding delivery times, order accuracy, and responsiveness. Effective logistics systems incorporate robust customer service strategies to enhance satisfaction and loyalty by ensuring timely and reliable delivery of goods.

Demand forecasting plays a pivotal role in logistics by using historical data, market trends, and other relevant factors to predict future demand for products. Accurate forecasting helps businesses optimize inventory levels, production schedules, and transportation resources, thereby reducing costs and minimizing the risk of stockouts or excess inventory.

Warehousing is another critical aspect of logistics management, involving the storage and management of inventory. Warehouses serve as distribution hubs where goods are stored, sorted, and dispatched as per demand. Effective warehouse management ensures that products are readily available for order fulfillment while optimizing space, handling, and operational costs.

Material handling within logistics refers to the movement, control, and protection of materials and products throughout the supply chain. It encompasses activities such as loading and unloading shipments, packaging, and internal transportation within facilities. Efficient material handling processes streamline operations, reduce handling times, and enhance overall productivity.

Inventory control is essential for maintaining optimal stock levels to meet customer demand without overstocking or understocking. Effective inventory management practices involve monitoring stock levels, tracking inventory movements, and implementing strategies such as just-in-time (JIT) inventory systems to minimize carrying costs and maximize operational efficiency.

Order processing within logistics involves the systematic handling of customer orders from receipt to fulfillment. This includes order entry, verification, picking, packing, and shipping. Streamlining order processing procedures ensures accurate and timely order fulfillment, contributing to customer satisfaction and operational efficiency.

Transportation is a cornerstone of logistics, encompassing the physical movement of goods between suppliers, manufacturers, warehouses, retailers, and ultimately to end consumers. It involves selecting the appropriate modes of transport (road, rail, air, sea) based on factors like cost, speed, and reliability. Efficient transportation logistics optimize delivery times and costs, supporting timely market responsiveness and competitive advantage.

Logistics plays a pivotal role across various business models and industries, each tailored to meet specific needs and challenges. Understanding different examples of logistics illustrates its diverse applications and critical functions within supply chain management [17].

In manufacturing, efficient logistics are crucial for operations relying on just-in-time (JIT) inventory management [17]. This approach minimizes storage costs by synchronizing raw material deliveries with production schedules. For instance, a manufacturer needs meticulous demand planning to ensure it receives materials exactly when required, avoiding excess inventory and storage expenses. Logistics efforts are focused on selecting reliable suppliers capable of timely deliveries, optimizing material handling processes upon receipt, and swiftly transitioning finished products to packaging and distribution points. This end-to-end logistics management ensures streamlined operations from procurement through to delivery to customers or distributors.

In retail, logistics are essential for both traditional brick-and-mortar stores and e-commerce operations. Consider a boutique clothing retailer sourcing inventory from designers and manufacturers. Upon receipt at their distribution centre, logistics involve unitizing items, adding barcodes for tracking, and organizing products for shipment to stores. The focus is on efficient intake processes, inventory management, and accurate fulfillment to meet customer demands in physical retail settings.

For retailers adopting an online sales model, logistics expand to include order fulfillment centres. These facilities receive goods from suppliers, manage inventory, and fulfill customer orders directly. This scenario requires precise logistics coordination, including real-time inventory tracking, order processing, and collaboration with third-party logistics providers (3PLs) like UPS or FedEx for efficient delivery to customers [17]. Logistics here ensure that products move swiftly from supplier to end consumer, optimizing speed and accuracy throughout the supply chain.

Furthermore, retail logistics encompass strategies for inventory redistribution based on demand forecasts. If certain stores experience higher demand for specific products, logistics involve transferring inventory between locations to meet customer needs and prevent markdowns. Conversely, sluggish sales may necessitate swift markdowns or offloading excess inventory to discount retailers. Logistics in these situations encompass inventory control, strategic planning for product movements, and efficient transportation logistics to minimize costs and maximize profitability.

Beyond traditional retail scenarios, logistics also address product disposal and recycling. If products remain unsold or are damaged beyond resale viability, logistics managers coordinate their transport to recycling facilities or donation centres. This process not only manages waste responsibly but also leverages tax incentives for charitable donations, demonstrating the broader scope of logistics in managing the entire lifecycle of products [17].

The logistics industry has undergone profound transformations since the advent of computerized inventory management and forecasting systems in the 1960s. These innovations revolutionized the way orders are tracked, inventory is managed, and goods are distributed globally [18]. Today, the logistics landscape is shaped by advanced technologies such as AI and machine learning, which enable more precise forecasting and efficient order management. This technological evolution has propelled logistics into one of the fastest-growing sectors worldwide, catering to diverse types of logistics companies each specializing in different facets of the supply chain.

Among the prominent types of logistics companies are e-commerce logistics firms, which have surged in response to the exponential growth of online shopping. Companies like Amazon exemplify how e-commerce logistics has transformed consumer expectations, offering rapid delivery times through a sophisticated network of distribution, sortation, and fulfillment centres [18]. Amazon's logistics strategy relies on efficient movement of goods from suppliers to fulfillment centres, followed by meticulous sorting and rapid transportation using diverse modes such as trucks and airplanes.

Figure 13: Amazon's new one million square-foot fulfilment centre in Fife. Scottish Government. CC BY 2.0, via Flickr.

Third-party logistics (3PL) providers also play a pivotal role in the logistics ecosystem. These companies, including industry giants like UPS and FedEx, offer comprehensive supply chain solutions that encompass warehousing, packaging, and transportation services. By outsourcing logistics to 3PL providers, businesses can benefit from economies of scale, access to global networks, and enhanced customer service capabilities. This outsourcing allows companies to focus on core competencies while leveraging the logistics expertise of specialized providers.

Freight logistics and freight forwarders constitute another crucial segment within logistics. Freight logistics companies specialize in physical transportation of goods, ensuring they are moved efficiently from point A to point B. On the other hand, freight forwarders focus on optimizing transport solutions and managing documentation for international shipments. Companies like Flexport and Transfix have introduced innovative models in freight forwarding, leveraging technology to simplify processes and enhance visibility across the supply chain [18].

The logistics industry thrives on collaboration among these diverse players, creating a complex yet interconnected web of services that drive efficiency and reduce costs throughout the supply chain. This interconnectedness ensures that goods move seamlessly from production facilities to consumers, supported by a blend of technological innovation, logistical expertise, and global infrastructure. As logistics continues to evolve, driven by advancements in technology and changing consumer expectations, the industry remains poised for further growth and transformation, shaping the future of global commerce.

The logistics industry is structured around various service providers that cater to different aspects of the supply chain. Among these are the distinctions between 1PL, 2PL, 3PL, and 4PL logistics providers, each serving specific roles in the movement and management of goods and services [19].

Starting with 1PL, or First Party Logistics, this model involves a manufacturer handling its own logistics operations internally, without relying on third-party assistance. In a 1PL setup, the manufacturer takes full responsibility for transporting goods directly to customers or distribution points using its own fleet and resources. This approach gives the manufacturer direct control over the logistics process, enabling them to tailor operations closely to their specific needs and ensuring alignment with their production and customer service strategies.

Moving to 2PL, or Second Party Logistics, these companies specialize in transporting goods via various modes such as road, rail, sea, or air. Examples include shipping lines that operate cargo vessels between global ports and air freight companies that manage shipments by plane. Unlike 1PL, 2PL companies do not produce goods themselves but focus solely on transporting products efficiently and securely according to client requirements. They may own their transportation assets or operate on a contractual basis, depending on the scope and scale of their operations.

Next, 3PL, or Third Party Logistics, represents a highly popular arrangement where companies engage third-party providers to handle specific logistics functions or even entire supply chain operations. These providers offer comprehensive services ranging from warehousing and inventory management to transportation, customs clearance, and distribution. 3PL companies leverage their expertise and infrastructure to streamline logistics processes, reduce costs, and enhance operational flexibility for their clients. This model allows businesses to focus on core competencies while outsourcing logistical complexities to specialized partners.

Lastly, 4PL, or Fourth Party Logistics, takes outsourcing to another level by acting as a lead logistics provider and consultant. 4PL companies assume responsibility for managing and optimizing the entire supply chain on behalf of their clients. They integrate multiple logistics service providers (including 3PLs) and technologies to orchestrate seamless operations, improve supply chain visibility, and achieve strategic objectives. Beyond traditional logistics services, 4PLs also offer advanced capabilities such as data analytics, market research, and strategic planning to continuously optimize supply chain performance. Importantly, 4PLs maintain impartiality in recommending logistics solutions, prioritizing the best interests of their clients' supply chain efficiency and effectiveness.

The distinctions between 1PL, 2PL, 3PL, and 4PL logistics providers illustrate a spectrum of logistical capabilities and service offerings within the industry. Each type of logistics provider plays a crucial role in ensuring goods move efficiently from production to consumption, tailored to the unique needs and scale of businesses across various sectors globally [19].

Logistics Activities

Customer service is a critical component of business operations aimed at ensuring customer satisfaction and loyalty. It encompasses various activities designed to address customer needs and concerns promptly and effectively. For example, in the context of computer software manufacturers, customer service may involve a dedicated hotline where customers can call to discuss issues they encounter with the software [20]. This direct interaction allows companies to troubleshoot problems, provide technical support, and enhance the overall user experience. Additionally, customer service extends to on-site equipment servicing and training for new users, further bolstering customer confidence and usability.

A pivotal aspect of customer service is its role in cultivating a user-friendly reputation for the company. Businesses strive to develop a positive perception among customers as being easy to engage with and responsive to their inquiries and support needs. This reputation contributes significantly to customer retention and acquisition, as satisfied customers are more likely to continue using a company's products and services and recommend them to others.

Monitoring and measuring customer service performance is essential for companies to maintain high standards and stay competitive. They employ various metrics to assess their service levels, such as tracking the number of rings before calls are answered, response times for inquiries, and the percentage of repair parts delivered within agreed-upon timeframes. By analysing these metrics, businesses can identify areas for improvement, address bottlenecks in customer service processes, and benchmark their performance against industry standards and competitors.

Demand forecasting is another crucial activity closely intertwined with logistics operations within businesses. It involves predicting future demand for products or services based on historical data, market trends, and insights from marketing efforts. Logistics teams collaborate closely with marketing departments to gather and analyse customer order patterns and preferences. This early intelligence is invaluable for logistics professionals as they plan and coordinate the movement of goods to meet anticipated customer demand.

For logistics staff, demand forecasting provides essential input for planning transportation, inventory management, and warehouse operations. By anticipating customer orders and production schedules, logistics teams can optimize supply chain activities, ensuring timely delivery of products to customers while minimizing excess inventory holding costs. This proactive approach not only enhances operational efficiency but also supports overall business agility and responsiveness to fluctuating market demands.

In essence, customer service and demand forecasting are integral functions that contribute to the success and competitiveness of businesses across industries. Effective customer service builds trust and loyalty among customers, while demand forecasting empowers logistics teams to align their operations with anticipated market needs, ultimately driving operational efficiency and customer satisfaction. These interconnected activities underscore the importance of integrating customer-centric strategies with logistics planning to achieve business objectives effectively.

Documentation flow in logistics refers to the systematic management of paperwork that accompanies the movement of physical goods throughout the supply chain. It involves a series of documents that serve as contracts, verification tools, and proof of transactions between various parties involved in the shipment process [20]. A fundamental document in logistics is the bill of lading, which acts as a contract between the shipper and the carrier, detailing the terms and conditions of transportation. This document is crucial for establishing liability and ownership during transit.

Accompanying the bill of lading is the packing list, which itemizes the contents of each shipment package. This list is prepared by the shipper and serves as a reference for both the carrier and the consignee upon receipt of the goods. Upon delivery, the consignee verifies the accuracy of the shipment against the waybill provided by the carrier and the entries on the packing list. This verification ensures that the shipment is complete and accurate, mitigating potential disputes over missing or damaged items.

For international shipments, the documentation requirements are more extensive and can include a wide range of documents, often varying based on the destination country's regulations. These documents may include commercial invoices, certificates of origin, inspection certificates, export licenses, and customs declarations.

Each document serves a specific purpose in complying with legal and regulatory requirements, facilitating smooth customs clearance, and ensuring the seamless movement of goods across borders.

In modern logistics practices, electronic data interchange (EDI) has become increasingly prevalent as a means to streamline the documentation process. EDI allows for the electronic exchange of business documents, such as purchase orders, invoices, and shipping notices, between trading partners. This digital approach enhances accuracy, efficiency, and speed in processing transactions, reducing paperwork errors and administrative costs associated with traditional paper-based documentation.

Order processing in logistics is a critical function that involves the systematic handling of customer orders from receipt to fulfillment. The process typically begins with the receipt of an order, which can come through various channels such as salespersons, phone calls, emails, or electronic systems for regular buyers and sellers. Electronic data interchange (EDI) plays a significant role in modern order processing by facilitating seamless communication and transaction processing between trading partners.

The first step in order processing is to verify the accuracy of the order details. This ensures that the order document is free from internal errors and discrepancies that could lead to misunderstandings or incorrect shipments. Once verified, the next step often involves checking the customer's credit or financial capability to pay for the goods. This step is crucial in managing financial risks and ensuring that transactions are conducted with reliable customers.

After confirming the order and customer details, logistics personnel determine the optimal inventory point from which to fulfill the order. Instructions are then relayed to the warehouse where the goods are stored. A warehouse worker receives an "order picking list," which specifies the items and quantities to be picked from inventory to assemble the customer's order. This process, known as order picking, ensures that the correct items are selected for packaging and shipment.

In the packing area, the assembled order undergoes a final check to verify completeness and accuracy. Once verified, the order is packed securely and labelled for shipment. Simultaneously, the traffic manager prepares transportation documents such as the bill of lading and notifies a carrier to pick up the shipment from the warehouse or distribution centre.

An important aspect of order processing is the generation of an invoice for the goods, which is sent to the buyer along with the shipment. This document serves as a formal request for payment and includes details of the purchased items, quantities, prices, and any applicable taxes or discounts. Additionally, various inventory and financial records are updated to reflect the outgoing shipment and the corresponding financial transaction.

Throughout the entire order processing cycle, logistics professionals monitor the "order cycle," which refers to the duration between receiving the order and shipping it out. This timeline is critical for assessing operational efficiency and meeting customer expectations for delivery times. From the buyer's perspective, the "order cycle" refers to the time span between placing an order and receiving the goods, highlighting the importance of timely and accurate order fulfillment in maintaining customer satisfaction.

Packaging serves dual purposes within the logistics and retail environments: promotion and protection. Primarily, packaging is designed to attract consumers' attention and persuade them to purchase the product. Whether through eye-catching designs, vibrant colours, or informative labels, packaging plays a crucial role in distinguishing a product from its competitors on store shelves. Effective packaging not only enhances brand recognition but also communicates essential product information to consumers, such as ingredients, usage instructions, and brand identity.

Equally important is the protective function of packaging, which safeguards the product during storage, handling, and transportation. Packaging materials are selected based on their ability to shield the product from physical damage, environmental factors (e.g., moisture, light, temperature), and potential tampering. For instance, food and pharmaceutical packages are often designed to be tamperproof, ensuring consumer safety and product integrity. Moreover, packaging may need to prevent products from damaging surrounding items, especially in cases where goods are stored or transported in bulk quantities.

Environmental considerations increasingly influence the choice of packaging materials. There is a growing demand for containers that are recyclable, biodegradable, or made from recycled materials, driven by consumer preferences for sustainable products and regulatory requirements promoting recycling initiatives. Many jurisdictions have enacted laws and regulations that encourage or mandate the recycling of beverage containers and other packaging materials to reduce waste and minimize environmental impact.

Packaging in retail logistics operates within a hierarchical structure. Products are typically packaged in multiple layers: individual retail containers that consumers purchase, which are nested within larger boxes or cartons. These cartons, usually about one cubic foot in size, facilitate efficient handling during stocking and distribution. They are transported and stored on pallets, standardized wooden platforms approximately 6 inches high and 40 inches by 48 inches in dimension. Pallets enable

STRATEGIC MANAGEMENT FOR TRANSPORT AND LOGISTICS 71

mechanical handling using forklift trucks, which have lifting prongs that fit into slots on the pallets to lift and move them.

Palletised loads, also referred to as "unit loads," are a standard method for handling packaged freight across various logistics operations. They are loaded onto and unloaded from warehouses, railcars, and trucks using forklift trucks, ensuring efficient movement and storage of goods. For bulk materials that are not packaged, such as iron ore, coal, and grains, bulk handling methods are employed. These materials are transported in large quantities by train, truck, or ship, and they are loaded and unloaded using specialized mechanical equipment tailored to handle bulk goods efficiently. Similarly, liquids like petroleum are transported through pipelines or specialized tankers, while dry bulk materials such as flour and cement are moved pneumatically through dry tanks using vacuum devices.

Figure 14: Pallets ready for shipping at the UNICEF world warehouse in Copenhagen. heb@Wikimedia Commons (mail), CC BY-SA 3.0, via Wikimedia Commons.

Parts and service support are critical aspects of logistics and operations management, ensuring that equipment sold to customers remains functional and operational over its lifespan. For industries like automotive and manufacturing, maintaining an inventory of spare parts for all models and products is essential. Automakers, for instance, typically stock parts for their vehicles up to a decade after production ceases, ensuring that customers can access replacement components and repairs as needed. This commitment to parts availability is crucial for customer satisfaction and retention, as buyers of capital equipment often base their purchasing decisions on the assurance of long-term serviceability and support.

Prompt delivery of repair parts is another key component of parts and service support. In situations where equipment breaks down unexpectedly, such as farm machinery in the middle of harvesting season, manufacturers may resort to expedited shipping methods like chartering small planes to deliver critical parts directly to the field. This ensures minimal downtime and operational disruptions, highlighting the logistical agility required to support field service operations effectively.

Plant and warehouse site selection is a strategic decision-making process that businesses undertake to optimize their logistics and supply chain operations. When establishing new facilities, firms conduct comprehensive system analysis and design to determine the optimal number and locations of warehouses or production plants. For example, a company needing to distribute repair parts across a large country within tight timelines might opt for a centralized warehouse location accessible by air express services for overnight deliveries. Conversely, if surface deliveries via trucks are preferred, multiple warehouse sites spread throughout the country may be necessary to ensure timely and cost-effective distribution.

The site selection process involves several layers of analysis, starting with identifying regions that align with market demand, labour availability and costs, tax incentives, climate conditions, and transportation infrastructure. Once a region is chosen, specific cities are evaluated based on factors such as land-use regulations, traffic accessibility, expansion potential, soil stability, utility capacities, and proximity to transportation hubs like rail lines. Each criterion plays a crucial role in ensuring the operational efficiency and resilience of the facility in serving its intended market or region.

Moreover, firms operating in dynamic markets must also consider factors such as market contraction or expansion. In scenarios where market demand shifts or operational efficiencies dictate, firms may need to consolidate or close existing production or distribution facilities. The decision to close a facility requires careful planning to mitigate adverse impacts on overall operations and to optimize resource allocation in line with evolving business strategies and market conditions.

Production scheduling is a critical function within manufacturing operations, integrating the efforts of various departments including logistics to optimize efficiency and meet customer demand. At its core, production scheduling aims to align the demand for products with the capacity of the production facility and the availability of raw materials and components. This process involves detailed planning to ensure that inbound materials are synchronized with the production timeline, minimizing idle time and maximizing utilization of resources. Logistics staff play a pivotal role in advising on transportation costs and strategies, often aiming to establish efficient material movement patterns that reduce overall logistics expenses.

The production scheduling process encompasses several key activities. Firstly, it involves coordinating the production process itself to fulfill both current orders and anticipated future demand. Manufacturers must ensure that production runs smoothly and on schedule, adhering to predefined production quotas and quality standards. Additionally, products must be scheduled for timely shipment to wholesalers, retailers, and end customers, taking into account factors such as transportation lead times and customer delivery preferences.

In scenarios where special events or promotional campaigns require increased product availability, production schedules must be flexible enough to accommodate these fluctuations in demand. This flexibility is crucial to responding promptly to unforeseen events or market changes, ensuring that production remains agile and responsive to customer needs.

The concept of just-in-time (JIT) manufacturing principles influences modern production scheduling strategies significantly. JIT emphasizes lean production practices that minimize inventory holding costs by synchronizing production with demand. This approach requires disciplined adherence to on-time deliveries of raw materials and components to avoid disruptions in the production flow. Logistics teams often collaborate closely with production planners to establish efficient delivery schedules and optimize material flows, aiming to reduce waste and enhance operational efficiency.

Moreover, routing plays a critical role in production scheduling and logistics management. Routing decisions determine the optimal paths for transportation vehicles, such as trucks, considering factors like traffic conditions, distance, fuel efficiency, and delivery deadlines. Modern routing systems leverage advanced technologies and real-time data to dynamically adjust routes, avoiding congestion and optimizing delivery times. By deploying sophisticated routing algorithms, businesses can streamline logistics operations, reduce transportation costs, and enhance overall supply chain efficiency.

Parts and service support are crucial aspects of maintaining equipment functionality and customer satisfaction over its lifecycle. For instance, automakers typically maintain extensive inventories of parts to support their models for up to a decade after production ceases. This commitment reassures customers that repair parts will be available, facilitating long-term ownership and reducing downtime. Prompt delivery of repair parts is essential across various industries; in agriculture, for example, farm implement manufacturers might deploy small aircraft to deliver urgently needed parts to equipment like combines in remote fields during critical harvesting periods.

Selecting optimal plant and warehouse sites involves a meticulous process of system analysis and design. Companies evaluate factors such as market reach, labour availability, tax implications, climate conditions, and transportation infrastructure to determine suitable locations. For example, a company needing to distribute repair parts swiftly nationwide might opt for a centralized warehouse using air-express services for overnight deliveries. Conversely, a strategy relying on surface transport might require multiple warehouses scattered geographically to ensure efficient regional coverage. Such decisions are critical in optimizing supply chain efficiency and reducing operational costs while meeting customer service expectations.

Production scheduling integrates logistics expertise with production planning to harmonize product demand with manufacturing capabilities and resource availability. Logistics professionals collaborate closely with production planners to coordinate inbound materials, production processes, and outbound shipments to customers and distributors. This alignment ensures that manufacturing operations remain responsive to market demands while minimizing inventory holding costs through just-in-time delivery philosophies. Flexible scheduling strategies accommodate unforeseen events, maintaining agility in production processes to adapt quickly to changing market conditions or special promotional campaigns.

Purchasing is closely intertwined with production scheduling, as it involves procuring materials and components essential for manufacturing. Logistics teams advise on transportation strategies to ensure timely delivery of purchased materials. Monitoring carrier performance and consolidating shipments are common practices to optimize transportation efficiency and reduce costs. Effective purchasing practices contribute significantly to supply chain management by enhancing inventory control and supplier relationships, thereby supporting seamless production operations.

Returned products present another facet of logistics management, encompassing recalls due to safety concerns or product expiration. Reverse distribution processes manage the return of goods from retailers or consumers to manufacturers for repair, replacement, or refund. Salvage centres handle unsellable items by sorting and redistributing them for reuse or recycling, thereby minimizing waste and supporting sustainable practices in product disposal.

Traffic management plays a pivotal role in logistics operations, encompassing the planning, procurement, and coordination of transportation services. Traffic managers oversee freight consolidation, carrier selection, and route optimization to streamline logistics operations and reduce transportation costs. They negotiate contracts with carriers and monitor their performance to ensure efficient and reliable delivery of goods. Advanced technologies like computerized routing systems enable precise route planning, optimizing delivery times and mitigating risks associated with traffic congestion or unforeseen delays.

Finally, managing a firm's own fleet of vehicles involves compliance with extensive federal and state regulations governing vehicular operations and safety. Traffic managers ensure adherence to these regulations while overseeing the operation and maintenance of company-owned trucks, planes, or ships. This responsibility includes managing vehicle fleets efficiently, optimizing utilization, and ensuring compliance with environmental and safety standards. By integrating these elements effectively, logistics professionals contribute to enhancing supply chain efficiency, reducing costs, and improving overall customer service levels.

Warehouse and distribution centre management is a critical logistics function that revolves around the efficient handling and storage of a firm's inventories. While warehouses and distribution centres share similarities, they serve distinct purposes based on the nature of the goods and the logistical needs of the firm. Warehouses primarily focus on storing goods over extended periods, serving as repositories for products that may have seasonal demand patterns or slow turnover rates. For instance, warehouses are essential for storing canned foods produced during harvest seasons, ensuring a steady supply throughout the year. Conversely, items like Christmas decorations are stored until peak demand periods, showcasing the warehouse's role in managing inventory cycles efficiently.

Distribution centres, on the other hand, emphasize rapid turnover and throughput of goods. These facilities are strategically positioned to streamline the distribution process, particularly for retail chains and businesses with high-volume products. Grocery chains, for example, use distribution centres to receive bulk shipments via railcars and trucks. Upon arrival, products are organized into stacks and picked for individual retail stores' orders. This process involves meticulous inventory management and order fulfillment strategies to ensure timely and accurate delivery to each location. Distribution centres are crucial in optimizing supply chain operations by consolidating shipments, reducing transportation costs, and enhancing overall efficiency in meeting consumer demands.

Managing the logistics of moving people also falls under the purview of warehouse and distribution centre management, albeit in a different context. When large groups of individuals need to be relocated, firms may charter buses or airplanes and coordinate accommodations to facilitate smooth transitions. This approach is common during large-scale projects like the construction of infrastructure such as the Trans-Alaska Pipeline, where housing and logistical support were provided to accommodate workers over an extended period. Similarly, on an international scale, governments and corporations often manage the movement of labour forces across borders, recruiting workers from their home countries and deploying them to where they are needed most.

Effective warehouse and distribution centre management involves a range of tasks, from optimizing storage space and inventory levels to implementing efficient picking and packing processes. Technology plays a crucial role, with inventory management systems and automated picking technologies enhancing operational efficiency and accuracy. Moreover, strategic location selection based on market proximity, transportation infrastructure, and operational costs is key to achieving competitive advantages in logistics. By mastering these aspects, logistics professionals ensure that warehouses and distribution centres operate seamlessly, supporting supply chain objectives of timely delivery, cost efficiency, and customer satisfaction.

International logistics refers to the management and coordination of movements across national borders, presenting a more intricate set of challenges compared to domestic logistics. One of the primary complexities in international logistics stems from border crossings, where goods undergo inspections and are subject to various regulatory checks. Import duties and charges are commonly assessed, adding a layer of financial consideration that doesn't exist in domestic trade. Furthermore, stringent inspections may be conducted to ensure compliance with the importing country's health, safety, environmental protection, and labelling standards. This regulatory landscape necessitates meticulous planning and documentation to navigate successfully.

Documentation plays a pivotal role in international logistics, often posing more significant challenges than the physical movement of goods itself. Numerous documents are required for international shipments, including invoices, packing lists, certificates of origin, and customs declarations. Each document must be meticulously prepared and presented accurately at customs and inspection points to facilitate smooth clearance. The logistics of assembling, verifying, and coordinating these documents demand attention to detail and adherence to specific international trade regulations and protocols.

Many international shipments are transported via sea routes, involving complex port operations and maritime logistics. Moving goods through ports and managing sea transport can be time-consuming due to processes such as container loading and unloading, customs inspections, and compliance with maritime regulations. Additionally, international logistics must contend with the challenges posed by different time zones, which can restrict the hours available for communications and coordination between parties involved in the shipment process. These time zone differences necessitate careful scheduling and coordination to ensure timely responses and operational efficiency across global supply chains.

The use of metric measurements is another aspect of international logistics that requires adaptation. While the United States primarily uses customary units, most other countries enforce the use of metric measurements for consistency and standardization in international trade. This necessitates conversion and compliance with metric standards for packaging, labelling, and documentation, adding another layer of complexity to international logistics operations.

Service industry logistics, although distinct from traditional manufacturing logistics in terms of physical goods movement, are equally critical for ensuring efficient operations. In the service sector, logistical needs often revolve around timely and reliable transportation of documents, parcels, and sometimes perishable items such as medical supplies. Unlike manufacturing, where large quantities of tangible products are moved, service industries rely on carriers for small parcel deliveries and postal services for essential communications and document handling. For instance, banks require prompt processing and delivery of checks to maintain financial transactions smoothly, while hospitals must ensure that medical supplies and medications are readily available for patient care.

Coordination and management of logistics within service industries are essential to maintain operational efficiency and customer satisfaction. While some larger organizations may have dedicated logistics departments with equal status to other major functions like finance and marketing, many firms integrate logistical activities across various departments. Historically, logistics functions in manufacturing were often split between inbound materials management and outbound physical distribution management, with each handled by different departments. Today, the trend leans towards integrating these functions more holistically, sometimes through third-party logistics providers who manage and coordinate logistics activities comprehensively.

Effective communication systems play a crucial role in modern service industry logistics. Advanced technology such as linked computers and real-time scanning systems at checkout counters in retail stores enable instant transmission of sales data to central offices. This real-time data allows companies to manage inventory levels efficiently by restocking merchandise promptly based on actual sales rather than projections. Such systems reduce the need for large inventory buffers and enhance responsiveness to customer demand, thereby improving overall logistical efficiency.

Control systems are another vital component of service industry logistics, especially concerning security and inventory management. Given the valuable nature of goods and materials in transit, robust control systems are necessary to prevent pilferage and unauthorized access. These systems track the movement of goods throughout the logistical chain, ensuring that every item leaving the facility is properly documented and accounted for. Integrated with modern technologies, these control systems utilize computerized tracking and authentication mechanisms to maintain the integrity and security of logistical operations.

Logistics Strategies

A logistics strategy encompasses a structured approach involving rules, processes, and policies aimed at optimizing the distribution of goods in a business. It focuses on coordinating plans to achieve efficiency and cost-effectiveness while prioritizing the maintenance of high business performance and customer service standards. This strategy addresses the entire spectrum of logistics operations, from procurement and production to distribution and delivery, aiming to streamline these processes for maximum effectiveness.

The importance of a logistics strategy cannot be overstated for any company, irrespective of its size or industry. It serves as a critical framework for navigating the complexities of the supply chain and responding to changes effectively. By engaging in thorough logistics planning, companies can anticipate potential impacts, such as disruptions or shifts in demand, and develop strategies to mitigate risks and maintain operational continuity. This proactive approach not only helps in meeting current logistics demands but also prepares the business to adapt swiftly to future challenges.

It's essential to distinguish between logistics strategy and supply chain management, although these terms are sometimes used interchangeably. Supply chain management encompasses the entire journey of goods, from sourcing raw materials through production to delivering finished products to customers. In contrast, logistics strategy specifically focuses on the movement and control of goods within this broader supply chain context. It ensures that logistics operations are efficiently planned and executed to support overall supply chain goals of cost-efficiency, responsiveness, and customer satisfaction.

Here are five key tips for developing an effective logistics strategy:
- Use accurate data: Leveraging accurate data is crucial for informed decision-making in logistics. It helps in forecasting demand, planning for sea-

sonal variations, and optimizing inventory levels. Accurate data also supports cost reduction efforts and ensures that logistics plans can adapt to changing market conditions and customer needs.

- Stay connected with stakeholders: Maintaining open communication channels with suppliers, manufacturers, distributors, and customers fosters collaboration and transparency across the supply chain. Strong stakeholder relationships enhance responsiveness to changes and enable quicker problem-solving, thereby improving overall supply chain efficiency.

- Focus on customer satisfaction: A customer-centric approach ensures that logistics strategies align with customer expectations and demands. By understanding and meeting customer needs promptly and efficiently, companies can build customer loyalty and gain a competitive edge in the market.

- Utilize available technology: Embracing technological advancements such as IoT for real-time tracking, AI for predictive analytics, and automated systems for inventory management enhances operational efficiencies in logistics. These technologies improve accuracy, reduce costs, and optimize resource allocation, thereby supporting the logistics strategy's objectives.

- Regularly review and adapt: Continuous evaluation and adjustment of logistics strategies are essential to maintain relevance and effectiveness. Regular reviews help identify areas for improvement, capitalize on opportunities for optimization, and ensure alignment with evolving business goals and market conditions.

Standards play a pivotal role in logistics planning by providing benchmarks and best practices for logistics operations. Standards such as EN 14943:2005 and ISO 23354:2020 define terminology, logistics performance measures, and visibility requirements. They ensure consistency, efficiency, and quality across logistics processes, enabling organizations to enhance their operational performance and meet industry standards effectively.

Logistic Technical Developments

The logistics industry has undergone a significant evolution driven by technological advancements that have reshaped how supply chains operate across various sectors. From optimizing delivery processes to enhancing warehouse efficiencies, logistics tech developments have revolutionized the field, making it more agile and responsive to the demands of modern commerce [18].

One of the pivotal advancements in logistics technology is the integration of AI and optimization tools. These innovations have become essential in managing the complexities of supply chains, particularly as consumer expectations for online delivery speed and reliability continue to rise. Real-time visibility software platforms like FourKites, project44, and FreightVerify have empowered logistics managers to monitor shipments, identify bottlenecks, and resolve issues promptly [18]. Such tools not only streamline operations but also enhance overall efficiency by reallocating resources effectively across the supply chain. Similarly, fleet management solutions such as those offered by Motive leverage technology to track cargo and optimize routes, thereby improving logistics efficiency and ensuring safer operations.

Amazon, a leader in e-commerce logistics, exemplifies how advanced technologies like AI and machine learning are leveraged to optimize logistics operations. From AI-powered product recommendations to warehouse automation, Amazon has pioneered the use of technology to enhance customer experience and operational efficiency. The acquisition of Kiva Systems in 2012 marked a significant milestone, introducing warehouse automation with thousands of robots that optimize processes like picking and packing. This automation has not only accelerated order fulfillment but also reduced operational costs, demonstrating the transformative impact of technology on logistics management.

The rise of autonomous vehicles represents another frontier in logistics technology. These vehicles are poised to revolutionize last-mile delivery by making it faster and more cost-effective. Companies like Starship Technologies are at the forefront, developing self-driving vehicles capable of navigating urban environments and delivering goods directly to consumers' doorsteps. Autonomous vehicles not only promise to streamline logistics operations but also offer significant potential for reducing carbon emissions and improving sustainability in transportation.

Drones have also emerged as a disruptive technology in logistics, particularly for aerial inspection and small-item delivery. Companies like Zipline have pioneered the use of drones for medical supply delivery in remote areas, showcasing the potential for drones to revolutionize logistics beyond traditional delivery methods. In warehouse settings, drones are used for inventory management, inspection tasks, and maintenance, significantly enhancing operational efficiency and reducing labour costs.

Furthermore, 3D printing has introduced a paradigm shift in logistics by enabling on-demand manufacturing and customization of products. This technology has the potential to decentralize production processes, allowing for localized manufacturing and rapid prototyping. By reducing lead times and minimizing waste, 3D printing offers logistics companies the ability to meet consumer demand for personalized products while optimizing supply chain efficiency.

Logistics Information and Information Systems

Logistics information systems (LIS) play a crucial role in the modern supply chain by managing, processing, and disseminating information essential for the efficient movement of goods from suppliers to consumers. These systems encompass a wide array of technologies and processes designed to streamline logistics operations, improve decision-making, and enhance overall supply chain performance.

At its core, logistics information systems gather data from various sources within the supply chain, including suppliers, manufacturers, warehouses, transportation providers, and retailers. This data encompasses everything from inventory levels and order statuses to transportation schedules and customer demand forecasts. By integrating this data into a centralized platform, LIS enables real-time visibility into the entire logistics network, facilitating better coordination and planning across all stages of the supply chain.

One of the primary benefits of logistics information systems is their ability to improve operational efficiency. By automating routine tasks such as order processing, inventory management, and shipment tracking, these systems reduce the likelihood of errors and delays. Automated alerts and notifications help logistics managers proactively address potential disruptions, such as delays in shipments or shortages in inventory, thereby minimizing their impact on overall supply chain performance.

Moreover, logistics information systems enhance decision-making capabilities through advanced analytics and reporting functionalities. These systems can analyse historical data and perform predictive analytics to forecast demand trends, optimize inventory levels, and identify opportunities for cost savings. By providing actionable insights into supply chain operations, LIS empower logistics managers to make informed decisions that drive efficiency, reduce costs, and improve customer service levels.

In addition to internal operational benefits, logistics information systems facilitate collaboration and communication across supply chain partners. Cloud-based LIS platforms enable real-time data sharing and collaboration among suppliers, manufacturers, distributors, and retailers, fostering greater transparency and responsiveness. This collaborative approach not only strengthens relationships between stakeholders but also enhances the agility of the supply chain in responding to changes in market demand or unforeseen disruptions.

Furthermore, logistics information systems contribute to regulatory compliance and sustainability initiatives within the logistics industry. By maintaining accurate records and documentation of shipments, LIS help ensure adherence to international trade regulations, customs requirements, and environmental standards. This capability is particularly critical for global supply chains that involve cross-border shipments and compliance with diverse regulatory frameworks.

Overall, logistics information systems represent a cornerstone of modern supply chain management, driving operational efficiency, informed decision-making, collaboration, and compliance. As technologies such as artificial intelligence, machine learning, and Internet of Things continue to evolve, the capabilities of LIS are expected to expand further, offering new opportunities for optimizing supply chain performance and meeting the evolving demands of global commerce.

Logistics Information Systems (LIS) are sophisticated digital platforms built on integrated software infrastructure designed to streamline and optimize logistics operations through smart management and data-driven decision-making. These systems are pivotal for businesses engaged in supply chain management, providing comprehensive tools to manage various facets including procurement, storage, order fulfillment, shipment tracking, and transportation logistics.

The importance of Logistics Information Systems lies in their ability to ensure a seamless flow of information across the entire supply chain ecosystem. By integrating stakeholders such as manufacturers, logistics service providers (LSPs), 3PL partners, carriers, freight forwarders, and last-mile operators, LIS facilitates enhanced visibility, transparency, and efficiency in logistics operations. This integration enables real-time data sharing and collaboration, which are essential for timely decision-making and proactive management of logistics processes.

Depending on specific operational needs, Logistics Information Systems incorporate diverse components tailored to manage different aspects of logistics. These components may include Transport Management Systems (TMS), Last Mile Delivery Management Systems, Shipment Tracking Systems, Freight Procurement Systems, Container Tracking Systems, and more. Each component plays a crucial role in optimizing its respective area of logistics, contributing to overall operational efficiency and cost-effectiveness.

Incorporating advanced computing technologies such as Artificial Intelligence (AI), Machine Learning (ML), Data Analytics, Big Data, and Data Visualization, LIS enhances its functionalities by offering predictive analytics, demand forecasting, route optimization, and inventory management capabilities. These technologies empower logistics managers to make informed decisions, optimize resource allocation, and improve service levels.

Real-time monitoring and control are fundamental capabilities of Logistics Information Systems. They enable stakeholders to track shipments, monitor inventory levels, and manage logistics operations remotely and in real-time. This capability is crucial for responding swiftly to disruptions, adjusting routes, or reallocating resources to ensure efficient delivery and customer satisfaction.

Moreover, Logistics Information Systems can seamlessly integrate with existing enterprise systems such as Warehouse Management Systems (WMS), Order Management Systems (OMS), Enterprise Resource Planning (ERP), and Customer Management Systems (CMS). This integration provides a centralized dashboard-like interface for comprehensive management, monitoring, communication, and collaboration across all logistics functions. It facilitates cross-functional coordination, reduces redundancies, and enhances overall organizational efficiency.

The role of a Logistics Information System (LIS) extends beyond mere data management; it serves as a pivotal tool in modern supply chain management, offering centralized records and reports that aggregate, analyse, validate, and visualize data from various supply chain components. This capability is essential for strategic decision-making, enabling businesses to gain comprehensive insights into their operations and optimize their logistics processes.

One of the primary functions of LIS is to empower businesses to deliver optimized services and manage efficient deliveries that enhance customer satisfaction while minimizing costs. By integrating functionalities such as order fulfillment, shipment tracking, and real-time status updates for shipments, riders, or orders, LIS ensures smooth operational workflows. This real-time visibility and control over logistics operations are crucial for meeting customer expectations and maintaining service levels.

Advanced LIS incorporates dynamic optimization capabilities, enabling route planning based on multiple constraints such as traffic conditions, delivery priorities, and resource availability. This feature enhances operational efficiency by ensuring optimal route selection and resource allocation, thereby reducing transportation costs and improving delivery timelines. Furthermore, LIS facilitates on-the-go order consolidation, which enhances efficiency by combining multiple orders into cohesive delivery routes.

Customer experience (CX) is significantly enhanced through LIS functionalities that provide dynamic Estimated Time of Arrival (ETA) updates. These updates enable businesses to communicate accurate delivery times to customers, fostering transparency and trust. In cases of delays or unforeseen circumstances, automated alerts and notifications are generated, keeping customers informed about the status of their shipments and the reasons for any disruptions. This proactive communication helps manage customer expectations and mitigate dissatisfaction.

In addition to operational efficiencies and customer communication, LIS plays a critical role in digitalizing documentation and automating processes such as customs clearance. By securely handling online documents and automating compliance procedures, LIS reduces paperwork, minimizes errors, and accelerates the clearance process. This digital transformation not only improves efficiency but also enhances regulatory compliance and reduces administrative overheads associated with logistics operations.

The Logistics Information System (LIS) comprises several critical components that collectively streamline and optimize various facets of logistics operations within businesses. One of these components is the Transport Management System (TMS), which automates transportation processes. TMS solutions provide a centralized platform for planning, monitoring, tracking, and managing logistics operations. By offering a unified dashboard, TMS allows enterprises to efficiently oversee logistics partners and gain comprehensive visibility into their logistics operations, thereby enhancing overall efficiency and cost-effectiveness.

Another essential component of LIS is the Last Mile Delivery Management System, which focuses on managing the final leg of delivery from the warehouse to the end customer. Integrated with existing ERP systems, this system facilitates faster deliveries through smart routing and zone/geofence-based driver allocation. By managing orders, delivery professionals, and customer communications from a single interface, businesses can reduce costs associated with last-mile logistics while ensuring high standards of customer experience.

Shipment Tracking System is another pivotal component that enables businesses to track and monitor shipments in real-time, providing granular updates on the movement of goods throughout the supply chain. This capability not only enhances operational visibility but also helps in minimizing incidental costs like detention and demurrage. Automated alerts and notifications, including predictive and analytical insights, further empower businesses to proactively manage risks and potential delays, improving overall logistics efficiency and customer service.

Freight Procurement System within LIS automates the procurement process for freight services, managing RFQs, shipping lines, spot inquiries, bookings, and transactions. By engaging with multiple vendors and leveraging competitive bidding, businesses can secure optimal shipping rates and gain market intelligence for effective rate management. This component significantly reduces freight costs, streamlines invoicing, and enhances the efficiency of freight management operations.

For containerized shipments, Container Tracking System provides real-time location tracking and visibility. It consolidates data from various sources to offer a comprehensive view of container movements, supporting efficient logistics planning and management. This system's customizable dashboard allows businesses to monitor container status and ensure timely delivery, thereby improving supply chain reliability and responsiveness.

End-to-end Delivery Orchestration and Management System integrates multiple logistics functions such as route planning, order management, optimization, and 3PL management into a cohesive platform. It spans across the entire supply chain from the First Mile to the Last Mile, employing AI-driven routines to optimize operations, enhance visibility, and streamline logistics processes. This comprehensive approach enables businesses to achieve operational efficiency and meet customer demands effectively.

Dispatch Management System focuses on coordinating the movement of goods and transportation assets within the supply chain. It encompasses planning, managing, tracking, and controlling logistics operations to ensure accurate and timely deliveries at minimal costs. This system plays a crucial role in optimizing on-field performance, managing logistics assets efficiently, and maintaining operational consistency across the supply chain.

Analytics and Reporting capabilities within LIS enable businesses to gather, process, and leverage organizational data for informed decision-making. This component generates data-rich reports across various system components and time frames, facilitating agility and reliability in business operations. By visualizing and exporting data in multiple formats, businesses can derive actionable insights, drive continuous improvement, and foster data-driven growth within their logistics operations.

Finally, the 3PL/Courier Aggregator Management System centralizes the management of multiple logistics partners from a single dashboard. It enables businesses to optimize partner selection, negotiate competitive rates, and enforce service standardization across different logistics providers. By expanding serviceability and enhancing operational efficiency through effective partner management, this component supports business growth and competitiveness in the logistics industry. Together, these components form an integrated Logistics Information System that plays a crucial role in modernizing logistics operations, enhancing efficiency, and delivering superior customer experiences.

Implementing Logistics Information Systems (LIS) presents several challenges that businesses must navigate to ensure successful integration and operation within their logistics operations [21]. One of the primary challenges is the integration with existing systems. Many businesses operate with legacy systems that have been developed and customized over years to suit specific operational needs. Integrating LIS with these systems requires careful planning to ensure compatibility and seamless data exchange. This process can be complex, as different systems may have varying data formats, protocols, and interfaces. Ensuring that LIS integrates effectively without disrupting ongoing operations is crucial to maintain continuity and efficiency.

Cost considerations represent another significant challenge in implementing LIS. The upfront investment in acquiring and implementing the system, along with ongoing maintenance and support costs, can be substantial. Businesses need to evaluate the return on investment (ROI) of implementing LIS against the benefits it promises to deliver, such as improved operational efficiency, reduced costs, and enhanced customer service. Cost-benefit analysis plays a crucial role in decision-making, as companies weigh the potential long-term gains against immediate financial outlay [21].

Change management is another critical aspect of implementing LIS successfully. Introducing new technologies and processes often requires a cultural shift within the organization. Employees may resist changes due to fear of the unknown, reluctance to learn new systems, or concerns about job security. Effective change management involves clear communication about the benefits of LIS, providing training programs to upskill employees, and addressing concerns proactively. Leadership support and involvement are essential to champion the implementation process and demonstrate the benefits of adopting LIS for both the organization and its employees.

Training employees to use LIS effectively is crucial for maximizing its benefits. Without adequate training, employees may struggle to adapt to new workflows and functionalities, leading to underutilization of the system's capabilities. Training programs should be comprehensive, covering not only technical aspects but also operational procedures and best practices for leveraging LIS to streamline logistics operations. Investing in continuous training and support ensures that employees are proficient in using LIS and can contribute to its successful implementation and ongoing optimization.

While Logistics Information Systems offer significant benefits such as enhanced efficiency, improved decision-making, and better customer service, their implementation is not without challenges. Overcoming integration complexities, managing costs effectively, navigating change within the organization, and ensuring comprehensive employee training are critical steps in successfully implementing LIS. By addressing these challenges systematically and proactively, businesses can harness the full potential of LIS to transform their logistics operations and gain a competitive edge in the marketplace [21].

Implementing Logistics Information Systems (LIS) successfully requires adherence to best practices that ensure clarity, stakeholder involvement, and comprehensive training. Firstly, defining a clear project scope and objectives is essential. This involves outlining the specific goals of implementing LIS, such as improving operational efficiency, enhancing visibility in the supply chain, or reducing logistics costs. Clear objectives help in setting realistic expectations, establishing a timeline for implementation, and aligning stakeholders across the organization. This clarity ensures that all parties involved understand the purpose of LIS and are committed to achieving its goals.

Stakeholder involvement is another critical best practice for successful LIS implementation. Engaging relevant departments such as IT, supply chain management, operations, finance, and customer service ensures that diverse perspectives are considered during the planning and execution phases. Involving stakeholders from the outset allows for better decision-making, as different teams can contribute their expertise and insights. It also fosters ownership of the project among stakeholders, increasing their commitment to supporting the implementation process and addressing any challenges that may arise along the way.

Comprehensive training programs are indispensable for ensuring smooth adoption and effective utilization of LIS within the organization. Investing in training initiatives tailored to different user groups, from frontline logistics staff to senior management, is crucial. Training should cover not only the technical aspects of using the LIS but also operational procedures, best practices, and troubleshooting techniques. This equips employees with the knowledge and skills needed to navigate the new system confidently, reducing resistance to change and accelerating the integration of LIS into daily operations.

Moreover, ongoing support and communication are integral to the success of LIS implementation. Providing continuous support after the initial rollout helps address user queries, resolve technical issues promptly, and fine-tune system configurations based on feedback from users. Clear communication about the benefits of LIS and its impact on workflows encourages buy-in from employees and reinforces the organization's commitment to leveraging technology for strategic advantage.

Lastly, monitoring and evaluating the implementation process are essential best practices. Regularly assessing progress against predefined objectives allows stakeholders to identify any deviations from the plan and take corrective actions as necessary. This iterative approach enables continuous improvement and ensures that LIS aligns with evolving business needs and industry trends over time.

The Distribution Network

The distribution network has evolved significantly in the 21st century, largely driven by the shift from traditional in-person shopping to the dominance of e-commerce [19]. This transformation has not only reshaped consumer behaviour but also posed new challenges to logistics management. Today, supply chains face mounting pressure as the variety and volume of goods increase, raw materials become more diverse, and consumer expectations for faster delivery options escalate. This has created a complex operational environment where logistics efficiency is crucial for maintaining competitive advantage in a consumer-driven market.

Fundamentally, a distribution network encompasses the infrastructure and processes involved in the movement of physical goods from their point of origin to the end consumer. It includes storage facilities, transportation routes, and logistics systems tailored to meet specific business needs. Larger corporations like Amazon and Apple exemplify sophisticated distribution networks designed to handle vast quantities of diverse products while meeting stringent delivery timelines across global markets. The effectiveness of these networks directly impacts customer satisfaction, product availability, and overall operational efficiency.

Logistics, closely intertwined with distribution, refers to the comprehensive planning, execution, and control of operations involved in the supply, transaction, and transportation of goods. Key logistics functions encompass a wide range of activities such as bulk shipments, packaging, transportation management, order tracking, inventory management, and ensuring product quality through measures like temperature control and security protocols. Effective logistics management ensures smooth physical distribution of goods, which is foundational to the success of any distribution network [19].

Employing a distribution management system (DMS) is critical for optimizing the distribution network and overcoming logistical challenges. A well-implemented DMS enhances operational efficiency by minimizing wastage, reducing storage costs, and enabling just-in-time inventory management. By streamlining logistics operations, DMS solutions also facilitate faster order processing and delivery, thereby improving overall customer satisfaction and loyalty [19]. Moreover, these systems enhance visibility across the supply chain, providing real-time insights to internal teams and external stakeholders alike.

Despite the benefits, implementing and maintaining an efficient distribution network and DMS comes with its own set of challenges. Natural disruptions such as severe weather events, raw material shortages, or global pandemics can disrupt supply chains and impact distribution capabilities. Human factors like protests, strikes, or geopolitical conflicts can also cause significant logistical disruptions. Moreover, transportation disruptions such as vehicle breakdowns, maintenance delays, or regulatory compliance issues further complicate logistics operations. Economic fluctuations, including recessions or sudden shifts in market demand, add another layer of complexity to maintaining a resilient distribution network capable of adapting to changing conditions.

A distribution network serves as a crucial element of a company's strategic framework, essential for ensuring products reach customers efficiently and cost-effectively, thereby enhancing profit margins. Depending on the nature of the product and the geographic spread of customers, distribution networks can vary significantly in complexity. At its core, a distribution network encompasses the pathways through which goods move from production facilities to end consumers.

In a comprehensive distribution network, goods typically flow through multiple stages, starting from manufacturers to wholesalers, then to retailers, and finally reaching consumers. Each stage may involve its own distribution network optimized for its specific role in the supply chain. For instance, manufacturers may operate centralized distribution centres to serve multiple wholesalers or retailers, while retailers themselves may manage distribution centres to cater directly to local consumers. This multi-tiered approach ensures that products are efficiently managed and delivered at each step of the supply chain.

The effectiveness of a distribution network hinges on two critical factors: proximity to consumers and the quality of its infrastructure. Distribution centres strategically located close to major consumer markets minimize transportation costs and reduce delivery times, enhancing customer satisfaction. Furthermore, the infrastructure within these distribution centres, including storage facilities, handling equipment, and transportation logistics, is tailored to meet specific operational requirements and to efficiently manage the flow of products throughout the network.

Managing a distribution network entails careful planning and coordination across various aspects of operations, including equipment procurement, staffing, implementation of information technology systems, and management of transportation fleets. Companies must make strategic decisions regarding the configuration of their distribution network, choosing between centralized hubs that serve as distribution points for broader regions (hub-and-spoke model) or decentralized networks where smaller distribution centres are dispersed closer to consumer clusters.

Distribution networks primarily function within the post-manufacturing stage of the supply chain, where they play a pivotal role in moving finished goods to end users. This involves meticulous handling of inventory, efficient order fulfillment processes, and adherence to delivery schedules to meet customer expectations. Moreover, an effective distribution network expands a company's reach, enabling it to penetrate new geographic markets and seize growth opportunities.

Ultimately, a well-designed distribution network not only accelerates the speed at which products reach consumers but also optimizes operational efficiencies across the supply chain. By enhancing logistical capabilities and adapting to the complexities of modern supply chains, companies can establish competitive advantages in delivering superior customer experiences while maximizing profitability [19].

Chapter 5

Maintaining Operational Procedures for Transport and Logistics Enterprises

In the realm of transport and logistics enterprises, operational procedures play a pivotal role in ensuring efficiency, cost-effectiveness, and overall success. Logistics, encompassing various facets such as warehousing, transportation, and information management, is crucial for the seamless flow of goods within the supply chain [22]. Supply chain management integrates marketing and manufacturing with distribution functions to enhance competitive advantage [22]. As international trade burgeons, the environmental implications of transport and logistics operations become increasingly significant, necessitating a thorough understanding and integration of sustainability practices into business operations [23].

Operational procedures for transport and logistics enterprises encompass a structured framework of guidelines, protocols, and practices designed to facilitate the efficient and safe movement of goods from suppliers to consumers. These procedures are essential for ensuring that logistical operations run smoothly, meet regulatory requirements, and achieve optimal performance in terms of cost-effectiveness, reliability, and customer satisfaction.

Key Components of Operational Procedures:

- Order Processing and Fulfillment: This involves the systematic handling of customer orders, including order receipt, processing, picking, packing, and shipping. Standardized procedures ensure accuracy, timeliness, and traceability throughout the order fulfillment process.

- Inventory Management: Effective inventory management procedures govern the storage, tracking, and replenishment of goods within warehouses or distribution centres. These procedures optimize inventory levels to meet demand while minimizing carrying costs and stockouts.

- Transportation Planning and Execution: Procedures for transportation involve route planning, carrier selection, scheduling, and dispatching vehicles or modes of transport. They aim to maximize vehicle utilization, minimize transit times, and ensure on-time delivery while adhering to safety and regulatory standards.

- Warehousing and Distribution: Operational procedures for warehousing and distribution cover receiving, storage, and outbound processing of goods. They include procedures for inventory control, space utilization, order picking methods (e.g., batch picking, zone picking), and loading/unloading operations.

- Safety and Security Protocols: These procedures focus on ensuring the safety of personnel, facilities, and cargo. They encompass guidelines for handling hazardous materials, securing facilities against theft or unauthorized access, and adhering to occupational health and safety regulations.

- Quality Control and Assurance: Procedures for quality control aim to maintain product integrity throughout the supply chain. This includes inspections, testing procedures, and compliance checks to ensure goods meet specified quality standards before shipment to customers.

- Customer Service and Communication: Operational procedures emphasize clear communication with customers regarding order status, delivery schedules, and any potential issues or delays. Customer service protocols ensure prompt resolution of inquiries or complaints to enhance customer satisfaction.

- Compliance and Regulatory Requirements: Enterprises must adhere to various regulatory requirements and industry standards governing transport and logistics operations. Operational procedures include measures to ensure compliance with laws, regulations, permits, and environmental standards.

Importance of operational procedures:
- Efficiency: Standardized procedures streamline operations, reduce inefficiencies, and minimize costs associated with errors or delays in logistics processes.
- Consistency: Consistent procedures ensure that tasks are performed uniformly across different locations or teams, promoting reliability in service delivery and customer experience.
- Risk Management: Defined procedures mitigate risks associated with inventory loss, transportation delays, safety incidents, and regulatory non-compliance.
- Continuous Improvement: By documenting procedures and monitoring performance metrics, enterprises can identify areas for improvement and implement corrective actions to enhance operational effectiveness over time.

In today's dynamic business environment, transport and logistics enterprises must also focus on adaptability and innovation within their operational procedures. This includes leveraging technology (e.g., GPS tracking, warehouse management systems), adopting sustainable practices (e.g., green logistics), and responding agilely to market changes and customer expectations.

Operational procedures form the backbone of transport and logistics enterprises, providing a structured framework for efficient, safe, and compliant movement of goods. By establishing clear guidelines, embracing technology, and fostering a culture of continuous improvement, enterprises can optimize their logistics operations and maintain a competitive edge in the global marketplace.

At its core, the focus of these systems is to ensure that products are transported timely, safely, and cost-effectively, meeting the demands of customers while optimizing resource utilization across various stages of the supply chain.

The primary focus of transport and logistics systems is on the seamless coordination of activities involved in transporting goods. This encompasses planning routes, selecting appropriate modes of transport (such as trucks, ships, airplanes, or trains), and executing the movement of goods from origin to destination. Operations must consider factors like distance, terrain, infrastructure availability, regulatory requirements, and customer delivery expectations to achieve efficient logistics management.

Resources: Effective operation of transport and logistics systems relies heavily on a range of resources. These include physical assets like vehicles, warehouses, and distribution centres, as well as human resources such as logistics managers, warehouse staff, drivers, and administrative personnel. Furthermore, technological resources such as transportation management systems (TMS), GPS tracking, inventory management software, and communication tools play a crucial role in enhancing operational efficiency, real-time monitoring, and decision-making capabilities within the logistics framework.

Management: Management within transport and logistics systems involves overseeing the entire supply chain process to ensure smooth operations and optimal performance. This includes strategic planning, resource allocation, risk management, and continuous improvement initiatives. Logistics managers are tasked with coordinating logistics activities, optimizing routes to minimize costs and transit times, negotiating contracts with carriers and suppliers, and maintaining high standards of service delivery and customer satisfaction. Effective management also entails addressing challenges such as disruptions in supply, changing regulatory landscapes, and technological advancements that impact logistics operations.

Workplace Operating Systems: Workplace operating systems in transport and logistics enterprises encompass the procedural frameworks and operational protocols that guide day-to-day activities. These systems ensure consistency, compliance with safety standards, and adherence to operational procedures across different teams and locations. They include protocols for order processing, inventory management, warehouse operations, transportation scheduling, safety procedures, quality assurance, and customer service. By standardizing workflows and integrating technology where applicable, workplace operating systems streamline operations, reduce errors, and enhance overall productivity within logistics environments.

In essence, the focus of operation within transport and logistics systems revolves around efficiently managing the movement of goods through strategic planning, resource utilization, and effective management practices. By leveraging a combination of physical, human, and technological resources, and implementing robust workplace operating systems, enterprises can optimize their logistics operations, mitigate risks, and meet the dynamic demands of global supply chains effectively.

Transport and Equipment Applications, Capacities, Configurations, Safety Hazards and Control Mechanisms

Transport and equipment applications in logistics and supply chain operations encompass a wide range of vehicles, machinery, and technologies designed to facilitate the movement and handling of goods across various stages of the supply chain. These applications vary in capacities, configurations, and safety considerations, each tailored to specific operational needs and environmental conditions. Here's an overview of key aspects related to transport and equipment in logistics:

Applications and Types: Transport and equipment in logistics include a diverse array of vehicles and machinery used for different purposes:

1. Road Transport: Trucks, vans, and specialized vehicles (e.g., refrigerated trucks, tanker trucks) are commonly used for land transport, offering flexibility in delivering goods door-to-door.

2. Rail Transport: Trains and railcars are utilized for long-distance freight transport, offering high capacity and energy efficiency over land routes.

3. Maritime Transport: Cargo ships, container vessels, and bulk carriers transport goods across oceans and seas, handling large volumes of cargo in standardized containers.

4. Air Transport: Cargo planes and freighter aircraft provide fast and efficient transport for time-sensitive goods over long distances.

5. Material Handling Equipment: Forklifts, conveyors, pallet jacks, and automated guided vehicles (AGVs) are essential for loading, unloading, and moving goods within warehouses and distribution centres.

Capacities and Configurations: The capacities and configurations of transport and equipment vary based on the type of goods being transported, operational requirements, and infrastructure constraints:

- Vehicle Capacities: Trucks and ships have varying load capacities measured in weight (tonnes) or volume (cubic meters), accommodating different types of cargo from bulk commodities to specialized goods.

- Containerization: Standardized containers (e.g., 20-foot and 40-foot containers) enable efficient intermodal transport, facilitating seamless transfer between different modes of transportation (e.g., ship to truck).

- Handling Equipment: Forklifts and AGVs come in different sizes and lifting capacities to handle diverse loads, from small packages to heavy pallets.

Safety Hazards and Control Mechanisms: Transport and equipment operations pose inherent safety hazards that require robust control mechanisms to mitigate risks to personnel, cargo, and infrastructure:

- Traffic Accidents: Road transport involves risks such as collisions, rollovers, and hazardous material spills. Safety measures include driver training, vehicle maintenance, and compliance with traffic laws.

- Loading and Unloading: Manual handling during loading/unloading poses risks of injuries and damage to goods. Use of proper lifting techniques, mechanized equipment, and safety protocols (e.g., personal protective equipment) minimizes risks.

- Material Handling Operations: Forklift operations in warehouses require adherence to safety protocols, including operational training, designated traffic lanes, and pedestrian safety measures.

- Equipment Failures: Mechanical failures in vehicles or machinery can lead to accidents or operational disruptions. Preventive maintenance, equipment inspections, and emergency response plans mitigate risks associated with equipment malfunctions.

Control Mechanisms: Effective control mechanisms ensure safe transport and equipment operations:

- Safety Regulations: Compliance with national and international safety standards (e.g., International Maritime Organization regulations for shipping) establishes minimum safety requirements.

- Training and Certification: Operator training programs certify personnel to operate specific equipment safely and proficiently.

- Technology Integration: Advanced technologies such as GPS tracking, telematics, and automated safety systems enhance real-time monitoring of vehicle operations, promoting safer driving practices and proactive maintenance.

- Risk Assessments: Regular risk assessments identify potential hazards and implement preventive measures to mitigate risks in transport and equipment operations.

Transport and equipment applications, along with their capacities, configurations, safety hazards, and control mechanisms, have a profound impact on operational procedures within transport and logistics enterprises. These factors influence how goods are transported, stored, and handled throughout the supply chain, directly affecting efficiency, safety, and overall operational effectiveness.

Impact on Operational Procedures:
- **Efficiency in Transport and Handling:**
  - **Applications and Types:** The choice of transport modes (road, rail, maritime, air) and equipment types (trucks, ships, forklifts, AGVs) determines the efficiency of transporting goods from suppliers to customers. Operational procedures must align transport and equipment selection with the specific requirements of goods, distances, and delivery timelines.
  - **Capacities and Configurations:** Understanding the capacities (volume, weight) and configurations (e.g., containerization) of transport and equipment is crucial. This knowledge allows for optimal utilization of resources, minimizing empty space and maximizing cargo volume or weight capacity per trip.

- **Safety Considerations and Control Mechanisms:**
  - **Safety Hazards:** Transport and equipment operations pose various safety hazards, such as vehicle accidents, material handling injuries, and equipment malfunctions. These hazards can disrupt operations, cause injuries, damage goods, and incur financial losses.
  - **Control Mechanisms:** Implementing robust control mechanisms, including safety protocols, training programs, equipment inspections, and compliance with safety regulations, is essential. Operational procedures

must integrate these controls to mitigate risks and ensure a safe working environment for personnel and the protection of assets.

- **Regulatory Compliance:**

  - **Impact on Procedures:** Regulatory requirements, such as transportation laws, environmental standards, and occupational safety regulations, directly influence operational procedures. Compliance with these regulations dictates how transport and equipment are managed, maintained, and operated within legal boundaries.

  - **Adaptation and Documentation:** Operational procedures must adapt to regulatory changes, ensuring that transport and equipment practices align with updated standards. Documentation of compliance efforts, audits, and adherence to safety protocols is integral to maintaining operational continuity and regulatory compliance.

- **Operational Efficiency and Cost Management:**

  - **Efficiency Gains:** Properly configured transport and equipment applications contribute to operational efficiency by reducing transportation costs, minimizing delays, and optimizing resource utilization (e.g., fuel efficiency, labour productivity).

  - **Cost Management:** Effective control mechanisms help manage operational costs associated with maintenance, repairs, insurance, and compliance. Operational procedures should incorporate cost-effective strategies to optimize transport routes, reduce downtime, and enhance overall logistics performance.

- **Integration of Technology:**

  - **Technological Advancements:** Integration of advanced technologies (e.g., GPS tracking, WMS, TMS, RFID) enhances operational procedures by providing real-time visibility, data analytics for performance monitoring, and automation of routine tasks.

  - **Impact on Efficiency:** Technology-driven solutions improve decision-making, optimize route planning, and streamline inventory management. Operational procedures benefit from enhanced transparency, accuracy, and responsiveness to customer demands.

Planning and Developing Operational Procedures

Developing and maintaining operational procedures for transport and logistics enterprises requires a systematic approach to identify and confirm processes that need development or modification. This includes:

Step 1: Process Identification

- **Engage Relevant Personnel**: The first step is to engage with key personnel across different departments within the transport and logistics enterprise. This includes operations managers, logistics coordinators, fleet managers, and other stakeholders who are directly involved in executing and overseeing operational processes.

- **Process Mapping**: Conduct thorough process mapping sessions where current operational procedures are documented in detail. This involves identifying every step involved in various processes such as order processing, shipment handling, warehouse management, transportation scheduling, and delivery logistics.

- **Gather Input and Feedback**: During process mapping, gather input from frontline staff who execute these processes daily. Their insights are invaluable in understanding practical challenges, inefficiencies, and areas needing improvement.

Step 2: Validation and Confirmation

- **Review Current Procedures**: Once processes are mapped, review existing operational procedures against industry standards, regulatory requirements, and best practices. Identify gaps, redundancies, or areas where procedures are outdated or ineffective.

- **Identify Areas for Development or Modification**: Based on the review, pinpoint specific processes that require development (for new procedures) or modification (for existing procedures). This could include improving efficiency, enhancing safety protocols, reducing costs, or addressing compliance issues.

- **Prioritize Changes**: Prioritize the identified areas based on criticality, impact on operations, and alignment with strategic objectives. Some changes may be urgent (e.g., addressing safety concerns), while others may be aimed at optimizing efficiency or enhancing customer service.

Step 3: Confirmation with Relevant Personnel and Business Units

- **Stakeholder Consultation**: Engage relevant personnel and business units in discussions to confirm the identified processes requiring development or modification. This ensures alignment with organizational goals, operational feasibility, and resource availability.

- **Communicate Proposed Changes**: Clearly communicate proposed changes to all stakeholders involved. Provide detailed explanations of why changes are necessary, expected benefits, and how these changes align with broader business objectives.

- **Obtain Buy-in and Feedback**: Seek buy-in from key stakeholders, including managers, supervisors, and frontline employees. Address any concerns or resistance by highlighting potential improvements in efficiency, safety enhancements, or other benefits resulting from the proposed changes.

- **Document Agreement**: Document agreements reached during stakeholder consultations. This includes capturing feedback, modifications based on discussions, and consensus on the final scope and implementation timeline for developing or modifying operational procedures.

Step 4: Implementation and Monitoring

- **Develop New Procedures**: Develop detailed operational procedures based on the agreed-upon changes. Document step-by-step instructions, roles and responsibilities, decision points, and key performance indicators (KPIs) for monitoring effectiveness.

- **Training and Awareness**: Conduct training sessions to ensure all personnel understand the new procedures. Provide training materials, conduct workshops, and offer hands-on demonstrations where applicable. Build awareness of the benefits of the changes and how they contribute to overall organizational success.

- **Monitor Implementation**: Monitor the implementation of new procedures closely. Track performance metrics to evaluate effectiveness, identify any teething issues, and make adjustments as necessary.

- **Continuous Improvement**: Establish a framework for continuous improvement. Regularly review operational procedures, gather feedback from stakeholders, and make refinements based on lessons learned and changing business needs.

Process identification within a transport and logistics enterprise involves several critical steps aimed at understanding and documenting current operational procedures in detail. Here's a comprehensive explanation:

Engage Relevant Personnel

The initial step in process identification is to engage with key personnel across different departments within the organization. This includes operations managers, logistics coordinators, fleet managers, and other stakeholders who have direct involvement in executing and overseeing operational processes. Engaging these stakeholders is crucial as they possess in-depth knowledge of day-to-day operations, challenges faced, and potential areas for improvement. Their perspectives provide valuable insights into the practical aspects of operations, ensuring that all relevant processes are identified and understood comprehensively.

Process Mapping

Once relevant personnel are engaged, the next step is to conduct thorough process mapping sessions. Process mapping involves documenting current operational procedures in detail. This includes identifying and mapping out every step involved in various processes such as order processing, shipment handling, warehouse management, transportation scheduling, and delivery logistics. The goal is to create visual representations or flowcharts that depict how each process unfolds, from initiation to completion. This exercise helps in visualizing the sequence of activities, dependencies between different steps, and potential bottlenecks or inefficiencies within the processes.

Gather Input and Feedback

During the process mapping sessions, it is essential to gather input and feedback from frontline staff who are directly responsible for executing these processes on a daily basis. Frontline staff, including warehouse workers, drivers, logistics coordinators, and other operational personnel, offer invaluable insights into the practical challenges they encounter, inefficiencies they observe, and suggestions for improvement. Their firsthand knowledge plays a critical role in identifying areas where processes may not align with operational realities or where there are opportunities to streamline workflows, reduce costs, enhance safety, or improve customer service.

Step 2 in developing and maintaining operational procedures for transport and logistics enterprises involves validation and confirmation of identified processes. Here's a detailed explanation of each sub-step:

Review Current Procedures

The first sub-step in validation and confirmation is to thoroughly review the current operational procedures that have been mapped out. This review process is critical as it evaluates existing procedures against industry standards, regulatory requirements, and best practices. It involves assessing whether the documented procedures align with established benchmarks and whether they comply with relevant laws and regulations governing the transport and logistics industry. The review also identifies any gaps, redundancies, or areas where procedures may be outdated or ineffective in meeting current operational needs. By conducting a comprehensive review, organizations can pinpoint areas that require improvement or updating to ensure operational efficiency and compliance.

Identify Areas for Development or Modification

Based on the review of current procedures, the next step is to identify specific areas that require either development of new procedures or modification of existing ones. This identification process focuses on improving operational effectiveness, enhancing safety protocols, reducing costs, addressing compliance issues, or meeting strategic objectives. Areas for development could include implementing new technologies to streamline processes, introducing standardized safety protocols for handling hazardous materials, or revising inventory management procedures to optimize warehouse operations. Modification may involve refining existing procedures to eliminate inefficiencies, integrating new regulatory requirements, or adapting to changes in customer expectations or market conditions.

Prioritize Changes

Once areas for development or modification have been identified, the next critical task is to prioritize these changes. Prioritization involves assessing the criticality of each identified area, evaluating its potential impact on operations, and aligning it with strategic objectives. Urgent changes, such as addressing safety concerns or regulatory compliance issues, may be prioritized higher due to their immediate impact on business operations and legal obligations. Similarly, changes aimed at optimizing efficiency, reducing operational costs, or enhancing customer service may be prioritized based on their potential to deliver significant benefits to the organization. Prioritization ensures that resources are allocated effectively and that changes are implemented in a systematic manner that aligns with organizational priorities and goals.

Step 3 in developing and maintaining operational procedures for transport and logistics enterprises focuses on confirming identified processes through consultation with relevant personnel and business units. Here's a detailed explanation of each sub-step:

Stakeholder Consultation

The first sub-step involves engaging relevant personnel and business units in discussions to validate and confirm the identified processes requiring development or modification. This consultation phase is crucial as it ensures that proposed changes align with organizational goals, operational feasibility, and resource availability. Stakeholders typically include operations managers, logistics coordinators, fleet managers, and other key personnel who have direct involvement or oversight of the processes in question. By involving these stakeholders early in the process, organizations can gather diverse perspectives, identify potential challenges, and assess the impact of proposed changes on day-to-day operations.

Communicate Proposed Changes

Clear and effective communication of proposed changes is essential during this phase. Stakeholders need to be informed about why changes are necessary, the expected benefits, and how these changes align with broader business objectives. Detailed explanations should outline how the proposed modifications will address identified gaps, improve operational efficiency, enhance safety protocols, or ensure compliance with regulatory requirements. Transparent communication helps build understanding and support among stakeholders, fostering a collaborative approach to developing or modifying operational procedures.

Obtain Buy-in and Feedback

Seeking buy-in from key stakeholders is critical to the success of implementing operational changes. This sub-step involves actively engaging with managers, supervisors, and frontline employees to obtain their support for the proposed changes. It's important to address any concerns or resistance by addressing potential implications, clarifying misconceptions, and highlighting the benefits of the proposed modifications. Feedback from stakeholders should be carefully considered to incorporate valuable insights and perspectives into the final decision-making process. This iterative approach ensures that proposed changes are well-received and aligned with the operational realities and needs of the organization.

Document Agreement

Documenting agreements reached during stakeholder consultations is the final sub-step in this process. This includes capturing feedback received from stakeholders, modifications made based on discussions, and consensus on the final scope and implementation timeline for developing or modifying operational procedures. Documentation should be comprehensive and transparent, outlining agreed-upon changes, responsibilities, and any action items required for implementation. Clear documentation serves as a reference point for all stakeholders involved, ensuring accountability, tracking progress, and facilitating effective communication throughout the implementation phase.

Step 4 in developing and maintaining operational procedures for transport and logistics enterprises focuses on the implementation and ongoing monitoring of newly developed or modified procedures. Here's a detailed explanation of each sub-step:

Develop New Procedures

The first sub-step involves developing detailed operational procedures based on the agreed-upon changes from previous steps. This includes documenting step-by-step instructions that outline how the revised processes should be executed. Each procedure should clearly define roles and responsibilities, decision points, and key milestones or checkpoints. It's crucial to incorporate measurable metrics or Key Performance Indicators (KPIs) into the procedures to monitor their effectiveness over time. Developing comprehensive procedures ensures consistency in operations and provides a clear roadmap for employees to follow.

Training and Awareness

Conducting training sessions is essential to ensure that all personnel understand and are capable of implementing the new procedures effectively. Training should encompass a variety of methods, including formal sessions, workshops, hands-on demonstrations, and e-learning modules where applicable. Training materials should be comprehensive and accessible, covering not only the procedural steps but also the rationale behind the changes and their expected benefits. Building awareness among employees about how the new procedures contribute to overall organizational success helps foster buy-in and a culture of continuous improvement.

Monitor Implementation

Monitoring the implementation of new procedures is critical to identifying any initial challenges or areas needing adjustment. Organizations should establish mechanisms to track performance metrics and assess the effectiveness of the newly implemented procedures. This includes measuring KPIs related to efficiency, productivity, quality, safety, and compliance. Regular monitoring allows stakeholders to promptly address any issues that arise, provide additional support or training where necessary, and ensure that the procedures are being followed consistently across the organization.

Continuous Improvement

Establishing a framework for continuous improvement is the final sub-step in Step 4. This involves creating processes for regularly reviewing operational procedures, gathering feedback from stakeholders, and making refinements based on lessons learned and evolving business needs. Continuous improvement fosters agility and responsiveness within the organization, allowing it to adapt to changing market conditions, technological advancements, or regulatory requirements. By soliciting feedback from frontline employees, managers, and other stakeholders, organizations can identify opportunities for further optimization and enhancement of operational procedures.

Discussing and validating the scope, focus, and extent of operational procedures with affected personnel is crucial in the context of developing and maintaining operational excellence in transport and logistics enterprises for several key reasons:

Ensuring Alignment with Operational Needs

By involving affected personnel in discussions, you ensure that the operational procedures are designed to meet the specific needs and challenges faced by the organization. Frontline staff and managers who are directly involved in executing these procedures on a daily basis bring valuable insights into operational realities, constraints, and opportunities for improvement. Their input helps in shaping procedures that are practical, effective, and aligned with the operational environment.

Enhancing Practicality and Feasibility

Operational procedures that are developed without input from affected personnel may overlook critical operational nuances or practical considerations. By engaging these stakeholders, you can validate the feasibility of proposed procedures within the existing operational framework. This validation process helps in identifying potential barriers, resource constraints, or logistical challenges that need to be addressed to ensure smooth implementation and adherence to procedures.

Promoting Ownership and Accountability

Involving personnel in discussions about operational procedures fosters a sense of ownership and accountability among team members. When employees understand the rationale behind the procedures and have contributed to their development, they are more likely to adhere to them conscientiously. This ownership enhances overall operational efficiency and reliability, as employees feel empowered to take responsibility for their roles in executing the procedures effectively.

Improving Employee Buy-in and Morale

Discussions and validation sessions provide an opportunity for employees to voice their opinions, concerns, and suggestions regarding operational procedures. When their feedback is taken into account and integrated into the development process, it demonstrates that their perspectives are valued. This inclusivity contributes to higher levels of employee satisfaction, morale, and engagement, as employees feel respected and recognized for their expertise and contributions.

Driving Continuous Improvement

Continuous improvement is essential for adapting to changing market conditions, technological advancements, and customer expectations in the transport and logistics sector. Engaging affected personnel in discussions ensures that procedures remain dynamic and responsive to evolving needs. Stakeholders can identify areas for refinement or enhancement based on ongoing feedback and performance metrics, driving continuous improvement in operational efficiency and effectiveness.

Mitigating Risks and Enhancing Safety

Transport and logistics operations involve inherent risks related to safety, compliance, and regulatory requirements. By discussing procedures with safety officers, compliance managers, and other relevant personnel, you can identify and address potential risks proactively. Validating procedures ensures that safety protocols are robust, regulatory requirements are met, and risks are mitigated effectively, safeguarding both personnel and operational assets.

In terms of the key risks in transport and logistics, accidents and collisions pose significant risks in the transportation sector due to their multifaceted impacts. Primarily caused by human error, equipment malfunction, infrastructure deficiencies, or adverse weather conditions, these incidents result in dire consequences globally [24]. The foremost impact of accidents is the loss of life and physical injuries, affecting victims directly and causing emotional and economic repercussions for their families and communities. Moreover, accidents lead to substantial property damage, including vehicles, infrastructure, and cargo, necessitating costly repairs, insurance claims, and potential loss of goods. Economically, these incidents cause delivery delays, increased insurance premiums, and legal liabilities, thereby disrupting supply chains and inflating costs for businesses and consumers alike.

Infrastructure wear and tear presents another critical risk to transportation and logistics operations. As roads, bridges, railways, and ports deteriorate over time due to heavy use and environmental factors, they become less reliable, contributing to operational inefficiencies. Worn-out infrastructure results in delays and bottlenecks, impacting delivery schedules and transit times. Additionally, the increased need for maintenance incurs higher costs for both public authorities and transportation companies, potentially raising consumer prices. Moreover, compromised infrastructure poses safety risks, such as road accidents from potholes or structural failures of bridges, endangering public safety and further complicating logistics operations [24].

Environmental hazards represent a significant risk factor affecting transportation routes and infrastructure integrity. Events like hurricanes, floods, earthquakes, and wildfires can disrupt transport corridors by damaging or blocking roads, railways, ports, and airports. Such disruptions halt the movement of goods, causing delays or complete stoppages in supply chains. Environmental disasters also inflict direct damage on transportation mediums like vehicles, ships, trains, and aircraft, as well as critical infrastructure such as bridges and tunnels, necessitating extensive repairs or replacements. Consequently, these events lead to increased transportation costs due to rerouting efforts, heightened demand for alternative routes, and repair expenses, impacting global trade and local economies alike.

Cybersecurity threats have emerged as a modern risk facing the transportation and logistics industry, as digitalization becomes increasingly integral to operational efficiency [24]. From GPS systems to cargo tracking software, digital tools present vulnerabilities that malicious actors exploit through data breaches, compromising sensitive information such as customer details and financial records. Such breaches not only jeopardize privacy and lead to financial losses but also disrupt operations by targeting software systems, causing delays and affecting service delivery timelines. In extreme cases, cyber-attacks can escalate to sabotage operations, manipulating digital controls to alter shipment details or reroute goods, thereby posing physical and financial risks to both companies and consumers.

Regulatory and compliance challenges add another layer of risk for transportation and logistics enterprises operating within a complex regulatory landscape. Compliance failures with safety standards, environmental regulations, customs procedures, and other legal requirements can result in substantial fines, impacting financial viability and profitability. Operational disruptions may occur if shipments fail to meet import/export regulations, leading to delays at customs checkpoints and disrupting supply chain flows. Severe instances of non-compliance could even result in the suspension or revocation of operating licenses, halting business operations and tarnishing the company's reputation within the industry and among stakeholders. Thus, navigating regulatory frameworks and ensuring adherence to evolving compliance standards are critical to maintaining operational continuity and competitiveness in the global logistics market [24].

A step-by-step process to discuss and validate the scope, focus, and extent of operational procedures with affected personnel includes:

- **Engage Relevant Personnel:** The first step is to identify and engage with all relevant personnel who will be affected by or involved in the operational procedures. This includes operations managers, logistics coordinators, frontline staff, safety officers, IT personnel, and any other stakeholders who have expertise or are impacted by the procedures. In larger organizations, this might also involve representatives from different departments or regions where the procedures will be implemented.

- **Define Scope and Objectives:** Conduct discussions to clearly define the scope and objectives of the operational procedures. This involves outlining what specific processes or activities the procedures will cover, such as order processing, warehouse management, transportation logistics, safety protocols, and compliance requirements. Define the boundaries of the procedures to ensure they address the identified needs without unnecessary complexity or overlap with existing processes.

- **Gather Input and Feedback:** Facilitate sessions or meetings where affected personnel can provide input and feedback on the proposed scope, focus, and extent of the operational procedures. This step is crucial as it allows frontline staff and subject matter experts to share their insights, experiences, and concerns related to the procedures. Their input helps in identifying potential gaps, refining the scope to be more comprehensive, and ensuring that the procedures are practical and feasible to implement.

- **Validate Feasibility and Alignment:** During discussions, validate the feasibility of implementing the proposed procedures within the operational context of the organization. Assess whether the procedures align with existing workflows, infrastructure capabilities, and resource availability. Consider operational constraints, such as budgetary limitations, technological capabilities, and regulatory requirements, to ensure that the procedures are realistic and achievable.

- **Document Agreement and Modifications:** Document agreements reached during the discussions, including any modifications or adjustments made based on feedback from stakeholders. Ensure that there is consensus on the scope, focus areas, and extent of the operational procedures among all relevant personnel. This documentation serves as a reference point and helps in maintaining clarity throughout the development and implementation phases.

- **Align with Strategic Objectives:** Throughout the validation process, ensure that the scope, focus, and extent of the operational procedures align with broader strategic objectives of the organization. Consider how the procedures contribute to enhancing efficiency, improving service delivery, reducing costs, ensuring compliance, and supporting overall business growth. Alignment with strategic goals ensures that the procedures are not only functional but also contribute to the long-term success and sustainability of the transport and logistics enterprise.

Key Considerations:

- **Communication:** Effective communication is essential throughout the discussions and validation process. Ensure that all stakeholders are informed about the purpose, benefits, and implications of the operational procedures.

- **Flexibility:** Be open to adjustments and refinements based on feedback and changing business needs. Flexibility allows for continuous improvement and adaptation to evolving circumstances.

- **Training and Support:** Plan for training sessions to familiarize personnel with the finalized operational procedures. Provide ongoing support to address any challenges or questions that arise during the implementation phase.

The transportation and logistics industry is inherently exposed to a variety of risks, ranging from infrastructure vulnerabilities to modern-day cyber threats. To effectively mitigate these risks and ensure safer and more efficient operations, company policies and procedures can adopt several proactive measures.

Firstly, proactive safety measures are paramount. Regular training programs should be implemented to educate staff on safety protocols specific to transportation and logistics. This includes emergency procedures, safe handling practices, and operational guidelines aimed at minimizing accidents and injuries. Investing in modern equipment that meets stringent safety standards further reduces the risk of malfunctions and enhances operational safety. Establishing and enforcing strict safety protocols, continually updated to address emerging risks, ensures a culture of safety throughout the organization [24].

Infrastructure investment plays a critical role in mitigating risks associated with deteriorating infrastructure. Regular maintenance schedules should be implemented to identify and address wear and tear before they escalate into significant issues that could disrupt operations or compromise safety. Strategic upgrades to transportation routes, facilities, and supporting infrastructure are also essential to enhance efficiency, safety, and capacity to meet evolving demands.

Preparedness for environmental hazards is another key aspect. Developing robust contingency plans that outline alternative transportation routes and methods in the event of natural disasters or severe weather conditions is crucial [24]. Regular risk assessments should be conducted to identify vulnerable points in the transportation chain, enabling proactive measures to minimize potential damages and ensure continuity of operations during adverse environmental events.

In today's digital age, cybersecurity best practices are indispensable for protecting sensitive data and maintaining operational continuity. Companies should prioritize regular updates and patches for all software and systems to safeguard against known vulnerabilities and emerging cyber threats. Educating employees about cybersecurity risks and implementing stringent access controls and authentication measures are essential components of a multi-layered defence strategy. This strategy should encompass robust firewalls, encryption protocols, intrusion detection systems, and incident response plans to swiftly mitigate any cyber incidents that may occur [24].

Staying updated on regulatory requirements is equally crucial. Continuous monitoring of regulatory changes across all regions of operation helps companies adapt swiftly and ensure compliance with evolving standards. Active engagement with industry associations and lobbying efforts can provide insights into upcoming regulatory changes, enabling proactive adjustments to operational practices. Conducting routine compliance checks ensures that all aspects of operations, from safety protocols to environmental standards and cybersecurity practices, remain in alignment with current regulations, thereby mitigating legal risks and potential fines.

In the dynamic field of transport and logistics, ensuring that new developments in operational procedures are not duplicating previous work is crucial to optimizing resources, maintaining efficiency, and avoiding confusion among personnel. Here's a detailed approach to evaluate current procedures effectively:

- Document Existing Procedures: Start by documenting all current operational procedures comprehensively. This involves capturing step-by-step processes, workflows, responsibilities, and any associated documentation or guidelines. Having a clear and centralized repository of existing procedures is essential for thorough evaluation.

- Conduct Stakeholder Interviews: Engage with key stakeholders across various departments involved in the operational procedures. This includes operations managers, logistics coordinators, frontline staff, and other relevant personnel. Conduct interviews or workshops to gather insights into how current procedures are perceived, any identified shortcomings, and areas for improvement.

- Process Mapping and Analysis: Utilize process mapping techniques to visually represent the current operational workflows. This helps in understanding the sequence of activities, decision points, dependencies, and interactions between different stages of the process. Analyse these maps to identify redundancies, inefficiencies, bottlenecks, and areas where procedures may be outdated or no longer effective.

- Gap Analysis: Perform a comprehensive gap analysis to compare current procedures against industry standards, best practices, and organizational goals. Identify gaps where existing procedures do not adequately address current needs or where improvements could yield significant benefits in terms of efficiency, safety, or cost-effectiveness.

- Cross-Functional Review: Facilitate cross-functional reviews where different departments and stakeholders come together to evaluate current procedures holistically. This collaborative approach helps in identifying overlaps or duplications across departments and ensures that all perspectives are considered before proceeding with any new developments.

- Benchmarking: Compare current procedures with benchmarks from industry peers or leading organizations. This external benchmarking provides insights into innovative practices or technological advancements that could be adapted to enhance existing procedures without unnecessary duplication of effort.

- Feedback and Iteration: Seek feedback from stakeholders on proposed changes or improvements identified through the evaluation process. Incorporate their input to refine and validate the findings. This iterative approach ensures that any developments in procedures are aligned with practical needs and operational realities.

- Documentation and Communication: Document the outcomes of the evaluation process, including identified gaps, proposed changes, and reasons for proceeding with new developments. Communicate these findings clearly to all stakeholders involved to ensure transparency and alignment of expectations.

- Continuous Monitoring and Review: Establish mechanisms for continuous monitoring and review of operational procedures. Implement regular audits or assessments to track the effectiveness of new developments and to identify any emerging issues or areas for further refinement.

Developing and maintaining operational procedures for transport and logistics enterprises requires a thorough understanding of the various factors that can influence the development process. To identify these factors and incorporate them into the procedures:

1. Identifying Relevant Factors: Begin by identifying factors that are likely to impact the development of operational procedures. These factors can include regulatory requirements, technological advancements, market trends, customer expectations, operational risks, environmental considerations, and internal organizational goals. Each of these factors plays a crucial role in shaping how procedures should be designed and implemented to ensure alignment with broader strategic objectives.

2. Stakeholder Engagement: Engage with stakeholders across different levels and departments within the organization. This includes operations managers, logistics coordinators, IT specialists, compliance officers, and frontline staff who are directly involved in executing or affected by the procedures. By involving stakeholders early in the process, you can gather diverse perspectives and insights into how these factors influence day-to-day operations and procedural requirements.

3. Risk Assessment and Mitigation: Conduct a comprehensive risk assessment to identify potential risks associated with the development and implementation of new procedures. This involves evaluating both internal risks (e.g., operational disruptions, safety hazards) and external risks (e.g., regulatory changes, economic shifts). Once risks are identified, develop techniques and strategies to mitigate these risks and incorporate them into the procedural framework. For instance, if new regulations are expected, ensure procedures are flexible enough to adapt to these changes swiftly.

4. Technological Integration: Evaluate technological advancements that can

impact operational efficiency and effectiveness. Incorporate techniques for leveraging technology into procedures, such as automation, real-time tracking systems, data analytics for decision-making, and digital communication tools. Integration of these technologies not only enhances operational performance but also improves responsiveness to customer demands and market dynamics.

5. Compliance and Regulatory Requirements: Stay abreast of regulatory requirements specific to the transport and logistics industry. Incorporate techniques for ensuring compliance into procedural development, such as regular audits, documentation standards, safety protocols, and reporting procedures. Adherence to regulatory standards not only mitigates legal risks but also enhances credibility and trust with customers and stakeholders.

6. Environmental and Sustainability Considerations: Recognize the impact of operational procedures on the environment and adopt techniques for promoting sustainability. This may include optimizing routes to reduce fuel consumption, implementing eco-friendly packaging practices, or integrating renewable energy sources into transportation operations. By incorporating techniques for environmental stewardship into procedures, enterprises can align with global sustainability goals and enhance their reputation as responsible corporate citizens.

7. Continuous Improvement Culture: Foster a culture of continuous improvement within the organization. Implement techniques such as feedback loops, performance metrics, and regular reviews to continuously monitor and refine operational procedures. Encourage stakeholders to provide feedback on the effectiveness of procedures and identify opportunities for further enhancement based on evolving factors and emerging trends.

Here are examples of each of the factors that can impact the development of operational procedures for transport and logistics enterprises:

- **Regulatory Requirements:**

    a. **Example**: Changes in international shipping regulations regarding emissions standards can impact fleet management procedures. New requirements for reporting or safety protocols mandated by transportation authorities can necessitate updates in operational procedures to ensure compliance and avoid penalties.

- **Technological Advancements:**

    a. **Example:** Introduction of blockchain technology for supply chain transparency and security. Operational procedures may need to incorporate new data management protocols and integration methods to leverage blockchain's capabilities in tracking shipments and ensuring authenticity across the supply chain.

- **Market Trends:**

    a. **Example:** Shift towards e-commerce and omnichannel retailing. Logistics procedures may need to prioritize faster delivery times, real-time tracking, and flexible warehousing solutions to meet the growing demand for same-day or next-day delivery services driven by online shopping trends.

- **Customer Expectations:**

    a. **Example:** Increasing demand for sustainable practices in logistics. Operational procedures may include guidelines for using eco-friendly packaging materials, optimizing delivery routes to minimize carbon footprint, and offering transparency in environmental impact reporting to meet customer expectations for corporate responsibility.

- **Operational Risks:**

    a. **Example:** Risks associated with supply chain disruptions due to natural disasters. Procedures may need contingency plans for alternative sourcing, rerouting shipments, and activating emergency response teams to mitigate delays and maintain continuity in logistics operations during unforeseen events.

- **Environmental Considerations:**

    a. **Example:** Growing awareness of climate change impacts. Procedures may require adherence to stricter emissions standards, adoption of electric or hybrid vehicles in fleets, and implementation of sustainability practices such as recycling and reducing packaging waste to align with corporate sustainability goals and regulatory expectations.

- **Internal Organizational Goals**:

    a. **Example**: Objective to improve operational efficiency and reduce costs. Procedures may focus on optimizing inventory management through lean principles, streamlining warehouse operations with automated picking systems, and implementing performance metrics to track and achieve operational targets set by the organization.

Each of these factors influences how operational procedures are developed, modified, and implemented within transport and logistics enterprises. By proactively identifying and addressing these factors, organizations can ensure that their procedures are not only effective in meeting current needs but also adaptable to future changes and aligned with strategic objectives for sustainable growth and competitive advantage.

Developing and maintaining operational procedures for transport and logistics enterprises involves thorough research and consideration of various inputs to ensure effectiveness and alignment with organizational goals. Here's a detailed approach on how to research proposed operational procedures and incorporate user input:

- Researching Operational Procedures: Conducting comprehensive research is essential to understand industry best practices, regulatory requirements, technological advancements, and emerging trends. Here's how this can be approached:

    o Industry Best Practices: Begin by reviewing established standards and practices within the transport and logistics industry. This can include studying guidelines from industry associations, publications, and case studies of successful implementations by peer organizations. For example, researching how leading logistics companies manage last-mile delivery or optimize warehouse operations can provide insights into effective procedures.

    o Regulatory Requirements: Stay updated on local, national, and international regulations that govern transport and logistics operations. Regulatory bodies such as the Department of Transportation (DOT), International Maritime Organization (IMO), and Federal Aviation Administration (FAA) provide guidelines on safety, environmental compliance, and operational standards that must be integrated into procedures.

- Technological Advancements: Research current and emerging technologies relevant to logistics operations, such as GPS tracking systems, warehouse automation, and real-time data analytics platforms. Understanding how these technologies can enhance efficiency, reduce costs, and improve service delivery informs the procedural framework.

- Market and Customer Trends: Analyse market trends and customer expectations shaping the logistics landscape. This includes studying consumer preferences for faster delivery, sustainable practices, and enhanced transparency. Market research reports, customer feedback surveys, and industry forecasts help identify evolving demands that should be addressed in operational procedures.

- Incorporating User Input: User input is crucial for developing operational procedures that are practical, user-friendly, and aligned with operational realities. Here's how to effectively incorporate user feedback:

  - Engage Stakeholders: Involve key stakeholders from various departments and levels within the organization. This includes operations managers, logistics coordinators, warehouse staff, and frontline employees who directly execute or oversee logistics operations. Conduct workshops, focus groups, or interviews to gather insights into current challenges, pain points, and suggestions for improvement.

  - Feedback Mechanisms: Establish formal and informal channels for ongoing feedback from users. This could include suggestion boxes, digital feedback platforms, or regular meetings where employees can voice concerns and provide input on proposed procedures. Actively encourage participation and ensure anonymity if necessary to promote candid feedback.

  - Prototype Testing: Develop prototypes or pilot projects for new procedures and involve users in testing and refining them. This allows for hands-on evaluation of procedural effectiveness, identification of potential bottlenecks, and adjustment based on real-world scenarios. User testing helps validate procedures before full implementation, minimizing risks and ensuring usability.

- Training and Education: Provide training sessions and workshops to educate users on new procedures and gather further input on usability and practicality. Training should emphasize the rationale behind procedural changes, expected outcomes, and how users can contribute to continuous improvement. Encourage open dialogue and address concerns raised during training sessions to foster a supportive environment for procedural adoption.

Regulatory requirements related to transport and logistics vary significantly across different countries and regions, reflecting local laws, international agreements, and industry standards. Here's an outline of the key regulatory areas that typically impact transport and logistics operations globally:

- **Safety Regulations**:

    - **Vehicle Safety**: Regulations governing vehicle standards, maintenance, and safety inspections to ensure roadworthiness and minimize accidents.

    - **Driver Safety**: Requirements for driver qualifications, training, rest periods, and limits on driving hours to prevent fatigue-related incidents.

    - **Cargo Handling**: Guidelines for safe loading, unloading, and securement of cargo to prevent shifting, damage, or hazards during transportation.

- **Environmental Regulations**:

    - **Emissions Standards**: Regulations on vehicle emissions to mitigate air pollution and comply with environmental targets.

    - **Waste Management**: Requirements for the handling and disposal of hazardous materials and waste generated during transport operations.

- **Transportation Security**:

    - **Cargo Security**: Measures to secure cargo against theft, tampering, or terrorism risks, including screening procedures and secure supply chain practices.

    - **Facility Security**: Regulations for securing transportation facilities such as airports, ports, and warehouses against unauthorized access or threats.

- **Customs and Trade Compliance:**

    o **Import and Export Controls:** Regulations governing the movement of goods across borders, including customs clearance procedures, tariffs, and trade sanctions.

    o **Documentation:** Requirements for accurate and timely documentation, including invoices, bills of lading, and import/export declarations.

- **Labour Laws and Employment Practices:**

    o **Employment Standards:** Regulations related to wages, working hours, and working conditions for employees in the transport and logistics sector.

    o **Health and Safety:** Requirements for workplace safety, including provisions for ergonomic standards, personal protective equipment (PPE), and accident reporting.

- **Insurance and Liability:**

    o **Liability Coverage:** Requirements for insurance coverage to protect against liabilities arising from accidents, cargo damage, or third-party claims.

    o **Surety Bonds:** Regulations mandating surety bonds or financial guarantees for carriers to ensure financial responsibility and compliance with contractual obligations.

- **International Agreements and Treaties:**

    o **International Transport Agreements:** Compliance with international treaties and agreements governing cross-border transport, such as the United Nations Convention on Contracts for the International Carriage of Goods by Road (CMR) or the International Maritime Organization (IMO) regulations for shipping.

- **Technology and Data Protection:**

- **Data Privacy**: Regulations concerning the collection, storage, and processing of personal data, particularly relevant in logistics operations that involve customer information or tracking data.

- **Cybersecurity**: Requirements for protecting digital infrastructure and data systems from cyber threats and ensuring secure transmission of information.

These regulatory requirements are essential for transport and logistics companies to navigate effectively to ensure compliance, operational efficiency, and the safety of personnel and cargo. Adherence to these regulations not only mitigates legal risks but also contributes to sustainable and responsible business practices in the global supply chain.

Here are some specific examples of regulatory requirements related to transport and logistics from different countries around the world:

Safety Regulations

United States:

- **Vehicle Safety:** Governed by the Federal Motor Carrier Safety Administration (FMCSA), which sets standards for vehicle maintenance, safety inspections (e.g., annual inspections), and equipment requirements such as brake systems and lighting.

- **Driver Safety:** Regulations under the FMCSA include requirements for driver qualifications, hours of service (HOS) limitations to prevent driver fatigue, and mandatory rest periods.

- **Cargo Handling:** Guidelines include securement requirements for cargo to prevent shifting during transport, outlined in the FMCSA's Cargo Securement Rules.

European Union:

- **Vehicle Safety:** Regulated under the European Union Roadworthiness Package, which includes standards for vehicle inspections, emissions, and technical roadside checks.

- **Driver Safety:** Covered by EU legislation on working time, driving hours, and rest periods for professional drivers, aimed at preventing fatigue-related accidents.

- **Cargo Handling:** EU regulations ensure safe loading and unloading practices to prevent damage and hazards during transportation.

Environmental Regulations

Japan:

- **Emissions Standards:** Governed by strict regulations under the Japanese Automobile Standards Internationalization (JAS) law, which sets emission standards for vehicles to reduce air pollution.

- **Waste Management:** Regulations mandate proper handling and disposal of hazardous materials and waste generated during transport operations, ensuring compliance with environmental protection laws.

Germany:

- **Emissions Standards:** Enforced through the German Federal Motor Transport Authority (KBA), which sets emissions limits and requirements for vehicle registration and emissions testing.

- **Waste Management:** Strict regulations under Germany's Waste Management Act (KrWG) govern the handling, recycling, and disposal of hazardous and non-hazardous waste in transport and logistics operations.

Transportation Security

United Kingdom:

- **Cargo Security:** Regulated under the UK Border Force, which oversees cargo security measures including screening procedures and secure supply chain practices to prevent smuggling and terrorism risks.

- **Facility Security:** Requirements for securing transportation facilities like ports and airports are governed by the Department for Transport (DfT) and enforced through specific security regulations.

Customs and Trade Compliance

China:

- **Import and Export Controls:** Governed by the General Administration of Customs of the People's Republic of China (GACC), which mandates customs clearance procedures, tariffs, and enforces trade sanctions.

- **Documentation:** Strict requirements for accurate and timely documentation such as invoices, bills of lading, and import/export declarations under China's customs regulations.

Labour Laws and Employment Practices
Australia:
- **Employment Standards:** Regulated by the Fair Work Act, which sets national employment standards covering wages, working hours, and working conditions in the transport and logistics sector.

- **Health and Safety:** Managed by Safe Work Australia, which enforces workplace safety regulations including ergonomic standards, PPE requirements, and accident reporting protocols.

Insurance and Liability
Canada:
- **Liability Coverage:** Governed by the Insurance Bureau of Canada (IBC), which mandates liability insurance coverage for carriers to protect against accidents, cargo damage, and third-party claims.

- **Surety Bonds:** Regulations require carriers to post surety bonds or financial guarantees to ensure financial responsibility and compliance with contractual obligations under Canada's transportation laws.

International Agreements and Treaties
International:
- **International Transport Agreements:** Compliance with treaties like the United Nations Convention on Contracts for the International Carriage of Goods by Road (CMR) and the International Maritime Organization (IMO) regulations for shipping, which establish uniform rules for international transport and maritime operations.

Technology and Data Protection
European Union (EU):
- **Data Privacy:** Regulated under the General Data Protection Regulation (GDPR), which sets strict rules on the collection, storage, and processing of personal data, affecting logistics operations handling customer information and tracking data.

- **Cybersecurity:** GDPR also mandates cybersecurity measures to protect digital infrastructure and data systems from cyber threats, ensuring secure transmission of information in logistics and transport operations.

These examples illustrate the diversity and complexity of regulatory requirements that transport and logistics companies must navigate globally. Adhering to these regulations is crucial not only for compliance but also for maintaining operational efficiency, ensuring the safety of personnel and cargo, and promoting sustainable business practices in the global supply chain.

To develop, document, and verify operational procedures in accordance with workplace procedures:

Initial Planning and Scope Definition

The process begins by clearly defining the scope and objectives of the operational procedures. This involves identifying the specific processes within transport and logistics operations that require procedural documentation. For example, this could include order processing, warehouse management, vehicle maintenance, or customs clearance procedures. Engaging with key stakeholders from relevant departments such as operations, logistics, safety, and compliance is crucial at this stage to understand their requirements and ensure comprehensive coverage of all operational aspects.

Process Mapping and Documentation

Once the scope is defined, conduct detailed process mapping sessions. This involves documenting current practices, workflows, and decision points involved in each operational process. Process mapping helps in visualizing the flow of activities, identifying potential bottlenecks, and understanding dependencies between different steps. During this phase, it's important to gather input from frontline staff who are directly involved in executing these procedures. Their practical insights and feedback are invaluable for ensuring that the documented procedures are practical, effective, and aligned with actual operational realities.

Development of Operational Procedures

Based on the process mapping and stakeholder input, develop the operational procedures in a structured and standardized format. Each procedure should include:

- **Step-by-step Instructions:** Clear and concise instructions outlining each task and activity involved in the process.

- **Roles and Responsibilities:** Define the roles of personnel involved in executing or overseeing the procedure.

- **Decision Points:** Identify critical decision-making points and specify criteria or guidelines for making decisions.

- **Key Performance Indicators (KPIs):** Establish measurable KPIs to monitor the effectiveness and efficiency of the procedure.

It's essential to ensure that the procedures are documented in accordance with workplace procedures and formatting standards. This promotes consistency, clarity, and ease of reference for employees who will use these procedures in their daily tasks.

Verification and Validation

Once drafted, the operational procedures should undergo thorough verification and validation processes:

- **Internal Review:** Share the draft procedures with internal stakeholders, including department heads, supervisors, and frontline staff. Encourage feedback and review to validate the accuracy, clarity, and practicality of the procedures.

- **External Consultation:** Depending on the complexity or industry-specific requirements, seek input from external experts or consultants. This could include regulatory bodies, industry associations, or external auditors who can provide expertise and ensure alignment with industry best practices and regulatory requirements.

Documentation and Approval

After incorporating feedback and making necessary revisions, finalize the operational procedures. Ensure that they are formally documented and stored in a centralized location accessible to all relevant personnel. Document control procedures should be in place to manage revisions, updates, and version control of the procedures over time.

Training and Implementation

Implement a comprehensive training program to ensure that all personnel are familiar with the new or updated operational procedures. Training sessions should cover the content of the procedures, explain the rationale behind each step, and provide practical examples or simulations where applicable. Training helps in fostering understanding, compliance, and adherence to the documented procedures across the organization.

Continuous Improvement and Review

Finally, establish a framework for continuous improvement of operational procedures. Regularly review procedures to assess their effectiveness, identify areas for optimization or updates based on feedback, changing regulations, or evolving industry standards. Encourage a culture of continuous improvement where employees are encouraged to suggest improvements and participate in refining operational procedures to enhance efficiency and maintain compliance.

Trialling new operational procedures in transport and logistics with a target group involves a methodical approach to ensure feasibility, effectiveness, and minimal disruption to daily operations. Here's a detailed explanation of how to conduct such trials:

Firstly, identify the specific operational area or process where the new procedures will be implemented. This could range from optimizing delivery routes to improving inventory management systems or enhancing safety protocols in warehousing. By pinpointing the area of focus, you can ensure that the trial remains targeted and manageable.

Secondly, select a representative target group within your organization or operational environment. This group should include key stakeholders who are directly involved in or impacted by the processes being trialled. This typically includes drivers, warehouse staff, logistics coordinators, and other relevant personnel. Their participation is crucial as they provide first-hand insights into the practicality and effectiveness of the new procedures.

Thirdly, communicate the objectives and expectations of the trial clearly to the selected target group. It's essential that everyone understands why the new procedures are being trialled, what specific outcomes are expected, and how their participation contributes to the process improvement efforts. Clear communication helps in gaining buy-in and commitment from the participants.

Fourthly, provide comprehensive training to the target group before the trial begins. This training should cover the details of the new procedures, any changes in workflows or technologies, safety protocols, and their roles and responsibilities during the trial period. Training ensures that participants are well-prepared and confident in executing the new procedures correctly.

Next, implement the new procedures on a small scale initially. Start with a pilot phase in a controlled environment or specific operational segment rather than rolling out changes across the entire organization at once. This approach allows for careful monitoring and evaluation of the procedures in real-world conditions, while minimizing potential disruptions to overall operations.

During the trial period, gather quantitative and qualitative data to assess the performance of the new procedures. Quantitative data may include metrics like time saved, cost-effectiveness, or productivity gains, while qualitative data could involve feedback from participants regarding usability, challenges encountered, and suggestions for improvement. This data forms the basis for evaluating the success of the trial against predefined objectives.

After the trial period concludes, conduct a comprehensive evaluation of the trial results. Analyse the gathered data to determine whether the new procedures have achieved the desired outcomes and effectively addressed the identified needs or challenges. Evaluate any unexpected issues or benefits that emerged during the trial, as these insights can inform further refinements or adjustments.

Based on the evaluation findings, iterate and refine the new operational procedures as necessary. This may involve making adjustments to workflows, providing additional training or resources, or revising implementation strategies based on feedback from the target group. Continuous improvement ensures that the procedures are optimized for maximum efficiency and effectiveness.

Finally, document the finalized procedures and prepare for wider rollout across the organization if the trial proves successful. Develop comprehensive guidelines, manuals, or standard operating procedures (SOPs) based on the refined procedures and ensure that all relevant stakeholders are informed and trained accordingly.

Throughout the entire process, ongoing communication and feedback with the target group and other stakeholders are crucial. Regularly solicit input, address concerns, and maintain transparency about the progress and outcomes of the trial. This collaborative approach fosters a culture of continuous improvement and ensures that operational procedures are tailored to meet the specific needs and challenges of the transport and logistics environment.

Developing performance indicators to measure the effectiveness of transport and logistics operational procedures involves a structured approach to ensure that key aspects of performance are quantitatively assessed. Here's a detailed explanation of how to develop such indicators:

Identify Key Objectives and Outcomes

Begin by identifying the primary objectives of the operational procedures you want to measure. These objectives could include improving efficiency, reducing costs, enhancing safety, or improving customer satisfaction. Each objective should be clearly defined and aligned with the overall goals of the organization.

Define Measurable Metrics

For each objective, define specific metrics or Key Performance Indicators (KPIs) that will be used to measure performance. Metrics should be measurable, relevant, and directly tied to the objectives identified. Examples of KPIs in transport and logistics might include:

- **On-time Delivery Rate:** Percentage of deliveries made on or before the scheduled time.

- **Inventory Turnover:** How quickly inventory is sold or used up within a given period.

- **Vehicle Utilization Rate:** Percentage of time vehicles are actively transporting goods versus idle or waiting.

- **Fuel Efficiency:** Litres of fuel consumed per mile or kilometre travelled.

- **Safety Incident Rate:** Number of safety incidents per thousand hours worked or per number of deliveries.

Set Targets and Benchmarks

Establish realistic targets or benchmarks for each KPI based on historical data, industry standards, or desired improvements. Targets provide a clear goalpost for performance measurement and help in assessing whether the operational procedures are meeting expectations.

Establish Data Collection Methods

Determine how data will be collected for each KPI. This may involve utilizing existing systems and software, implementing new tracking mechanisms, or relying on manual data entry depending on the availability of resources and the complexity of the metrics.

Implement Monitoring and Reporting Systems

Develop a system for monitoring and reporting KPIs regularly. This could involve creating dashboards or reports that automatically update with real-time data, allowing stakeholders to track performance trends and deviations from targets.

Evaluate and Interpret Data

Regularly evaluate the collected data against established KPIs and targets. Look for trends, patterns, and anomalies that may indicate areas of success or areas needing improvement. Interpretation of data should consider both quantitative metrics and qualitative feedback from stakeholders.

Continuous Improvement and Adjustment

Use the insights gained from performance indicators to drive continuous improvement efforts. Identify areas where operational procedures can be adjusted or refined to better achieve desired outcomes. Engage with stakeholders to solicit feedback and ideas for improvement based on the performance data.

Communicate Results and Adjust Strategies

Communicate performance results and insights to relevant stakeholders within the organization. Use this information to adjust strategies, allocate resources effectively, and make informed decisions about future operational procedures.

Review and Refine Performance Indicators

Periodically review the effectiveness of chosen KPIs and performance measurement methods. As operational procedures evolve or organizational priorities shift, ensure that performance indicators remain relevant and aligned with current objectives.

Document and Standardize

Document the chosen performance indicators, measurement methods, targets, and reporting processes in standardized procedures or manuals. This ensures consistency in measurement across different teams or departments and facilitates alignment with organizational goals.

Here are some specific examples of how you can develop performance indicators for transport and logistics operational procedures based on the structured approach outlined:

Identify Key Objectives and Outcomes

Begin by identifying primary objectives aligned with the overall goals of the organization, such as:

- **Objective:** Improve efficiency in delivery operations.

- **Objective:** Enhance safety across all transport activities.

- **Objective:** Reduce operational costs related to fuel consumption.

Define Measurable Metrics (KPIs)

For each objective, define specific KPIs that can quantitatively measure performance:

- **KPI:** On-time Delivery Rate

  - **Metric:** Percentage of deliveries made on or before the scheduled time.

- **KPI:** Inventory Turnover

  - **Metric:** How quickly inventory is sold or used up within a given period.

- **KPI:** Vehicle Utilization Rate

- **Metric:** Percentage of time vehicles are actively transporting goods versus idle or waiting.

- **KPI:** Fuel Efficiency

  - **Metric:** Litres of fuel consumed per mile or kilometre travelled.

- **KPI:** Safety Incident Rate

  - **Metric:** Number of safety incidents per thousand hours worked or per number of deliveries.

Set Targets and Benchmarks
Establish realistic targets or benchmarks for each KPI:

- **Target:** Achieve an on-time delivery rate of 95%.

- **Benchmark:** Maintain an inventory turnover ratio of 8 times per year.

- **Target:** Increase vehicle utilization rate to 85%.

- **Target:** Improve fuel efficiency by 10% compared to the previous year.

- **Target:** Reduce safety incident rate to less than 1 incident per 10,000 hours worked.

Establish Data Collection Methods
Determine how data will be collected for each KPI:

- **Data Collection Method:** Utilize GPS tracking systems for delivery times.

- **Data Collection Method:** Use warehouse management systems for inventory turnover.

- **Data Collection Method:** Install telematics devices in vehicles for utilization rates.

- **Data Collection Method:** Monitor fuel consumption through vehicle telematics or fuel cards.

- **Data Collection Method:** Maintain incident logs and safety reports.

Implement Monitoring and Reporting Systems
Develop systems for monitoring and reporting KPIs:

- **System:** Implement dashboard software for real-time tracking of delivery performance.

- **System:** Use ERP systems to generate inventory turnover reports monthly.

- **System:** Utilize fleet management software for monitoring vehicle utilization rates.

- **System:** Create monthly fuel efficiency reports using telematics data.

- **System:** Regularly update safety incident logs and report quarterly.

Evaluate and Interpret Data

Regularly evaluate collected data against established KPIs and targets:

- **Evaluation:** Analyse monthly on-time delivery rates against the 95% target.

- **Evaluation:** Compare quarterly inventory turnover ratios to the benchmark.

- **Evaluation:** Track vehicle utilization rates weekly and adjust scheduling as needed.

- **Evaluation:** Review quarterly fuel efficiency reports and identify areas for improvement.

- **Evaluation:** Conduct quarterly safety reviews and implement corrective actions as necessary.

Continuous Improvement and Adjustment

Use insights from performance indicators for continuous improvement:

- **Action:** Implement route optimization software to improve delivery efficiency.

- **Action:** Conduct regular driver training programs to enhance safety practices.

- **Action:** Pilot hybrid vehicles to test fuel efficiency improvements.

- **Action:** Enhance maintenance schedules to improve vehicle utilization rates.

- **Action:** Upgrade safety equipment and procedures based on incident reviews.

Communicate Results and Adjust Strategies
Communicate performance results and insights to stakeholders:

- **Communication:** Share quarterly performance reports with management and operations teams.

- **Adjustment:** Allocate resources based on fuel efficiency and safety improvement priorities.

- **Strategies:** Develop new operational procedures based on data-driven insights.

Review and Refine Performance Indicators
Periodically review and refine selected KPIs and measurement methods:

- **Review:** Assess effectiveness of current KPIs in capturing desired outcomes.

- **Refinement:** Update KPIs based on evolving operational priorities and technological advancements.

Document and Standardize
Document chosen KPIs, measurement methods, and reporting processes:

- **Documentation:** Maintain standardized procedures in an operations manual.

- **Standardization:** Ensure consistency in data collection and reporting across departments.

Monitoring the Implementation of the Operational Procedures

Introducing new operational procedures within transport and logistics enterprises requires careful planning and engagement with affected personnel to ensure successful adoption and compliance. Here's a detailed explanation of how to approach this process:

Firstly, identify the specific units or job functions within the organization that will be affected by the new operational procedures. This could include drivers, warehouse staff, logistics coordinators, and administrative personnel involved in planning and oversight. Understanding the scope and impact of the procedures on these units is crucial for effective planning.

Once the affected units or job functions are identified, plan a structured communication strategy. Schedule meetings or sessions with personnel to introduce the new operational procedures. Clearly communicate the objectives, benefits, and expected outcomes of the procedures. Emphasize how the changes align with organizational goals such as improving efficiency, enhancing safety standards, or reducing operational costs.

During the introduction phase, facilitate open discussions and provide opportunities for questions and clarifications. Ensure that affected personnel understand the rationale behind the new procedures and how they contribute to overall organizational success. Use visual aids, demonstrations, or simulations if applicable to enhance comprehension and illustrate practical implications.

Acknowledge potential concerns or challenges that personnel may have regarding the new procedures. Encourage feedback to gather insights into practical considerations and potential implementation obstacles. Addressing concerns proactively demonstrates commitment to employee well-being and ensures that the procedures are realistically tailored to operational realities.

Provide comprehensive training sessions tailored to the specific needs of each unit or job function. Training should cover not only the procedural aspects but also the underlying principles, expected behaviours, and any new tools or technologies being introduced. Hands-on training sessions or workshops can enhance practical understanding and build confidence among personnel.

Ensure that all affected personnel have access to detailed documentation of the operational procedures. This could include manuals, standard operating procedures (SOPs), checklists, and reference guides. Centralize resources in easily accessible formats to facilitate ongoing reference and compliance.

Implement a monitoring and support system to track the initial implementation of the procedures. Assign designated personnel or teams responsible for providing guidance, troubleshooting issues, and ensuring adherence to the new processes. Regularly check in with personnel to assess their comfort level with the procedures and address any emerging challenges promptly.

Periodically evaluate the effectiveness of the introduced procedures through feedback mechanisms and performance metrics. Solicit input from personnel on their experiences and suggestions for improvement. Use this feedback to refine procedures, update training materials, and address any unforeseen issues that may arise during initial implementation.

Recognize and reinforce compliance with the new procedures through positive reinforcement strategies. Highlight successes and improvements resulting from the procedures to reinforce their importance and encourage continued adherence. Celebrate milestones and achievements to maintain momentum and foster a culture of continuous improvement.

Providing effective induction and supervision is important to support personnel in successfully implementing new transport and logistics procedures.

Begin by designing a comprehensive induction program that introduces personnel to the new transport and logistics procedures. This program should cover the following aspects:

- Introduction to Procedures: Provide an overview of why the new procedures are being implemented, their benefits, and how they align with organizational goals.

- Training Sessions: Conduct detailed training sessions that explain each step of the procedures, including practical demonstrations or simulations where applicable. Ensure that training is tailored to different roles within the organization to address specific responsibilities and tasks.

- Documentation and Resources: Distribute comprehensive documentation such as manuals, standard operating procedures (SOPs), checklists, and flowcharts that personnel can refer to as they familiarize themselves with the procedures.

- Q&A and Clarifications: Encourage questions and discussions during the induction process to clarify doubts and ensure personnel have a clear understanding of their roles and responsibilities.

Effective supervision is essential to reinforce learning and provide ongoing support as personnel begin implementing the new procedures:

- Assigned Mentors or Supervisors: Assign experienced personnel or supervisors as mentors to support individuals or teams during the initial phases of procedure implementation. These mentors can provide guidance, answer questions, and offer practical insights based on their experience.

- Regular Check-ins: Schedule regular check-in meetings or sessions to monitor progress, address challenges, and provide feedback. These sessions should be structured to review adherence to procedures, discuss any issues encountered, and identify areas for improvement.

- Feedback Mechanisms: Establish formal and informal feedback mechanisms where personnel can provide input on their experiences with the new procedures. Encourage open communication to identify potential gaps or inefficiencies early on and take corrective actions promptly.

Provide hands-on support and practical guidance to ensure that personnel feel confident and competent in applying the new procedures:

- On-the-Job Training: Offer on-the-job training opportunities where personnel can apply the procedures in real-world scenarios under supervision. This hands-on approach helps reinforce learning and build practical skills.

- Problem-Solving Skills: Equip personnel with problem-solving skills to effectively address unexpected challenges or deviations from standard procedures. Foster a mindset of continuous improvement by encouraging personnel to propose solutions and adaptations as needed.

Recognize and reinforce adherence to the new procedures to motivate personnel and reinforce their importance:

- Acknowledgment of Achievements: Celebrate successes and achievements resulting from effective implementation of the procedures. Recognize individuals or teams who demonstrate exemplary adherence and contribute positively to operational efficiency.

- Feedback Loops: Close the feedback loop by acknowledging and incorporating valuable suggestions and improvements proposed by personnel. This fosters a sense of ownership and encourages ongoing engagement in the improvement process.

Continuously monitor the implementation of the new procedures and be prepared to make adjustments based on feedback and evolving operational needs:

- Performance Metrics: Establish performance metrics and key performance indicators (KPIs) to track the effectiveness of the new procedures over time. Regularly analyse these metrics to identify trends, areas for improvement, and opportunities to optimize processes further.

- Iterative Improvement: Embrace a culture of iterative improvement where procedures are refined based on real-world feedback and evolving best practices in the transport and logistics industry. Engage personnel in the improvement process to leverage their insights and expertise.

Monitoring personnel performance to ensure adherence to operational procedures and assessing the need for process modifications is essential for maintaining efficiency and effectiveness in transport and logistics enterprises. Here's a detailed approach on how to effectively manage this aspect:

Begin by defining clear performance metrics and Key Performance Indicators (KPIs) that align with the operational procedures. These metrics should be measurable, specific, and relevant to the objectives of the procedures. Examples include on-time delivery rates, error rates in order processing, safety compliance, productivity metrics like units picked per hour, or customer satisfaction scores related to service levels.

Utilize technology and systems to monitor performance in real-time or near real-time. This may involve:

- **Tracking Software:** Implementing tracking software or systems that provide data on key metrics such as delivery times, inventory accuracy, or vehicle utilization rates.

- **Dashboards and Reports:** Developing dashboards or automated reporting systems that highlight performance against established KPIs. These tools allow for quick identification of trends, deviations, or areas requiring attention.

Conduct regular performance reviews with personnel to discuss adherence to procedures and assess overall performance:

- **Scheduled Reviews:** Establish regular review periods (e.g., weekly, monthly, quarterly) where performance data is analysed and discussed with individual team members or departments.

- **Feedback Sessions:** Use these reviews as opportunities to provide constructive feedback on performance, acknowledge achievements, and identify areas for improvement.

When deviations from procedures are identified:

- **Root Cause Analysis:** Conduct thorough root cause analysis to understand why deviations occur. This may involve reviewing operational processes, identifying training gaps, or examining external factors impacting performance.

- **Corrective Actions:** Implement corrective actions promptly to address non-adherence. This could include additional training, revising procedures to enhance clarity, adjusting resource allocation, or providing necessary support.

Embrace a culture of continuous improvement where feedback from performance monitoring drives enhancements to operational procedures:

- **Feedback Integration:** Incorporate feedback from performance monitoring into the review and refinement of operational procedures. Solicit input from personnel who are directly involved in executing procedures to leverage their frontline insights.

- **Iterative Adjustments:** Continuously evaluate the effectiveness of procedures based on performance data and stakeholder feedback. Make iterative adjustments to optimize processes, improve efficiency, and address evolving business needs.

Document performance monitoring processes, findings, and adjustments made to operational procedures:

- **Documentation:** Maintain records of performance reviews, corrective actions taken, and outcomes achieved. This documentation serves as a reference for future assessments and ensures consistency in monitoring practices.

- **Standardization:** Standardize performance monitoring protocols across departments or units to maintain fairness and transparency in evaluating adherence to procedures.

Invest in ongoing training and development initiatives to support personnel in meeting performance expectations:

- **Skills Enhancement:** Offer targeted training programs to improve skills related to executing operational procedures effectively. This may include technical skills, compliance training, or leadership development to support supervisors in overseeing adherence.

Actively seeking feedback from personnel who are directly involved in implementing operational procedures is another important aspect for their successful development and maintenance in transport and logistics enterprises. Here's a detailed approach on how to effectively solicit and utilize feedback:

To begin, foster an environment where feedback is valued and encouraged. Communicate to personnel that their input is essential for improving processes and achieving organizational goals. Emphasize transparency and openness in soliciting feedback to ensure that all voices are heard and considered.

Implement structured feedback mechanisms that facilitate the collection of constructive input from personnel:

- **Surveys and Questionnaires:** Develop surveys or questionnaires tailored to gather insights on specific aspects of the operational procedures. Ensure questions are clear, focused, and allow for both quantitative ratings and qualitative comments.

- **Focus Groups or Workshops:** Arrange periodic focus groups or workshops where personnel can discuss their experiences, challenges, and suggestions in a group setting. This allows for interactive discussions and the exploration of ideas among peers.

- **One-on-One Interviews:** Conduct individual interviews with personnel, particularly those in key roles or with specialized knowledge, to delve deeper into specific issues or areas of improvement. This approach can yield detailed insights that may not emerge in group settings.

When soliciting feedback, prioritize active listening and genuine engagement:

- **Listen Actively:** Pay close attention to what personnel are saying without interruption or judgment. Demonstrate empathy and respect for their perspectives, fostering trust and openness.

- **Ask Probing Questions:** Seek clarification or additional details where needed to fully understand the feedback provided. Encourage personnel to elaborate on their experiences and ideas for improvement.

Collect feedback regularly and promptly after implementation or updates to operational procedures:

- **Timing:** Gather feedback at strategic intervals, such as after initial implementation, during pilot phases, or following significant process changes. This allows for timely adjustments and improvements based on real-world experiences.

- **Continuous Monitoring:** Establish ongoing feedback loops where personnel can provide input as they encounter operational procedures in their daily tasks. This real-time feedback helps identify emerging issues and opportunities for immediate action.

Once feedback is collected, analyse it systematically to identify recurring themes, trends, or specific suggestions for improvement:

- **Data Analysis:** Use quantitative data from surveys and qualitative insights from interviews or focus groups to identify patterns in feedback. Prioritize areas where improvements can have the most significant impact on operational efficiency or personnel satisfaction.

- **Actionable Insights:** Translate feedback into actionable insights by developing clear action plans and prioritizing changes based on feasibility and expected benefits. Involve relevant stakeholders, such as managers and process owners, in decision-making to ensure alignment with organizational goals.

Communicate outcomes and actions taken in response to feedback to personnel:

- **Feedback Dissemination:** Share summaries of feedback findings, along with proposed actions or changes, with all personnel involved in implementing operational procedures. Transparency in this process fosters accountability and demonstrates responsiveness to personnel input.

- **Recognition and Appreciation:** Acknowledge and appreciate personnel contributions to process improvement efforts. Celebrate successes and recognize individuals or teams whose feedback led to significant enhancements or positive outcomes.

Evaluating the Implementation of Operational Procedures

Assessing the effectiveness of operational procedures against developed performance indicators is critical for transport and logistics enterprises to ensure they meet organizational goals and deliver optimal outcomes. Here's a detailed exploration of how this assessment can be effectively carried out:

To begin, it's essential to establish clear and relevant performance indicators (KPIs) that align with the objectives of the operational procedures. These KPIs should be measurable, specific, and directly tied to desired outcomes such as efficiency improvements, cost reductions, safety enhancements, or customer satisfaction levels. For example, KPIs could include on-time delivery rates, inventory turnover times, fuel consumption per mile, or safety incident rates.

Implement robust systems for data collection and monitoring that allow for accurate measurement of the established KPIs. This may involve leveraging technology such as GPS tracking systems, warehouse management software, telematics devices in vehicles, or automated reporting tools. Regularly collect relevant data points to track performance over time and ensure that data quality is maintained to facilitate meaningful analysis.

Conduct periodic evaluations to assess how well operational procedures are performing against the defined KPIs. This evaluation should involve:

- **Comparative Analysis:** Compare actual performance data against predefined targets or benchmarks set during the development phase of the procedures. Identify any deviations or areas where performance falls short of expectations.

- **Root Cause Analysis:** Investigate underlying reasons for performance variations or discrepancies. This may include reviewing operational processes, analysing data trends, or conducting surveys and interviews with personnel involved in executing the procedures.

Interpret performance data comprehensively to derive actionable insights and inform decision-making:

- **Trend Identification:** Identify trends or patterns in performance data that indicate areas of success or concern. For example, increasing on-time delivery rates may indicate the effectiveness of route optimization procedures, while rising safety incident rates may highlight the need for enhanced safety protocols.

- **Quantitative and Qualitative Assessment:** Combine quantitative metrics with qualitative feedback from stakeholders to gain a holistic understanding of operational procedure effectiveness. Qualitative insights can provide context and nuances that quantitative data alone may not capture.

Use assessment findings to drive continuous improvement efforts:

- **Actionable Recommendations:** Develop actionable recommendations based on assessment findings to optimize operational procedures. Prioritize initiatives that promise the highest impact on KPIs and align with strategic organizational objectives.

- **Iterative Refinement:** Implement iterative refinements to operational procedures based on assessment outcomes and stakeholder feedback. Continuously monitor the impact of changes made to ensure ongoing improvement and alignment with evolving business needs.

Communicate assessment results and improvement initiatives effectively within the organization:

- **Reporting:** Prepare clear and concise reports summarizing assessment findings, trends, and recommended actions. Tailor reports to different audiences, such as senior management, operational teams, or external stakeholders, to ensure relevance and impact.

- **Stakeholder Engagement:** Engage stakeholders in discussions around assessment outcomes to foster understanding, alignment, and support for improvement initiatives. Encourage a collaborative approach to problem-solving and decision-making.

Modifying or deleting operational procedures in transport and logistics enterprises plays a crucial role in maintaining efficiency, safety, and responsiveness to evolving business needs. A structured approach is essential for effective management of this process.

To begin, establishing a robust evaluation mechanism is paramount. This involves systematically assessing the effectiveness and relevance of current operational procedures. Key components include defining performance metrics such as on-time delivery rates, cost-effectiveness, safety records, customer satisfaction scores, and compliance metrics. Reliable methods for data collection, including automated systems and qualitative insights from personnel and customer surveys, help in gathering comprehensive performance data. Regular reviews at scheduled intervals, like quarterly or annually, analyse trends, strengths, weaknesses, and areas for improvement across all operational procedures.

Clear criteria must be defined for determining when operational procedures should be modified or deleted. These criteria should be aligned with enterprise goals, regulatory requirements, industry best practices, and stakeholder feedback. Factors considered include performance issues against established KPIs, changes in the business environment such as technological advancements or shifts in market demands, feedback from personnel involved in procedure execution, and the evaluation of cost-efficiency in resource utilization and operational overheads.

Establishing a transparent decision-making process is crucial. This involves fostering cross-functional collaboration among stakeholders from relevant departments such as operations, safety, quality assurance, and logistics management. Data-driven decisions are made by conducting comprehensive analyses of performance data, trends, and stakeholder feedback, ensuring a balanced assessment. Risk assessments evaluate potential impacts of proposed modifications or deletions on operational efficiency, safety, compliance, and customer satisfaction.

Effective implementation and communication strategies are key to ensuring changes are smoothly integrated. This includes developing clear implementation plans outlining steps for modifications or phasing out procedures, assigning responsibilities, setting timelines, and allocating resources accordingly. Training and transition plans are vital to support personnel affected by changes, ensuring understanding of revised processes, guidelines, and implications for their roles. Transparent communication strategies are employed to inform relevant stakeholders of changes, explain rationales, highlight anticipated benefits, and address concerns or questions proactively.

Monitoring the implementation of changes and gathering feedback are critical steps in the process. Post-implementation reviews evaluate effectiveness by comparing performance against pre-defined KPIs and benchmarks, measuring improvement. Continuous improvement initiatives utilize feedback and performance data to iteratively refine procedures, fostering a culture of ongoing enhancement aligned with evolving business needs.

Finally, documenting all modifications or deletions in accordance with organizational policies ensures transparency and facilitates future reference or audits. Detailed records include rationales, decision-making processes, implementation details, and outcomes. Compliance assurance ensures modified procedures adhere to relevant laws, regulations, and industry standards through periodic audits, identifying opportunities for further optimization.

In transport and logistics enterprises, keeping relevant personnel informed of the evaluation process and advising them of subsequent changes to operational procedures is crucial for maintaining organizational alignment, fostering engagement, and ensuring smooth transitions. Here's an in-depth exploration of how this can be effectively achieved:

Communication is foundational to this process. At the outset, it's essential to establish clear channels and protocols for disseminating information to personnel directly involved in executing operational procedures. This includes frontline staff, managers, supervisors, and other stakeholders whose roles are directly impacted by procedural changes. By establishing transparent communication channels early on, such as regular team meetings, digital platforms, or dedicated communication tools, organizations can ensure that all personnel are aware of the evaluation process and its objectives.

Once the evaluation process is underway, timely updates and progress reports should be provided to keep personnel informed of developments. This involves sharing insights gathered from performance metrics, data analysis, and stakeholder feedback. Transparency in sharing both successes and areas needing improvement fosters a culture of openness and accountability among teams.

When changes to operational procedures are identified as necessary based on evaluation outcomes, it's crucial to communicate these changes clearly and comprehensively. This communication should outline the rationale behind the modifications, detailing how they align with organizational goals, enhance operational efficiency, or address identified challenges. Providing this context helps personnel understand the significance of the changes and their role in implementing them effectively.

Moreover, advisories on subsequent changes should not only convey what changes are being made but also explain how these changes will impact daily operations, roles, responsibilities, and interactions across different teams or departments. This proactive approach minimizes ambiguity and resistance, encouraging buy-in from personnel who are essential to the successful implementation of revised procedures.

Throughout the communication process, it's important to encourage feedback and questions from personnel. Actively soliciting input demonstrates respect for their expertise and insights, which can uncover valuable perspectives on the practical implications of proposed changes. This feedback loop also enhances the overall quality of decision-making by incorporating frontline experiences and perspectives into procedural adjustments.

Training and support mechanisms should accompany communication efforts to ensure that personnel are equipped to navigate and implement new procedures effectively. This may involve conducting training sessions, workshops, or providing access to instructional materials that clarify the revised processes, outline expectations, and address any operational or technical aspects that require clarification.

Lastly, maintaining ongoing communication throughout the implementation phase and beyond is essential for monitoring progress, addressing emerging challenges, and making any necessary refinements. This iterative approach not only supports the initial transition but also reinforces a culture of continuous improvement where operational procedures evolve in response to feedback and changing organizational needs.

managing records, reports, and recommendations for improvement within workplace information systems and processes is essential for ensuring transparency, compliance, and continuous enhancement of operational procedures. Here's a detailed exploration of how this can be effectively achieved:

The foundation of managing records, reports, and recommendations begins with establishing robust information systems and processes. This involves implementing digital platforms, databases, or integrated software systems tailored to capture, store, and organize data related to operational procedures. These systems should be designed to accommodate various types of information, including performance metrics, incident reports, compliance documentation, and improvement recommendations.

Effective management starts with capturing comprehensive data relevant to operational procedures. This includes detailed records of procedure performance, safety incidents, customer feedback, and operational efficiency metrics. Utilizing standardized formats and protocols ensures consistency in data entry and facilitates easier retrieval and analysis when evaluating procedures or preparing reports.

Documentation plays a pivotal role in maintaining accurate records and generating insightful reports. Each phase of procedure evaluation, from initial implementation to periodic reviews and improvement cycles, should be meticulously documented. Reports should not only summarize performance data but also highlight trends, areas for improvement, and recommendations based on findings. These reports serve as a critical tool for decision-making and strategic planning within the enterprise.

Recommendations for improvement should be integrated into the information systems and processes seamlessly. This involves categorizing recommendations based on urgency, feasibility, and potential impact on operational outcomes. Prioritization ensures that actionable improvements are addressed promptly, aligning with organizational goals and enhancing overall efficiency.

Maintaining accessibility and transparency in information management is vital. Personnel involved in operational procedures should have appropriate access to relevant records, reports, and improvement recommendations as needed for their roles. This fosters accountability and empowers employees to contribute to continuous improvement efforts through informed decision-making and proactive problem-solving.

Adhering to compliance and regulatory requirements is non-negotiable in managing workplace information systems. This includes safeguarding sensitive data, ensuring data privacy, and complying with industry-specific regulations and standards.

Regular audits and assessments can help verify compliance, identify potential gaps, and implement corrective actions to mitigate risks.

Regular monitoring and evaluation of information systems are essential to ensure their effectiveness and relevance over time. This involves conducting periodic reviews of system performance, usability, and alignment with evolving business needs. Feedback from users regarding system functionality and data accuracy should be incorporated into ongoing system enhancements and updates.

Providing adequate training and support to personnel on information system usage is crucial. This ensures that employees understand how to navigate the systems, input data correctly, retrieve information efficiently, and utilize reports effectively for decision-making. Continuous training also facilitates a culture where employees are proactive in contributing to data integrity and system optimization.

Establishing feedback mechanisms allows stakeholders to contribute insights and suggestions for enhancing information systems and processes. This iterative approach to improvement ensures that the systems evolve alongside operational procedures, addressing emerging needs and technological advancements effectively.

Licence and Permit Requirements Relevant to Transport and Logistics Operations

License and permit requirements play a crucial role in governing transport and logistics operations worldwide, ensuring compliance with safety standards, environmental regulations, and operational protocols. These requirements vary significantly across countries and regions, reflecting local laws, international agreements, and specific industry needs. Some specific examples include:

United States: In the United States, transport and logistics operations are subject to a complex array of federal, state, and local regulations. Key licenses and permits include:

- Federal Motor Carrier Safety Administration (FMCSA) Operating Authority: Required for interstate trucking companies engaged in transporting goods across state lines. Companies must obtain operating authority through a process that includes proving financial responsibility and compliance with safety regulations.

- Commercial Driver's License (CDL): Truck drivers must possess a CDL issued by their state of residence, demonstrating competence and compliance with federal safety standards.

- Environmental Protection Agency (EPA) Permits: Required for companies transporting hazardous materials or pollutants, ensuring compliance with environmental regulations such as the Clean Air Act and Clean Water Act.

European Union: In the European Union (EU), transport and logistics are governed by harmonized regulations aimed at facilitating cross-border trade and ensuring environmental sustainability. Key requirements include:

- Community License for Road Haulage: Issued by EU member states, this license authorizes carriers to transport goods across EU borders and ensures compliance with EU road transport regulations.

- ADR Certification: Required for transporting dangerous goods by road, verifying that drivers and vehicles meet stringent safety standards outlined in the European Agreement concerning the International Carriage of Dangerous Goods by Road (ADR).

- Customs Authorizations: Companies engaged in international transport must obtain customs authorizations, such as Authorized Economic Operator (AEO) status, which streamline customs procedures and enhance supply chain security.

China: China's transport and logistics sector is governed by regulations issued by the Ministry of Transport and other relevant authorities. Key requirements include:

- Road Transport Permit: Issued for different types of road transport operations, including freight transport, passenger transport, and dangerous goods transport. Permits specify vehicle types, routes, and operational conditions.

- Customs Declarations: Required for imports and exports, ensuring compliance with China's customs regulations and tariffs. Transport companies must adhere to customs clearance procedures and documentation requirements to facilitate smooth international trade.

Australia: In Australia, transport and logistics operations are regulated at the federal and state levels, ensuring safety, environmental protection, and compliance with national standards. Key requirements include:

- Heavy Vehicle National Law (HVNL) Compliance: Governs heavy vehicle operations across states and territories, requiring operators to obtain permits for oversize or over-mass vehicles and comply with fatigue management regulations.

- Dangerous Goods Transport License: Required for transporting hazardous materials, ensuring adherence to strict safety protocols and emergency response procedures outlined by state authorities.

Global Perspective: Across the globe, transport and logistics enterprises must navigate a diverse regulatory landscape that includes licensing and permitting requirements tailored to specific industry sectors, transport modes, and types of cargo. Compliance with these requirements is essential for ensuring operational legality, minimizing risks, and maintaining the safety and security of goods in transit.

Problems that may Occur when Developing and Maintaining Operational Procedures for Transport and Logistics Enterprises

Complex regulatory compliance in transport and logistics operations poses significant challenges due to the diverse and often stringent requirements imposed by various jurisdictions worldwide. These regulations encompass a wide range of aspects, including permits, licenses, environmental standards, and safety protocols, each designed to ensure the safety of operations, protect the environment, and maintain industry standards. Navigating these complexities requires a deep understanding of local, national, and international laws, as well as proactive management strategies to avoid potential pitfalls.

Diverse Requirements and Jurisdictions: Regulatory requirements can vary widely between different regions, countries, and even states or provinces within a single country. For example, transport regulations in the European Union (EU) are harmonized to some extent under common directives and regulations, but still allow for some national variations. In contrast, regulations in the United States are governed by federal agencies like the Federal Motor Carrier Safety Administration (FMCSA), alongside state-specific requirements that can differ significantly in terms of licensing, vehicle standards, and operational limits.

Permits and Licenses: Obtaining the necessary permits and licenses is critical for legal operation within each jurisdiction. These may include road transport permits, hazardous materials permits, customs authorizations, and certifications for specialized transport (e.g., oversized loads). Each type of permit typically involves specific application processes, documentation requirements, and compliance checks to ensure that vehicles, drivers, and operations meet safety and operational standards.

Environmental Standards: Environmental regulations impose strict requirements on transport and logistics operations to minimize environmental impact. These standards may cover emissions controls, waste management, noise pollution, and the handling of hazardous materials. Compliance often requires implementing technology and practices that reduce carbon emissions, promote fuel efficiency, and ensure proper disposal of waste, all while adhering to local environmental laws and international agreements.

Safety Protocols: Safety is paramount in transport and logistics, where stringent protocols govern vehicle maintenance, driver qualifications, load securement, and emergency response procedures. Non-compliance with safety regulations can lead to accidents, injuries, and legal liabilities, underscoring the importance of rigorous training, regular inspections, and adherence to established safety standards.

Consequences of Non-Compliance: Failure to comply with regulatory requirements can have serious consequences for transport and logistics enterprises. These may include fines, penalties, suspension of operating licenses or permits, legal disputes, and reputational damage. Operational disruptions resulting from non-compliance can lead to delays in deliveries, loss of customer trust, and financial losses due to halted operations or increased insurance premiums.

To effectively manage complex regulatory compliance in transport and logistics:

- Stay Informed: Keep abreast of regulatory updates and changes across jurisdictions where operations are conducted. Engage with industry associations, legal advisors, and regulatory agencies to understand evolving requirements and implications for business operations.

- Develop Compliance Programs: Establish robust compliance programs that include regular audits, training programs, and internal controls to ensure adherence to regulatory standards. Implement technology solutions for tracking compliance metrics and maintaining accurate records.

- Proactive Risk Management: Identify potential compliance risks and develop mitigation strategies to address them before they escalate. This includes conducting risk assessments, developing contingency plans, and establishing clear communication channels for reporting and addressing compliance issues.

- Engage Stakeholders: Foster collaboration with stakeholders, including employees, suppliers, customers, and regulatory authorities, to promote a culture of compliance and address shared challenges proactively.

Navigating complex regulatory frameworks in transport and logistics operations requires a strategic approach that integrates legal expertise, operational diligence, and proactive compliance management. By prioritizing compliance, enterprises can mitigate risks, ensure operational continuity, and uphold their commitment to safety, environmental stewardship, and regulatory adherence in a globalized marketplace.

Technological integration in transport and logistics, encompassing systems like Warehouse Management Systems (WMS), Transportation Management Systems (TMS), and GPS tracking, presents both opportunities and challenges for enterprises aiming to enhance operational efficiency and customer service. The integration process involves deploying new technologies into existing infrastructures, which can be complex due to several key factors.

Compatibility Challenges: One of the primary challenges is ensuring compatibility with existing systems. Many transport and logistics enterprises operate with legacy systems that may not easily integrate with newer technologies. Compatibility issues can arise from differences in data formats, protocols, or software architecture, necessitating custom integration solutions or middleware to bridge the gap between systems. This can prolong implementation timelines and require careful planning to minimize disruption to ongoing operations.

Data Security Concerns: Introducing new technologies also raises concerns about data security and integrity. WMS, TMS, and GPS tracking systems involve collecting, storing, and transmitting sensitive information such as inventory data, customer details, and operational schedules. Ensuring robust cybersecurity measures, including encryption, access controls, and regular audits, is essential to protect against data breaches, unauthorized access, and potential disruptions to operations due to cyber threats.

Training and Skills Development: The adoption of advanced technologies often necessitates training and upskilling for personnel to effectively utilize these systems. Training programs are crucial to ensure that employees understand how to operate new software interfaces, interpret data generated by systems like TMS for route optimization or inventory management, and troubleshoot common issues. Adequate training reduces the learning curve, enhances user proficiency, and supports smoother integration into daily operations.

Impact on Implementation Timelines: Integrating new technologies can impact implementation timelines and operational efficiency. Delays may occur during the initial setup phase, particularly if customization or configuration is required to align systems with specific operational needs. Moreover, unexpected technical challenges or software bugs may arise, necessitating additional testing and refinement before full deployment. Effective project management and collaboration between IT teams, operations managers, and external vendors are crucial to mitigate these risks and ensure successful implementation within projected timelines.

Benefits and Strategic Considerations: Despite the challenges, technological integration offers significant benefits to transport and logistics enterprises. WMS enhances inventory accuracy and warehouse productivity by optimizing storage space and streamlining picking processes. TMS improves route planning, reduces fuel costs, and enhances delivery efficiency through real-time tracking and logistics coordination. GPS tracking systems provide visibility into fleet operations, enabling better decision-making, route optimization, and customer service.

To navigate the complexities of technological integration effectively, transport and logistics enterprises should adopt a strategic approach. This includes conducting thorough needs assessments to identify technological requirements, evaluating vendor capabilities, and selecting systems that align with long-term business objectives. Developing a phased implementation plan, prioritizing critical functionalities, and allocating resources for training and support are essential steps to ensure smooth integration and maximize return on investment in new technologies.

In conclusion, while technological integration in transport and logistics presents challenges such as compatibility issues, data security concerns, and training needs, proactive planning, and strategic management can mitigate these challenges. By leveraging advanced systems like WMS, TMS, and GPS tracking effectively, enterprises can enhance operational efficiency, improve customer service, and maintain a competitive edge in a rapidly evolving industry landscape.

Supply chain disruptions represent a significant challenge for transport and logistics enterprises, impacting the seamless flow of goods and services from suppliers to consumers. These disruptions can stem from a variety of external factors, each posing unique challenges to supply chain operations.

Natural Disasters and Environmental Factors: Natural disasters such as hurricanes, earthquakes, floods, or wildfires can severely impact transportation infrastructure, including roads, ports, and airports. These events disrupt supply chain networks by causing physical damage, delaying shipments, and necessitating rerouting of transportation routes. For example, a hurricane affecting coastal regions can lead to port closures and delays in cargo handling, affecting the timely delivery of goods.

Geopolitical Tensions and Trade Policies: Geopolitical tensions, trade disputes, and changes in trade policies between countries can introduce uncertainty and volatility into supply chains. Tariffs, sanctions, and political instability can disrupt the flow of goods across borders, leading to delays at customs, increased costs due to tariffs, and supply chain reconfiguration to comply with new regulations. For instance, changes in trade agreements between major trading partners can impact logistics planning and sourcing strategies for international shipments.

Supplier Issues and Disruptions: Supplier-related disruptions such as raw material shortages, production delays, or quality issues can ripple through the supply chain, affecting downstream operations. Dependency on a single supplier or limited supplier diversity increases vulnerability to disruptions. For example, a supplier experiencing labour strikes may struggle to fulfill orders, leading to delays in manufacturing and subsequent delivery delays to customers.

Unexpected Demand Fluctuations: Fluctuations in consumer demand, seasonal spikes, or sudden shifts in market trends can strain supply chain capacities and logistics networks. Underestimating demand can result in stockouts, while overestimating can lead to excess inventory and increased storage costs. Forecasting accuracy and inventory management are critical to mitigating the impact of demand fluctuations on supply chain operations.

Impact on Operations and Mitigation Strategies: Supply chain disruptions have profound implications for transport and logistics enterprises, affecting operational efficiency, customer satisfaction, and overall business performance. Delays in delivery times can lead to financial penalties, loss of customer trust, and competitive disadvantage in the market. Increased costs due to expedited shipping, inventory holding, or sourcing alternative suppliers further strain profitability.

To mitigate supply chain disruptions, enterprises can adopt several strategies:

- Risk Assessment and Contingency Planning: Conducting risk assessments to identify potential disruptions and developing contingency plans with alternative suppliers, transport routes, or storage facilities to maintain continuity of operations during crises.

- Diversification of Suppliers and Supply Sources: Cultivating relationships with multiple suppliers and sourcing from geographically diverse regions reduces reliance on single sources and mitigates the impact of localized disruptions.

- Advanced Technology and Data Analytics: Implementing advanced technology such as predictive analytics, real-time tracking systems, and inventory management software enhances visibility into supply chain operations, enabling proactive decision-making and rapid response to disruptions.

- Collaboration and Communication: Strengthening collaboration with stakeholders including suppliers, customers, and logistics partners facilitates timely information exchange and coordinated responses to mitigate disruptions and minimize impact on operations.

While supply chain disruptions are inevitable due to external factors such as natural disasters, geopolitical tensions, supplier issues, and demand fluctuations, proactive planning, risk management strategies, and technological integration enable transport and logistics enterprises to build resilience, maintain operational continuity, and sustain competitive advantage in a dynamic global marketplace.

Labour issues present significant challenges in the transport and logistics industry, impacting workforce management, operational efficiency, and overall business continuity. These challenges encompass various aspects related to recruitment, retention, skills development, and compliance with labour laws and safety regulations.

Driver Shortages and Recruitment Difficulties: One of the most pressing labour issues in transport and logistics is the shortage of qualified drivers. This shortage is exacerbated by factors such as an aging workforce, stringent licensing requirements, and competition from other industries offering potentially more attractive working conditions. Recruitment efforts often face challenges in attracting and retaining skilled drivers, leading to increased competition among employers and higher costs associated with recruitment and retention strategies.

Skills Gaps in Logistics Planning and Management: Effective logistics planning and management require specialized skills in areas such as route optimization, inventory management, supply chain analytics, and regulatory compliance. However, there is often a skills gap where the demand for these specialized skills exceeds the available talent pool. Training programs and professional development initiatives are essential to bridge these gaps and ensure that logistics personnel possess the knowledge and expertise needed to perform their roles effectively.

Compliance with Labour Laws and Safety Regulations: Transport and logistics enterprises must adhere to stringent labour laws and safety regulations governing employee working conditions, hours of service, rest periods, and occupational health and safety standards. Non-compliance can result in legal liabilities, fines, and reputational damage. Ensuring compliance requires ongoing monitoring, training, and implementation of policies and procedures that prioritize employee welfare and mitigate operational risks associated with regulatory violations.

High Turnover Rates and Retention Strategies: High turnover rates are a persistent challenge in the transport and logistics industry, driven by factors such as demanding work schedules, job stress, and limited career advancement opportunities. Retaining skilled personnel is crucial for maintaining operational continuity and reducing recruitment costs. Implementing retention strategies, such as competitive compensation packages, career development pathways, work-life balance initiatives, and recognition programs, can enhance employee satisfaction and loyalty.

Impact on Operational Efficiency: Labour issues directly impact operational efficiency and service delivery within transport and logistics enterprises. Driver shortages or turnover can lead to delays in deliveries, increased transit times, and higher operational costs associated with recruiting and training replacements. Skills gaps in logistics planning can hinder optimization efforts, affecting inventory management, fleet utilization, and overall supply chain efficiency.

Addressing Labour Issues: To address labour challenges effectively, transport and logistics enterprises can implement several strategies:

- Investment in Training and Development: Offer ongoing training programs to enhance employee skills in logistics planning, safety protocols, and regulatory compliance. Support career progression through certifications and professional development opportunities to attract and retain talent.

- Enhanced Recruitment Strategies: Develop targeted recruitment campaigns, collaborate with educational institutions to promote careers in logistics, and leverage technology for recruiting and screening candidates. Offer competitive salaries, benefits, and incentives to attract skilled drivers and logistics professionals.

- Improvement in Working Conditions: Prioritize workplace safety, provide ergonomic equipment, and promote a positive organizational culture that values employee well-being. Address concerns related to job stress and work-life balance to improve job satisfaction and reduce turnover rates.

- Utilization of Technology: Implement advanced technologies such as telematics, route optimization software, and real-time tracking systems to streamline operations, improve fleet management, and enhance productivity. Automation of repetitive tasks can also alleviate workforce pressures and increase operational efficiency.

Addressing labour issues in transport and logistics requires a multifaceted approach that encompasses recruitment strategies, skills development, compliance with labour regulations, and initiatives to enhance workplace conditions and employee retention. By investing in their workforce and adopting proactive measures, enterprises can mitigate labour-related challenges, improve operational efficiency, and foster sustainable growth in a competitive industry landscape.

Environmental sustainability has emerged as a critical imperative for transport and logistics enterprises, driven by global efforts to mitigate climate change, reduce carbon footprints, and adopt eco-friendly practices across supply chain operations. However, achieving sustainability goals while maintaining operational efficiency and cost-effectiveness presents significant challenges within the industry.

Carbon Emissions Reduction: Transport and logistics operations are major contributors to carbon emissions, primarily through fuel consumption in road, air, sea, and rail transportation. Reducing emissions requires strategies such as optimizing routes to minimize mileage, adopting fuel-efficient vehicles, investing in alternative fuels (e.g., electric or hybrid vehicles), and implementing eco-driving practices. These initiatives aim to lower greenhouse gas emissions and comply with regulatory standards aimed at curbing environmental impact.

Waste Minimization and Circular Economy Practices: Minimizing waste generation and promoting circular economy principles are essential for enhancing environmental sustainability in logistics. This involves optimizing packaging materials, implementing reverse logistics for product returns and recycling, and reducing packaging waste through innovative design and material choices. By adopting circular economy practices, enterprises can reduce resource consumption, landfill waste, and environmental pollution associated with logistics operations.

Challenges in Balancing Sustainability and Operational Efficiency: A key challenge lies in balancing sustainability objectives with operational efficiency and cost-effectiveness. For instance, transitioning to eco-friendly vehicles or alternative fuels may involve higher upfront costs for vehicle acquisition or infrastructure development. Additionally, optimizing routes to reduce emissions must also consider factors such as delivery schedules, customer preferences, and regulatory compliance, which may impact operational timelines and costs.

Regulatory Compliance and Stakeholder Expectations: Meeting environmental standards and complying with regulatory requirements is crucial for transport and logistics enterprises. Regulations often mandate emission limits, waste disposal practices, and sustainability reporting, imposing legal obligations and potential penalties for non-compliance. Stakeholders, including customers, investors, and regulatory bodies, increasingly demand transparency and accountability regarding environmental performance, influencing business decisions and operational strategies.

Technological and Innovation Solutions: Advancements in technology play a pivotal role in enhancing environmental sustainability within logistics operations. Innovations such as smart logistics platforms, real-time monitoring systems, and data analytics enable enterprises to optimize fleet management, track carbon emissions, and identify opportunities for efficiency improvements. Integration of renewable energy sources, such as solar-powered warehouses or electric vehicle charging stations, further supports sustainable practices across logistics infrastructures.

Strategic Planning and Collaboration: To effectively address environmental sustainability challenges, transport and logistics enterprises should adopt a strategic approach that includes:

- Long-term Sustainability Goals: Establishing clear sustainability goals aligned with global environmental targets, such as carbon neutrality or zero-waste initiatives, to guide organizational strategies and investments.

- Collaboration with Stakeholders: Engaging with suppliers, logistics partners, and regulatory agencies to foster collaboration and collective action towards shared sustainability objectives. Partnerships can facilitate knowledge sharing, resource pooling, and joint initiatives to address common environmental challenges.

- Continuous Improvement: Implementing a culture of continuous improvement through regular monitoring, performance measurement, and feedback loops to evaluate the effectiveness of sustainability initiatives. Investing in employee training and awareness programs promotes sustainability awareness and commitment across the organization.

Addressing environmental sustainability in transport and logistics requires a holistic approach that integrates technological innovation, regulatory compliance, stakeholder engagement, and strategic planning. By prioritizing sustainability alongside operational efficiency and cost-effectiveness, enterprises can mitigate environmental impact, enhance brand reputation, and position themselves as leaders in sustainable logistics practices amidst evolving global expectations and regulatory landscapes.

Example Operational Procedure

The following provides an example of a operational procedure for transporting and delivering goods using road transport:

Operational Procedure: Road Transport and Delivery

Objective: To ensure safe, efficient, and timely delivery of goods from the warehouse to customers while maintaining compliance with regulatory standards and optimizing operational efficiency.

Scope: This procedure applies to all road transport activities conducted by [Company Name] for delivering goods to customers within [Region/Country].

Responsibilities:

- **Transport Manager:** Responsible for overseeing the execution of transport operations, including route planning, vehicle allocation, and compliance with safety regulations.

- **Drivers:** Responsible for operating vehicles safely, adhering to traffic laws, and ensuring the secure loading and unloading of goods.

- **Warehouse Staff:** Responsible for preparing goods for dispatch, ensuring accurate inventory records, and coordinating with transport personnel.

Procedure:

- **Pre-Transport Preparation:**

    - **Order Receipt and Processing:** Upon receiving customer orders, the warehouse staff verifies stock availability and prepares goods for dispatch.

    - **Route Planning:** The Transport Manager or logistics team plans optimal delivery routes based on customer locations, traffic conditions, and delivery schedules to minimize transit time and fuel consumption.

    - **Vehicle Inspection:** Drivers conduct pre-trip inspections of assigned vehicles to ensure roadworthiness, including checking brakes, lights, tires, and securing cargo.

- **Loading and Securing Goods:**

    - Warehouse staff loads goods onto designated vehicles according to delivery routes and schedules.

- Ensure proper stacking, secure fastening of goods using appropriate restraints (e.g., straps, pallets), and adherence to weight distribution guidelines to prevent shifting during transit.

- **Transport and Delivery:**
    - Drivers operate vehicles safely, adhering to speed limits, traffic regulations, and road conditions.
    - Communicate with dispatch or central control for updates on route adjustments, delays, or customer-specific instructions.
    - Upon arrival at customer locations, drivers coordinate with recipients for unloading procedures, verifying goods against delivery notes, and obtaining signatures for confirmation of receipt.

- **Safety and Compliance:**
    - Drivers and transport personnel adhere to safety protocols, including wearing seat belts, avoiding distractions, and following company policies on alcohol and drug use.
    - Ensure compliance with transportation laws, including vehicle weight restrictions, hours of service regulations, and environmental standards (e.g., emissions control).

- **Post-Delivery Procedures:**
    - Upon completion of deliveries, drivers report back to the warehouse or central operations for debriefing.
    - Document any delivery discrepancies, customer feedback, or incidents encountered during transit.
    - Vehicles undergo post-trip inspections and maintenance checks as needed, with any defects or issues reported for immediate rectification.

- **Continuous Improvement:**
    - Conduct regular reviews and analysis of transport operations to identify areas for improvement in efficiency, cost-effectiveness, and customer

service.

- ○ Implement feedback from drivers, customers, and stakeholders to refine operational procedures, optimize routes, and enhance overall logistics performance.

Documentation and Record-Keeping:
- Maintain accurate records of all transport activities, including delivery schedules, vehicle maintenance logs, driver certifications, and incident reports.

- Ensure compliance with record-keeping requirements for regulatory audits and internal performance evaluations.

Emergency Procedures:
- Outline procedures for handling emergencies such as vehicle breakdowns, accidents, or adverse weather conditions.

- Provide drivers with emergency contact information and protocols for immediate response and support.

Conclusion: By following this operational procedure, [Company Name] aims to achieve consistent and reliable delivery services that meet customer expectations, uphold safety standards, and contribute to overall operational efficiency in road transport logistics. Regular training, adherence to protocols, and continuous monitoring ensure that the procedure remains effective and adaptable to changing business needs and regulatory requirements.

Chapter 6

Monitoring the Safety of Transport Activities

Monitoring the safety of transport activities is crucial for ensuring compliance with regulatory standards, protecting personnel, and maintaining the integrity of transported goods.

Establish Safety Policies and Procedures

Begin by developing comprehensive safety policies and procedures tailored to your specific transport activities. These should cover all aspects of transport operations, including vehicle maintenance, driver behaviour, cargo handling, and emergency response protocols. Ensure these policies are clearly communicated to all employees and integrated into daily operations.

Establishing comprehensive safety policies and procedures is foundational to ensuring the safety and security of transport activities within logistics operations. These policies not only mitigate risks but also promote a culture of safety among employees.

Assessment of Transport Activities: The first step involves conducting a thorough assessment of all transport activities. This assessment should identify potential hazards and risks associated with vehicle operations, driver behaviour, cargo handling, and emergency situations. By understanding these risks, logistics managers can develop targeted policies that address specific safety concerns relevant to their operations.

Development of Safety Policies: Based on the assessment, develop clear and concise safety policies that outline the expected standards and procedures for safe transport operations. These policies should be comprehensive, covering every aspect from vehicle maintenance schedules to emergency response protocols. For example, policies may include guidelines on regular vehicle inspections, safe loading and unloading practices, defensive driving techniques, and procedures for handling hazardous materials.

Integration into Daily Operations: Once developed, it is critical to ensure that these safety policies are integrated into daily operations seamlessly. This involves:

- Training and Education: Provide comprehensive training programs for all employees involved in transport activities. Training should encompass understanding safety policies, recognizing potential hazards, and implementing safe practices. Regular refresher courses should reinforce these principles and update employees on any changes to policies or regulations.

- Documentation and Communication: Clearly communicate safety policies to all employees through handbooks, training sessions, and signage in the workplace. Ensure that policies are easily accessible and regularly reviewed to maintain relevance and effectiveness. Documenting procedures for easy reference ensures that employees can access information promptly when needed.

Enforcement and Accountability: Establish mechanisms for enforcing safety policies and holding employees accountable for adherence. This may include:

- Monitoring and Auditing: Regularly monitor compliance with safety policies through audits, inspections, and performance reviews. Audits can identify areas of non-compliance or gaps in implementation that require corrective action.

- Feedback and Improvement: Encourage employees to provide feedback on safety policies and procedures. This feedback can help identify practical challenges in implementation and suggest improvements that enhance safety and efficiency.

Adaptation to Regulatory Requirements: Stay abreast of regulatory requirements and ensure that safety policies align with local, national, and international standards. Compliance with regulations not only ensures legal adherence but also enhances overall safety practices by incorporating best practices and industry standards.

Promotion of Safety Culture: Lastly, promote a culture of safety throughout the organization. Safety should be prioritized at all levels of management, with leaders actively demonstrating their commitment to safety through actions and decisions. Recognize and reward employees who exemplify safety practices and encourage open communication about safety concerns.

Implement Regular Vehicle Inspections and Maintenance

Regular inspections and maintenance of vehicles are vital for preventing accidents and ensuring operational reliability. Implement a scheduled maintenance program that includes:

- **Pre-Trip Inspections:** Require drivers to conduct pre-trip inspections, checking key aspects such as brakes, lights, tires, and fluid levels.

- **Periodic Maintenance:** Schedule regular maintenance checks according to manufacturer guidelines and operational demands, covering all vehicle systems and components.

- **Post-Trip Inspections:** Conduct post-trip inspections to identify any issues that may have arisen during transport and address them promptly.

Implementing regular vehicle inspections and maintenance is critical to ensuring the safety, reliability, and longevity of transport vehicles within logistics operations. This practice not only helps prevent accidents but also enhances operational efficiency by minimizing downtime and costly repairs.

Pre-Trip Inspections: Before embarking on any journey, drivers should conduct thorough pre-trip inspections of their vehicles. This step ensures that all essential components are in proper working condition and identifies potential issues that could compromise safety or performance. Key aspects checked during pre-trip inspections typically include:

- **Brakes:** Inspecting brake pads, discs, and hydraulic systems to ensure proper functionality and responsiveness.

- **Lights:** Checking headlights, taillights, turn signals, and brake lights to ensure visibility and compliance with road safety regulations.

- **Tires:** Examining tire tread depth, inflation levels, and overall condition to prevent blowouts and ensure optimal grip on the road.

- **Fluid Levels:** Verifying levels of engine oil, coolant, brake fluid, and windshield washer fluid to maintain proper vehicle operation and prevent mechanical failures.

Drivers should document the results of pre-trip inspections using standardized checklists, noting any abnormalities or required maintenance actions. Immediate attention should be given to any issues identified before commencing the journey.

Periodic Maintenance: In addition to pre-trip inspections, establish a structured schedule for periodic maintenance checks based on manufacturer guidelines and operational demands. This proactive approach helps prevent mechanical breakdowns and extends the lifespan of vehicles. Periodic maintenance tasks typically include:

- **Engine Maintenance:** Changing oil and filters, inspecting belts, hoses, and engine mounts to ensure optimal performance and fuel efficiency.

- **Transmission and Drivetrain:** Checking transmission fluid levels, inspecting drivetrain components (e.g., axles, driveshafts) for wear and tear.

- **Suspension and Steering:** Examining shock absorbers, ball joints, and steering components to maintain vehicle stability and responsiveness.

- **Electrical System:** Testing battery condition, inspecting wiring, fuses, and alternator output to ensure reliable operation of electrical components.

Maintain detailed records of all maintenance activities, including dates of service, parts replaced, and technician signatures. This documentation aids in tracking vehicle history, identifying recurring issues, and scheduling future maintenance tasks proactively.

Post-Trip Inspections: Following each journey, conduct post-trip inspections to identify any new issues that may have arisen during transport. Post-trip inspections serve as a complementary check to pre-trip inspections and allow for prompt identification and resolution of emerging problems. Key areas to inspect during post-trip inspections include:

- **Fluid Leaks:** Checking for leaks or spills of engine oil, coolant, brake fluid, or hydraulic fluids that may indicate underlying mechanical issues.

- **Exterior Damage:** Assessing the vehicle for any new scratches, dents, or signs of external damage that could compromise safety or vehicle integrity.

- **Cargo Handling Equipment:** Verifying the condition of tie-downs, lift-gates, or other cargo handling equipment to ensure they are operational and secure for future use.

Any issues identified during post-trip inspections should be promptly reported to maintenance personnel for evaluation and necessary repairs. Documenting post-trip inspection findings contributes to comprehensive vehicle maintenance records and informs ongoing maintenance schedules and practices.

Continuous Improvement: To optimize the effectiveness of regular vehicle inspections and maintenance, establish a culture of continuous improvement within the organization. Encourage feedback from drivers and maintenance personnel regarding the effectiveness of inspection procedures and potential areas for enhancement. Regularly review inspection protocols and update them as needed to reflect changes in vehicle technology, regulatory requirements, or operational conditions.

Utilize Telematics and GPS Tracking

Leveraging technology such as telematics and GPS tracking systems provides real-time data on vehicle location, speed, driving behaviour, and overall performance. These systems can monitor:

- **Driving Behaviour:** Track speed, acceleration, braking patterns, and adherence to routes. Identify unsafe driving behaviours and provide corrective feedback.

- **Vehicle Diagnostics:** Monitor engine performance, fuel efficiency, and mechanical health, enabling proactive maintenance and reducing the risk of breakdowns.

- **Route Adherence:** Ensure drivers follow planned routes, avoiding unauthorized deviations that could lead to safety risks.

Utilizing telematics and GPS tracking systems in transport and logistics operations offers significant advantages by providing real-time insights into vehicle performance, driver behaviour, and operational efficiency. These technologies integrate advanced data analytics with satellite navigation, enabling comprehensive monitoring and management capabilities. Here's a detailed explanation of how telematics and GPS tracking systems can enhance

Figure 15: Fleet Board Telematics. Travelerz, CC BY-SA 3.0 PL, via Wikimedia Commons.

Real-Time Monitoring of Driving Behaviour: Telematics and GPS tracking systems enable continuous monitoring of driving behaviour, including speed, acceleration, braking patterns, and adherence to planned routes. By collecting and analysing this data in real-time, fleet managers can identify unsafe driving behaviours such as harsh braking or speeding. This information allows for immediate intervention through coaching and training programs aimed at improving driver safety and reducing the risk of accidents. For example, if a driver consistently exceeds speed limits or engages in aggressive driving manoeuvres, managers can provide corrective feedback and implement targeted interventions to promote safer driving practices.

Vehicle Diagnostics and Maintenance Management: These systems also facilitate ongoing monitoring of vehicle diagnostics and health. By tracking engine performance metrics, fuel efficiency, and mechanical conditions such as tire pressure or engine temperature, telematics help identify potential issues before they escalate into costly breakdowns or operational disruptions. Proactive maintenance scheduling based on real-time data ensures that vehicles receive timely servicing, reducing downtime and enhancing overall fleet reliability. For instance, alerts for low oil pressure or abnormal engine temperatures can prompt immediate action to prevent mechanical failures and extend vehicle lifespan.

Ensuring Route Adherence and Efficiency: GPS tracking capabilities within telematics systems ensure drivers adhere to planned routes and schedules. Real-time tracking enables fleet managers to monitor vehicle locations, anticipate arrival times, and detect unauthorized deviations from designated routes. This functionality not only enhances operational efficiency by optimizing route planning and minimizing unnecessary mileage but also improves customer satisfaction through accurate delivery timelines. By analysing historical route data and identifying optimal routes, logistics companies can streamline operations, reduce fuel consumption, and mitigate risks associated with unforeseen delays or detours.

Integration and Data Utilization: Integrating telematics and GPS tracking data with fleet management software enables comprehensive performance analysis and decision-making. Advanced analytics tools provide actionable insights into operational trends, driver productivity, and vehicle utilization rates. By leveraging data-driven insights, logistics managers can make informed decisions to optimize fleet operations, allocate resources efficiently, and improve overall business performance. For example, identifying high-traffic routes or inefficient driving habits allows for route optimization strategies that reduce operational costs and environmental impact.

Compliance and Safety Benefits: Telematics systems also support regulatory compliance by recording and reporting driver hours of service, ensuring adherence to legal driving limits and rest periods. Compliance with industry regulations and safety standards is enhanced through accurate data documentation and reporting capabilities. By maintaining compliance with regulations, logistics companies mitigate legal risks and uphold their reputation as responsible operators within the industry.

Conduct Safety Audits and Inspections

Regular safety audits and inspections are essential for assessing compliance with safety policies and identifying areas for improvement:

- **Internal Audits:** Conduct periodic internal audits to review adherence to safety procedures, vehicle maintenance records, and driver compliance with regulations.

- **Third-Party Inspections:** Engage external auditors or regulatory bodies to conduct independent inspections, providing an unbiased assessment of your safety practices.

Conducting regular safety audits and inspections is a fundamental practice in ensuring the safety and compliance of transport and logistics operations. These audits and inspections serve to evaluate adherence to safety policies, identify potential hazards, and implement corrective measures to mitigate risks. Here's a detailed exploration of how safety audits and inspections contribute to enhancing safety standards within logistics enterprises:

Internal Audits for Comprehensive Safety Review: Internal safety audits are conducted periodically within the organization to assess compliance with established safety procedures and protocols. These audits are typically carried out by qualified personnel within the safety or compliance departments. The objectives of internal audits include:

- Review of Safety Policies and Procedures: Auditors examine the effectiveness and implementation of safety policies, ensuring that they align with regulatory requirements and industry best practices. This includes policies related to vehicle maintenance, driver behaviour, cargo handling, and emergency response protocols.

- Evaluation of Vehicle Maintenance Records: Auditors review vehicle maintenance records to verify that scheduled maintenance tasks are performed according to manufacturer guidelines and operational requirements. This ensures that vehicles are in optimal condition to operate safely on the road and reduces the risk of mechanical failures.

- Assessment of Driver Compliance: Audits assess driver compliance with safety regulations, including adherence to driving hours, use of personal protective equipment (PPE), and completion of mandatory safety training programs. Identifying non-compliance issues allows for corrective actions such as additional training or disciplinary measures to reinforce safety standards.

Third-Party Inspections for Objective Evaluation: Engaging external auditors or regulatory bodies to conduct third-party inspections provides an unbiased assessment of safety practices and compliance. These inspections offer an independent perspective and validate the effectiveness of internal safety measures. Key aspects of third-party inspections include:

- Objective Assessment: External auditors bring expertise and objectivity to evaluate safety protocols, procedures, and compliance with regulatory standards. They identify potential gaps or deficiencies that may not have been identified internally, offering recommendations for improvement.

- Verification of Regulatory Compliance: Inspections ensure that the organization complies with local, national, and international safety regulations governing transport and logistics operations. This includes adherence to vehicle safety standards, driver licensing requirements, and environmental regulations.

- Benchmarking Against Industry Standards: Comparing audit findings with industry benchmarks helps organizations benchmark their safety performance against peers and identify opportunities for improvement. This fosters a culture of continuous improvement and accountability in maintaining high safety standards.

Implementation of Audit Findings and Continuous Improvement: Upon completion of audits and inspections, it is essential to implement findings and recommendations promptly. This involves:

- Corrective Actions: Addressing identified deficiencies through corrective actions, such as revising safety procedures, enhancing training programs, or upgrading equipment and infrastructure.

- Monitoring and Follow-Up: Monitoring the effectiveness of corrective actions and conducting follow-up audits to ensure sustained compliance and continuous improvement. This iterative process reinforces safety culture and enhances operational resilience against potential risks.

Benefits of Safety Audits and Inspections: Regular safety audits and inspections offer numerous benefits to transport and logistics enterprises:

- Enhanced Safety Performance: By identifying and addressing safety risks proactively, audits reduce the likelihood of accidents, injuries, and property damage.

- Compliance Assurance: Ensuring compliance with regulatory requirements and industry standards mitigates legal risks and enhances organizational reputation.

- Cost Savings: Preventing accidents and downtime through effective safety measures reduces operational costs associated with repairs, insurance premiums, and legal liabilities.

Implement Driver Training Programs

Ongoing training and education are crucial for maintaining a culture of safety within transport operations:

- **Initial Training:** Provide comprehensive training for new drivers, covering safe driving techniques, vehicle operation, cargo handling, and emergency procedures.

- **Refresher Courses:** Offer regular refresher courses to update drivers on new regulations, safety technologies, and best practices.

- **Behavioural Training:** Address specific safety concerns through targeted training programs, such as defensive driving courses or fatigue management workshops.

Implementing driver training programs is essential for fostering a culture of safety and enhancing operational efficiency within transport and logistics operations. These programs not only equip drivers with essential skills and knowledge but also promote adherence to safety protocols and regulatory compliance.

Initial Training for New Drivers: Effective driver training begins with comprehensive programs designed to onboard new drivers and familiarize them with essential safety practices and operational procedures. Initial training typically covers a range of topics, including:

- Safe Driving Techniques: Educating drivers on defensive driving techniques, hazard awareness, and proper vehicle handling practices to minimize risks on the road.

- Vehicle Operation: Providing detailed instruction on operating company vehicles, including understanding vehicle controls, performing pre-trip inspections, and responding to mechanical issues or emergencies.

- Cargo Handling and Securement: Training drivers on proper loading and securing of cargo to prevent shifting or damage during transit, ensuring compliance with weight distribution and load securement regulations.

- Emergency Procedures: Equipping drivers with protocols for responding to accidents, breakdowns, hazardous material spills, or other emergencies encountered during transport operations.

Figure 16: Driver training. Lucylonghauler, CC BY-SA 3.0, via Wikimedia Commons.

Refresher Courses to Maintain Knowledge and Skills: Continued learning through refresher courses is vital for keeping drivers updated on evolving regulations, technologies, and best practices in the transport industry. These courses serve several purposes:

- Regulatory Updates: Updating drivers on changes to local, national, or international regulations governing road safety, hours of service, and environmental standards.

- Safety Technologies: Introducing drivers to new safety technologies integrated into company vehicles, such as collision avoidance systems, telematics, and GPS tracking, and providing training on their use.

- Best Practices: Reinforcing best practices in areas like fuel efficiency, route optimization, and customer service to improve operational efficiency and customer satisfaction.

Behavioural Training to Address Safety Concerns: Targeted training programs address specific safety concerns and behavioural issues among drivers, aiming to mitigate risks associated with human factors:

- Defensive Driving Courses: Teaching defensive driving techniques to anticipate and react to potential hazards on the road, reducing the likelihood of accidents caused by aggressive or reckless driving behaviours.

- Fatigue Management Workshops: Educating drivers on recognizing signs of fatigue, managing sleep schedules, and adopting strategies to prevent drowsy driving, which is a leading cause of accidents in the transport industry.

- Customer Interaction and Service Excellence: Providing guidance on professional conduct during customer interactions, emphasizing communication skills, problem-solving abilities, and adherence to service standards.

Implementation and Evaluation of Training Effectiveness: Effective implementation of driver training programs involves several key steps to ensure their success:

- Training Delivery: Utilizing a mix of classroom instruction, hands-on practice, simulations, and e-learning modules to accommodate different learning styles and maximize engagement.

- Evaluation and Feedback: Assessing driver performance and knowledge retention through quizzes, practical assessments, and feedback sessions to identify areas needing improvement or additional training.

- Continuous Improvement: Using evaluation data to refine training curricula, update materials, and tailor programs to address emerging safety challenges or operational needs.

Benefits of Driver Training Programs: Implementing robust driver training programs offers numerous benefits to transport and logistics enterprises:

- Improved Safety Performance Equipping drivers with skills and knowledge to handle diverse road conditions and emergencies reduces the likelihood of accidents and promotes a safer work environment.

- Regulatory Compliance: Ensuring drivers understand and adhere to regulatory requirements minimizes legal risks and penalties associated with non-compliance.

- Enhanced Operational Efficiency: Well-trained drivers contribute to improved vehicle performance, fuel efficiency, and on-time delivery rates, enhancing overall operational efficiency and customer satisfaction.

Monitor Compliance with Safety Regulations

Ensure compliance with all relevant safety regulations and standards:

- **Regulatory Compliance:** Stay updated on local, national, and international transport safety regulations. Implement changes in procedures and practices as required to meet new regulatory standards.

- **Documentation:** Maintain accurate and up-to-date records of all safety-related activities, including vehicle maintenance logs, driver training certifications, and safety audit reports.

Monitoring compliance with safety regulations is crucial for ensuring the safety and regulatory adherence of transport and logistics operations. It involves staying updated on applicable safety standards, implementing necessary changes in procedures, and maintaining meticulous documentation.

Understanding Regulatory Compliance Requirements:

Effective compliance monitoring begins with a thorough understanding of local, national, and international safety regulations that govern transport operations. Regulations can encompass a wide range of areas, including vehicle safety standards, driver qualifications and hours of service, cargo handling practices, environmental protections, and emergency response protocols. Regulatory requirements can vary significantly between jurisdictions and may be subject to frequent updates or changes.

Implementation of Regulatory Changes:

Once regulations are identified and understood, the next step is to implement changes in procedures and practices to ensure compliance. This may involve:

- Policy and Procedure Updates: Reviewing existing safety policies and procedures to align them with current regulatory requirements. Updating policies as needed to reflect new standards or guidelines issued by regulatory authorities.

- Training and Awareness: Providing ongoing training and awareness programs to educate employees about regulatory changes, their implications for operations, and the importance of compliance. This includes training on new safety protocols, technologies, and best practices.

- Integration with Operations: Embedding compliance into daily operations by incorporating regulatory requirements into operational processes, such as vehicle inspections, driver dispatch protocols, and cargo handling procedures.

Documentation and Record-Keeping:
Maintaining accurate and up-to-date documentation is essential for demonstrating compliance with safety regulations. Key documentation includes:

- Vehicle Maintenance Logs: Recording regular inspections, maintenance activities, repairs, and replacements to ensure vehicles meet safety standards and perform reliably on the road.

- Driver Training Certifications: Documenting completion of initial training programs, refresher courses, and ongoing education to verify that drivers possess the necessary skills and knowledge to operate safely and legally.

- Safety Audit Reports: Keeping records of internal and external safety audits, including findings, corrective actions taken, and follow-up measures implemented to address identified deficiencies.

Monitoring and Auditing Compliance:
Monitoring compliance involves ongoing oversight and evaluation to ensure that safety regulations are consistently followed. Key aspects of monitoring include:

- Regular Audits and Inspections: Conducting regular audits of safety practices, procedures, and documentation to assess compliance with regulatory requirements. Internal audits provide an opportunity to identify gaps or areas needing improvement, while third-party audits offer an objective assessment of compliance status.

- Performance Metrics: Establishing key performance indicators (KPIs) related to safety compliance, such as the frequency of vehicle inspections, incident rates, or compliance with driver rest periods. Monitoring KPIs helps track progress, identify trends, and prioritize areas for corrective action.

- Feedback and Continuous Improvement: Soliciting feedback from employees, stakeholders, and regulatory authorities to identify potential compliance issues or opportunities for enhancement. Using feedback to refine procedures, implement corrective actions, and continuously improve safety performance.

Benefits of Monitoring Compliance:
Effective monitoring of safety compliance offers numerous benefits to transport and logistics enterprises:

- Risk Mitigation: Minimizing the risk of accidents, injuries, and legal liabilities associated with non-compliance with safety regulations.

- Operational Efficiency: Enhancing operational efficiency by ensuring that procedures are aligned with regulatory requirements, reducing disruptions and downtime caused by regulatory violations.

- Enhanced Reputation: Demonstrating a commitment to safety and regulatory compliance enhances the organization's reputation among customers, stakeholders, and regulatory authorities.

Establish a Reporting System for Safety Incidents

Create a robust reporting system for safety incidents that encourages prompt and transparent reporting of any accidents, near-misses, or safety concerns:

- **Incident Reporting:** Develop a clear process for reporting safety incidents, ensuring that all employees understand how and when to report issues.

- **Investigation and Analysis:** Investigate reported incidents thoroughly to determine root causes and implement corrective actions. Use data from incident reports to identify trends and areas for improvement.

Establishing a robust reporting system for safety incidents is essential in transport and logistics operations to promote a culture of safety, mitigate risks, and continuously improve safety practices.

Developing a Clear Incident Reporting Process:
A well-defined incident reporting process is the foundation of an effective safety reporting system. It should be straightforward, accessible, and clearly communicated to all employees across the organization. Key components of the process include:

- Procedures and Guidelines: Develop written procedures outlining how and when to report safety incidents, near-misses, injuries, or other safety concerns. Ensure these guidelines are easily accessible to employees through digital platforms, manuals, or posters in common areas.

- Reporting Channels: Establish multiple reporting channels to accommodate different communication preferences and ensure prompt reporting. This may include online reporting forms, direct contact with safety officers or supervisors, and anonymous reporting options to encourage open communication without fear of reprisal.

- Timeliness and Responsiveness: Emphasize the importance of timely reporting to capture accurate details and facilitate prompt response and investigation. Encourage employees to report incidents as soon as they occur or as soon as they become aware of a safety concern.

Investigation and Root Cause Analysis:

Upon receiving a safety incident report, conduct thorough investigations to identify root causes and contributing factors. The investigation process should be systematic and involve:

- Immediate Response: Promptly respond to reported incidents to ensure the safety of personnel and mitigate immediate risks. This may involve securing the scene, providing medical assistance if necessary, and preventing further incidents from occurring.

- Gathering Evidence: Collect relevant evidence, such as witness statements, photographs, video footage, and equipment involved in the incident. Ensure confidentiality and sensitivity when handling personal information or sensitive data.

- Root Cause Analysis: Use established methodologies, such as Fishbone (Ishikawa) diagrams, 5 Whys analysis, or Fault Tree Analysis (FTA), to systematically determine the underlying causes of the incident. Identify contributing factors related to equipment failure, human error, procedural deficiencies, or environmental conditions.

Implementing Corrective and Preventive Actions:

Based on findings from the investigation, implement corrective actions to address immediate safety concerns and preventive actions to reduce the likelihood of similar incidents in the future. This may include:

- Process Improvement: Revise existing safety procedures, workflows, or protocols to enhance safety measures and prevent recurrence of similar incidents. Ensure that revised procedures are communicated effectively to all relevant personnel and integrated into daily operations.

- Training and Awareness: Provide targeted training programs to educate employees on lessons learned from incident investigations, emphasizing safe work practices, hazard recognition, and emergency response protocols.

- Equipment and Facility Upgrades: Consider upgrading equipment, implementing engineering controls, or modifying facilities to mitigate identified risks and improve overall safety performance.

Utilizing Incident Data for Continuous Improvement:
Collect and analyse data from incident reports to identify trends, patterns, and recurring issues. This data-driven approach enables proactive safety management and continuous improvement initiatives:

- Trend Analysis: Conduct periodic reviews of incident data to identify trends or emerging patterns that may indicate systemic issues requiring further investigation or targeted interventions.

- Performance Metrics: Establish key performance indicators (KPIs) related to safety incident rates, response times, and effectiveness of corrective actions. Monitor KPIs to gauge the impact of safety initiatives and track progress toward safety objectives.

- Feedback and Communication: Foster a culture of continuous improvement by soliciting feedback from employees, safety committees, and stakeholders. Encourage open dialogue on safety concerns and encourage suggestions for improving safety procedures and practices.

Benefits of Establishing a Reporting System for Safety Incidents:
Implementing a robust reporting system for safety incidents offers several benefits to transport and logistics enterprises:

- Enhanced Safety Culture: Promotes transparency, accountability, and a proactive approach to safety management across the organization.

- Risk Mitigation: Identifies and addresses potential hazards and risks before they escalate into more significant incidents or accidents.

- **Compliance and Legal Protection:** Demonstrates compliance with regulatory requirements and mitigates legal liabilities associated with safety incidents through thorough documentation and proactive risk management.

Foster a Safety Culture

Promote a culture of safety within the organization, emphasizing the importance of safe practices and continuous improvement:

- **Safety Leadership:** Encourage leaders and managers to model safe behaviour and prioritize safety in decision-making.
- **Employee Engagement:** Involve employees in safety initiatives, seeking their input on safety practices and recognizing their contributions to maintaining a safe work environment.
- **Continuous Improvement:** Regularly review and update safety policies and procedures based on feedback, incident reports, and new safety technologies.

Fostering a safety culture within transport and logistics organizations is paramount to ensuring the well-being of personnel, protecting assets, and maintaining operational continuity. This approach goes beyond mere compliance with safety regulations; it involves instilling a mindset where safety is ingrained in every aspect of operations.

Safety Leadership:

Leadership plays a crucial role in shaping organizational culture and setting the tone for safety. Effective safety leaders prioritize safety as a core value and demonstrate their commitment through actions and decisions. They actively participate in safety initiatives, visibly support safety programs, and hold themselves and others accountable for adhering to safety standards. By modelling safe behaviours and emphasizing the importance of safety in all communications, leaders create an environment where safety is not seen as a separate initiative but as integral to overall business success.

Employee Engagement:

Engaging employees in safety initiatives is key to building a strong safety culture. Employees are often the frontline observers of safety hazards and are essential in identifying and mitigating risks. Organizations can involve employees by:

- Participation in Safety Committees: Establishing safety committees or forums where employees from different departments can discuss safety concerns, share ideas for improvement, and collaborate on safety initiatives.

- Training and Education: Providing comprehensive training on safety protocols, hazard recognition, emergency procedures, and the proper use of safety equipment. Encouraging ongoing education ensures that employees remain informed about best practices and regulatory changes.

- Recognition and Incentives: Recognizing and rewarding employees who demonstrate exemplary safety practices or contribute innovative ideas for enhancing safety. Incentives can range from verbal recognition in team meetings to tangible rewards that reinforce a safety-first culture.

Continuous Improvement:
Safety is a dynamic aspect of organizational management that requires continuous improvement efforts. To foster a culture of safety, organizations should:

- Regularly Review Policies and Procedures: Conduct periodic reviews of safety policies and procedures to ensure they are up to date with current regulations and industry best practices. Solicit feedback from employees and safety committees to identify areas for improvement or clarification.

- Learn from Incidents: Encourage a proactive approach to incident reporting and investigation. Analyse incident data to identify trends, root causes, and systemic issues that require corrective actions. Use lessons learned to revise procedures, implement preventive measures, and enhance training programs.

- Embrace Technology: Leverage advancements in safety technologies, such as wearable devices, real-time monitoring systems, and predictive analytics, to proactively identify and mitigate safety risks. Incorporating technology not only enhances operational efficiency but also strengthens safety management practices.

Chain of Responsibility

The concept of "Chain of Responsibility" (CoR) is a legal and regulatory framework designed to ensure that all parties involved in transport and logistics operations share responsibility for compliance with safety and regulatory requirements. Originating from Australian law, particularly in the context of heavy vehicle transport, the principle has since been adopted and adapted in various forms globally to enhance safety and accountability across supply chains.

Key Elements of Chain of Responsibility:

- **Shared Responsibility:** CoR recognizes that responsibility for safety extends beyond just the driver and vehicle operator. It includes all parties in the supply chain who have influence or control over transport tasks, such as consignors, consignees, loaders, schedulers, and operators.

- **Legal Obligations:** Under CoR, these parties have legal obligations to ensure compliance with safety standards, fatigue management, load restraint, vehicle maintenance, and other regulations. Each party is expected to take reasonable steps to prevent breaches of these regulations.

- **Safety Focus:** The primary aim of CoR is to improve safety outcomes within the transport industry by holding all parties accountable for their roles in ensuring safe practices. This includes mitigating risks associated with fatigue, speeding, overloading, and unsafe transport practices.

- **Enforcement and Penalties:** Regulatory authorities enforce CoR through inspections, audits, and investigations. Penalties for non-compliance can be severe and may include fines, license suspensions, or legal action against individuals or companies found responsible for safety breaches.

Application and Impact:

- **Industry Compliance:** Implementing CoR requires robust systems and processes within organizations to monitor and manage compliance across the supply chain. This includes documentation of responsibilities, training programs, and regular audits to ensure adherence to safety standards.

- **Risk Management:** By clarifying responsibilities and accountability, CoR helps mitigate risks associated with transport operations. It encourages proactive risk management practices and promotes a culture of safety within organizations.

- **Legal Clarity:** CoR provides clarity on legal obligations and expectations for all parties involved in transport operations. This helps in resolving disputes and improving communication and cooperation within the supply chain.

Examples of CoR in Practice:
- **Australia:** In Australia, CoR is governed by the Heavy Vehicle National Law (HVNL), which places legal duties on all parties in the supply chain to ensure safe transport operations. This includes obligations related to loading, vehicle maintenance, driver fatigue management, and safe driving practices.

- **United States:** While not explicitly labelled as "Chain of Responsibility," similar principles are embedded in U.S. regulations governing transportation, particularly in sectors such as trucking and logistics. Responsibilities for safety and compliance are distributed among various stakeholders involved in transport operations.

- **Europe and Beyond:** Countries in Europe and other regions have adopted variations of CoR principles to improve safety and regulatory compliance in transport and logistics. These frameworks aim to enhance operational efficiency while prioritizing safety and environmental sustainability.

Chain of Responsibility is a vital concept in transport and logistics management, emphasizing shared accountability for safety and compliance across the supply chain. By clarifying roles, promoting proactive safety measures, and enforcing legal obligations, CoR helps mitigate risks, improve industry standards, and ensure the safe and efficient movement of goods and people globally.

Here's an overview of how responsibility and accountability are managed in the U.S. transport sector:

Federal Regulations and Standards
- **Federal Motor Carrier Safety Administration (FMCSA):** The FMCSA is a key federal agency responsible for regulating and overseeing commercial motor vehicles (CMVs) in interstate commerce. It sets standards for driver qualifications, hours of service, vehicle maintenance, and safety equipment.

- **Federal Regulations:** Various federal regulations under the Department of Transportation (DOT) mandate safety standards for CMVs and their operations. These regulations cover areas such as vehicle weight limits, hazardous materials transportation, driver licensing, and compliance with safety protocols.

State Regulations

- **State Transportation Agencies:** Each state in the U.S. has its own transportation department or agency responsible for overseeing transportation within its jurisdiction. States may adopt and enforce additional regulations beyond federal standards to address specific local needs and conditions.

- **State-Specific Laws:** States may have specific laws governing issues such as weight restrictions, traffic regulations, environmental standards, and safety requirements applicable to commercial vehicles operating within their boundaries.

Industry Standards and Best Practices

- **American Trucking Associations (ATA):** The ATA and other industry associations develop voluntary standards, guidelines, and best practices for safe and efficient transport operations. These standards often align with federal regulations but may provide additional guidance to enhance safety and operational effectiveness.

- **Safety Management Systems (SMS):** Many transport companies in the U.S. implement Safety Management Systems tailored to their operations. SMS frameworks focus on risk management, compliance with regulations, driver training, vehicle maintenance, and incident reporting.

Legal Principles

- **Liability and Accountability:** In cases of accidents or safety violations involving commercial vehicles, U.S. legal principles establish liability and accountability. Responsible parties may include drivers, vehicle operators, owners, shippers, and other stakeholders involved in the transport chain.

- **Litigation and Enforcement:** Legal actions, including civil lawsuits and regulatory enforcement actions by federal and state authorities, address violations of safety regulations. Penalties for non-compliance can include fines, license suspensions, and other sanctions aimed at promoting compliance and improving safety outcomes.

Practical Application

In practice, the U.S. approach to ensuring safety and regulatory compliance in transport operations involves a combination of federal oversight, state-specific regulations, industry standards, and legal principles. This multifaceted framework aims to promote safety, protect public interests, and ensure the efficient movement of goods while holding stakeholders accountable for their roles in transport operations.

In Europe, the concept similar to Chain of Responsibility (CoR) is addressed through various regulatory frameworks and directives that emphasize shared responsibility, accountability, and compliance with safety standards across the transport and logistics sectors. While there isn't a single unified term like "Chain of Responsibility" used throughout Europe, several key principles and regulatory approaches achieve similar objectives. Here's an overview of how responsibility and accountability are managed in the European Union (EU) and its member states:

European Union Regulations and Directives

- **Road Transport Legislation:** The EU regulates road transport through directives and regulations aimed at harmonizing safety standards and operational practices across member states. Key directives include:

    - **Directive 2006/126/EC (Driver Licensing):** Sets out requirements for obtaining and maintaining driver licenses for various vehicle categories.

    - **Directive 2003/59/EC (Driver Certificate of Professional Competence - CPC):** Establishes requirements for professional qualifications and ongoing training for drivers of commercial vehicles.

    - **Directive 2006/22/EC (Drivers' Hours):** Specifies rules on driving times, breaks, and rest periods to combat driver fatigue and improve road safety.

    - **Directive 96/53/EC (Weights and Dimensions):** Establishes standards for maximum weights and dimensions of commercial vehicles to ensure safety and infrastructure protection.

- **Transport Safety Agencies:** The European Union Agency for Railways (ERA), European Maritime Safety Agency (EMSA), and the European Aviation Safety Agency (EASA) play crucial roles in regulating and overseeing safety standards in their respective transport modes.

National Regulations and Standards

- **Member State Laws:** EU member states implement and enforce EU directives through national legislation and regulations. They may also establish additional requirements and standards to address specific local conditions and needs.

- **Enforcement and Compliance:** Regulatory authorities in each member state enforce safety standards through inspections, audits, and enforcement actions. Penalties for non-compliance can include fines, license suspensions, and other sanctions to ensure adherence to safety regulations.

Industry Practices and Best Practices

- **Industry Associations:** Organizations such as the International Road Transport Union (IRU) and national transport associations develop industry standards, guidelines, and best practices to promote safety and operational efficiency.

- **Safety Management Systems (SMS):** Transport companies in Europe often implement SMS frameworks tailored to their operations. These systems focus on risk management, compliance with regulations, training, vehicle maintenance, and incident reporting to enhance safety outcomes.

Practical Application

In practice, the European approach to ensuring safety and regulatory compliance in transport operations emphasizes a harmonized regulatory framework across member states, supported by national laws and industry standards. The overarching goal is to promote safety, protect the environment, and ensure the efficient movement of goods and passengers while holding all parties accountable for their roles in transport operations.

In the context of the Heavy Vehicle National Law (HVNL) in Australia, the principle of shared responsibility within the Chain of Responsibility (CoR) framework is crucial for ensuring safety and compliance across the transport industry. Here's an explanation of how shared responsibilities are determined within the HVNL or applicable state/territory laws and regulations:

The HVNL is a national framework that governs the operation of heavy vehicles over 4.5 tonnes gross vehicle mass (GVM) across most Australian states and territories. It aims to improve road safety, promote productivity, and ensure fair competition in the transport sector. The CoR provisions under the HVNL extend liability beyond

STRATEGIC MANAGEMENT FOR TRANSPORT AND LOGISTICS

just the driver of a heavy vehicle to other parties in the transport chain who have influence or control over transport operations.

Principles of Shared Responsibility:

- **Primary Duties:** Under the HVNL, all parties in the transport chain have primary duties to ensure safety and compliance. These duties are not limited to the driver but extend to:

    - **Operators:** Those who operate or manage the use of heavy vehicles.

    - **Consignors and Consignees:** Parties responsible for the consignment of goods.

    - **Loading Managers:** Those responsible for loading or unloading goods onto/from the vehicle.

    - **Schedulers and Employers:** Those involved in planning and scheduling transport operations.

    - **Executive Officers:** Senior management or directors who have the ability to influence the company's conduct.

- **Shared Responsibility Obligations:** The HVNL mandates that all parties in the transport chain must take all reasonable steps to prevent breaches of road transport laws. This includes ensuring that their actions or decisions do not contribute to unsafe practices or breaches of legal requirements such as:

    - Ensuring vehicles are roadworthy and properly maintained.

    - Preventing driver fatigue through safe scheduling and monitoring practices.

    - Securing loads properly to prevent shifting or falling during transit.

    - Compliance with speed limits, vehicle dimensions, and other operational regulations.

    - Providing adequate training and supervision for drivers and other personnel involved in transport operations.

Determining Shared Responsibilities:

- **Risk Assessment:** Parties must conduct risk assessments to identify potential risks and hazards associated with their transport operations. This involves assessing the likelihood and consequences of breaches occurring within their sphere of influence.

- **Control and Influence:** Responsibility is attributed based on the level of control or influence each party has over the transport activities. This can include operational decisions, contractual arrangements, financial incentives, and managerial oversight.

- **Contractual Agreements:** Contracts and agreements between parties often specify roles, responsibilities, and expectations regarding safety and compliance. These agreements can influence how responsibilities are allocated within the transport chain.

Compliance and Enforcement:

- **Enforcement:** Regulatory authorities enforce CoR obligations through inspections, audits, and investigations. They may issue fines, penalties, or sanctions for breaches of the HVNL or related regulations.

- **Education and Awareness:** Authorities also promote education and awareness campaigns to inform stakeholders about their CoR obligations and encourage proactive compliance measures.

In practice, the principle of shared responsibility within the HVNL ensures that all parties in the transport chain are accountable for safety and compliance, not just the driver of the heavy vehicle. By assigning responsibilities based on influence and control, the CoR framework aims to improve safety outcomes, reduce risks on the road, and foster a culture of proactive risk management within the transport industry in Australia.

This framework assigns specific primary duties to various parties involved in transport operations.

Firstly, drivers of heavy vehicles bear a fundamental responsibility to operate safely and adhere strictly to road transport laws. This encompasses driving in a manner that ensures their fitness to operate, compliance with speed limits and rest requirements, and adherence to all relevant road rules. They are also required to conduct thorough pre-trip inspections to verify the roadworthiness and proper maintenance of their vehicles, and to secure loads adequately to prevent shifting or falling during transit.

Operators, who manage the use of heavy vehicles, are tasked with maintaining vehicles to a safe operational standard through regular servicing and maintenance. They must implement robust safety management systems to address risks such as driver fatigue and speed compliance. Additionally, operators are responsible for providing comprehensive training and supervision to drivers and other personnel involved in transport operations, ensuring they are well-equipped to uphold safety standards.

Consignors and consignees, responsible for the consignment of goods, play a crucial role in ensuring safe loading and unloading practices. They must adhere to best practices and regulatory requirements to ensure goods are handled securely. Providing accurate information about the goods, including their weight, dimensions, and any special handling requirements, is essential to facilitating safe transport operations.

Loading managers oversee the loading and unloading of heavy vehicles, focusing on proper load restraint to prevent instability or hazards on the road. They must comply strictly with relevant standards and guidelines governing load handling and restraint to ensure safety throughout the transportation process.

Schedulers and employers involved in planning and scheduling transport operations are responsible for managing driver fatigue and ensuring compliance with rest breaks and working hours. They must meticulously plan routes that minimize risks and adhere to regulatory requirements concerning vehicle dimensions and weight limits.

At the executive level, senior management and directors hold accountability for overall CoR compliance within their organizations. They are obligated to provide leadership in promoting a culture of safety and compliance, allocating adequate resources to support effective CoR compliance systems, and ensuring that all aspects of the transport operations align with regulatory standards.

Implementation and compliance with the HVNL and related regulations require each party in the transport chain to take proactive measures to prevent breaches of road transport laws. This involves conducting rigorous risk assessments to identify potential hazards and risks associated with transport activities, developing and maintaining documented policies and procedures that outline responsibilities and compliance measures, providing ongoing training and education to employees to enhance their understanding of safety responsibilities, and regularly monitoring and reviewing compliance with CoR obligations through audits and inspections to identify areas for improvement.

Regulatory authorities enforce CoR obligations through a variety of means, including inspections, audits, and investigations. Penalties for non-compliance can be severe, encompassing fines, sanctions, and other enforcement actions. The overarching objective of the CoR framework is to ensure that all parties in the transport chain share responsibility for safety and compliance, thereby enhancing road safety, protecting the environment, and promoting fair competition within the transport industry.

Monitoring Obligations to Law and Regulations

Monitoring the safety of transport activities involves several key steps to ensure that workplace policies, procedures, and other safety documents are identified and effectively monitored as they apply to specific job functions. Here's how you can approach it:

- **Identification of Relevant Documents:**
  - **Policies:** Identify workplace policies related to transport safety, which may include vehicle use policies, driver safety protocols, maintenance schedules, and emergency procedures.
  - **Procedures:** Understand the specific procedures that govern transport activities, such as loading and unloading protocols, route planning, vehicle inspection routines, and reporting procedures for accidents or incidents.
  - **Safety Documents:** Gather relevant safety documents like risk assessments, safety data sheets (SDS) for hazardous materials being transported, and any regulatory compliance documents.
- **Job Function Analysis:**
  - Determine how each job function within the transport operation interacts with these policies, procedures, and safety documents. This includes drivers, supervisors, maintenance personnel, and logistics coordinators.

- Clearly define responsibilities and expectations for each role in relation to safety protocols.

- **Monitoring Process:**

  - **Regular Reviews:** Schedule regular reviews of policies, procedures, and safety documents to ensure they are up-to-date with current regulations and industry best practices.

  - **Audits and Inspections:** Conduct periodic audits and inspections to verify compliance with established policies and procedures. This may involve checking vehicle maintenance records, driver logs, and adherence to safety protocols during operations.

  - **Feedback Mechanisms:** Establish feedback mechanisms where employees can report safety concerns or suggest improvements to existing policies and procedures.

- **Training and Awareness:**

  - Provide ongoing training to employees on the importance of adhering to safety policies and procedures.

  - Ensure that all employees, especially those involved directly in transport activities, are aware of their responsibilities and the potential consequences of non-compliance.

- **Documentation and Record-Keeping:**

  - Maintain comprehensive records of all safety-related activities, including training sessions, audits, inspections, and incidents.

  - Document any changes or updates made to policies and procedures, and ensure these are communicated effectively to all relevant personnel.

- **Continuous Improvement:**

  - Foster a culture of continuous improvement by reviewing incidents or near misses to identify areas where policies or procedures can be enhanced.

- Encourage proactive suggestions from employees for improving safety measures based on their experiences and observations.

In the transport and logistics industry, managing speed and fatigue is critical to ensuring both safety and regulatory compliance. Several methods and requirements are employed to facilitate and monitor these aspects according to job functions and workplace procedures.

Speed Management:

Effective speed management begins with clear policies and procedures that outline speed limits, safe driving practices, and the consequences of exceeding speed limits. These policies are typically based on regulatory requirements and best practices in road safety. In the transport industry, speed is often monitored through various methods:

- Speed Limiters: Vehicles may be equipped with speed limiters that restrict maximum speeds to comply with legal limits and company policies. These devices help prevent drivers from exceeding safe speeds, especially on highways or within urban areas.

- GPS and Telematics Systems: Many companies utilize GPS and telematics systems to monitor vehicle speed in real-time. These systems provide data on actual driving speeds, allowing for immediate intervention if drivers exceed set limits. They also enable managers to track historical speed data for analysis and compliance reporting.

- Driver Training and Monitoring: Regular training sessions educate drivers on the importance of adhering to speed limits and safe driving practices. Supervisors may conduct periodic assessments or ride-alongs to observe driver behaviour and reinforce compliance with speed regulations.

- Feedback and Reporting Systems: Implementing feedback mechanisms where drivers receive alerts or reports on their driving behaviour regarding speed violations encourages self-awareness and accountability. These systems can also notify management of persistent issues that require corrective action.

STRATEGIC MANAGEMENT FOR TRANSPORT AND LOGISTICS

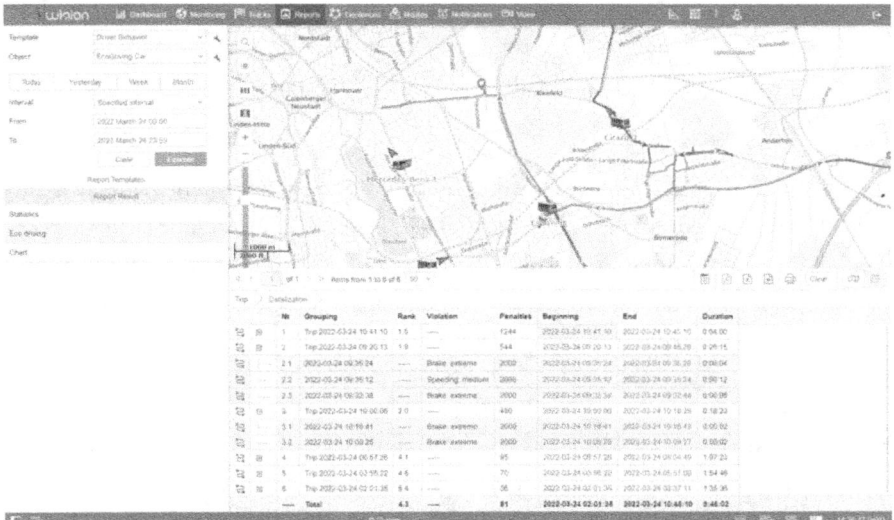

Figure 17: Wialon telematics solution. AldiDi, CC BY-SA 4.0, via Wikimedia Commons.

Fatigue Management:

Fatigue management is crucial to prevent accidents caused by drowsy driving, which can be as dangerous as driving under the influence of alcohol. The transport industry implements several strategies to address fatigue among drivers:

- Hours of Service Regulations: Regulatory bodies often mandate maximum allowable driving hours within specific periods, ensuring drivers take adequate rest breaks and adhere to daily and weekly limits. Companies must track and enforce these regulations to prevent driver fatigue.

- Driver Scheduling and Rostering: Effective scheduling practices aim to distribute workloads evenly among drivers, minimizing the risk of fatigue. Rosters should consider factors like consecutive driving hours, overnight shifts, and rest periods to promote alertness and compliance with legal requirements.

- Fatigue Risk Management Systems (FRMS): FRMS utilize data-driven approaches to assess and mitigate fatigue risks within transport operations. These systems may involve predictive modelling, fatigue monitoring technologies, and comprehensive fatigue management plans tailored to specific job functions and operational contexts.

- Education and Awareness Programs: Ongoing training programs educate drivers and logistics personnel about the signs and risks of fatigue. They promote strategies for recognizing fatigue symptoms, managing sleep hygiene, and adopting healthy lifestyle habits that support alertness on the road.

- Incident Analysis and Continuous Improvement: Analysing incidents related to fatigue and near-misses provides insights into systemic issues and opportunities for improvement. Companies can implement corrective actions, such as adjusting schedules or enhancing rest facilities, to enhance fatigue management strategies.

In the transport and logistics industry, accurately calculating and assessing vehicle dimension and mass limits is crucial for ensuring compliance with legal regulations and operational safety standards. Several methods are employed to monitor these limits effectively, tailored to specific job functions within the industry.

Dimension Limits:

Calculating and monitoring vehicle dimensions involves precise measurements of length, width, height, and axle spacing to ensure compliance with road regulations and operational constraints. Methods include:

- Pre-Trip Inspections: Drivers and logistics personnel conduct pre-trip inspections to verify that vehicles comply with dimensional limits set by local authorities. This includes checking overall vehicle height, width including any protruding loads, and ensuring compliance with bridge height restrictions.

- Load Planning and Optimization: Utilizing load planning software helps optimize cargo placement within permissible dimensions. This ensures that vehicles are loaded within legal limits and that loads are distributed evenly to maintain stability and safety during transit.

- Vehicle Modification Compliance: Any modifications to vehicles that affect dimensions, such as installing rooftop equipment or extending trailer lengths, must comply with regulatory guidelines. Monitoring these modifications ensures that vehicles remain within legal limits.

- Real-Time Monitoring Systems: Some companies employ real-time tracking and monitoring systems that alert drivers and dispatchers if a vehicle exceeds preset dimensional limits during transit. These systems help prevent inadvertent violations and allow for immediate corrective action.

Mass Limits:

Monitoring vehicle mass limits involves accurately calculating the weight of the vehicle itself (tare weight) and the combined weight of its cargo (gross vehicle mass or gross combination mass). Methods for monitoring mass limits include:

- Weighbridge Checks: Vehicles are periodically weighed at designated weighbridges to ensure compliance with legal mass limits. This process verifies that the vehicle's load is within permissible weight thresholds, preventing overloading which can lead to mechanical strain and safety hazards.

- Payload Management Software: Utilizing specialized software helps calculate and monitor payload distribution to ensure that vehicles operate within legal mass limits. This includes considering axle weight distribution to prevent overloading on specific axles, which can affect vehicle stability and road safety.

- Axle Load Monitoring: Monitoring individual axle loads during operation helps ensure that no single axle exceeds legal weight limits. This approach is critical for compliance with axle weight restrictions imposed by regulatory authorities.

- Driver Education and Training: Educating drivers on the importance of adhering to mass limits and providing training on load securement techniques helps prevent overloading and ensures compliance with weight regulations. Drivers are also trained to recognize signs of overloading and take corrective measures as necessary.

In the transport and logistics sector, ensuring the secure fastening of loads is paramount for upholding road safety standards and meeting regulatory obligations. Various methods are employed to effectively monitor and enforce load security, all designed to align with rigorous workplace procedures and mitigate the risks associated with load shifting or cargo spillage.

One of the foundational approaches is the establishment of Standard Operating Procedures (SOPs) specifically tailored for load securing. These SOPs provide clear guidelines on how to safely secure different types of cargo using appropriate equipment such as straps, chains, dunnage, and edge protectors. They also detail the necessary tension or torque specifications for securing devices, ensuring that loads remain stable throughout transit.

Before embarking on journeys, drivers and logistics personnel conduct meticulous inspections of both the load and the securing devices. This pre-departure check includes verifying the correct placement, tension, and condition of straps or chains. Throughout the journey, regular inspections are essential to monitor load stability continuously and promptly detect any signs of loosening or shifting that could compromise safety.

A critical aspect of ensuring load security involves calculating the required restraint force to withstand various forces such as cargo weight, braking or acceleration forces, and road conditions. These calculations are crucial in selecting and implementing appropriate securing methods that can effectively prevent load movement and maintain stability during transportation.

Comprehensive training and ongoing education programs are integral to equipping drivers and loading personnel with the necessary skills for effective load securing. Training covers a range of topics including proper techniques for securing different types of loads, hazard recognition, and protocols for responding to emergencies or load shifting incidents. Regular refresher courses ensure that employees are updated on the latest safety standards and technological advancements in load securing equipment.

Technological advancements play a pivotal role in modern load security monitoring. Tools like load monitoring sensors provide real-time feedback on changes in load distribution or tension levels in securing devices. Telematics systems integrated with GPS can issue alerts if loads exceed safe parameters during transit, enabling immediate corrective action to be taken to mitigate potential risks.

Documenting and maintaining accurate records of load securing procedures and inspections are essential for compliance and accountability. Detailed documentation includes records of pre-trip inspections, methods employed for load securing, and any adjustments made during transit. This documentation not only facilitates internal audits but also ensures adherence to workplace procedures and regulatory requirements.

Establishing a feedback mechanism within the organization encourages drivers and personnel to report incidents and provide suggestions for improving load securing practices. Analysing feedback, along with reviewing near misses or incidents, helps identify systemic issues and implement corrective measures to continuously enhance load security protocols. This proactive approach not only enhances safety but also strengthens operational efficiency and reinforces a culture of safety awareness throughout the organization.

In the transport and logistics industry, adhering to robust safety standards for heavy vehicles is paramount to ensure both operational efficiency and the safety of drivers, passengers, and other road users. Comprehensive methods are employed to identify and monitor these safety standards in accordance with workplace procedures, addressing various aspects of vehicle design, maintenance, and operational practices.

Firstly, identifying heavy vehicle safety standards begins with a thorough understanding of regulatory requirements set forth by governmental authorities. These standards encompass a wide range of criteria, including vehicle dimensions, weight limits, braking systems, lighting and visibility requirements, emission controls, and structural integrity. Workplace procedures are aligned with these standards to ensure full compliance, which may involve regular updates and training sessions to keep personnel informed of any regulatory changes.

Monitoring heavy vehicle safety standards involves several proactive measures. Routine inspections and maintenance checks play a crucial role in ensuring that vehicles meet prescribed safety criteria. These inspections cover essential components such as brakes, tires, suspension systems, and engine performance, conducted by qualified technicians trained to identify and rectify any potential safety issues promptly.

Additionally, implementing a systematic approach to vehicle inspections is essential. Pre-departure inspections, for instance, are conducted to verify that all safety features are functional and in compliance with standards before vehicles enter service. Regular scheduled maintenance intervals are also established to address wear and tear, ensuring that vehicles remain in optimal condition and capable of operating safely under varying conditions.

Workplace procedures are further reinforced through the adoption of technological advancements in vehicle monitoring and safety systems. Advanced telematics systems, for example, provide real-time data on vehicle performance and driver behaviour, allowing fleet managers to identify potential safety risks such as excessive speeding, harsh braking, or unauthorized vehicle operation. These systems also facilitate remote diagnostics, enabling timely maintenance interventions to uphold safety standards.

Training and education are integral components of ensuring compliance with heavy vehicle safety standards. Drivers and maintenance personnel receive comprehensive training on safe driving practices, emergency response protocols, and the proper use of safety equipment. Continuous education programs keep them updated on the latest safety innovations and regulatory requirements, empowering them to contribute effectively to maintaining high safety standards within the organization.

Documentation and record-keeping are critical to demonstrating adherence to workplace procedures and regulatory standards. Detailed records of vehicle inspections, maintenance activities, safety audits, and compliance certifications are maintained for internal audits and regulatory compliance purposes. This documentation not only serves as a reference for future inspections but also provides transparency and accountability within the organization.

In the realm of transport and logistics, identifying, assessing, and effectively managing risks associated with transport activities is crucial for ensuring safety, operational efficiency, and compliance with regulatory requirements. This process involves systematic steps aligned with workplace procedures to mitigate potential hazards and minimize the impact of risks on personnel, cargo, and the environment.

Identification of Risks: The first step in managing transport activity risks is to identify potential hazards and risks inherent in the operation. This includes analysing various factors such as vehicle operations, loading and unloading procedures, road conditions, weather patterns, and potential human errors. Workplace procedures typically involve conducting comprehensive risk assessments that consider historical incident data, industry best practices, and regulatory guidelines to identify all possible risks associated with transport activities.

Driver fatigue is a critical issue in the transport industry, posing significant risks to both drivers and public safety. Fatigue often stems from inadequate sleep, driving during typical sleep hours such as late at night or early morning, and prolonged periods of wakefulness. Studies show that being awake for 17 hours straight can impair driving ability equivalent to having a blood alcohol concentration of 0.05%, resulting in reactions that are 50% slower [25]. This is especially concerning given the size and weight of some trucks, which can exceed 40 tons, making them particularly hazardous when operated by fatigued drivers.

To address these risks, in Australia for example, the National Heavy Vehicle Regulator (NHVR) has implemented stringent fatigue management laws for heavy vehicle operators. These regulations stipulate limits on daily driving hours and mandatory rest periods between shifts, forming part of the broader Chain of Responsibility law aimed at enhancing road safety [25].

Monitoring and managing driver fatigue is facilitated through various methods. Traditionally, paper-based logbooks or electronic journey management systems track driving hours and rest breaks. Advanced technologies, such as in-vehicle systems that monitor driver eye movements for signs of drowsiness (like prolonged blinks or rapid eye movements), offer real-time alerts to mitigate fatigue-related risks.

For interstate hauls, some heavy vehicles are equipped with sleeper berths behind the driver's cabin, providing a designated rest area complete with a bed and privacy curtain [25]. Additionally, transport companies may establish on-site rest facilities resembling small motor inns, enabling drivers to recuperate after extended shifts.

Given the high incidence of work-related injuries in the transport industry, particularly musculoskeletal disorders (MSDs), effective risk management is crucial. MSDs often result from repetitive manual tasks like loading trucks and ergonomic challenges such as prolonged static seating during driving [25]. Implementing robust procedures and ergonomic interventions can mitigate these risks, although the dynamic nature of transport operations can complicate consistent risk management practices.

Stress management is also paramount for heavy vehicle drivers due to the demanding nature of their work. Manoeuvring large trucks across vast distances under tight schedules and handling diverse cargo, including hazardous materials, contributes to elevated stress levels. Research indicates that stressed drivers are significantly more likely to be involved in accidents, highlighting the need for effective stress reduction strategies and supportive workplace environments.

Figure 18: Road conditions can add to driver stress and fatigue such as ice road trucking. MJ Preston, CC BY-SA 3.0, via Wikimedia Commons.

Figure 19: Oversize loads can also create additional stress. 111 Emergency from New Zealand, CC BY 2.0, via Wikimedia Commons.

Risk Assessment: Once risks are identified, the next phase involves assessing their likelihood and potential consequences. Risk assessment methodologies may vary but generally involve qualitative and quantitative analysis to prioritize risks based on their severity and likelihood of occurrence. This step helps in understanding which risks pose the greatest threat and where resources should be allocated for effective risk management.

Implementation of Risk Control Measures: After identifying and assessing risks, appropriate risk control measures are implemented to mitigate or eliminate identified hazards. These measures are designed to reduce the likelihood of incidents and minimize their impact if they occur. Examples of risk control measures include:

- Engineering Controls: Modifying equipment or infrastructure to enhance safety, such as installing vehicle safety features, improving road signage, or implementing automated safety systems.

- Administrative Controls: Establishing policies, procedures, and guidelines that govern safe transport practices, including driver training programs, scheduling practices that minimize fatigue, and protocols for emergency response.

- Personal Protective Equipment (PPE): Providing drivers and personnel with appropriate PPE, such as reflective vests or safety helmets, to reduce the risk of injury during transport activities.

Monitoring and Review: Once risk control measures are implemented, continuous monitoring and review are essential to ensure their effectiveness and adapt to changing conditions. Regular inspections, audits, and performance evaluations help identify any gaps or emerging risks that require adjustment or enhancement of existing controls. This iterative process ensures that risk management strategies remain relevant and effective over time.

Integration with Workplace Procedures: Throughout this entire process, adherence to workplace procedures is critical. These procedures provide a structured framework for identifying, assessing, implementing, and monitoring risk control measures consistently across all transport activities. They also ensure that all employees are aware of their roles and responsibilities in maintaining a safe working environment and complying with regulatory standards.

Documentation and Communication: Documenting all aspects of risk management activities, including risk assessments, control measures, monitoring results, and incident reports, is essential for accountability and compliance. Clear communication of safety protocols and updates ensures that all stakeholders, including drivers, management, and regulatory authorities, are informed and aligned with the organization's commitment to safety.

Monitoring and reviewing workplace records related to transport activities is essential for ensuring compliance, identifying trends, and improving overall operational efficiency and safety within the transport and logistics industry. These records encompass a wide range of documentation that detail various aspects of transport operations, including vehicle maintenance logs, driver records, trip reports, incident reports, and compliance documents.

Workplace records serve as a crucial repository of information that reflects the daily operations and regulatory compliance of transport activities. Vehicle maintenance records, for instance, document scheduled maintenance checks, repairs, and inspections conducted on each vehicle. These records not only ensure that vehicles are maintained in optimal condition but also demonstrate compliance with safety standards and regulatory requirements.

Monitoring workplace records is particularly vital for ensuring adherence to regulatory requirements set by authorities such as the National Heavy Vehicle Regulator (NHVR) or local transportation agencies. These regulations may dictate standards for driver qualifications, hours of service, vehicle inspections, and load securement. Regular review of records helps verify compliance with these regulations, thereby mitigating legal risks and potential penalties.

Records related to driver performance, including training certifications, driving logs, and incident reports, provide insights into individual driver behaviour and competence. Monitoring these records allows management to identify potential training needs, recognize exemplary performance, and address any issues related to driver conduct or safety violations promptly.

Analysing transport activity records can also yield insights into operational efficiency and resource allocation. Trip reports and delivery logs, for example, provide data on routes taken, delivery times, fuel consumption, and vehicle utilization. This information enables management to optimize logistics processes, reduce turnaround times, and streamline resource allocation for improved cost-effectiveness.

Beyond compliance and efficiency, regular monitoring and review of workplace records support a culture of continuous improvement. By identifying trends in incidents, near misses, or equipment failures, organizations can implement proactive measures to prevent recurrence. This includes updating procedures, enhancing training programs, or investing in new technologies that enhance safety and operational performance.

Adhering to industry best practices involves benchmarking against standards set by leading organizations and adopting proven methodologies for record-keeping and review. This ensures that transport operations align with current industry standards and strive for excellence in safety, efficiency, and customer satisfaction.

Advancements in digital technologies have revolutionized record-keeping in the transport sector. Electronic systems, including fleet management software and telematics solutions, automate data collection and analysis. These technologies provide real-time insights into vehicle performance, driver behaviour, and compliance metrics, facilitating proactive decision-making and enhancing overall transparency.

Managing workplace policies, procedures, safety documents, and operational practices in sea transport involves several systematic steps to ensure safety, regulatory compliance, and operational efficiency. Here's a detailed approach to addressing each aspect:

Workplace Policies, Procedures, and Safety Documents:

- **Identification:** Begin by identifying relevant workplace policies, procedures, and safety documents specific to sea transport. These may include international maritime regulations (e.g., SOLAS, MARPOL), company-specific safety protocols, emergency response plans, and operational procedures.

- **Monitoring:** Establish a structured process for monitoring adherence to these documents. This involves regular reviews to ensure policies are up-to-date with regulatory changes and industry best practices. Utilize audits, inspections, and feedback mechanisms to verify compliance across all levels of maritime operations.

Management of Speed and Fatigue:
- **Methods and Requirements:** Determine methods and requirements for managing vessel speed and mitigating crew fatigue. This includes adhering to international standards for watchkeeping, rest hours as per STCW regulations, and utilizing voyage planning software to optimize routes and minimize fatigue-inducing conditions.

- **Monitoring:** Implement systems to monitor vessel speed and crew fatigue levels. This may involve onboard monitoring systems for crew rest hours, fatigue assessment tools, and regular performance evaluations to ensure compliance with operational standards and safety protocols.

Calculation and Assessment of Vehicle Dimension and Mass Limits:
- **Methods:** Develop procedures for calculating and assessing the dimensions and mass limits of vessels. This includes using naval architecture principles, stability calculations, and cargo loading software to determine safe operating limits.

- **Monitoring:** Regularly review and update vessel loading plans, conduct stability tests, and utilize onboard sensors or draft surveys to monitor actual versus planned load conditions. Ensure compliance with load line regulations and safety margins during loading and unloading operations.

Ensuring Secure Loads:
- **Methods:** Establish protocols and procedures for securing cargo and ensuring it remains stable during transit. Use lashing plans, container securing devices, and stowage arrangements in accordance with IMO guidelines and vessel-specific requirements.

- **Monitoring:** Conduct pre-voyage inspections of cargo securing arrangements, monitor sea fastenings during transit using onboard surveillance systems, and implement continuous checks to prevent cargo shifting or damage.

Heavy Vessel Safety Standards:
- **Identification:** Identify applicable safety standards and regulations for sea transport, including those governing vessel construction, equipment, fire safety, and emergency preparedness.

- **Monitoring:** Regularly assess vessel compliance through inspections, surveys, and classification society audits. Maintain records of safety equipment inspections, maintenance activities, and crew training to ensure adherence to safety standards and regulatory requirements.

Figure 20: Loading freight for transport by sea. CC0 Public Domain, via PxHere.

Identification, Assessment, and Control of Transport Activity Risks:
- **Identification:** Conduct comprehensive risk assessments for sea transport activities, considering factors such as weather conditions, navigational hazards, cargo handling risks, and human factors.

- **Assessment and Control:** Implement risk control measures through safety management systems (SMS), emergency response drills, and crew training programs. Monitor risks through incident reporting, near-miss investigations, and safety audits to continuously improve safety practices and mitigate operational risks.

Monitoring and Review of Workplace Records:
- **Monitoring:** Establish procedures for monitoring and reviewing records related to sea transport activities. This includes voyage reports, crew training records, maintenance logs, incident reports, and compliance documentation.

- **Review:** Regularly review records to identify trends, assess compliance with regulatory requirements, and implement corrective actions. Utilize data analytics and reporting tools to enhance decision-making and ensure transparency in operational performance.

Managing workplace policies, procedures, safety documents, and operational practices in air transport involves rigorous adherence to safety regulations, operational standards, and industry best practices. This includes:

Workplace Policies, Procedures, and Safety Documents:
- **Identification:** Identify and compile relevant workplace policies, procedures, and safety documents specific to air transport. These may include airline operations manuals, aircraft handling procedures, emergency response plans, and regulatory compliance documents (e.g., FAA regulations in the US, EASA regulations in Europe).

- **Monitoring:** Implement a systematic approach to monitor adherence to these documents. Conduct regular audits, inspections, and reviews to ensure alignment with current regulations, industry standards, and company-specific protocols. Update documents as necessary to reflect changes in regulatory requirements or operational practices.

Management of Speed and Fatigue:
- **Methods and Requirements:** Define methods and requirements for managing aircraft speed and mitigating crew fatigue. This includes adherence to flight duty and rest regulations (e.g., FAR Part 117 in the US), scheduling practices that minimize fatigue, and utilization of fatigue risk management

systems (FRMS) or crew resource management (CRM) principles.

- **Monitoring:** Monitor flight crew duty schedules, rest periods, and adherence to operational limits using crew scheduling software or FRMS. Conduct regular fatigue risk assessments and audits to ensure compliance with regulatory requirements and safety standards.

Calculation and Assessment of Aircraft Dimension and Mass Limits:
- **Methods:** Develop procedures for calculating and assessing aircraft dimensions, weight limits, and centre of gravity. Utilize aircraft performance manuals, load planning software, and weight and balance calculations to ensure safe operating conditions.

- **Monitoring:** Implement checks and balances to verify accuracy of load manifests, conduct weight and balance calculations before each flight, and monitor actual versus planned load distribution during loading operations. Maintain records of weight and balance calculations and compliance with aircraft limitations.

Ensuring Secure Loads:
- **Methods:** Establish protocols and procedures for securing cargo, baggage, and equipment on aircraft. Utilize cargo loading manuals, palletisation techniques, and restraint systems compliant with IATA regulations and aircraft manufacturer guidelines.

- **Monitoring:** Conduct pre-flight inspections of cargo loading and securing procedures. Utilize load monitoring sensors or visual inspections to verify the integrity of cargo restraints during flight. Implement corrective actions and continuous checks to prevent load shifting or damage.

STRATEGIC MANAGEMENT FOR TRANSPORT AND LOGISTICS 201

Figure 21: ULD loader lifting a ULD from apron dollies level to aircraft cargo bay level. Unit Load Device (ULD) is standardized size air cargo container. Jamesshliu, CC BY-SA 3.0, via Wikimedia Commons.

Aircraft Safety Standards:
- **Identification:** Identify applicable safety standards and regulations for aircraft operations and maintenance. This includes airworthiness directives, maintenance requirements, and safety management systems (SMS) guidelines.
- **Monitoring:** Monitor aircraft compliance through scheduled maintenance inspections, airworthiness checks, and audits conducted by regulatory authorities or internal safety teams. Maintain records of maintenance activities, safety inspections, and compliance with safety standards.

Identification, Assessment, and Control of Transport Activity Risks:
- **Identification:** Conduct comprehensive risk assessments for air transport activities, considering factors such as weather conditions, airspace congestion, airport operations, and human factors (e.g., pilot error).
- **Assessment and Control:** Implement risk control measures through safety

assessments, emergency response drills, and crew training programs. Utilize safety data analysis, incident reporting systems, and safety audits to monitor risks and implement proactive measures to mitigate operational hazards.

Monitoring and Review of Workplace Records:
- **Monitoring:** Establish procedures for monitoring and reviewing records related to air transport activities. This includes flight operation records, maintenance logs, incident reports, crew training records, and compliance documentation.

- **Review:** Conduct regular reviews of records to identify trends, assess compliance with regulatory requirements, and evaluate operational performance. Utilize data analytics and reporting tools to enhance decision-making and ensure transparency in safety and operational practices.

Due Diligence

In the dynamic world of transportation logistics, every decision carries significant weight, impacting the smooth flow of goods and the financial health of stakeholders throughout the supply chain. Whether you operate as a shipper, carrier, or broker, success hinges on meticulous preparation and thorough research. Recent disruptions across the industry underscore the critical importance of due diligence in shielding against potential risks and liabilities [26].

Due diligence in transport and logistics refers to the comprehensive process of conducting thorough research, investigation, and analysis before entering into agreements, partnerships, or transactions within the industry. It involves systematically gathering relevant information, assessing risks, and verifying compliance with regulatory requirements and industry standards. Due diligence aims to ensure that all parties involved in transport and logistics operations make informed decisions that mitigate risks, uphold legal and safety standards, and protect their financial interests.

Key aspects of due diligence in transport and logistics include:
- Financial and Operational Assessments: Evaluating the financial stability and operational capabilities of potential partners, including carriers, brokers, and service providers. This may involve reviewing financial statements,

assessing creditworthiness, and verifying insurance coverage to ensure they can fulfill contractual obligations.

- Compliance and Regulatory Checks: Verifying compliance with local, national, and international regulations governing transport operations. This includes adherence to safety standards, environmental regulations (such as emissions controls), and transportation laws specific to different modes (road, rail, air, sea).

- Safety and Risk Management: Assessing safety records, risk management practices, and incident histories to gauge the level of risk associated with a potential partnership. This includes evaluating safety protocols, training programs, and emergency response plans to ensure they meet industry best practices.

- Contractual and Legal Review: Reviewing contracts, agreements, and terms of service to clarify responsibilities, liabilities, and dispute resolution mechanisms. Legal experts often play a crucial role in identifying potential legal risks and ensuring that contractual terms protect the interests of all parties.

- Operational Performance and Reputation: Investigating operational performance metrics, customer reviews, and industry reputation to gauge reliability and service quality. This includes checking references, conducting site visits, and assessing operational capabilities to verify claims made by potential partners.

- Environmental and Social Considerations: Assessing the environmental impact of transport activities, adherence to sustainability practices, and social responsibility commitments. This aspect is increasingly important as stakeholders prioritize ethical business practices and sustainable development goals.

Due diligence in transport and logistics is essential for mitigating risks such as financial loss, operational disruptions, safety incidents, regulatory non-compliance, and reputational damage. It provides stakeholders with the necessary information and confidence to make informed decisions, establish reliable partnerships, and ensure the efficient and safe movement of goods and passengers across global supply chains.

For all parties involved in transportation agreements, conducting comprehensive due diligence is non-negotiable. This process entails vetting potential partners rigorously and assessing their financial stability and operational reliability. Ignoring these steps can expose stakeholders to substantial risks, including financial losses, operational disruptions, and even legal disputes [26].

Carriers, entrusted with the responsibility of transporting goods, play a pivotal role in maintaining the integrity of supply chains. They face inherent risks, especially when engaging with brokers or shippers whose financial standing may be uncertain. By conducting thorough background checks and continuously monitoring the financial health of their business partners, carriers can mitigate these risks and safeguard their operations against potential pitfalls.

Similarly, shippers must exercise caution in selecting transportation providers. While cost considerations are crucial, prioritizing price over due diligence can lead to unforeseen complications [26]. By thoroughly evaluating the financial stability, track record, and adherence to safety standards of carriers and brokers, shippers can minimize risks to their supply chains and uphold their commitments to customers.

Legal ramifications loom large in disputes between carriers, brokers, and shippers, underscoring the need for clear contractual terms and proactive risk management [26]. The importance of weighing the significance of disputes against the value of ongoing business relationships is important. This strategic approach helps stakeholders navigate disputes effectively while preserving crucial partnerships.

Continuous vigilance and proactive risk mitigation are paramount in an industry characterized by rapid changes and regulatory complexities. Regular contract reviews, monitoring of financial indicators, and prompt action on potential red flags enable stakeholders to stay ahead of risks and uphold their operational commitments [26].

Due diligence isn't merely a best practice in the transport industry—it's an indispensable requirement. By prioritizing thorough research, effective communication, and prudent risk management, stakeholders can navigate the complexities of transportation logistics with confidence and integrity.

The due diligence process is a critical investigation conducted by businesses to thoroughly examine another company s financial records, operations, and potential risks before entering into agreements such as mergers, acquisitions, or partnerships. It serves to protect the interests of the acquiring or merging entity by ensuring transparency, identifying potential liabilities, and verifying the accuracy of representations made by the target company.

In scenarios where one company intends to merge with or acquire another, due diligence becomes essential. This comprehensive research encompasses various aspects, including the financial health of the target company, its operational capabilities, legal compliance, and adherence to industry standards. For instance, buyers in mergers and acquisitions (M&A) typically engage professionals such as accountants, investment bankers, and lawyers to conduct due diligence [27]. These experts scrutinize financial statements, assess market position, evaluate customer and supplier relationships, and review legal agreements to mitigate risks associated with the transaction.

An illustrative example is Dropoff's acquisition of Rightaway Delivery, Inc., where thorough due diligence would involve examining Rightaway's financial records, assessing its client base and operational efficiency, and ensuring alignment with Dropoff's strategic goals [27]. This process not only helps in identifying potential synergies but also uncovers any financial or operational red flags that could impact the success of the acquisition.

The necessity of due diligence extends beyond financial considerations. It plays a crucial role in compliance with regulations pertaining to anti-money laundering, bribery, and corruption [27]. By verifying compliance with these regulations, companies mitigate legal risks and uphold ethical standards, thus safeguarding their reputation and avoiding potential legal consequences.

In logistics and courier companies, due diligence takes on added significance due to the high-value nature of shipments and the critical need for reliability and security in operations. These companies must ensure that all parties involved in their supply chain—from suppliers and subcontractors to delivery agents—are legitimate, reliable, and compliant with industry regulations. The process involves rigorous checks, including background screenings, financial audits, and assessments of operational capabilities. This helps mitigate risks such as cargo theft, regulatory non-compliance, and reputational damage, which could arise from associations with untrustworthy or non-compliant partners.

In the context of rail transport, due diligence plays a crucial role in ensuring the safety, reliability, and legal compliance of operations before entering into agreements or partnerships. Here's how due diligence is applied specifically within the rail industry, mirroring the comprehensive process outlined for transport and logistics more broadly:

Financial and Operational Assessments: Before engaging with rail carriers or service providers, due diligence involves evaluating their financial stability and operational capabilities. This includes reviewing financial statements to assess profitability, liquidity, and debt levels. Operational assessments may entail examining track records of on-time performance, capacity utilization, and maintenance practices to ensure they can meet service requirements without disruptions.

Compliance and Regulatory Checks: Rail transport is heavily regulated, requiring thorough checks to ensure compliance with federal, state, and local regulations. This includes adherence to safety standards set by regulatory bodies like the Federal Railroad Administration (FRA) in the United States or equivalent agencies in other countries. Due diligence verifies that rail operators comply with rules governing track maintenance, equipment safety, crew certifications, and environmental protection measures such as noise and emissions controls.

Safety and Risk Management: Safety is paramount in rail operations due to the potential consequences of accidents. Therefore, due diligence includes assessing safety records, incident histories, and risk management practices of rail operators. This involves reviewing safety protocols, emergency response plans, and employee training programs to ensure they meet industry standards and mitigate operational risks effectively.

Contractual and Legal Review: Legal experts are often involved in reviewing contracts, agreements, and terms of service between rail operators, clients, and regulatory authorities. This ensures clarity on responsibilities, liabilities, insurance coverage, and dispute resolution mechanisms in case of unforeseen events or contractual breaches. Understanding legal obligations and protections is critical to safeguarding financial interests and maintaining operational continuity.

Operational Performance and Reputation: Rail due diligence includes evaluating operational performance metrics such as reliability, frequency of service, and customer satisfaction. Site visits and references from other clients provide firsthand insights into the reliability of rail operators and their ability to deliver consistent service quality. Assessing industry reputation helps gauge reliability and ethical standards, crucial for maintaining trust within the supply chain and among stakeholders.

Environmental and Social Considerations: Rail transport impacts the environment through emissions, noise pollution, and land use. Due diligence includes assessing environmental compliance with regulations and commitments to sustainable practices. This involves reviewing sustainability initiatives, adherence to energy efficiency standards, and efforts to minimize environmental impacts through technology adoption and operational practices.

Monitoring Heavy Vehicle Operation Safety

When potential risks in heavy vehicle transport activities are identified, immediate and systematic actions are necessary to mitigate these risks effectively. First, conduct a comprehensive risk assessment to evaluate the severity and likelihood of the identified risks. This involves gathering data on incidents, analysing patterns, and consulting with experienced personnel. Implement immediate control measures such as adjusting routes, modifying operational practices, or enhancing safety protocols. Communicate the risks and the actions being taken to all relevant stakeholders, ensuring that drivers, managers, and support staff understand their roles in mitigating these risks. Regularly review and update the risk management plan to incorporate new information and continuously improve safety measures.

Managing speed and fatigue in heavy vehicle operations requires careful consideration of external factors such as weather conditions, traffic density, and road infrastructure. Weather can significantly impact driving conditions, necessitating adjustments in speed to maintain safety. For instance, during adverse weather conditions like rain, fog, or snow, reduced visibility and road grip require slower speeds to prevent accidents. Traffic density affects driving time and stress levels, contributing to driver fatigue. Heavy traffic can lead to prolonged driving hours and increased pressure to meet delivery deadlines, necessitating breaks and careful scheduling to avoid fatigue. Road infrastructure, including the condition of roads and availability of rest areas, also plays a crucial role. Poor road conditions can cause physical strain and vehicle damage, while well-maintained rest areas provide necessary stops for rest and recuperation.

Staying informed about the latest developments in transport safety involves regular training, attending industry seminars, and subscribing to relevant publications. Engaging with professional associations and regulatory bodies provides access to updates on best practices and new regulations. Companies should implement ongoing education programs to ensure that all employees are aware of current safety standards and procedures.

Conduct a detailed analysis of the company's transport activities to identify specific hazards and risks. This includes reviewing the types of goods transported, the routes taken, and the operational procedures followed. Risk assessments should be performed regularly, focusing on potential hazards such as cargo shifts, mechanical failures, and human factors like driver fatigue.

Allocating resources effectively involves investing in advanced safety equipment, regular vehicle maintenance, and comprehensive training programs. Financial resources should be directed towards upgrading vehicle fleets with the latest safety technologies, such as collision avoidance systems and fatigue monitoring devices. Human resources should be allocated to monitor compliance and implement safety protocols consistently.

Regular audits and inspections are essential to verify the effectiveness of control measures. This includes reviewing incident reports, conducting safety drills, and collecting feedback from drivers and other personnel. Data from these activities should be analyzed to identify trends and areas for improvement, ensuring that safety measures are continuously refined and effective.

Drivers play a critical role in transport activities, directly influencing safety and operational efficiency. They are responsible for vehicle operation, compliance with safety regulations, and timely delivery of goods. Their influence extends to decision-making during unforeseen circumstances, such as route changes due to traffic or weather conditions. Ensuring drivers are well-trained and equipped to make safe decisions is crucial for overall transport safety.

Each individual within the transport chain has specific duties that contribute to overall safety and efficiency. For drivers, this includes vehicle inspection, adherence to driving schedules, and compliance with traffic laws. For managers, it involves planning routes, scheduling maintenance, and ensuring compliance with regulatory requirements.

Supervisors must ensure that those under their supervision understand and fulfill their responsibilities. This includes providing adequate training, monitoring performance, and addressing any issues that arise. Supervisors play a key role in maintaining a culture of safety and accountability within the organization.

Individuals in positions of influence must communicate effectively with other parties in the chain of responsibility, such as suppliers, clients, and regulatory bodies. Their duties include negotiating contracts, ensuring compliance with safety standards, and coordinating activities to ensure smooth and safe transport operations.

Adhering to industry standards and requirements involves implementing specific methods for managing fatigue, such as regulated work-rest schedules, and using technologies like electronic logging devices (ELDs) to monitor driving hours. Speed management can be enhanced through GPS-based tracking systems that alert drivers and dispatchers to speed violations. Load restraint involves using proper securing techniques and equipment, while mass and dimension compliance requires accurate measurements and adherence to legal limits. Regular vehicle maintenance, guided by manufacturer recommendations and regulatory standards, ensures vehicle safety and reliability.

The chain of responsibility (CoR) in transport activities includes all parties involved in the supply chain, such as consignors, consignees, packers, loaders, and operators. Each party has a specific level of influence and control over various aspects of transport safety and compliance. Understanding the CoR ensures that all parties are accountable for their roles and responsibilities, reducing the risk of accidents and non-compliance.

Non-compliance with heavy vehicle laws and regulations can result in severe consequences, including hefty fines, legal sanctions, and reputational damage. It can also lead to increased scrutiny from regulatory bodies and higher insurance premiums. In severe cases, non-compliance can result in accidents, injuries, and fatalities, leading to significant financial and legal repercussions for the company.

A shared duty refers to responsibilities held by multiple parties within the transport chain. Reasonably practicable actions are those that a person can reasonably take to ensure safety. A risk is a potential threat that could cause harm, while a heavy vehicle transport activity includes all tasks related to the operation and management of heavy vehicles.

An unreasonable request in the context of transport activities is any demand that compromises safety, violates regulations, or exceeds the capacity or legal limits of the vehicle or driver. For example, asking a driver to exceed legal driving hours or overload a vehicle is unreasonable and unsafe.

Current codes of practice can be found through industry associations, regulatory bodies, and government websites. These codes provide guidelines on best practices and compliance standards.

Heavy vehicle standards are typically published by regulatory authorities and industry organizations. These standards outline technical and operational requirements for heavy vehicles.

Information on securing loads, load placement, and load restraint can be obtained from regulatory guidelines, training programs, and industry best practice documents. These resources provide detailed instructions on how to safely secure and transport cargo.

Vehicle dimension and mass limits are specified in regulatory documents and guidelines provided by transportation authorities. Regular updates on these limits can be found on government websites and through industry bulletins.

Each job function within the transport industry has specific policies and procedures designed to ensure safety and compliance. It is essential to be familiar with these policies and understand how they apply to one's role and responsibilities.

Regular training and updates on workplace procedures help maintain high standards of operational safety and efficiency.

Chapter 7

Managing International Freight Transfer

International freight transfer refers to the process of transporting goods across international borders from one country to another. It involves the movement of cargo by various modes of transport, such as ships, airplanes, trucks, and trains, depending on the distance, urgency, and type of goods being transported.

Key aspects of international freight transfer include:

- Modes of Transport: Goods can be transported internationally by sea (maritime shipping), air (airfreight), road (trucking), or rail (rail freight), each with its own logistics and considerations.

- Logistics and Supply Chain Management: International freight transfer requires careful coordination of logistics and supply chain management to ensure goods are picked up, transported, and delivered efficiently and on time.

- Customs Clearance: Import and export regulations vary between countries, and international freight transfer involves navigating customs procedures and obtaining necessary documentation for clearance.

- Packaging and Handling: Proper packaging and handling are crucial to protect goods during transit, especially over long distances and varying environmental conditions.

- Documentation and Compliance: Compliance with international trade regulations, including documentation such as invoices, packing lists, and certificates of origin, is essential for smooth international freight transfer.

- Insurance and Risk Management: International shipments may involve risks such as damage, loss, or theft, necessitating insurance coverage and risk management strategies to protect the value of the goods.

- Cost Considerations: Freight costs for international transport vary based on factors such as distance, mode of transport, urgency, and the nature of the goods. Factors like fuel prices and currency exchange rates also impact costs.

International transport of goods involves various modes, each tailored to different logistical needs and considerations. These modes include sea (maritime shipping), air (airfreight), road (trucking), and rail (rail freight), each playing a critical role in global trade and commerce.

Maritime Shipping: Maritime shipping is the backbone of international trade, handling the majority of global freight. It involves transporting goods via ships across oceans and seas. Maritime shipping is suitable for large volumes of goods that are not time-sensitive. Cargo ships vary in size and capacity, accommodating diverse types of goods from raw materials to finished products. Logistics in maritime shipping include port operations, containerization, and adherence to international maritime regulations and safety standards. Factors such as transit times, weather conditions, and sea routes significantly impact the efficiency and cost-effectiveness of maritime transport.

Airfreight: Airfreight is the fastest mode of international transport, ideal for perishable goods, high-value items, and time-sensitive shipments. Air transport offers rapid delivery, often measured in hours or days compared to weeks for sea transport. Major airports worldwide serve as hubs for air cargo operations, handling a wide range of goods from electronics to pharmaceuticals. Logistics in airfreight focus on cargo handling, customs clearance, and compliance with air transport regulations. Cost considerations in airfreight are influenced by factors such as fuel prices, airport charges, and capacity availability.

Trucking: Road transport, or trucking, plays a crucial role in connecting ports, airports, and rail terminals to final destinations. It is flexible and offers door-to-door delivery options, making it suitable for short to medium-distance shipments within and between countries. Trucking logistics involve route planning, loading and unloading operations, and adherence to road transport regulations. Factors affecting trucking efficiency include traffic conditions, road infrastructure quality, and driver availability. Specialized trucks are used for transporting various goods, including refrigerated trucks for perishable items and flatbed trucks for oversized cargo.

Rail Freight: Rail transport is efficient for transporting large volumes of goods over land, especially for long distances and bulk commodities like minerals, grains, and manufactured goods. Rail freight is known for its cost-effectiveness and lower environmental impact compared to road transport for long-haul shipments. Logistics in rail freight include terminal operations, rail network coordination, and compliance with rail transport regulations. Rail transport is integrated into multimodal logistics chains, connecting ports and industrial centres. Challenges in rail freight logistics include infrastructure maintenance, scheduling, and ensuring compatibility between different rail networks.

Each mode of transport in international trade offers distinct advantages and challenges, influencing decisions based on factors such as shipment urgency, cost considerations, volume of goods, and environmental impact. Effective logistics management and adherence to regulatory requirements are crucial for optimizing the efficiency, reliability, and sustainability of international freight transport across these diverse modes.

Logistics and supply chain management form the backbone of international freight transfer, encompassing the intricate processes and strategies necessary to ensure the seamless movement of goods from origin to destination. This field involves the planning, execution, and control of the flow of goods, information, and finances across the global supply chain.

Planning and Coordination: Effective logistics and supply chain management begins with meticulous planning. This includes determining optimal routes, selecting appropriate modes of transport (sea, air, road, rail), and scheduling shipments to meet customer demand while optimizing efficiency and minimizing costs. Logistics planners consider factors such as transportation lead times, transit routes, and potential risks along the supply chain.

Transportation Management: Once shipments are planned, transportation management becomes crucial. This involves coordinating the movement of goods through various stages, from pickup at the point of origin to delivery at the final destination. Logistics managers oversee carrier selection, negotiate freight rates, arrange bookings with shipping lines or airlines, and manage customs clearance procedures. Real-time tracking and monitoring systems are often employed to provide visibility into shipment progress and ensure timely delivery.

Inventory Management: Effective logistics includes managing inventory levels throughout the supply chain. Inventory management ensures that sufficient stock is available to meet customer demand without overstocking, which ties up capital and storage space. Techniques such as just-in-time (JIT) inventory and cross-docking are used to streamline inventory flows and minimize holding costs.

Warehousing and Distribution: Warehousing plays a critical role in logistics by providing storage facilities for goods during transit. Distribution centres strategically located near transportation hubs facilitate efficient order fulfillment and enable rapid response to market demands. Warehouse operations include inventory control, order picking, packing, and shipping, all managed to optimize space utilization and minimize handling costs.

Risk Management and Contingency Planning: Logistics professionals must assess and mitigate risks throughout the supply chain. These risks include disruptions due to weather events, political instability, labour strikes, or supplier failures. Contingency plans are developed to address potential disruptions and ensure continuity of operations, such as alternative transport routes or backup suppliers.

Technology Integration: Modern logistics heavily relies on technology to enhance efficiency and visibility across the supply chain. This includes logistics software for route optimization, warehouse management systems (WMS) for inventory tracking, and electronic data interchange (EDI) for seamless communication between trading partners. Advanced analytics and artificial intelligence (AI) are increasingly used to forecast demand, optimize logistics processes, and improve decision-making.

Customs clearance is a pivotal process in international freight transfer, encompassing the procedures and documentation required to facilitate the legal import and export of goods across national borders. This process is essential for ensuring compliance with each country's customs regulations, tariffs, and trade policies while facilitating the smooth flow of goods through the supply chain.

Understanding Customs Procedures Each country maintains its own set of customs procedures and regulations, which govern the entry and exit of goods. Importers and exporters must familiarize themselves with these regulations to ensure adherence and avoid delays or penalties. Customs procedures typically include documentation submission, inspection of goods, assessment of duties and taxes, and clearance for release into or out of the country.

Documentation Requirements: Successful customs clearance hinges on accurate and complete documentation. Key documents typically required include commercial invoices, packing lists, bills of lading (for sea freight), air waybills (for air freight), certificates of origin, import/export licenses, and any special permits or certificates applicable to specific goods (such as sanitary certificates for food products). These documents serve to verify the nature, quantity, and value of goods being imported or exported and ensure compliance with regulatory requirements.

Tariffs and Duties: Customs authorities assess tariffs and duties on imported goods based on factors such as the product's classification under the Harmonized System (HS) code, its declared value, and any applicable trade agreements or preferences. Importers are responsible for paying these duties and taxes, which can significantly impact the landed cost of goods and affect pricing strategies and profitability in international trade.

Customs Inspections and Clearance Process: Upon arrival at the port, airport, or border crossing, goods undergo customs inspection to verify compliance with regulations and documentation accuracy. Inspections may include physical examination of goods, sampling for testing purposes (e.g., for quality or safety standards), and verification of packaging and labelling requirements. Clearance is granted once customs officials are satisfied that all requirements have been met, allowing goods to be released for further transport to their final destination.

Challenges and Considerations: Customs clearance can pose challenges due to the complexity of regulations, potential language barriers, differing interpretations of rules, and occasional discrepancies in documentation. Delays in customs clearance can impact supply chain efficiency, lead to storage costs, and affect customer satisfaction. As such, effective management of customs processes, proactive communication with customs authorities, and leveraging technology for streamlined documentation and compliance tracking are critical for minimizing delays and ensuring smooth operations in international freight transfer.

Role of Customs Brokers and Agents: Many importers and exporters engage customs brokers or agents who specialize in navigating customs procedures on behalf of their clients. These professionals possess expertise in customs regulations, maintain relationships with customs officials, and facilitate the timely and compliant clearance of goods. They play a vital role in advising on tariff classifications, preparing accurate documentation, managing duty payments, and resolving customs-related issues to expedite the movement of goods across borders.

Packaging and handling play integral roles in ensuring the safe and efficient transport of goods across various modes of transportation, including road, sea, air, and rail. Proper packaging is essential not only for protecting goods from physical damage but also for preserving their quality and integrity throughout the supply chain.

Protection Against Physical Damage: Effective packaging shields goods from potential hazards such as impacts, vibrations, compression forces, and temperature fluctuations encountered during transit. Packaging materials and techniques are selected based on the nature of the goods being transported, their fragility, weight, and sensitivity to environmental conditions. For instance, fragile items may require cushioning materials like foam or bubble wrap, while perishable goods may need insulated containers to maintain temperature control.

Preservation of Product Quality: Certain goods, such as food products, pharmaceuticals, electronics, and chemicals, require specific packaging considerations to prevent contamination, degradation, or spoilage. Packaging solutions may include moisture barriers, anti-static materials, UV protection, and gas-tight seals to maintain product freshness and efficacy. Compliance with regulatory standards for packaging and handling ensures that goods meet safety and quality requirements throughout their journey.

Optimization of Space and Weight: Efficient packaging not only protects goods but also optimizes space utilization within transport containers, such as shipping containers, pallets, and air freight containers. Maximizing packing density minimizes wasted space and reduces transportation costs per unit of goods. Moreover, lightweight packaging materials contribute to overall freight cost savings and environmental sustainability by reducing fuel consumption and carbon emissions during transport.

Handling Practices: Proper handling procedures are equally crucial to prevent damage during loading, unloading, and transfer between modes of transport. Training personnel in correct handling techniques reduces the risk of mishandling that can lead to product breakage, spills, or other forms of damage. Use of appropriate equipment, such as forklifts, pallet jacks, and conveyor systems, further enhances safety and efficiency in material handling operations.

Environmental Considerations: Sustainable packaging practices are gaining importance in global supply chains. Companies are increasingly adopting eco-friendly packaging materials, such as biodegradable plastics, recyclable cardboard, and reusable containers, to minimize environmental impact. Sustainable packaging not only aligns with corporate social responsibility goals but also meets consumer expectations for environmentally friendly products.

Regulatory Compliance: Packaging and handling must comply with international, national, and industry-specific regulations governing the transport of hazardous materials, dangerous goods, and controlled substances. Compliance ensures safety for workers, transportation personnel, and the general public, while also mitigating legal risks associated with non-compliance.

Continuous Improvement and Innovation: In response to evolving logistics challenges and customer demands, packaging and handling practices continue to evolve.

Innovations in packaging technology, such as smart packaging with built-in sensors for monitoring conditions like temperature and humidity, enhance visibility and control over product integrity throughout the supply chain. Continuous improvement initiatives focus on reducing packaging waste, enhancing efficiency, and improving overall supply chain resilience.

Documentation and compliance are crucial components of international trade and freight transfer, ensuring that goods move seamlessly across borders while adhering to regulatory requirements. This process involves preparing and managing various documents that validate the legality, origin, nature, and destination of goods being transported. Here's a detailed exploration of documentation and compliance in international freight transfer:

Types of Documentation: Several key documents are required to facilitate international freight transfer. These include:

- Commercial Invoice: A detailed document issued by the seller to the buyer that itemizes the goods being sold, their prices, terms of sale, and other pertinent information. It serves as the basis for customs valuation and determines import duties and taxes.

- Packing List: A document that provides a detailed inventory of the contents of each package or container being shipped. It specifies the quantity, weight, dimensions, and packaging type of each item to aid in cargo handling and customs clearance.

- Bill of Lading (B/L): A contract between the shipper and the carrier that serves as a receipt for the goods shipped, evidence of the contract of carriage, and a document of title. It outlines the terms under which the goods are transported and acts as proof of ownership during transit.

- Certificate of Origin: A document that certifies the country of origin of the goods being exported. It may be required for customs clearance, tariff determination, and compliance with trade agreements or preferential trade arrangements that offer tariff benefits based on origin.

- Insurance Certificate: Provides evidence of insurance coverage for the goods during transit, protecting against risks such as loss, damage, or theft.

- Export License or Permit: Depending on the nature of the goods and destination country, an export license or permit may be required to authorize the exportation of specific goods subject to export controls, sanctions, or licensing requirements.

Importance of Documentation and Compliance: Proper documentation and compliance with international trade regulations serve several critical purposes:

- Facilitating Customs Clearance: Accurate and complete documentation streamlines the customs clearance process by providing authorities with necessary information to assess duties, taxes, and regulatory compliance.

- Ensuring Legal Compliance: Compliance with import and export regulations, including licensing, labelling, and packaging requirements, helps avoid penalties, delays, and potential seizure of goods by customs authorities.

- Mitigating Risks: Proper documentation reduces the risk of disputes, discrepancies, and legal challenges during transit and at destination ports. It provides a clear record of transaction terms, shipment details, and compliance with contractual obligations.

- Supporting Trade Finance: Documentation such as the commercial invoice and bill of lading serves as key documents in trade finance transactions, including letters of credit, ensuring payment security for exporters and financial institutions.

- Enabling Trade Facilitation: Standardized documentation practices and compliance with international trade norms contribute to smoother cross-border trade, enhancing supply chain efficiency and global market access for businesses.

Challenges and Considerations: Despite the importance of documentation, international trade poses challenges such as varying regulatory requirements across countries, language barriers, and the complexity of managing multiple documents for each shipment. Automated document management systems and electronic data interchange (EDI) platforms help mitigate these challenges by improving accuracy, efficiency, and compliance in document preparation and submission.

Insurance and risk management play critical roles in safeguarding international shipments against potential losses, damages, or theft during transit. Given the complexities and uncertainties of global trade, businesses involved in international freight transfer must adopt robust insurance policies and risk management strategies to protect the value of their goods. Here's a detailed exploration of insurance and risk management in the context of international shipments:

Importance of Insurance Coverage: International shipments are exposed to various risks throughout the supply chain, including:

- Physical Damage: Goods can sustain damage due to mishandling, accidents during transportation, or environmental factors such as temperature fluctuations or rough seas.

- Loss or Theft: Cargo may be lost or stolen during transit, especially in regions with higher incidence of theft or inadequate security measures.

- Third-Party Liability: Liability risks arise from incidents causing damage or injury to third parties, including property damage or bodily injury caused by cargo or transport operations.

Types of Insurance Coverage:

- Marine Cargo Insurance: Specifically designed for goods transported by sea, marine cargo insurance covers risks such as damage, loss, or theft from the time the goods leave the seller's premises until they reach the buyer's designated destination. It typically includes coverage for both ocean transit and inland transit segments.

- Air Cargo Insurance: Similar to marine cargo insurance but tailored for airfreight shipments, covering risks associated with air transportation, including damage, loss, or theft during air transit.

- Inland Transit Insurance: Covers goods transported by road or rail within a country, protecting against risks during domestic transportation before or after international shipment.

- Customs Bonds and Duty Insurance: Provides coverage for customs duties and taxes payable in the event goods are lost or damaged during transit, ensuring financial protection against unexpected costs.

Risk Management Strategies:

- Risk Assessment: Conducting thorough risk assessments to identify potential hazards and vulnerabilities at each stage of the supply chain, from packing to final delivery. This includes evaluating transportation routes, storage facilities, and handling procedures.

- Loss Prevention Measures: Implementing proactive measures to mitigate risks, such as using secure packaging, employing tracking and monitoring technologies, and adhering to best practices in cargo handling and storage.

- Contractual Protections: Including robust insurance clauses in contracts with carriers, freight forwarders, and logistics providers to clarify responsibilities, liabilities, and insurance coverage terms in case of loss or damage.

- Emergency Response Plans: Developing contingency plans and procedures to respond promptly to incidents such as accidents, theft, or natural disasters affecting cargo during transit.

Benefits of Insurance and Risk Management:
- Financial Protection: Insurance coverage provides financial compensation for the value of lost or damaged goods, helping businesses avoid significant financial losses and maintain profitability.

- Operational Continuity: Effective risk management strategies ensure uninterrupted supply chain operations by minimizing disruptions caused by unforeseen events or accidents.

- Compliance and Assurance: Demonstrating compliance with regulatory requirements and customer expectations regarding cargo security and risk mitigation enhances business reputation and credibility in global markets.

Challenges and Considerations:
- Cost vs. Benefit: Balancing the cost of insurance premiums against the potential financial losses from uninsured risks requires careful consideration and risk assessment.

- Complexity of Coverage: Understanding and selecting appropriate insurance policies tailored to specific shipment types, routes, and cargo values can be complex, requiring expertise in international trade and logistics.

Cost considerations in international freight transport encompass a range of factors that influence the overall expenses incurred by businesses when shipping goods across borders. Understanding these factors is crucial for effective budgeting, pricing strategies, and decision-making in global supply chain management. Here's an in-depth exploration of the key cost considerations:

Factors Influencing Freight Costs:

- Distance and Route: The geographical distance between the origin and destination of the shipment significantly affects freight costs. Longer distances generally entail higher transportation costs due to increased fuel consumption, transit time, and operational complexities.

- Mode of Transport: The choice between sea freight, airfreight, road transport, or rail transport has a profound impact on costs. Sea freight is typically more cost-effective for large volumes and non-perishable goods but involves longer transit times. Airfreight, while faster, is generally more expensive, making it suitable for urgent or high-value shipments.

- Urgency and Transit Time: Urgency plays a critical role in determining freight costs. Expedited or time-sensitive shipments often incur higher costs due to prioritized handling, faster transit times, and potentially premium service charges.

- Nature of Goods: The type, size, weight, and characteristics of the goods being transported influence freight costs. Perishable or fragile items may require specialized handling, packaging, or temperature-controlled environments, adding to transportation expenses.

- Fuel Prices: Fluctuations in global fuel prices directly impact transportation costs, particularly for modes like road transport and airfreight, where fuel constitutes a significant portion of operational expenses.

- Currency Exchange Rates: International trade involves transactions in different currencies. Exchange rate fluctuations between currencies used for pricing and payments can affect the cost of goods and freight charges, impacting overall import/export costs.

Additional Cost Considerations:

- Insurance: The cost of insurance coverage to protect against risks such as damage, loss, or theft during transit is an essential component of freight costs, particularly for high-value shipments or goods prone to risk.

- Customs Duties and Taxes: Import/export duties, tariffs, and taxes imposed by customs authorities in both the exporting and importing countries contribute to the total cost of international trade transactions.

- Handling and Storage Fees: Charges associated with loading/unloading, warehousing, and storage facilities at ports, airports, or transit hubs add to transportation costs, especially for shipments requiring temporary storage.

- Regulatory Compliance: Costs related to compliance with international trade regulations, documentation requirements, and certification standards must be factored into freight budgets to avoid delays, penalties, or non-compliance issues.

Strategies for Managing Freight Costs:
- Optimizing Transportation Routes: Choosing efficient and cost-effective transportation routes based on distance, infrastructure, and transit times can reduce overall freight expenses.

- Negotiating Rates: Establishing long-term partnerships with reliable freight forwarders, carriers, and logistics providers allows businesses to negotiate competitive rates and service agreements tailored to their shipping needs.

- Consolidation and Optimization: Consolidating smaller shipments into larger, full container loads (FCL) or combining multiple shipments through freight consolidation services can achieve economies of scale and reduce per-unit transportation costs.

- Utilizing Technology: Leveraging transportation management systems (TMS) and logistics software for route optimization, real-time tracking, and performance analytics helps streamline operations and minimize costs.

Analysing Freight Transfer Requirements

To effectively manage international freight transfer, especially when dealing with diverse regulations and customer requirements, several steps should be followed:
- Identifying Local and International Codes and Regulations, and Workplace Policies: Begin by thoroughly researching and understanding the applicable local and international codes and regulations governing freight transfer. This includes regulations related to customs, import/export requirements, transport of dangerous goods, and any industry-specific standards. Identify workplace policies that dictate compliance with these regulations, ensuring

all activities align with legal and operational standards.

- Obtaining and Analysing Customer Requirements: Gather comprehensive information on current and potential customers, focusing on their international freight requirements. This involves understanding the nature of their shipments, frequency of shipments, destinations, special handling needs (such as temperature control or hazardous materials), and any specific documentation requirements. Analyse this data to tailor freight solutions that meet customer expectations and regulatory obligations.

- Identifying Special Characteristics and Customer Requirements: Evaluate and interpret the special characteristics and unique requirements associated with the types of freight to be transferred. This includes identifying specific handling protocols, packaging standards, labelling requirements, and compliance certifications for various categories of goods, including dangerous goods and hazardous substances. Ensure interpretations align with workplace procedures to mitigate risks and ensure safe handling throughout the transportation process.

- Evaluating Options for International Freight Transfer: Assess available options for international freight transfer based on identified special requirements, customer needs, and relevant regulatory frameworks. Consider factors such as transit times, transport modes (air, sea, road, rail), cost-effectiveness, security measures, and environmental considerations. Evaluate each option against Australian and international codes and regulations applicable to the transportation of goods, particularly hazardous substances and dangerous goods.

- Documenting Selected Freight Transfer Arrangements: Once the optimal freight transfer options are identified, document these arrangements thoroughly in accordance with workplace policies and regulatory requirements. Documentation should include detailed transport plans, contracts with carriers or freight forwarders, shipping schedules, compliance certificates, and any special instructions or handling procedures. Ensure that all documentation is accurate, up-to-date, and accessible to relevant stakeholders throughout the shipment process.

Analysing data to customize freight solutions requires a methodical approach aimed at comprehending both customer expectations and regulatory prerequisites, ensuring that proposed solutions are viable and compliant. The process begins with gathering comprehensive details about the customer's freight requirements, encompassing specifics such as the nature of goods (e.g., perishable or hazardous materials), shipment volumes, frequency, preferred delivery schedules, and any special handling instructions. Direct engagement with customers or deploying detailed questionnaires helps in capturing all essential information upfront.

Concurrently, a thorough understanding of the regulatory landscape governing global freight transportation is essential. This entails familiarizing oneself with local, national, and international regulations pertinent to the goods being transported. Key considerations include packaging stipulations, labelling requirements, necessary documentation (like customs forms and certificates of origin), permissible transport modes (air, sea, road, rail), and constraints related to hazardous substances or controlled items.

Effective data analysis techniques play a pivotal role in processing and interpreting the collected information. Tools such as spreadsheets, databases, and specialized software enable the organization and analysis of data points such as shipment volumes, delivery frequencies, destination preferences, and regulatory compliance data. Identifying patterns, trends, and correlations in this data informs strategic decision-making regarding freight solutions.

Next, aligning customer needs with regulatory obligations involves a meticulous comparison to pinpoint potential challenges or constraints. Proposed freight solutions must not only meet customer expectations in terms of cost-effectiveness, transit times, and service quality but also adhere rigorously to applicable laws and regulations. Factors like adherence to packaging standards, meticulous handling procedures, temperature control requirements (where relevant), and environmental considerations are critical aspects to address.

Customizing freight solutions based on the analysed data ensures a harmonious balance between compliance and customer satisfaction. This phase may necessitate recommending specific transport modes tailored to the goods' characteristics (e.g., recommending refrigerated containers for perishable items), optimizing routing to minimize transit durations and costs, and selecting reputable carriers or freight forwarders known for their adherence to compliance standards and operational excellence.

Finally, establishing mechanisms for continuous monitoring and adjustment is crucial for sustaining compliance and meeting evolving customer expectations. Regular evaluation of metrics such as on-time delivery rates, customer feedback, and updates in regulatory requirements enables proactive adjustments to freight solutions. Maintaining transparent communication with customers facilitates prompt responses to changing needs or regulatory revisions, ensuring ongoing satisfaction and adherence to best practices in international freight management.

Shipping Labels

An international shipping label is a crucial component of the logistics process when sending packages abroad. Typically, it consists of a printed paper or sticker affixed to the package, containing essential information necessary for the shipment's smooth transportation, processing, and delivery to its international destination. This label serves as the primary identifier throughout the shipment's journey, enabling logistical and customs authorities to handle and track the package efficiently across borders.

The core function of an international shipping label revolves around streamlining the shipping process by providing vital details. These include the sender's and recipient's addresses, package contents, shipping method, tracking number, and any necessary customs declarations. Such information is indispensable for carriers and customs officials to correctly process the shipment, comply with international shipping regulations, and ensure smooth customs clearance at the destination.

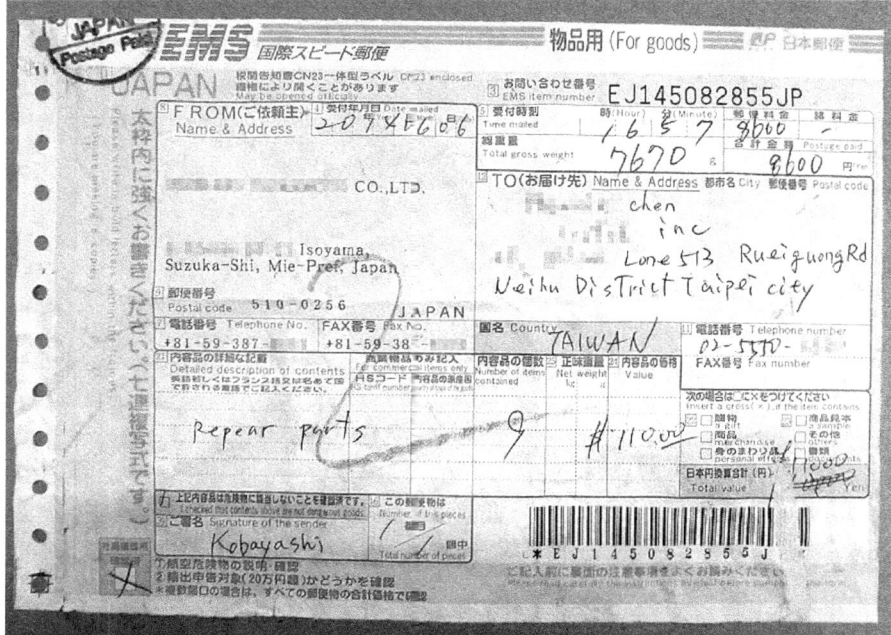

Figure 22: Japan Post EMS label for goods. Solomon203, CC BY-SA 4.0, via Wikimedia Commons.

Compared to domestic shipping labels, international shipping labels differ significantly in detail and compliance requirements. One of the primary distinctions lies in the inclusion of comprehensive customs information. International labels must detail the nature and value of the goods being shipped, the country of origin, and other pertinent customs-related data. This information is critical for customs authorities to assess duties, taxes, and compliance with import regulations, ensuring the legality and smooth flow of goods across borders.

Another critical aspect is regulatory compliance. International shipments are subject to diverse regulations that vary by country. Shipping labels must adhere to these regulations, which may include specific labelling requirements, language preferences, and adherence to international shipping agreements. Labels often incorporate features like barcodes or QR codes for enhanced tracking and security, crucial for monitoring the package's progress and ensuring accountability throughout its journey.

The importance of international shipping labels cannot be overstated in the context of global trade and logistics. They play a pivotal role in ensuring efficient delivery by providing accurate routing information, thereby minimizing the risk of delivery errors, delays, or loss. Moreover, these labels facilitate compliance with complex customs regulations, helping to avoid penalties or seizure of goods. They also serve as a communication tool, conveying handling instructions and ensuring transparency among all stakeholders involved in the shipping process, from senders to recipients and everyone in between.

In essence, international shipping labels are indispensable tools in the logistics chain, ensuring that goods traverse international boundaries seamlessly while adhering to legal requirements and facilitating effective communication across global supply chains. Their accurate preparation and adherence to regulatory standards are fundamental to successful international trade operations.

Understanding the anatomy of international shipping labels is essential for anyone involved in global trade, as these labels serve as critical tools for the efficient and compliant movement of goods across international borders. Designed with meticulous detail, international shipping labels contain specific components that are vital for logistical operations, regulatory compliance, and ensuring accurate delivery to the intended destination.

Sender and recipient information is foundational on international shipping labels. The sender's name and address clearly identify the origin of the package, while the recipient's details ensure the package reaches the correct destination without errors or delays. This information is crucial for carriers and customs officials to process the shipment accurately and efficiently.

Package information, such as weight and dimensions, is essential for calculating shipping costs and determining how the package will be handled throughout its journey. A clear description of the package contents is also included, aiding customs authorities in assessing duties, taxes, and import restrictions based on the nature of the goods being shipped.

Tracking and identification features are integral to international shipping labels. A unique tracking number allows both the sender and recipient to monitor the package's progress in real-time. Barcodes or QR codes provide additional scanning capabilities at various points along the shipment route, enabling automated updates and enhancing transparency in logistics operations.

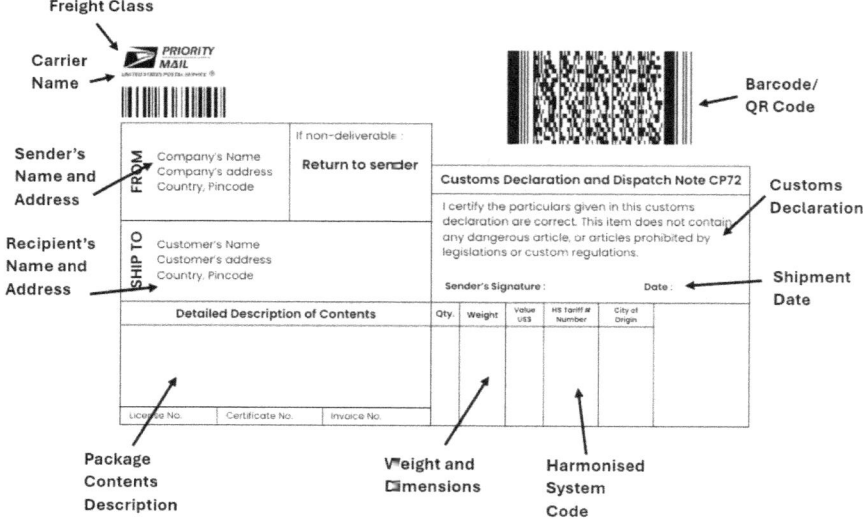

Figure 23: International Shipping Label components.

Customs and regulatory information is perhaps the most critical aspect of an international shipping label. It includes a detailed customs declaration listing the contents of the package, their value, and the country of origin. Harmonized System (HS) codes, internationally recognized classification codes, assist customs authorities in accurately identifying and categorizing the goods for proper duty assessment and regulatory compliance.

Special handling instructions are indicated on the label through symbols or explicit instructions. These denote if the contents are fragile, perishable, or hazardous, ensuring that carriers and handlers exercise appropriate caution and follow specific handling protocols throughout transit.

Carrier and route information on the label specify the shipping company responsible for transportation, the freight class indicating the cargo's characteristics for handling and pricing purposes, and sometimes the route with transit points for multi-leg journeys. This information helps in coordinating logistics and ensuring that the package moves smoothly from origin to destination.

Additional elements like the date of shipment and return instructions provide supplementary information that aids in managing logistics contingencies. Knowing when the package was dispatched helps in estimating delivery times, while clear return instructions facilitate the handling of undeliverable packages, reducing potential disruptions in the shipping process.

Each element on an international shipping label is meticulously curated to ensure accuracy, compliance with international shipping regulations, and efficient delivery. Any misinformation or omission of these critical details can lead to delays, additional costs, or the loss of the package during transit. Therefore, understanding and correctly utilizing international shipping labels are paramount for successful global trade operations, safeguarding both the sender's and recipient's interests in the complex world of international logistics.

Filling out international shipping labels correctly is crucial to ensure smooth and efficient delivery of shipments across borders, adhering to carrier requirements and international customs regulations. The following steps apply:

Step 1: Sender and Recipient Information Firstly, provide accurate sender details, including the full name, address, and contact information. It's essential that this information matches precisely with the details registered on your shipping account or invoice to avoid any confusion or delivery issues. Similarly, for the recipient, ensure their full name, complete address, including postal code and country, and contact information are correctly entered.

When writing addresses, use block letters and avoid punctuation. For instance, write "456 Market Blvd, Unit 789" instead of "456 Market Blvd., Unit 789." If the address is long, use standard abbreviations like "CA" for California to save space and ensure clarity.

Step 2: Package Information Accurately record and provide the weight and dimensions of the package. This information is critical for carriers to determine shipping costs and for handling the package correctly throughout its journey. Additionally, clearly describe the contents of the package in detail. Instead of vague terms like "electronics," specify items with specifics such as "2 wireless earbuds, Bluetooth" or "1 digital wristwatch, waterproof." This detailed description helps customs authorities accurately assess the contents for compliance purposes.

Step 3: Customs Declaration Include the declared value of the items being shipped and their country of origin. It's crucial to accurately state the value to comply with customs regulations. Under-declaring the value can lead to penalties and delays in customs clearance. Also, include the appropriate Harmonized System (HS) codes for each item. These internationally recognized codes assist customs in identifying the products and applying the correct tariffs or duties.

Additionally, if applicable, include any relevant warranties or certifications for specific items being shipped, particularly for electronics or specialized goods that require additional documentation for customs clearance.

Step 4: Additional Information If the package contains fragile, perishable, or hazardous materials, ensure to mark this clearly on the label. Use symbols or explicit instructions such as "Handle with care – fragile" or "Keep upright – contain liquids." These instructions help ensure proper handling throughout transit and minimize the risk of damage.

Provide clear return instructions on the label in case the package cannot be delivered to the recipient. This ensures the carrier knows how to manage undeliverable packages effectively.

Step 5: Review and Attach the Label Before printing the label, carefully review all the information entered for accuracy and completeness. Ensure that all details, including sender and recipient information, package contents, customs declaration, and special handling instructions, are correct.

Print the shipping label on durable, adhesive paper suitable for the size of the package. Attach the label securely to the largest side of the package, ensuring it is fully visible and won't become detached during transit. Proper attachment helps carriers and customs officials easily identify and process the package.

Step 6: Supporting Documentation Include any necessary supporting documents, such as commercial invoices or certificates of origin, with the package. These documents should be securely enclosed in a visible pouch on the package to facilitate customs clearance processes. Ensuring all required paperwork is readily accessible streamlines customs procedures and helps prevent delays or issues during international shipping.

Understanding how international shipping works is essential for anyone engaged in global trade, as it involves a complex series of steps to ensure packages move smoothly from sender to recipient across international borders. The process is facilitated by the meticulous preparation and use of international shipping labels, which serve as the key document guiding the package throughout its journey. This includes:

Step 1: Label Creation and Package Dispatch

The process begins with the creation of an international shipping label. This label is filled out by the sender and contains critical information such as the sender's and recipient's details, package contents, weight, dimensions, and any necessary customs declarations. Once the label is securely attached to the package, the shipment is dispatched. This can involve dropping off the package at a designated shipping carrier's facility or arranging for a carrier pickup.

Step 2: Initial Processing and Transit

Upon receipt of the package, the shipping carrier processes it at their facility. The information on the shipping label, including unique identifiers like barcodes or QR codes, is scanned and entered into the carrier's tracking system. This tracking system allows both the sender and recipient to monitor the package's progress throughout its journey.

Before leaving the origin country, the package undergoes export clearance. Customs officials review the shipping label and accompanying export documentation to ensure compliance with export regulations. This step is crucial as it verifies that the package's contents and documentation align with international trade laws.

The package is then transported to its destination based on the routing information provided on the shipping label. Depending on the distance and destination, this transit can involve transportation by air, sea, or land, often passing through various international transit hubs along the way.

Step 3: Customs Clearance

Upon arrival in the destination country, the package enters customs clearance. Customs officials inspect the shipping label and accompanying documents to verify the declared contents, assess any applicable duties or taxes, and ensure compliance with local import regulations. The accuracy and completeness of the shipping label and accompanying documentation are critical during this stage to prevent delays or issues with customs clearance.

If the package meets all regulatory requirements and no additional inspections or duties are necessary, it proceeds to clearance. Any applicable duties and taxes, as indicated by the information on the shipping label, are calculated and charged at this stage.

Step 4: Final Delivery

Once customs clearance is obtained, the package is transferred to a local carrier (if different from the initial carrier) for final delivery. The local carrier transports the package to the recipient's specified address as indicated on the shipping label. Throughout this process, the carrier's tracking system updates the package's status, providing real-time information on its location and expected delivery time.

Upon successful delivery, the tracking system confirms the receipt of the package by the recipient, completing the international shipping process. Both the sender and recipient can access this information online, ensuring transparency and accountability throughout the shipment's journey.

Barcodes and QR codes are pivotal tools in the realm of international shipping, offering multifaceted advantages in tracking, data management, and operational efficiency throughout the entire journey of a shipment. Here's a detailed exploration of their roles and benefits within the context of global logistics:

Tracking and Traceability: Barcodes serve as fundamental identifiers in shipping due to their simplicity and reliability. Each package is assigned a unique barcode that encodes essential information such as origin, destination, tracking number, and pertinent details. These barcodes are scanned at key points along the shipping route—starting from the sender's facility, through transit phases, at customs checkpoints, and upon arrival at the recipient's distribution centre. This scanning process updates the package's status in real-time, providing both senders and recipients with accurate location tracking and estimated delivery times.

QR codes expand upon traditional barcodes by offering enhanced functionality. They can store more extensive data sets, including URLs, textual information, and even images. In international shipping contexts, QR codes are employed to offer supplementary details beyond basic tracking information. For instance, QR codes might link to comprehensive product descriptions, handling instructions, or necessary customs documentation. This versatility proves invaluable when intricate data accompanies a shipment.

Data Management and Accuracy: Barcodes and QR codes play crucial roles in bolstering data management within international shipping operations. By scanning these codes at various checkpoints, shipping carriers and logistics providers ensure seamless flow of accurate information through their systems. This automation reduces the incidence of manual data entry errors, streamlines paperwork, and enhances overall operational efficiency. As packages progress through different stages—from initial dispatch to customs clearance and final delivery—barcode and QR code scans ensure that all stakeholders access consistent, up-to-date information about each shipment, fostering reliability in logistics operations.

Compliance and Security: In the realm of international shipping, adherence to customs regulations and security protocols is paramount. Barcodes and QR codes affixed to shipping labels facilitate compliance by granting customs officials instant access to critical information. This includes specifics such as the nature of the goods, their declared value, country of origin, and any requisite special handling instructions. Rapid access to such information streamlines the customs clearance process, mitigates delays, and ensures that shipments comply with all regulatory stipulations. This adherence to regulatory standards is essential for maintaining the integrity and efficiency of global supply chains.

Customer Transparency and Service: Both barcodes and QR codes significantly contribute to enhancing customer service in international shipping. Through online tracking tools provided by shipping carriers, customers can monitor their shipments in real-time. This transparency builds trust and confidence as customers can anticipate delivery timelines and plan accordingly. In instances where issues arise, such as delays or package diversions, carriers can promptly update customers through their tracking systems. This proactive communication not only mitigates concerns but also reinforces customer satisfaction by providing clarity and support throughout the shipping process.

Operational Efficiency and Cost Savings: The integration of barcodes and QR codes into international shipping operations yields substantial gains in operational efficiency and cost-effectiveness. Automation of tracking and data management processes reduces reliance on manual labour, consequently cutting down associated costs related to tracking and paperwork. Enhanced data accuracy and transparency diminish the likelihood of misplaced or mishandled packages, thereby minimizing operational disruptions and the resultant financial impacts. Overall, the adoption of barcode and QR code technologies optimizes logistics operations, ensuring smoother workflows and improved cost management within global shipping networks.

Obtaining Customer Information and Requirements

Obtaining and analysing information on current and potential customers, along with their international freight requirements, is crucial for businesses involved in global trade. This is achieved through:

- Market Research and Outreach: Begin by conducting comprehensive market research to identify potential customers who may require international freight services. This involves using various sources such as industry databases, trade publications, online platforms, and networking events to gather leads and contacts. Engaging in proactive outreach through direct communication, email campaigns, or attending industry-specific conferences can also help in establishing initial contact with potential clients.

- Customer Needs Assessment: Once initial contact is established, initiate a thorough assessment of each customer's specific international freight requirements. This process entails conducting structured interviews, surveys, or meetings with key stakeholders within the customer's organization. The goal is to gather detailed information regarding their shipping volumes, frequency of shipments, preferred transport modes (air, sea, road, rail), special handling requirements (e.g., temperature-controlled shipping for perishable goods), and any specific regulatory or compliance needs.

- Documenting Requirements: Document all gathered information systematically in accordance with workplace procedures. This includes recording customer preferences, logistical challenges, budget constraints, and any unique demands related to international shipping. Use standardized forms or digital systems to ensure accuracy and consistency in data capture, facilitating easy retrieval and analysis during subsequent stages.

- Analysing Data and Patterns: Analyse the compiled data to identify recurring patterns, trends, and customer preferences. Look for commonalities such as preferred shipping routes, peak shipping seasons, specific product categories frequently shipped internationally, and any emerging market demands. Use analytical tools and methodologies to derive actionable insights that can inform strategic decision-making and tailored service offerings.

- Regulatory and Compliance Review: Ensure that the gathered information includes insights into customers' regulatory and compliance requirements for international shipments. This involves understanding specific customs procedures, import/export regulations, documentation requirements (e.g., certificates of origin, customs declarations), and adherence to international shipping standards (e.g., Incoterms). Verify that all customer needs align with legal and regulatory frameworks applicable to international freight transport.

- Developing Tailored Solutions: Based on the analysis, develop customized freight solutions that align with each customer's unique requirements and preferences. Propose comprehensive shipping plans that optimize cost-efficiency, transit times, and service levels while ensuring compliance with regulatory obligations. Present these solutions in detailed proposals or presentations that clearly articulate the benefits and value-add propositions tailored to each customer's international shipping needs.

- Continuous Feedback and Improvement: Establish mechanisms for ongoing customer feedback and performance evaluation to refine and improve service offerings over time. Solicit feedback regarding service satisfaction, operational efficiencies, and areas for enhancement. Incorporate this feedback into continuous improvement initiatives aimed at refining service delivery, strengthening customer relationships, and adapting to evolving market dynamics.

Identifying and interpreting special characteristics and customer requirements for various types of freight is a critical aspect of ensuring efficient and compliant international shipping operations.

Initiate direct communication with customers to gather preliminary information about their freight requirements. This could involve engaging with key stakeholders such as procurement managers, logistics coordinators, or operations personnel within the customer's organization. Understand the nature of the goods they intend to ship internationally, including any special characteristics such as perishability, fragility, hazardous nature, or specific handling requirements.

Conduct a thorough needs assessment to delve deeper into the specific characteristics and requirements of the freight to be transferred. Use structured questionnaires, interviews, or surveys to capture detailed insights regarding the physical attributes of the goods (e.g., dimensions, weight), packaging requirements (e.g., temperature-controlled packaging for perishable items), and any unique handling instructions (e.g., fragile items needing careful handling).

Incorporate regulatory and compliance considerations into the assessment process. Understand the applicable international shipping regulations, including customs requirements, import/export restrictions, and hazardous materials regulations if relevant. Ensure that customer requirements align with these regulatory frameworks to avoid delays, fines, or operational disruptions during the shipping process.

Document all identified special characteristics and customer requirements meticulously using standardized templates or digital systems as per workplace procedures. Ensure accuracy and clarity in recording details such as product specifications, packaging specifications, required certifications or permits, and any specific instructions for handling, storage, or transport.

Interpret the gathered information to analyse the implications for shipping logistics and operational planning. Assess how the identified special characteristics and customer requirements will impact factors such as transportation mode selection (air, sea, road, rail), route planning, packaging materials, and scheduling of shipments. Consider operational feasibility, cost implications, and compliance with international standards throughout this analysis.

Collaborate internally within the organization and consult with relevant stakeholders such as logistics specialists, regulatory experts, and shipping carriers to validate interpretations and gather additional insights. Leverage their expertise to ensure comprehensive understanding and accurate interpretation of customer requirements, especially in complex cases involving specialized or regulated goods.

Based on the analysis and interpretation, develop tailored shipping solutions that meet the specific needs and preferences of each customer. Propose comprehensive logistics plans that optimize transportation efficiency, minimize risks associated with special characteristics (e.g., minimizing exposure to temperature fluctuations for pharmaceuticals), and ensure compliance with all relevant regulations. Present these solutions to customers in clear, detailed proposals that outline the benefits and value-add propositions of the proposed shipping arrangements.

Establish mechanisms for continuous review and adaptation of processes to incorporate evolving customer requirements and regulatory changes. Maintain open communication channels with customers to solicit feedback and address any emerging needs or challenges promptly. Continuously improve internal processes and procedures based on lessons learned and feedback received to enhance service delivery and customer satisfaction.

Evaluating appropriate options for international freight transfer involves a meticulous process that considers a range of factors, from specific customer requirements to stringent regulatory standards for transporting goods globally. Here's a comprehensive approach to effectively evaluate these options:

Begin by thoroughly understanding the unique requirements of the customer. Engage in detailed discussions or utilize structured questionnaires to gather information about the nature of the goods, their volume, frequency of shipments, preferred transit times, and any special handling instructions. This step is crucial as it forms the foundation for identifying suitable transport options that align with the customer's specific needs.

Next, identify any special characteristics or requirements associated with the freight. This includes considerations such as whether the goods are hazardous substances, perishable items requiring temperature control, oversized or heavy cargo needing specialized handling equipment, or high-value items necessitating enhanced security measures. These specifications must be clearly defined to guide the selection of appropriate transport methods and logistics solutions.

Familiarize yourself with relevant local and international regulations governing the transportation of goods, particularly hazardous substances and dangerous goods. Understand requirements related to packaging, labelling, documentation, and handling procedures specified by bodies like the International Maritime Organization (IMO), International Air Transport Association (IATA), or national customs authorities. Ensure that all proposed freight transfer options comply with these regulatory standards to avoid legal penalties and operational disruptions.

Assess different transport modes—such as air freight, sea freight, road transport, and rail freight—in terms of their suitability for meeting the identified special requirements and regulatory obligations. Consider factors like transit times, cost-effectiveness, reliability, environmental impact, and infrastructure availability for each mode. For instance, air freight may be preferred for perishable goods requiring rapid delivery, while sea freight might be more economical for bulk shipments over longer distances.

Conduct a comprehensive risk assessment to identify potential risks associated with each transport option. Evaluate risks related to safety, security, environmental impact, and regulatory compliance. Develop mitigation strategies to address identified risks, such as implementing additional security measures for high-value goods or selecting carriers with robust safety records and compliance protocols.

Perform a detailed cost analysis for each proposed transport option. Consider factors such as freight rates, handling fees, insurance premiums, customs duties, and potential additional costs associated with compliance requirements (e.g., specialized packaging for hazardous materials). Balance the cost implications against the value provided in terms of service levels, reliability, and adherence to customer expectations to determine the most cost-effective and viable option.

Based on the evaluation criteria—customer requirements, special characteristics, regulatory compliance, transport mode suitability, risk assessment, and cost analysis—select the optimal freight transfer option. Document the selected option in detail, including all agreed-upon terms, conditions, and responsibilities of each party involved. Ensure that documentation complies with internal policies, contractual obligations, and regulatory requirements to facilitate smooth execution and accountability throughout the shipping process.

Establish mechanisms for ongoing monitoring and evaluation of selected freight transfer options. Continuously gather feedback from customers and stakeholders to assess performance against expectations and identify opportunities for improvement. Stay updated on changes in regulatory requirements and industry best practices to proactively adapt strategies and optimize international freight transfer operations over time.

Documenting selected options for freight transfer arrangements is a critical step in ensuring clarity, compliance, and accountability throughout the logistics process. Here's a detailed approach on how to effectively document these arrangements in accordance with workplace policy and regulations:

Start by maintaining comprehensive records of all communications, decisions, and agreements related to freight transfer options. Document details such as the chosen transport mode (e.g., air, sea, road), specific carriers or freight forwarders selected, agreed-upon delivery schedules, and any special handling requirements identified during the evaluation process. Ensure that these records are accurate, up-to-date, and easily accessible to authorized personnel involved in logistics management.

Adhere strictly to workplace policies and procedures governing the documentation of freight transfer arrangements. Familiarize yourself with internal guidelines regarding record-keeping standards, approval processes, and documentation formats. Ensure that all documented information aligns with these policies to maintain consistency and transparency in operational practices.

Ensure that documentation complies with relevant regulatory requirements applicable to international freight transport. This includes adherence to local and international laws governing the shipment of goods, such as customs regulations, import/export controls, hazardous materials handling guidelines, and transportation security protocols. Include necessary details on shipping labels, invoices, customs declarations, and other required documentation to facilitate smooth customs clearance and regulatory compliance.

Formalize freight transfer arrangements through detailed contracts or service agreements with chosen carriers or logistics service providers. Clearly outline terms and conditions, responsibilities of each party, pricing structures, liability clauses, insurance coverage, and dispute resolution mechanisms. Review contracts carefully to ensure they accurately reflect negotiated terms and protect the interests of your organization in the event of unforeseen circumstances or disputes.

Communicate documented freight transfer arrangements effectively with all relevant stakeholders, including internal teams, external partners, and customers. Provide clear instructions and expectations regarding shipment handling, tracking procedures, delivery timelines, and reporting requirements. Obtain written confirmation or acknowledgment from involved parties to confirm understanding and acceptance of documented arrangements, reducing the risk of misunderstandings or operational errors.

Implement robust version control measures to manage revisions and updates to freight transfer documentation over time. Maintain a centralized repository or electronic system for storing documents, ensuring that the latest versions are readily accessible and identifiable. Regularly review and update documentation as needed to reflect changes in operational practices, regulatory requirements, or business priorities.

Conduct training sessions or workshops for personnel involved in logistics and freight management to ensure awareness of documentation requirements and adherence to workplace policies. Monitor compliance through regular audits or reviews of documentation practices, seeking opportunities for continuous improvement in documentation accuracy, completeness, and regulatory alignment.

Planning International Freight Transfer Systems and Processes

Expanding your customer base through international shipping is a critical strategy for business growth. While many companies begin their operations locally, expanding globally offers access to a vast pool of potential customers and significantly enhances a company's growth prospects. International shipping facilitates the movement of goods across borders, whether by ocean, air, or road, enabling businesses to reach customers in different countries. However, navigating international shipping involves a complex process that requires adherence to various regulations and logistical considerations [28].

International shipping encompasses the import and export of goods between countries, involving meticulous planning and compliance with specific international trade policies and customs regulations. Businesses must meticulously prepare paperwork and documentation to ensure their shipments clear customs smoothly. Each country has its own set of rules governing imports and exports, including restrictions on certain products and requirements for tariffs and duties. For instance, countries like Canada maintain strict lists of prohibited items and impose tariffs on specific goods, necessitating careful attention to compliance or engagement with professional freight forwarding services to navigate these complexities [28].

Beyond regulatory challenges, international shipping presents logistical hurdles such as navigating different time zones, language barriers, and currency exchanges. These factors add layers of complexity compared to domestic shipping but can be managed effectively through thorough preparation and understanding of international logistics processes. Businesses that invest in learning these intricacies can optimize their shipping operations, ensuring efficient and cost-effective delivery solutions for their customers worldwide [28].

The duration of international shipping varies widely depending on factors such as the shipping mode (air, sea, road), distance, and customs processing times. Air freight typically offers faster delivery times, often within days, but at a higher cost compared to sea freight, which may take several weeks to reach its destination. Regardless of the mode chosen, the international shipping process generally comprises five key stages: export haulage, export customs clearance, transportation, import customs clearance, and import haulage (last-mile delivery). Each stage requires careful coordination to ensure smooth transit and compliance with regulatory requirements at both ends of the shipment's journey [28].

For businesses new to international shipping, leveraging the expertise of freight forwarding companies can be invaluable. These firms specialize in managing the complexities of global logistics, offering services that include route planning, documentation preparation, customs brokerage, and shipment tracking. Whether outsourcing to a freight forwarder or managing shipping processes in-house, businesses must prioritize accurate information gathering, thorough customs clearance procedures facilitated by customs brokers, and robust shipment tracking systems. These steps not only ensure regulatory compliance but also enhance customer trust by providing transparent and reliable shipping services [28].

Shipping goods internationally involves navigating a complex series of steps and considerations, making it essential to work with a knowledgeable freight forwarder to streamline the process [29]. Understanding each phase of international shipping is crucial to ensuring goods are transported efficiently and without complications. These steps include:

- Step 1: Importer orders goods from a supplier The process begins when the importer places an order for goods from a supplier. This initiates the need for international shipping arrangements.

- Step 2: Pro forma invoice is provided The supplier provides a pro forma invoice, which acts as an estimate similar to a quote. This document outlines the terms and estimated costs associated with the purchase.

- Step 3: Purchase order is created The importer creates a purchase order based on the pro forma invoice. This document formalizes the agreement and specifies the details of the goods to be purchased.

- Step 4: Buyer hires a freight forwarder To handle the transportation logistics, the buyer hires a freight forwarder. The freight forwarder manages the complex process of shipping the goods from the supplier to the buyer.

- Step 5: Freight forwarder confirms Incoterms The freight forwarder confirms the Incoterms with both the buyer and the supplier. Incoterms define the responsibilities and obligations of each party concerning the shipment, including costs and risks.

- Step 6: Buyer obtains a Letter of Credit To secure payment for the goods, the buyer obtains a Letter of Credit from their bank. This financial document guarantees that the supplier will receive payment once the terms of the shipment are met.

- Step 7: Supplier's bank approves the Letter of Credit The supplier's bank reviews and approves the Letter of Credit, ensuring that it meets the agreed-upon terms and conditions for payment.

- Step 8: Manufacturing of the goods begins With the financial arrangements in place, the supplier begins the manufacturing process for the goods ordered by the buyer.

- Step 9: Supplier provides an order confirmation and a Commercial Invoice After the goods are manufactured, the supplier provides the buyer with an order confirmation and a Commercial Invoice. The Commercial Invoice details the final cost and is used for customs clearance.

- Step 10: Freight forwarder contacts their overseas partner The freight forwarder coordinates with their overseas partner to arrange the local movement of the goods, ensuring smooth logistics management.

- Step 11: Agent contacts the supplier locally The local agent contacts the supplier to arrange the collection and transportation of the goods to the nearest port or depot for export.

- Step 12: Supplier provides export documentation The supplier prepares all necessary export documents, which the freight forwarder will handle on behalf of the buyer. These documents are crucial for customs clearance.

- Step 13: Supplier books the shipment With all documents in order, the supplier books the shipment for export, ensuring space on the necessary transport modes is reserved.

- Step 14: Bill of Lading is issued When the carrier arrives to pick up the goods, a Bill of Lading is issued. This document acts as a receipt and confirms that the goods have been received by the carrier in acceptable condition.

- Step 15: Buyer secures the Bill of Lading The buyer will need to present the Bill of Lading to claim ownership of the shipment upon its arrival. The freight forwarder can manage this process on the buyer's behalf.

- Step 16: Goods are customs cleared and delivered Once the goods pass through export customs clearance, they are delivered to the agreed location, as determined by the Incoterms.

- Step 17: Supplier completes the Export Declaration The supplier completes the Export Declaration, which is required for the goods to leave the country of origin.

- Step 18: Goods are placed in international transit After clearing customs, the goods are placed in international transit. This step involves transporting the goods via the chosen shipping method.

- Step 19: Goods arrive in the buyer's country for import clearance Upon arrival in the destination country, the goods undergo import clearance. Customs authorities check all documentation and ensure compliance with local regulations.

- Step 20: Goods are delivered to the buyer After import clearance, the goods are finally delivered from the destination country port to the buyer's specified location, completing the shipping process.

The initial step in the shipping process begins with the importer, or consignee, requesting quotes and ordering goods from a supplier, also known as the consignor. This transaction typically starts with the importer seeking quotes from various suppliers, which may include details such as pricing, quantities, and shipping terms. These quotes often come in the form of a proforma invoice, which serves as an estimate rather than a final invoice for customs purposes [29].

Upon approving the quote, the consignee proceeds to create a purchase order, which formalizes the agreement between the importer and the supplier [29]. A purchase order outlines the specifics of the order, including the goods' description, quantities, pricing, projected shipping date, origin and destination addresses, and dimensions of the freight. This document plays a crucial role in managing the logistics of the shipment and ensuring clarity between all parties involved.

For businesses engaged in international trade, the accuracy and completeness of the purchase order are critical. It serves not only as a contractual agreement but also as a foundation for subsequent steps in the shipping process, including customs clearance and freight transportation. The purchase order helps to align expectations and responsibilities, ensuring that the supplier prepares the goods for shipment according to agreed-upon terms and conditions [29].

Moreover, the purchase order facilitates efficient coordination with the freight forwarder. Freight forwarders specialize in managing the logistics of international shipping, offering expertise in navigating regulatory requirements, choosing optimal shipping routes, and handling documentation. Working closely with a freight forwarder ensures that the shipment progresses smoothly from origin to destination, minimizing delays and compliance issues [29].

In essence, while shipping goods internationally can present challenges such as customs regulations, documentation requirements, and logistical complexities, following a structured approach starting with a clear and comprehensive purchase order sets the foundation for a successful shipping experience. Collaborating with a trusted freight forwarder further enhances this process by leveraging their knowledge and resources to manage every aspect of the shipment, thereby facilitating efficient and hassle-free international trade operations. This approach not only enhances operational efficiency but also contributes to maintaining positive supplier relationships and meeting customer expectations regarding delivery timelines and product quality.

Incoterms, short for International Commercial Terms, are a set of internationally recognized standard trade terms used in international sales contracts. They were first introduced by the International Chamber of Commerce (ICC) in 1936 and have since been periodically updated to reflect changes in global trade practices. Incoterms define the rights and obligations of both the buyer and the seller in international trade transactions, specifically regarding the delivery of goods, transfer of risks, and division of costs between parties.

The main purpose of Incoterms is to clarify who is responsible for the various tasks, costs, and risks associated with the transportation and delivery of goods from the seller to the buyer. These terms are crucial as they help avoid misunderstandings and disputes by clearly outlining the responsibilities of each party involved in the transaction.

Key aspects of Incoterms include:
- **Standardization**: Incoterms provide a common language and framework that facilitate international trade negotiations and transactions. They ensure consistency and clarity in contracts across different countries and legal jurisdictions.

- **Types of Terms**: Incoterms are divided into different categories, each specifying different levels of responsibility and obligations for both the seller and the buyer. For example, some terms are more favourable to the seller (where the seller bears less risk and responsibility), while others are more favourable to the buyer (where the buyer assumes greater control and risk).

- **Components**: Each Incoterm specifies:

  - The point at which the seller's responsibility for costs and risks ends.

  - The point at which the buyer takes on responsibility for costs and risks.

  - The point at which the goods are considered delivered (i.e., when the delivery obligation is fulfilled).

  - Which party is responsible for various tasks such as transportation, insurance, customs clearance, and payment of duties and taxes.

- **Commonly Used Terms**: Some of the commonly used Incoterms include EXW (Ex Works), FOB (Free on Board), CIF (Cost, Insurance, and Freight), and DAP (Delivered at Place). Each of these terms specifies different levels of involvement and obligations for both parties.

- **Applicability**: Incoterms are not legally binding unless expressly incorporated into a sales contract. Therefore, it's essential for businesses to clearly specify which Incoterm applies to their transactions to avoid misunderstandings.

Agreeing on shipping Incoterms is a crucial step in international trade transactions, setting out the responsibilities and liabilities between the buyer and seller during the shipment process. Incoterms, short for International Commercial Terms, are standardized rules established by the International Chamber of Commerce (ICC) that define the allocation of costs, risks, and tasks involved in the delivery of goods from the seller to the buyer. Before finalizing any purchase order, it is essential for both parties to agree on the appropriate Incoterm that best suits their specific transaction and circumstances [29].

The selection of the correct Incoterm is paramount because it determines several critical factors, including when ownership and risk transfer occur, who is responsible for arranging transportation, insurance, and customs clearance, and who bears the costs associated with these activities. For instance, if a buyer opts for Ex Works (EXW) terms, they take responsibility for all stages of the shipping process from the seller's premises to the final destination [29]. This includes arranging for transportation, insurance, and handling customs procedures, highlighting the importance of understanding the implications of each Incoterm choice.

Engaging a freight forwarder is often a necessary step once the Incoterms are agreed upon, especially if the terms require the buyer to manage the shipping process. A freight forwarder specializes in coordinating the transportation and logistics of goods from the point of origin to the destination, ensuring smooth transit and compliance with international shipping regulations. Their expertise is invaluable in navigating the complexities of global logistics, which can involve multiple modes of transport and varying regulatory requirements across different countries.

In international transactions, particularly those involving significant financial commitments, obtaining a Letter of Credit (LC) is a common practice to secure payment for the goods. A Letter of Credit is issued by a bank on behalf of the buyer, guaranteeing payment to the seller upon presentation of specified documents that conform to the terms and conditions outlined in the LC. This financial instrument provides assurance to both parties that payment will be made once the goods are shipped and documents are in order, mitigating risks associated with non-payment or disputes [29].

Once the order is confirmed and arrangements are made, the supplier issues a commercial invoice detailing the goods' price, quantity, and other relevant details. This document is crucial for customs clearance and serves as proof of the transaction's commercial value. Importers must keep the commercial invoice securely as it supports compliance with customs regulations and facilitates smooth clearance of goods upon arrival at the destination country. Proper documentation management is essential to avoid delays and ensure that all regulatory requirements are met during the importation process.

Step 2 in the international shipping process involves the crucial role of the freight forwarder in arranging the export of goods from the supplier's location to the buyer's destination [29]. This step is pivotal in ensuring that all necessary preparations and documentation are in place for smooth customs clearance and transit of the goods.

When working with an independent freight forwarder, the agent responsible for handling the shipment will initiate contact with their overseas counterpart. This overseas representative then coordinates with the supplier to arrange for the collection and export of the goods. Central to this process is the preparation of several key documents that are essential for customs purposes and regulatory compliance.

Firstly, the supplier prepares a Packing List, which details comprehensive information about the shipment. This document includes essential details such as the exporter's and buyer's contact information, how the goods are packed, and the quantity of each item. It serves as a vital reference for the freight forwarder in managing the logistics of the shipment.

Additionally, if the goods are destined for a free-trade country, the supplier must prepare a Certificate of Origin. This certificate certifies the origin of the goods, confirming where they were produced. It plays a critical role in ensuring that the buyer can benefit from any applicable preferential trade agreements that reduce or eliminate import duties.

Another important document is the Shipper's Letter of Instruction (SLI), which provides detailed shipping instructions to the local shipping agent. This document ensures clarity and accuracy in the handling and transportation of the goods throughout the shipping process.

For shipments to Australia as an example, specific documents like the Australian Packing Declaration may be required, especially if shipping goods by sea [29]. This declaration details the packing materials used in the shipment and is crucial for Australian customs to assess biosecurity risks associated with the importation of goods.

Furthermore, if the goods are classified as dangerous goods according to international regulations (IATA or IMO), the supplier must complete and include relevant Dangerous Goods Forms. These forms provide critical information about the nature of the hazardous materials being shipped and ensure compliance with safety regulations during transportation.

On the buyer's end, particularly when importing goods into Australia, there are several documents and permits they must obtain for export customs clearance. This includes an Export Declaration for goods exceeding AUD$2,000 in value or requiring an export permit. Importers may also need specific permits like an Import Declaration or Biosecurity Import Conditions (BICON) permit, depending on the nature of the goods being imported and their associated risks.

Navigating the complexities of export and import documentation requires expertise and compliance with local and international regulations. Many businesses opt to work with licensed customs brokers and freight forwarders who specialize in managing these processes efficiently. These professionals ensure that all required documents are prepared accurately, regulatory requirements are met, and the shipment moves smoothly through customs, minimizing delays and ensuring compliance with international trade laws. Their involvement helps streamline the shipping process, reduce risks, and facilitate successful international transactions.

Step 3 in the international shipping process involves the crucial step of booking the freight once all necessary documentation for export is in order [29]. This step is pivotal in ensuring that the shipment moves forward smoothly and reaches its destination on time, especially during peak shipping seasons.

Booking freight involves securing space on a vessel or an aircraft for transporting the goods from the supplier's location to the buyer's destination. This process requires careful planning and coordination to accommodate the volume of goods and the specific requirements of the shipment.

Timing is critical when booking freight, particularly during peak shipping seasons, which typically occur from September to January. During these periods, demand for shipping space is high due to increased consumer demand, holidays, and various economic factors. It's essential for suppliers to book freight early to avoid potential delays or difficulties in securing space on preferred shipping routes.

Early booking not only ensures that there is adequate space available but also allows sufficient time for logistical preparations, such as arranging for transportation to the port or airport, preparing cargo for shipment, and completing final checks on documentation and compliance requirements.

For sea freight, booking typically involves securing a slot on a container vessel or bulk carrier. Factors such as container availability, vessel schedules, and transit times to the destination port are considered when making these arrangements. Suppliers must also ensure that the booked vessel can accommodate the size and nature of their cargo, whether it's containerized goods, bulk commodities, or specialized cargo requiring specific handling.

Similarly, for air freight, booking involves reserving space on an aircraft that meets the shipment's timeline and service level requirements. Air freight bookings are influenced by factors such as flight schedules, cargo capacity, and airline-specific regulations for transporting goods, including hazardous materials or perishable items.

Effective communication and collaboration between the supplier, freight forwarder, and shipping carrier are essential during the booking process. Clear instructions regarding shipment details, including departure and arrival dates, shipping preferences (direct or transshipment), and any special handling requirements, ensure that the booking meets the supplier's expectations and operational needs.

By booking freight early and proactively managing logistics, suppliers can mitigate risks associated with shipping delays, maximize efficiency in supply chain operations, and maintain customer satisfaction by ensuring timely delivery of goods to their destination. This proactive approach helps suppliers navigate challenges posed by peak shipping seasons and other logistical complexities inherent in international trade.

Step 4 in the international shipping process involves transporting the goods from the supplier's location to an international depot or port for export, a critical phase facilitated by the logistics chain established earlier [29]. Depending on the agreed shipping incoterms, this step may be managed either by the supplier directly or by the consignee with the assistance of their appointed freight forwarder. This phase is essential as it sets the stage for export clearance and subsequent international transit.

Once the goods are packed and prepared for shipment, they are transported to a designated depot or port. This leg of the journey marks the transition from domestic handling to international logistics. The choice of depot or port depends on factors such as proximity, shipping routes, and the mode of transport selected under the incoterms.

During this phase, export clearance procedures commence. Export clearance ensures that all regulatory requirements, documentation, and inspections are completed in compliance with both domestic regulations and international trade laws. This process may involve verifying the accuracy of documentation, confirming the declared value of goods, and ensuring adherence to export control measures.

A pivotal document issued during this step is the Bill of Lading (B/L). The B/L serves as a contract of carriage between the shipper (supplier) and the carrier (transporter), confirming that the carrier has received the goods in acceptable condition and undertakes responsibility for their safe delivery to the destination port or depot. The B/L also serves as a crucial legal document that establishes ownership of the goods during transit.

In the context of international shipping, multiple bills of lading may be involved, reflecting different stages and modes of transport within the overall shipment journey. For example, an inland bill of lading may be issued for goods transported from a supplier's warehouse to a local seaport, while a separate ocean bill of lading is issued by the ocean carrier for goods transported across international waters.

Upon receiving the bill of lading from the carrier, the supplier transfers its legal rights over the goods to the consignee (buyer). The consignee must present the bill of lading to claim ownership of the shipment and facilitate its release at the destination port or depot. This process underscores the importance of accurate documentation and timely coordination to ensure smooth and efficient shipment handling.

Effective management of this step often involves leveraging the expertise of freight forwarding companies who specialize in navigating complex international logistics. These professionals facilitate the transportation arrangements, manage documentation requirements, and coordinate with carriers and regulatory authorities to streamline the export process and mitigate potential delays or complications.

Step 5 in the international shipping process involves crucial steps that ensure goods are processed through export customs clearance and placed in international transit, ready for their journey to the destination [29]. This phase is pivotal in international logistics as it involves regulatory compliance and the transition from domestic to international shipping environments.

Export customs clearance is a critical checkpoint where all documentation related to the shipment is meticulously reviewed and verified by government agencies. This process ensures compliance with export regulations, verifies the accuracy of declared goods and values, and confirms adherence to trade policies and restrictions. Suppliers are typically required to complete an Export Declaration, which provides authorities with essential information about the nature, value, and destination of the goods being exported.

Upon successful clearance of export customs, the goods are then prepared for international transit. At this stage, a separate bill of lading may be issued by the carrier handling the international leg of the journey. The bill of lading serves as a contract of carriage and a receipt for the goods, detailing the terms under which the goods are transported from the port of departure to the port of destination.

In international shipping, there are various modes of transport available depending on the volume and nature of the goods [29]:

- Full Container Load (FCL): This option is chosen when a buyer's shipment fills an entire shipping container. FCL shipments are ideal for large quantities of goods or when the buyer requires exclusive use of a container to prevent mixing with other consignments.

- Less than Container Load (LCL): When a buyer's goods do not occupy an entire container, they are consolidated with shipments from other buyers in the same container. LCL shipments are cost-effective for smaller volumes of cargo and allow for shared container space.

- Reefer: Refrigerated containers, known as reefers, are used to transport temperature-sensitive goods such as fruits, vegetables, dairy products, meat, and seafood. Reefer containers maintain specific temperature and humidity conditions throughout transit to ensure the integrity and freshness of perishable goods.

- Out of Gauge (OOG): Out of Gauge or break bulk shipments refer to goods that are oversized or irregularly shaped and cannot fit into standard shipping containers. These shipments often require special handling and may incur additional surcharges due to their size or weight.
- Flat Racks: Flat racks are specialized containers that lack sides and have collapsible or removable ends They are suitable for goods that are oversized, bulky, or awkwardly shaped and cannot be accommodated in standard containers. Flat racks offer flexibility in loading and securing cargo that does not conform to standard container dimensions.

Choosing the appropriate mode of transport depends on factors such as the nature of the goods, shipping budget, urgency of delivery, and specific requirements outlined in the agreed incoterms. Each mode of transport comes with its advantages and considerations, impacting factors such as transit time, cost-effectiveness, and logistical complexity.

Step 6 in the international shipping process involves the critical stage where the buyer's goods arrive in the destination country and undergo import clearance procedures [29]. This phase is essential to ensure compliance with local regulations, facilitate the entry of goods into the country, and prepare for their onward distribution to the buyer.

Upon arrival in the buyer's country, imported goods must undergo import clearance procedures overseen by customs authorities. In Australia as an example, this responsibility falls under the jurisdiction of the Australian Border Force (ABF). The ABF ensures that all imported goods meet regulatory requirements and are properly documented before entering the Australian market [29].

Import clearance involves several key processes and considerations:
- Regulatory Compliance: Importers must comply with Australian laws and regulations governing the importation of goods. Depending on the nature of the goods, specific regulations may apply, such as those concerning motor vehicles, animals, human remains, or intellectual property. Compliance ensures that imported goods meet safety, environmental, health, and quality standards set by Australian authorities.
- Tariffs, Taxes, and Charges: Imported goods may be subject to customs duties, tariffs, and other charges imposed by the Australian government. These fees vary depending on the type and value of the goods being imported. Importers must calculate and pay these duties to clear their goods through

customs.

- Quarantine Inspection: Certain goods imported into Australia, such as plants, animals, certain minerals, and human products like human remains, may require quarantine inspection upon arrival. The Australian Department of Agriculture and Water Resources conducts these inspections to prevent the introduction of pests and diseases that could harm agriculture, wildlife, or public health. Depending on the inspection findings, goods may require treatment or additional documentation to meet quarantine requirements.

- Documentation Requirements: Importers must provide accurate and complete documentation to facilitate import clearance. Key documents include the commercial invoice, packing list, bill of lading or air waybill, and any certificates or permits required for specific types of goods. These documents serve as proof of the transaction, establish ownership, and assist customs officials in verifying the nature and value of the imported goods.

Navigating the import clearance process requires careful planning and adherence to procedural requirements outlined by the ABF and other relevant Australian agencies. Importers often work with licensed customs brokers who specialize in handling import procedures and ensuring compliance with regulatory obligations. Customs brokers facilitate the submission of required documentation, coordinate inspections, calculate duties and taxes, and assist importers in resolving any issues that may arise during the clearance process.

Successful import clearance is crucial for ensuring timely delivery of goods to the buyer and avoiding delays or penalties associated with non-compliance. By understanding and fulfilling import requirements, importers can maintain the integrity of their supply chains, uphold regulatory standards, and facilitate seamless international trade operations into Australia [29].

Step 7 in the international shipping process involves the final leg of transporting goods from the port of entry to the buyer's designated delivery point [29]. This step is crucial for completing the logistics chain and ensuring that the goods reach their final destination safely and efficiently.

Once the goods have cleared customs and obtained necessary approvals, they are ready for transportation to the buyer. The method of transport and delivery logistics are determined by the agreed incoterms (International Commercial Terms) specified in the sales contract. Incoterms define the responsibilities and obligations of buyers and sellers regarding transportation, insurance, and risk ownership during the shipping process.

Depending on the type of shipment—whether by air, full container load (FCL), or less than container load (LCL) for international sea freight—various transport options become available. These options cater to different types of cargo and delivery preferences:

- Trucking and Ground Delivery: Goods can be transported via truck directly from the port to the buyer's location or designated delivery point. This method is common for both loose cargo and containerized shipments. Trucks equipped with side loaders or roller doors facilitate the unloading process, ensuring efficient handling and placement of goods at the delivery site.

- Container Delivery: For containerized shipments (FCL or LCL), containers can be delivered intact to the buyer's premises or another specified location. Depending on accessibility and logistical considerations, containers may be unloaded using specialized equipment such as cranes or forklifts. Container delivery methods ensure that goods remain secure and protected throughout the transportation process.

- Customized Delivery Arrangements: Buyers and transport providers may discuss specific delivery preferences before shipment arrival to streamline the delivery process. This could include considerations such as time constraints, site accessibility, and special handling requirements. Coordination with a freight forwarder or logistics provider helps ensure that delivery arrangements align with buyer expectations and operational capabilities.

Effective communication between the buyer, transport company, or freight forwarder is essential during this phase. Clear instructions regarding delivery preferences, timing, and any special requirements (e.g., live unload at a designated roller door) help minimize delays and ensure smooth execution of the delivery process.

Furthermore, adherence to incoterms clarifies which party—buyer or seller—is responsible for arranging and bearing the costs of transportation, insurance, and risk management up to the point of delivery. This clarity avoids misunderstandings and disputes, promoting efficient international trade operations.

Step 7 marks the culmination of the international shipping journey, where goods transition from port clearance to final delivery to the buyer. By leveraging appropriate transport options and adhering to agreed incoterms, importers ensure seamless logistics execution, timely delivery, and customer satisfaction in receiving their goods as per contractual agreements.

Interpreting workplace policies and mission statements to define process requirements for international freight transfer involves aligning organizational objectives with operational practices to ensure consistency, compliance, and efficiency in global logistics. This can be effectively achieved by:

Understanding Workplace Policies and Mission Statement: Begin by thoroughly reviewing and understanding the workplace policies and mission statement related to international freight transfer. Workplace policies typically outline guidelines, procedures, and standards that govern various aspects of logistics operations, including freight handling, documentation, compliance with regulations, and customer service. The mission statement provides strategic direction and overarching goals that the organization aims to achieve through its logistics activities.

Identifying Process Requirements: Based on the workplace policies and mission statement, identify specific process requirements for international freight transfer. This involves breaking down the broad goals and guidelines into actionable steps and procedures. For example, policies may stipulate requirements for accurate documentation, adherence to customs regulations, handling of hazardous materials, and maintaining transparency in communication with stakeholders.

Integrating Compliance and Regulatory Standards: Ensure that the defined process requirements align with relevant compliance and regulatory standards governing international freight transfer. This includes understanding local and international laws, trade agreements, import/export controls, and industry-specific regulations (e.g., handling of perishable goods or dangerous goods). Integrate these standards into the process requirements to mitigate legal risks and ensure smooth operations across borders.

Defining Operational Procedures: Translate the process requirements into clear and detailed operational procedures that outline step-by-step actions for executing international freight transfers. Specify responsibilities, timelines, documentation protocols, quality control measures, and contingency plans for unforeseen circumstances. Ensure that each procedure is practical, achievable, and supports the organization's goals of efficiency, customer satisfaction, and cost-effectiveness.

Communicating and Training: Communicate the defined process requirements and operational procedures to all relevant stakeholders, including logistics personnel, managers, suppliers, and partners. Provide comprehensive training to ensure that employees understand their roles, responsibilities, and the importance of adhering to workplace policies. Training should cover areas such as the use of technology systems, compliance with regulatory requirements, customer service standards, and handling of sensitive information.

Monitoring and Continuous Improvement: Establish mechanisms for monitoring the effectiveness of the defined process requirements through key performance indicators (KPIs) and regular performance reviews. Monitor metrics such as on-time delivery rates, accuracy of documentation, customer feedback, and compliance with regulatory standards. Use data analytics and feedback mechanisms to identify areas for improvement and implement corrective actions to enhance operational efficiency and effectiveness.

Review and Adaptation: Regularly review workplace policies, mission statements, and process requirements to ensure they remain aligned with evolving business goals, industry trends, and regulatory changes. Adapt procedures as necessary to address new challenges, optimize workflows, and capitalize on opportunities for innovation and improvement in international freight transfer operations.

Establishing appropriate systems to facilitate the organization of international freight transfer involves a strategic approach to ensure efficiency, compliance, and risk management throughout the logistics process. Begin by conducting a thorough needs assessment to identify specific requirements and challenges associated with international freight transfer. Evaluate existing systems, processes, and technologies used within your organization for freight logistics. Consider factors such as the volume of shipments, types of goods handled (including any hazardous materials), geographical reach, regulatory complexities, and customer expectations.

Select and implement appropriate technology solutions and infrastructure to support international freight operations effectively. This may include transportation management systems (TMS), enterprise resource planning (ERP) software with logistics modules, electronic data interchange (EDI) systems for seamless communication with partners, and tracking and monitoring tools. Evaluate these options based on their ability to streamline processes, enhance visibility, and integrate with existing IT systems.

Conduct a comprehensive risk analysis to identify potential threats and vulnerabilities in international freight operations. Consider risks related to transportation delays, cargo damage or loss, regulatory non-compliance, security breaches, and financial implications. Develop risk mitigation strategies and integrate them into your systems. For example, implement contingency plans for alternate shipping routes or carriers, enhance cargo tracking capabilities, and ensure compliance with international safety and security standards.

Establish a robust regulatory compliance framework to ensure adherence to local and international laws governing freight transport. This includes understanding customs regulations, import/export controls, trade agreements, and industry-specific standards (e.g., handling of perishable goods or hazardous materials). Integrate compliance checks into your systems to automate documentation, customs clearance processes, and reporting requirements.

Coordinate with reliable suppliers, carriers, freight forwarders, and other logistics partners to establish seamless communication and collaboration. Evaluate potential partners based on their track record, capabilities, service levels, and adherence to regulatory standards. Establish clear contractual agreements outlining roles, responsibilities, service level expectations, and contingency plans for emergencies or disruptions.

Implement systems for monitoring performance metrics related to international freight transfer, such as transit times, on-time delivery rates, shipment accuracy, and customer satisfaction. Use key performance indicators (KPIs) to measure system effectiveness and identify areas for improvement. Regularly review data analytics and feedback to refine processes, optimize routes, reduce costs, and enhance service quality.

Provide comprehensive training programs for employees involved in international freight logistics to ensure proficiency in using systems, understanding regulatory requirements, and implementing best practices. Foster a culture of continuous learning and skill development to adapt to evolving industry trends, technological advancements, and regulatory changes.

Organizing international freight transfers involves a meticulous process that begins with identifying and documenting the human resources needed for the task. Firstly, personnel responsible for logistics management are crucial. These individuals oversee the entire transfer process, from coordinating shipments to ensuring compliance with international regulations. They must possess a deep understanding of logistics operations, customs procedures, and transportation logistics.

Secondly, customs brokers play a pivotal role in navigating the complex regulatory requirements of different countries. They ensure that all necessary documentation, such as customs declarations and permits, is accurately prepared and submitted to facilitate smooth border crossings. Their expertise in tariff classifications and trade agreements helps minimize delays and potential fines.

Thirdly, freight forwarders are essential in organizing the physical movement of goods. They arrange transportation, handle packaging, and manage warehousing needs. Their network of carriers and knowledge of transportation modes (air, sea, land) ensure efficient and cost-effective delivery options based on the specific requirements of each shipment.

Additionally, legal experts specializing in international trade law provide guidance on contractual agreements, insurance coverage, and risk management strategies. Their role is crucial in mitigating legal risks and ensuring compliance with international trade laws and agreements such as Incoterms.

Furthermore, IT professionals are increasingly vital in managing data integration and information flow across different stakeholders and systems. They implement and maintain technology solutions for tracking shipments in real-time, managing inventory levels, and optimizing supply chain efficiency.

Lastly, project managers oversee the entire process, ensuring coordination among all stakeholders involved in the international freight transfer. They develop comprehensive project plans, allocate resources effectively, monitor progress, and resolve any issues that may arise during transit.

Initiating action to ensure staff are assigned, recruited, and/or trained in accordance with identified human resource requirements is a critical phase in organizational planning, particularly in the context of complex tasks such as international freight transfer. This process begins with a thorough assessment of the identified human resource needs, taking into account specific skills, qualifications, and experience required for each role involved in the freight transfer process.

Assigning staff involves aligning existing employees with the identified roles based on their expertise and capabilities. This may entail reassigning individuals from within the organization who possess relevant experience or skills that can be applied to international logistics and freight management. Clear communication of responsibilities and expectations is crucial during this phase to ensure that all team members understand their roles in supporting the successful execution of international freight transfers.

Recruitment plays a pivotal role in filling any gaps identified in the current workforce. Organizations may seek external candidates who bring specialized knowledge in areas such as customs compliance, logistics coordination, or international trade regulations. Recruitment efforts should be targeted towards attracting candidates with a proven track record in similar roles and a strong understanding of the global supply chain dynamics. This process typically involves conducting interviews, assessing candidates' technical competencies, and evaluating their ability to adapt to the organization's culture and values.

Training and development are integral components of ensuring staff are equipped with the necessary skills and knowledge to perform their roles effectively. This includes providing specialized training programs on international shipping procedures, customs documentation requirements, and the use of logistics management software. Continuous learning opportunities also help employees stay updated with evolving industry trends and regulatory changes, enhancing their ability to navigate complex international logistics challenges.

Moreover, establishing a structured onboarding process is essential for new hires to quickly integrate into their roles and become productive members of the international freight transfer team. This process includes orientation sessions to familiarize them with organizational policies, procedures, and team dynamics. Mentoring and coaching programs can further support their professional growth and development within the organization.

Identifying and procuring office, computer, and communications equipment is a fundamental step in ensuring operational efficiency and effective communication within any organization, particularly those involved in managing international freight transfers. This process begins with a comprehensive assessment of the specific equipment requirements tailored to the needs of the logistics and administrative teams responsible for overseeing freight operations.

Office equipment encompasses a range of essential tools such as desks, chairs, filing cabinets, and ergonomic accessories that contribute to a productive work environment. These items are selected based on factors like space availability, functional requirements, and ergonomic standards to support the comfort and well-being of employees engaged in tasks ranging from administrative duties to logistics coordination.

Computer equipment plays a crucial role in facilitating various aspects of international freight transfer operations, including data management, communication, and real-time tracking of shipments. This includes desktop computers, laptops, tablets, and mobile devices equipped with software applications tailored to logistics management, inventory tracking, and communication platforms. The selection criteria often prioritize compatibility with existing IT infrastructure, security protocols, and scalability to accommodate future growth and technological advancements.

Communications equipment is essential for maintaining seamless connectivity across dispersed teams, suppliers, and clients involved in international freight transfers. This may involve procuring telecommunications systems such as VoIP phones, video conferencing equipment, and satellite communication devices to ensure reliable communication channels regardless of geographical location or operational challenges. Integration with cloud-based collaboration tools and secure communication protocols further enhances efficiency and data security in managing cross-border logistics operations.

Actions initiated for appropriate assignment or procurement of office, computer, and communications equipment typically involve several key steps. This includes conducting a needs assessment to determine specific equipment requirements based on operational workflows and user preferences. Budgetary considerations play a crucial role in identifying cost-effective solutions that align with financial constraints while meeting functional specifications and quality standards.

Essential equipment typically needed:

- **Office Equipment:**

    - **Desks and Chairs:** Ergonomically designed furniture to provide comfort during long hours of administrative tasks and logistics coordination.

    - **Filing Cabinets:** Secure storage for important documents, including shipping manifests, customs declarations, and contracts.

    - **Printers and Scanners:** Devices for generating hard copies of shipping documents and scanning receipts, invoices, and other paperwork.

    - **Whiteboards and Noticeboards:** Tools for visual communication and displaying critical information such as shipment schedules and logistics updates.

    - **Stationery and Supplies:** Pens, paper, folders, and other office supplies essential for administrative tasks and record-keeping.

- **Computer Equipment:**

    - **Desktop Computers and Laptops:** Essential for administrative staff, logistics coordinators, and IT professionals to manage logistics software, track shipments, and handle documentation electronically.

    - **Monitors:** Dual monitors or large screens for enhanced productivity and multitasking capabilities.

    - **Printers and Copiers:** High-speed printers for generating shipping labels, invoices, and other documents, as well as copiers for duplicating paperwork.

- **Barcode Scanners:** Tools for inventory management and tracking shipments throughout the logistics process.

- **External Hard Drives and Backup Systems:** Secure storage solutions for backing up critical data and ensuring continuity in case of hardware failure or data loss.

- **Communications Equipment:**

    - **Telecommunication Systems:** VoIP phones, video conferencing equipment, and headsets for seamless communication with international partners, clients, and suppliers.

    - **Mobile Devices:** Smartphones and tablets equipped with logistics management apps for real-time communication and tracking of shipments.

    - **Satellite Phones:** Reliable communication tools for remote locations or areas with limited cellular coverage, ensuring continuous connectivity during international operations.

    - **Cloud-Based Collaboration Tools:** Platforms for sharing documents, project management, and team collaboration across different time zones and locations.

    - **Secure Network Infrastructure:** Firewalls, VPNs (Virtual Private Networks), and encryption software to safeguard sensitive data transmitted over the internet and protect against cyber threats.

Once equipment needs are identified, organizations proceed with vendor selection, negotiations, and procurement processes to acquire necessary items within specified timelines. This may involve evaluating multiple suppliers based on factors such as product quality, reliability, warranty support, and after-sales service. Installation, configuration, and testing procedures ensure that all equipment is operational and integrated seamlessly into existing infrastructure, minimizing disruption to daily operations and optimizing functionality.

Further. managing international freight transfers efficiently requires specialized software to handle various aspects of logistics, documentation, and communication. Here are the key types of software typically used in this field:

- **Transportation Management Systems (TMS):**

  - TMS software helps coordinate and optimize the movement of goods across different transportation modes (air, sea, land).

  - It includes features for route planning, carrier selection, freight booking, and shipment tracking.

  - TMS systems ensure efficient logistics operations by automating processes and providing real-time visibility into shipment status.

- **Customs Management and Compliance Software:**

  - This software assists in managing customs documentation and compliance requirements.

  - It automates the preparation of customs declarations, invoices, and other required documentation.

  - It integrates with customs authorities' systems to facilitate smooth clearance of goods across international borders.

- **Warehouse Management Systems (WMS):**

  - WMS software tracks and manages inventory within warehouses or distribution centres.

  - It optimizes storage space, manages picking, packing, and shipping processes, and provides real-time inventory visibility.

  - Integration with TMS and ERP (Enterprise Resource Planning) systems ensures seamless coordination between warehouse operations and transportation logistics.

- **Enterprise Resource Planning (ERP) Systems:**

  - ERP software integrates various business processes, including finance, procurement, inventory management, and logistics.

  - It provides a centralized platform for managing international freight operations, tracking costs, and maintaining regulatory compliance.

- ERP systems often include modules or integration capabilities with TMS, WMS, and financial management software.

- **Supply Chain Visibility Software:**

  - This software provides end-to-end visibility into supply chain operations, including inbound and outbound logistics.

  - It enables real-time tracking of shipments, monitors inventory levels, and predicts delivery times.

  - Supply chain visibility software enhances decision-making by providing insights into potential disruptions and optimizing supply chain performance.

- **Document Management Systems (DMS):**

  - DMS software centralizes and manages documents related to international freight transfers, such as shipping contracts, bills of lading, and insurance certificates.

  - It ensures document accessibility, version control, and compliance with document retention policies.

  - Integration with other systems facilitates document exchange and workflow automation.

- **Collaboration and Communication Tools:**

  - Tools like email clients, instant messaging platforms, and video conferencing software facilitate communication with international partners, clients, and logistics providers.

  - Collaboration tools enable real-time interaction, file sharing, and project management across distributed teams.

- **Risk Management and Compliance Software:**

  - This software monitors regulatory changes, assesses compliance risks, and implements risk mitigation strategies.

○ It ensures adherence to international trade regulations, sanctions, and export controls to avoid penalties and disruptions.

Implementing and integrating these software solutions into the organization's IT infrastructure supports efficient operations, improves decision-making capabilities, enhances customer service, and ensures compliance with international trade regulations throughout the freight management process.

Documenting and updating quality standards and procedures for proposed international freight transfer processes is crucial for ensuring consistency, reliability, and compliance throughout the logistics operations. This process begins with a thorough assessment of existing procedures and industry best practices, aiming to establish a framework that aligns with the organization's goals, regulatory requirements, and customer expectations.

Quality standards and procedures are essential in international freight transfer to ensure efficiency, reliability, and compliance throughout the logistics process. These standards encompass various practices aimed at enhancing the accuracy of shipment documentation, timeliness of delivery, adherence to packaging and handling requirements, appropriate selection of transportation modes, customs compliance, security and risk management, and customer service and communication. By adhering to these standards, organizations can minimize risks, enhance reliability, and deliver consistent value to stakeholders involved in global logistics operations [30].

Quality standards and procedures applicable to international freight transfer encompass a wide range of practices aimed at ensuring efficiency, reliability, and compliance throughout the logistics process. Here are some specific examples:

- **Accuracy of Shipment Documentation:**

    ○ **Standard:** All shipping documents, including invoices, packing lists, and bills of lading, must accurately reflect the contents, quantities, and values of goods being transported.

    ○ **Procedure:** Document verification processes are implemented to ensure that all information is correctly recorded and corresponds with regulatory requirements at the point of origin and destination.

- **Timeliness of Delivery:**

    ○ **Standard:** Shipments must arrive at their destination within agreed-upon transit times or delivery windows.

- **Procedure:** Monitoring and tracking systems are used to provide real-time visibility of shipment progress, enabling proactive management of potential delays and timely communication with stakeholders.

- **Packaging and Handling Requirements:**

  - **Standard:** Goods must be packaged securely and in accordance with international packaging standards to prevent damage during transit.

  - **Procedure:** Standard operating procedures (SOPs) are established for proper handling, stacking, and securing of goods to minimize risks of breakage, spoilage, or loss.

- **Transportation Mode Selection:**

  - **Standard:** The selection of transportation modes (air, sea, road, rail) must consider factors such as cost, transit time, capacity, and environmental impact.

  - **Procedure:** Evaluation criteria and decision-making protocols are documented to guide the selection of the most appropriate transportation mode based on shipment characteristics and customer requirements.

- **Customs Compliance and Documentation:**

  - **Standard:** All customs declarations, permits, licenses, and certificates required for international shipments must be accurately completed and submitted in accordance with local and international regulations.

  - **Procedure:** Clear guidelines and checklists are established for preparing and submitting customs documentation, including adherence to tariff classifications, trade agreements (e.g., Incoterms), and import/export controls.

- **Security and Risk Management:**

  - **Standard:** Measures must be in place to mitigate risks related to theft, tampering, or terrorism threats during international transit.

  - **Procedure:** Security protocols, such as container sealing procedures, cargo screening, and compliance with international security standards (e.g., International Ship and Port Facility Security Code - ISPS Code), are implemented and regularly reviewed.

- **Customer Service and Communication:**

    ○ **Standard:** Proactive communication with customers regarding shipment status, delays, and resolution of issues is essential for maintaining service excellence.

    ○ **Procedure:** Customer service protocols outline communication channels, response times, and escalation procedures to address customer inquiries and ensure satisfaction throughout the freight transfer process.

These examples illustrate how quality standards and procedures in international freight transfer encompass aspects ranging from documentation accuracy and regulatory compliance to operational efficiency, security, and customer service. By adhering to these standards and procedures, organizations can enhance reliability, minimize risks, and deliver consistent value to stakeholders involved in global logistics operations.

One critical aspect of quality standards in international freight transfer is the accuracy of shipment documentation. It is essential that all shipping documents, such as invoices, packing lists, and bills of lading, accurately reflect the contents, quantities, and values of the goods being transported. To ensure this accuracy, document verification processes are implemented to guarantee that all information is correctly recorded and aligns with regulatory requirements at both the point of origin and destination [30].

Timeliness of delivery is another key standard in international freight transfer. Shipments are expected to arrive at their destination within agreed-upon transit times or delivery windows. Monitoring and tracking systems are utilized to provide real-time visibility of shipment progress, enabling proactive management of potential delays and facilitating timely communication with stakeholders [30].

Packaging and handling requirements also form a crucial part of quality standards in international freight transfer. Goods must be securely packaged according to international standards to prevent damage during transit. Standard operating procedures are established for proper handling, stacking, and securing of goods to minimize risks of breakage, spoilage, or loss [30].

Moreover, the selection of transportation modes is a significant standard in international freight transfer. Factors such as cost, transit time, capacity, and environmental impact are considered when choosing between air, sea, road, or rail transport. Evaluation criteria and decision-making protocols are documented to guide the selection of the most suitable transportation mode based on shipment characteristics and customer requirements [30].

Customs compliance and documentation are also vital components of quality standards in international freight transfer. It is imperative that all customs declarations, permits, licenses, and certificates required for international shipments are accurately completed and submitted in line with local and international regulations. Clear guidelines and checklists are established to ensure the accurate preparation and submission of customs documentation, including adherence to tariff classifications, trade agreements, and import/export controls ([30].

Security and risk management standards are essential to mitigate risks related to theft, tampering, or terrorism threats during international transit. Security protocols, such as container sealing procedures, cargo screening, and compliance with international security standards like the International Ship and Port Facility Security Code (ISPS Code), are implemented and regularly reviewed to ensure the safety of shipments [30].

Furthermore, customer service and communication standards are crucial for maintaining service excellence in international freight transfer. Proactive communication with customers regarding shipment status, delays, and issue resolution is vital. Customer service protocols outline communication channels, response times, and escalation procedures to address customer inquiries and ensure satisfaction throughout the freight transfer process [30].

Firstly, defining quality standards involves specifying benchmarks and performance metrics that outline the expected outcomes of each stage in the freight transfer process. This may include criteria such as shipment accuracy, timeliness of deliveries, and adherence to safety protocols. These standards serve as a guideline for assessing and improving operational efficiency while meeting customer satisfaction goals.

Secondly, documenting procedures details step-by-step instructions for executing each aspect of the international freight transfer process. This includes procedures for order processing, inventory management, packaging requirements, transportation modes selection, and customs clearance. Documented procedures provide clarity to employees regarding their roles and responsibilities, ensuring consistency in operations and minimizing errors or delays.

Updating these standards and procedures involves a systematic review and revision process to incorporate feedback from stakeholders, industry changes, and lessons learned from past operations. This iterative approach ensures that procedures remain relevant and effective in addressing evolving challenges and opportunities in international logistics.

Adherence to workplace procedures ensures compliance with regulatory requirements governing international freight transfers. This includes customs regulations, import/export laws, trade agreements, and security protocols mandated by international bodies and national authorities. Documenting these procedures helps mitigate risks associated with non-compliance, such as customs delays, fines, or disruptions in supply chain operations.

Integrating quality management principles such as continuous improvement and risk assessment enhances the effectiveness of documented procedures. Regular audits, performance reviews, and employee training programs support ongoing refinement and optimization of processes to meet changing customer demands and industry standards.

Monitoring and Coordinating Systems and Processes for International Freight Transfer

Monitoring international freight forwarding operations against identified quality standards and compliance with local and international regulatory requirements is essential to ensure efficiency, reliability, and adherence to legal obligations throughout the logistics process. This monitoring process begins with establishing clear quality standards that define the expectations and benchmarks for each stage of freight forwarding operations, from initial booking to final delivery.

Firstly, quality standards encompass aspects such as accuracy in documentation, timeliness of deliveries, proper handling and packaging of goods, and adherence to agreed-upon service levels. For instance, documentation accuracy ensures that all shipping documents, including invoices, packing lists, and bills of lading, are correctly prepared and comply with regulatory requirements both at the origin and destination countries. Timeliness of deliveries involves monitoring shipments to ensure they arrive within agreed transit times, minimizing delays and disruptions to supply chains.

Secondly, compliance with local and international regulatory requirements is crucial in international freight forwarding operations. This includes adherence to customs regulations, import/export controls, trade agreements (such as Incoterms), and security protocols mandated by international bodies and national authorities. For example, freight forwarders must ensure that all necessary customs declarations, permits, licenses, and certificates are accurately completed and submitted in accordance with applicable laws and regulations. Monitoring involves regular audits, inspections, and reviews to verify compliance and identify any potential gaps or areas for improvement.

Thirdly, monitoring against quality standards and regulatory compliance involves implementing robust monitoring and tracking systems throughout the logistics process. These systems provide real-time visibility into shipment status, allowing freight forwarders to proactively manage and address issues such as delays, damages, or regulatory discrepancies. Monitoring may include performance metrics, KPIs (Key Performance Indicators), and regular reporting to measure operational efficiency and compliance levels.

Moreover, continuous improvement is integral to the monitoring process. By analysing data and feedback from monitoring activities, freight forwarders can identify trends, root causes of issues, and opportunities for enhancing operational processes. This may involve refining standard operating procedures (SOPs), conducting training programs for staff on regulatory changes, or implementing technology upgrades to enhance tracking and reporting capabilities.

Identifying and addressing non-compliance with quality standards or regulatory requirements is a critical aspect of ensuring the integrity and reliability of international freight forwarding operations. When instances of non-compliance are detected, it is essential to initiate prompt and appropriate actions in accordance with established workplace procedures to rectify the issue and mitigate potential risks.

Firstly, the process begins with robust monitoring and auditing mechanisms designed to systematically assess adherence to quality standards and regulatory requirements throughout the freight forwarding process. This may involve regular inspections, internal audits, and performance reviews conducted by qualified personnel who are trained to identify deviations from established protocols.

Once non-compliance is identified, immediate actions are taken to document and report the findings using standardized reporting procedures. This includes detailing the nature of the non-compliance, its potential impact on operations or regulatory compliance, and any corrective measures already implemented or planned. Clear and transparent reporting ensures that all stakeholders, including management, regulatory authorities, and customers, are informed promptly and accurately.

Next, appropriate actions are initiated to rectify the non-compliance in accordance with predefined workplace procedures. These actions may vary depending on the nature and severity of the issue but typically involve:

- Root Cause Analysis: Investigating the underlying reasons for the non-compliance to prevent recurrence. This may involve conducting interviews, reviewing documentation, and analysing data to identify gaps in processes, training deficiencies, or systemic issues.

- Corrective Actions: Implementing immediate corrective measures to address the non-compliance and mitigate any potential adverse effects. This could include reprocessing shipments, revising documentation, or revisiting training programs for staff involved.

- Preventive Actions: Developing and implementing long-term solutions to prevent similar incidents from occurring in the future. This may include updating SOPs, enhancing training programs, or implementing new technologies to improve monitoring and compliance capabilities.

- Communication and Follow-up: Communicating openly with affected parties, stakeholders, and regulatory authorities regarding the actions taken and the steps being implemented to prevent recurrence. Regular follow-up and monitoring ensure that corrective and preventive measures are effective and sustainable over time.

It's important to maintain documentation throughout this process to demonstrate compliance efforts and facilitate future audits or inspections. This documentation includes records of non-compliance reports, corrective actions taken, preventive measures implemented, and outcomes of follow-up assessments.

Monitoring customer satisfaction with international freight transfer services is crucial for maintaining competitiveness, improving service delivery, and fostering long-term relationships with clients in the global logistics industry. This process begins with establishing clear workplace procedures designed to systematically measure, assess, and respond to customer feedback and perceptions throughout the freight transfer journey.

Firstly, customer satisfaction monitoring involves defining key performance indicators (KPIs) and metrics that reflect the quality, reliability, and responsiveness of freight forwarding services. These metrics may include on-time delivery performance, accuracy of documentation, communication effectiveness, handling of inquiries and complaints, and overall service reliability. Establishing measurable benchmarks allows freight forwarding companies to objectively evaluate their performance and identify areas for improvement.

Secondly, collecting customer feedback occurs through various channels such as surveys, interviews, direct communication, and online platforms. Feedback collection methods should be accessible, user-friendly, and tailored to capture insights across different stages of the customer experience—from initial booking and shipment tracking to final delivery and post-delivery support. This ensures a comprehensive understanding of customer perceptions and expectations throughout the entire freight transfer process.

Thirdly, analysing customer satisfaction data involves systematic review and interpretation of feedback gathered from multiple sources. This analysis helps identify trends, recurring issues, and areas of strength or weakness in service delivery. By examining customer comments, ratings, and satisfaction scores, freight forwarding companies can pinpoint specific operational areas that require attention or enhancement to better meet customer needs and expectations.

As such, monitoring customer satisfaction with international freight transfer services involves a systematic approach to gather, analyse, and respond to customer feedback effectively including:

- **Define Key Performance Indicators (KPIs):**

    o Start by identifying specific KPIs that measure aspects of the customer experience relevant to international freight transfer. This may include:

    - On-time delivery performance

    - Accuracy of documentation (e.g., invoices, bills of lading)

    - Communication effectiveness

    - Handling of inquiries and complaints

    - Overall service reliability

- **Establish Feedback Collection Channels:**

    o Implement various channels for collecting customer feedback throughout the freight transfer process. Options include:

    - Customer satisfaction surveys sent via email or accessible through customer portals

    - Direct interviews or feedback sessions with key customers

- Online review platforms or feedback forms on the company's website
- Customer service interactions and post-delivery follow-ups

- **Design Feedback Mechanisms:**
  - Ensure that feedback mechanisms are user-friendly, accessible, and tailored to capture insights at different touchpoints of the customer journey. Consider using:
    - Rating scales or Likert scales to quantify satisfaction levels
    - Open-ended questions to gather qualitative feedback and suggestions
    - Net Promoter Score (NPS) surveys to gauge customer loyalty and likelihood to recommend the service

- **Collect and Record Feedback:**
  - Regularly collect customer feedback using the established channels and mechanisms. Ensure that feedback is recorded systematically and categorized based on relevant criteria such as service type, shipment destination, or customer segment.

- **Analyse Feedback Data:**
  - Conduct thorough analysis of the collected feedback to identify trends, patterns, and areas for improvement. Pay attention to both quantitative metrics (scores, ratings) and qualitative insights (comments, suggestions).
  - Use statistical tools or software to aggregate data and generate reports that highlight performance against KPIs and benchmarks.

- **Act on Insights:**
  - Based on the analysis, prioritize actions to address identified issues and capitalize on strengths. Actions may include:

- Implementing corrective measures to resolve recurring issues (e.g., process improvements, training initiatives)

- Enhancing communication protocols to improve transparency and responsiveness

- Recognizing and replicating best practices identified through positive feedback

- **Communicate Findings and Actions:**

  - Share feedback findings, analysis results, and planned actions with relevant stakeholders, including management, customer service teams, and frontline staff.

  - Provide clear communication to customers regarding the steps taken to address feedback and improve service quality.

- **Continuous Monitoring and Improvement:**

  - Establish a continuous feedback loop by regularly monitoring customer satisfaction metrics and revisiting KPIs to ensure they remain relevant.

  - Engage in ongoing dialogue with customers to stay attuned to evolving expectations and market trends, adjusting strategies and service offerings as needed.

Moreover, responding to customer feedback involves implementing appropriate actions based on the findings of the satisfaction monitoring process. This includes addressing identified concerns promptly, implementing corrective measures to resolve issues, and communicating transparently with customers regarding the steps taken to improve service quality. Proactive customer engagement and follow-up demonstrate commitment to continuous improvement and customer-centric service delivery.

Furthermore, integrating customer satisfaction monitoring into ongoing quality management systems ensures alignment with organizational goals and objectives. By regularly reviewing performance against established KPIs and benchmarks, freight forwarding companies can track progress, measure success, and refine strategies to enhance overall customer satisfaction and loyalty. This continuous monitoring and improvement cycle not only strengthen relationships with existing clients but also position companies competitively in attracting new business opportunities in the global marketplace.

Addressing customer concerns and implementing suggestions for service improvements in international freight transfer operations is crucial for maintaining customer satisfaction, improving service quality, and fostering long-term relationships. This process involves several key steps outlined within workplace procedures to ensure systematic handling and effective resolution of customer feedback.

Firstly, receiving customer concerns and suggestions occurs through various channels, including direct communication, surveys, feedback forms, and customer service interactions. These channels serve as critical touchpoints for capturing both positive feedback and areas where customers perceive shortcomings or opportunities for enhancement in service delivery.

Secondly, workplace procedures dictate the systematic recording and categorization of customer feedback. This involves documenting the nature of concerns or suggestions, identifying specific issues related to service quality, logistics operations, or customer interactions, and assigning appropriate tags or categories for easy tracking and analysis.

Thirdly, upon receipt of customer feedback, immediate actions are initiated to acknowledge and investigate each concern or suggestion. This includes:

- **Assessment and Analysis:** Reviewing the feedback to understand the root causes and implications for service delivery. This may involve cross-referencing with existing performance data, customer history, or operational metrics to gain a comprehensive understanding of the issue.

- **Prioritization:** Prioritizing concerns based on severity, frequency, and potential impact on customer satisfaction and business operations. Urgent issues affecting critical shipments or recurring problems are often addressed with higher priority.

- **Resolution Planning:** Developing a plan of action to address identified concerns or implement suggested improvements. This may involve collaborating with relevant departments such as logistics, customer service, IT, or quality assurance to devise effective solutions.

Moreover, workplace procedures typically include mechanisms for escalation and decision-making. For complex or high-impact issues, involving senior management or cross-functional teams ensures that adequate resources and expertise are allocated to resolve challenges promptly and effectively.

Furthermore, implementing corrective actions and service improvements involves:

- **Implementation:** Executing planned actions to rectify identified issues or introduce enhancements. This may include process adjustments, system upgrades, training programs for staff, or procedural updates to prevent recurrence.

- **Communication:** Transparently communicating with customers regarding the steps taken to address their concerns or suggestions. Providing updates on progress, timelines for resolution, and measures implemented helps build trust and demonstrates commitment to customer satisfaction.

Lastly, monitoring the outcomes of implemented actions is essential to evaluate their effectiveness and measure improvements in service quality. This may involve ongoing tracking of key performance indicators (KPIs), conducting follow-up surveys or feedback sessions with customers, and revisiting feedback mechanisms to ensure continuous alignment with evolving customer expectations.

Completing and documenting reports related to international freight transfer operations is essential for maintaining transparency, accountability, and operational efficiency within logistics organizations. These reports serve as crucial records that provide insights into various aspects of freight operations, compliance with regulations, and performance metrics. Following workplace procedures ensures that reports are accurately compiled, disseminated to relevant personnel, and utilized effectively across the organization.

Firstly, workplace procedures outline the types of reports required and the frequency of their completion. These may include:

- **Shipment Reports:** Detailing specifics of each shipment such as origin, destination, contents, and transportation mode used.

- **Performance Reports:** Assessing key performance indicators (KPIs) like on-time delivery rates, cargo damage rates, and customer satisfaction metrics.

- **Compliance Reports:** Documenting adherence to regulatory requirements, including customs declarations, import/export documentation, and security protocols.

Secondly, compiling reports involves gathering data from various sources within the organization's operational and administrative systems. This data collection process ensures that reports are comprehensive and reflective of actual operations. It may involve collaboration between logistics personnel, customer service teams, compliance officers, and IT specialists to gather and verify data accuracy.

Thirdly, once compiled, reports are reviewed for accuracy, completeness, and compliance with established standards and procedures. Quality checks are conducted to ensure that data is consistent, calculations are correct, and information is presented in a clear and understandable format. Reports may also undergo internal audits or peer reviews to validate findings and ensure reliability.

Moreover, workplace procedures specify the distribution of reports to relevant personnel and stakeholders. This includes:

- **Management:** Providing operational and performance reports to senior management for strategic decision-making, resource allocation, and performance evaluation.

- **Operations Teams:** Sharing detailed shipment reports with logistics coordinators, warehouse managers, and transportation personnel to facilitate operational planning and coordination.

- **Compliance Officers:** Distributing compliance reports to ensure adherence to regulatory requirements and prompt resolution of any identified issues.

Furthermore, documentation practices ensure that reports are archived and stored securely in accordance with data protection policies and regulatory guidelines. This includes maintaining records of past reports for historical reference, audit purposes, and future analysis. Digital storage solutions and document management systems help streamline access to archived reports while safeguarding sensitive information.

Ongoing review and utilization of reports play a vital role in driving continuous improvement within international freight transfer operations. Analysing trends, identifying areas for enhancement, and implementing corrective actions based on report findings contribute to optimizing efficiency, reducing costs, and enhancing customer satisfaction over time.

Accessing Contacts and Sources of Information/Documentation Needed when Managing International Freight Transfer Systems

Managing international freight transfer systems effectively requires access to a variety of contacts and sources of information/documentation to ensure smooth operations, regulatory compliance, and timely resolution of logistical challenges. These contacts and sources of information are essential for obtaining critical updates, coordinating logistics, and addressing issues that may arise during the transportation of goods across borders.

Customs Authorities and Agencies are pivotal contacts when managing international freight transfers. They provide essential information regarding customs regulations, import/export documentation requirements, duty rates, and clearance procedures. Establishing direct communication channels with customs officials helps expedite the clearance process and ensures compliance with local and international trade laws.

Transportation Providers and Freight Forwarders serve as key contacts for coordinating the physical movement of goods. Freight forwarders offer expertise in selecting optimal transportation modes (air, sea, road, rail), negotiating freight rates, and managing logistics operations. Building strong relationships with reliable transportation providers ensures competitive pricing, efficient transit times, and secure handling of shipments throughout the supply chain.

Trade Associations and Industry Networks provide valuable resources and networking opportunities for staying informed about industry trends, best practices, and regulatory updates affecting international freight transfers. Membership in trade associations facilitates access to training programs, seminars, and industry events where professionals can exchange knowledge and discuss emerging challenges in global logistics.

Legal and Compliance Advisors offer guidance on navigating complex regulatory frameworks governing international trade. They provide interpretations of trade agreements, sanctions, export controls, and compliance with environmental and safety standards. Collaborating with legal experts ensures adherence to legal requirements, mitigates risks associated with non-compliance, and facilitates prompt resolution of regulatory issues.

Technology Providers and Software Platforms offer innovative solutions for managing international freight transfer systems. Transportation Management Systems (TMS), Customs Management Software, and Supply Chain Visibility Platforms streamline operations by automating processes, tracking shipments in real-time, and enhancing communication across global supply chains. Integrating these technologies improves efficiency, reduces costs, and enhances visibility throughout the logistics process.

Financial Institutions and Insurance Providers play a crucial role in managing financial transactions and mitigating risks associated with international trade. Banks offer trade finance services such as letters of credit and payment guarantees, facilitating secure financial transactions between buyers and sellers. Insurance providers offer cargo insurance coverage against loss or damage during transit, providing financial protection and peace of mind to stakeholders involved in international freight transfers.

Government Agencies and Regulatory Bodies oversee compliance with international trade regulations and safety standards. Contacts within these agencies provide information on licensing requirements, cargo security measures (e.g., ISPS Code), and crisis management protocols for handling emergencies such as natural disasters or geopolitical disruptions. Establishing relationships with government officials enhances transparency, facilitates regulatory compliance, and ensures swift response to regulatory inquiries or audits.

Here are specific examples from around the world that illustrate the importance of various contacts and sources of information/documentation in managing international freight transfer systems effectively:

- **Customs Authorities and Agencies:**

    - **United States (US Customs and Border Protection - CBP):** CBP provides detailed information on customs regulations, tariff classifications, import/export documentation requirements, and duty rates. Establishing direct communication with CBP officials helps expedite customs clearance processes at ports of entry such as Los Angeles/Long Beach and New York/New Jersey, ensuring compliance with US trade laws.

- **Transportation Providers and Freight Forwarders:**

    - **Europe (DHL, Kuehne + Nagel):** DHL and Kuehne + Nagel are key freight forwarders and logistics providers in Europe. They offer comprehensive services for coordinating air, sea, road, and rail transport across the continent. Establishing partnerships with these companies ensures efficient transit times and reliable handling of shipments, crucial for moving goods between major hubs like Frankfurt, London, and Rotterdam.

- **Trade Associations and Industry Networks:**

- **Asia-Pacific (Asia-Pacific Economic Cooperation - APEC):** APEC facilitates trade and economic cooperation among 21 member economies across the Asia-Pacific region. It provides valuable resources and networking opportunities through working groups and forums focused on harmonizing customs procedures, sharing best practices, and addressing regulatory updates affecting international freight transfers.

- **Legal and Compliance Advisors:**

  - **Middle East (Dubai Customs):** Dubai Customs plays a pivotal role in the UAE by providing guidance on navigating complex regulatory frameworks governing international trade. They offer interpretations of trade agreements, export controls, and compliance with local and international standards. Collaborating with legal experts ensures adherence to Dubai's stringent customs regulations at ports like Jebel Ali, a major hub for trade in the region.

- **Technology Providers and Software Platforms:**

  - **Global (SAP Global Trade Services):** SAP Global Trade Services offers software solutions for managing international trade processes, including transportation management, customs compliance, and supply chain visibility. Integrating SAP GTS improves efficiency and reduces costs by automating regulatory compliance checks and providing real-time tracking capabilities across global supply chains.

- **Financial Institutions and Insurance Providers:**

  - **Latin America (Banco Santander, Mapfre Insurance):** Banco Santander in Latin America offers trade finance solutions such as letters of credit and payment guarantees to facilitate secure financial transactions for importers and exporters. Mapfre Insurance provides cargo insurance coverage against risks like loss or damage during transit, ensuring financial protection for stakeholders involved in international freight transfers across the region.

- **Government Agencies and Regulatory Bodies:**

  - **Australia (Australian Border Force - ABF):** ABF oversees compliance with Australia's customs and border protection laws, including licensing requirements and cargo security measures under the ISPS Code. Contacts within ABF provide guidance on crisis management protocols for handling emergencies at ports like Sydney and Melbourne, enhancing transparency and ensuring regulatory compliance in international trade operations.

These examples demonstrate how access to diverse contacts and sources of information/documentation is essential for navigating the complexities of international freight transfer systems. By leveraging these relationships and resources, logistics professionals can ensure smooth operations, regulatory compliance, and timely resolution of logistical challenges across different regions and trade corridors worldwide.

Applying Operational Requirements for The Safe Transfer and Storage of Dangerous Goods and Hazardous Substances

The safe transfer and storage of dangerous goods and hazardous substances are critical operational requirements in logistics and supply chain management. These substances, which can range from flammable liquids and corrosive materials to explosives and radioactive substances, pose significant risks to human health, the environment, and property if not handled with utmost care and compliance with stringent regulations.

Compliance with Regulatory Requirements forms the foundation of safe operations. Each country has its own set of regulations governing the transportation and storage of dangerous goods. For example, in the United States, the Department of Transportation (DOT) issues regulations under Title 49 of the Code of Federal Regulations (CFR), while in Europe, the European Agreement concerning the International Carriage of Dangerous Goods by Road (ADR) sets the standards. Compliance with these regulations entails proper classification, packaging, labelling, and documentation of hazardous materials, ensuring they are handled and transported safely.

Risk Assessment and Management are crucial steps in ensuring the safe transfer and storage of dangerous goods. Before transport or storage, thorough risk assessments are conducted to identify potential hazards associated with the specific substances involved. This includes assessing factors such as toxicity, flammability, reactivity, and environmental impact. Based on these assessments, risk management strategies are developed to mitigate identified risks through appropriate control measures, including specialized packaging, handling procedures, and emergency response plans.

Figure 24: Dangerous goods storage and labelling. Mr Thinktank, CC BY 2.0, via Flickr.

Packaging and Handling Procedures are tailored to the characteristics of each hazardous substance. Packaging requirements are stringent to prevent leaks, spills, or exposure during transport. This may involve using containers made of materials compatible with the substance's properties, such as corrosion-resistant metals or high-density plastics. Additionally, handling procedures include guidelines for loading and unloading, securing shipments to prevent movement, and using equipment like forklifts or cranes designed for hazardous materials handling.

Figure 25: Dangerous goods transport by rail. Kecko, CC BY 2.0, via Flickr.

Training and Certification of personnel involved in the transfer and storage of dangerous goods are essential to ensure competency and adherence to safety protocols. Training programs cover topics such as hazard recognition, emergency response procedures, and regulatory compliance specific to the substances being handled. Certifications, such as the Hazardous Materials Endorsement (HME) for commercial drivers in the US or ADR training for drivers in Europe, validate competence in safely transporting hazardous materials.

Emergency Preparedness and Response plans are critical to promptly address incidents involving hazardous substances. These plans outline procedures for responding to spills, leaks, fires, or other emergencies that may occur during transport or storage. They include protocols for notifying authorities, evacuating personnel, containing spills, and mitigating environmental impacts. Regular drills and exercises ensure readiness and familiarity with emergency procedures among personnel.

Furthermore, Environmental Protection Measures are integrated into operational requirements to minimize the impact of hazardous substances on ecosystems and communities. This includes implementing spill containment measures, wastewater treatment protocols, and compliance with environmental permits and regulations governing air, water, and soil quality. Environmental considerations are integral to maintaining sustainability and corporate responsibility in hazardous materials management.

Ensuring the safe transfer and storage of dangerous goods and hazardous substances requires a comprehensive approach that encompasses regulatory compliance, rigorous risk management, specialized packaging and handling procedures, ongoing training, emergency preparedness, and environmental stewardship. By adhering to these operational requirements, logistics and supply chain professionals can mitigate risks, protect personnel and the environment, and uphold safety standards in the global movement of hazardous materials.

Chapter 8

Managing a Supply Chain

Managing a supply chain involves a multifaceted approach that encompasses various interconnected elements. The contemporary landscape of supply chain management has evolved to include global supply chains for innovative products, highlighting the crucial role intermediaries play in facilitating these complex networks [31]. Supply chain management is increasingly recognized as the orchestration of essential business processes across a network of organizations within the supply chain [32]. Sustainable supply chain management (SSCM) is a critical aspect that involves actions aimed at achieving sustainable development through the interconnections and coordination of elements within the supply chain [33]. In the healthcare sector, managing supply chains presents unique challenges that offer opportunities for research in areas such as coordination, mass customization, and incentives, which can provide insights applicable to traditional supply chains [34].

Managing a supply chain involves overseeing and optimizing the entire process of sourcing, producing, and delivering products or services to customers. It encompasses a range of activities and responsibilities aimed at ensuring efficiency, cost-effectiveness, and responsiveness throughout the supply chain network. Managing a supply chain entails:

- **Strategic Planning and Design:**

    ○ **Network Design:** Determining the optimal configuration of supply chain activities, including sourcing locations, production facilities, distribution centres, and transportation routes to minimize costs and maximize efficiency.

- **Supplier Management:** Selecting and managing suppliers based on criteria such as quality, reliability, cost, and sustainability to ensure a reliable supply of materials and components.

- **Demand Planning:** Forecasting customer demand and aligning production and inventory levels to meet customer needs while minimizing excess inventory and stockouts.

- Sourcing and Procurement:

  - **Supplier Relationship Management:** Establishing strong relationships with suppliers through effective communication, collaboration, and contract negotiations to achieve favourable terms and conditions.

  - **Procurement:** Purchasing raw materials, components, and services required for production or resale at competitive prices, while maintaining quality standards and compliance with regulations.

- Production and Manufacturing:

  - **Production Planning and Control:** Planning production schedules, allocating resources, and managing manufacturing processes to optimize efficiency, minimize lead times, and ensure quality standards are met.

  - **Inventory Management:** Monitoring inventory levels, implementing Just-in-Time (JIT) or lean principles to reduce carrying costs, and ensuring availability of materials to support production and customer demand.

- Logistics and Distribution:

  - **Transportation Management:** Selecting the appropriate modes of transportation (e.g., trucking, rail, air, sea) and logistics providers to ensure timely and cost-effective delivery of goods to customers.

  - **Warehouse Management:** Efficiently managing warehouse operations, including receiving, storing, picking, packing, and shipping goods, to optimize space utilization and streamline order fulfillment processes.

- Information Systems and Technology:

- **Supply Chain Visibility:** Implementing technology solutions (e.g., Enterprise Resource Planning - ERP, Supply Chain Management - SCM systems) to provide real-time visibility into inventory levels, order status, and supply chain performance metrics.
- **Data Analytics:** Utilizing data analytics and business intelligence tools to analyse supply chain data, identify trends, forecast demand more accurately, and make data-driven decisions to improve efficiency and responsiveness.

- **Risk Management and Sustainability:**
  - **Risk Mitigation:** Identifying potential risks (e.g., supply disruptions, geopolitical instability, natural disasters) and implementing strategies to mitigate their impact on supply chain operations.
  - **Sustainability Initiatives:** Incorporating environmental, social, and governance (ESG) criteria into supply chain practices to promote ethical sourcing, reduce carbon footprint, and enhance corporate social responsibility.

- **Continuous Improvement and Collaboration:**
  - **Performance Measurement:** Establishing key performance indicators (KPIs) to monitor supply chain performance, identify areas for improvement, and drive continuous optimization efforts.
  - **Collaboration:** Working closely with internal departments (e.g., marketing, sales, finance) and external stakeholders (e.g., suppliers, logistics providers, customers) to align supply chain activities with business goals and enhance overall organizational performance.

In essence, managing a supply chain requires a holistic approach that integrates strategic planning, operational execution, technology utilization, risk management, and collaboration across the entire network. It aims to create value for customers, optimize costs, and ensure sustainability in a competitive global marketplace. Effective supply chain management enables organizations to adapt to changing market conditions, mitigate risks, and achieve operational excellence in delivering products and services to end-users.

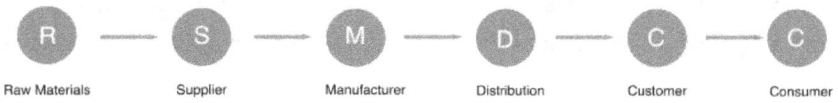

Figure 26: Basic diagram of supply chain network showing the movement of goods from the raw materials stage into the hands of the end consumer. David pogrebeshsky, CC BY-SA 4.0, via Wikimedia Commons.

Strategic partnerships play a vital role in sustainable supply chain management, aiming to integrate an organization's social, environmental, and economic goals transparently across inter-organizational processes to enhance long-term economic performance [35]. Green supply chain management is another essential aspect that involves integrating environmental considerations into every stage of supply chain implementation to enhance environmental management efficiency and reduce pollution [36]. Supply chain management in various industries, such as the red chili industry in Indonesia, involves partner selection, transaction systems, contractual agreements, government support, and collaboration among supply chain actors [37]. Supplier selection is a key component of sustainable supply chain management, as suppliers' performance impacts downstream enterprises significantly [38].

Global supply chain management emphasizes a comprehensive and coordinated cooperative management model that focuses on resource utilization, cooperation among different entities in the supply chain, market development, and system efficiency improvement to achieve mutual benefits [39]. Supply chain management entails managing the flow of supply and demand, as well as information, to meet end-user needs efficiently [40]. Sustainable supply chain design and management require organizations to consider economic, environmental, and social performance measures across strategic, tactical, and operational decision-making processes [41]. The coordination of corporate partners, internal departments, processes, and customers along a supply chain is fundamental to effective supply chain management [42].

Successful supply chain management necessitates a shift from managing individual functions to integrating activities into key supply chain processes [43]. Managing a sustainable supply chain involves focusing on environmental aspects, such as sustainable raw material management and eco-friendly consumption, to ensure sustainability throughout the supply chain [44]. Strategic decisions in supply chain management, such as facility location, resource allocation, and product transportation, are crucial for enhancing organizational performance and gaining a competitive advantage [45]. Supply chain management encompasses the regulation and optimization of various flows, including logistics, information, capital, value, and business, to provide maximum value to customers efficiently and cost-effectively [46].

Supply chain management involves the strategic coordination of business functions within a company and across businesses in the supply chain to enhance long-term performance [47]. The integration of key business processes from end-users through original suppliers to provide value-added products, services, and information is at the core of supply chain management [48]. Managing supply chain tasks, such as planning, control, organizational structuring, and risk management, is essential for effective supply chain operations [49]. Reducing delivery costs is a critical aspect of managing supply chain costs and improving overall supply chain efficiency [50]. Supply chain management aims to achieve integrated effects across entities in the supply chain by optimizing processes and relationships [51].

Risk management is a crucial component of supply chain management, allowing decision-makers to understand and mitigate the impact of risks within the supply chain network [52]. Sustainable supply chain management involves the integration of sustainability principles for both internal and external organizational processes to achieve sustainability goals [53]. Managing operational risks within the supply chain has become imperative for ensuring smooth operations and mitigating potential disruptions [54]. Blockchain technology offers transparency in supply chain management by enhancing information sharing and trust among supply chain members [55, 56]. Knowledge sharing plays a vital role in supply chain collaborative innovation, enhancing efficiency and cost-effectiveness within the supply chain [57].

Developing and Implementing a Supply Chain Strategy

A supply chain strategy is a comprehensive plan or framework that guides how an organization manages and optimizes its supply chain activities to achieve its business objectives effectively. It involves making strategic decisions about sourcing, production, inventory management, logistics, and distribution to ensure that goods or services are delivered to customers in a timely, cost-effective manner while meeting quality standards and maximizing profitability. Here are key elements and components of a supply chain strategy:

- Alignment with Business Goals: A supply chain strategy must align closely with the overall strategic goals and objectives of the organization. This alignment ensures that supply chain activities contribute directly to achieving broader business priorities such as revenue growth, market expansion, cost reduction, or customer satisfaction improvement.

- Network Design and Configuration: It involves determining the optimal configuration of the supply chain network, including the number and location of suppliers, production facilities, warehouses, distribution centres, and retail outlets. This decision impacts factors like transportation costs, lead times, and responsiveness to customer demand.

- Sourcing and Procurement Strategies: These strategies focus on selecting suppliers, negotiating contracts, managing relationships, and ensuring a reliable supply of materials or components. They aim to achieve cost savings, quality assurance, sustainability goals, and resilience against supply chain disruptions.

- Production and Operations Planning: This aspect of the strategy involves decisions related to production scheduling, capacity management, process improvements, and technology adoption to enhance efficiency, reduce waste, and meet production targets while maintaining product quality.

- Inventory Management: Strategies for inventory management aim to balance the costs associated with holding inventory against the risks of stockouts or excess inventory. Techniques such as Just-in-Time (JIT), Vendor Managed Inventory (VMI), and safety stock management are employed to optimize inventory levels across the supply chain.

- Logistics and Transportation: These strategies focus on selecting transportation modes (e.g., road, rail, air, sea), optimizing routes, managing freight costs, and improving the efficiency of goods movement from suppliers to customers. They also include warehousing, distribution, and fulfillment operations.

- Risk Management and Resilience: Supply chain strategies incorporate measures to identify, assess, and mitigate risks such as supplier disruptions, natural disasters, geopolitical instability, or regulatory changes. Strategies may include diversifying suppliers, creating contingency plans, and improving supply chain visibility.

- Technology and Digitalization: Leveraging technology and digital tools such as Enterprise Resource Planning (ERP), Supply Chain Management (SCM) systems, Internet of Things (IoT), and data analytics plays a crucial role in modern supply chain strategies. These technologies improve visibility, decision-making, collaboration, and responsiveness across the supply chain network.

- Continuous Improvement and Innovation: Supply chain strategies emphasize ongoing optimization and innovation to adapt to changing market conditions, customer expectations, and technological advancements. Continuous improvement initiatives focus on enhancing processes, reducing costs, and increasing agility to maintain competitive advantage.

In essence, a supply chain strategy serves as a roadmap that guides the operational activities of an organization's supply chain, aligning them with business objectives and enabling efficient and effective management of resources, processes, and relationships across the entire supply chain network. By developing and implementing a well-defined supply chain strategy, organizations can improve performance, reduce costs, mitigate risks, and enhance overall competitiveness in the marketplace.

Developing and implementing a supply chain strategy begins with a clear understanding of the organization's objectives and aligning these with strategies that optimize the entire supply chain network. This includes:

- **Identifying Organizational Objectives:**

    ○ **Strategic Goals:** Start by defining the overarching strategic goals of the organization. These may include objectives such as increasing market share, expanding into new markets, enhancing product quality, reducing costs, or improving customer service levels.

    ○ **Operational Priorities:** Understand specific operational priorities that support these strategic goals, such as lean operations, agility in responding to customer demand, or sustainability initiatives.

- **Assessing Supply Chain Capabilities:**

    ○ **Current State Analysis:** Conduct a comprehensive assessment of the organization's current supply chain capabilities, including sourcing, manufacturing, logistics, and distribution. This involves evaluating existing processes, infrastructure, technology systems, and human resources.

- **Gap Analysis:** Identify gaps between current capabilities and desired outcomes based on organizational objectives. Determine areas where improvements or realignment are needed to support the strategic goals effectively.

- **Developing Supply Chain Strategies:**

  - **Strategic Alignment:** Formulate supply chain strategies that are closely aligned with the organization's strategic objectives. For example, if the goal is to reduce time-to-market for new products, strategies might focus on improving supply chain agility and responsiveness.

  - **Risk Management:** Incorporate risk management strategies to mitigate potential disruptions in the supply chain, such as diversifying supplier networks, implementing contingency plans, or leveraging technology for real-time monitoring and response.

- **Collaboration and Integration:**

  - **Cross-Functional Collaboration:** Foster collaboration between different functional areas within the organization (e.g., procurement, operations, marketing, finance) to ensure alignment of supply chain strategies with overall business objectives. This collaborative approach helps in integrating supply chain considerations into decision-making processes across the organization.

  - **Supplier and Customer Collaboration:** Engage proactively with key suppliers and customers to enhance collaboration and align supply chain strategies with their needs and expectations. This may involve joint planning sessions, sharing of information, and exploring opportunities for innovation and value creation.

- **Implementing Supply Chain Initiatives:**

  - **Implementation Plan:** Develop a detailed implementation plan that outlines specific actions, timelines, responsibilities, and performance metrics for executing supply chain strategies. Assign clear roles and responsibilities to stakeholders involved in the implementation process.

  - **Change Management:** Address potential challenges related to organizational culture, resistance to change, or resource constraints through effective change management strategies. Communicate the benefits of the new supply chain initiatives and provide training and support to facilitate adoption.

- **Monitoring and Continuous Improvement:**

  - **Performance Metrics:** Establish key performance indicators (KPIs) to monitor the effectiveness of supply chain strategies in achieving organizational objectives. KPIs may include metrics such as inventory turnover, on-time delivery performance, supply chain cost efficiency, and customer satisfaction levels.

  - **Continuous Evaluation:** Regularly evaluate supply chain performance against established KPIs and conduct periodic reviews to assess the alignment of strategies with evolving business needs. Use data analytics and feedback mechanisms to identify areas for improvement and opportunities for optimization.

Reviewing the current supply chain management (SCM) strategy involves assessing how effectively it aligns with and supports the overarching organizational strategies and objectives. This process is crucial for evaluating performance, identifying areas of strength and weakness, and making informed decisions to optimize the supply chain's contribution to organizational success.

Alignment with Organizational Objectives: The review begins by revisiting the organization's strategic goals and priorities. These could encompass objectives such as cost reduction, enhancing customer satisfaction, expanding market reach, improving product quality, or achieving sustainability targets. The SCM strategy should be assessed based on its ability to directly support these goals. For example, if the organizational strategy emphasizes rapid market expansion, the SCM strategy should focus on agility, scalability, and efficient distribution networks to support this objective.

Performance Metrics and KPIs: Establishing clear performance metrics and key performance indicators (KPIs) is essential for evaluating the effectiveness of the SCM strategy. Metrics may include inventory turnover rates, order fulfillment accuracy, lead times, supply chain costs as a percentage of revenue, and customer service levels. By comparing actual performance against these benchmarks, organizations can gauge how well the SCM strategy is delivering against organizational expectations.

Operational Efficiency and Effectiveness: Assessing operational efficiency involves evaluating how well the SCM strategy optimizes resources and processes to minimize costs and maximize productivity. This includes analysing procurement practices, inventory management techniques, production scheduling, and transportation logistics. Effectiveness, on the other hand, measures the SCM strategy's ability to meet customer demand accurately and promptly while maintaining high product quality standards.

Risk Management and Resilience: Evaluating the SCM strategy should include an assessment of its resilience in mitigating supply chain risks. This involves identifying vulnerabilities such as supplier disruptions, geopolitical factors, natural disasters, or regulatory changes. A robust SCM strategy integrates risk management practices like dual sourcing, inventory buffers, and contingency planning to ensure continuity of operations and minimize potential disruptions.

Customer and Stakeholder Satisfaction: Assessing customer and stakeholder satisfaction provides critical feedback on how well the SCM strategy meets their expectations and requirements. Feedback mechanisms, customer surveys, and supplier performance evaluations are used to gather insights into areas for improvement. A well-aligned SCM strategy enhances overall stakeholder satisfaction by improving service levels, reducing lead times, and enhancing product availability.

Continuous Improvement Initiatives: The review should identify opportunities for continuous improvement within the SCM strategy. This involves leveraging data analytics, adopting emerging technologies (such as AI and IoT for supply chain optimization), and implementing best practices from industry benchmarks. Continuous improvement initiatives ensure that the SCM strategy remains adaptive to changing market dynamics, technological advancements, and evolving customer expectations.

Assessing supply chain opportunities that add value to an organization involves a systematic approach to identify and capitalize on strategic initiatives within the framework of the organization's overall strategy and budgetary constraints. Here's a detailed process on how to effectively carry out this assessment:

- Understand Organizational Strategy and Goals: Begin by gaining a thorough understanding of the organization's strategic objectives and priorities. These may include goals such as increasing market share, improving product quality, expanding into new markets, reducing costs, or enhancing customer service. Aligning supply chain opportunities with these goals ensures that initiatives contribute directly to achieving broader business objectives.

- Conduct a Current State Assessment: Evaluate the existing supply chain capabilities, processes, and performance metrics. This involves analysing key areas such as sourcing and procurement practices, production and operations efficiency, inventory management, logistics and transportation, and overall supply chain resilience. Identify strengths, weaknesses, inefficiencies, and potential areas for improvement or optimization.

- Identify Potential Value-Adding Opportunities: Look for areas within the supply chain where improvements or new initiatives can create significant value for the organization. Opportunities may arise from technological advancements, process innovations, strategic partnerships, supplier collaborations, or operational efficiencies. For example, adopting new technology for supply chain visibility or implementing sustainable sourcing practices could lead to cost savings or enhanced customer satisfaction.

- Prioritize Opportunities Based on Strategic Fit and Impact: Prioritize identified opportunities based on their alignment with the organization's strategic priorities, potential impact on key performance indicators (KPIs), and feasibility within budgetary constraints. Consider factors such as scalability, risks associated with implementation, and timeline for realizing benefits. Opportunities that offer high strategic value with manageable risks and costs should be given priority.

- Develop Business Cases and Financial Analysis: Develop detailed business cases for prioritized opportunities, outlining the expected benefits, costs, resource requirements, and implementation timelines. Conduct financial analysis to quantify potential cost savings, revenue growth, or other measurable benefits. Consider factors like return on investment (ROI), payback period, and net present value (NPV) to justify investments and secure budgetary approval.

- Engage Stakeholders and Obtain Buy-In: Engage stakeholders across various departments, including senior management, operations, finance, IT, and procurement, to gain support and alignment for identified supply chain opportunities. Communicate the strategic rationale, expected benefits, and risks associated with each initiative. Address concerns, gather feedback, and collaborate on refining the proposed plans to ensure alignment with organizational goals.

- Define Implementation Plans and Metrics: Develop detailed implementation plans for selected opportunities, outlining specific actions, responsibilities, milestones, and performance metrics. Define KPIs to measure progress and success, such as cost savings achieved, inventory turnover improvements, lead time reductions, or customer satisfaction enhancements. Establish monitoring mechanisms to track performance and make adjustments as needed.

- Monitor, Evaluate, and Adjust: Continuously monitor the implementation of supply chain initiatives, track performance against established metrics, and evaluate the impact on organizational goals and financial outcomes. Conduct regular reviews to assess the effectiveness of implemented strategies, identify lessons learned, and make adjustments to optimize results over time.

Designing and implementing a supply chain strategy that enhances effectiveness and aligns with organizational objectives requires a systematic and integrated approach across various facets of the supply chain. The process begins with a thorough understanding of the organization's strategic goals, market position, and customer needs. This foundational understanding helps in shaping the supply chain strategy to not only meet current requirements but also to anticipate future demands and challenges.

Firstly, a comprehensive analysis of the current state of the supply chain is conducted. This assessment involves evaluating existing processes, capabilities, performance metrics, and the overall efficiency of the supply chain network. Areas for improvement are identified, such as optimizing sourcing and procurement practices, enhancing production and operations efficiency, improving inventory management, and streamlining logistics and distribution channels.

Based on the analysis, strategic priorities are identified that the supply chain strategy should address. These priorities could include enhancing customer responsiveness, reducing lead times, lowering costs, improving product quality, or expanding market reach. Clear objectives are defined for each priority area, ensuring alignment with broader organizational goals and measurable outcomes.

Next, strategic initiatives are developed to address identified priorities and opportunities. This involves designing specific action plans and initiatives that leverage technology, process improvements, supplier relationships, and operational efficiencies to achieve desired outcomes. For example, implementing advanced analytics for demand forecasting or adopting lean manufacturing principles to reduce waste and improve production efficiency.

Collaboration across departments and functions is crucial during the design phase. Stakeholders from operations, finance, marketing, IT, and procurement collaborate to ensure that the supply chain strategy is integrated with other organizational functions and supported by cross-functional alignment. This collaborative approach helps in gaining buy-in, leveraging diverse expertise, and overcoming potential barriers to implementation.

Once the strategy is designed, it is important to focus on implementation. Implementation involves translating strategic plans into actionable steps, allocating resources, defining timelines, and assigning responsibilities. Clear communication of the strategy and its objectives to all levels of the organization fosters understanding, engagement, and commitment to the strategy's success.

Monitoring and evaluation are integral throughout the implementation process. Key performance indicators (KPIs) are established to track progress, measure performance against objectives, and identify areas needing adjustment. Regular reviews and assessments allow for continuous improvement, ensuring that the supply chain strategy remains adaptive and responsive to changing market conditions, customer expectations, and internal capabilities.

Lastly, the success of the supply chain strategy hinges on continuous learning and adaptation. Organizations should foster a culture of innovation and agility, encouraging experimentation with new technologies, processes, and business models. Lessons learned from both successes and setbacks are incorporated into future iterations of the strategy, driving ongoing improvements and sustaining competitive advantage in the marketplace.

The COVID-19 pandemic has fundamentally reshaped how supply chain management (SCM) is perceived and executed, shifting the focus from lean efficiency to resilience [58]. Traditionally, businesses prioritized lean strategies aimed at minimizing waste and maximizing efficiency to deliver products quickly and cost-effectively. However, the global disruptions caused by the pandemic exposed vulnerabilities in supply chains worldwide, prompting a critical reassessment of SCM strategies.

Organizations quickly realized that efficiency alone was insufficient to navigate the unprecedented challenges posed by the pandemic. Instead, resilience emerged as a crucial factor in ensuring continuity and mitigating risks across supply chains. Resilience in this context refers to the ability of organizations to rapidly adapt sourcing, manufacturing, and distribution activities in response to sudden disruptions, whether caused by supply chain interruptions, transportation delays, or shifts in consumer demand [58].

According to a survey by Gartner, only a minority of organizations reported having highly resilient supply chains at the outset of the pandemic. This highlighted the need for proactive measures to enhance resilience moving forward. Many organizations recognized that while increasing supply chain resilience may involve additional costs in the short-term, it is a necessary investment to safeguard long-term profitability and sustainability.

To bolster supply chain resilience, several strategic approaches have gained prominence. One critical strategy is the strategic placement of buffers along the supply chain. These buffers include inventory buffers, which involve maintaining safety stock to buffer against unexpected delays or demand spikes. Time buffers ensure that materials arrive ahead of demand, protecting critical processes, while capacity buffers utilize underutilized space like warehouses to maintain operational flexibility [58].

Another key strategy is diversifying manufacturing and sourcing networks. Relying on a single source for critical components or materials proved risky during the pandemic, as disruptions in one region could halt production globally. Multi-sourcing involves categorizing suppliers based on cost and potential impact, then forging relationships with additional suppliers or those with operations in diverse geographic locations to mitigate risks.

Investing in advanced demand forecasting capabilities has also become essential. Accurate demand forecasting, driven by data analytics rather than intuitive guesswork, enables organizations to anticipate fluctuations in demand and adjust supply chain operations accordingly. This proactive approach not only improves lead times and reduces costs but also enhances customer satisfaction by ensuring product availability [58].

Furthermore, standardizing processes across the supply chain enhances reliability and efficiency. Standardization simplifies operations and promotes consistency, particularly in global supply chains where suppliers and manufacturers operate across diverse locations [58]. By adopting standardized platforms, products, and production processes, organizations can streamline operations, improve collaboration, and ensure compliance with regulatory requirements.

In recent years, companies across various industries have demonstrated agility and strategic foresight in adapting their supply chain strategies to respond to market dynamics and global challenges. Two notable examples highlight how organizations have leveraged innovative approaches to optimize supply chain operations and mitigate risks:

Walgreens, a prominent pharmacy chain, exemplifies the power of big data analytics in transforming supply chain management. In 2016, Walgreens made significant investments in advanced supply chain technology that harnesses consumer data to predict future purchasing trends [58]. By analysing these metrics, Walgreens can anticipate customer demand more accurately and adjust their inventory levels accordingly. This proactive approach not only helps in reducing excess inventory but also optimizes warehousing and transportation costs. By aligning supply chain operations closely with consumer behaviour insights, Walgreens enhances operational efficiency while ensuring sufficient stock availability to meet customer demands promptly [58].

Another compelling example comes from Bob's Discount Furniture, a US-based retailer specializing in affordable furniture products. In 2018, amidst escalating trade tensions between the United States and China, Bob's Discount Furniture took proactive measures to mitigate potential impacts on their supply chain [58]. Recognizing the looming threat of higher tariffs on goods imported from China, which could disrupt their business operations and increase costs, the company swiftly pivoted its sourcing strategy. Within a remarkably short timeframe of 3-4 months in early 2019, Bob's Discount Furniture successfully relocated 25-30% of its furniture sourcing away from China to other countries with more favourable trade conditions [58]. This strategic move not only diversified their supplier base but also ensured continuity in product availability and minimized tariff-related risks.

Both examples illustrate key principles of effective supply chain strategy: responsiveness to market changes, proactive risk management, and leveraging technology and data-driven insights to optimize operations. By embracing these strategies, Walgreens and Bob's Discount Furniture not only navigated challenges effectively but also positioned themselves for sustainable growth in competitive markets. These cases underscore the importance for businesses to continuously evaluate and evolve their supply chain strategies to maintain resilience, mitigate risks, and capitalize on emerging opportunities in an increasingly interconnected global economy.

Companies, both large and small, harness various supply chain strategies to drive efficiency, resilience, and growth in their operations. These strategies are crucial for navigating complexities, optimizing processes, and responding to dynamic market conditions. Several notable examples highlight how organizations have successfully implemented supply chain strategies tailored to their specific needs and challenges [59].

Boeing exemplifies the power of collaborative improvement through its adoption of the ASCM SCOR model (Supply Chain Operations Reference). By implementing this framework and educating employees across functions, Boeing created a unified approach to addressing supply chain challenges [59]. Within a short span of 90 days, Boeing's SCOR team identified deficiencies in its fighter planes program, aligned them with industry best practices, and proposed actionable recommendations [59]. This strategic initiative led to a significant 44% reduction in critical shortages, showcasing the immediate impact of a structured supply chain approach.

Similarly, Univar Solutions embarked on a corporate transformation following its merger with Nexeo Solutions [59]. The company focused on enhancing efficiency and agility by leveraging the ASCM SCOR model to streamline operations across planning, sourcing, manufacturing, delivery, returns, and enabling functions. By consolidating systems, eliminating redundancies, and optimizing legacy contracts, Univar achieved substantial savings exceeding $100 million [59]. This transformation not only improved operational efficiency but also positioned Univar for sustained growth and agility, critical during the disruptions brought by the COVID-19 pandemic.

Eaton, amidst the challenges of the pandemic, prioritized resilience in its supply chain strategy. Educating employees on supply chain fundamentals and best practices enabled Eaton to proactively address disruptions such as material shortages, labour constraints, and logistics bottlenecks [59]. Strengthening multi-sourcing strategies, enhancing supplier collaboration, and optimizing end-to-end supply chain processes bolstered Eaton's ability to maintain continuity and meet customer demands during volatile times.

Intel, on the other hand, focuses on ethical sourcing through its supply chain strategy [59]. Leveraging digital tools and protocols like the smelter audit, Intel ensures that metals such as tin, tungsten, gold, and tantalum are sourced from conflict-free origins. This commitment to ethical practices not only aligns with Intel's corporate values but also enhances transparency and trust with stakeholders, including customers and regulatory bodies.

These examples underscore the diverse applications of supply chain strategy in achieving operational excellence, cost efficiency, and customer satisfaction. Whether through collaborative frameworks like SCOR, agility in response to market shifts, resilience amidst disruptions, or ethical sourcing initiatives, organizations deploy supply chain strategies to provide clear operational direction. Fine-tuning these strategies over time ensures adaptability to changing environments while consistently driving business success through optimized efficiencies and minimized costs. A well-prepared and effectively executed supply chain strategy thus remains pivotal in guiding organizations toward sustained growth and leadership in their respective industries [59].

Gaining commitment from stakeholders to implement a supply chain strategy is crucial for its successful execution and alignment with organizational goals. This process involves engaging stakeholders at various levels within the organization, including senior management, department heads, operational teams, and external partners or suppliers.

Firstly, it's essential to clearly communicate the strategic vision and objectives of the supply chain strategy. This involves articulating how the proposed strategy aligns with broader organizational goals such as enhancing customer satisfaction, improving operational efficiency, reducing costs, or expanding market reach. By demonstrating the strategic relevance and potential benefits of the supply chain strategy, stakeholders can better understand its importance and impact on overall business performance.

Engagement with stakeholders should be inclusive and collaborative. Involve key stakeholders early in the strategy development process to gather input, insights, and concerns. This collaborative approach fosters a sense of ownership and encourages stakeholders to actively participate in shaping the strategy according to their expertise and perspectives. It also helps in addressing potential resistance or scepticism by ensuring that all voices are heard and considered in the decision-making process.

Another critical aspect is to clearly define roles, responsibilities, and expectations for each stakeholder involved in implementing the supply chain strategy. By outlining specific roles and the contributions expected from each stakeholder group, clarity is established regarding their involvement and accountability. This clarity minimizes confusion, avoids duplication of efforts, and ensures coordinated action towards achieving common goals.

Effective communication plays a pivotal role throughout the implementation process. Regularly communicate updates, progress, milestones, and successes related to the supply chain strategy to stakeholders. Use various communication channels such as meetings, presentations, workshops, newsletters, and digital platforms to keep stakeholders informed and engaged. Transparent communication builds trust, maintains momentum, and reinforces commitment to the strategy's objectives.

Addressing concerns and overcoming resistance is an inevitable part of gaining stakeholder commitment. Actively listen to stakeholders' feedback, acknowledge their concerns, and provide evidence-based explanations or solutions where possible. Engage in constructive dialogue to resolve issues, clarify misunderstandings, and demonstrate the benefits of the supply chain strategy in mitigating risks or achieving desired outcomes.

Furthermore, align the supply chain strategy with incentives and recognition mechanisms to motivate stakeholders. Recognize and reward individuals or teams that contribute significantly to the strategy's success. Incentives may include performance bonuses, career advancement opportunities, or public recognition within the organization. By linking individual or team achievements to the strategic objectives of the supply chain strategy, stakeholders are encouraged to remain committed and actively contribute to its implementation.

Lastly, monitor progress and evaluate outcomes regularly. Establish key performance indicators (KPIs) aligned with the supply chain strategy's objectives to measure success and identify areas for improvement. Share performance metrics and insights with stakeholders to demonstrate the impact of their efforts and to reinforce the importance of continued commitment to the strategy's long-term success.

Assigning responsibility to monitor a supply chain strategy involves defining clear roles, establishing accountability, and ensuring continuous oversight to ensure alignment with organizational objectives and operational effectiveness.

Firstly, identify key stakeholders and personnel who will be responsible for monitoring and overseeing the implementation of the supply chain strategy. This typically includes supply chain managers, logistics experts, procurement officers, and cross-functional teams involved in various stages of the supply chain process. It's crucial to select individuals with the requisite skills, experience, and authority to effectively manage and monitor strategic initiatives.

Once personnel are identified, clearly define their roles and responsibilities in relation to monitoring the supply chain strategy. This involves outlining specific tasks, milestones, and deliverables expected from each role. For instance, supply chain managers may be responsible for overall strategy execution, monitoring KPIs, and coordinating with internal teams and external partners. Procurement officers might focus on supplier performance management, contract negotiations, and ensuring compliance with sourcing strategies.

Establishing accountability is paramount to ensure that responsibilities are taken seriously and commitments are met. Assign clear ownership of key performance indicators (KPIs) and metrics that will be used to measure the success of the supply chain strategy. Define metrics such as cost savings, inventory turnover, on-time delivery rates, customer satisfaction scores, and sustainability targets that align with strategic objectives. This clarity helps in setting benchmarks for performance evaluation and provides a basis for continuous improvement efforts.

Promote cross-functional collaboration and communication among personnel responsible for monitoring the supply chain strategy. Encourage regular meetings, status updates, and information sharing to foster a cohesive approach to strategy implementation. Cross-functional collaboration ensures that insights from different departments are integrated, potential issues are addressed promptly, and decisions are made collaboratively to optimize supply chain performance.

Provide adequate resources and tools to support personnel in their monitoring roles. This includes access to data analytics platforms, supply chain management software, and reporting mechanisms that enable real-time monitoring of KPIs and performance metrics. These tools facilitate informed decision-making, early identification of deviations from planned targets, and proactive responses to changes in market conditions or operational challenges.

Implement a feedback loop to gather insights and lessons learned from monitoring activities. Encourage personnel to provide feedback on the effectiveness of the supply chain strategy, identify areas for improvement, and propose adjustments based on performance data and stakeholder input. Regularly review monitoring processes and adjust responsibilities as needed to ensure alignment with evolving organizational priorities and strategic goals.

Lastly, foster a culture of accountability and continuous improvement within the supply chain management team. Recognize and celebrate successes, address performance gaps constructively, and provide opportunities for professional development and skills enhancement. By nurturing a proactive and accountable environment, organizations can ensure that personnel responsible for monitoring the supply chain strategy are empowered to drive operational excellence, mitigate risks, and contribute to long-term business success.

By means of a summative example, here's an example of a basic supply chain strategy for a fictional company, ABC Electronics:

ABC Electronics Supply Chain Strategy:

Objective: ABC Electronics aims to enhance customer satisfaction, optimize operational efficiency, and achieve sustainable growth through a robust and agile supply chain strategy.

Key Initiatives:
- Demand Forecasting and Planning: Implement advanced demand forecasting models using historical data, market trends analysis, and customer feedback to accurately predict product demand. Collaborate closely with sales and marketing teams to align production schedules with anticipated demand fluctuations.

- Supplier Relationship Management: Strengthen strategic partnerships with key suppliers through regular performance reviews, joint innovation initiatives, and risk mitigation strategies. Develop a supplier scorecard system to evaluate performance based on criteria such as quality, reliability, cost, and sustainability practices.

- Inventory Optimization: Adopt lean inventory management principles to minimize carrying costs while ensuring sufficient stock levels to meet customer demand. Implement just-in-time (JIT) inventory systems and safety stock buffers to mitigate supply chain disruptions and reduce excess inventory.

- Logistics and Distribution: Enhance logistics efficiency by optimizing transportation routes, consolidating shipments, and leveraging technology for real-time tracking and tracing of shipments. Explore opportunities for modal shift to environmentally friendly transportation options to reduce carbon footprint.

- Sustainability and Ethical Sourcing: Integrate sustainable practices throughout the supply chain by sourcing materials from ethical suppliers who adhere to environmental and social responsibility standards. Implement a comprehensive supplier code of conduct and conduct regular audits to ensure compliance.

- Technology Integration: Invest in supply chain management software and analytics tools to improve visibility, transparency, and decision-making capabilities across the supply chain. Leverage data analytics for predictive maintenance of equipment, route optimization, and proactive risk management.

- Continuous Improvement and Innovation: Promote a culture of continuous improvement by fostering cross-functional collaboration, encouraging employee feedback, and implementing lean manufacturing principles. Embrace innovation in product design, packaging, and supply chain processes to drive efficiency and customer value.

Measurement and Evaluation: Establish key performance indicators (KPIs) such as inventory turnover rate, on-time delivery performance, supply chain cost-to-sales ratio, and customer satisfaction scores. Conduct regular performance reviews and benchmarking against industry standards to monitor progress and identify areas for improvement.

By implementing this comprehensive supply chain strategy, ABC Electronics aims to strengthen its competitive position, mitigate risks, and achieve sustainable growth in the dynamic electronics industry landscape.

Managing the Flow of Supplies through the Supply Chain

Understanding the flows of supply chain management involves grasping the intricacies of five critical elements: product, information, cash, demand, and returns. Each of these flows plays a pivotal role in ensuring the smooth and efficient operation of a supply chain, thereby influencing the overall performance and success of a business.

Firstly, the product flow encompasses the physical movement of goods from suppliers to customers [60]. This flow involves logistics, transportation, and warehousing activities aimed at delivering products on time and in optimal condition. The efficiency of product flow directly impacts factors such as product availability, lead times, and customer satisfaction. A well-managed product flow ensures that goods move swiftly through the supply chain minimizing delays and optimizing inventory levels.

Secondly, information flow is crucial for enabling effective communication and data sharing across the supply chain. It involves the transmission of information between various stakeholders, including suppliers, manufacturers, distributors, retailers, and customers. Timely and accurate information flow supports decision-making processes related to production planning, inventory management, and responding to changes in market demand. For instance, real-time data on inventory levels can help businesses adjust procurement strategies or production schedules to meet fluctuating customer demands efficiently [60].

Thirdly, cash flow represents the movement of money within the supply chain ecosystem. This flow includes payments to suppliers for raw materials or finished goods, collection of payments from customers, and management of working capital. Efficient cash flow management is essential for maintaining financial stability, liquidity, and the ability to invest in growth opportunities. Delays or disruptions in cash flow can hinder operations, affect supplier relationships, and limit a business's ability to innovate or expand [60].

Fourthly, demand flow focuses on forecasting and managing customer demand throughout the supply chain. It involves analysing historical data, market trends, and customer preferences to anticipate future demand accurately. Effective demand flow management helps businesses optimize inventory levels, minimize stock-outs, and align production schedules with anticipated sales volumes. By understanding customer demand patterns, businesses can enhance their responsiveness to market changes and improve overall supply chain efficiency [60].

Lastly, returns flow addresses the management of product returns and reverse logistics processes. This flow includes handling returned goods, processing refunds or replacements, and managing inventory disposition. Efficient returns management is crucial for maintaining customer satisfaction, reducing operational costs associated with returns processing, and ensuring that returned products are reintegrated into inventory or disposed of responsibly [60].

Managing the flow of supplies through the supply chain involves overseeing the movement of raw materials, components, and finished products from suppliers to customers efficiently and effectively. This process ensures that goods are delivered on time, in the right quantity and quality, while minimizing costs and maximizing customer satisfaction. This includes:

- Supply Chain Planning and Forecasting: Begin by conducting thorough demand forecasting and supply planning. Use historical data, market trends, and customer insights to predict demand accurately. Collaborate closely with sales, marketing, and production teams to align supply chain activities with anticipated demand fluctuations. Establish inventory levels and safety stock buffers to mitigate supply chain risks and ensure continuity of supply.

- Supplier Relationship Management (SRM): Cultivate strong relationships with suppliers to enhance supply chain efficiency. Regularly communicate with suppliers to understand their capabilities, lead times, and potential challenges. Implement supplier performance metrics and conduct regular reviews to evaluate reliability, quality, and adherence to delivery schedules. Foster collaboration and innovation with key suppliers to drive continuous improvement and reduce supply chain disruptions.

- Inventory Management: Implement robust inventory management practices to optimize stock levels and minimize carrying costs. Utilize inventory control techniques such as ABC analysis, economic order quantity (EOQ), and just-in-time (JIT) inventory systems. Maintain visibility across the supply chain through inventory tracking and real-time data analytics to facilitate proactive decision-making and prevent stockouts or overstock situations.

- Logistics and Transportation Efficiently manage logistics and transportation activities to streamline the flow of supplies. Optimize transportation routes, modes of transport, and shipment consolidation to reduce lead times and transportation costs. Leverage technology solutions for route optimization, real-time tracking, and visibility into shipment status. Ensure compliance with regulatory requirements and adopt sustainable transportation practices to minimize environmental impact.

- Warehouse Management: Implement effective warehouse management practices to facilitate the smooth flow of supplies within facilities. Utilize warehouse layout optimization, automation, and digital inventory management systems to improve storage efficiency and order fulfillment accuracy. Implement lean principles to reduce waste, improve productivity, and enhance overall operational efficiency within warehouses.

- Risk Management and Contingency Planning: Identify potential risks and develop contingency plans to mitigate supply chain disruptions. Conduct risk assessments across the supply chain, including supplier risks, geopolitical factors, natural disasters, and economic uncertainties. Establish alternative sourcing strategies, dual sourcing arrangements, and business continuity plans to maintain supply chain resilience and ensure continuity of supply during crises.

- Continuous Improvement and Adaptation: Foster a culture of continuous improvement and adaptation within the supply chain management team. Encourage cross-functional collaboration, innovation, and knowledge sharing to identify opportunities for process optimization and efficiency gains. Regularly review supply chain performance metrics and KPIs to monitor progress, identify areas for improvement, and implement corrective actions as needed.

- Technology Integration: Leverage supply chain management software, advanced analytics, and digital tools to enhance visibility, transparency, and decision-making capabilities. Implement integrated systems for demand forecasting, inventory management, procurement, and logistics to facilitate seamless flow of information and materials across the supply chain. Embrace emerging technologies such as blockchain for enhanced supply chain traceability and transparency.

Supply Chain Management (SCM) encompasses several key elements that are essential for orchestrating the seamless flow of goods and services from suppliers to customers and managing related activities. These elements are interconnected and collectively contribute to the efficiency, effectiveness, and responsiveness of the supply chain [61]:

- Planning: The planning phase sets the foundation for SCM by defining the overarching supply chain strategy. This includes forecasting demand, aligning resources (such as raw materials, production capacities, and workforce) with requirements, and establishing communication channels both internally among departments and externally with suppliers and customers. Metrics are set to measure the performance and effectiveness of the supply chain, ensuring that it delivers value to customers while achieving company objectives. Effective planning prevents inefficiencies and minimizes the risk of disruptions like the bullwhip effect, where small fluctuations in demand amplify along the supply chain due to poor coordination.

- Sourcing: Sourcing involves selecting and managing suppliers who provide the necessary goods and services to support production and operations. Key activities include developing a robust supplier network, negotiating supplier agreements, purchasing goods, receiving shipments, and managing inventory levels. Efficient sourcing practices are crucial for maintaining quality, managing costs, and ensuring timely availability of materials. Poor sourcing decisions can lead to increased costs, delays in production, and shortages in raw materials or components.

- Making: The making element focuses on transforming raw materials into finished products through manufacturing processes. This includes accepting raw materials, conducting manufacturing operations, implementing quality control measures to ensure product integrity, packaging products for shipment, scheduling production, and managing production facilities and equipment. Effective manufacturing practices are essential for meeting customer specifications, maintaining product quality, and optimizing production efficiency.

- Delivering: Delivering encompasses all activities involved in fulfilling customer orders and delivering products or services to customers. Key activities include coordinating customer orders, scheduling deliveries, managing transportation logistics, handling customs requirements for international shipments, invoicing customers, and managing payment processing. Efficient delivery processes are critical for ensuring on-time delivery, meeting customer expectations, and enhancing overall customer satisfaction.

- Returning: The returning element addresses the management of returned items from customers or suppliers, also known as reverse logistics. This involves handling post-delivery customer support, managing returns of defective or excess products, processing refunds or replacements, and ensuring compliance with regulatory requirements related to product returns. Effective management of returns helps minimize losses, maintain customer loyalty, and optimize inventory management processes.

Supply chain management operates on three distinct levels—strategic, tactical, and operational—each essential for ensuring the smooth and efficient flow of goods and services from suppliers to customers.

Firstly, at the strategic level, the emphasis is on long-term planning and goal-setting. Strategic supply chain management involves making high-level decisions that shape the overall direction of the supply chain [60]. This includes identifying market opportunities, analysing customer demands, and setting overarching objectives. Key strategic decisions often revolve around selecting suppliers and partners, determining distribution channels, and optimizing the supply chain network to enhance competitiveness and profitability. For example, strategic initiatives may involve entering new markets, adopting new technologies, or implementing sustainable practices to align with corporate objectives.

Secondly, the tactical level of supply chain management focuses on translating strategic plans into actionable steps. Here, the emphasis is on planning and executing specific activities to achieve strategic goals effectively. Tactical decisions typically involve detailed planning of production schedules, inventory management strategies, and procurement processes. Forecasting demand accurately, adjusting production capacities, and optimizing inventory levels are critical tasks at this level. Tactical decisions ensure that the supply chain operates efficiently by balancing supply and demand, minimizing costs, and optimizing resource utilization.

Lastly, the operational level of supply chain management deals with the day-to-day execution of activities and processes. At this level, the focus is on implementing the plans and strategies developed at the strategic and tactical levels. Operational management involves overseeing activities such as order processing, transportation management, warehousing operations, and quality control. It also includes monitoring key performance indicators (KPIs), ensuring compliance with regulations and standards, and resolving operational issues promptly to maintain smooth operations. Operational decisions are geared towards maximizing efficiency, improving productivity, and enhancing customer satisfaction by delivering products and services on time and in optimal condition [60].

Supply chain management (SCM) also encompasses various types of strategies and models that businesses adopt to optimize their operations and meet customer demands effectively. These different types of SCM are tailored to specific industries and market conditions, each emphasizing different aspects such as efficiency, responsiveness, flexibility, or specialization. Supply chain models include [61]:

- Continuous Flow Model: The continuous flow model is characterized by a steady and uninterrupted flow of goods through the supply chain. It is best suited for industries with high-volume production of standardized products, such as chemicals, paper, and basic commodities. This model relies on efficient production processes and Just-in-Time (JIT) inventory practices to minimize waste and maximize operational efficiency. Manufacturers using this model typically have predictable demand patterns and focus on cost reduction through economies of scale and streamlined operations.

- Fast Chain Model: The fast chain model is designed for industries where product lifecycles are short and demand is volatile. This model emphasizes agility and speed in responding to market trends and customer preferences. It is commonly found in industries like fashion, electronics, and consumer goods, where being first to market with new products can confer a competitive advantage. The fast chain model integrates rapid product development, flexible manufacturing processes, and responsive supply chain networks to capitalize on market opportunities and minimize the risk of obsolete inventory.

- Efficient Chain Model: The efficient chain model focuses on maximizing operational efficiency and reducing costs throughout the supply chain. It is suitable for hypercompetitive markets where price competitiveness and operational excellence are critical. This model relies on accurate demand forecasting, efficient production planning, and optimization of logistics and distribution networks. Industries such as automotive, appliances, and basic manufacturing often adopt the efficient chain model to maintain profitability through lean practices and continuous improvement initiatives.

- Agile Model: The agile supply chain model is characterized by its ability to quickly adapt to changes in customer demand and market conditions. It is commonly employed in industries that produce highly customized or make-to-order products, such as aerospace, pharmaceuticals, and high-tech manufacturing. The agile model emphasizes flexibility in production processes, rapid response capabilities, and close collaboration with suppliers and customers. This model enables businesses to meet specific customer requirements efficiently while minimizing inventory levels and operational overhead.

- Custom-Configured Model: The custom-configured model allows for extensive customization and personalization of products during the assembly or production process. It is prevalent in industries where products require varying configurations or specifications based on customer preferences, such as automotive, electronics, and industrial equipment manufacturing. This model combines elements of both continuous flow and agile models, managing standardized processes efficiently while accommodating unique customer requirements through flexible manufacturing capabilities.

- Flexible Model: The flexible supply chain model is characterized by its ability to scale production capacity up or down rapidly in response to fluctuating demand patterns. It is suitable for seasonal industries or businesses facing unpredictable demand cycles, such as agriculture, retail, and seasonal consumer goods. The flexible model requires adaptable production processes, agile workforce management, and robust supply chain partnerships to ensure responsiveness and operational resilience during peak and off-peak periods.

Each type of supply chain management model offers distinct advantages depending on the industry dynamics, market conditions, and strategic priorities of the organization. Successful implementation of these SCM models requires aligning operational strategies with business objectives, leveraging technology and analytics for decision-making, and fostering collaborative relationships across the supply chain ecosystem. By selecting the appropriate SCM model, businesses can enhance competitiveness, improve customer satisfaction, and achieve sustainable growth in today's dynamic global marketplace.

Supply chain management (SCM) best practices are crucial for businesses aiming to enhance operational efficiency, reduce costs, and improve customer satisfaction. These practices encompass a range of strategies that address various aspects of the supply chain, from procurement to delivery. Here's an in-depth exploration of these SCM best practices:

Recruiting Supply Chain Professionals: Recruiting skilled professionals is foundational to effective supply chain management. Businesses should seek individuals with expertise in logistics, procurement, inventory management, and strategic planning. Developing partnerships with supply chain recruitment agencies and fostering relationships with universities for internships and graduate programs can help attract and retain top talent. Ongoing training and career development ensure that supply chain professionals stay abreast of evolving technologies and industry trends, enabling them to make informed decisions that optimize supply chain performance.

Building Strong Supplier Relationships: Strong supplier relationships are essential for supply chain resilience and efficiency. Collaborative partnerships built on trust and mutual benefit help mitigate risks, reduce costs, and improve reliability. Beyond transactional aspects such as pricing and delivery schedules, businesses should align with suppliers who share similar values regarding sustainability, ethical practices, and innovation. Effective communication and problem-solving capabilities within these relationships foster agility and responsiveness, enabling both parties to adapt to changing market conditions and customer demands.

Diversifying Supplier Networks: To mitigate supply chain disruptions, businesses should diversify their supplier networks. Relying on a single supplier increases vulnerability to disruptions caused by natural disasters, geopolitical issues, or regulatory changes. Diversification involves identifying alternative suppliers and maintaining transparent communication to anticipate and address potential challenges. This approach not only enhances supply chain resilience but also provides flexibility in sourcing raw materials and components, ensuring continuity of operations during unforeseen circumstances.

Utilizing Economies of Scale: Leveraging economies of scale enables businesses to reduce costs by purchasing goods in bulk. This approach lowers per-unit costs through volume discounts and streamlines administrative and warehousing expenses. Strategies such as blanket orders and standing orders help stabilize inventory levels and protect against price fluctuations. By optimizing procurement practices and consolidating purchasing power, businesses can achieve cost efficiencies while maintaining supply chain agility and responsiveness to fluctuating market demands.

Improving Demand Forecasting: Accurate demand forecasting is critical to aligning inventory levels with customer demand. Forecasting errors can lead to overstocking, tying up capital in excess inventory, or understocking, resulting in lost sales opportunities. Advanced forecasting techniques, including data analytics and predictive modelling, help businesses anticipate demand patterns based on historical sales data, market trends, and promotional activities. Enhanced demand forecasting capabilities enable proactive inventory management, minimizing stockouts and reducing carrying costs while improving overall supply chain efficiency.

Enhancing Inventory Management: Effective inventory management ensures optimal levels of stock to meet customer demand without excessive holding costs. Real-time visibility into inventory levels, coupled with automated replenishment systems, enables businesses to synchronize supply with demand accurately. Adopting inventory optimization strategies, such as just-in-time (JIT) and lean inventory principles, minimizes waste and maximizes operational efficiency. By aligning inventory management practices with supply chain objectives, businesses can improve order fulfillment rates, reduce lead times, and enhance customer satisfaction.

Integrating Supply Chain Planning and Enterprise Planning: Integrating supply chain planning with enterprise resource planning (ERP) systems facilitates seamless coordination between operational and strategic business processes. This integration enables real-time updates to inventory forecasts, production schedules, and procurement activities, aligning short-term operational plans with broader business objectives. By leveraging integrated planning capabilities, stakeholders can anticipate disruptions, simulate scenarios, and optimize resource allocation to achieve maximum profitability and responsiveness in dynamic market environments.

Considering Total Cost of Ownership (TCO): Total Cost of Ownership (TCO) analysis evaluates the comprehensive expenses associated with supply chain activities, including acquisition, storage, transportation, and operational costs. By accounting for all cost components and factors such as trade incentives, currency fluctuations, and storage requirements, businesses can make informed sourcing decisions that optimize cost-efficiency and operational effectiveness. TCO analysis informs strategic decision-making, helping businesses identify opportunities to reduce costs, improve resource utilization, and enhance supply chain performance across the entire value chain.

Investing in SCM Software: Investing in SCM software solutions enhances supply chain visibility, efficiency, and decision-making capabilities. Advanced SCM software provides real-time data analytics, predictive insights, and collaborative tools that enable proactive management of supply chain operations. These technologies facilitate demand forecasting, inventory optimization, supplier relationship management, and logistics coordination, empowering businesses to streamline processes, reduce lead times, and meet customer expectations effectively. By embracing digital transformation through SCM software, businesses can achieve operational excellence, drive growth, and maintain competitive advantage in today's global marketplace.

Incorporating these SCM best practices into business operations fosters resilience, agility, and sustainability within the supply chain, positioning businesses to adapt to evolving market dynamics and deliver superior value to customers. By continuously refining and optimizing supply chain strategies, businesses can achieve operational efficiency, mitigate risks, and capitalize on growth opportunities in an increasingly competitive business environment.

Obtaining detailed information on the specifications of supplies within the supply chain is crucial for ensuring smooth operations, maintaining quality standards, and meeting customer expectations. This process involves gathering comprehensive data about the characteristics, features, and requirements of each supply item used in manufacturing, assembly, or distribution processes.

Firstly, initiating this process typically begins with clear communication and collaboration between procurement teams and suppliers. Suppliers play a pivotal role in providing accurate specifications of the supplies they offer. This information includes technical details such as dimensions, materials, tolerances, performance criteria, and compliance standards that the supplies must meet. Establishing transparent communication channels with suppliers helps clarify any ambiguities and ensures alignment on specifications before procurement decisions are made.

Secondly, leveraging technology and digital tools can streamline the collection and management of supply specifications. Supply chain management systems (SCM) and enterprise resource planning (ERP) software often include modules dedicated to supplier management and product specifications. These tools enable procurement teams to store and access detailed information centrally, facilitating easy retrieval and reference during decision-making processes.

Thirdly, conducting thorough inspections and audits of supply specifications is essential to verify compliance and quality. Quality assurance teams or designated inspectors may perform on-site visits or audits at supplier facilities to assess production processes and confirm that supplies meet specified requirements. These audits help identify potential issues early, mitigate risks, and ensure that supplies consistently meet performance expectations throughout the supply chain.

Moreover, documenting and maintaining up-to-date records of supply specifications is critical for traceability and regulatory compliance. This documentation includes records of tests, certifications, and any deviations or modifications to specifications over time. By maintaining a comprehensive database of specifications, businesses can respond quickly to inquiries, resolve disputes, and adapt to changes in market conditions or regulatory requirements.

Lastly, fostering a culture of continuous improvement and feedback loops within the supply chain enhances the accuracy and relevance of supply specifications. Regularly soliciting feedback from stakeholders, including production teams, quality assurance personnel, and end-users, helps identify opportunities for refinement or enhancement of supply specifications. This iterative process promotes agility and responsiveness, enabling businesses to adapt quickly to emerging trends, customer preferences, or technological advancements.

In essence, obtaining and managing information on the specifications of supplies in the supply chain involves a systematic approach that integrates communication, technology, verification, documentation, and continuous improvement practices. By adhering to these principles, businesses can optimize supply chain efficiency, maintain high product quality, and ultimately enhance customer satisfaction.

To clarify the aims, objectives, and plans of supplies against organizational policies and procedures, it's essential to follow a structured approach that aligns supply activities with overarching business goals and compliance requirements.

Firstly, understanding the aims involves grasping the overarching purpose or mission of the organization. This could include profitability goals, market expansion targets, customer satisfaction metrics, or sustainability commitments. Aims provide a broad direction for the organization and serve as the foundation for setting specific objectives within the supply chain context.

Objectives, on the other hand, translate these aims into actionable and measurable outcomes. In the context of supply chain management, objectives might include reducing procurement costs by a certain percentage, improving supplier lead times, enhancing product quality standards, or achieving higher inventory turnover ratios. These objectives should be SMART (Specific, Measurable, Achievable, Relevant, Time-bound) to provide clarity and accountability.

Plans outline the detailed strategies and tactics to achieve these objectives. They involve mapping out the steps, timelines, resources, and responsibilities required to execute supply chain activities effectively. Plans may encompass sourcing strategies, inventory management protocols, logistics optimization, supplier relationship management frameworks, and risk mitigation strategies. Each plan should be aligned with organizational policies and procedures to ensure compliance with legal, ethical, and operational guidelines.

To effectively clarify and align the aims, objectives, and plans of supplies with organizational policies and procedures, several key steps can be taken:

- Comprehensive Understanding: Begin by thoroughly understanding the organization's strategic goals, operational constraints, and regulatory requirements. This involves reviewing mission statements, strategic plans, and policies that govern supply chain operations.

- Stakeholder Alignment: Engage stakeholders across departments, including procurement, finance, operations, and legal teams, to ensure consensus on objectives and plans. Alignment ensures that supply chain strategies complement broader organizational goals and adhere to established policies.

- Risk Assessment: Conduct a risk assessment to identify potential compliance risks associated with supply chain activities. Factors such as supplier reliability, product safety standards, environmental regulations, and labour practices should be evaluated to mitigate risks and ensure adherence to policies.

- Policy Integration: Integrate supply chain plans with organizational policies and procedures. This includes incorporating guidelines for ethical sourcing, sustainability practices, quality assurance, and contractual obligations into procurement processes and supplier agreements.

- Performance Metrics: Define key performance indicators (KPIs) that measure the effectiveness of supply chain activities in achieving objectives. KPIs could include cost savings, supplier performance ratings, inventory turnover rates, on-time delivery metrics, and compliance audit results.

- Continuous Monitoring and Improvement: Establish mechanisms for ongoing monitoring and review of supply chain performance against objectives and policies. Regular audits, performance reviews, and feedback loops help identify areas for improvement and ensure continuous alignment with organizational aims.

By clarifying the aims, setting SMART objectives, developing detailed plans, and aligning these with organizational policies and procedures, businesses can optimize their supply chain operations. This structured approach not only enhances operational efficiency and effectiveness but also fosters sustainable growth and competitive advantage in the marketplace.

Allocating supply chain tasks effectively involves careful planning, clear communication, and strategic delegation to ensure smooth operations and optimal performance within the organization.

Firstly, it's crucial to understand the scope of supply chain tasks that need to be allocated. This includes identifying specific responsibilities such as procurement, inventory management, logistics coordination, supplier relationship management, demand forecasting, and quality control. Each task should be clearly defined in terms of objectives, timelines, and expected outcomes to provide clarity to personnel involved.

Once tasks are identified, the next step is to assess the skills, capabilities, and availability of personnel within the supply chain team. This involves evaluating individual strengths, expertise in specific areas of supply chain management, experience with relevant tools or technologies, and capacity to handle assigned responsibilities effectively. Matching tasks to personnel based on their competencies ensures that tasks are completed efficiently and mitigates risks associated with inadequate skills or knowledge.

Communication plays a crucial role in the allocation process. Clearly communicate the allocated tasks to each team member, emphasizing their roles, responsibilities, and expectations. Provide context regarding how their tasks contribute to overall supply chain objectives and organizational goals. Open communication channels allow team members to ask questions, seek clarification, and provide feedback, fostering a collaborative environment conducive to success.

Delegation should be strategic and consider workload distribution to prevent overburdening individuals or teams. Assess workload capacity and prioritize tasks based on urgency, complexity, and strategic importance. Balance workload distribution to optimize productivity and minimize bottlenecks in supply chain operations. Additionally, consider factors such as time zones, geographical locations, and language proficiency if tasks involve global supply chain activities to ensure seamless coordination and communication across borders.

Furthermore, establish accountability mechanisms to monitor progress and evaluate task completion. Define key performance indicators (KPIs) relevant to each task to measure performance objectively. Regularly review KPIs, provide constructive feedback, and recognize achievements to motivate team members and maintain engagement in supply chain tasks.

Finally, support ongoing professional development and training opportunities for personnel involved in supply chain tasks. Continuous learning ensures that team members stay updated with industry trends, best practices, and emerging technologies, enhancing their skills and improving overall supply chain performance.

Supporting personnel to achieve supply chain tasks and milestones involves creating an environment where team members are empowered, equipped with necessary resources, and motivated to excel in their roles.

Provide comprehensive training and development opportunities tailored to the specific requirements of supply chain tasks. This includes initial onboarding sessions to familiarize new hires with organizational policies, procedures, and systems. Ongoing training should cover technical skills such as using supply chain management software, understanding logistics processes, and mastering inventory control methods. Soft skills training in communication, problem-solving, and negotiation is also essential to enhance interpersonal capabilities critical for effective supply chain management.

Mentorship and coaching play a crucial role in supporting personnel. Assign experienced mentors who can provide guidance, share industry insights, and offer practical advice based on their own experiences. Coaching sessions can focus on setting achievable goals, monitoring progress, and addressing challenges encountered during task execution. This personalized support helps build confidence, accelerates learning curves, and fosters a culture of continuous improvement within the supply chain team.

Access to reliable resources and tools is fundamental to task achievement. Ensure that personnel have access to state-of-the-art supply chain management systems, software applications, and technological platforms that streamline processes and enhance productivity. Provide adequate infrastructure and logistical support to facilitate seamless communication with suppliers, distributors, and other stakeholders across the supply chain network. Investing in robust IT infrastructure and maintaining up-to-date equipment ensures that personnel can perform their tasks efficiently without technological constraints.

Clear communication channels are essential for effective task support. Establish open lines of communication where personnel can seek guidance, report challenges, and share progress updates with supervisors and colleagues. Regular team meetings, one-on-one sessions, and virtual communication platforms facilitate real-time collaboration, problem-solving, and decision-making. Encourage an open-door policy where personnel feel comfortable raising concerns or suggesting improvements to optimize supply chain operations.

Recognition and rewards motivate personnel to achieve supply chain milestones and exceed performance expectations. Acknowledge individual and team achievements through formal recognition programs, awards ceremonies, or peer-to-peer commendations. Recognize contributions that align with organizational values, promote teamwork, and drive innovation within the supply chain function. Incentive programs such as bonuses, promotions, or career advancement opportunities based on performance metrics further reinforce a culture of excellence and commitment to achieving supply chain goals.

Foster a supportive organizational culture that values employee well-being, work-life balance, and professional growth. Implement policies and initiatives that prioritize health and safety in supply chain operations, particularly in physically demanding or high-risk environments. Encourage work flexibility, provide opportunities for skill development, and promote a healthy work-life integration to sustain personnel motivation and engagement over the long term.

Monitoring and controlling the achievement of supply chain objectives against cost and timescales is crucial for ensuring efficiency, meeting customer demands, and achieving organizational goals. Here's how organizations can effectively carry out this process:

Establish clear and measurable supply chain objectives aligned with broader organizational goals. These objectives should be specific, measurable, achievable, relevant, and time-bound (SMART). For instance, objectives could include reducing transportation costs by 10% within the next fiscal year or improving order fulfillment times by 20% by the end of the quarter. Clear objectives provide a benchmark against which progress can be monitored and evaluated.

Implement robust performance metrics and key performance indicators (KPIs) to track progress towards supply chain objectives. Metrics may include cost per unit shipped, on-time delivery rates, inventory turnover ratios, lead times, and customer satisfaction scores. These KPIs should be regularly monitored through automated systems or manual tracking processes, depending on the organization's technological capabilities and the complexity of supply chain operations.

Utilize supply chain management software and enterprise resource planning (ERP) systems to gather real-time data and analytics. These tools provide visibility into various supply chain activities, from procurement and production to distribution and logistics. Real-time data enables proactive decision-making, allowing supply chain managers to identify potential bottlenecks, mitigate risks, and optimize processes to stay on track with cost and timescale objectives.

Conduct regular performance reviews and assessments to evaluate supply chain performance against predetermined benchmarks. Schedule periodic meetings or reviews where stakeholders across departments can analyse KPIs, discuss challenges, and propose solutions to improve efficiency and cost-effectiveness. These reviews should be collaborative, involving input from logistics managers, procurement specialists, warehouse supervisors, and other relevant personnel to ensure comprehensive oversight.

Supply chain management KPIs (Key Performance Indicators) play a critical role in assessing and optimizing the efficiency and effectiveness of supply chain operations. These metrics provide valuable insights into various aspects of the supply chain, helping organizations identify strengths, weaknesses, and areas for improvement. Here are some essential supply chain management KPIs and their significance [60]:

- Cash-to-Cycle Time: This KPI measures the average length of time between paying for raw materials and receiving payment for goods delivered. It is crucial for managing working capital efficiently. A shorter cash-to-cycle time indicates better liquidity management and reduced financial risk, as it minimizes the time funds are tied up in the supply chain process.

- Perfect Order Rate: The perfect order rate calculates the percentage of orders that are delivered in full, on time, and without errors. This metric directly impacts customer satisfaction, reflecting the supply chain's ability to meet customer expectations consistently. A high perfect order rate indicates efficient order processing, accurate inventory management, and effective logistics coordination.

- Landed Costs: Landed costs encompass all additional expenses incurred in importing goods, such as freight charges, customs duties, taxes, and handling fees. Understanding landed costs is essential for accurately assessing the total cost of inventory and making informed pricing decisions. It helps in optimizing sourcing strategies and controlling supply chain expenditures.

- Fill Rate: The fill rate measures the percentage of orders that are successfully completed with the initial shipment. It indicates how well the supply chain meets demand promptly and completely. A high fill rate signifies strong inventory availability and fulfillment capabilities, contributing to enhanced customer satisfaction and retention.

- Inventory Days of Supply: This KPI calculates how many days inventory will last based on current inventory levels and average daily usage. It helps in managing inventory levels efficiently by ensuring that sufficient stock is available to meet demand without excessive carrying costs. A lower inventory days of supply indicates efficient inventory management and reduced capital tied up in unsold inventory.

- Inventory Turnover: Inventory turnover measures how often inventory is sold and replaced within a specific period. It is calculated by dividing the cost of goods sold (COGS) by average inventory. A high inventory turnover ratio suggests that inventory is moving quickly, reducing holding costs and minimizing the risk of obsolete inventory. It reflects effective inventory control and demand forecasting accuracy.

- On-Time Delivery: This metric assesses the percentage of orders delivered to customers on or before the promised date. On-time delivery performance is crucial for maintaining customer trust and satisfaction. It highlights the reliability of transportation and logistics operations in meeting customer expectations and fulfilling service level agreements.

- On-Time Shipment: Similar to on-time delivery, on-time shipment measures the percentage of orders that are shipped according to schedule. It indicates the efficiency of order processing, packing, and dispatching activities within the supply chain. Deviations between on-time delivery and on-time shipment metrics can pinpoint areas needing improvement in logistics management.

- Supply Chain Costs as a Percentage of Sales: This KPI compares the total cost of supply chain activities (including procurement, production, warehousing, and transportation) to the organization's total sales revenue. It helps in assessing the cost efficiency of the supply chain relative to business performance. A lower percentage indicates effective cost management and improved profitability.

Implement corrective actions and continuous improvement initiatives based on performance insights. When deviations from cost or timescale objectives occur, promptly identify root causes through root cause analysis techniques such as Fishbone diagrams or Pareto charts. Once identified, develop action plans with specific steps, responsibilities, and timelines to address the issues and bring performance back on track. Continuous improvement fosters a culture of innovation and efficiency within the supply chain team.

Communicate progress and challenges transparently to stakeholders at all levels of the organization. Regularly update senior management, department heads, and team members on supply chain performance metrics, achievements, and areas needing improvement. Effective communication ensures alignment with organizational goals and encourages collaboration across functions to collectively work towards achieving supply chain objectives within cost and timescale constraints.

Lastly, adapt and adjust supply chain strategies in response to changing market conditions, customer preferences, or external disruptions. Flexibility and agility are key to maintaining competitiveness in a dynamic business environment. Monitor industry trends, technological advancements, and regulatory changes that may impact supply chain operations, and proactively adjust strategies to optimize performance while balancing cost considerations and delivery timelines.

By systematically monitoring and controlling the achievement of supply chain objectives against cost and timescales, organizations can optimize efficiency, enhance customer satisfaction, and drive sustainable growth. This disciplined approach not only improves operational performance but also strengthens the organization's overall competitive position in the marketplace.

Presenting reports on supply chain outcomes to stakeholders is a critical task that requires clear communication, strategic alignment, and the ability to convey complex information effectively. This includes:

Understand Stakeholder Needs: Before preparing the report, it's essential to understand the needs and expectations of your stakeholders. Different stakeholders, such as executives, investors, operational managers, and customers, may have varying interests in supply chain outcomes. Tailor your report to address their concerns, whether it's financial performance, operational efficiency, customer satisfaction, or risk management.

Define Objectives and Scope: Clearly define the objectives of the report and its scope. Identify the key metrics and KPIs (Key Performance Indicators) relevant to supply chain outcomes that align with organizational goals. This ensures that the report focuses on meaningful data and insights that stakeholders can use to make informed decisions.

Organize the Report Structure: Structure the report logically to present information in a coherent and understandable manner. Start with an executive summary that provides a concise overview of the main findings and recommendations. Follow with detailed sections covering different aspects of supply chain performance, such as:

- **Financial Performance**: Include metrics like cost savings, cost-to-serve, and return on investment (ROI) from supply chain initiatives.

- **Operational Efficiency**: Discuss metrics such as on-time delivery, fill rate, inventory turnover, and cycle time reductions achieved through process improvements.

- **Customer Satisfaction**: Highlight metrics related to perfect order rate, customer complaints, and feedback on supply chain responsiveness.

- **Risk Management**: Address supply chain risks identified and mitigation strategies implemented to ensure continuity and resilience.

Visualize Data Effectively: Utilize graphs, charts, and tables to visualize data and trends effectively. Visual representations make complex information easier to understand and facilitate quicker decision-making by stakeholders. Ensure that visuals are clear, labelled appropriately, and support the narrative of your report.

Provide Context and Analysis: Interpret the data presented in the report to provide meaningful insights and actionable recommendations. Explain the reasons behind trends or deviations from targets, highlighting both successes and areas needing improvement. Use benchmarks or comparisons with industry standards to provide context and validate achievements.

Focus on Impact and Future Outlook: Emphasize the impact of supply chain improvements on overall business performance. Discuss how enhancements in supply chain efficiency have contributed to cost savings, revenue growth, competitive advantage, or customer satisfaction. Provide a forward-looking perspective by outlining future initiatives, potential challenges, and opportunities for further optimization.

Engage Stakeholders: During the presentation, actively engage stakeholders by encouraging questions and discussions. Address concerns promptly and provide additional context or data as needed to clarify points. Tailor your communication style and level of detail to suit the audience's expertise and interests, ensuring they grasp the implications of supply chain outcomes on broader organizational goals.

Follow-Up and Feedback: After the presentation, solicit feedback from stakeholders to gauge their understanding and satisfaction with the report. Use feedback to refine future presentations and reports, ensuring continuous improvement in communication and transparency regarding supply chain outcomes.

Managing Supply Chain Relationships and Activities

Applying portfolio analysis techniques to assess relationships in supply chains involves a structured approach to evaluating and managing supplier relationships based on strategic goals and performance metrics.

Define Strategic Objectives: Begin by clarifying the strategic objectives of your supply chain management strategy. These objectives could include reducing costs, improving quality, enhancing innovation, ensuring sustainability, or mitigating risks. Understanding these goals is crucial as they will guide the selection and evaluation of supplier relationships.

Segment Suppliers: Segment your suppliers based on criteria relevant to your strategic objectives. Common segmentation criteria include spend volume, criticality of supply, risk exposure, innovation potential, geographical location, and supplier performance. This segmentation helps prioritize resources and efforts based on the strategic importance of each supplier to your organization.

Select Portfolio Analysis Tools: Choose appropriate portfolio analysis tools to assess supplier relationships. Two widely used techniques are the Boston Consulting Group (BCG) Matrix and the Kraljic Matrix:

- BCG Matrix: This matrix categorizes suppliers into four quadrants based on two dimensions: market growth rate (indicative of future opportunities and risks) and relative market share (indicative of current contribution and dependency). Suppliers are classified as Strategic (high market share, high growth), Bottleneck (low market share, high growth), Routine (high market share, low growth), or Passive (low market share, low growth). Strategic suppliers warrant heavy investment and close collaboration, while passive suppliers may require minimal attention.

- Kraljic Matrix: This matrix categorizes suppliers based on two dimensions: supply risk (likelihood of supply disruption) and profit impact (financial impact on the organization). Suppliers are classified as Strategic (high risk, high impact), Leverage (low risk, high impact), Non-critical (low risk, low impact), or Bottleneck (high risk, low impact). Strategic suppliers require proactive management to mitigate risks and leverage opportunities, while non-critical suppliers may focus more on transactional relationships.

Boston Consulting Group (BCG) Matrix

The Growth Share Matrix, often referred to as the Boston Consulting Group (BCG) Matrix, is a strategic tool used by businesses to manage their portfolio of products or business units. It categorizes these entities into four quadrants based on two key factors: relative market share and market growth rate. This matrix provides a framework for executives to make informed decisions about resource allocation, prioritization, and strategic direction.

Quadrants and Strategies:

1. Cash Cows (Low Growth, High Share): This quadrant represents products or business units with a high relative market share in a low-growth market. Cash cows generate significant cash flows due to their established market position, but their growth potential is limited. Companies are advised to "milk" these cash cows by maximizing profits and minimizing investments. Resources from cash cows can be redeployed into other areas of the business with higher growth potential.

2. Stars (High Growth, High Share): Stars are products or business units that enjoy both a high market share in a rapidly growing market. These entities have strong potential for future profitability and market leadership. Companies should invest heavily in stars to capitalize on their growth opportunities and solidify their competitive position. This may involve investing in innovation, marketing, or expanding production capacity to sustain growth and maximize returns.

3. Question Marks (High Growth, Low Share): Question marks, also known as "problem children," are products or business units with a low market share in a high-growth market. These entities have potential for growth but are not yet dominant in their market. Companies face a strategic choice with question marks: invest to increase market share and turn them into stars, or consider divesting if growth prospects do not justify further investment. The decision hinges on the likelihood of achieving market leadership and sustainable profitability.

4. Pets (Low Growth, Low Share): Pets are products or business units with a low market share in a low-growth market. They neither generate significant cash flow nor offer growth potential. These entities are typically candidates

for divestment, liquidation, or repositioning efforts. Keeping pets can tie up resources that could be better utilized elsewhere in the business. Companies should assess whether to exit these markets entirely or find alternative strategies to minimize losses.

Strategic Implications:

The Growth Share Matrix underscores the importance of achieving market leadership, as this position often translates into sustainable competitive advantages and superior returns. Companies with high relative market share are better positioned to achieve economies of scale, pricing power, and operational efficiencies that competitors find challenging to replicate.

Long-term Considerations:

While the matrix provides a snapshot of current market dynamics, it also emphasizes the need for ongoing strategic evaluation and adaptation. Products or business units can move between quadrants as market conditions evolve, necessitating continuous monitoring and adjustment of resource allocation strategies. This flexibility allows companies to respond effectively to changes in competitive landscapes, technological advancements, and shifting consumer preferences.

In essence, the Growth Share Matrix serves as a strategic compass for businesses to navigate their portfolio management decisions. It guides executives in identifying where to invest resources for growth, where to sustain profitability, and where to make tough decisions about divestment or restructuring to optimize overall business performance. By aligning investments with market opportunities and competitive strengths, companies can enhance their market position and drive sustained value creation over time.

Kraljic Matrix

The Kraljic Matrix, developed by Peter Kraljic in the 1980s, is a strategic procurement tool widely used by supply chain and procurement professionals to categorize and manage supplier relationships based on supply risk and profit impact. This matrix helps organizations identify vulnerabilities in their supply chain, develop appropriate strategies for different types of products and services, and mitigate potential disruptions.

Key Elements of the Kraljic Matrix:

The Kraljic Matrix evaluates suppliers and their offerings based on two key dimensions:

- Risk Impact: This dimension assesses the level of difficulty associated with sourcing a particular product or service and the potential vulnerability this creates for the organization. Products or services with high risk impact may face supply disruptions due to factors like supplier reliability, geopolitical risks, or scarcity of resources.

- Cost Impact: This dimension measures the financial impact of the product or service on the organization's profitability. It evaluates how significant the costs are in relation to overall expenses and profitability goals. Lowering costs through effective procurement strategies can enhance profitability and competitiveness.

Four Quadrants of the Kraljic Matrix:
- Critical (Strategic): Products or services in this quadrant are characterized by high risk impact and high cost impact. These are critical to the organization's operations or strategic goals, often with limited alternative suppliers. Examples include specialized components or technologies crucial for product assembly. Strategic management of these items involves forming strong partnerships with suppliers, managing risks through supplier diversification or contingency plans, and negotiating for stable supply and favourable terms.

- Leverage (Non-Critical): Products or services in this quadrant have high cost impact but low risk impact. They are typically commodities or items with numerous alternative suppliers and competitive pricing. Organizations can leverage their purchasing power to negotiate lower prices, use competitive bidding processes, and explore product substitutions without significant supply chain risks.

- Bottleneck (Supply Chain Vulnerable): Bottleneck products have low cost impact but high risk impact. They are often specialized items or materials with limited availability or susceptible to market fluctuations, such as rare minerals or specialized chemicals. Managing bottleneck items requires securing alternative suppliers, maintaining buffer stocks, and monitoring market conditions closely to mitigate supply disruptions and price volatility.

- Routine (Non-Critical): Products or services in this quadrant have low risk impact and low cost impact. They are typically standard, easily replaceable items with multiple suppliers and stable prices. Examples include office supplies, basic maintenance materials, or generic consumables. Routine products benefit from efficient procurement processes, standardization, and automated purchasing systems to optimize cost-effectiveness and streamline supply chain operations.

Application and Strategic Insights:

The Kraljic Matrix guides procurement and supply chain professionals in tailoring their strategies based on the unique characteristics of each product or service category. It facilitates proactive management of supply chain risks, enhances negotiation strategies with suppliers, and ensures alignment with organizational goals and priorities. By categorizing suppliers and products into these four quadrants, organizations can allocate resources effectively, prioritize strategic investments, and optimize their supply chain performance to achieve sustainable competitive advantage in the marketplace.

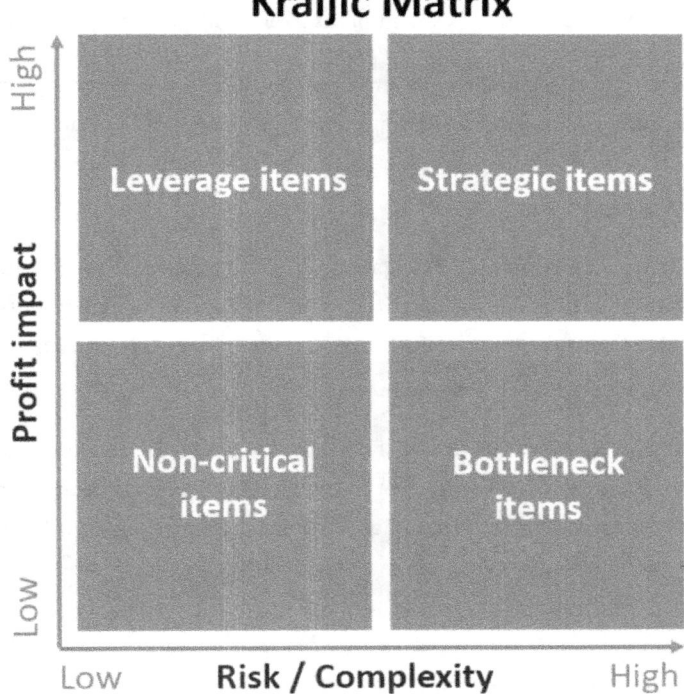

Figure 27: Illustration of the Kraljic matrix. 7804j, CC0, via Wikimedia Commons.

Evaluate Supplier Performance: Assess each supplier's performance against predefined KPIs and metrics aligned with your strategic objectives. Performance metrics may include on-time delivery, quality performance, cost competitiveness, responsiveness, innovation capability, sustainability practices, and compliance with contractual terms. Use both quantitative data (e.g., performance metrics, financial impact) and qualitative assessments (e.g., relationship dynamics, communication) to gain a comprehensive view of supplier performance.

Allocate Resources and Strategies: Based on the analysis from portfolio tools, allocate appropriate resources and develop tailored strategies for each supplier category:

- Strategic Suppliers: Engage in collaborative partnerships, joint innovation initiatives, and long-term contracts to ensure alignment with strategic goals. Invest in supplier development programs to enhance capabilities and mitigate risks.

- Leverage Suppliers: Focus on improving operational efficiencies, negotiating favourable terms, and leveraging economies of scale. Implement supplier performance improvement plans to enhance reliability and reduce costs.

- Non-critical Suppliers: Streamline transactional processes, automate interactions where feasible, and monitor performance at a basic level. Consider consolidating spend or exploring alternative suppliers to optimize resource allocation.

- Bottleneck Suppliers: Mitigate supply chain risks through contingency planning, dual sourcing strategies, and risk-sharing agreements. Develop robust supplier monitoring and escalation procedures to manage potential disruptions effectively.

Monitor and Review: Continuously monitor supplier performance and revisit portfolio analysis periodically to adapt to evolving business conditions and strategic priorities. Regularly review the supplier portfolio to identify emerging trends, risks, and opportunities that may necessitate adjustments in supplier relationships and strategies.

Communicate and Collaborate: Foster open communication and collaboration with suppliers across all categories. Share insights from portfolio analysis to align expectations, clarify mutual goals, and strengthen relationships based on transparency and trust. Engage stakeholders internally to ensure alignment between supply chain strategies and broader organizational objectives.

Evaluating the financial, technical, and performance data of suppliers is a critical process within supply chain management that ensures organizations make informed decisions aligned with their strategic goals and operational needs. This evaluation involves gathering and analysing data across various dimensions to assess suppliers' capabilities, reliability, and suitability to meet the organization's requirements.

Financial Evaluation: Financial stability and health are crucial indicators when evaluating suppliers. This assessment involves reviewing suppliers' financial statements, such as balance sheets, income statements, and cash flow statements, to gauge their profitability, liquidity, and overall financial health. Key financial ratios like liquidity ratios (e.g., current ratio, quick ratio), profitability ratios (e.g., gross profit margin, net profit margin), and solvency ratios provide insights into suppliers' ability to manage financial obligations, invest in capabilities, and sustain operations over the long term.

Technical Evaluation: The technical evaluation focuses on suppliers' technical capabilities, expertise, and innovation potential relevant to the products or services they provide. This assessment includes reviewing their technological infrastructure, manufacturing processes, quality control measures, and adherence to industry standards and regulations. Evaluating technical capabilities ensures that suppliers can consistently deliver products or services that meet quality standards, specifications, and performance requirements demanded by the organization and its customers.

Performance Evaluation: Supplier performance evaluation involves assessing how well suppliers have met contractual obligations and performance metrics over time. This evaluation typically includes metrics such as on-time delivery performance, product quality, lead times, responsiveness to inquiries or issues, and overall customer satisfaction ratings. Performance data is gathered through supplier scorecards, performance reviews, customer feedback, and internal performance tracking systems. It provides insights into suppliers' reliability, consistency, and ability to align with the organization's operational needs and customer expectations.

Integration with Supply Chain Strategies: Effective evaluation of supplier data is integral to aligning with supply chain strategies. Organizations must first define their strategic objectives, whether it's cost reduction, innovation, risk mitigation, or operational efficiency. The evaluation process then focuses on identifying suppliers whose financial health, technical capabilities, and performance align with these strategic priorities.

For instance, if the strategy emphasizes innovation and product differentiation, the evaluation may prioritize suppliers with strong R&D capabilities and a track record of introducing new technologies or products. Conversely, if cost reduction is a priority, suppliers offering competitive pricing and efficient cost structures may be prioritized.

Tools and Techniques: Various tools and techniques support the evaluation process, including supplier audits, site visits, benchmarking against industry standards, and conducting interviews with supplier management teams. Advanced analytics and supplier management software also play a crucial role in aggregating and analysing data efficiently, identifying trends, and generating actionable insights to support decision-making.

Continuous Improvement: Evaluation of supplier data is not a one-time exercise but a continuous process aimed at fostering long-term supplier relationships and driving continuous improvement within the supply chain. Regularly reviewing and updating supplier evaluations ensures that organizations adapt to changing market conditions, technological advancements, and evolving customer preferences while maintaining alignment with supply chain strategies.

Identifying opportunities to adjust supply chain strategies in response to evolving customer needs, supply chain dynamics, and organizational objectives is crucial for maintaining competitiveness and sustainability. This process involves a strategic approach to recognize shifts in market demands, technological advancements, regulatory changes, and internal business goals. Here's a detailed exploration of how to effectively identify and capitalize on these opportunities:

Understanding evolving customer needs is foundational to adjusting supply chain strategies. This analysis involves gathering qualitative and quantitative data through market research, customer surveys, focus groups, and feedback mechanisms. By identifying emerging trends, preferences, and pain points among customers, organizations can align supply chain strategies to enhance customer satisfaction and loyalty. For example, if customers increasingly prioritize sustainable products, the supply chain strategy may need to incorporate eco-friendly sourcing practices or enhance transparency in product traceability.

Assessing supply chain dynamics involves evaluating the performance of existing suppliers, logistics partners, and distribution channels. This assessment includes monitoring key performance indicators (KPIs) such as lead times, inventory turnover, supplier reliability, and transportation costs. By analysing these metrics, organizations can pinpoint inefficiencies, bottlenecks, or areas of improvement within the supply chain. Adjusting strategies may involve optimizing sourcing strategies, enhancing warehousing capabilities, or implementing advanced technologies like IoT (Internet of Things) for real-time visibility and predictive analytics.

Aligning supply chain strategies with organizational objectives requires a clear understanding of strategic priorities such as cost reduction, innovation, market expansion, or risk management. This alignment ensures that supply chain adjustments support broader business goals and contribute to overall organizational success. For instance, if the organizational objective is to penetrate new markets, the supply chain strategy may prioritize agility and scalability to quickly adapt to varying market demands and regulatory requirements.

The process of identifying opportunities to adjust supply chain strategies involves cross-functional collaboration across departments such as operations, procurement, sales, and marketing. Regular strategic meetings, brainstorming sessions, and workshops can facilitate the identification of emerging opportunities and challenges. Leveraging data analytics and scenario planning techniques allows organizations to anticipate future trends and proactively adjust supply chain strategies before disruptions occur.

Maintaining flexibility and responsiveness in supply chain strategies is essential to effectively respond to changing external and internal factors. This agility enables organizations to capitalize on opportunities swiftly, mitigate risks, and maintain competitive advantage. Implementing agile supply chain practices, such as demand-driven planning, vendor-managed inventory (VMI), and just-in-time (JIT) manufacturing, enhances responsiveness to fluctuating market demands and customer expectations.

Continuous improvement is integral to adapting supply chain strategies over time. Regularly evaluating the effectiveness of adjusted strategies through performance metrics, benchmarking against industry standards, and feedback from stakeholders ensures ongoing optimization. This iterative process allows organizations to refine supply chain strategies based on lessons learned, emerging trends, and evolving business priorities.

Designing and implementing a framework to promote collaboration with suppliers is essential for organizations aiming to achieve a competitive advantage in their supply chain. This process involves establishing structured approaches and fostering relationships that go beyond traditional buyer-supplier interactions.

Establish Clear Objectives and Goals: Begin by defining clear objectives and goals for collaboration with suppliers. These should align with the overall strategic objectives of the organization, such as improving product quality, reducing costs, enhancing innovation, or increasing supply chain resilience. Clearly articulated goals provide a shared understanding and motivation for both parties involved, fostering commitment and alignment from the outset.

Select Key Suppliers Strategically: Identify and prioritize key suppliers based on their strategic importance to your organization. Consider factors such as their impact on product quality, delivery reliability, innovation capabilities, and market position.

Building collaborative relationships with strategically chosen suppliers allows for deeper integration and mutual benefits, contributing significantly to achieving competitive advantage.

Foster Trust and Transparency: Trust is the cornerstone of successful supplier collaboration. Establishing open communication channels, sharing relevant information, and maintaining transparency about goals, challenges, and expectations build trust over time. This trust encourages suppliers to invest in the relationship, share insights, and proactively address issues, thereby enhancing collaboration and driving joint improvements.

Co-create Value Through Joint Initiatives: Collaborate with suppliers to co-create value through joint initiatives that leverage each party's strengths and capabilities. This could involve joint product development, process improvement projects, or sustainability initiatives. By pooling resources, knowledge, and expertise, both organizations can innovate faster, optimize processes, and deliver superior products or services to customers.

Implement Performance Metrics and Continuous Improvement: Define key performance indicators (KPIs) and metrics to measure the success of supplier collaboration efforts. These metrics should align with the objectives set earlier and include aspects such as quality metrics, on-time delivery performance, cost savings, and innovation outcomes. Regularly review performance against these metrics and collaborate with suppliers on continuous improvement initiatives to drive ongoing enhancements in efficiency and effectiveness.

Leverage Technology and Tools: Utilize technology platforms and tools to facilitate collaboration and communication with suppliers. This may include supplier relationship management (SRM) systems, collaborative planning tools, and shared data analytics platforms. These tools enable real-time information sharing, visibility into supply chain activities, and collaborative decision-making, thereby enhancing efficiency and responsiveness.

Establish Governance and Conflict Resolution Mechanisms: Establish a governance structure that outlines roles, responsibilities, and escalation paths for resolving conflicts or disputes that may arise during collaboration. Clear governance ensures that both parties adhere to agreements, manage risks effectively, and address issues promptly, thereby maintaining the momentum of collaborative efforts towards achieving competitive advantage.

Cultivate a Collaborative Culture: Promote a collaborative culture within your organization and among supplier relationships. Encourage cross-functional teams to collaborate with suppliers, share insights, and participate in joint workshops or training sessions. This collaborative mindset fosters innovation, knowledge sharing, and continuous learning, driving long-term competitive advantage through adaptive and responsive supply chain practices.

Evaluate and Adapt Over Time: Regularly evaluate the effectiveness of the collaboration framework and make necessary adjustments based on performance insights, market changes, and evolving organizational priorities. Continuous adaptation ensures that the collaboration framework remains relevant, responsive, and aligned with current business needs, maintaining its ability to contribute to sustained competitive advantage.

Consulting with organizational management to confirm progress of supply chain activities in alignment with organizational objectives involves a systematic and collaborative approach to ensure that supply chain initiatives contribute effectively to overall strategic goals. Here's a detailed exploration of how to conduct this process effectively:

Establish Clear Communication Channels: Begin by establishing clear communication channels with organizational management. This includes scheduling regular meetings, defining reporting structures, and identifying key stakeholders involved in supply chain management and strategic decision-making. Open and transparent communication is essential to ensure alignment between supply chain activities and organizational objectives.

Review Strategic Objectives and KPIs: Before consulting with management, thoroughly review the organization's strategic objectives and key performance indicators (KPIs) related to supply chain management. Understand how supply chain activities are expected to contribute to broader organizational goals such as cost reduction, operational efficiency, customer satisfaction, or market expansion. This review provides a framework for evaluating progress and highlighting areas of alignment or potential improvement.

Prepare Comprehensive Progress Reports: Compile comprehensive progress reports that detail the current status of supply chain activities, achievements against set objectives, challenges encountered, and upcoming milestones or initiatives. These reports should be data-driven, utilizing relevant metrics and KPIs to provide a clear picture of performance trends and outcomes. Visual aids such as charts, graphs, and trend analyses can enhance the clarity and impact of the reports.

Seek Feedback and Input: During consultations, actively seek feedback and input from organizational management regarding the progress of supply chain activities. Encourage discussions on areas of success, opportunities for improvement, resource allocation priorities, and any strategic shifts or emerging challenges that may impact supply chain effectiveness. This dialogue fosters a collaborative environment where management insights contribute to refining supply chain strategies and tactics.

Align Resource Allocation and Priorities: Discuss resource allocation and priorities with organizational management to ensure that sufficient resources, both financial and human, are allocated to support key supply chain initiatives. Evaluate the balance between short-term operational needs and long-term strategic investments, ensuring that resource allocation aligns with the organization's overall priorities and competitive positioning.

Address Challenges and Mitigate Risks: Highlight any challenges or risks identified during the progress review and consultation process. Work collaboratively with management to develop proactive strategies and contingency plans to mitigate risks, address operational bottlenecks, or capitalize on emerging opportunities. This proactive approach demonstrates responsiveness and ensures that supply chain activities remain resilient and adaptable to changing business conditions.

Foster a Culture of Continuous Improvement: Emphasize the importance of continuous improvement in supply chain activities and processes. Discuss initiatives for optimizing supply chain efficiency, enhancing supplier relationships, leveraging technology advancements, and adopting best practices in industry standards. Encourage management to support initiatives that promote innovation, sustainability, and resilience within the supply chain ecosystem.

Document Agreed Action Plans: Document agreed action plans and decisions resulting from consultations with organizational management. Clarify responsibilities, timelines, and deliverables to ensure accountability and follow-through on strategic initiatives. Documenting these agreements provides a reference point for tracking progress, evaluating outcomes, and revisiting strategic discussions in future consultations.

Monitor and Report Progress Regularly: Establish a framework for ongoing monitoring and reporting of supply chain progress to organizational management. Define regular intervals for progress updates, performance reviews, and strategic reviews to maintain visibility and accountability. Adapt reporting formats and content based on management preferences and evolving organizational priorities to ensure relevance and effectiveness.

As such, managing supplier relationships effectively requires a strategic approach aimed at fostering long-term partnerships that contribute positively to organizational objectives. This includes [62]:

1. See Interactions as Relationships: To manage supplier relationships effectively, it's crucial to view interactions beyond mere transactions. Each interaction con-

tributes to the broader relationship, influencing trust, collaboration, and mutual benefit. By shifting focus to long-term relationships, organizations can align supplier interests with their own strategic goals, fostering stability and reliability in the supply chain.

2. Track Every Interaction: Tracking every interaction with suppliers is essential for gaining insights into relationship dynamics. Utilizing a supplier relationship management (SRM) system allows organizations to record and manage emails, phone calls, meetings, contracts, and agreements systematically. This centralized approach not only enhances transparency but also ensures continuity even when personnel change, preserving valuable institutional knowledge.

3. Assign Responsibility: Clearly defining roles and responsibilities for supplier relationship management is critical. Designating specific individuals or teams to oversee supplier interactions ensures consistency and accountability. Depending on the organization's structure, responsibilities may include negotiation, contract management, performance evaluation, and strategic alignment with procurement goals.

4. Ensure Visibility Into All Suppliers: Achieving end-to-end visibility into all supplier relationships is a foundational strategy for effective supply chain management. Organizations should leverage technology and data analytics to consolidate supplier information in a centralized platform. This includes supplier locations, performance metrics, risk assessments, and contractual obligations, facilitating informed decision-making and proactive risk management.

5. Segment Suppliers: Not all suppliers have equal impact on organizational operations. Segmenting suppliers based on criteria such as operational impact, frequency of interaction, type of goods/services supplied, and strategic importance allows organizations to prioritize resource allocation and tailor engagement strategies accordingly. This segmentation ensures that critical suppliers receive appropriate attention and resources.

6. Track Relationship Health: Monitoring the health of supplier relationships goes beyond tracking interactions; it involves assessing factors like communication frequency, sentiment analysis, feedback loops, and collaborative initiatives. Tools for relationship health tracking enable organizations to identify strengths, address potential issues proactively, and cultivate stronger, more resilient partnerships over time.

7. Discover New Suppliers: Continuously exploring new supplier relationships enhances supply chain resilience and agility. This proactive approach mitigates risks associated with supply chain disruptions and strengthens negotiating positions. Engaging with potential new suppliers diversifies sourcing options, fosters innovation,

and prepares organizations to respond effectively to market changes and unforeseen challenges.

8. Communicate Regularly: Effective communication is fundamental to maintaining healthy supplier relationships Regular updates on market conditions, operational changes, and strategic priorities enable both parties to align their efforts and anticipate challenges. Transparent communication builds trust, enhances collaboration, and facilitates swift resolution of issues, ultimately driving mutual value creation.

9. Ask for Feedback: Actively seeking feedback from suppliers demonstrates a commitment to continuous improvement and mutual success. Regularly soliciting input on collaboration effectiveness, service quality, and process efficiency helps identify areas for enhancement and strengthens partnership dynamics. Implementing feedback-driven improvements fosters a culture of responsiveness and innovation within supplier relationships.

Evaluating and Improving Supply Chain Effectiveness

To effectively review the effectiveness of current relationships within the supply chain and align them with the supply chain management strategy, organizations need to undertake a comprehensive evaluation process. This begins with defining clear objectives and performance metrics that reflect the strategic goals of the organization. Metrics may include supplier performance, reliability, responsiveness, cost-effectiveness, and alignment with organizational values such as sustainability and innovation.

Next, organizations should conduct a thorough assessment of current relationships against these metrics. This involves gathering data through supplier performance reviews, surveys, and stakeholder feedback. It's essential to analyse not only quantitative metrics but also qualitative aspects such as communication effectiveness, collaborative problem-solving, and alignment of goals.

Comparing supply chain management models is crucial to determine the most appropriate infrastructure that supports organizational objectives effectively. This comparison typically involves evaluating different frameworks or methodologies such as lean supply chain, agile supply chain, and resilient supply chain models. Each model offers unique advantages based on factors like operational flexibility, responsiveness to market changes, risk management capabilities, and cost efficiency.

Assessing techniques to support the development of innovation in the supply chain involves identifying opportunities for improvement and fostering a culture of continuous innovation. Techniques may include collaborative product development with suppliers, implementing advanced technologies like AI and IoT for supply chain optimization, and exploring new market trends and customer demands. Innovation in the supply chain can lead to competitive advantages such as improved product quality, faster time-to-market, and enhanced customer satisfaction.

Analysing cost reduction activities within the supply chain is essential for achieving organizational objectives, especially in optimizing operational efficiency and profitability. This involves identifying cost drivers across the supply chain, such as procurement costs, transportation costs, inventory carrying costs, and overhead expenses. Strategies for cost reduction may include supplier consolidation, negotiation for better pricing terms, implementing lean practices to minimize waste, and optimizing inventory management through just-in-time principles.

Consolidating analysis and evaluation results from the above activities is critical to improving future supply chain management strategies. By synthesizing findings and identifying trends or patterns, organizations can make informed decisions to enhance supplier relationships, adopt more effective supply chain management models, foster innovation, and achieve cost reduction goals. Seeking feedback from organization management throughout this process ensures alignment with overall business objectives and promotes continuous improvement in supply chain management strategies.

Improving supply chain efficiency involves a multifaceted approach that encompasses various strategies and practices aimed at optimizing processes, enhancing collaboration, and leveraging technology. One of the primary recommendations is to increase supply chain visibility. This entails tracking products from production through warehousing to delivery, enabling organizations to monitor inventory levels, streamline operations, and respond swiftly to disruptions. Technologies like IoT and advanced analytics provide real-time data, facilitating proactive decision-making and operational adjustments [63].

Building strong relationships with dependable suppliers is another critical aspect of enhancing efficiency. Beyond cost considerations, reliable suppliers ensure consistent delivery and quality, minimizing supply chain disruptions. Effective communication plays a pivotal role here, enabling prompt issue resolution and alignment on strategic goals. Consistent vendor management ensures uniformity in dealing with suppliers, optimizing processes and cost efficiencies across the supply chain [63].

Strategic partnerships that are mutually beneficial further enhance efficiency. These partnerships involve crafting contracts that align incentives and goals, fostering collaboration and innovation. Automation of supply chain processes is instrumental in reducing errors and operational costs. By automating routine tasks like inventory management and order processing, organizations can allocate resources more efficiently and focus on strategic initiatives [63].

Integrated supply chain software provides a centralized platform for managing operations across multiple warehouses and improving order fulfillment processes. This software integrates supply chain analytics, offering insights into performance metrics and areas for improvement. Optimizing inventory management through technology helps maintain optimal stock levels, reduces stockouts, and improves forecasting accuracy, enhancing overall operational efficiency [63].

Implementing a robust returns management system is crucial for customer satisfaction and operational efficiency. Streamlined returns processes not only improve customer loyalty but also provide valuable insights into product quality and supplier performance. Real-time supply chain data analytics enable organizations to monitor performance metrics continuously, enabling agile responses to changing market dynamics and operational challenges [63].

Embracing new technologies and engaging with IT departments regularly are essential for staying ahead in supply chain efficiency. IT collaboration ensures alignment of technology investments with business objectives and facilitates the adoption of innovative solutions. Moreover, investing in employee development and training ensures that staff are equipped with the necessary skills to operate and optimize supply chain processes effectively [63].

Incorporating green shipping and packaging practices aligns with environmental expectations and enhances brand reputation. Using biodegradable materials and reducing packaging waste not only supports sustainability goals but also reduces logistics costs. Finally, establishing a supply chain efficiency plan and continuous improvement processes ensures ongoing optimization. This includes forming supply chain councils to oversee efficiency initiatives, track performance metrics, and evaluate new technologies, thereby fostering a culture of continuous improvement within the organization [63].

By implementing these strategies comprehensively and adapting to evolving market conditions, organizations can achieve significant improvements in supply chain efficiency, driving operational excellence and competitive advantage in the marketplace.

Chapter 9

Manage Facility and Inventory Requirements

Managing a facility and its inventory requirements within the transport and logistics industry involves intricate planning, efficient operations, and meticulous oversight to ensure smooth operations and meet customer demands. This process is crucial across various contexts, from warehousing to distribution centres and transportation hubs.

Firstly, effective facility management begins with strategic planning. This includes selecting an optimal location that balances proximity to suppliers, customers, and transportation networks. The facility layout should be designed to maximize operational efficiency, with considerations for storage capacity, workflow optimization, and safety regulations. For instance, warehousing facilities may utilize various storage systems such as pallet racks, mezzanines, or automated storage and retrieval systems (AS/RS) depending on inventory characteristics and throughput requirements.

Inventory management within these facilities involves maintaining optimal stock levels to meet demand while minimizing carrying costs and stockouts. This requires implementing robust inventory control systems that track goods in real-time, from receipt to dispatch. Technologies like barcode scanning, RFID, and warehouse management systems (WMS) play a crucial role in accurate inventory tracking, reducing errors, and improving efficiency.

In the context of transportation logistics, managing inventory extends beyond storage to include efficient handling and distribution. Cross-docking facilities, for instance, streamline the process by transferring goods directly from inbound to outbound transportation vehicles, reducing storage time and handling costs. Effective load planning and routing strategies optimize transportation resources, ensuring timely deliveries while minimizing fuel consumption and environmental impact.

Moreover, facility managers must consider regulatory compliance and safety standards specific to the transport and logistics industry. This includes adhering to transportation regulations, hazardous materials handling protocols, and maintaining facilities that are conducive to worker safety and operational efficiency. Regular inspections, employee training on safety procedures, and adherence to Health and Safety guidelines are essential components of facility management in this sector.

Another critical aspect of managing facilities in transport and logistics is adapting to seasonal fluctuations and market trends. For instance, during peak seasons or promotional periods, facilities may experience increased demand, requiring temporary storage solutions, additional staff, or extended operating hours. Flexibility in facility operations and inventory management practices allows companies to respond promptly to market demands and maintain service levels.

Furthermore, leveraging data analytics and performance metrics is becoming increasingly important in optimizing facility operations. Monitoring key performance indicators (KPIs) such as inventory turnover rates, order fulfillment accuracy, and facility utilization rates provides insights into operational efficiency and areas for improvement. Continuous improvement initiatives based on data-driven insights enable facilities to streamline processes, reduce costs, and enhance customer satisfaction.

Warehouse systems are intricate operational environments that necessitate efficient resource management, effective workplace operating systems, and adept management practices to ensure smooth functioning and optimal productivity. The integration of technologies such as RFID-based systems, warehouse management systems (WMS), automation, and AI-driven solutions plays a crucial role in enhancing warehouse performance [64-66]. These systems are designed to streamline operations, improve inventory management, optimize order picking processes, and enhance overall productivity [67-69].

Human and technological factors significantly impact warehouse productivity, with the efficiency of operators and the optimization of WMS systems playing key roles in determining operational success [70]. The utilization of advanced algorithms in AI-driven warehouse automation systems helps in optimizing various aspects of warehouse operations, from inventory management to order fulfillment, leading to increased efficiency and cost-effectiveness [66]. Additionally, the development of

RFID-based automatic warehouse management systems has been shown to improve storage location arrangements, inventory management, and the flow of goods within warehouses, ultimately contributing to operational success [71].

Warehouse management systems (WMS) are pivotal in managing and monitoring warehouse processes, assisting in the efficient flow of products from receipt to shipping [72]. These systems encompass various functionalities such as pick operations, shelf management, receive processing, replenishment management, and cycle counting, all of which are essential for effective warehouse operations [73]. Moreover, the implementation of cloud-based location assignment systems and real-time analytics in warehouse operations has been highlighted as beneficial for storage location assignments and operational efficiency [74].

Efficient order picking systems are crucial for warehouse operations, as they significantly impact labour costs and customer service levels [67]. The design and application of data analytics, IoT-enabled solutions, and automated route-planning systems in warehouses have been shown to enhance operational efficiency and management effectiveness [75]. Furthermore, the integration of product intelligence and the use of multi-expert systems in warehouse management can aid in addressing operational challenges and improving overall performance [76].

Warehouse layout design, energy-aware models, and green warehouse performance monitoring systems are essential considerations for optimizing warehouse operations and promoting sustainability [77]. The development of automated storage systems, dynamic route-planning systems, and intelligent agent-based frameworks can help warehouses adapt to dynamic demand environments and improve operational control [78]. Additionally, the utilization of radio frequency identification (RFID) technology, mobile voice picking systems, and IoT-enabled solutions can enhance warehouse efficiency and streamline operations [73].

Identifying Space Requirements

Assessing medium-term and long-term storage needs within an organization involves a detailed and strategic approach to ensure that storage capabilities align with business goals and regulatory requirements. This process begins by integrating insights from the enterprise business plan, which outlines growth projections, market expansion strategies, and product diversification plans. Legislative requirements, such as safety regulations and environmental standards, also play a critical role in shaping storage strategies.

A crucial aspect of this assessment is understanding the characteristics of the products being stored. Factors such as product type (e.g., perishable goods, electronics), picking frequencies (how often items are retrieved from storage), value (high-value items requiring secure storage), fragility, weight, handling characteristics, quantity, and holding periods (duration of storage) are evaluated. This comprehensive analysis helps determine the appropriate type and amount of storage needed, whether it's temperature-controlled facilities for perishables or secure warehouses for high-value goods.

Simultaneously, the assessment extends to evaluating the facility itself. Existing infrastructure, including warehouse layout, storage systems (e.g., racks, shelving), and handling equipment (forklifts, automated systems), is scrutinized to determine its capacity to accommodate the stock holding and handling requirements of each inventory item. This step ensures that the facility can effectively manage the diverse storage needs identified during the product assessment phase.

Volume requirements are another critical consideration in this process. Calculating the ongoing stock holding needs involves forecasting demand based on historical data, market trends, and business projections. This helps determine the quantity of goods that must be stored at any given time to meet customer demand and operational requirements without overstocking or understocking.

Once the individual storage needs for different product types and volumes are established, the total space requirement is calculated. This involves aggregating the space needed for each category of goods based on their respective characteristics and volume requirements. The result is a comprehensive space utilization plan that outlines how different areas of the facility will be allocated and utilized to optimize storage efficiency and accessibility.

The space utilization plan not only considers the physical dimensions but also incorporates operational factors such as workflow optimization, aisle widths for efficient material handling, and safety protocols. It serves as a blueprint for organizing the facility's layout to ensure that storage space is maximized without compromising accessibility or operational efficiency.

Calculating warehouse space requirements involves a meticulous assessment of various factors that collectively determine the optimal storage capacity for your company's inventory. One of the primary considerations is pallet size, as pallets serve as the standard unit for storing and transporting goods in warehouses. Understanding the dimensions of your pallets, whether they are standard 48 inches by 40 inches or square, directly influences how much floor and vertical space each unit of inventory occupies on warehouse shelves [79].

Equally crucial is determining the number of pallets your inventory requires. This entails forecasting or estimating the quantity of goods you anticipate storing at any given time. Accurate projections ensure that the warehouse space is neither underutilized, leading to inefficiencies, nor overutilized, risking congestion and accessibility issues.

Stacking height is another critical factor in warehouse space planning. While vertical stacking optimizes space utilization, it must comply with safety regulations, such as those set by the Occupational Safety and Health Administration (OSHA). These guidelines prescribe maximum stacking heights based on pallet size, material characteristics, and weight to prevent hazards such as collapses or instability.

Many warehouses struggle with underutilized capacity, often due to a combination of factors that hinder efficient storage management. Businesses frequently overlook the need to calculate and optimize their space utilization, assuming there isn't enough room without realizing the potential for better space management strategies [80].

One of the primary challenges contributing to inefficient warehouse space utilization is an inadequate layout. A poorly configured warehouse setup can severely limit capacity. For instance, using horizontal racking systems exclusively may consume floor space excessively while creating narrow aisles that restrict movement and accessibility. By neglecting to utilize vertical space effectively, businesses miss out on opportunities to store more inventory without expanding their physical footprint [80].

Seasonal demand fluctuations also pose significant challenges. Failing to anticipate and plan for peaks in demand leads to overstocking issues. When last-minute inventory replenishment orders coincide with already fully stocked warehouses, congestion ensues, exacerbating storage problems and compromising operational efficiency. Without proactive planning and adaptable storage solutions, warehouses struggle to accommodate varying inventory volumes efficiently [80].

Another common issue affecting warehouse capacity is outdated training and protocols. As businesses evolve and expand, they often introduce new storage solutions or modify existing layouts to optimize space. However, inadequate training for warehouse staff on these changes can lead to inefficient use of available space. Workers may not be familiar with new storage locations or handling procedures, resulting in suboptimal storage practices and potential safety hazards. Effective training programs are crucial to ensuring that warehouse personnel can maximize storage capacity while maintaining operational safety and efficiency [80].

Furthermore, the absence of appropriate warehouse technology can significantly hinder space utilization efforts. A lack of inventory visibility, which can be addressed through a robust warehouse management system (WMS), makes it challenging to track and manage inventory effectively. Without real-time data on inventory levels and locations, businesses struggle to make informed decisions about space allocation and utilization. Similarly, inadequate material handling equipment limits the ability to leverage vertical storage space efficiently. Investments in modern warehouse technologies and equipment are essential for optimizing space usage and enhancing overall warehouse productivity [80].

Warehouse space utilization refers to how effectively the warehouse layout and inventory placement maximize available area. Efficient space utilization involves strategic placement of goods based on factors like demand frequency, access requirements, and storage conditions [79]. Factors beyond direct control, such as irregularly shaped inventory or specialized storage needs, can also impact space utilization efficiency.

Moreover, the layout of your warehouse plays a crucial role in determining space requirements. Factors such as aisle width, shelving systems, and the arrangement of storage zones (e.g., bulk storage, picking areas) significantly influence how efficiently space is utilized. A well-designed layout facilitates smooth material flow, minimizes travel distances for picking operations, and enhances overall operational efficiency.

Warehouse space utilization is a critical metric that measures how effectively the available storage area in a warehouse is being used. It's essentially the ratio of the actual storage space being utilized to the total available storage space. A 100% utilization ratio would mean that every square foot or meter of usable warehouse space is occupied by inventory or equipment.

The optimal warehouse space utilization ratio varies depending on several factors specific to the type of inventory and operational requirements of the business. One significant factor is the shape and stackability of the inventory. Products that cannot be neatly stacked or have irregular shapes naturally occupy more space and require wider aisles for manoeuvrability during picking and retrieval. Consequently, warehouses handling such inventory may have a lower utilization ratio, perhaps around 40% to 50%, to ensure efficient movement and accessibility [79].

Another crucial consideration is the presence of expiration dates on products. Goods with limited shelf lives, such as food or cosmetics, require careful management to ensure that older stock is rotated out first (FIFO - first in, first out). This necessitates more space for orderly storage and retrieval, often resulting in a warehouse utilization ratio around 50%. This ratio allows enough room for safe handling and quick access to products nearing expiration.

For businesses managing a diverse range of products with moderate turnover rates but no expiration constraints, a higher utilization ratio of around 60% to 70% may be feasible [79]. This level of utilization accommodates multiple stock-keeping units (SKUs) and facilitates efficient inventory turnover, typically up to six times a year. It strikes a balance between space efficiency and operational flexibility, enabling the warehouse to handle a broader range of products effectively.

In scenarios where the inventory consists of few SKUs, does not expire, and turnover is relatively low, warehouses might aim for an utilization ratio of up to 80%. This higher ratio maximizes storage capacity while still allowing adequate space for operational activities such as picking, packing, and replenishment [79].

It's crucial to note that maintaining a warehouse space utilization ratio of 100% is not advisable. A fully packed warehouse makes it challenging for staff to move around freely, increasing the risk of accidents and slowing down operations. Adequate aisle space, clear pathways, and efficient layout design are essential to ensure smooth workflow and maintain safety standards within the warehouse environment [79].

Calculating warehouse capacity is essential for ensuring efficient storage and operational planning within logistics and supply chain management. Whether using a warehouse space calculator or performing calculations manually, the process involves several key steps to determine the required storage area based on specific inventory and operational needs [79].

Firstly, gather information on the number of pallets that need to be stored in the warehouse. If exact numbers are unavailable, estimates can suffice initially, with adjustments made as more precise data becomes available. Understanding the volume of pallets is crucial as it forms the basis for calculating overall space requirements.

Next, consider the stacking height of pallets. This refers to how many pallets can be safely stacked on top of each other. For instance, if the stacking height is two pallets high, divide the total number of pallets by two. If stacking is not feasible, use a divisor of one.

Calculate the square footage of each pallet to determine the space occupied on the warehouse floor. Standard pallet dimensions often measure 48 inches by 40 inches. Convert these dimensions into square feet by multiplying width by length and then dividing by 144 (since there are 144 square inches in a square foot) [79].

Once the square footage per pallet is established, multiply this figure by the stacking height to ascertain the total square footage required for the stacked pallets. For example, if you have 16 pallets and can stack them two high, multiply eight (stacking height) by the calculated square footage per pallet to get the total square footage needed [79].

After calculating the total square footage needed for the pallets, consider the desired warehouse utilization ratio. This ratio indicates the percentage of available space that will be utilized for storage. For instance, if aiming for 50% utilization, divide the total square footage by 0.5 (which is 50% expressed as a decimal) to determine the actual warehouse space required [79].

It's prudent to plan for future growth and flexibility when determining warehouse capacity. Allocate additional space beyond current needs to accommodate potential increases in inventory or the addition of new product types. Adjust calculations accordingly by increasing the number of pallets or modifying the utilization ratio to ensure adequate space reserves.

Identifying Safety and Security Requirements

Warehouse safety is critically important for maintaining a healthy and productive work environment that prioritizes the well-being of employees and protects valuable assets. Accidents and injuries in warehouses can have far-reaching consequences, including costly downtime, legal liabilities, and reputational damage [81]. Therefore, organizations must not only understand the importance of warehouse safety but also implement robust safety procedures and best practices to mitigate risks effectively.

First and foremost, ensuring safety in a warehouse environment is essential for safeguarding employees. By providing a safe workplace, organizations demonstrate their commitment to the health and security of their workforce. This commitment not only protects employees from physical harm but also fosters a sense of trust and loyalty. When warehouse workers feel safe and valued, they are more likely to be motivated, focused, and engaged in their work, ultimately leading to improved productivity [81].

Moreover, a safe warehouse environment contributes to reduced absenteeism and turnover rates. Employees are less likely to miss work due to injuries or illnesses sustained in unsafe conditions. This continuity in workforce presence enhances operational efficiency and reduces the costs associated with hiring and training new personnel. Lower turnover rates also contribute to greater stability and consistency in warehouse operations.

Financially, investing in warehouse safety can yield significant savings. By preventing accidents and injuries, organizations can potentially lower their insurance premiums and workers' compensation costs. Insurance providers often reward businesses with strong safety records by offering reduced premiums. Furthermore, minimizing workplace injuries reduces the financial burden of medical expenses and compensation claims, contributing to overall cost-effectiveness [81].

Compliance with regulatory requirements is another crucial aspect of warehouse safety. Warehouses are subject to various safety regulations and standards imposed by governmental bodies like OSHA (Occupational Safety and Health Administration) in the United States [81]. Adhering to these regulations not only ensures legal compliance but also protects businesses from fines, penalties, and legal liabilities resulting from non-compliance. Regular audits and assessments help organizations stay updated with evolving safety standards and maintain a safe working environment.

Beyond regulatory compliance, prioritizing warehouse safety enhances the company's reputation. Businesses known for their commitment to safety are viewed as responsible corporate citizens by customers, suppliers, and potential employees. A positive safety culture enhances trust and credibility, strengthening relationships with stakeholders and contributing to long-term business success. Moreover, a strong reputation for safety can attract top talent seeking a secure and supportive work environment, further enhancing the organization's competitive edge in the market [81].

Assessing risks and ensuring safety and security within a warehouse environment is paramount to protecting personnel, inventory, and facilities. This process begins with a comprehensive risk assessment that identifies potential hazards and evaluates their likelihood and potential impact. Risks can vary widely, including physical dangers like slips, trips, and falls, as well as more specific risks such as chemical hazards from stored products or fire hazards from electrical systems.

Once risks are identified, prioritization is key. This involves determining which risks pose the highest threat to safety and security and require immediate attention. Factors considered include the frequency of exposure to the risk, the severity of potential consequences, and existing control measures in place. For example, a warehouse storing flammable materials would prioritize fire hazards and ensure stringent fire prevention measures.

Next, storage handling security procedures are established and documented for each class or type of product. This involves categorizing products based on their characteristics such as flammability, toxicity, or sensitivity to temperature changes. Each category then requires specific handling protocols to minimize risks during storage, handling, and transportation. For instance, hazardous materials might need to be stored in designated areas with adequate ventilation and fire suppression systems.

Fire prevention is a critical aspect of warehouse safety. Identifying and implementing appropriate firefighting systems is essential and must comply with building code regulations and specific storage material requirements. This includes installing fire detection systems such as smoke detectors and fire alarms, as well as fire suppression systems like sprinklers or specialized extinguishing agents tailored to the types of materials stored. Regular inspections and maintenance of these systems ensure they are functional and ready to respond in case of emergencies.

An evacuation plan is another fundamental component of warehouse safety. It should be developed in alignment with the enterprise safety program and consider the layout of the facility, the number of personnel, and the types of hazards present. The plan outlines clear procedures for evacuating personnel safely in various emergency scenarios, such as fires, chemical spills, or structural collapses. It includes designated evacuation routes, assembly points, and responsibilities for personnel involved in managing the evacuation process.

Throughout this process, continuous monitoring and review are essential. Regular safety audits and inspections help identify any new risks or gaps in existing safety measures. Training programs for personnel ensure they are familiar with safety procedures, emergency protocols, and the proper use of safety equipment. By prioritizing safety and security through comprehensive risk assessment, documented procedures, appropriate firefighting systems, and a well-defined evacuation plan, warehouses can minimize risks and create a safer environment for everyone involved.

Several key standards and regulations play a significant role in governing warehouse safety, each focusing on different aspects of workplace hazards and safety management [81].

First and foremost, the Occupational Safety and Health Administration (OSHA) sets forth comprehensive regulations that warehouses in the United States must follow. These regulations cover various aspects such as walking-working surfaces (29 CFR 1910.22), personal protective equipment (29 CFR 1910.132), material handling (29 CFR 1910.176), powered industrial trucks (29 CFR 1910.178), and hazard communication (29 CFR 1910.1200). Compliance with OSHA standards is essential for ensuring the safety of warehouse personnel and avoiding penalties for non-compliance.

In addition to OSHA regulations, the American National Standards Institute (ANSI) and the American Society of Safety Professionals (ASSP) have developed standards specific to fall protection systems. ANSI/ASSP Z359.1 outlines safety requirements for personal fall arrest systems, including harnesses, lanyards, and anchorages [81]. Warehouses where employees work at heights must implement fall protection measures that meet or exceed these standards to prevent fall-related injuries and fatalities.

Fire safety is another critical aspect addressed by standards such as NFPA 13, developed by the National Fire Protection Association (NFPA) [81]. NFPA 13 sets forth guidelines for the installation of fire sprinkler systems in warehouses and other structures. Properly designed and maintained sprinkler systems are crucial for suppressing fires effectively, minimizing property damage, and ensuring the safety of warehouse occupants in case of a fire emergency.

Furthermore, the International Organization for Standardization (ISO) has developed ISO 45001, which provides a framework for occupational health and safety management systems [81]. ISO 45001 helps organizations establish a systematic approach to managing workplace safety hazards, promoting a proactive safety culture, and continuously improving safety performance. Implementing ISO 45001 in warehouses demonstrates a commitment to maintaining high safety standards and protecting employees from workplace hazards.

Overall, adhering to these warehouse safety standards not only helps organizations comply with legal requirements but also enhances workplace safety, reduces the risk of accidents and injuries, and improves overall operational efficiency. By investing in comprehensive safety measures and staying updated with evolving standards, warehouses can create a safer work environment, protect their workforce, and mitigate potential risks associated with non-compliance and workplace incidents.

Warehouses, while essential for storing goods, can indeed be hazardous environments if safety protocols are not rigorously followed. The consequences of neglecting warehouse safety can be severe, ranging from injuries and fatalities to legal liabilities and damage to company reputation. Recent statistics show a concerning trend with fatalities in the warehouse industry increasing by over 100% since 2019, highlighting the urgency for robust safety measures [82].

One of the most significant risks in warehouses involves equipment, particularly forklifts and other Powered Industrial Trucks (PITs). Forklift accidents alone cause around 87 fatalities annually in the United States, underscoring the critical need for thorough training in safe operation and maintenance of these vehicles. Failure to adhere to safety protocols can result in serious injuries or death, making comprehensive training and strict adherence to operational guidelines imperative [82].

Figure 28: Forklift operation in a warehouse setting around loading dock. ELEVATE, via Pexels.

Another hidden but lethal threat in warehouses is carbon monoxide (CO) build-up from mobile equipment such as forklifts and trucks [82]. These vehicles emit CO as exhaust, which, without proper ventilation, can accumulate to dangerous levels, leading to symptoms like impaired vision, headaches, and even fatal poisoning. Training employees to recognize early signs of CO poisoning and implementing effective ventilation systems are crucial preventive measures.

Loading docks also pose significant safety challenges, including risks of forklifts driving off docks and objects falling on employees. Proper training and adherence to safety protocols around loading and unloading activities are essential to mitigate these risks. Ensuring that equipment is properly maintained and that employees are trained to identify and report hazardous conditions can significantly enhance safety at loading docks [82].

Pedestrian safety is another critical concern in warehouses where the interaction between pedestrians and mobile equipment poses a high risk of accidents. Employees must be trained to maintain awareness of their surroundings, make eye contact with equipment operators, and follow designated walkways [82]. Conversely, forklift operators should be trained to yield to pedestrians, reduce speed in congested areas, and avoid risky manoeuvres that could endanger others.

Figure 29: Narrow Walkway Between Metal Shelves. Daniel Andraski, via Pexels.

Conveyor systems, vital for efficient warehouse operations, present their own set of safety hazards. These include pinch points, falling products, and risks associated with maintenance activities. Regular inspections, proper guarding of pinch points, and thorough training in lockout/tagout procedures are essential to prevent accidents related to conveyors. Adequate lighting in conveyor areas and clear signage also contribute to a safer working environment.

Handling hazardous materials in warehouses requires strict adherence to safety protocols to prevent spills, fires, or chemical exposures. Proper storage procedures, including maintaining clear aisles, stacking loads evenly, and using appropriate signage for hazardous materials, are critical. Employees should receive thorough training on handling procedures, emergency response protocols, and the use of personal protective equipment (PPE) [82].

Ergonomic safety is another important aspect of warehouse operations, as repetitive tasks and improper lifting techniques can lead to musculoskeletal injuries over time. Implementing ergonomic principles such as using lifting aids, optimizing workplace design, and providing ergonomic training can reduce the risk of injuries and improve overall worker well-being [82].

Finally, fire hazards remain a constant concern in warehouses due to the storage of flammable materials and the presence of electrical equipment. Installing and maintaining fire detection and suppression systems, training employees in fire safety procedures, and conducting regular fire drills are essential measures to minimize the risk of fires and ensure prompt response in case of emergencies [82].

Effective warehouse safety procedures are crucial for maintaining a secure work environment and minimizing the risk of accidents that could lead to injuries, downtime, and financial losses. A comprehensive approach begins with implementing a robust warehouse safety program that addresses all aspects of operations. This program should include regular hazard identification, risk assessment, and control measures tailored to the specific risks inherent in warehouse environments. Regular review and updates to the safety program ensure it remains relevant and effective as operations evolve, equipment changes, or new regulations are introduced [81].

Central to warehouse safety procedures is the provision of regular safety training and drills for employees. Training should cover safety protocols, equipment operation, hazard recognition, and emergency response procedures. Conducting regular safety drills, including fire drills and emergency evacuation exercises, ensures that employees are prepared to respond effectively in case of emergencies, thereby reducing panic and improving overall safety outcomes during critical situations [81].

Clear communication protocols are vital in maintaining warehouse safety. Establishing channels for reporting hazards, near-misses, and incidents encourages proactive safety awareness among employees. Regular safety briefings, updates on safety procedures, and sharing of lessons learned from incidents contribute to a culture where safety is a top priority and everyone feels responsible for maintaining a safe workplace [81].

Routine safety inspections and audits play a crucial role in identifying potential hazards before they lead to accidents. Inspections should be conducted regularly by knowledgeable personnel who can thoroughly assess all aspects of warehouse operations, including equipment condition, storage practices, housekeeping standards, and adherence to safety protocols. Addressing identified hazards promptly through corrective actions prevents accidents and improves overall safety performance [81].

Personal Protective Equipment (PPE) is another critical component of warehouse safety procedures. Providing appropriate PPE and ensuring employees wear it correctly significantly reduces the risk of injuries from workplace hazards. Common types of PPE used in warehouses include safety footwear, protective eyewear, gloves, hearing protection, hard hats, and high-visibility clothing. Proper training on the selection, use, maintenance, and disposal of PPE is essential to maximize its effectiveness and ensure compliance with safety regulations [81].

Occupational safety in warehouses encompasses broader aspects beyond PPE, including ergonomic considerations, chemical safety, electrical safety, fall protection, and vehicle/equipment safety. Ergonomic solutions help prevent musculoskeletal disorders by promoting proper work postures, using adjustable workstations, and implementing safe lifting techniques. Chemical safety protocols ensure the safe handling, storage, and disposal of hazardous materials, accompanied by thorough employee training and provision of necessary PPE.

Electrical safety measures include adherence to codes and standards for electrical installations, training on safe practices like lockout/tagout procedures, and regular inspections to prevent electrical hazards. Fall protection systems, such as guardrails and personal fall arrest systems, protect employees working at heights, while vehicle and equipment safety protocols involve training on safe operation, traffic management plans, and maintenance schedules to mitigate the risk of accidents [81].

Fire safety in warehouses is a paramount concern due to the potential for devastating consequences such as property damage, injuries, and loss of life. Effective fire safety measures encompass several critical elements that collectively aim to prevent fires, detect them early, and facilitate safe evacuation procedures.

Firstly, fire detection and suppression systems are essential components of warehouse fire safety. Installing fire alarms and smoke detectors throughout the facility ensures early detection of fires, enabling swift response actions to mitigate their spread. Additionally, sprinkler systems play a crucial role in controlling and extinguishing fires before they escalate, thereby minimizing damage to inventory and infrastructure [81].

Accessible fire extinguishers strategically placed throughout the warehouse are indispensable tools for immediate firefighting efforts. It's vital that employees are trained regularly on how to properly use fire extinguishers, including the types of fires they are effective against and safe firefighting techniques. This training not only enhances preparedness but also empowers employees to respond effectively in emergency situations, potentially preventing small fires from becoming major incidents.

Emergency exits and evacuation routes must be meticulously planned and maintained to ensure quick and safe evacuation of personnel in the event of a fire. These exits should be clearly marked, unobstructed, and designed to accommodate the maximum occupancy of the warehouse during an evacuation. Regular drills and simulations of emergency evacuation procedures are critical to familiarize employees with escape routes and to test the efficiency of evacuation plans under realistic conditions [81].

Fire safety training is integral to preparing warehouse staff to respond calmly and effectively during a fire emergency. Training programs should cover not only firefighting procedures but also evacuation protocols, the importance of early detection, and the roles and responsibilities of employees during a fire incident. By instilling a culture of fire safety awareness among employees, warehouses can significantly enhance their overall preparedness and resilience against fire hazards.

Proper storage and handling of flammable and combustible materials are fundamental aspects of fire prevention in warehouses. These materials should be stored in designated areas that are segregated from ignition sources such as electrical equipment or heating systems. Following strict handling procedures, including the use of appropriate containers and equipment further reduces the risk of accidental ignition and minimizes the potential for fire outbreaks [81].

A robust warehouse safety policy is fundamental to creating a workplace environment where employees can perform their duties safely and effectively. This policy serves as a foundational document that outlines the organization's commitment to prioritizing safety, defines responsibilities for all personnel, and establishes procedures to prevent accidents and mitigate risks [81].

Central to any warehouse safety policy is management's unequivocal commitment to safety. This commitment should be articulated clearly within the policy, emphasizing that safety is a core value of the organization. Management should pledge to provide the necessary resources, support, and leadership to ensure a safe working environment. This includes allocating budget for safety initiatives, appointing designated safety personnel, and fostering a culture where safety is prioritized at all levels of the organization.

Employee responsibilities and accountability form another critical component of the safety policy. It should clearly outline the specific safety obligations of every employee, from warehouse workers to supervisors and managers. Employees are expected to adhere strictly to safety procedures, use required personal protective equipment (PPE), and promptly report any hazards or incidents they encounter. Accountability measures should be in place to evaluate and reinforce compliance with safety protocols, ensuring that employees understand the consequences of non-compliance through regular evaluations and disciplinary actions as necessary.

Hazard identification, assessment, and control procedures are integral to preventing accidents and injuries in warehouses. The safety policy should detail systematic methods for identifying potential hazards, assessing their risks, and implementing appropriate control measures. This involves conducting regular risk assessments of warehouse operations, equipment, and storage practices to proactively identify hazards such as trip hazards, machinery risks, or chemical exposures. Control measures may include engineering controls (e.g., barriers, ventilation systems), administrative controls (e.g., procedures, signage), and personal protective equipment (PPE) requirements tailored to specific hazards.

Training and competency development are pivotal elements of warehouse safety policies. The policy should stipulate requirements for initial safety training for new hires, ongoing refresher courses, and specialized training for tasks involving specialized equipment or hazardous materials. Training programs should equip employees with the knowledge and skills necessary to perform their duties safely, emphasizing proper handling of equipment, emergency procedures, and safe work practices. Regular competency assessments ensure that employees maintain proficiency and adapt to changes in procedures or equipment.

Incident reporting and investigation protocols are essential for learning from safety incidents and preventing future occurrences. The safety policy should establish clear procedures for reporting incidents, near-misses, and injuries promptly. Investigations should be conducted promptly and thoroughly to determine the root causes of incidents, whether they involve equipment failures, procedural lapses, or human errors. Corrective actions should be identified and implemented to address underlying issues and prevent recurrence, demonstrating a commitment to continuous improvement in safety performance [81].

Emergency preparedness and response planning are critical components of a comprehensive warehouse safety policy. This includes developing and maintaining an emergency response plan tailored to warehouse-specific hazards, such as fires, chemical spills, or structural failures. The policy should outline procedures for evacuations, medical emergencies, and other critical incidents, ensuring that all employees are trained in emergency procedures and participate in regular drills to test response readiness. By fostering a proactive approach to emergency preparedness, warehouses can mitigate risks and protect the safety of their workforce effectively.

Warehouse safety inspections are a critical component of maintaining a safe and compliant work environment in warehouses. These inspections are designed to systematically identify potential hazards, assess safety practices, and ensure that regulations are adhered to. Conducting regular safety inspections is essential to proactively mitigate risks, prevent accidents, and uphold the well-being of warehouse personnel [81].

Firstly, the frequency of safety inspections should be tailored to the specific needs and operations of the warehouse. Typically, inspections are conducted at regular intervals, such as monthly, quarterly, or semi-annually, depending on factors like the size of the warehouse, the complexity of operations, and the level of risk associated with the activities conducted. More frequent inspections may be necessary in high-risk areas or during periods of increased activity.

During inspections, the scope should encompass all facets of warehouse operations. This includes examining the storage and handling of materials, assessing equipment maintenance and operational safety, evaluating housekeeping standards, and observing employee work practices. Comprehensive inspections ensure that potential hazards, from improperly stored materials to unsafe operating practices, are identified promptly.

Standardized inspection checklists are invaluable tools for ensuring consistency and thoroughness during inspections. These checklists guide inspectors through a systematic evaluation of various safety aspects within the warehouse. They help inspectors document findings objectively and identify deviations from safety standards or procedures. Checklists may cover areas such as fire safety, electrical hazards, ergonomics, personal protective equipment (PPE) usage, and emergency preparedness.

Qualified personnel should conduct safety inspections to ensure effectiveness and reliability of findings. This may include designated safety managers, trained safety officers within the organization, or external safety consultants who bring specialized expertise and objectivity to the inspection process. Personnel conducting inspections should possess adequate knowledge of warehouse operations, safety regulations, and hazard identification techniques.

Following up on inspection findings is crucial to maintaining safety standards. Identified hazards and deficiencies must be addressed promptly through corrective actions. These actions may involve implementing immediate corrective measures to mitigate imminent risks, scheduling repairs or upgrades to equipment or facilities, revising safety procedures, or providing additional training to employees. Documenting inspection findings and tracking the progress of corrective actions ensure accountability and continuous improvement in safety performance.

Ultimately, the goal of warehouse safety inspections is to proactively manage risks, enhance safety awareness among employees, and cultivate a culture of safety within the organization. By systematically identifying and addressing potential hazards, warehouse operators can minimize the likelihood of accidents, injuries, and regulatory violations. Regular safety inspections not only protect the well-being of employees but also contribute to operational efficiency, regulatory compliance, and overall organizational resilience in the face of potential safety challenges.

Monitoring warehouse safety metrics is crucial for organizations aiming to maintain a safe work environment and improve safety outcomes systematically. These metrics provide quantitative insights into various aspects of safety performance, allowing warehouse operators to track trends, identify areas for improvement, and make informed decisions based on data.

One of the fundamental metrics used in warehouse safety monitoring is the Total Recordable Incident Rate (TRIR). This metric calculates the number of recordable incidents, including injuries and illnesses, per 100 full-time employees over a specific period. TRIR serves as a key indicator of overall safety performance, reflecting the frequency and severity of incidents within the warehouse environment.

Similarly, the Lost Time Incident Rate (LTIR) measures the number of incidents that result in lost work time per 100 full-time employees over a defined timeframe. LTIR provides insight into the impact of workplace incidents on productivity and employee well-being, highlighting areas where safety improvements are necessary to reduce downtime and associated costs.

Near-miss reporting rate is another critical metric that warehouses monitor. Near-misses are incidents or situations that have the potential to cause harm but did not result in injury or damage. By encouraging employees to report near-misses and tracking these incidents, warehouses can identify underlying hazards and proactively implement preventive measures before accidents occur.

Safety inspection findings also play a significant role in safety monitoring efforts. This metric involves tracking the number and types of hazards identified during routine safety inspections. It reflects the effectiveness of hazard identification processes and the diligence of safety protocols in place. Monitoring safety inspection findings allows warehouses to prioritize corrective actions and ensure continuous improvement in safety standards.

Furthermore, the safety training completion rate is essential for assessing the effectiveness of safety training programs within the warehouse. This metric measures the percentage of employees who have completed required safety training courses. A high completion rate indicates a robust training culture and better-prepared workforce, reducing the likelihood of incidents caused by inadequate knowledge or skills.

By monitoring these safety metrics and others specific to their operations, warehouse operators can gain actionable insights into their safety performance. These metrics enable them to benchmark against industry standards, set realistic safety goals, and allocate resources effectively to address identified risks. Continuous monitoring and analysis of safety metrics facilitate a proactive approach to safety management, fostering a culture of safety where prevention and improvement are prioritized. Ultimately, leveraging safety metrics empowers warehouses to reduce the risk of accidents and injuries, enhance operational efficiency, and cultivate a safer and more productive work environment for all employees.

Proper first aid procedures are critical in warehouse environments where the risk of injuries is inherent despite safety measures in place. Ensuring that every employee undergoes first aid training is essential as it equips them with the skills needed to respond effectively in emergencies, potentially saving lives [83].

According to Occupational Safety and Health Administration (OSHA) guidelines, a well-equipped first-aid kit is a fundamental requirement in warehouses. It should include items such as adhesive bandages, medical gloves, antibiotic ointment, bandages of various sizes, antiseptic wipes, scissors, burn dressings, splints, cold packs, sterile pads, eye wash, a tourniquet, a first aid guide, triangular bandages, and hand sanitizer. Having these supplies readily available ensures prompt and effective response to injuries [83].

Basic first-aid procedures recommended by organizations like the American Heart Association and American Red Cross cover a range of scenarios that may occur in warehouses. For instance, in cases of cardiac arrest, immediate initiation of chest compressions and use of an automated external defibrillator (AED) are crucial steps that can significantly improve outcomes if performed promptly [83].

In the event of crush injuries, it's vital to control bleeding by applying direct pressure and elevating the affected area to minimize swelling. For fractures, stabilizing the injury with a splint and padding, along with providing pain relief and avoiding unnecessary movement of the injured limb, are key steps before medical help arrives [83].

Managing bleeding involves applying pressure to the wound with sterile gauze or cloth and maintaining pressure until bleeding stops. Burns, another common warehouse injury, require immediate cooling under running water and covering with a sterile bandage to prevent infection [83].

Warehouse operators must emphasize the importance of these first aid procedures through regular training sessions and ensuring that all employees are familiar with emergency protocols. This proactive approach not only prepares employees to respond effectively to injuries but also instils confidence and a sense of security among the workforce.

Warehouse safety communication is crucial for ensuring that employees understand and adhere to safety protocols, thereby fostering a secure work environment. Effective communication strategies in warehouses encompass various methods and practices designed to inform, engage, and empower employees in safety awareness and compliance.

One of the primary strategies is conducting regular safety meetings. These meetings provide a platform to discuss pertinent safety topics, review safety procedures, and address any emerging safety concerns. By involving employees in safety discussions, warehouse management can ensure that safety messages are communicated effectively and that employees feel valued and informed about their role in maintaining a safe workplace [81].

Another critical aspect of safety communication is the use of safety signage. Clear and visible signage plays a pivotal role in alerting employees to potential hazards, indicating emergency exits, and delineating safe pedestrian pathways. Properly placed signage ensures that safety information is readily accessible and reinforces safe behaviours throughout the warehouse environment.

Safety bulletin boards also serve as a centralized communication hub for safety-related information. These boards typically display safety policies, procedures, training schedules, and safety performance metrics. By keeping important safety information visible and accessible, warehouse operators facilitate ongoing education and awareness among employees, promoting a culture of safety.

An open-door policy is essential for encouraging transparent communication between employees and management regarding safety matters. This policy allows employees to voice safety concerns, provide feedback on safety initiatives, and report hazards or incidents promptly. Establishing multiple communication channels, such as suggestion boxes or anonymous reporting systems, further facilitates employee engagement in safety communication efforts.

Moreover, soliciting safety feedback from employees is integral to continuous improvement in safety practices. Employees on the front lines often possess valuable insights into potential hazards or inefficiencies that may go unnoticed during formal inspections. By actively involving employees in safety initiatives and decision-making processes, warehouse operators demonstrate a commitment to fostering a collaborative and safety-conscious workplace culture.

In parallel to these communication strategies, leveraging modern warehouse safety technologies can significantly enhance safety efforts. Technologies such as collision avoidance systems on forklifts, automated guided vehicles (AGVs), and fall protection systems provide tangible safeguards against common workplace hazards. These technologies mitigate risks associated with vehicle accidents, manual handling injuries, and falls from heights, thereby bolstering overall safety performance [81].

Safety monitoring software is another valuable tool for warehouse operators, enabling them to track safety metrics, manage safety inspections and audits, and streamline incident reporting and investigation processes. By leveraging data-driven insights from safety software, warehouses can identify trends, proactively address safety issues, and continuously improve safety protocols [81].

Wearable technology, such as smart helmets or vests equipped with sensors, offers real-time monitoring of environmental conditions and worker behaviour. These devices can alert employees to potential hazards, track their location within the warehouse, and provide immediate feedback on safety compliance, enhancing situational awareness and response capabilities [81].

Developing and Implementing a Documentation System

Developing and implementing a robust system for recording and tracing stock location, receival, throughput, and dispatch in a warehouse environment is crucial for ensuring operational efficiency and meeting various business requirements. This system serves multiple purposes, including facilitating accurate reporting, maintaining quality assurance standards, and fulfilling financial obligations.

Firstly, the system should be designed to accurately record the location of every item within the warehouse. This involves assigning unique identifiers to each stock item and utilizing technology such as barcode scanning or RFID (Radio Frequency Identification) to track their movement from receival through to dispatch. By maintaining a real-time inventory database, warehouse managers can quickly locate specific items, optimize storage space, and prevent stockouts or overstock situations.

Tracking throughput involves monitoring the flow of goods through the warehouse, from the moment they are received from suppliers to when they are shipped out to customers. This not only ensures timely order fulfillment but also helps in identifying bottlenecks or inefficiencies in the warehouse operations. By analysing throughput data, warehouse managers can streamline workflows, adjust staffing levels, and improve overall productivity.

For dispatch operations, the system should integrate with shipping carriers to generate accurate shipping labels, track shipments in transit, and provide delivery confirmations. This capability is essential for meeting customer expectations regarding delivery times and for ensuring compliance with service level agreements (SLAs).

Moreover, implementing such a system supports quality assurance efforts by enabling regular audits and inspections of inventory accuracy and condition. It allows for the identification of discrepancies or damaged goods, facilitating prompt corrective actions and minimizing potential losses.

From a financial perspective, the recorded data on stock movement and throughput provides valuable insights for cost management and budgeting. It helps in forecasting inventory needs, optimizing inventory levels, and calculating accurate cost-of-goods-sold (COGS) figures. This information is crucial for financial reporting purposes, aiding in decision-making related to pricing strategies, inventory investments, and resource allocation.

In a similar vein, developing and implementing a system for recording communication with carriers, customers, and employees is essential for assessing operational effectiveness and driving continuous improvement. This system should capture and store all relevant communications, including emails, phone calls, and notes, in a centralized repository.

Effective communication tracking helps in evaluating the efficiency of interactions with external parties, such as carriers and customers. For instance, it allows managers to monitor response times to customer inquiries, track delivery performance, and identify areas for service enhancement. By analysing communication data, warehouses can improve customer satisfaction levels and strengthen relationships with business partners.

Internally, tracking employee communications provides insights into team collaboration, customer service interactions, and adherence to operational procedures. It enables managers to identify training needs, recognize exemplary performance, and address any communication gaps or issues promptly.

Furthermore, the system should facilitate the analysis of communication patterns and trends over time. This data-driven approach helps in identifying recurring challenges or opportunities for process improvement. For example, recognizing frequent customer inquiries about shipment statuses may prompt warehouses to enhance tracking capabilities or provide proactive shipment notifications.

Ultimately, both systems—stock recording and tracing, and communication recording—are integral to the efficient and effective management of warehouse operations. They support strategic decision-making, enable compliance with regulatory requirements, and contribute to overall business success by enhancing operational transparency, customer satisfaction, and financial performance. By continually refining these systems based on data insights and feedback, warehouses can adapt to evolving market demands and maintain a competitive edge in the logistics industry.

Designing Storage Zones

Warehouse zoning is a fundamental strategy in warehouse management that involves dividing the warehouse space into distinct functional areas, each designated for specific tasks such as receiving, storage, picking, packing, and shipping. The primary goal of warehouse zoning is to optimize operational efficiency by organizing workflows and minimizing unnecessary movement and downtime. By clearly defining and allocating areas for each task, warehouse operators can streamline operations, enhance productivity, and improve overall operational effectiveness [84].

One of the key benefits of warehouse zoning is its ability to facilitate efficient movement within the facility. By assigning specific areas for different functions, such as receiving areas for unloading goods, storage areas for housing inventory, and picking areas for retrieving items, employees can navigate the warehouse with greater ease and efficiency. This structured approach reduces the time spent searching for items and moving between tasks, thereby increasing the throughput of goods and orders [84].

Moreover, proper warehouse zoning significantly contributes to effective inventory management. Each zone is optimized to handle specific types of activities and goods, ensuring that items are stored, picked, and processed in accordance with their unique requirements. This systematic organization minimizes the risk of errors such as misplaced items or inventory discrepancies, which can lead to delays in order fulfillment and dissatisfaction among customers. By maintaining accurate inventory records and improving inventory visibility, warehouse zoning supports better decision-making processes and enables businesses to respond more quickly to customer demands and market fluctuations [84]

From a customer perspective, efficient warehouse zoning translates into improved service levels and enhanced satisfaction. Orders can be processed and fulfilled more promptly and accurately, reducing lead times and ensuring timely delivery of goods. This reliability contributes to customer loyalty and retention, which are crucial for sustaining long-term business success and profitability [84].

Furthermore, warehouse zoning plays a vital role in resource optimization and cost management. By strategically planning the layout and allocation of space, businesses can maximize the utilization of available storage capacity and minimize wastage of resources such as time, labour, and energy. This efficiency not only reduces operational costs but also enhances profitability by increasing throughput and minimizing operational inefficiencies [84].

Accurately assessing space requirements and equipment operation is a foundational step in planning warehouse zones effectively. This process involves a thorough evaluation of both current operational needs and future growth projections.

Initially, warehouse managers must gather detailed information on the types and volumes of goods to be stored and processed. This includes considering the dimensions, weight, and characteristics of the inventory, as well as factors like turnover rates and seasonal fluctuations in demand. By analysing historical data and forecasting future trends, managers can determine the spatial requirements for different types of storage, such as bulk storage, shelving systems, or specialized racks for fragile items.

Simultaneously, assessing equipment operation entails evaluating the types and quantities of machinery and tools needed to handle the inventory efficiently. This may include forklifts, pallet jacks, conveyor systems, and automated handling equipment. Understanding how these machines function and interact with storage configurations is crucial for optimizing workflow and minimizing operational bottlenecks.

Once space and equipment needs are identified, the next step is assessing the facility itself to maximize space utilization. This involves evaluating the layout, dimensions, and structural features of the warehouse. Managers should consider factors such as ceiling height, column placement, floor load capacity, and access points (such as doors and docks). This assessment helps determine where different storage areas, bays, workstations, and other operational zones should be positioned within the warehouse.

The positioning of storage areas, bays, and workstations is guided by the data gathered during the planning process. Strategic placement is essential for optimizing workflow efficiency and minimizing unnecessary movement of goods and personnel. For instance, high-demand items may be placed closer to shipping areas to expedite order fulfillment, while bulk storage areas can be located further away to accommodate larger quantities without impeding daily operations.

Moreover, planning for maintenance and cleaning is a critical aspect often overlooked during warehouse design and layout. Adequate provision must be made for routine maintenance of equipment and infrastructure to ensure operational reliability and safety. This includes allocating space for maintenance workshops, storage of spare parts, and easy access to utilities such as electrical outlets and water supply for cleaning purposes.

Similarly, incorporating cleaning protocols into the warehouse layout is essential for maintaining a hygienic and safe working environment. Designated cleaning stations, storage for cleaning supplies, and clear pathways for cleaning equipment ensure that cleanliness standards are consistently met. Implementing these provisions not only enhances workplace safety but also contributes to compliance with regulatory requirements and industry standards.

A well-designed warehouse operates like a well-oiled machine, where each zone serves a distinct purpose crucial to overall efficiency and productivity. Warehouse zoning, structured around functionality and purpose, is pivotal in organizing operations seamlessly. Among the key zones—Receiving, Storage, Picking, Packing, and Shipping—each plays a critical role tailored to specific requirements and objectives [84].

Starting with the Receiving Area, it serves as the entry point where incoming goods are received from suppliers or production facilities. Here, meticulous processes ensure accuracy and quality control. Items are carefully unloaded, cross-checked against purchase orders, and inspected for any damages or defects. This initial scrutiny is vital in preventing inventory discrepancies and delays downstream.

Efficient functioning of the Receiving Area involves several key functions: unloading shipments, verifying contents, assessing quality, and updating inventory records. These tasks demand precision and attention to detail to maintain accurate stock levels and ensure that only high-quality goods proceed to the next stages of storage or processing.

Optimizing the Receiving Area involves strategic approaches such as designating specific docks for different types of shipments to streamline unloading processes and reduce congestion. Implementing technologies like barcode scanners or RFID enhances efficiency by automating data capture and minimizing errors. Techniques like cross-docking expedite the flow of goods directly from inbound to outbound shipments, reducing handling and storage costs.

Moving to the Storage Area, its purpose is to house items after they are received until they are needed for further processing or shipment. This zone requires systematic organization to maximize space utilization and ensure efficient retrieval. Storage solutions such as selective pallet racks or automated storage systems optimize vertical space, while inventory labelling and tracking systems maintain accuracy.

In the Picking Area, items are retrieved from storage based on order requirements. This zone is crucial for order fulfillment, focusing on accurate and timely item selection, packing, and inventory updates. Technologies such as warehouse management systems (WMS) and order-picking technologies enhance picking efficiency by providing real-time data and optimizing workflow routes.

The Packing Area ensures that picked items are securely packed and prepared for shipment. Here, attention to detail is key in ensuring that orders are correctly packed, labelled, and protected for transit. Quality control checks in this zone verify order accuracy and packaging integrity before items move to the final zone—Shipping.

Lastly, the Shipping Area serves as the gateway where prepared orders are dispatched to customers. It integrates staging zones, loading docks, labelling stations, and quality control points to streamline the shipping process. Efficient organization here facilitates timely deliveries, enhances customer satisfaction, and ensures operational success [84].

In addition to the core operational zones like receiving, storage, picking, packing, and shipping, warehouses often include several other critical areas that play essential roles in ensuring smooth operations and maintaining high standards of efficiency and safety. These areas are strategically designed and allocated within the warehouse facility to support various ancillary functions necessary for comprehensive logistics management [85].

One of the primary ancillary areas in a warehouse is the office and service spaces. This section typically houses administrative functions critical to warehouse operations, such as inventory management, order processing, accounting, customer service, and carrier management. Equipped with computer systems, communication tools, and administrative resources, this area serves as the nerve centre for coordinating logistics activities, handling paperwork, and ensuring smooth communication between different departments and external stakeholders [85].

Adjacent to the office area, warehouse facilities often include amenities zones that cater to the needs of employees. These amenities may include changing rooms, restrooms, a cafeteria, and meeting rooms. Providing comfortable and functional amenities is essential for maintaining employee well-being, promoting productivity, and fostering a positive work environment within the warehouse [85].

Another vital area within warehouse facilities is the maintenance area. This space is dedicated to the maintenance and repair of machinery, equipment, and warehouse infrastructure. It may include a workshop equipped with tools and diagnostic equipment, storage for spare parts, and facilities for charging batteries used in material handling equipment. Regular maintenance activities conducted in this area help ensure the operational efficiency of machinery and prevent costly breakdowns that could disrupt warehouse operations [85].

Handling returns efficiently is another crucial function in many warehouses, facilitated by a designated returns zone. In this area, warehouse personnel receive, inspect, and process merchandise that customers have returned. Quality control procedures are implemented to assess the condition of returned items and determine whether they can be reintegrated into inventory for resale or if they need to be discarded or sent for further processing.

For warehouses involved in repackaging operations, there is a specific repackaging area where products are handled to rework them into different containers or smaller units. This area is essential for meeting specific customer requirements, optimizing storage and distribution processes, or preparing goods for retail sale in smaller, consumer-friendly packaging formats. Efficient operations in the repackaging area contribute to reducing waste and enhancing overall supply chain flexibility.

In warehouses dealing with sensitive products such as food and pharmaceuticals, a quarantine area is often designated. This space is specially designed to isolate and quarantine goods that require special handling due to quality control issues, regulatory compliance, or contamination concerns. The quarantine area is equipped with controls and procedures to prevent cross-contamination and ensure that quarantined products do not come into contact with other inventory, maintaining product integrity and regulatory compliance standards [85].

Overall, these ancillary areas in warehouses play critical roles beyond the core operational zones, supporting administrative functions, maintenance activities, returns management, repackaging operations, and specialized handling requirements. By strategically designing and allocating these areas within the warehouse facility, logistics operators can enhance operational efficiency, maintain regulatory compliance, and meet customer expectations for timely and accurate order fulfillment. Each area contributes to the overall functionality and success of the warehouse, ensuring that it operates as a well-coordinated hub for logistics and distribution activities [85].

Evaluating Facility Utilisation

Maintaining an efficient and optimized warehouse operation requires a continual system of review and assessment across various critical areas. One key aspect is ensuring that storage areas and systems are functioning at their optimum levels. This involves regular checks and evaluations to identify any inefficiencies, bottlenecks, or areas where improvements can be made. Warehouse operators typically conduct routine inspections and performance reviews to assess factors such as storage capacity utilization, inventory turnover rates, and the effectiveness of shelving and racking systems in maximizing space.

Similarly, the assessment of receiving and dispatching systems is crucial to ensuring smooth and efficient warehouse operations. These systems are evaluated to determine their capability in handling incoming shipments promptly and accurately, as well as expediting the outbound shipping process. Factors such as dock utilization, turnaround times, and accuracy in order fulfillment are scrutinized to identify opportunities for streamlining processes and reducing cycle times.

Storage and handling systems also undergo assessment to ensure they provide ease of access and comply with ergonomic principles. This involves evaluating the layout of storage areas, the efficiency of material handling equipment such as forklifts and conveyors, and the ergonomic design of workstations. Ensuring ergonomic compliance helps mitigate risks of injuries and strains among warehouse personnel while enhancing overall operational efficiency by facilitating quicker and safer movement of goods.

Another critical aspect of warehouse management is assessing the product handling and storage processes to minimize product damage, contamination, and stock losses. This assessment involves examining handling procedures, storage conditions (such as temperature and humidity controls for perishable goods), and the implementation of quality control measures. By identifying potential areas of product damage or contamination risks, warehouse operators can implement corrective actions to improve handling practices and enhance product integrity throughout the storage and distribution cycle.

Maintaining flexibility in facility layout to meet changing storage and handling requirements is essential for adapting to evolving business needs and market demands. Warehouse layouts should be designed with scalability and adaptability in mind, allowing for easy reconfiguration of storage areas, expansion of capacity, or integration of new technologies as required. This flexibility ensures that the warehouse can efficiently accommodate fluctuations in inventory volumes, seasonal demand changes, or shifts in product lines without disruptions to operations.

Establishing appropriate reporting systems is crucial for capturing and maintaining data that can inform the design of improved facilities and systems. Modern warehouses rely on data-driven insights to optimize operational performance and strategic decision-making. Reporting systems should capture key performance indicators (KPIs) such as inventory turnover rates, order fulfillment accuracy, labour productivity, and equipment uptime. Regular analysis of these metrics helps identify trends, pinpoint areas for improvement, and guide investments in new technologies or process enhancements to drive continuous improvement initiatives.

Warehouse space utilization is a critical metric that directly impacts the efficiency, productivity, and profitability of warehouse operations. It quantifies how effectively a warehouse is using its available storage space relative to its total capacity. This metric can be expressed as a percentage or decimal, providing a clear indicator of whether the warehouse is maximizing its storage potential or underutilizing valuable space.

High warehouse space utilization, such as 75% or 0.75 in the example of a 10,000 square feet warehouse using 7,500 square feet, signifies efficient use of storage capacity. Maximizing space utilization minimizes wasted storage areas, optimizing the use of every square foot available. This efficiency not only reduces overhead costs like rent, utilities, and maintenance per stored unit but also enhances inventory management. With more storage capacity effectively utilized, warehouses can maintain higher stock levels, reduce the risk of stockouts, and improve overall inventory visibility and control.

Conversely, low warehouse space utilization indicates underutilization of storage capacity, potentially leading to wasted space and increased operational costs. When significant portions of a warehouse remain unused or underused, businesses incur unnecessary expenses for space that could otherwise be utilized to store additional inventory or accommodate operational expansions. Poor space utilization can also hinder effective inventory management by complicating stock tracking, increasing the likelihood of overstocking or understocking, and reducing overall operational efficiency.

Calculating warehouse space utilization involves determining the ratio of occupied storage space to total storage space. Various methods can be employed depending on the warehouse's layout and storage systems, including the cube method (measuring volume in cubic feet), floor method (measuring area in square feet), or slot method (counting storage slots or locations). Each method provides insights into how efficiently the warehouse is using its available storage space.

To improve warehouse space utilization, businesses can implement several strategies. Optimizing warehouse layout through the use of efficient storage systems like racking, shelving, or mezzanines can maximize vertical and horizontal space utilization. Adjusting aisle widths and organizing inventory based on size, shape, weight, or frequency of use can further enhance space efficiency and picking operations. Adopting lean inventory management practices such as JIT (Just-in-Time) inventory and cycle counting helps reduce excess inventory and frees up storage space for more productive uses.

Regular monitoring of warehouse space utilization is essential to ensure ongoing efficiency. Warehouse Management Systems (WMS) provide real-time data on occupancy rates, fill rates, and cube utilization, enabling timely adjustments to space allocation and layout. Key Performance Indicators (KPIs) such as storage cost per unit, inventory turnover ratio, and order fulfillment rate serve as benchmarks to evaluate performance against set targets and industry standards. Benchmarking against other warehouses in the same sector can provide valuable insights and best practices for further optimizing space utilization and operational efficiency.

Calculating and optimizing warehouse space utilization is crucial for maximizing efficiency and minimizing operational costs. The process involves several key steps that help warehouse managers accurately assess their storage capacity and identify areas for improvement [86].

Firstly, determining the total size of the warehouse involves more than just measuring the floor area. It requires accounting for all usable storage space while excluding areas like offices, restrooms, and other non-storage zones. This total square footage is then multiplied by the warehouse's clear height, which is the vertical distance from the floor to the lowest overhead obstruction. This calculation yields the warehouse's storage capacity in cubic feet, a vital metric that influences storage stacking, forklift manoeuvrability, and overall safety within the facility [86].

Next, calculating the inventory cube size involves assessing the cubic volume occupied by racks and shelving where inventory is stored. This step considers the footprint of each storage area, multiplying the length, width, and height of racks to determine the total volume of inventory storage. This metric, known as the inventory cube size, provides insights into how effectively space within the racks is utilized for storing goods [86].

Once both the warehouse storage capacity and inventory cube size are established, it's essential to calculate the storage cube size. This figure represents the actual storage capacity within the warehouse racks and shelves. Typically, the storage cube size should ideally range between 22% to 27% of the warehouse's total storage capacity. This range allows sufficient space for workers to move efficiently during loading, unloading, and picking operations. If the storage cube size exceeds 27%, it may indicate cramped conditions that hinder operational efficiency and increase labour costs. Conversely, a cube size below 22% suggests inefficient rack placement and underutilization of warehouse space [86].

Evaluating warehouse utilization space involves comparing the inventory cube size to the storage cube size. This step helps determine how effectively the available storage space is utilized. It's crucial to factor in operational needs such as aisle width, rack orientation, and clear heights to ensure optimal space utilization without compromising safety or efficiency. Adjustments may include reconfiguring aisle layouts, optimizing rack sizes and orientations, or even reconsidering the warehouse's clear height in specific areas to enhance storage efficiency.

Continuous evaluation and adjustment are essential for maintaining optimal warehouse space utilization. By regularly monitoring and analysing space utilization metrics, warehouse managers can identify opportunities for improvement. Implementing efficient storage and retrieval systems, adopting lean inventory management practices, and optimizing warehouse layout and organization contribute to maximizing space utilization and improving overall warehouse performance [86].

Optimizing warehouse space utilization involves a systematic approach that considers the physical dimensions of the warehouse, the efficiency of storage systems, and operational requirements. By understanding and managing these factors, warehouse operators can enhance productivity, reduce costs, and ensure that their facilities operate at peak efficiency levels [85].

Chapter 10

Implementing and Monitoring Transport Logistics

Mobilising resources, coordinating multi-modal transport activities, monitoring consignments, and implementing a contingency management strategy are essential components of effective logistics and transport management. This includes:

- **Mobilising Resources:** Mobilising resources in logistics involves gathering and deploying the necessary assets and personnel to execute transportation operations efficiently. This includes:

    - **Human Resources:** Ensuring that skilled personnel, such as drivers, warehouse staff, and logistics coordinators, are available and properly trained.

    - **Transportation Assets:** Mobilising vehicles, trailers, containers, and other equipment required for transporting goods.

    - **Financial Resources:** Allocating funds for fuel, maintenance, insurance, and other operational expenses.

    Effective mobilization ensures that resources are deployed in a timely manner to meet transportation demands and operational schedules.

- **Coordinating Multi-Modal Transport Activities:** Coordinating multi-modal transport involves managing the seamless movement of goods across different modes of transportation, such as road, rail, sea, and air. This includes:

- **Route Planning:** Determining the optimal combination of transport modes and routes to minimize costs and delivery times.

- **Intermodal Coordination:** Ensuring smooth transitions between different modes of transport, such as from truck to train or ship to truck, without delays or disruptions.

- **Documentation and Compliance:** Managing the paperwork and regulatory requirements associated with each mode of transport, including customs clearance for international shipments.

Effective coordination ensures that goods are transported efficiently across various transportation networks, optimizing supply chain performance.

- **Monitoring Consignments:** Monitoring consignments involves tracking and overseeing the movement of goods throughout the transportation process. This includes:

  - **Real-Time Tracking:** Using technology such as GPS systems and RFID tags to monitor the location and status of shipments.

  - **Condition Monitoring:** Checking the condition of goods to ensure they are handled and transported according to specifications, especially for sensitive or perishable items.

  - **Performance Monitoring:** Evaluating key performance indicators (KPIs) such as on-time delivery rates, transit times, and inventory levels to assess logistics efficiency.

Continuous monitoring enables logistics managers to identify potential issues early and take corrective actions to prevent delays or disruptions.

- **Implementing a Contingency Management Strategy:** A contingency management strategy involves preparing for and responding to unexpected events or disruptions that may impact transportation operations. This includes:

  - **Risk Assessment:** Identifying potential risks such as weather disruptions, accidents, strikes, or supplier delays that could affect transport logistics.

- **Contingency Planning:** Developing plans and procedures to mitigate risks and minimize their impact on operations, such as alternative routes or backup suppliers.

- **Emergency Response:** Mobilising resources and personnel swiftly in response to emergencies to ensure minimal disruption to transportation activities.

Effective contingency management ensures resilience in the face of unforeseen events, maintaining continuity in supply chain operations and meeting customer expectations.

To effectively mobilize resources, coordinate multi-modal transport activities, monitor consignments, and implement a contingency management strategy in the transportation sector, a comprehensive approach involving various stakeholders such as senders, consignors, carriers, shippers, and buyers is crucial [87]. Multimodal supply chains, characterized by multiple changes of transport modes, vehicles, and operators, are associated with increased risks of theft, untimely delivery, and deterioration in freight quality [88]. Monitoring and tracking consignments, addressing obstacles in port, rail, and road projects, as well as managing issues related to banking channels are essential in such supply chains [89].

Efficient resource mobilization in transportation operations can be achieved by leveraging technology, such as blockchain-based frameworks for privacy-preserving business process mining from distributed event logs [87]. The digitization of rail transport has been identified as a key factor in delivering faster and more efficient services, emphasizing the importance of integrated technological solutions in the sector [90]. Information and communication technology has also been shown to enhance the efficiency of border posts in Africa, streamlining processes [91].

Community involvement is vital in mobilising resources for emergency care access, especially in remote areas, where community organizations can facilitate emergency transportation and mutual aid, improving access to emergency care services [92]. Smart mobility solutions have been recognized as a means to enhance transportation efficiency by reducing costs and improving public transit, ridesharing, and active transportation services [93].

Implementing a contingency management strategy in transportation involves addressing challenges and risks. For example, in livestock air transport, considering the welfare impacts on animals throughout the journey is crucial, from road transport to the airport and ending at the importing premises [94]. Monitoring stress levels of horses during transportation to sales events using faecal glucocorticoid metabolites provides insights into the physiological impact of transportation on animals, aiding in understanding and mitigating stressors [95].

Real-time monitoring of freight vehicle movements is essential, particularly in the transportation of hazardous materials, to prevent large-scale accidents in urban areas [96]. Digital twins in refrigerated supply chains enable stakeholders to quantify trade-offs in maintaining product quality and marketability, emphasizing data-driven decision-making in transportation processes [97].

Smart mobility solutions offer a promising avenue to enhance the efficiency of transportation systems, especially in food distribution, by meeting transportation demands effectively through improved service delivery and cost-cutting measures [93]. Integrating new mobility services like ride-sharing and bike-sharing with traditional public transport systems contributes to a more sustainable and efficient transportation ecosystem [98].

Mobilising Resources

Mobilising resources in logistics is a critical aspect of ensuring that transportation operations run smoothly and efficiently. It encompasses the strategic gathering and deployment of various assets and personnel necessary to facilitate the movement of goods from origin to destination. At its core, mobilising resources involves careful planning and coordination across multiple fronts to meet operational demands and ensure timely delivery.

To ensure smooth and efficient operations, acquiring an optimal resource level that aligns with operational schedules is crucial for any organization. This process begins with a thorough assessment of the current operational demands, including production schedules, customer orders and logistical requirements. Understanding these factors allows managers to determine the precise quantity of resources needed, whether it involves personnel, equipment, or materials.

Once the resource needs are identified, the next step is to evaluate relevant regulatory and insurance requirements. This involves understanding the legal framework and industry standards that govern resource deployment. For example, in transportation and logistics, regulations may dictate driver qualifications, vehicle maintenance schedules, or safety protocols. Insurance requirements ensure that adequate coverage is in place to protect against risks associated with operations, such as liability for accidents or damage to goods.

After acquiring and implementing the necessary resources, continuous assessment and monitoring are essential to ensure operational effectiveness and efficiency. This involves tracking resource utilization against predefined performance metrics and benchmarks. For personnel, it includes evaluating productivity levels, adherence to safety protocols, and overall performance quality. For equipment and materials, monitoring may involve uptime, maintenance schedules, and cost-effectiveness.

In the dynamic environment of logistics and operations management, adjustments to resource allocation are often necessary. This step requires proactive management where deficiencies or oversupply of resources are identified through ongoing monitoring and performance evaluation. For instance, if a warehouse consistently experiences delays due to insufficient forklifts, management may decide to increase the fleet size or optimize shift schedules. Conversely, if certain equipment or personnel are underutilized, adjustments may involve reallocating resources to areas of greater demand or reducing surplus capacity.

Changes to resource allocation should always adhere to enterprise procedures and guidelines. This ensures that decisions are made in a structured and transparent manner, taking into account operational needs, budget constraints, and regulatory compliance. Effective communication within the organization is essential during this process to align stakeholders and ensure smooth transitions without compromising operational continuity.

Human resources play a pivotal role in logistics mobilization. This includes ensuring that skilled personnel are available and adequately trained to handle various tasks within the transportation process. For example, logistics coordinators oversee the entire logistics chain, from planning routes to managing schedules and resolving operational issues. Drivers are essential for physically transporting goods, while warehouse staff manage inventory, loading, and unloading processes. Effective mobilization of human resources ensures that each role is filled with competent individuals who understand their responsibilities and can contribute to efficient operations.

Transportation assets are another critical component of logistics mobilization. This includes vehicles, trailers, containers, and any specialized equipment needed for transporting goods safely and efficiently. Mobilising these assets involves ensuring that they are in optimal condition, properly maintained, and available when needed. For example, a logistics manager must coordinate the deployment of trucks and trailers based on shipment volumes, route requirements, and delivery schedules.

Effective asset mobilization minimizes downtime and maximizes utilization, thereby enhancing overall operational efficiency.

Firstly, logistics managers must assess the current inventory of transportation assets. This includes determining the number and types of vehicles (trucks, vans, etc.), trailers, containers, and any specialized equipment such as refrigerated units or flatbeds that are available for use. It's crucial to have a clear understanding of the capabilities and capacities of each asset to match them effectively with the transportation needs.

Next, planning and scheduling play a pivotal role in asset mobilization. Logistics managers need to coordinate the deployment of these assets based on several factors:

- **Shipment Volumes:** The quantity and type of goods being transported influence the choice of vehicles and equipment. For instance, larger shipments might require trucks with greater capacity or specialized handling equipment.

- **Route Requirements:** Different routes may necessitate specific types of vehicles or equipment due to road conditions, terrain, or regulatory restrictions. Logistics managers must select assets that are suitable for the intended route to ensure efficient and safe transportation.

- **Delivery Schedules:** Timeliness is critical in logistics. Assets must be deployed in alignment with delivery schedules to meet customer expectations and operational deadlines.

Financial resources are essential for supporting logistics operations. Mobilising financial resources involves allocating funds for fuel, maintenance, insurance, and other operational expenses associated with transportation. This includes budgeting for ongoing costs such as vehicle upkeep, driver salaries, and regulatory compliance fees. Effective financial mobilization ensures that adequate resources are available to sustain day-to-day operations and respond to unforeseen challenges or fluctuations in demand.

In practice, mobilising resources requires a cohesive approach that integrates human, asset, and financial resources seamlessly. It begins with forecasting operational needs based on customer orders, inventory levels, and market trends. Planning involves assessing resource availability, identifying potential constraints, and developing contingency plans to mitigate risks. Coordination across departments ensures that all stakeholders are aligned with operational objectives and timelines.

Successful mobilization of resources also involves leveraging technology and data analytics to optimize resource allocation and utilization. Advanced logistics systems provide real-time visibility into asset availability, performance metrics, and cost efficiencies. This enables proactive decision-making and continuous improvement in resource management practices.

Overall, effective mobilization of resources in logistics is essential for achieving operational excellence, meeting customer expectations, and maintaining competitiveness in the marketplace. By prioritizing strategic planning, coordination, and investment in key resources, logistics providers can enhance efficiency, reduce costs, and deliver superior service to their clients.

Coordinating Multi-modal Transport Activities

Multimodal transportation, also known as intermodal transportation, is a pivotal strategy in supply chain and logistics management that integrates various modes of transport—such as rail, road, water, and air—into a cohesive and efficient network. This approach optimizes the movement of goods across different geographical regions by leveraging the strengths of each mode to achieve enhanced efficiency, cost-effectiveness, and sustainability [99].

One of the primary advantages of multimodal transportation lies in its ability to capitalize on the unique capabilities of each transport mode. For instance, rail transport excels in long-distance haulage of bulk commodities due to its high carrying capacity and energy efficiency. Meanwhile, trucks offer flexibility and accessibility for last-mile deliveries to customer doorsteps. By seamlessly combining these modes, companies can reduce transportation costs, improve delivery times, and enhance overall logistics efficiency [99].

Efficiency gains in multimodal transportation are facilitated through several mechanisms. Intermodal terminals serve as pivotal hubs where cargo can be smoothly transferred between different modes of transport. These terminals streamline operations, minimize handling delays, and optimize the flow of goods. Containerization further enhances efficiency by standardizing cargo packaging, enabling seamless transfer between modes without the need for manual handling, thus reducing the risk of damage and loss [99].

Moreover, multimodal transportation helps alleviate congestion on congested roadways by diverting traffic to less crowded modes such as rail or waterways. This not only improves traffic flow and reduces travel times but also lowers fuel consumption and enhances air quality—a critical consideration in urban areas and environmentally sensitive regions [99].

Cost-effectiveness is another significant benefit of multimodal transportation. By selecting the most economical mode of transport for each leg of the journey, companies can optimize their transportation expenses. For example, utilizing rail or water transport for long-distance hauls can be more cost-effective than relying solely on trucks. Additionally, the consolidation of goods at intermodal terminals and economies of scale achieved through standardized containers contribute to cost savings and operational efficiency [99].

Sustainability is increasingly becoming a priority for businesses. Multimodal transportation supports sustainability goals by reducing carbon emissions and minimizing environmental impact. By shifting some transportation activities from road to rail or water, companies can achieve substantial reductions in greenhouse gas emissions and energy consumption. This aligns with regulatory requirements and corporate sustainability initiatives, enhancing overall environmental stewardship [99].

In terms of customer satisfaction, multimodal transportation plays a crucial role in meeting diverse customer needs and expectations. Faster transit times, improved reliability, and flexible delivery options contribute to enhanced service levels and customer loyalty. Businesses can offer expedited air transport for time-sensitive shipments or cost-effective rail transport for bulk goods, catering to varying customer requirements effectively [99].

Furthermore, multimodal transportation expands the global reach of supply chain businesses. By seamlessly integrating different transport modes, companies can navigate complex international supply chains, overcome geographic barriers, and access new markets. This global connectivity facilitates trade, supports economic growth, and strengthens competitiveness in a globalized marketplace [99].

Improved inventory management is also a significant benefit of multimodal transportation. Faster transit times and reliable transport options enable businesses to optimize inventory levels, reduce holding costs, and improve inventory turnover. Enhanced visibility and accuracy in tracking shipments across different modes contribute to better supply chain coordination and inventory control, ultimately improving operational efficiency and customer satisfaction [99].

Preparing facilities, personnel, and equipment for interchange functions involves careful planning and execution in logistics and supply chain operations. First and foremost, facilities must be readied to ensure they meet the specific requirements for handling goods efficiently. This includes setting up intermodal terminals or other designated areas where goods can be seamlessly transferred between different modes of transport such as trucks, trains, ships, or planes. These facilities need to be equipped with appropriate infrastructure, such as loading docks, ramps, and handling equipment like forklifts or cranes, tailored to the types of goods being transferred.

Personnel readiness is equally critical. Skilled personnel, including logistics coordinators, warehouse staff, and equipment operators, must be deployed and adequately trained to handle loading and unloading operations safely and efficiently. Training ensures they understand operational procedures, safety protocols, and the use of specialized equipment, thereby minimizing risks and ensuring smooth operations during interchange activities.

Equipment readiness is another essential aspect. Vehicles, handling machinery, and other equipment required for loading and unloading operations must be maintained in optimal condition. Regular inspections, maintenance schedules, and timely repairs are essential to prevent breakdowns and delays that could disrupt operations. For instance, ensuring that trucks have functioning lifting mechanisms and that forklifts are properly maintained enhances operational efficiency and reduces downtime.

Security arrangements play a crucial role in interchange functions, especially for handling valuable or sensitive goods. Security protocols must be invoked as required to safeguard goods against theft, damage, or unauthorized access. This involves implementing access control measures, surveillance systems, and securing storage areas to prevent incidents that could compromise the integrity of the goods being transferred.

Loading and unloading operations must be conducted thoroughly in accordance with operational schedules, statutory requirements, industry codes of practice, and enterprise procedures. This includes adhering to designated loading times, sequence of operations, and safety regulations to ensure compliance and minimize operational disruptions. For example, goods must be loaded in a manner that maintains balance and stability within transport vehicles or containers, adhering to weight distribution guidelines and securing loads to prevent shifting during transit.

Furthermore, completing and updating relevant documentation is essential to record and track the movement of goods accurately. This includes preparing shipping manifests, bills of lading, customs documentation, and any other required paperwork. Documentation must be completed in accordance with operational schedules, reporting requirements, and regulatory standards to facilitate efficient logistics operations and compliance with legal and administrative procedures.

Monitoring Consignment Tracking

Consignment tracking is a fundamental process within businesses that operate with consignment inventory models. In this arrangement, a consignor entrusts their goods to a consignee, who holds and sells the inventory on behalf of the consignor. The consignee is responsible for tracking the inventory's status, ensuring it is properly managed, and accounting for sales accurately until the products are sold, at which point profits are shared with the consignor. This process is pivotal for the smooth operation and success of consignment businesses, as it ensures transparency, accountability, and effective management of inventory throughout its lifecycle [100].

The significance of consignment tracking cannot be overstated. Firstly, it facilitates accurate record-keeping of consigned inventory. This is critical for businesses to maintain visibility into their stock levels, track what has been sold, and monitor what needs replenishing. Accurate records help prevent issues such as overstocking, which ties up capital unnecessarily, or understocking, which can lead to missed sales opportunities and dissatisfied customers [100].

For consignors, effective consignment tracking provides essential insights into their inventory's status. They can monitor inventory levels, track sales performance, and determine when to replenish stock. This visibility allows consignors to make informed decisions about production, purchasing, and overall inventory management strategies, thereby optimizing their supply chain operations [100].

Consignees also benefit significantly from consignment tracking systems. They can monitor sales activities in real-time, track revenues generated from consigned goods, and ensure timely and accurate payments to consignors based on the agreed-upon terms. This not only fosters trust and transparency between consignors and consignees but also helps in maintaining strong business relationships over the long term [100].

The methods for consignment tracking can vary. Traditionally, it was managed manually using pen-and-paper records or spreadsheets, which are labour-intensive and prone to errors. However, with advancements in technology, many businesses now utilize specialized software systems or integrated point-of-sale (POS) solutions. These tools automate inventory tracking, sales monitoring, and reporting processes, enhancing efficiency, accuracy, and overall operational effectiveness [100].

Implementing effective consignment tracking practices involves adopting suitable tracking methods and ensuring that all transactions and inventory movements are accurately recorded and updated. Regular audits and reconciliations of inventory records against physical counts are also essential to maintain accuracy and integrity in the tracking process [100].

Consignment tracking stands as a critical operational pillar for businesses engaged in the sale and distribution of goods, ensuring efficient management of inventory, timely deliveries, and enhanced customer satisfaction. At its core, consignment tracking involves monitoring the movement of goods from one location to another, encompassing the entire logistics chain from shipment to delivery. This meticulous tracking is essential to prevent losses from lost or stolen goods, mitigate delays in deliveries, and avoid errors in fulfilling customer orders, thereby safeguarding both the business's operational efficiency and its reputation among customers [100].

From a customer perspective, consignment tracking plays a pivotal role in enhancing the overall purchasing experience. Customers expect transparency and reliability in tracking their orders, wanting to know precisely when their purchases will arrive. By providing real-time updates on shipment statuses and expected delivery times, businesses can significantly bolster customer satisfaction levels. This transparency builds trust and loyalty, as customers feel informed and assured throughout the entire delivery process, from placement of the order to its final receipt [100].

Moreover, consignment tracking facilitates efficient inventory management for businesses. By continuously monitoring inventory levels and tracking the movement of goods, businesses can optimize stock levels to meet demand without overstocking or understocking. This strategic management not only prevents potential losses from perishable goods or excess inventory but also ensures that products are available when customers place orders. Efficient inventory management is crucial for cost reduction, operational efficiency, and maintaining competitiveness in the market [100].

Timely deliveries are another critical benefit of effective consignment tracking. Businesses can monitor the progress of shipments in real-time, allowing them to anticipate potential delays and take proactive measures to ensure on-time deliveries. This reliability in delivery schedules enhances customer satisfaction by meeting their expectations for prompt and dependable service. It also minimizes the risk of disruptions in supply chains, thereby maintaining smooth operations and reducing the likelihood of customer dissatisfaction due to late deliveries [100].

Cost reduction is yet another advantage derived from consignment tracking. By optimizing delivery routes based on real-time tracking data, businesses can reduce transportation costs, fuel consumption, and vehicle wear and tear. Additionally, insights gained from tracking shipments allow businesses to identify opportunities for streamlining operations, such as consolidating shipments or improving warehouse efficiency. These cost-saving measures contribute to overall profitability and financial health by minimizing unnecessary expenditures associated with logistics and fulfillment [100].

Monitoring consignment tracking systems against workplace quality standards is a crucial aspect of ensuring smooth and efficient logistics operations. It involves continuously overseeing the processes and systems used to track the movement and status of consignments throughout their journey within the supply chain.

To begin with, implementing a robust consignment tracking system is essential. This system should be designed to capture and record key information such as shipment origins, destinations, transit times, handling conditions, and delivery statuses. It may utilize various technologies including barcode scanning, RFID (Radio Frequency Identification), GPS (Global Positioning System), or integrated software platforms that provide real-time updates.

Once the consignment tracking system is in place, ongoing monitoring against workplace quality standards becomes imperative. This involves regular checks and audits to ensure that the system functions as intended and meets predetermined performance metrics. Quality standards may include accuracy in tracking information, timeliness of updates, reliability of data, and adherence to operational protocols.

During monitoring, any variations from workplace quality standards must be promptly identified. This requires vigilant observation and comparison of actual system performance against established benchmarks. For instance, discrepancies such as delayed or erroneous tracking updates, missing data points, or inconsistencies in reported information should be flagged for further investigation.

Upon identifying deviations from quality standards, appropriate actions must be initiated without delay. This could involve troubleshooting technical issues with the tracking system, conducting root cause analysis to determine underlying reasons for discrepancies, and implementing corrective measures to rectify identified problems.

In cases where improvements are needed to enhance system performance or compliance with standards, proactive steps should be taken. This may include revising standard operating procedures (SOPs), providing additional training to personnel responsible for using the tracking system, upgrading technology or software, or integrating new features to enhance functionality and reliability.

Furthermore, instituting a continuous improvement mindset is crucial. Regular feedback loops and performance reviews can help in identifying recurring issues or areas for enhancement. This allows logistics managers and teams to implement iterative improvements over time, ensuring that consignment tracking systems evolve to meet changing operational demands and industry standards.

Managing a consignment business effectively requires robust tools for tracking inventory, sales, and payments to consignors. Consignment tracking, a pivotal aspect of inventory management, ensures that businesses can monitor the movement and status of consigned items from receipt to sale, thereby maintaining accurate records and facilitating smooth transactions. Several tools are available to assist businesses in this endeavour, each offering unique capabilities tailored to streamline and enhance the consignment tracking process.

Consignment software stands out as a specialized solution designed explicitly for consignment businesses. These software platforms automate many labour-intensive tasks associated with consignment tracking, such as recording sales, tracking inventory levels, and managing payments to consignors. By providing real-time visibility into inventory movements and financial transactions, consignment software improves accuracy, efficiency, and operational transparency. Popular options in the market include ConsignCloud, SimpleConsign, and ConsignmentTill, each offering features tailored to meet the specific needs of consignment operations [100].

Additionally, inventory management software proves beneficial for tracking consignment inventory, albeit it is more generalized compared to consignment-specific solutions. These software tools enable businesses to manage overall inventory levels, track stock movements, and monitor sales across different channels. While not designed exclusively for consignment, inventory management software like TradeGecko, Zoho Inventory, and Fishbowl can still be customized to accommodate consignment tracking needs effectively. They provide comprehensive inventory insights and streamline inventory control processes, contributing to overall operational efficiency [100].

For smaller businesses or those starting with consignment operations, spreadsheet templates offer a cost-effective alternative. Spreadsheet templates can be customized to track consignment items, sales transactions, and payments to consignors. While they may lack the automation and integration capabilities of software solutions, spreadsheet templates are flexible and accessible, making them suitable for businesses with simpler tracking requirements. However, they require diligent manual updating and may be prone to human errors, particularly as the volume of consigned items and transactions grows [100].

Barcode scanners represent another indispensable tool for enhancing consignment tracking accuracy and efficiency. By integrating barcode scanning technology with consignment or inventory management software, businesses can streamline the process of receiving, tracking, and selling consignment items. Barcode scanners enable quick and error-free data entry, reducing manual handling errors and expediting inventory updates. This technology is particularly advantageous in fast-paced environments where rapid inventory turnover is essential for maintaining operational efficiency and customer satisfaction [100].

Choosing the right tool for consignment tracking depends on the specific needs and scale of the business. Larger operations may benefit from dedicated consignment software or integrated inventory management solutions that offer scalability and advanced features. Smaller businesses or those with simpler tracking requirements may find spreadsheet templates and basic inventory tools sufficient to meet their needs. Barcode scanners, regardless of the chosen tracking method, enhance accuracy and efficiency across all stages of consignment management, from receipt to sale [100].

As technology advances, the landscape of consignment tracking is undergoing significant transformations, driven by the need for more reliable, efficient, and transparent tracking systems. This evolution is particularly pronounced in response to the burgeoning e-commerce industry, where the ability to accurately monitor consignment movements from origin to destination is crucial for operational success and customer satisfaction. The future of consignment tracking technology is poised to leverage several innovative technologies, each offering unique benefits that enhance visibility, efficiency, and security throughout the supply chain.

RFID (Radio Frequency Identification) technology stands out as a cornerstone of future consignment tracking solutions. RFID tags utilize radio waves to transmit unique identifiers stored within the tag, enabling real-time tracking and monitoring of individual items. In retail and logistics settings, RFID tags are affixed to consignment packages, enabling automated scanning and inventory management across warehouses and distribution centers. This technology enhances accuracy in inventory control, reduces manual handling errors, and speeds up the retrieval of consignment items, thereby optimizing operational efficiency.

GPS (Global Positioning System) tracking represents another pivotal advancement in consignment tracking technology. GPS devices attached to consignment packages provide continuous location updates, allowing businesses to monitor the precise whereabouts of shipments throughout their journey. Particularly valuable for high-value or time-sensitive consignments like medical supplies or perishable goods, GPS tracking ensures adherence to delivery schedules, minimizes the risk of loss or theft, and enhances overall supply chain visibility. Businesses benefit from improved logistics planning and better customer service, as real-time tracking information enables proactive communication with customers regarding delivery status.

Blockchain technology is revolutionizing consignment tracking by introducing unparalleled transparency and security into supply chain operations. As a decentralized digital ledger, blockchain records every transaction or event related to a consignment in a secure, immutable manner. This technology enables stakeholders across the supply chain—from manufacturers and distributors to retailers and consumers—to access a transparent record of consignment movements, ensuring authenticity and preventing tampering or fraud. By enhancing trust and accountability, blockchain technology bolsters supply chain resilience and supports regulatory compliance, particularly in industries where provenance and authenticity are critical.

Artificial Intelligence (AI) is increasingly integrated into consignment tracking systems to optimize operational processes and enhance decision-making capabilities. AI-powered algorithms analyse vast amounts of data generated from consignment tracking, enabling predictive analytics for demand forecasting, route optimization, and inventory management. Machine learning algorithms can identify patterns and anomalies in consignment behaviour, allowing businesses to pre-emptively address potential issues such as delays or disruptions. By automating routine tasks and providing actionable insights, AI empowers businesses to streamline operations, reduce costs, and improve overall efficiency in managing consignment inventory.

The future of consignment tracking technology is characterized by a convergence of these advanced technologies, each contributing to greater operational agility, enhanced customer satisfaction, and sustainable business practices. By adopting RFID for real-time item tracking, GPS for location-based monitoring, blockchain for secure and transparent transactions, and AI for predictive analytics, businesses can achieve unprecedented levels of efficiency and reliability in their consignment operations. As these technologies continue to evolve and become more accessible, businesses across industries stand to benefit from improved supply chain management, reduced operational costs, and enhanced competitiveness in a rapidly evolving marketplace.

Blockchain technology offers several compelling advantages when applied to consignment tracking within supply chains. Essentially, blockchain serves as a decentralized and transparent digital ledger that records transactions across multiple computers in a secure and immutable manner. This unique architecture makes blockchain particularly suitable for enhancing trust, transparency, and efficiency in consignment tracking scenarios.

- **Immutable Recordkeeping**: One of the primary benefits of blockchain in consignment tracking is its ability to maintain an immutable record of transactions. Each transaction or event related to the consignment, such as its origin, transportation milestones, and delivery, is recorded as a block in the chain. Once recorded, these blocks cannot be altered retroactively without altering all subsequent blocks, which requires the consensus of the network participants. This immutability ensures that the data regarding consignment movements and transactions remains tamper-proof and transparent.

- **Enhanced Transparency**: Blockchain promotes transparency by providing all stakeholders with real-time access to a single, shared source of truth. This transparency is crucial in supply chains where multiple parties, such as manufacturers, distributors, logistics providers, and customers, are involved. Each participant can view the entire history of consignment transactions and movements, ensuring that everyone operates on the same information. This transparency reduces disputes, improves accountability, and strengthens trust among supply chain partners.

- **Improved Traceability and Provenance**: Consignment tracking using blockchain enables enhanced traceability and provenance verification. Each consignment item can be assigned a unique identifier (e.g., a digital token or RFID tag) recorded on the blockchain. As the consignment moves through different stages of the supply chain—from production to distribution and final delivery—the blockchain records each interaction and transfer of ownership. This end-to-end traceability helps identify inefficiencies, locate lost or stolen items, and verify the authenticity and origin of products, which is crucial for compliance with regulatory requirements and quality assurance standards.

- **Smart Contracts for Automation**: Blockchain platforms often support smart contracts, which are self-executing contracts with predefined rules and conditions written into code. In consignment tracking, smart contracts can automate various aspects of transactions and logistics operations. For example, smart contracts can automatically trigger payments to consignors upon successful delivery of consignment items, based on predefined conditions such as confirmation of receipt or adherence to delivery schedules. This automation reduces administrative overhead, minimizes disputes, and ensures faster settlement of transactions.

- **Security and Fraud Prevention**: Blockchain's decentralized architecture and cryptographic techniques ensure robust security for consignment tracking data. Unlike traditional centralized databases vulnerable to cyber-attacks or unauthorized access, blockchain networks distribute data across multiple nodes, making it extremely difficult for malicious actors to alter or manipulate the data. Furthermore, cryptographic algorithms used in blockchain ensure that transactions are securely validated and authenticated, reducing the risk of fraud and ensuring data integrity throughout the consignment tracking process.

- **Efficiency and Cost Savings**: By streamlining recordkeeping, reducing paperwork, and automating processes, blockchain can significantly enhance operational efficiency and reduce costs in consignment tracking. The elimination of intermediaries, faster settlement times, and improved visibility into supply chain operations contribute to overall cost savings. Moreover, blockchain facilitates smoother coordination and collaboration among supply chain participants, leading to faster decision-making and improved responsiveness to market demands.

Blockchain technology offers a transformative solution for consignment tracking by providing immutable recordkeeping, enhanced transparency, improved traceability, automated processes through smart contracts, robust security, and operational efficiency. As industries increasingly adopt digital transformation strategies, blockchain's potential to revolutionize consignment tracking is poised to create more resilient, transparent, and efficient supply chains in the future.

Implementing a Contingency Management Strategy

In recent years, global events such as the COVID-19 pandemic, the Suez Canal blockage, and regional crises have underscored the volatility and unpredictability of the business environment. These events have prompted businesses worldwide to re-evaluate their logistics strategies and prioritize flexibility and resilience. Contingency planning has emerged as a critical component to mitigate risks and ensure operational continuity in the face of unexpected disruptions [101].

The shift from a "just-in-time" to a "just-in-case" logistics approach reflects this evolving mindset. Traditionally, businesses focused on minimizing inventory holding costs and relied heavily on streamlined, efficient supply chains to deliver goods precisely when needed. However, the emphasis is now shifting towards building redundancies and preparedness into supply chain operations. This involves diversifying supply chain routes, modes of transport, sourcing locations, and ports to create robustness against disruptions. By maintaining a portfolio of options, businesses can swiftly pivot to alternative solutions when unforeseen events threaten primary logistics routes or modes [101].

Multimodal transport exemplifies this adaptive strategy. By integrating multiple modes of transport—such as sea, air, road, and rail—businesses can leverage the strengths of each mode to ensure continuity even amid disruptions affecting specific transport routes or modes [101].

Flexibility and customer awareness are also pivotal in effective contingency planning. While logistics providers can offer expertise and alternative solutions, businesses must remain open to unconventional or non-standardized approaches during crises. Unpredictable events like strikes, accidents, or economic downturns necessitate agility and a willingness to explore new avenues to maintain operations and meet customer demands [101].

Visibility and control over shipments play a crucial role in mitigating disruptions. Advanced digital tools provide real-time insights into shipment status and location, enabling businesses to monitor goods throughout the supply chain. This end-to-end visibility empowers proactive decision-making, allowing stakeholders to identify potential challenges early and implement timely interventions. With comprehensive data at their fingertips, businesses can make informed choices, manage risks effectively, and maintain operational efficiency even in challenging circumstances [101].

Effective communication is another cornerstone of successful contingency planning. Clear and transparent communication channels ensure that all stakeholders in the supply chain are informed and aligned during disruptions. A well-defined communication strategy facilitates rapid coordination, enabling swift adjustments in roles and responsibilities across the supply chain network. Whether liaising with suppliers, transportation partners, or customers, transparent communication fosters trust, enhances collaboration, and facilitates a cohesive response to unexpected events [101].

Managing operational schedules in logistics requires a dynamic approach that involves continual review, assessment of incidents, contingency planning, strategic processing of information, and clear documentation of actions. Here's how each aspect is approached in detail:

Continual Review of Operational Schedule: To effectively manage operational schedules in logistics, it's crucial to continually review and update schedules based on the latest information, reports, and feedback. This process involves monitoring key metrics such as delivery times, inventory levels, and resource availability. By staying proactive and responsive to changes, logistics managers can optimize schedules to improve efficiency and meet customer demands effectively.

Identification and Assessment of Issues or Incidents: In logistics, unforeseen issues or incidents can disrupt schedules and impact operations. It's essential to swiftly identify the nature, extent, and potential impact of these issues. This involves assessing them against a predefined contingency management strategy. For example, if there's a delay due to weather conditions or mechanical failures, logistics managers must evaluate how these incidents affect delivery timelines and customer commitments.

Processing Relevant Information to Establish Priorities: Upon identifying issues or incidents, logistics managers process relevant information to establish priorities and responses. This step involves gathering data from various sources, such as operational reports, customer feedback, and real-time updates. By analysing this information, managers can prioritize tasks, allocate resources effectively, and implement timely solutions to mitigate disruptions.

Redirecting and Controlling Operations: To adapt to changes in the transport environment and tasks, logistics managers redirect and control operations according to enterprise procedures. This may involve reallocating resources, adjusting routes, or modifying delivery schedules to maintain service levels. By maintaining flexibility and responsiveness, logistics operations can effectively navigate unexpected challenges while minimizing disruptions to customers and stakeholders.

Initiating and Maintaining Liaison with Stakeholders: Effective communication and liaison with organizations and individuals affected by changed operational schedules are critical. Logistics managers initiate and maintain contacts with stakeholders, including suppliers, customers, and transport partners. Clear communication ensures that all parties are informed of schedule changes, expectations, and any necessary adjustments. This proactive approach fosters collaboration and enhances the ability to resolve issues promptly.

Documenting Actions Clearly and Filing: Throughout the process, it's essential to document all actions taken clearly and systematically. This includes recording incident details, responses, decisions made, and outcomes. Clear documentation ensures accountability, facilitates continuous improvement, and provides a reference for future analysis or audits. By maintaining comprehensive records, logistics managers can track the effectiveness of strategies, identify recurring issues, and implement preventive measures to enhance operational resilience.

Designing a logistics contingency plan begins with identifying potential disruptions that could impact supply chain and logistics operations. This initial step is crucial as it sets the foundation for anticipating and preparing for various events that could disrupt normal business activities. Methods such as risk assessment, scenario analysis, SWOT analysis, and brainstorming are employed to evaluate the likelihood and severity of disruptions. These disruptions can stem from internal factors like operational processes, staffing issues, or equipment failures, as well as external factors such as supplier delays, natural disasters, regulatory changes, or geopolitical instability.

During this phase, it's essential to comprehensively assess all aspects of the logistics operations, including suppliers, customers, transportation modes, infrastructure, regulatory requirements, technological dependencies, security vulnerabilities, and environmental factors. Prioritizing critical areas that are most susceptible to disruptions ensures that resources are allocated effectively to protect these vulnerabilities.

Following the identification of potential disruptions, the next step involves developing alternative solutions. This phase focuses on creating strategies and contingency measures that can mitigate the negative impacts of disruptions. Decision-making tools such as decision trees, flowcharts, or matrices are utilized to map out various response options for each identified scenario. Factors like feasibility, cost-effectiveness, timeliness, quality implications, and alignment with business objectives are considered in evaluating these alternatives.

Establishing roles and responsibilities forms the third step in the contingency planning process. Clear delineation of responsibilities ensures that there is a structured approach to managing disruptions when they occur. This includes defining who within the organization is responsible for initiating the plan, coordinating response efforts, communicating with stakeholders, and executing specific tasks. A robust communication plan is crucial, outlining communication channels, escalation procedures, reporting requirements, and access to necessary information and resources.

The final step in designing a logistics contingency plan is testing and regular updating. Testing the plan through simulations, drills, or exercises helps assess its effectiveness and identify any gaps or weaknesses. Feedback from participants and stakeholders provides valuable insights into refining and improving the plan. Regular updates are essential to ensure that the plan remains relevant and responsive to changes in the business environment, logistics operations, regulations, and emerging risks.

Continuous monitoring and periodic reviews of the contingency plan are necessary to adapt to evolving challenges and ensure readiness for unforeseen disruptions. This iterative process of identification, development, implementation, and evaluation strengthens the organization's resilience and ability to maintain operational continuity in the face of disruptions in the logistics landscape. By diligently following these steps, businesses can enhance their preparedness and minimize the impact of disruptions on their supply chain and logistics operations.

Chapter 11

Managing Export Logistics

Export logistics encompasses the intricate processes involved in managing the movement of goods from their point of origin to their destination in international markets. It is a comprehensive supply chain discipline that integrates various activities including order handling, transportation, inventory management, storage, packaging, and customs clearance. Efficient export logistics management is pivotal for businesses aiming to gain a competitive edge by enhancing order fulfillment and reducing product cycles [102].

The export logistics process begins once the goods are ready for dispatch. An essential early decision for exporters is the selection of a reliable ocean freight forwarder or export logistics company. These partners play a crucial role in coordinating the transportation mode and handling customs clearance, ensuring smooth delivery to the final destination. Depending on the shipping method chosen—such as sea/ocean freight—options like consolidation, less than container load (LCL), full container load (FCL), or project cargo are considered to optimize shipping efficiency and cost-effectiveness [102].

Preparing goods for export involves meticulous packing that adheres to international shipping standards. Each package must be appropriately marked and labelled, with a packing list detailing the contents of multiple packages if applicable. Once excise formalities are completed, the goods are cleared from the exporter's premises, marking the initiation of the logistical journey [102].

Documentation is a critical aspect of export logistics to ensure compliance with international trade regulations and facilitate smooth transit. Key documents include the commercial invoice, bill of lading, certificate of origin, packing list, insurance certificate, and various other certificates and licenses depending on the nature of the goods and destination country requirements. These documents are managed and processed by the export logistics coordinator or freight forwarder to facilitate seamless transportation and customs procedures [102].

The transportation phase of export logistics involves multiple stakeholders collaborating to ensure the timely and secure delivery of goods. Beyond the exporter and importer, this includes banks, insurance companies, customs house agents, port authorities, shipping companies, and transit transport providers. Coordinated efforts are essential to handle shipping logistics, customs clearance, and comply with regulatory requirements at both ends of the shipment journey [102].

Optimizing the export logistics process requires strategic planning and effective management across various dimensions. Proper planning ensures that products are available on schedule, transportation options are assessed for efficiency and cost-effectiveness, and potential disruptions are mitigated. Efficient people management and interpersonal skills enhance collaboration among stakeholders, streamlining operations and improving overall productivity [102].

Figure 30: Efficient export logistics are required to manage the complexity of export. CC0 Public Domain, via PxHere.

Storage management is another critical consideration in export logistics, particularly for goods with perishable or fragile attributes. Maximizing warehouse capacity through efficient storage practices ensures that goods remain in optimal condition before shipping. The choice of transportation mode directly impacts delivery speed and cost, highlighting the importance of selecting the most suitable option based on specific business requirements and market conditions [102].

In today's digital age, automation plays a crucial role in optimizing export logistics processes. Advanced software solutions enable real-time tracking of goods, automated updates on shipment status, and streamlined communication among stakeholders. Automation reduces manual intervention, enhances accuracy, and improves overall operational efficiency, thereby supporting businesses in meeting customer demands and maintaining competitive advantage in global markets [102].

In essence, effective export logistics management involves a combination of strategic planning, meticulous execution, stakeholder collaboration, and leveraging technology to navigate the complexities of international trade and ensure seamless supply chain operations from origin to destination.

Planning Efficient Export Logistics

In the realm of export logistics, navigating local and international codes, regulations, and workplace policies is crucial to ensuring compliance and smooth operations. These regulations encompass a wide range of requirements from customs declarations to packaging standards, import/export tariffs, and environmental considerations. Identifying and understanding these regulations is the foundational step in planning export logistics activities. This process involves extensive research, consultation with regulatory bodies, and staying updated with any changes that may impact operations.

Once regulatory frameworks are understood, consignment loads undergo thorough evaluation based on critical parameters and specific customer instructions. This evaluation includes factors such as weight, volume, fragility, perishability, and any special handling requirements. Customer instructions are meticulously reviewed to ensure that the logistics plan aligns with their expectations and meets contractual obligations. Clear communication with customers is essential to confirm understanding and address any concerns upfront.

Assessing the capacity and capability of local and overseas transport modes is integral to designing an efficient logistics strategy. Different transport modes such as road, rail, sea, and air each offer distinct advantages in terms of speed, cost-effectiveness, and suitability for different types of cargo. Evaluating these options involves analysing factors like transit times, reliability, accessibility of routes, and infrastructure compatibility. This assessment ensures that the chosen transport modes align with the proposed logistics tasks and operational requirements.

Preliminary schedules are then aligned with the operational capacity and capability of available transport systems, equipment, and staff. This step involves matching the planned export logistics activities with the resources and capabilities at hand, considering factors such as vehicle availability, warehouse space, handling equipment, and workforce expertise. Balancing these elements optimizes resource utilization and minimizes operational disruptions, enhancing overall efficiency.

Planning for export logistics involves strategic decisions aimed at achieving efficient and effective delivery and load handling while adhering to regulatory and workplace procedures. This planning phase integrates all identified requirements, customer instructions, and logistical capabilities into a cohesive operational plan. Key considerations include route planning, shipment consolidation, scheduling of loading/unloading activities, and contingency planning for unexpected events. The goal is to ensure that every step of the logistics process is meticulously planned to achieve timely delivery and meet customer expectations.

Addressing identified deficiencies in operational capability and availability requires proactive strategies in accordance with workplace procedures. This may involve training programs to enhance staff skills, investing in upgraded equipment or technology, or establishing partnerships with reliable transport providers. By addressing deficiencies pre-emptively, organizations can mitigate risks, improve operational readiness, and maintain high standards of service delivery in the dynamic field of export logistics.

Effective planning and execution of export logistics rely on a thorough understanding of regulatory requirements, meticulous evaluation of consignment loads and customer instructions, assessment of transport modes, strategic alignment of schedules with operational capabilities, and proactive strategies to address operational deficiencies. This comprehensive approach ensures compliance, enhances efficiency, and enables organizations to navigate the complexities of global trade with confidence.

Ensuring quality standards and procedures in export logistics processes is crucial for maintaining efficiency, reliability, and compliance with regulatory requirements. This begins with confirming or updating existing quality standards in accordance with workplace procedures. Quality standards encompass a range of factors including packaging requirements, handling protocols, documentation accuracy, and adherence to international trade regulations. Updating these standards involves reviewing current practices, integrating feedback from stakeholders, and incorporating any changes in regulations or industry best practices to enhance operational effectiveness.

Assessing the nature, extent, and potential impact of issues or incidents in planned export logistics is a proactive measure aimed at risk management. This assessment involves identifying various scenarios that could disrupt the logistics process, such as transportation delays, customs clearance issues, adverse weather conditions, or geopolitical tensions. Each scenario is evaluated based on its likelihood and potential impact on shipment timelines, costs, and customer satisfaction. Understanding these factors allows logistics managers to prioritize risks and allocate resources accordingly to minimize disruptions.

Developing contingency management strategies for identified issues and incidents is a critical aspect of export logistics planning. These strategies draw upon previous experiences and lessons learned from similar scenarios to formulate effective responses. By referencing past incidents, logistics teams can identify successful approaches and refine strategies that mitigate risks and expedite resolution. Contingency plans may include alternative transport routes, emergency communication protocols, backup suppliers, or temporary storage solutions, all aimed at maintaining operational continuity despite unforeseen challenges.

Documenting implementation procedures for contingency plans ensures clarity and consistency in response to disruptions. This documentation outlines specific actions to be taken, roles and responsibilities of personnel involved, and necessary resource allocations. It also includes protocols for updating and refining plans based on ongoing evaluations and changes in the operating environment. Continual upgrades to implementation procedures involve monitoring industry trends, technological advancements, and regulatory updates that may impact export logistics operations.

Incorporating resource and infrastructure support into implementation procedures ensures that logistics operations are adequately equipped to meet established quality standards. This includes maintaining up-to-date facilities, investing in reliable transport vehicles, and leveraging digital tools for real-time tracking and communication. Aligning infrastructure support with quality standards and international operating environments involves adapting to evolving customer expectations, regulatory requirements, and global trade dynamics. By continually upgrading infrastructure and resources, organizations can enhance operational resilience, improve service delivery, and uphold their reputation in the competitive export logistics landscape.

Planning and managing export logistics involves numerous complexities that can lead to various challenges. Some common problems that may occur include:

- **Customs Delays and Compliance Issues**: Customs clearance processes can be lengthy and complicated, leading to delays in shipments. Issues may arise due to incorrect documentation, tariff classifications, or regulatory changes. To resolve these problems, exporters can ensure accurate and complete documentation, engage customs brokers for expertise, and stay updated on regulatory changes through regular communication with authorities.

- **Transportation and Infrastructure Issues**: Problems such as transportation delays, breakdowns, or infrastructure limitations (like port congestion or inadequate road conditions) can disrupt logistics schedules. Mitigating actions include diversifying transportation modes and routes, maintaining contingency plans for alternative routes, and partnering with reliable logistics providers who offer robust infrastructure support.

- **Supply Chain Disruptions**: Unexpected disruptions like natural disasters, political instability, or supplier failures can impact supply chain continuity. Actions to mitigate these include maintaining buffer stocks, fostering relationships with alternative suppliers, and implementing risk management strategies like insurance coverage for contingencies.

- **Communication and Coordination Challenges**: Poor communication between stakeholders (exporters, carriers, customs officials, etc.) can lead to misunderstandings, delays, or errors in logistics operations. Establishing clear communication channels, using technology for real-time updates, and conducting regular meetings or briefings can enhance coordination and resolve issues promptly.

- **Quality Control and Product Compliance**: Issues related to product quality, compliance with export regulations, or customer specifications can lead to rejections or delays. Implementing robust quality assurance processes, conducting pre-shipment inspections, and ensuring adherence to international standards can prevent these problems.

- **Financial and Cost Management**: Budget overruns, unexpected costs (like tariffs or duties), and inefficient cost management practices can strain financial resources. Actions include conducting thorough cost-benefit analyses, negotiating favourable terms with suppliers and carriers, and leveraging technology for cost monitoring and optimization.

- **Legal and Documentation Errors**: Errors in contracts, shipping documents, or insurance coverage can lead to legal disputes or financial liabilities. To avoid these issues, exporters should engage legal experts for contract reviews, ensure compliance with export documentation requirements, and maintain accurate records throughout the logistics process.

Producing Operation Schedules for Export Logistics

Establishing local and overseas transportation modes, times, and routes to maximize effective and efficient operations is fundamental to successful logistics management. This process begins with thorough research and planning to identify the most suitable transport options based on factors such as cost-effectiveness, reliability, transit times, and regulatory compliance. For instance, selecting between road, rail, sea, or air transport involves evaluating each mode's capacity, infrastructure availability, and environmental impact. Routes are then mapped out to optimize delivery times and minimize logistical challenges, taking into account factors like traffic patterns, weather conditions, and potential geopolitical risks.

Arranging resources in collaboration with relevant Australian and overseas personnel is essential for ensuring operational schedules are met consistently. This collaborative effort involves coordinating with local partners, suppliers, transport providers, and international agents to align resources with logistical requirements. This may include securing necessary permits, customs clearances, and ensuring workforce availability to support smooth operations across borders. Effective communication and strategic partnerships play a crucial role in synchronizing efforts and mitigating potential disruptions that could impact delivery timelines or operational efficiency.

Identifying and accounting for local and international regulatory requirements, codes of practice, and workplace procedures within operational schedules are critical steps in compliance management. This involves staying abreast of evolving regulations governing trade, transportation, and safety standards in both domestic and international markets. Compliance with these standards ensures legal adherence, minimizes risks of penalties or delays, and fosters a reputation for reliability and integrity in global supply chains. Adapting operational schedules to accommodate regulatory changes and industry best practices requires continuous monitoring and adjustment to maintain alignment with prevailing legal frameworks.

Applying tracking procedures to consignments using relevant technology and systems is essential for maintaining visibility and control throughout the logistics process. Modern tracking technologies, such as GPS systems, RFID tags, and real-time tracking software, enable logistics operators to monitor consignments from origin to destination accurately. These systems facilitate proactive management by providing real-time updates on shipment status, location, and condition. By adhering to workplace procedures for tracking, logistics teams can promptly address any deviations or issues that may arise, ensuring timely interventions to uphold service commitments and customer expectations.

Consolidating and forwarding schedules to appropriate personnel ensures effective coordination and communication across all stakeholders involved in logistics operations. This step involves compiling comprehensive schedules that outline transport modes, routes, departure times, and delivery deadlines. Clear and concise communication of schedules to relevant personnel, including drivers, warehouse staff, and customer service teams, enhances operational transparency and alignment of efforts. Storing schedules in accordance with workplace procedures, whether digitally or in physical formats, ensures accessibility for future reference, audits, or adjustments based on evolving operational needs.

Establishing local and overseas transportation modes, times, and routes to maximize effective and efficient operations involves a systematic approach that integrates several key considerations:

- **Mode Selection**: The first step is to evaluate and select the most suitable transportation modes based on factors such as the nature of the goods, distance, urgency of delivery, cost-effectiveness, and environmental impact. For example, choosing between road, rail, sea, or air transport depends on factors like speed, capacity, reliability, and infrastructure availability.

- **Route Planning**: Once the transportation modes are determined, the next step is to plan optimal routes. Route planning involves considering various factors such as distance, traffic conditions, potential hazards, transit times, and geopolitical considerations. Efficient route planning aims to minimize transit times, reduce fuel consumption, and avoid unnecessary delays or risks.

- **Transit Times**: Estimating transit times accurately is crucial for logistics planning. This involves understanding the time required for each leg of the journey, including loading/unloading, customs clearance, and potential delays due to weather or other factors. Transit times impact scheduling, inventory management, and customer service commitments.

- **Cost Efficiency**: Maximizing cost efficiency involves balancing transportation costs with service levels and operational requirements. This includes evaluating factors like fuel costs, tolls, tariffs, taxes, and labour expenses associated with different transportation modes and routes. Cost-effective transportation solutions contribute to overall profitability and competitiveness.

- **Regulatory Compliance**: Compliance with local and international regulations is essential for smooth operations. Transportation modes and routes must align with regulatory requirements related to safety standards, vehicle emissions, weight restrictions, customs procedures, and documentation. Non-compliance can lead to penalties, delays, and reputational damage.

- **Environmental Impact**: Considering the environmental impact of transportation modes and routes is increasingly important. Efforts to minimize carbon emissions and adopt sustainable practices, such as using cleaner fuels or optimizing routes to reduce mileage, align with corporate social responsibility goals and regulatory mandates.

- **Technological Integration**: Leveraging technology, such as GPS tracking systems, route optimization software, and real-time monitoring tools, enhances operational efficiency. These technologies provide visibility into shipments, enable proactive management of delays or disruptions, and support data-driven decision-making for continuous improvement.

- **Risk Management**: Identifying and mitigating risks associated with transportation modes and routes is critical. This includes assessing potential hazards such as political instability, natural disasters, strikes, or supply chain disruptions that could impact operations. Developing contingency plans and alternative routes helps minimize risks and ensures continuity of operations.

By systematically evaluating these factors and integrating them into logistics planning processes, organizations can establish local and overseas transportation modes, times, and routes that maximize efficiency, reliability, and customer satisfaction. Continuous monitoring, feedback mechanisms, and adaptation to changing circumstances further optimize operations and support long-term business success in the global marketplace.

Navigating local and international regulatory, permit, and license requirements is essential for businesses engaged in export logistics. These requirements form a complex framework of rules and procedures that govern the movement of goods across borders, ensuring compliance with legal standards, safety protocols, and trade agreements. Understanding and adhering to these regulations are crucial to avoiding delays, penalties, and reputational damage while facilitating smooth and lawful export operations.

Local regulatory requirements vary widely by country and can encompass a range of issues such as customs procedures, documentation requirements, tax obligations, and environmental standards. For instance, exporters may need to obtain specific permits or licenses to export certain types of goods deemed sensitive or controlled by local authorities. Compliance often involves detailed paperwork, including export declarations, certificates of origin, and inspection certificates, which must be submitted accurately and on time to ensure clearance through customs.

On an international level, export logistics are governed by global trade agreements and treaties that establish uniform standards and procedures among participating countries. Organizations must stay informed about these agreements, such as free trade agreements (FTAs) or regional economic partnerships, which may provide preferential tariff rates or streamlined customs procedures for qualifying exports. Compliance with international regulations also includes adherence to sanctions and embargoes imposed by international bodies or individual countries, restricting trade with certain nations or entities for political or security reasons.

Permit requirements further complicate export logistics, as they may vary not only by product type but also by destination country. Exporters may need licenses for goods considered dual-use, with both civilian and military applications, or for products subject to environmental protection regulations. Ensuring proper documentation and certification is crucial, as failure to comply with permit requirements can lead to shipment delays, fines, or even legal consequences.

Moreover, export logistics must align with transportation regulations governing different modes of transport, such as maritime, air, rail, or road transportation. Each mode has its own set of regulations concerning safety standards, cargo handling procedures, and liability, which exporters must adhere to for the secure and lawful transport of goods.

Successfully managing local and international regulatory requirements in export logistics demands meticulous planning, continuous monitoring of legal developments, and strong partnerships with experienced customs brokers, legal advisors, and logistics providers. Organizations that prioritize compliance not only mitigate risks but also enhance their reputation as reliable and responsible international traders, fostering smoother operations and sustainable growth in global markets.

As examples illustrating how organizations can systematically evaluate and integrate key considerations into their logistics planning to establish local and overseas transportation modes, times, and routes effectively and efficiently:

Mode Selection: An international pharmaceutical company needs to transport temperature-sensitive vaccines from its manufacturing facility in Europe to distribution centres across Asia. After evaluating speed, capacity, and reliability, they choose air transport due to its fast transit times and ability to maintain temperature control. Despite higher costs compared to sea freight, air transport ensures timely delivery, maintaining product efficacy and meeting urgent healthcare needs.

Local and overseas transport involves a variety of applications, equipment, capacities, configurations, safety hazards, and control mechanisms that are essential for efficient logistics operations:

- **Applications**: Local transport typically includes road and rail for shorter distances, while overseas transport often relies on sea and air freight for longer distances. Each mode is chosen based on factors like speed, cost, and the nature of the goods being transported.

- **Equipment**: Equipment used varies widely. For local transport, trucks, vans, and trains are common, equipped with loading docks and secure fastening systems. Overseas transport utilizes containers, pallets, and specialized handling equipment like cranes for loading/unloading containers from ships.

- **Capacities and Configurations**: Capacities range from small parcel deliveries to large-scale container shipments. Configurations include standardized container sizes for international shipping and customizable options for local transport to accommodate various cargo types.

- **Safety Hazards and Control Mechanisms**: Hazards include accidents during loading/unloading, cargo shifting, and exposure to weather conditions. Control mechanisms involve stringent safety protocols, secure packaging, training for personnel, and compliance with transportation regulations.

Route Planning: A logistics firm in South America plans routes for transporting perishable goods from agricultural regions to export hubs on the coast. Route planning considers factors like road conditions, seasonal weather patterns affecting mountain passes, and distance to ports. By optimizing routes to avoid traffic congestion and reduce mileage, they minimize transit times and fuel consumption. This approach ensures fresher produce reaches international markets promptly, enhancing customer satisfaction and minimizing waste.

Transit Times: A global electronics manufacturer in Asia schedules shipments of new product releases to retail outlets in North America. Estimating transit times involves accounting for loading/unloading, customs clearance, and potential delays due to weather or regulatory inspections. By factoring in these variables and using historical data, they create accurate delivery schedules that align with promotional campaigns and customer demand, ensuring timely availability of products in stores.

Cost Efficiency: A European fashion retailer evaluates transportation options for importing apparel from manufacturing hubs in Southeast Asia. They analyse fuel costs, shipping tariffs, and taxes associated with sea freight versus air freight. Opting for sea freight despite longer transit times, they achieve significant cost savings per unit, allowing them to offer competitive pricing in a highly price-sensitive market segment while maintaining profitability.

Regulatory Compliance: An Australian mining company plans transportation routes for exporting minerals to Europe, adhering to stringent environmental and safety regulations. They ensure that transportation modes and routes comply with international standards for hazardous materials, emissions control, and cargo handling. Compliance with regulations mitigates risks of fines or operational delays, safeguarding their reputation and maintaining smooth logistics operations.

Environmental Impact: A logistics provider in North America integrates sustainability into their transportation planning for delivering goods nationwide. They invest in hybrid vehicles and optimize routes to minimize carbon emissions and reduce fuel consumption. By adopting eco-friendly practices, such as consolidating shipments and using renewable energy sources, they meet corporate sustainability goals, attract environmentally conscious clients, and comply with increasingly stringent regulatory requirements.

Technological Integration: A global shipping company employs GPS tracking systems and route optimization software to manage container shipments from ports in Asia to distribution centres in Europe. Real-time monitoring tools allow them to track vessel locations, optimize routes based on weather conditions and traffic patterns, and provide customers with accurate shipment status updates. This technological integration enhances operational efficiency, reduces transit times, and improves overall service reliability.

Risk Management: An American automotive supplier assesses risks associated with transporting sensitive automotive components from manufacturing facilities to assembly plants across the country. They develop contingency plans for potential disruptions like strikes or natural disasters, establishing alternative transportation routes and suppliers. By proactively managing risks, they ensure uninterrupted supply chain operations, minimize production downtime, and maintain high customer satisfaction levels.

By systematically evaluating these factors and integrating them into their logistics planning processes, organizations can establish local and overseas transportation modes, times, and routes that maximize efficiency, reliability, and customer satisfaction. Continuous monitoring, feedback mechanisms, and adaptation to changing circumstances further optimize operations and support long-term business success in the competitive global marketplace.

Applying tracking procedures to consignments using relevant technology and systems involves a systematic approach to ensure visibility, accountability, and efficiency throughout the shipment process. This typically includes:

Selection of Tracking Technology: Organizations begin by selecting appropriate tracking technology based on the nature of the consignments, regulatory requirements, and operational needs. This could include GPS tracking systems, RFID tags, barcode scanning systems, or advanced logistics software that integrates with global positioning systems and databases.

Integration into Workflow: Once the tracking technology is chosen, it is integrated into the organization's workflow and operational processes. This may involve training personnel on how to use the tracking devices or software, establishing protocols for when and how to apply tracking identifiers (such as RFID tags or barcodes) to consignments, and ensuring that all relevant stakeholders understand the importance of accurate tracking.

Application of Tracking Identifiers: At the point of dispatch or packaging, tracking identifiers are applied to each consignment. For instance, RFID tags may be attached to pallets or individual items, while barcode labels are affixed to packages. This step ensures that each consignment is uniquely identified and can be tracked throughout its journey.

Real-Time Monitoring: Throughout transit, the consignments are monitored in real-time using the selected tracking technology. GPS tracking systems provide continuous updates on the location of vehicles or containers, while RFID or barcode systems allow for scanning at various checkpoints (such as warehouses, customs checkpoints, or delivery hubs). This real-time monitoring enables organizations to track the movement of consignments, detect any deviations from the planned route or schedule, and respond promptly to any issues or delays.

Data Collection and Analysis: The tracking technology collects data related to the consignments, including location, temperature (if applicable), handling conditions, and transit times. This data is stored in a centralized system or cloud-based platform, where it can be analysed to identify patterns, optimize routes, improve efficiency, and enhance decision-making processes.

Compliance with Workplace Procedures: Organizations ensure that tracking procedures comply with workplace procedures, industry standards, and regulatory requirements. This includes maintaining data privacy and security, adhering to protocols for handling sensitive information, and complying with international trade regulations related to customs declarations and documentation.

Exception Handling and Reporting: In case of any exceptions or deviations from the planned route or schedule, the tracking system alerts designated personnel. These exceptions could include delays, route diversions, or incidents affecting the consignment's integrity. Prompt reporting and communication allow for swift corrective actions to minimize disruptions and ensure timely delivery.

Continuous Improvement: Organizations regularly review and evaluate their tracking procedures to identify areas for improvement. This may involve feedback from stakeholders, analysis of performance metrics (such as on-time delivery rates or inventory accuracy), and technological advancements in tracking systems. Continuous improvement ensures that tracking procedures remain effective, responsive to changing business needs, and aligned with evolving industry standards.

Implementing tracking procedures with relevant technology and systems is crucial for ensuring smooth logistics operations. Let's delve into realistic examples of how organizations apply these procedures to consignments:

Selection of Tracking Technology: Organizations like a multinational electronics manufacturer may opt for RFID tags embedded in packaging to track high-value electronic components. This choice ensures real-time monitoring of inventory movement within global supply chains, enhancing visibility and reducing the risk of loss or theft during transit.

Integration into Workflow: A global pharmaceutical company integrates GPS tracking systems into its logistical workflow for shipping temperature-sensitive vaccines. Personnel are trained to affix temperature sensors alongside barcode labels on each shipment. This integration ensures compliance with stringent regulatory standards while providing real-time data on temperature deviations and shipment progress.

Application of Tracking Identifiers: In the automotive sector, manufacturers utilize barcode scanning systems at production facilities to label finished vehicle parts before shipping. Each part is scanned and assigned a unique barcode, facilitating accurate tracking from assembly lines to distribution centres worldwide. This method minimizes errors and ensures parts reach their destinations on schedule.

Real-Time Monitoring: A logistics provider specializing in perishable goods employs GPS-enabled containers to monitor shipments of fresh produce. Real-time updates on temperature, humidity, and location are transmitted via satellite to a central control centre. This allows proactive adjustments to transportation routes and storage conditions, ensuring optimal product quality upon arrival.

Data Collection and Analysis: A retail chain implements advanced logistics software integrated with AI-driven analytics to optimize its global supply chain. The system collects data on shipment volumes, transit times, and customer demand patterns. Through predictive analysis, the company identifies inefficiencies, adjusts inventory levels, and anticipates future logistical challenges to maintain competitive advantage.

Compliance with Workplace Procedures: An international shipping company adheres to strict workplace procedures and regulatory requirements when transporting hazardous materials. RFID tags are used to track chemical shipments, ensuring compliance with safety protocols and providing instant access to safety data sheets and emergency response plans during transport and delivery.

Exception Handling and Reporting: During peak holiday seasons, a global e-commerce retailer relies on automated alerts from its logistics software to manage unexpected delivery delays. This proactive approach allows customer service teams to notify affected customers promptly and arrange alternative shipping options to meet delivery deadlines, maintaining high customer satisfaction levels.

Continuous Improvement: A logistics consortium specializing in intermodal transport continuously evaluates its tracking procedures to enhance operational efficiency. Feedback from stakeholders, coupled with performance metrics on delivery accuracy and fuel consumption, drives ongoing improvements. Integration of blockchain technology further enhances transparency and security across the supply chain, ensuring compliance with evolving industry standards.

The following provides a basic sample Operation Schedule for Export Logistics:

Operation Schedule for Export Logistics

Date: [Insert Date]

Prepared by: [Your Name or Department]

Objective: To coordinate and manage the export logistics operations effectively and ensure timely delivery of consignments while adhering to regulatory requirements and workplace procedures.

Key Activities:

- **Pre-Dispatch Preparation:**

    a. Confirm availability of export-ready goods.

    b. Ensure all necessary documentation (commercial invoice, packing list, certificates) are complete and accurate.

    c. Verify compliance with export regulations and customs requirements.

- **Mode and Route Selection:**

    a. Evaluate transportation modes (air, sea, road) based on shipment volume, urgency, and cost-effectiveness.

    b. Select optimal routes considering transit times, geopolitical factors, and potential risks.

    c. Coordinate with freight forwarders and carriers for booking and scheduling.

- **Packaging and Labelling:**

    a. Ensure consignments are packed securely and labelled according to shipping standards.

    b. Incorporate tracking identifiers (RFID tags, barcode labels) as per tracking procedures.

- **Customs Clearance and Documentation:**

    a. Prepare and submit required export documentation (bill of lading, certificate of origin, export license).

    b. Coordinate with customs brokers for smooth clearance at origin and destination ports.

- **Transportation and Delivery:**

    a. Arrange for loading and transportation from warehouse/factory to port of departure.

    b. Monitor shipment in real-time using GPS tracking systems or other relevant technology.

    c. Ensure compliance with transit regulations and safety standards.

- **Risk Management and Contingency Planning:**

    a. Identify potential risks (weather delays, political instability) and establish contingency measures.

    b. Maintain communication channels open for swift response to unforeseen events.

    c. Implement alternative routes or transport modes as needed.

- **Communication and Reporting:**

    a. Maintain regular communication with stakeholders (suppliers, customers, logistics partners).

    b. Provide updates on shipment status, delays, or changes in schedule.

    c. Document all communications and actions taken for future reference.

Timeline:
- **Start Date:** [Insert Start Date]

- **End Date:** [Insert End Date]

Resources Required:
- Personnel: Export logistics coordinator, customs brokers, warehouse staff.

- Equipment: Forklifts, pallet jacks, packaging materials.

- Technology: GPS tracking systems, barcode scanners, computer systems.

Review and Evaluation:

- Conduct periodic reviews to assess operational efficiency and compliance with quality standards.

- Gather feedback from stakeholders and implement continuous improvement initiatives.

- Update operation schedules based on lessons learned and changing business needs.

Approval: This Operation Schedule is approved by [Name/Position] on [Date].

This sample Operation Schedule outlines the essential steps and considerations for managing export logistics operations effectively. Customize it according to your specific organizational requirements and operational context.

Monitoring and Coordinating Systems for Export Logistics

Monitoring export logistics against identified quality standards, planned processes, and regulatory requirements is crucial for ensuring smooth operations and compliance. This process involves continuous oversight to verify that all activities, from packaging and documentation to transportation and delivery, meet the predefined quality benchmarks and follow established procedures. Quality standards may include criteria for packaging integrity, accuracy of documentation, adherence to safety protocols, and compliance with international trade regulations such as Incoterms and customs procedures.

In the event of non-compliance with quality standards, planned processes, or regulatory requirements, it is essential to promptly identify deviations and initiate appropriate actions. This could involve conducting internal audits, inspections, or quality checks to pinpoint the root cause of the problem. Once identified, corrective actions are initiated to rectify the issues and prevent recurrence. This may include revising procedures, providing additional training to personnel, or implementing new controls to improve adherence to standards.

Customer satisfaction with export logistics operations is monitored using various methods to gauge their experience and feedback. This could involve customer surveys, feedback forms, or direct communication to gather insights on service levels, responsiveness, and overall satisfaction with the logistics services provided. Monitoring customer satisfaction helps identify areas for improvement and ensures that the logistics operations align with customer expectations and service agreements.

Addressing customer concerns and suggestions for service improvements is a critical part of maintaining customer satisfaction. Upon receiving feedback, whether positive or negative, organizations must follow workplace procedures to investigate issues, communicate with customers to understand their concerns, and take appropriate actions to resolve issues promptly. This could include improving communication channels, revising service protocols, or implementing customer-specific solutions to enhance service delivery.

Reports and documentation related to export logistics are completed systematically and referred to relevant personnel in accordance with workplace procedures. This involves compiling data on shipment volumes, transit times, compliance records, customer feedback, and any incidents or deviations encountered during operations. These reports provide insights into operational performance, facilitate decision-making, and ensure accountability across the logistics chain.

Monitoring changes in local and international regulations and codes of practice relevant to export logistics is essential to ensure ongoing compliance and operational efficiency. This involves staying updated with regulatory updates, trade agreements, customs procedures, and industry standards that may impact export operations. Upon identifying changes, organizations initiate appropriate actions such as updating procedures, training personnel, or adjusting systems to ensure continued adherence to legal and regulatory requirements. Proactively managing regulatory changes helps mitigate risks, maintain operational integrity, and uphold the organization's reputation in the global marketplace.

Measuring import/export logistics performance for shorter lead times involves monitoring key metrics that reflect efficiency, reliability, and customer satisfaction throughout the supply chain. Some of these include [103]:

Order Cycle Time: Order cycle time is critical in assessing the efficiency of logistics operations. It measures the average duration from order placement to customer receipt. Tracking order cycle time involves recording the initiation, processing, shipment, and delivery of each order. Tools such as order management software and shipment tracking systems are used to collect data, which is then analysed to identify bottlenecks and streamline processes. Strategies to reduce order cycle time include optimizing order processing workflows, selecting faster transportation modes, and consolidating shipments to minimize handling and transit times.

On-Time Delivery Rate: The on-time delivery rate indicates the percentage of orders delivered within the agreed-upon or expected timeframe. It directly impacts customer satisfaction and operational reliability. Monitoring this metric involves comparing actual delivery dates against promised or estimated dates for each order.

Tools like delivery confirmation systems and customer feedback surveys provide data for calculating and monitoring this rate. Improving on-time delivery involves setting realistic delivery expectations, maintaining clear communication with customers and suppliers, and swiftly addressing any delays or issues that arise during transit.

Customs Clearance Time: Customs clearance time measures how long it takes for goods to pass through customs at both origin and destination countries. This metric affects the speed, cost, and compliance of import/export operations. Monitoring customs clearance time requires tracking the timeline of customs declarations, inspections, and release processes. Customs management software and electronic data interchange systems facilitate data collection and optimization efforts. Strategies to reduce clearance time include preparing accurate documentation, ensuring proper goods classification, and leveraging preferential trade agreements or tariffs to expedite clearance procedures.

Inventory Turnover Ratio: The inventory turnover ratio indicates how quickly inventory is sold and replaced within a specific period. It reflects demand patterns and inventory management efficiency. Calculating this ratio involves dividing the cost of goods sold by the average inventory value over the same period. Tools such as inventory management software and financial reports provide the necessary data. Increasing inventory turnover requires accurate demand forecasting, adjusting inventory levels based on market trends, and adopting agile inventory management practices like just-in-time systems to minimize storage costs and optimize turnover.

Logistics Cost Per Unit: Logistics cost per unit measures the total expenses incurred in transporting, handling, storing, and delivering one unit of product. It directly impacts profitability and competitiveness. Tracking logistics cost per unit involves aggregating all logistics-related expenses and dividing by the number of units shipped. Accounting software, invoices, and receipts serve as sources for cost data. Strategies to lower logistics costs per unit include negotiating favourable terms with logistics providers, optimizing transportation routes and modes to minimize expenses, and implementing sustainable practices to reduce packaging waste and associated costs.

Chapter 12

Establishing International Distribution Networks

International distribution networks refer to the interconnected system of channels, logistics infrastructure, and partnerships established by companies to distribute their products or services across global markets. These networks are crucial for reaching customers in different countries efficiently and effectively. The key components and characteristics of international distribution networks include:

- **Channels and Routes**: International distribution networks encompass various channels and routes through which goods or services are transported from the manufacturer or supplier to end customers. This can include direct sales to retailers, wholesalers, distributors, agents, or directly to consumers via e-commerce platforms.

- **Logistics Infrastructure**: They rely on a robust logistics infrastructure that includes transportation modes (such as air, sea, road, rail), warehousing facilities, distribution centres, and fulfillment centres strategically located to optimize delivery times and minimize costs.

- **Partnerships and Alliances**: Companies often establish partnerships and alliances with local distributors, agents, freight forwarders, and logistics providers in different regions or countries. These partnerships help navigate local regulations, customs procedures, and cultural nuances, thereby facilitating smoother operations and market penetration.

- **Inventory Management**: Effective international distribution networks require sophisticated inventory management systems to ensure optimal stock levels at different locations. This includes balancing between centralized and decentralized inventory strategies to meet demand fluctuations and minimize stockouts.

- **Compliance and Regulations**: Navigating international trade regulations, customs requirements, and legal frameworks is essential. Distribution networks must comply with import/export laws, product standards, tax implications, and licensing requirements in each market they operate in.

- **Customer Service and Support**: Providing consistent customer service and support across borders is critical for maintaining customer satisfaction. This may involve multilingual support, localized marketing and sales efforts, and responsive handling of inquiries or issues.

- **Technology and Data Integration**: Leveraging technology such as supply chain management (SCM) systems, enterprise resource planning (ERP) software, and advanced analytics helps optimize operations, track shipments in real-time, and analyse market trends for better decision-making.

- **Risk Management**: International distribution networks face risks such as currency fluctuations, political instability, supply chain disruptions, and global pandemics. Effective risk management strategies involve contingency planning, diversification of suppliers and logistics routes, and insurance coverage.

International distribution networks are complex systems that facilitate the movement of goods or services from manufacturers or suppliers to end customers across global markets. Central to these networks are the channels and routes through which products are distributed. Channels refer to the different pathways or methods used to deliver goods or services, while routes denote the specific paths taken by these products through the supply chain.

In the context of international distribution networks, channels encompass a wide range of options tailored to meet diverse market needs and preferences. These channels can include direct sales to retailers or distributors, partnerships with wholesalers or agents who act as intermediaries, or direct-to-consumer sales via e-commerce platforms. Each channel serves a distinct purpose in reaching target markets efficiently and effectively.

Direct sales to retailers involve manufacturers selling products directly to retail stores or chains. This channel allows manufacturers to maintain control over pricing, branding, and customer relationships. It is common in industries where products require specialized knowledge or where brand reputation is crucial.

Wholesale distribution involves selling products in bulk quantities to wholesalers who then distribute them to retailers or other businesses. Wholesalers play a crucial role in aggregating demand from multiple retailers and providing logistical support such as storage and delivery. This channel is advantageous for manufacturers seeking broader market reach without managing individual retail relationships.

Distributors act as intermediaries between manufacturers and retailers or end consumers. They purchase goods from manufacturers in bulk and sell them to retailers or directly to consumers, handling logistics, marketing, and sales. Distributors often have established networks and expertise in specific markets, making them valuable partners for manufacturers expanding into new territories.

Agents represent manufacturers in foreign markets, negotiating sales and contracts on their behalf. They work on commission and facilitate market entry by leveraging local market knowledge and relationships. Agents are particularly useful in markets where cultural, regulatory, or logistical barriers may pose challenges.

E-commerce platforms have revolutionized distribution by enabling direct-to-consumer sales online. Manufacturers can reach global audiences without physical storefronts, utilizing digital marketing, online payment systems, and efficient shipping solutions. E-commerce channels offer scalability, convenience, and accessibility, appealing to modern consumers seeking convenience and diverse product offerings.

Each channel within international distribution networks serves unique purposes and comes with distinct advantages and challenges. Effective management of these channels involves understanding market dynamics, aligning distribution strategies with business goals, and adapting to changes in consumer behaviour and technological advancements. By leveraging a diverse mix of channels and optimizing distribution routes, businesses can enhance market penetration, improve customer satisfaction, and achieve sustainable growth in global markets.

International distribution networks rely heavily on a robust logistics infrastructure that encompasses various elements crucial for efficient operations and seamless supply chain management. At the core of this infrastructure are transportation modes, including air, sea, road, and rail, which serve as the arteries connecting manufacturers, suppliers, distributors, and ultimately, consumers across global markets.

Air transportation offers speed and efficiency, particularly for high-value or time-sensitive goods. It enables rapid delivery over long distances and is vital for industries like electronics, pharmaceuticals, and perishable goods where timely delivery is critical. Major airports around the world serve as key hubs facilitating the movement of goods between continents.

Sea transportation remains a cornerstone of international trade due to its cost-effectiveness and capacity for transporting large volumes of goods. Ports and shipping lanes connect major trade routes, facilitating the movement of goods between continents. Containerization has revolutionized sea freight, enabling standardized handling and reducing transit times.

Road transportation plays a pivotal role in connecting local and regional markets. It provides flexibility and door-to-door delivery capabilities, making it ideal for short-distance logistics and last-mile distribution. Road networks link manufacturing hubs with distribution centres and retail outlets, ensuring efficient supply chain operations.

Rail transportation offers an environmentally friendly and cost-effective alternative for transporting goods overland. It is particularly advantageous for transporting bulk commodities or goods over long distances within continents. Rail networks connect industrial centres and distribution hubs, complementing other modes of transport to create integrated logistics solutions.

Warehousing facilities form another critical component of logistics infrastructure within international distribution networks. These facilities serve as storage hubs where goods are temporarily housed before distribution. Warehouses are strategically located near transportation hubs and major markets to optimize inventory management, reduce transportation costs, and expedite order fulfillment.

Distribution centres act as pivotal nodes in the supply chain, facilitating the consolidation, sorting, and redistribution of goods to regional or local markets. They are equipped with advanced logistics technologies and systems to manage inventory, process orders, and coordinate shipments efficiently. Distribution centres enhance operational efficiency by minimizing storage costs and improving order accuracy and delivery speed.

Fulfillment centres are specialized facilities designed for e-commerce operations, where orders are processed, packed, and shipped directly to customers. These centres integrate automated picking, packing, and shipping processes to meet the demands of online retail, ensuring fast order processing and delivery times.

Strategically locating logistics infrastructure such as transportation modes, warehousing facilities, distribution centres, and fulfillment centres is crucial for optimizing delivery times and minimizing costs within international distribution networks. By leveraging a well-planned logistics infrastructure, businesses can enhance supply chain efficiency, improve customer satisfaction, and gain a competitive edge in global markets.

Partnerships and alliances play a pivotal role in the success of international distribution networks by enabling companies to navigate the complexities of global markets effectively. These collaborative relationships involve forging strategic connections with local distributors, agents, freight forwarders, and logistics providers in various regions or countries. Such partnerships are instrumental in overcoming barriers related to local regulations, customs procedures, and cultural nuances, thereby streamlining operations and enhancing market penetration strategies.

One of the primary benefits of partnerships in international distribution networks is their ability to leverage local expertise and networks. Local distributors and agents possess intimate knowledge of their markets, including consumer preferences, purchasing behaviours, and competitive landscapes. By partnering with these entities, companies can gain insights into market dynamics that might otherwise be challenging to navigate from a distance. This localized knowledge allows businesses to tailor their product offerings, pricing strategies, and marketing approaches to better suit local market conditions, thereby increasing their competitiveness and market share.

Moreover, partnerships and alliances facilitate compliance with local regulations and customs procedures. International trade involves navigating a complex web of regulations, tariffs, and import/export restrictions that vary from one country to another. Local partners are well-versed in these regulatory frameworks and can provide invaluable guidance on compliance requirements, documentation, and procedural intricacies. This ensures that shipments are processed smoothly through customs, reducing the risk of delays or penalties that could impact supply chain efficiency and customer satisfaction.

Cultural nuances and business practices also significantly influence market entry and operational success in foreign markets. Establishing partnerships with local entities fosters cultural competence and sensitivity, enabling companies to build trust and credibility with local stakeholders. This cultural alignment is crucial for effective communication, relationship building, and negotiation, which are essential for sustainable business growth in diverse global markets.

Furthermore, partnerships and alliances in international distribution networks enhance operational efficiency and flexibility. By collaborating with established logistics providers and freight forwarders, companies can access a reliable network of transportation and distribution channels. This allows for optimized supply chain management, including efficient inventory management, transportation scheduling, and order fulfillment. Shared resources and capabilities through partnerships can also reduce costs associated with warehousing, transportation, and logistics, thereby improving overall profitability and competitiveness.

In essence, partnerships and alliances are integral to navigating the complexities of international distribution networks. They enable companies to leverage local insights, comply with regulatory requirements, navigate cultural differences, and enhance operational efficiency. By forging strategic relationships with local distributors, agents, and logistics providers, businesses can effectively expand their global footprint, penetrate new markets, and sustain long-term growth in a competitive global landscape.

Effective inventory management is a cornerstone of successful international distribution networks, essential for ensuring seamless operations, meeting customer demands, and optimizing costs. These networks rely on sophisticated inventory management systems that strike a delicate balance between centralized and decentralized strategies to maintain optimal stock levels across different locations.

Centralized inventory management involves consolidating inventory in one or a few strategic locations. This approach offers several advantages, including lower holding costs, centralized control over inventory levels and distribution, and simplified logistics. For international distribution networks, centralized inventory hubs are typically located near major transportation hubs or markets, facilitating efficient distribution and minimizing transportation costs.

On the other hand, decentralized inventory management distributes stock across multiple locations, closer to end customers or regional markets. This approach reduces lead times, enhances responsiveness to local demand fluctuations, and mitigates risks associated with disruptions in supply chains or transportation. Decentralized inventory also supports faster order fulfillment and improves customer satisfaction by ensuring products are readily available closer to where they are needed.

A hybrid approach combining elements of both centralized and decentralized inventory strategies is often employed to optimize inventory management in international distribution networks. This hybrid model allows companies to leverage the benefits of centralized control and economies of scale while also maintaining flexibility and responsiveness at the local level. For instance, critical or high-demand products may be centrally stocked, while lower-demand items or regional-specific products are stored closer to end markets.

Advanced inventory management systems play a crucial role in supporting these strategies by providing real-time visibility into inventory levels, demand forecasts, and order statuses across the entire distribution network. Integrated with supply chain management software and ERP systems, these tools enable automated inventory replenishment, demand forecasting, and inventory optimization based on historical data, sales forecasts, and seasonal trends.

Inventory management in international distribution networks also involves managing complexities such as varying customs regulations, lead times for international shipments, and currency fluctuations. Companies must account for these factors when determining optimal inventory levels and distribution strategies to minimize risks and maintain cost-effectiveness.

Furthermore, effective inventory management is closely tied to customer satisfaction and operational efficiency. By ensuring the right products are available at the right locations and times, companies can reduce stockouts, improve order fulfillment rates, and enhance overall service levels. This not only strengthens customer relationships but also supports revenue growth and competitive advantage in global markets.

Navigating international trade regulations, customs requirements, and legal frameworks is a critical aspect of managing global distribution networks. For companies involved in international trade, compliance with import/export laws, product standards, tax regulations, and licensing requirements is not just a legal obligation but also a strategic imperative to ensure smooth operations and avoid potential risks and penalties.

At the core of compliance in international distribution networks is adherence to import/export laws of each country where goods are sourced from or delivered to. These laws govern the movement of goods across borders and include regulations on customs duties, tariffs, quotas, and trade agreements. For example, goods imported into the European Union must comply with EU regulations regarding product safety, labelling, and environmental standards.

Moreover, distribution networks must navigate specific product standards and certifications required by different markets. This may involve conformity assessment procedures, such as product testing, certification, and marking, to ensure compliance with local quality and safety standards. For instance, electronic products entering the United States must comply with FCC (Federal Communications Commission) regulations for electromagnetic interference.

Tax implications are another crucial consideration in international distribution. Companies must understand and comply with VAT (Value Added Tax), GST (Goods and Services Tax), customs duties, and other local taxes applicable in each market. Tax compliance not only affects the cost structure of products but also impacts pricing strategies, profitability, and competitiveness in global markets.

Licensing and permits are essential components of regulatory compliance in international distribution networks. Depending on the nature of the products and the countries involved, companies may need to obtain import/export licenses, permits for restricted goods (such as pharmaceuticals or hazardous materials), and certificates of origin. These documents authenticate the origin of goods and ensure compliance with trade regulations.

Managing compliance in international distribution networks requires a proactive approach and robust systems to stay updated with evolving regulations and requirements. Companies often employ compliance officers or engage legal experts and customs brokers who specialize in international trade to navigate complex regulatory landscapes effectively. These professionals provide guidance on regulatory interpretations, assist in obtaining necessary permits, and ensure that all documentation and procedures align with local and international standards.

Furthermore, technology plays a crucial role in compliance management within distribution networks. Integrated supply chain management systems, customs management software, and ERP (Enterprise Resource Planning) solutions help automate compliance processes, streamline documentation, and facilitate real-time visibility into shipments and regulatory updates. This technological integration enables companies to maintain accurate records, monitor transactional compliance, and respond promptly to regulatory changes or audits.

Navigating international trade regulations, customs requirements, and legal frameworks is a fundamental aspect of managing global distribution networks. For businesses engaged in international trade, compliance with these regulations is not just about avoiding legal pitfalls but also about ensuring operational efficiency, maintaining reputation, and fostering smooth market access worldwide.

At its core, compliance with international trade regulations involves adhering to the import and export laws of each country involved in the supply chain. These laws govern the movement of goods across borders and encompass a wide range of requirements, including customs duties, tariffs, quotas, and trade agreements. For instance, the World Trade Organization (WTO) oversees multilateral trade agreements that member countries must comply with, ensuring fair and transparent trade practices globally.

Product standards and regulations form another critical aspect of compliance. Different countries and regions have specific standards concerning product safety, quality, labelling, and environmental impact. These standards ensure that products entering a market meet local consumer protection laws and do not pose health or safety risks. Compliance often requires product testing, certification, and adherence to labelling requirements that vary across jurisdictions. For example, electronic products sold in the European Union must comply with CE marking standards to demonstrate conformity with EU safety, health, and environmental protection requirements.

Tax implications are also significant in international trade compliance. Companies must understand and comply with Value Added Tax (VAT), Goods and Services Tax (GST), customs duties, and other local taxes applicable in each market where they operate. Tax compliance not only affects the cost structure of goods but also influences pricing strategies, profit margins, and overall competitiveness. Ensuring accurate calculation and timely payment of taxes is crucial to avoid penalties and maintain financial health.

Licensing and permits are additional components of regulatory compliance in international distribution networks. Depending on the nature of the goods and the countries involved, companies may need to obtain import/export licenses, permits for restricted goods (such as pharmaceuticals or hazardous materials), and certificates of origin. These documents authenticate the origin of goods and ensure compliance with trade regulations designed to protect national security, public health, and the environment.

Navigating these complex regulatory landscapes requires a proactive approach and meticulous attention to detail. Many companies employ compliance officers, legal experts, or engage customs brokers who specialize in international trade to navigate these complexities effectively. These professionals provide expertise in interpreting regulations, obtaining necessary permits, and ensuring that all documentation and procedures align with local and international standards.

Moreover, technological advancements play a pivotal role in enhancing compliance management within distribution networks. Integrated supply chain management systems, customs management software, and Enterprise Resource Planning (ERP) solutions automate compliance processes, streamline documentation, and provide real-time visibility into shipments and regulatory updates. This technological integration enables companies to maintain accurate records, monitor transactional compliance, and promptly respond to regulatory changes or audits.

Ensuring excellent customer service and support across international borders is essential for businesses aiming to build and maintain strong customer relationships and drive growth in global markets. This aspect of managing international distribution networks goes beyond simply delivering products—it involves understanding and meeting diverse customer expectations, addressing cultural nuances, and effectively resolving issues in a timely manner.

One of the primary challenges in international customer service is overcoming language barriers. Operating in multiple countries means interacting with customers who speak different languages. Providing multilingual support is crucial for ensuring clear communication and addressing customer inquiries and concerns effectively. This often involves hiring bilingual or multilingual staff, utilizing translation services, or implementing customer service platforms that support multiple languages. By speaking the customer's language—both literally and figuratively—businesses can enhance customer satisfaction and loyalty.

Localizing marketing and sales efforts is another key aspect of effective international customer service. It entails adapting marketing campaigns, product messaging, and sales strategies to resonate with local cultures, preferences, and market conditions. This may involve tailoring promotional materials, advertisements, and product descriptions to reflect regional tastes and sensitivities. For instance, imagery, colours, and symbols that hold cultural significance may need to be adjusted to align with local norms and values, thereby enhancing the relevance and appeal of products to local customers.

Responsive handling of inquiries and issues is critical for maintaining customer satisfaction across borders. Customers expect prompt and efficient resolution of problems, whether related to product inquiries, order status updates, or post-purchase support. Establishing robust communication channels, such as dedicated customer service hotlines, email support, live chat, and social media platforms, allows customers to reach out easily and receive timely assistance. It's essential for customer service teams to be well-trained in handling diverse customer queries and equipped with the necessary information and tools to provide accurate and helpful responses.

Moreover, international customer service involves understanding and adhering to local regulations and practices related to customer rights, data privacy, and consumer protection. Compliance with these regulations builds trust with customers and demonstrates a commitment to ethical business practices. For example, businesses operating in the European Union must comply with the General Data Protection Regulation (GDPR), which governs the collection, use, and protection of personal data of EU residents. Adhering to such regulations not only avoids legal risks but also enhances the reputation of the company as a responsible global player.

Furthermore, leveraging technology can significantly enhance international customer service capabilities. Customer relationship management (CRM) systems, automated ticketing systems, and AI-powered chatbots can streamline customer interactions, improve response times, and provide personalized customer experiences. These tools enable businesses to track customer preferences, anticipate needs, and deliver targeted support efficiently across different time zones and regions.

In the realm of international distribution networks, leveraging advanced technology and integrating data across various platforms are crucial for optimizing operations and maintaining competitiveness in the global marketplace. Technology plays a pivotal role in enhancing efficiency, accuracy, and agility across the supply chain, from sourcing raw materials to delivering finished products to end customers.

Supply chain management (SCM) systems are at the core of modern logistics operations. These systems integrate and automate processes involved in sourcing, procurement, production planning, inventory management, logistics, and distribution. By centralizing and streamlining these operations, SCM systems enable real-time visibility into inventory levels, order status, and shipment tracking across multiple locations and countries. This visibility not only improves decision-making but also facilitates proactive management of supply chain disruptions and inventory fluctuations.

Enterprise resource planning (ERP) software complements SCM systems by integrating business processes such as finance, human resources, manufacturing, and sales into a single unified platform. In the context of international distribution networks, ERP systems provide a holistic view of business operations, enabling seamless coordination and collaboration across departments and geographies. This integration enhances data accuracy, reduces operational costs, and improves overall efficiency by eliminating redundant tasks and manual errors.

Advanced analytics and business intelligence tools play a critical role in leveraging the vast amount of data generated within international distribution networks. By analysing historical trends, market demand patterns, and customer behaviour, businesses can gain valuable insights to optimize inventory levels, forecast demand more accurately, and identify opportunities for cost savings and revenue growth. Predictive analytics capabilities enable proactive decision-making, allowing businesses to anticipate potential issues and adjust strategies in real-time to meet changing market conditions.

Real-time tracking and monitoring of shipments are essential components of effective international distribution. Technologies such as GPS tracking systems, RFID tags, and IoT sensors provide granular visibility into the movement and condition of goods throughout the supply chain. This real-time data allows businesses to mitigate risks, optimize route planning, and ensure on-time deliveries. Moreover, it enhances customer service by providing accurate information about shipment status and estimated arrival times.

Integration of technology also extends to customer-facing aspects of international distribution networks. E-commerce platforms, mobile apps, and customer portals enable seamless ordering, tracking, and communication with customers worldwide. These digital interfaces not only enhance the customer experience by offering convenience and transparency but also enable personalized marketing strategies based on customer preferences and purchasing behaviours.

However, successful integration of technology in international distribution networks requires careful planning and investment. Businesses must ensure that systems are scalable, adaptable to local regulations and market dynamics, and capable of interoperability with existing infrastructure and third-party systems. Training employees to effectively use and maximize the benefits of technology is equally important to drive adoption and ensure smooth operations.

In the realm of international distribution networks, navigating risks is a critical aspect of ensuring operational resilience and sustained success. These networks face a myriad of risks that can significantly impact supply chains and disrupt business operations on a global scale. Understanding and effectively managing these risks requires proactive strategies and robust contingency plans tailored to the complexities of international trade and logistics.

One of the foremost risks that international distribution networks contend with is currency fluctuations. Variations in exchange rates between currencies can affect the cost of goods, profitability margins, and overall financial stability. To mitigate these risks, businesses often employ hedging strategies or financial instruments that stabilize currency exposure, thereby minimizing the impact of volatile exchange rates on their bottom line. Additionally, maintaining diversified currency holdings or utilizing local currency invoicing where possible can provide further insulation against currency risks.

Political instability and regulatory changes in different countries pose significant challenges to international distribution networks. Shifts in government policies, trade agreements, or geopolitical tensions can disrupt supply chains, delay shipments, or lead to sudden market access restrictions. To manage these risks, businesses engage in thorough political risk assessments, monitor geopolitical developments, and establish alternative sourcing and distribution channels in regions prone to instability. Building strong relationships with local authorities and industry associations can also facilitate navigating regulatory complexities and ensuring compliance with evolving laws.

Supply chain disruptions are another critical risk that international distribution networks must anticipate and mitigate. Events such as natural disasters, supplier bankruptcies, labour strikes, or disruptions in transportation infrastructure can halt production and delay deliveries. Adopting a diversified supplier base spread across different regions or countries reduces dependence on single suppliers and minimizes the risk of prolonged disruptions. Moreover, implementing robust inventory management practices, maintaining safety stock levels, and establishing agile logistics networks enable swift responses to unforeseen disruptions without compromising on service levels.

Global pandemics, as exemplified by recent events, underscore the vulnerability of international distribution networks to widespread health crises. The COVID-19 pandemic, for instance, led to border closures, logistical bottlenecks, and unprecedented demand fluctuations. In response, businesses are increasingly integrating pandemic preparedness into their risk management frameworks. This includes developing continuity plans that address workforce safety, remote working capabilities, supply chain flexibility, and alternative logistics routes. Investing in advanced technologies for remote monitoring, virtual collaboration, and contactless operations also enhances resilience in the face of future health emergencies.

Insurance coverage plays a pivotal role in mitigating financial risks associated with international distribution networks. Businesses typically procure comprehensive insurance policies that cover various aspects of their operations, including cargo insurance for goods in transit, business interruption insurance for revenue losses due to disruptions, and liability insurance for legal protection against third-party claims. Conducting regular reviews of insurance policies and adjusting coverage levels based on evolving risk profiles and business expansion plans ensures adequate protection against unforeseen contingencies.

Source Potential Networks

Expanding internationally involves strategic decisions about how products or services will reach customers in foreign markets, and choosing the right international distribution channels is paramount to success. These channels constitute the network of intermediaries connecting producers to end-users across different countries and regions [104]. The selection of distribution channels is influenced by several critical factors, beginning with the nature of the product or service. Complex or specialized products might necessitate direct distribution channels to maintain quality control and provide adequate customer support, whereas standardized products might benefit from indirect channels to leverage economies of scale and market coverage [104].

Additionally, the characteristics of the target market play a crucial role. Factors such as market size, geographic dispersion, cultural preferences, and legal requirements impact channel choices. Larger and more diverse markets often require extensive distribution networks to ensure comprehensive market penetration and customer accessibility. Conversely, markets with specific cultural norms or regulatory environments may necessitate localized distribution approaches tailored to meet local expectations and compliance standards [104].

The level of market entry commitment also shapes distribution strategies. Companies testing new markets or aiming to minimize initial investment risks may opt for low-cost, flexible distribution channels such as exporting through agents or distributors. Conversely, those pursuing aggressive market entry strategies may establish direct channels like subsidiaries or joint ventures to secure greater control over operations and market positioning [104].

In practice, international distribution channels manifest in three primary types: direct, indirect, and hybrid channels. Direct channels involve direct interaction between the producer and end-users, leveraging methods like online sales, direct sales teams, or telemarketing. These channels offer control over customer relationships and distribution processes but require substantial investment in logistics and market development [104].

Indirect channels utilize intermediaries such as agents, distributors, wholesalers, or retailers to manage distribution tasks [104]. These channels reduce the producer's operational complexity and upfront costs while benefiting from intermediaries' local market knowledge and established networks. However, they involve relinquishing some control over the customer interface and distribution logistics.

Hybrid channels combine elements of both direct and indirect approaches. Strategies like franchising, licensing, or strategic alliances allow producers to customize distribution methods to suit specific market conditions. Hybrid channels offer flexibility and scalability, but they require careful coordination to manage the diverse interests and objectives of different channel partners effectively [104].

Managing international distribution partners presents both challenges and benefits. Challenges include identifying suitable partners aligned with the producer's goals and values, negotiating clear agreements that define roles and responsibilities, and overcoming communication barriers across diverse cultures and legal frameworks. Effective management entails continuous monitoring of partner performance, providing necessary support and training, and adapting strategies to evolving market conditions [104].

Despite challenges, managing international distribution partners offers significant benefits. It facilitates access to new markets and customer segments, enhances competitive advantage by leveraging partner strengths and resources, and increases profitability through expanded sales and reduced distribution costs. Moreover, effective partner management improves customer satisfaction by delivering localized products and services efficiently, thereby fostering brand loyalty and market growth.

Identifying and establishing an effective enterprise distribution network begins with a thorough assessment of current capabilities and future needs. This process involves evaluating existing distribution channels, logistics infrastructure, and operational efficiencies to identify areas for improvement and expansion. Organizations typically start by analysing their current distribution network performance metrics, such as delivery times, customer satisfaction levels, and operational costs. This analysis provides a baseline against which future network requirements can be evaluated.

Simultaneously, identifying potential agents capable of servicing current or anticipated operations is crucial. These agents could include logistics providers, freight forwarders, distribution centres, or third-party logistics (3PL) providers. Criteria for selection often encompass factors such as geographic coverage, service offerings, industry expertise, technological capabilities, and reputation in the market. Researching industry directories, networking within relevant trade associations, and leveraging professional networks help in compiling a list of potential service providers.

Once a list of potential service agents is compiled, organizations initiate contact through various means such as direct inquiries, requests for proposals (RFPs), or formal meetings. During these initial contacts, organizations seek to gather comprehensive information about each service provider's capacity, capabilities, and viability to meet specific operational requirements. Key questions typically revolve around the provider's experience in handling similar logistics challenges, their network reach, technological infrastructure, service level agreements (SLAs), and their ability to scale operations as needed.

Information sourcing involves conducting detailed discussions with potential service agents to assess their operational strengths and weaknesses. This includes evaluating their warehousing facilities, transportation fleet, IT systems for tracking and reporting, adherence to regulatory compliance, and their ability to handle specialized logistics requirements if applicable. Organizations may also request references or case studies to gauge the provider's track record and customer satisfaction levels.

Throughout this process, transparency and communication are essential. Clear articulation of organizational needs, expectations, and timelines ensures that potential service providers can respond effectively with tailored solutions. Moreover, establishing a collaborative relationship from the outset fosters mutual understanding and alignment on strategic objectives. This phase sets the foundation for selecting the most suitable service agents who can contribute to optimizing the enterprise distribution network, enhancing operational efficiency, and ultimately supporting business growth in competitive global markets.

When evaluating potential distribution partners for international expansion, businesses undertake a thorough assessment to ensure alignment with strategic goals and operational needs. This evaluation process involves scrutinizing various aspects that can significantly impact the success of the partnership and the effectiveness of distribution efforts [104].

One of the primary considerations is the partner's reputation, experience, and track record within the industry. A partner with a solid reputation and extensive experience in distributing similar products or services demonstrates reliability and competence. Their track record should reflect successful distribution operations, ideally in the target market or similar geographical regions, showcasing their capability to navigate local market dynamics and challenges [104].

Alignment with business goals and values is equally critical. This entails assessing whether the potential partner comprehends your brand identity, target audience, and market positioning. A partner who shares similar values and vision is more likely to contribute effectively to achieving mutual objectives. This alignment fosters a cohesive approach to market entry and expansion strategies, minimizing potential conflicts and maximizing collaborative efforts [104].

Market knowledge is another essential factor. Evaluating the partner's understanding of the target market includes their grasp of consumer preferences, cultural nuances, and compliance with local regulations. A partner with deep market insights can tailor distribution strategies to resonate with local consumer behaviours and preferences, thereby enhancing market penetration and acceptance of products or services [104].

The strength of the partner's distribution network is pivotal. An established and well-connected distribution network ensures efficient logistics and widespread market coverage. Assessing the partner's network involves examining the reach and capabilities of their distribution channels, warehouses, transportation systems, and fulfillment centres. A robust network enables timely delivery, minimizes supply chain disruptions, and supports scalability as business demands grow in the target market [104].

Financial stability and capability to invest in distribution activities are fundamental considerations. A financially stable partner possesses adequate resources, liquidity, and capital to sustain distribution operations and support growth initiatives. Their financial health not only ensures continuity in service but also indicates a commitment to long-term partnership and investment in expanding market presence [104].

Moreover, evaluating the partner's marketing and sales capabilities is crucial. A partner with strong marketing prowess and effective sales channels can drive product awareness, stimulate demand, and accelerate sales growth. Assessing their marketing strategies, sales team expertise, and customer relationship management practices provides insights into their ability to effectively promote and sell products or services to the target audience [104].

Communication and collaboration skills play a pivotal role in the success of international distribution partnerships. Effective communication fosters transparency, facilitates timely decision-making, and promotes a unified approach to resolving challenges. Collaborative skills ensure smooth coordination between partners, enabling proactive problem-solving and alignment on strategic initiatives to optimize distribution efficiencies and customer satisfaction [104].

Lastly, conducting thorough due diligence by seeking references and reviewing past performance is essential. Testimonials, case studies, or success stories from previous collaborations offer valuable insights into the partner's reliability, responsiveness, and ability to deliver results. This information validates their claims and provides confidence in their capacity to meet expectations and support business objectives effectively [104].

Establishing Potential Service Provider Profiles

When evaluating potential distributors or service providers, thorough assessment and documentation of their contact details, scope of operations, costs, and service standards are essential steps in establishing a reliable partnership. This process begins with gathering comprehensive information about the potential partner, including their organizational structure, geographical coverage, and the range of services they offer. Understanding the distributor's capabilities and limitations helps in determining whether they align with your business needs and operational requirements.

Cost analysis forms a crucial part of the evaluation process. This involves not only assessing the initial costs of engagement but also considering long-term expenses associated with the distributor's services. Factors such as pricing structures, fees, and any additional charges must be clearly understood and documented to ensure financial transparency and viability.

Service standards play a pivotal role in determining the quality of service delivery and customer satisfaction. Evaluating the distributor's service standards involves examining their track record in meeting deadlines, resolving issues, and maintaining communication throughout the distribution process. This assessment ensures that the distributor can uphold the level of service that aligns with your company's expectations and customer service commitments.

Assessing the technostructures and infrastructures of potential service providers involves evaluating their technological capabilities and operational systems. This includes assessing the compatibility of their systems with your own operational processes and technological platforms. Compatibility ensures seamless integration and efficient collaboration between your business and the distributor, minimizing disruptions and enhancing operational efficiency.

Another critical aspect is establishing the potential service provider's current credit ratings in accordance with enterprise procedures. This involves conducting a thorough credit assessment to evaluate their financial stability, creditworthiness, and ability to meet financial obligations. A reliable credit rating provides assurance that the distributor has the financial capacity to sustain operations and fulfill contractual commitments over the long term.

Security procedures are paramount when selecting potential service providers, especially in contexts involving sensitive or high-value goods. Establishing security protocols in accordance with workplace requirements ensures that the distributor adheres to industry-standard security practices to safeguard your products, information, and business interests. This may include assessing their physical security measures, data protection policies, and compliance with regulatory requirements related to security and confidentiality.

Developing a distribution strategy for international markets is a pivotal step for any business aiming to expand its reach beyond domestic borders. This strategy dictates how products or services will reach target customers and defines the management of relationships with distribution partners, crucially impacting market penetration, cost efficiencies, and customer satisfaction. However, crafting such a strategy is complex and multifaceted, requiring careful consideration of several key aspects tailored to the unique characteristics of each market [104].

One critical consideration in developing an international distribution strategy is the type of distribution channel to employ. Direct channels involve selling products or services directly to customers without intermediaries, fostering closer control over customer relationships and service quality. This approach is beneficial for companies with complex or customized offerings that require personalized support. In contrast, indirect channels utilize intermediaries like distributors, wholesalers, retailers, agents, or brokers to facilitate distribution. Indirect channels can leverage existing networks for broader market reach and operational efficiencies, making them suitable for standardized or mass-produced goods where economies of scale play a significant role. Hybrid or multi-channel approaches may also be adopted to cater to diverse customer segments or enhance market coverage [104].

Selecting the right distribution partners is another crucial aspect. Distributors, wholesalers, retailers, agents, and brokers each play distinct roles in the distribution process, influencing market access, customer reach, and operational dynamics. When evaluating potential partners, businesses must assess factors such as market presence, reliability, compatibility with brand values, local market expertise, and commitment to service excellence. Choosing partners aligned with these criteria enhances market entry strategies and mitigates risks associated with unfamiliar markets or regulatory landscapes [104].

Managing distribution relationships effectively is equally essential to the success of an international distribution strategy. This involves setting clear expectations, establishing performance metrics, providing necessary training and support, and fostering open communication channels. Effective relationship management ensures consistency in product/service delivery, enhances partner and customer satisfaction, optimizes distribution processes, and strengthens competitive positioning. For instance, clear communication of quality standards and regular performance evaluations help maintain product/service consistency, while proactive conflict resolution mechanisms ensure timely issue resolution, fostering trust and loyalty among partners [104].

Moreover, ongoing evaluation and adaptation of the distribution strategy are critical as market dynamics evolve. Market research, customer feedback, competitor analysis, and regulatory updates inform strategic adjustments to optimize distribution channels, enhance partner relationships, and capitalize on emerging opportunities. Flexibility and responsiveness to market changes enable businesses to stay competitive and sustain growth in international markets [104].

Selecting the right distribution channels and partners is a pivotal decision for businesses expanding internationally, as it directly impacts market reach, operational efficiency, and overall business success. Distribution channels serve as the pathways through which products or services reach end-customers in diverse markets, while distribution partners, such as wholesalers, retailers, agents, or distributors, facilitate this process by leveraging their networks and expertise. This strategic choice involves careful consideration of various factors to ensure alignment with business objectives and market dynamics.

Firstly, understanding the characteristics of your product or service is essential. Factors such as complexity, customization, and after-sales service requirements influence whether a direct, indirect, or hybrid distribution approach is suitable. For instance, high-tech products may benefit from direct channels to maintain control over quality and customer support, whereas consumer goods might leverage indirect channels for broader market access and cost efficiency.

Market characteristics also play a crucial role in channel selection. Factors like market size, growth potential, competitive landscape, consumer behaviours, and regulatory environments vary across markets and influence distribution strategies. For example, entering a highly regulated market may require partnering with distributors who understand local compliance and administrative procedures, ensuring smoother market entry and operations [104].

Equally important are the characteristics of potential distribution channels and partners themselves. Evaluating their reach, reputation, operational capabilities, communication protocols, cost structures, and alignment with your brand values is critical. This evaluation ensures that chosen partners can effectively enhance market penetration and customer satisfaction while minimizing risks associated with operational inconsistencies or reputational mismatches.

To guide the selection process, businesses should follow structured steps [104]:

1. **Define Distribution Objectives and Criteria:** Establish clear goals such as market share expansion, cost reduction, or brand enhancement. Criteria might include partner reputation, market coverage, cultural compatibility, or risk tolerance levels.

2. **Research Distribution Options:** Utilize market reports, industry publications, trade shows, and personal networks to explore available distribution channels and potential partners. Compare direct versus indirect approaches and assess the pros and cons of exclusive versus non-exclusive agreements based on your defined criteria.

3. **Evaluate and Select Partners:** Use scoring systems, decision matrices, or other evaluation frameworks to compare and prioritize potential partners. Conduct due diligence through references, site visits, or credential verification to confirm reliability and suitability.

4. **Negotiate and Formalize Agreements:** Once selected, negotiate terms that encompass roles, responsibilities, pricing, marketing support, training, performance metrics, and termination conditions. Formalize agreements through contracts or memoranda to protect mutual interests and ensure clarity.

5. **Manage and Monitor Relationships:** Establish robust communication channels, feedback mechanisms, and performance metrics to monitor partner performance regularly. Provide ongoing support, training, and incentives to optimize partner engagement and operational efficiency.

Throughout this process, continuous review and adaptation of the distribution strategy are essential to address evolving market dynamics, customer expectations, and competitive pressures. Regular performance evaluations enable businesses to make informed adjustments, refine distribution strategies, and capitalize on emerging opportunities for sustained growth and market leadership [104].

In essence, selecting the right distribution channels and partners demands a strategic approach tailored to product characteristics, market conditions, and partner capabilities. By meticulously assessing these factors and following structured steps, businesses can enhance their market entry strategies, optimize distribution efficiency, and foster long-term success in international markets.

Contracting Service Providers

Negotiating terms of operation and performance standards with selected service providers is a critical phase in establishing productive and compliant business relationships, particularly in international trade environments. This process involves defining clear expectations, responsibilities, and benchmarks for service delivery. Effective negotiation ensures that both parties align on crucial aspects such as service levels, quality standards, timelines, pricing structures, and dispute resolution mechanisms. It also sets the foundation for mutual understanding and accountability throughout the contractual period.

Once negotiations are finalized, completing contracts with selected service providers is the next step. This involves formalizing the agreed terms and conditions into legally binding agreements that outline rights, obligations, and liabilities of both parties. Contracts typically specify deliverables, milestones, payment terms, termination clauses, confidentiality obligations, and compliance with regulatory requirements. Completing contracts within the scope of authority ensures adherence to corporate governance and legal frameworks, safeguarding against unauthorized commitments and potential disputes.

Monitoring service provider performance against identified targets within the contract is essential for maintaining operational efficiency and achieving desired outcomes. This entails establishing key performance indicators (KPIs), conducting regular assessments, and measuring actual performance against agreed metrics. Monitoring allows proactive identification of issues or deviations from agreed standards, enabling timely corrective actions to ensure continuous improvement and alignment with business objectives.

In dynamic international and local trading environments, contract variances may arise due to changes in regulations, market conditions, or business priorities. It is crucial to renegotiate contract terms when necessary to accommodate these variances while complying with statutory requirements and adapting to evolving trade dynamics. This process involves assessing the impact of changes, proposing amendments, and reaching mutual agreement with service providers to realign expectations and contractual obligations effectively.

Finally, managing contracts and ancillary documentation in accordance with enterprise and regulatory requirements ensures proper governance and accountability. This includes securely storing contracts, amendments, correspondence, and supporting documentation in accessible formats. Compliance with regulatory frameworks ensures transparency, auditability, and legal validity, facilitating efficient contract management and mitigating risks associated with non-compliance or disputes.

Negotiating distribution agreements in the context of international markets is a strategic process that requires careful planning, clear communication, and a thorough understanding of market dynamics and partner capabilities. At its core, this negotiation aims to establish terms that facilitate efficient product or service distribution while protecting the interests of both parties involved [104].

Before initiating negotiations, it's crucial to define your distribution goals clearly. This includes identifying target markets, preferred distribution channels (direct, indirect, or hybrid), and specific objectives such as market penetration, sales growth, or brand visibility. Understanding these goals provides a framework for evaluating potential partners and shaping the negotiation process towards achieving mutually beneficial outcomes [104].

Thorough research into potential distribution partners is essential. Assessing their reputation, market presence, customer base, and operational capabilities helps ensure alignment with your brand values and market strategy. This research informs discussions on how each party can leverage strengths and mitigate weaknesses to maximize market reach and effectiveness [104].

Central to negotiating distribution agreements is defining roles and responsibilities. Clearly outlining what each party is expected to contribute—whether it's manufacturing and supply capabilities or distribution network management—minimizes ambiguity and sets expectations for operational efficiency and accountability. This clarity fosters a collaborative approach to achieving shared business objectives [104].

Pricing and payment terms are pivotal aspects of negotiations. Both parties must agree on pricing structures that reflect production costs, market demand, and competitive positioning while ensuring profitability. Negotiating payment schedules that accommodate cash flow needs and market realities can also contribute to a sustainable and mutually beneficial partnership [104].

Territorial rights and exclusivity are critical considerations in distribution agreements. Defining the geographic scope in which the distributor will operate helps prevent overlap and potential conflicts with other distribution channels. Exclusivity provisions, if granted, should align with market dynamics and strategic goals, balancing market coverage with competitive advantages [104].

Establishing clear performance metrics and KPIs is essential for monitoring and evaluating the success of the distribution agreement. Metrics such as sales targets, market share growth, customer satisfaction levels, and logistics performance enable ongoing assessment and adjustment of strategies to optimize outcomes. Regular review of these metrics facilitates proactive decision-making and fosters a responsive approach to market dynamics [104].

Intellectual property rights protection is another key area in negotiation. Safeguarding trademarks, patents, copyrights, and proprietary technology ensures brand integrity and prevents unauthorized use or infringement. Clear agreements on intellectual property usage and enforcement mechanisms provide legal recourse in case of disputes or breaches [104].

Including termination and dispute resolution clauses is vital for mitigating risks associated with unforeseen circumstances or disagreements. These clauses outline conditions under which the agreement can be terminated and specify procedures for resolving disputes swiftly and fairly. This proactive approach minimizes disruptions and preserves the integrity of the partnership over time [104].

Managing International Distribution Networks

Managing international distribution networks is a critical endeavour for businesses looking to expand globally. It involves a multifaceted approach encompassing strategic partner selection, clear agreement establishment, effective coordination, continuous performance monitoring, and adept handling of challenges that may arise in diverse international markets [104].

Managing international distribution networks involves overseeing and optimizing the flow of products or services from production or source locations to end-users across multiple countries or regions. This process requires careful planning, coordination, and continuous improvement to ensure efficiency, reliability, and responsiveness to market demands. Here's a detailed exploration of how to manage international distribution networks effectively:

Strategic Planning and Network Design: Effective management begins with strategic planning and network design. This involves:

- **Market Analysis and Segmentation:** Understanding target markets, customer preferences, and buying behaviours to tailor distribution strategies accordingly.

- **Channel Selection:** Choosing appropriate distribution channels (direct, indirect, hybrid) based on market characteristics, product type, and competitive landscape.

- **Network Optimization:** Designing an optimal distribution network that balances costs, service levels, and flexibility. This may include decisions on warehouse locations, transportation modes, and inventory positioning.

Partner Selection and Relationship Management: Selecting reliable distribution partners and managing relationships is crucial:

- **Due Diligence:** Conducting thorough assessments to evaluate partners' capabilities, reputation, financial stability, and alignment with business goals.

- **Contract Negotiation:** Negotiating clear agreements that define roles, responsibilities, performance metrics, pricing, and dispute resolution mechanisms.

- **Communication and Collaboration:** Establishing effective communication channels and fostering collaborative relationships to ensure alignment on goals, strategies, and operational practices.

Logistics and Supply Chain Management: Efficient logistics and supply chain management are essential:

- **Inventory Optimization:** Balancing inventory levels across locations to meet demand variability while minimizing carrying costs and stockouts.

- **Transportation Management:** Selecting and managing transportation modes (air, sea, road, rail) to optimize delivery times, costs, and sustainability.

- **Warehousing and Distribution Centres:** Ensuring warehouses and distribution centres are strategically located, well-equipped, and compliant with local regulations.

Technology Integration and Data Analytics: Leveraging technology enhances visibility and decision-making:

- **SCM and ERP Systems:** Implementing supply chain management (SCM) and enterprise resource planning (ERP) systems for real-time tracking, inventory management, and performance monitoring.

- **Advanced Analytics:** Utilizing data analytics to forecast demand, optimize routes, identify trends, and improve operational efficiency.

Compliance and Risk Management: Managing regulatory compliance and mitigating risks:

- **Legal and Regulatory Compliance:** Ensuring adherence to international trade laws, customs regulations, product standards, and licensing requirements in each market.

- **Risk Mitigation:** Developing contingency plans for currency fluctuations, political instability, supply chain disruptions, and global emergencies.

Performance Monitoring and Continuous Improvement: Monitoring network performance and driving continuous improvement:

- **KPIs and Metrics:** Establishing key performance indicators (KPIs) such as fill rates, on-time delivery, customer satisfaction, and cost per unit shipped.

- **Benchmarking and Evaluation:** Comparing performance against benchmarks, conducting regular reviews, and identifying opportunities for enhancement.

- **Adaptation and Flexibility:** Remaining agile to adapt strategies in response to market changes, customer feedback, and evolving business objectives.

Customer Service Excellence: Ensuring consistent service across borders:

- **Multilingual Support:** Providing language-specific customer service and support to address diverse customer needs and preferences.

- **Responsive Handling:** Promptly addressing inquiries, resolving issues, and maintaining high standards of service to enhance customer satisfaction and loyalty.

In essence, effective management of international distribution networks requires a holistic approach that integrates strategic planning, partnership management, logistics optimization, technological innovation, compliance assurance, risk mitigation, performance monitoring, and customer-centricity. By focusing on these aspects and continuously refining strategies, businesses can build resilient and efficient distribution networks that support sustainable growth and competitive advantage in global markets.

To begin with, selecting the right distribution channels and partners is foundational. This decision hinges on factors such as product characteristics, target market dynamics, and strategic objectives. Businesses may opt for distributors, agents, retailers, or direct sales depending on their specific needs and market conditions. Thorough research and due diligence are crucial to assess potential partners' capabilities, market presence, reputation, and alignment with the business's values and goals. This ensures that chosen partners can effectively represent and distribute products or services in their respective regions [104].

Once partnerships are established, clarity in agreements is paramount. Formalizing relationships through well-defined contracts helps mitigate misunderstandings and sets expectations regarding roles, responsibilities, exclusivity arrangements, pricing structures, delivery terms, service levels, and marketing efforts. Clear agreements foster trust and collaboration between business entities, paving the way for productive long-term partnerships.

Effective coordination and regular communication are essential components of managing international distribution networks. Operating across different time zones, languages, and cultures necessitates ongoing communication to ensure all partners are well-informed, trained, and supported. Businesses should provide partners with necessary updates on products, marketing materials, and operational changes. Equally important is soliciting feedback from partners to address concerns promptly and adapt strategies to local market needs. This proactive approach helps maintain strong relationships and enhances partner satisfaction and engagement.

Monitoring and evaluating performance are integral to assessing the effectiveness of distribution networks. Key performance indicators (KPIs) such as sales volume, revenue growth, market share, customer satisfaction, and adherence to service standards should be established and regularly reviewed. Analysing performance data allows businesses to identify areas for improvement, provide constructive feedback to partners, and recognize achievements. This iterative process ensures alignment with business objectives and drives continuous enhancement of distribution strategies.

Despite the benefits, managing international distribution networks presents challenges that require strategic navigation. One significant challenge is the potential loss of control and visibility over product distribution and customer service when relying on external partners. Issues such as varying product quality, delivery delays, inventory management discrepancies, pricing inconsistencies, or regulatory compliance gaps can impact brand reputation and customer satisfaction. To mitigate these risks, businesses should implement robust partner selection criteria, enforce contractual obligations rigorously, and conduct regular audits and performance reviews [104].

Cultural and linguistic differences pose another challenge, affecting communication and collaboration with international partners. Variances in norms, values, and business practices can lead to misunderstandings or conflicts. Overcoming these challenges involves fostering cultural sensitivity, investing in language support where necessary, and building mutual understanding and respect among diverse teams and partners.

Additionally, competition and conflict may arise among multiple partners operating in the same market or across overlapping territories. Issues such as price competition, channel conflicts, or customer acquisition battles can strain relationships and undermine collaborative efforts. To mitigate these conflicts, businesses should carefully segment markets, establish clear boundaries and incentives, and foster a cooperative environment where partners perceive mutual benefits in collaboration rather than rivalry.

Monitoring and evaluating performance in international distribution is a critical process that enables businesses to gauge the effectiveness of their strategies, optimize operations, and foster growth in global markets. By systematically tracking key performance indicators (KPIs) and leveraging data-driven insights, businesses can make informed decisions and continuously improve their distribution networks [104].

Firstly, defining clear KPIs is foundational. These indicators should align closely with strategic distribution goals and provide measurable benchmarks for success. Typical KPIs include sales revenue, market share, customer satisfaction ratings, on-time delivery rates, and return on investment (ROI). Each KPI offers a distinct perspective on distribution performance, allowing businesses to assess different facets of their operations comprehensively.

The following are some example KPIs used to measure distribution performance:

1. **Sales Revenue:** This KPI tracks the total revenue generated from product sales through different distribution channels over a specific period. It helps assess the effectiveness of sales strategies and channel performance in driving revenue growth.

2. **Market Share:** Market share indicates the percentage of total market sales that a company captures compared to its competitors. It provides insights into the company's competitive position and penetration within specific markets or segments.

3. **Customer Satisfaction Ratings:** Measuring customer satisfaction through surveys or feedback ratings helps gauge how well distribution channels are meeting customer expectations. High satisfaction levels typically correlate with repeat business and positive brand perception.

4. **On-time Delivery Rates:** This KPI measures the percentage of orders delivered on time to customers. It reflects the reliability and efficiency of distribution channels in meeting delivery commitments and fulfilling customer expectations.

5. **Return on Investment (ROI):** ROI calculates the profitability of investments made in distribution activities relative to the costs incurred. It con-

siders factors such as sales revenue generated, distribution costs, and investment in channel development or infrastructure.

6. **Inventory Turnover**: Inventory turnover ratio assesses how quickly inventory is sold and replaced within a given period. A higher turnover indicates efficient inventory management and effective sales through distribution channels.

7. **Fill Rate**: Fill rate measures the percentage of customer orders fulfilled completely from available inventory. It indicates inventory availability and distribution channel responsiveness to customer demand.

8. **Channel Partner Performance**: Assessing specific metrics related to channel partners, such as their sales volume, market coverage, and adherence to agreed-upon terms, helps evaluate their contribution to overall distribution effectiveness.

9. **Customer Lifetime Value (CLV)**: CLV estimates the total revenue a business can expect from a single customer over their entire relationship with the company. It helps prioritize customer acquisition and retention strategies through distribution channels.

10. **Cost per Order**: This metric calculates the average cost incurred to process and fulfill customer orders through distribution channels. Lowering the cost per order improves profitability and operational efficiency in distribution.

These KPIs provide a holistic view of distribution performance, enabling businesses to measure success, identify areas for improvement, and align distribution strategies with broader organizational goals effectively. Adjusting these metrics based on specific business objectives and market dynamics enhances their relevance and usefulness in evaluating distribution effectiveness [104].

Implementing robust tracking mechanisms is essential to effectively monitor distribution performance. Leveraging advanced technology solutions such as customer relationship management (CRM) systems, supply chain management software, and data analytics tools provides real-time visibility into sales trends, inventory levels, customer feedback, and operational efficiencies. These tools not only streamline data collection but also enable businesses to spot emerging issues promptly and capitalize on opportunities for improvement [104].

Regular performance reviews with distribution partners are integral to evaluating their contribution to overall performance. These reviews serve as structured checkpoints to assess partner adherence to KPIs, identify any performance gaps or bottlenecks, and foster collaborative problem-solving. Open and transparent communication during these reviews ensures alignment on expectations and enables swift corrective actions when necessary, reinforcing productive partnerships [104].

Analysing data collected from tracking mechanisms yields valuable insights into distribution performance trends. By scrutinizing patterns, correlations, and customer behaviour, businesses can uncover hidden opportunities and pinpoint areas for enhancement. For instance, analysis might reveal geographical regions where certain distribution channels excel or highlight opportunities to enhance customer satisfaction by optimizing delivery times or service quality [104].

Continuous improvement is the natural outcome of robust monitoring and evaluation processes. Armed with actionable insights from data analysis, businesses can initiate targeted improvements in various aspects of their distribution operations. This may involve refining inventory management practices, optimizing logistical processes to reduce lead times, enhancing training programs for partners, or exploring new distribution channels in emerging markets. Such proactive measures not only enhance operational efficiency but also strengthen competitive positioning in the global marketplace [104].

Ultimately, monitoring and evaluating distribution performance is not a one-time exercise but an ongoing commitment to operational excellence and strategic alignment. Regular assessment, analysis, and adaptation ensure that businesses remain responsive to market dynamics, customer expectations, and evolving business goals. By embracing a culture of continuous improvement and leveraging data-driven insights, businesses can optimize their international distribution networks to drive sustainable growth and achieve long-term success in global markets.

When navigating international distribution, ensuring compliance with legal considerations is crucial to avoiding risks and maintaining operational integrity across different markets. This includes [104]:

- Firstly, understanding local laws and regulations is foundational. Each country imposes its own regulatory framework governing product safety, labelling requirements, import/export restrictions, intellectual property rights, and consumer protection. For instance, some regions may have stringent safety standards for certain products, while others may require specific labelling in local languages. By thoroughly researching and comprehending these regulations, businesses can align their distribution practices accordingly to avoid penalties or market entry barriers.

- Establishing contracts and agreements with international distribution partners is equally critical. These legal documents should clearly delineate the terms of the partnership, including distribution rights, territories covered, pricing structures, payment terms, and mechanisms for resolving disputes. Clear and enforceable contracts not only protect the interests of all parties involved but also provide a framework for addressing potential disagreements or breaches that may arise during the distribution process.

- Protecting intellectual property (IP) rights is a paramount concern when expanding globally. Registering trademarks, patents, and copyrights in target countries ensures legal protection against unauthorized use or infringement. Prior research on existing IP protections in each market helps mitigate risks and preserves the brand's uniqueness and reputation. Robust IP protection strategies also involve monitoring and addressing any instances of infringement promptly to safeguard business interests.

- Compliance with export controls is essential for businesses engaged in international distribution, particularly when goods cross borders. Export control regulations aim to prevent sensitive goods or technologies from falling into unauthorized hands. Businesses must understand and adhere to both their home country's export laws and the regulations of target markets. This may involve obtaining necessary licenses or permits before exporting certain products, ensuring adherence to embargo restrictions, and complying with specific documentation requirements.

- Data privacy and security have emerged as critical considerations amid the digitalization of business operations. Businesses must align their international distribution practices with data protection laws applicable in each market. This includes implementing robust data security measures, such as encryption, secure storage, and stringent access controls, to protect sensitive customer information. Compliance with local data privacy regulations ensures that businesses uphold consumer trust and avoid potential legal repercussions related to data breaches or mishandling of personal information.

- Monitoring regulatory changes is an ongoing responsibility for businesses involved in international distribution. Laws and regulations governing commerce, trade, and consumer protection can evolve over time due to legislative updates or geopolitical shifts. Staying informed about these changes through regular monitoring, engaging with legal advisors, and participating in industry associations helps businesses adapt their distribution strategies proactively. By staying ahead of regulatory developments, businesses can maintain compliance, mitigate risks, and capitalize on emerging market opportunities effectively.

Chapter 13

Developing, Implementing and Reviewing Purchasing Strategies

In the realm of business operations the terms "purchasing" and "procurement" are often used interchangeably, yet they denote distinct aspects of the acquisition process that play crucial roles in organizational strategy and financial health. Understanding the nuances between these two concepts is essential for crafting effective strategies that balance short-term cost savings with long-term procurement benefits [105].

Purchasing Defined [105]: Purchasing specifically refers to the transactional activities involved in acquiring goods or services needed by a company. It encompasses the operational processes from identifying a requirement or need within the organization to the actual payment for the delivered product. Key activities in purchasing include defining the specifications (quantity, quality, type) of the needed items through purchase requisitions, conducting price comparisons and competitive analyses to secure favourable deals, negotiating prices and contract terms with suppliers, tracking the shipment and receiving goods, reconciling orders with invoices, and processing payments.

Procurement Defined [105]: Procurement, on the other hand, is a broader strategic function that encompasses both purchasing and sourcing activities within an organization. It involves a systematic approach to acquiring goods, services, or works that align with the organization's goals and objectives. Procurement strategies go beyond the transactional aspects of purchasing to include optimization of supplier relationships, management of third-party risks, strategic supply chain management and inventory control, competitive market analysis and benchmarking, negotiation of comprehensive contracts, considerations of sustainability and resilience in sourcing decisions, and ongoing evaluation of supplier performance throughout their lifecycle.

Key Differences and Integration [105]: The distinction between purchasing and procurement lies in their scope and strategic focus. Purchasing is primarily concerned with the tactical execution of acquiring goods or services at the best price and quality, while procurement extends beyond this to strategically managing the entire supply chain and vendor relationships to drive value and mitigate risks. While purchasing focuses on immediate cost efficiency and operational logistics, procurement emphasizes long-term strategic alignment with market dynamics, supplier capabilities, and organizational goals.

Balancing Short-term and Long-term Goals [105]: Effective procurement strategies integrate both purchasing and sourcing activities to achieve synergies that optimize cost savings, enhance operational efficiency, and foster innovation and resilience in supply chain management. Organizations should aim to strike a balance between short-term savings goals achieved through efficient purchasing practices and long-term procurement benefits derived from strategic supplier relationships, risk management strategies, and market intelligence.

In logistics and supply chain management, while procurement and purchasing are related terms, they have distinct meanings and functions:

Procurement Strategy: Procurement refers to the broader process of acquiring goods, services, or works from external sources. A procurement strategy encompasses the systematic approach and long-term plan that an organization follows to ensure it obtains the necessary resources at the right quality, quantity, price, and time to meet its operational needs and strategic objectives.

Key elements of a procurement strategy typically include:

- **Supplier Selection:** Choosing suppliers based on criteria such as capability, reliability, quality, and cost-effectiveness.

- **Negotiation:** Engaging in negotiations with suppliers to secure favourable terms and conditions, including pricing, delivery schedules, and contractual obligations.

- **Risk Management:** Identifying and mitigating risks associated with supply chain disruptions, supplier reliability, and market changes.

- **Supplier Relationship Management:** Cultivating and maintaining strong relationships with suppliers to foster collaboration, innovation, and mutual growth.

- **Compliance:** Ensuring adherence to legal, ethical, and regulatory requirements throughout the procurement process.

A procurement strategy focuses on optimizing the entire procurement lifecycle, from identifying needs and sourcing suppliers to finalizing contracts and managing supplier relationships. It aims to drive efficiency, reduce costs, manage risks, and support organizational objectives through strategic sourcing and supplier management practices.

Purchasing Strategy: Purchasing, on the other hand, refers specifically to the transactional aspect of acquiring goods or services. It involves the operational activities related to ordering, receiving, and paying for products or services as per the terms negotiated through the procurement process.

Key elements of a purchasing strategy include:

- **Ordering Process:** Efficiently processing purchase orders based on demand forecasts, inventory levels, and production schedules.

- **Supplier Performance Monitoring:** Monitoring and evaluating supplier performance based on metrics such as delivery times, product quality, and compliance with contractual terms.

- **Inventory Management:** Managing inventory levels to ensure adequate stock availability while minimizing carrying costs and stockouts.

- **Cost Control:** Implementing strategies to control purchasing costs, such as bulk purchasing, price negotiation, and vendor consolidation.

- **Procurement System Utilization:** Leveraging procurement systems and technologies to streamline purchasing workflows, automate repetitive tasks, and enhance data visibility.

While procurement strategy sets the overarching framework for sourcing and supplier management, purchasing strategy focuses on the operational execution of procurement activities to fulfill immediate requirements efficiently and cost-effectively. Both strategies are integral to achieving supply chain objectives and ensuring seamless logistics operations, albeit with different scopes and emphases within the procurement lifecycle.

A procurement strategy is a systematic approach that businesses use to acquire goods, services, or resources necessary for their operations [106]. It outlines the steps and objectives that procurement teams follow to ensure they obtain the right products at the right time and cost-effectively. By following a well-defined procurement strategy, organizations aim to optimize their supply chain processes, reduce costs, manage risks, and build sustainable supplier relationships.

Types of Procurement Strategies [106]:

- **Cost Reduction Strategy:** This is perhaps the most common procurement strategy, focusing on lowering costs and maximizing profits. It involves negotiating with suppliers for better pricing, implementing cost-saving measures such as automation or bulk purchasing, and scrutinizing internal expenses. Cost reduction strategies require continuous evaluation and decision-making across the organization to achieve financial efficiencies without compromising quality or service.

- **Risk Management Strategy:** In contrast to cost reduction, risk management strategies prioritize minimizing the impact of potential disruptions in the supply chain. This includes identifying and assessing risks such as supplier reliability, geopolitical instability, natural disasters, or economic fluctuations. Organizations develop contingency plans and strategies to mitigate these risks proactively, ensuring continuity of supply and business operations.

- **Supplier Management and Relationship Building:** This strategy emphasizes building strong, mutually beneficial relationships with suppliers. It involves selecting reliable suppliers who offer competitive pricing, quality products, and excellent service. Maintaining these relationships requires effective communication, performance monitoring, and addressing issues promptly. Suppliers that consistently meet expectations contribute to operational efficiency and customer satisfaction.

- **Vendor Development Strategy:** Vendor development focuses on nurturing strategic partnerships with suppliers to achieve shared goals and mutual growth. This approach is crucial when organizations depend heavily on specific suppliers for critical products or components. By collaborating closely with vendors, businesses can enhance product innovation, quality standards, and supply chain resilience.

- **Global Sourcing Strategy:** With global sourcing, organizations seek to find the most cost-effective and efficient suppliers worldwide. This strategy leverages international markets to access diverse sources of supply, reduce costs through competitive pricing, and capitalize on economies of scale. Effective global sourcing requires understanding regional regulations, logistics complexities, and cultural nuances to manage supply chain risks effectively.

- **Green Purchasing Strategy:** Increasingly popular, green purchasing focuses on sourcing goods and services from environmentally sustainable suppliers. This strategy aims to minimize ecological impact by reducing carbon footprints, conserving resources, and promoting sustainable practices throughout the supply chain. Green purchasing not only aligns with corporate sustainability goals but also enhances brand reputation and meets consumer demand for eco-friendly products.

- **Corporate Social Responsibility (CSR) Strategy:** CSR strategies reflect a company's commitment to ethical practices and social responsibility. Organizations prioritize partnering with suppliers who demonstrate ethical business practices, fair labour standards, and community engagement. CSR-driven procurement aligns with corporate values, enhances stakeholder trust, and contributes positively to society, thereby fostering long-term sustainability.

- **Quality Management Strategy:** Quality management in procurement focuses on ensuring consistent product quality and service excellence throughout the procurement process. This strategy emphasizes continuous improvement, adherence to quality standards, and proactive measures to address supplier performance issues. By maintaining rigorous quality control measures from procurement to delivery, organizations uphold customer satisfaction and brand reputation.

There is no one-size-fits-all approach to procurement strategy. Businesses must tailor their strategies based on their industry, operational needs, market dynamics, and strategic objectives. Often, a combination of multiple strategies may be necessary to achieve comprehensive procurement goals. By selecting and implementing the right mix of procurement strategies, organizations can optimize their procurement processes, drive efficiency, mitigate risks, and ultimately enhance overall business performance [106].

An effective purchasing strategy plays a pivotal role in the financial health and operational efficiency of any business. It goes beyond mere transactional procurement to encompass a systematic approach aimed at optimizing costs, minimizing inefficiencies, and ensuring that every purchasing decision contributes to the company's strategic objectives. At its core, a purchasing strategy defines how goods and services are acquired, setting forth guidelines, processes, and workflows that streamline purchasing activities and maximize cost savings [105].

Central to the success of a purchasing strategy is its ability to establish clear rules and procedures that govern procurement across the organization. By codifying these rules, businesses can mitigate common issues such as tail spend and maverick spending. Tail spend, which typically represents a small portion of total expenditures dispersed across a wide array of vendors and transactions, can often be overlooked in traditional procurement approaches focused on bulk purchases [105]. Addressing tail spend through a strategic purchasing framework involves analysing these smaller, fragmented expenditures to identify opportunities for consolidation, renegotiation with vendors, or even the adoption of new procurement strategies tailored to optimize these transactions.

Similarly, maverick spending poses significant challenges for businesses by circumventing established procurement processes and approvals. This rogue spending behaviour can lead to inflated costs, inconsistency in supplier relationships, and increased administrative burden as finance departments struggle to reconcile expenditures with purchase orders and invoices. Implementing a well-defined purchasing strategy helps combat maverick spending by enforcing compliance with established procurement protocols, ensuring that all purchases align with predetermined guidelines and approvals [105].

Furthermore, a robust purchasing strategy empowers finance and procurement teams to delve deeper into the root causes of tail spend and maverick spending. By leveraging data analytics and strategic sourcing practices, these teams can uncover insights into vendor performance, identify inefficiencies in procurement processes, and explore opportunities for supplier consolidation or diversification. For instance, they may evaluate whether tail spend is a result of inadequate vendor offerings or if adjustments are needed in contractual terms to better meet organizational needs [105].

In practice, the implementation of a purchasing strategy involves continuous evaluation and refinement. It requires ongoing monitoring of purchasing patterns, vendor relationships, and market dynamics to adapt to changing business conditions and optimize procurement outcomes. By systematically addressing tail spend and maverick spending through a well-crafted strategy, businesses not only achieve immediate cost savings but also foster a more agile and responsive procurement function capable of supporting long-term growth and competitiveness. Thus, investing in an effective purchasing strategy not only saves money in the short term but also contributes to sustained operational excellence and strategic value creation over time [105].

Logistics purchasing strategies encompass a variety of approaches aimed at efficiently acquiring goods and services necessary for the smooth operation of supply chains and logistical activities. These strategies are tailored to meet specific organizational goals, optimize costs, enhance operational efficiency, and ensure seamless supply chain management. Here are the key types of logistics purchasing strategies:

- **Cost-Based Purchasing Strategy:** Cost-based strategies focus primarily on reducing procurement expenses. This approach involves negotiating competitive prices with suppliers, seeking discounts for bulk purchases, and minimizing procurement costs without compromising quality or service levels. Cost-based strategies are crucial for organizations looking to maximize cost savings across their supply chains and logistics operations.

- **Quality-Based Purchasing Strategy:** Quality-based strategies prioritize the acquisition of high-quality goods and services that meet or exceed specified standards. In logistics, where reliability and consistency are critical, this strategy ensures that purchased items contribute to operational efficiency and customer satisfaction. Quality-based purchasing involves rigorous supplier evaluation, performance monitoring, and adherence to stringent quality control measures.

- **Time-Based Purchasing Strategy:** Time-based strategies emphasize the timely acquisition and delivery of goods to meet operational schedules and customer demands. This strategy is essential in logistics to minimize lead times, reduce inventory holding costs, and maintain efficient supply chain flow. Time-based purchasing often involves strategic partnerships with suppliers capable of rapid response times and reliable delivery schedules.

- **Risk-Based Purchasing Strategy:** Risk-based strategies aim to mitigate uncertainties and potential disruptions within the supply chain. In logistics, where external factors such as geopolitical events, natural disasters, or market fluctuations can impact operations, this strategy involves diversifying supplier bases, implementing contingency plans, and assessing supplier risk management capabilities. By identifying and addressing risks proactively, organizations can enhance supply chain resilience and minimize operational disruptions.

- **Relationship-Based Purchasing Strategy:** Relationship-based strategies prioritize long-term partnerships and collaborative relationships with suppliers. This approach fosters trust, communication, and mutual benefit between buyers and suppliers, leading to enhanced supply chain stability and responsiveness. Relationship-based purchasing strategies often involve joint development initiatives, shared risk management, and continuous improvement efforts to achieve common goals.

- **Sustainable Purchasing Strategy:** Sustainable strategies focus on environmentally and socially responsible procurement practices. In logistics, sustainable purchasing involves selecting suppliers that adhere to ethical standards, promote environmental conservation, and prioritize sustainable sourcing practices. This strategy not only aligns with corporate social responsibility objectives but also addresses growing consumer and regulatory demands for sustainability in supply chain operations.

- **Technology-Driven Purchasing Strategy:** Technology-driven strategies leverage digital tools and solutions to streamline procurement processes, enhance visibility, and improve decision-making. In logistics, technologies such as e-procurement systems, supply chain analytics, and automated inventory management facilitate real-time data access, optimize inventory levels, and support predictive purchasing capabilities. Technology-driven strategies enable organizations to achieve greater efficiency, accuracy, and agility in logistics purchasing operations.

Each type of logistics purchasing strategy offers distinct advantages depending on organizational priorities, market conditions, and supply chain requirements. Effective implementation of these strategies involves aligning procurement practices with overall business objectives, continuously evaluating supplier performance, and adapting to evolving industry trends and customer expectations. By selecting and integrating the most suitable purchasing strategies, organizations can optimize their logistics operations, reduce costs, mitigate risks, and enhance overall supply chain performance.

Developing, implementing, and reviewing purchasing strategies within the transport and logistics industry involves several strategic steps tailored to the specific contexts and challenges of this sector.

Developing Purchasing Strategies:

To begin, developing effective purchasing strategies in transport and logistics requires a deep understanding of the industry's dynamics, including market trends, supplier capabilities, regulatory requirements, and operational needs. Here's how this can be approached:

- **Market Analysis and Supplier Evaluation:** Conduct a thorough analysis of the market to identify potential suppliers who can meet your organization's needs. Evaluate suppliers based on criteria such as reliability, cost-effectiveness, service quality, geographical coverage, and technological capabilities. This evaluation should also consider the suppliers' track record in the transport and logistics sector to ensure they can meet industry-specific requirements.

- **Strategic Sourcing:** Determine the appropriate sourcing strategy based on your organization's objectives. This may involve decisions on whether to source globally or locally, use single or multiple suppliers, or employ direct procurement versus through intermediaries like distributors or brokers. Each decision should align with cost considerations, risk management, and supply chain efficiency goals.

- **Negotiation and Contracting:** Develop negotiation strategies that aim to achieve favourable terms and conditions with suppliers while maintaining a mutually beneficial relationship. Negotiations should cover pricing, payment terms, delivery schedules, quality standards, and contractual obligations. Contracts should be comprehensive, clearly defining roles, responsibilities, performance metrics, and mechanisms for dispute resolution.

Implementing Purchasing Strategies:

Once purchasing strategies are developed, effective implementation is crucial to realizing their intended benefits and optimizing supply chain operations:

- **Internal Alignment:** Ensure alignment across all organizational departments involved in purchasing and logistics. This includes collaboration with finance, operations, legal, and IT teams to integrate purchasing strategies seamlessly into overall business operations.

- **Supplier Relationship Management:** Establish robust processes for managing supplier relationships throughout the procurement lifecycle. This includes regular communication, performance reviews, feedback mechanisms, and joint improvement initiatives. Effective supplier relationship management fosters collaboration, transparency, and continuous improvement.

- **Technology Integration:** Leverage technology solutions such as procurement management systems, supply chain analytics, and digital platforms for procurement transactions. These tools enhance visibility, streamline processes, optimize inventory management, and support data-driven decision-making in purchasing operations.

Reviewing and Evaluating Purchasing Strategies:

Regular reviews and evaluations are essential to ensure purchasing strategies remain effective and responsive to changing market conditions and organizational goals:

- **Performance Metrics and KPIs:** Define key performance indicators (KPIs) aligned with strategic objectives, such as cost savings, supplier performance, delivery reliability, inventory turnover, and procurement cycle times. Monitor these metrics regularly to assess the effectiveness of purchasing strategies and identify areas for improvement.

- **Continuous Improvement:** Conduct periodic reviews and audits of purchasing processes and outcomes. Identify root causes of any issues or deviations from targets and implement corrective actions. Encourage feedback from stakeholders, including suppliers and internal teams, to drive continuous improvement in purchasing practices.

- **Adaptation to Industry Trends:** Stay abreast of emerging trends, technological advancements, regulatory changes, and market disruptions affecting the transport and logistics industry. Adjust purchasing strategies accordingly to capitalize on opportunities and mitigate risks proactively.

Optimizing procurement strategy is crucial for businesses aiming to enhance efficiency, reduce costs, and improve overall operational effectiveness. By following best practices, organizations can systematically develop and implement procurement strategies that align with their business goals and enhance competitiveness in the market.

Assess Current Business Standings: The first step in optimizing procurement strategy involves assessing the current internal and external business landscape. Internally, businesses should analyse their purchasing patterns, resource utilization, and cost structures across different departments. This assessment helps identify areas of inefficiency or overspending that can be targeted for improvement. Utilizing frameworks like the Kraljic Matrix allows businesses to categorize their procurement items based on profitability and supply risk, guiding strategic decision-making.

Externally, understanding competitors' strategies is essential. This involves evaluating how competitors manage procurement to achieve cost efficiencies or differentiate through quality and service. Benchmarking against industry standards and competitors can provide valuable insights into performance gaps and opportunities for improvement.

Define Procurement Goals and Draft Policy: With a clear understanding of current standings, businesses can define specific procurement goals that align with their strategic objectives. Goals should be SMART—Specific, Measurable, Attainable, Relevant, and Time-based—to ensure clarity and feasibility. For instance, a SMART goal could be to improve customer service levels to 98% within six months without increasing net inventory dollars.

Drafting a comprehensive procurement policy is equally important. This policy should outline the guidelines, procedures, and principles that govern procurement activities within the organization. It should be flexible enough to accommodate changing market conditions and operational needs while maintaining alignment with overarching business goals.

Integrate Procurement Strategy into a Transportation Management System (TMS): Integration of procurement strategy into a Transportation Management System (TMS) is critical for optimizing logistics and supply chain operations. A TMS facilitates the management of freight and carriers, streamlining processes such as rating, booking, and tracking shipments. By integrating procurement strategy with

TMS functionalities, businesses can achieve greater visibility into transportation costs, optimize route planning, and ensure timely deliveries.

Investing in a TMS can be a significant decision, considering the potential benefits in efficiency and cost savings. For businesses not ready to invest in a proprietary TMS, partnering with a third-party logistics (3PL) provider that offers TMS solutions can be a viable option. This allows businesses to leverage advanced logistics capabilities without the upfront costs and complexities associated with in-house TMS implementation.

Determining Purchasing Objectives

Researching and analysing industry benchmarks for purchasing involves a comprehensive examination of market standards, best practices, and performance metrics within the specific industry context. This process is crucial for understanding how peer organizations manage their procurement functions, optimize costs, and achieve operational efficiencies. Industry benchmarks provide valuable insights into key areas such as supplier relationships, procurement cycle times, cost savings initiatives, and technological advancements in procurement practices.

To begin, procurement professionals gather industry-specific data from reputable sources, industry reports, trade associations, and benchmarking studies. This data includes metrics like average procurement costs, supplier performance metrics, lead times, inventory turnover rates, and compliance benchmarks. Analysing this information helps organizations identify areas where they excel compared to industry peers and areas that may require improvement to enhance competitiveness and efficiency.

Simultaneously, internal purchasing data and information within the organization are analysed to establish a baseline for comparison against industry benchmarks. This involves reviewing historical purchasing patterns, expenditure data, supplier performance evaluations, contract compliance, and operational efficiencies. By analysing internal data, organizations can pinpoint strengths, weaknesses, and areas of opportunity within their procurement processes.

Consultations with relevant stakeholders and personnel are essential to inform the development of purchasing objectives aligned with organizational goals. Stakeholders may include procurement teams, finance departments, operations managers, and senior executives. These consultations facilitate a collaborative approach to identifying strategic priorities, addressing challenges, and setting realistic objectives that support broader organizational strategies.

During these consultations, stakeholders provide valuable input based on their functional expertise and operational insights. Discussions focus on understanding current procurement challenges, identifying emerging market trends, assessing supplier capabilities, and aligning purchasing objectives with corporate goals such as cost reduction, quality improvement, risk mitigation, and sustainability initiatives.

Once insights from industry benchmarks, internal data analysis, and stakeholder consultations are synthesized, purchasing objectives are drafted. These objectives outline specific targets, timelines, performance metrics, and action plans to achieve strategic procurement goals. Objectives should be SMART—Specific, Measurable, Achievable, Relevant, and Time-bound—to ensure clarity and accountability in execution.

Gaining approval from relevant personnel for purchasing objectives is the final critical step in the process. This involves presenting the drafted objectives to key decision-makers, such as senior management or the procurement steering committee, for review and endorsement. Approval signifies alignment with organizational priorities, resource allocation support, and commitment to achieving outlined procurement goals.

In conclusion, researching industry benchmarks, analysing internal data, conducting consultations with stakeholders, drafting SMART purchasing objectives, and gaining approval ensure a structured and strategic approach to procurement management. This systematic process not only enhances purchasing efficiency but also aligns procurement activities with organizational strategies, fosters stakeholder collaboration, and drives continuous improvement in procurement practices.

Collecting variable data in purchasing and logistics involves a systematic approach to gathering and analysing information that is crucial for improving operational efficiency and monitoring activities effectively. Initially, it's essential to clearly define each purchasing and logistics process, outlining their viability parameters comprehensively. This ensures that all aspects of these processes are considered for continuous improvement and accurate monitoring. Key data indicators such as financial volatility, demand fluctuations, insecurity factors, infrastructure stability, and workforce dynamics are identified and defined in terms of their purpose and relevance to procurement and logistics operations [107].

The purpose of these performance indicators lies in their ability to provide insights into various aspects of the purchasing and logistics processes. For instance, financial volatility metrics help in managing budgetary risks, while demand volatility indicators aid in forecasting and inventory management. Infrastructure and workforce volatility metrics ensure that operational resources are efficiently utilized and managed to support smooth logistics operations [107].

Once the indicators are established, the next step involves gathering data from all relevant processes and sources. This data collection phase is critical as it allows for scenario testing, event forecasting, and the formulation of preventive measures. Measuring these variables within each indicator is equally vital, providing a quantitative assessment of operational complexities and volumes across different facets of procurement and logistics. This includes evaluating warehouse operations based on inventory management policies and transport operations based on shipment volumes and geographical complexities [107].

Comparing these indicators involves benchmarking against industry standards and competitors' performance metrics. It helps in identifying areas where improvements can be made and resources can be allocated to enhance process maturity and efficiency. Continuous monitoring of these indicators through customized measurement systems ensures that real-time data is available to support decision-making processes. This involves maintaining updated performance tables for each operational area, facilitating informed decisions that contribute to competitive advantages through enhanced analysis capabilities, trend identification, and strategic procurement and logistics management [107].

In practical terms, integrating advanced information management systems plays a crucial role in leveraging collected data effectively. These systems enable quick analysis, pattern recognition, and streamlined decision-making processes across procurement and logistics functions. By adopting digital solutions and outsourcing management where feasible, organizations can eliminate errors and optimize productivity within their supply chains. This approach not only improves operational performance but also enhances overall competitiveness in the marketplace by addressing inefficiencies and supporting agile responses to dynamic market conditions [107].

Ultimately, implementing a robust data collection and analysis strategy in purchasing and logistics allows organizations to not only measure performance accurately but also to forecast and mitigate risks proactively. This strategic approach supports continuous improvement initiatives, strengthens operational resilience, and positions businesses to capitalize on emerging opportunities in the global marketplace.

Developing Purchasing Strategies

Developing effective purchasing strategies involves a methodical approach that integrates legal compliance, strategic objectives, resource planning, and stakeholder approval. Initially, it's crucial to conduct a thorough review of legal requirements pertaining to procurement activities. This includes understanding regulations related to procurement processes, contract laws intellectual property rights, and any industry-specific regulations that may impact purchasing decisions. By aligning strategies with legal frameworks, organizations ensure that their procurement practices not only meet compliance standards but also mitigate legal risks.

In parallel, developing purchasing strategies necessitates defining clear objectives that align with organizational goals. These objectives typically encompass achieving the "Five Rights" of procurement: procuring the right quality, quantity, item, place, and time. Each of these criteria ensures that purchased goods or services meet operational needs efficiently and effectively. For instance, ensuring the right quality involves specifying standards and expectations for products or services to meet operational requirements without compromising on performance or reliability.

The traditional description of the "Right" inputs includes [108]:

- Inputs of the appropriate "Quality".

- Delivered in the correct "Quantity".

- To the designated "Place".

- At the specified "Time".

- For the agreed-upon "Price".

These elements collectively form the "Five Rights" of procurement and supply, representing fundamental goals in procurement practices. They serve as standard criteria for evaluating procurement performance across industries. Even if not explicitly labelled as the "five rights," these principles are commonly addressed in procurement literature under terms like "key performance variables" or "procurement factors," essentially referring to the same fundamental objectives [108].

Ensuring the "Right Quality" of goods procured is critical to meeting both internal and external customer needs effectively Achieving this involves several key steps and considerations. First, it requires accurately specifying requirements and setting clear quality standards that align with the intended use and expectations of the goods. This involves detailed communication between the procurement team and stakeholders to ensure that all parties understand and agree upon the quality parameters.

On the supplier side, effective quality management practices are essential. This includes selecting suppliers with a proven track record of delivering high-quality goods, as well as establishing clear quality assurance processes within the procurement framework. Suppliers must be capable of consistently meeting the specified quality standards through rigorous inspections, testing, and adherence to agreed-upon quality control protocols.

When the "Right Quality" is not achieved, significant consequences can arise across various stages of the supply chain and business operations. Firstly, if goods do not meet the specified quality standards, they may need to be rejected or scrapped upon receipt. This not only leads to financial losses but also disrupts supply continuity and operational efficiency.

Moreover, inadequate quality can impact production machinery, potentially causing damage or inefficiencies that further escalate costs. If defective goods proceed to manufacturing stages without detection, finished products may themselves be flawed, necessitating rework or scrapping. This results in additional costs and delays in delivering products to market.

Furthermore, defective products reaching customers can lead to serious repercussions such as recalls, returns, and compensation claims. This not only damages customer trust and satisfaction but also tarnishes the company's reputation and goodwill in the market. Addressing these issues often involves significant financial outlays for rectification efforts, customer compensation, and initiatives to rebuild brand credibility.

Ultimately, ensuring the "Right Quality" in procurement is not just about meeting immediate operational needs but also safeguarding long-term business sustainability and competitiveness. It requires proactive quality management strategies, robust supplier relationships, and a commitment to continuous improvement across all stages of the procurement process to mitigate risks and deliver consistent value to customers and stakeholders alike.

Achieving the "Right Quantity" in procurement is crucial for maintaining operational efficiency, meeting customer demand, and optimizing inventory management. This involves several strategic approaches aimed at balancing supply with demand while minimizing the risks and costs associated with either surplus or insufficient stock.

Firstly, demand forecasting plays a pivotal role in determining the right quantity of goods to procure. This involves analysing historical data, market trends, and customer insights to predict future demand accurately. By leveraging sophisticated forecasting models and data analytics, procurement teams can anticipate fluctuations in demand and adjust their procurement plans accordingly. This proactive approach helps in preventing stockouts or excess inventory, thereby optimizing supply chain operations.

Effective inventory management is another key aspect of achieving the right quantity. It involves maintaining optimal stock levels that align with projected demand and service level agreements. Inventory management systems and techniques such as just-in-time (JIT) inventory, economic order quantity (EOQ) models, and safety stock calculations are utilized to ensure that goods are available when needed without excessive holding costs.

Moreover, implementing robust stock replenishment systems is essential. These systems automate the process of replenishing inventory based on predefined triggers such as reorder points or minimum stock thresholds. By automating this process, procurement teams can streamline operations, reduce manual errors, and ensure consistent availability of goods to meet ongoing demand.

When the "Right Quantity" is not achieved, significant challenges can arise across the supply chain and business operations. Insufficient stock levels can lead to stockouts, causing production bottlenecks, delays in fulfilling customer orders, and potentially damaging the company's credibility and customer relationships. This can result in lost sales opportunities and revenue, as well as increased costs due to expedited shipping or production adjustments to meet demand.

Conversely, over-ordering or holding excess stock can also pose risks and incur costs. Excess inventory ties up capital that could be used elsewhere in the business, occupies valuable storage space, and increases the risk of inventory obsolescence, deterioration, theft, or damage. Managing excess inventory requires effective inventory control measures and may involve markdowns or liquidation efforts to minimize financial losses.

Achieving the "Right Place" in procurement involves ensuring that goods are delivered to the intended destination efficiently, securely, and in optimal condition. This aspect of procurement is critical for maintaining supply chain integrity, minimizing costs associated with transportation and logistics, and safeguarding product quality throughout the delivery process.

Distribution planning plays a pivotal role in achieving the right place. It involves strategizing the optimal routes and methods for transporting goods from suppliers to their final destinations. This includes considerations such as geographic locations, delivery schedules, and logistical constraints. Effective distribution planning aims to streamline operations, reduce transit times, and minimize transportation costs while ensuring timely and accurate deliveries.

Similarly, transport planning focuses on selecting the appropriate modes of transportation and carriers to facilitate smooth and efficient delivery. Factors such as shipment size, distance, urgency, and environmental considerations influence transport planning decisions. Leveraging advanced logistics technologies and systems allows procurement teams to track shipments in real-time, optimize routes, and mitigate risks associated with transit delays or disruptions.

Packaging also plays a crucial role in ensuring goods arrive at the right place in good condition. Proper packaging protects products from damage, contamination, or theft during transit. Packaging design should consider the nature of the goods, transportation requirements, and environmental sustainability. Robust packaging practices contribute to minimizing product loss or damage, reducing return rates, and enhancing customer satisfaction.

When the "Right Place" is not achieved, various challenges can arise throughout the supply chain. Delivering goods to the wrong location can lead to delays in fulfillment, additional transportation costs to redirect shipments, and potential penalties for non-compliance with delivery agreements. Moreover, inadequate packaging or improper handling during transport can result in product damage, contamination, or theft, compromising product quality and customer trust.

Additionally, inefficient transport routes or methods can contribute to unnecessary environmental impact, such as increased carbon emissions or environmental damage from transportation activities. This underscores the importance of sustainable transport practices and compliance with environmental regulations in procurement and logistics operations.

Achieving the "Right Time" in procurement is crucial for ensuring goods are delivered precisely when needed to meet demand without incurring unnecessary inventory costs. This aspect of procurement involves strategic coordination of demand management and supplier management to optimize delivery schedules and maintain operational efficiency.

Demand management plays a pivotal role in determining the "Right Time" for procurement activities. It involves forecasting and analysing market demand patterns, seasonal variations, and customer preferences to anticipate when goods will be needed. By accurately predicting demand, procurement teams can adjust ordering schedules and inventory levels to align with anticipated requirements, thereby minimizing the risk of stockouts or excess inventory.

Supplier management is equally critical in achieving the "Right Time." Effective communication and collaboration with suppliers enable procurement teams to synchronize delivery schedules with production schedules or customer orders. This involves negotiating lead times, establishing reliable communication channels, and implementing robust supplier performance metrics to ensure timely deliveries.

When the "Right Time" is not achieved, several challenges can arise throughout the supply chain. Delayed deliveries can lead to production bottlenecks, causing idle production lines, increased labour costs, and potential disruptions in fulfilling customer orders on time. These delays can result in customer dissatisfaction, lost sales opportunities, and damage to the organization's reputation.

Conversely, goods delivered too early can impose unnecessary costs associated with inventory holding, such as storage expenses, depreciation of goods, and potential obsolescence. Excessive inventory ties up capital that could be allocated to other strategic initiatives and increases the risk of inventory write-offs due to product expiration or changes in market demand.

Effective procurement strategies mitigate these risks by establishing clear timelines, leveraging just-in-time inventory principles, and implementing agile supply chain practices. By aligning procurement activities with demand forecasts and maintaining close relationships with suppliers, organizations can optimize inventory levels, reduce carrying costs, and improve overall supply chain responsiveness.

Furthermore, leveraging digital tools and technologies for real-time data analytics and supply chain visibility enhances procurement agility. These tools enable proactive decision-making, rapid response to market fluctuations, and continuous improvement in delivery timing. By continuously refining procurement processes and adapting to changing market dynamics, organizations can achieve the "Right Time" consistently, enhancing operational efficiency and customer satisfaction.

Achieving the "Right Price" in procurement is essential for businesses aiming to balance cost-effectiveness with quality and reliability. This aspect of procurement involves strategic analysis, negotiation, and management of pricing to ensure that goods and services are acquired at a fair and competitive rate, optimizing profitability while maintaining supplier relationships.

Price analysis forms the cornerstone of securing the "Right Price." It involves evaluating market trends, benchmarking against industry standards, and assessing historical pricing data to determine a reasonable and competitive price point. Through thorough analysis, procurement professionals can identify opportunities for cost savings, negotiate better terms with suppliers, and ensure that pricing aligns with budgetary constraints and financial goals.

Supplier cost analysis complements price analysis by delving into the cost structures of suppliers. Understanding supplier cost components, such as raw materials, labor, overhead, and profit margins, enables procurement teams to negotiate pricing based on a clear understanding of supplier economics. By conducting detailed cost analyses, organizations can identify areas for potential cost reductions or efficiencies, fostering a collaborative approach to pricing negotiations that benefits both parties.

Competitive pricing and negotiation tactics are instrumental in achieving the "Right Price." This involves leveraging market competition and supplier relationships to secure favorable pricing terms. Procurement professionals use strategic negotiation techniques, such as bundling orders, volume discounts, or long-term contracts, to drive down costs while ensuring quality and reliability. Effective negotiation not only reduces procurement expenses but also strengthens supplier partnerships built on mutual trust and transparency.

When the "Right Price" is not achieved, several detrimental outcomes can impact the organization. Suppliers may exploit pricing discrepancies, leading to inflated costs that erode profit margins and strain supplier relationships. Unfair pricing practices can undermine supplier trust and compromise the reliability of the supply chain, potentially jeopardizing the continuity of goods and services essential for operations.

Moreover, rising material and supply costs driven by unfavourable pricing can diminish profitability, constrain financial resources available for reinvestment, and limit competitive advantages in the marketplace. Inadequate pricing strategies may force businesses to either absorb higher costs, reducing profitability, or pass these costs on to customers through increased prices, potentially resulting in lost sales and diminished market competitiveness.

To mitigate these risks, organizations should prioritize rigorous price analysis, continuous supplier cost evaluations, and proactive negotiation strategies. By fostering a collaborative approach with suppliers and maintaining transparency in pricing discussions, businesses can secure competitive pricing that supports sustainable growth, enhances financial performance, and reinforces long-term strategic objectives. This approach not only optimizes procurement outcomes but also strengthens the overall resilience and profitability of the organization in a dynamic business environment.

Human resources planning plays a crucial role in supporting the implementation of purchasing strategies within an organization. This process begins with assessing staffing needs based on the scope and complexity of procurement activities. It involves identifying the required skills, competencies, and experience levels essential for effective procurement management. By understanding these needs, organizations can strategically recruit, hire, and retain personnel who possess the expertise needed to execute procurement strategies successfully.

Furthermore, human resources planning encompasses the development of training programs tailored to enhance procurement capabilities across the organization. These programs aim to equip procurement professionals with the necessary knowledge of market trends, negotiation techniques, supplier relationship management, and regulatory compliance. Continuous training ensures that procurement teams remain agile and adept at adapting to evolving industry standards and organizational goals, thereby fostering a culture of continuous improvement and professional development.

Financial planning is equally critical in supporting purchasing strategies by allocating budgets effectively. It involves forecasting procurement expenses, setting financial targets, and identifying cost-saving opportunities without compromising quality or supplier relationships. Financial planners collaborate closely with procurement teams to align budgetary allocations with strategic priorities, ensuring that adequate funds are available to support procurement initiatives while adhering to financial constraints and optimizing cost management strategies.

Moreover, effective financial planning enables organizations to prioritize investments in technology, infrastructure, and resources necessary for streamlined procurement processes. It facilitates informed decision-making regarding capital expenditures, resource allocation, and contingency planning, thereby enhancing the overall efficiency and resilience of procurement operations.

Obtaining approval to implement purchasing plans and strategies involves engaging relevant stakeholders and decision-makers within the organization. This may include presenting detailed proposals that outline the rationale, objectives, expected outcomes, and resource requirements of the proposed strategies. Stakeholder approval ensures organizational buy-in and support, facilitating smoother implementation and alignment with broader corporate objectives.

Following approval, it's essential to incorporate any necessary changes or adjustments to the plans and strategies based on feedback or regulatory requirements. This iterative process allows for flexibility in adapting to evolving business needs, market conditions, or unforeseen challenges that may arise during implementation. Changes could involve revising procurement timelines, adjusting budget allocations, enhancing supplier selection criteria, or refining legal documentation to ensure compliance and efficiency.

Throughout this process, effective communication and collaboration across departments and with external partners play a crucial role in successful strategy development and implementation. By fostering a transparent and inclusive approach, organizations can leverage collective expertise and insights to refine purchasing strategies continuously. This iterative approach not only enhances operational effectiveness but also strengthens the organization's ability to navigate complexities and seize opportunities in an evolving business landscape.

The following is an example of a basic purchasing strategy:

Logistics Purchasing Strategy: Sample Document

Introduction: The logistics purchasing strategy outlined below is designed to optimize procurement processes within our organization, ensuring efficient supply chain management while achieving cost savings and maintaining high service levels. This strategy integrates key principles of procurement excellence to support our business objectives and enhance overall operational efficiency.

1. Objectives: The primary objectives of our logistics purchasing strategy include:

- Ensuring timely and reliable delivery of goods and services to meet operational demands.

- Optimizing procurement costs while maintaining quality standards.

- Enhancing supplier relationships and fostering strategic partnerships.

- Implementing sustainable procurement practices to minimize environmental impact.

- Strengthening internal procurement capabilities through training and development.

2. Scope: This strategy covers all aspects of logistics procurement, including:

- Sourcing and selecting suppliers based on quality, reliability, and cost-effectiveness.

- Negotiating favourable terms and conditions to maximize value for money.

- Managing inventory levels and optimizing stock replenishment processes.

- Monitoring supplier performance and conducting regular reviews to drive continuous improvement.

- Complying with legal and regulatory requirements related to procurement and logistics operations.

3. Key Strategies:

Supplier Relationship Management:

- Develop and maintain strong relationships with key suppliers to ensure reliable and consistent delivery.
- Conduct periodic supplier evaluations based on performance metrics such as quality, on-time delivery, and responsiveness.
- Collaborate with suppliers on innovation and process improvements to achieve mutual goals.

Cost Optimization:

- Implement cost-effective procurement practices without compromising quality or service levels.
- Conduct regular price benchmarking and negotiate competitive pricing with suppliers.
- Explore opportunities for volume discounts, consolidated shipments, and strategic sourcing.

Risk Management:

- Identify potential risks in the supply chain and develop mitigation strategies.
- Diversify supplier base to reduce dependency and minimize supply chain disruptions.
- Implement contingency plans to address unforeseen events such as natural disasters or geopolitical changes.

Sustainability Initiatives:

- Integrate sustainability criteria into supplier selection and procurement decisions.
- Promote environmentally friendly practices such as eco-friendly packaging

and transportation options.

- Monitor and report on sustainability performance to stakeholders and regulatory bodies.

4. Implementation Plan:
Human Resources:
- Assess staffing requirements and ensure procurement team has necessary skills and competencies.

- Provide ongoing training and development opportunities to enhance procurement capabilities.

- Foster a culture of collaboration and knowledge sharing within the procurement department.

Financial Planning:
- Allocate budgets effectively to support procurement activities and initiatives.

- Monitor expenditures closely and identify opportunities for cost savings and efficiency improvements.

- Align financial resources with strategic priorities to achieve long-term procurement objectives.

5. Monitoring and Evaluation:
- Establish key performance indicators (KPIs) to measure the success of the logistics purchasing strategy.

- Conduct regular reviews and audits to assess compliance with strategy objectives and performance targets.

- Implement feedback loops to incorporate lessons learned and make continuous improvements to the strategy.

Conclusion: This logistics purchasing strategy outlines our commitment to excellence in procurement practices, aiming to optimize supply chain efficiency, minimize costs, and enhance stakeholder value. By implementing these strategies and continuously monitoring our performance, we aim to achieve sustainable growth and operational resilience in a competitive marketplace.

Implementing Purchasing Strategies

Communicating purchasing strategies effectively to relevant personnel and stakeholders is crucial to ensure alignment and understanding across the organization. This process begins with clear and transparent communication channels that disseminate the strategy's goals, objectives, and expected outcomes. It involves engaging key stakeholders early on to garner buy-in and address any concerns or questions they may have. This communication should emphasize the strategic importance of the purchasing strategy in achieving organizational goals, whether it's cost savings, supplier relationship management, or operational efficiency improvements.

Identifying and accessing the necessary resources to implement purchasing strategies involves a comprehensive assessment of both human and financial resources. Human resources may include skilled procurement professionals, project managers, and support staff who will be instrumental in executing the strategy. Financial resources encompass budget allocations and funding necessary to procure goods and services, invest in technology, or conduct training programs. Accessing these resources requires collaboration between procurement leaders, finance departments, and possibly external partners or consultants to ensure adequate support throughout the implementation process.

Supporting the implementation of purchasing strategies entails providing the tools, training, and infrastructure needed for success. This includes equipping procurement teams with access to modern procurement tools and technologies, such as e-procurement systems or supplier management software, to streamline processes and enhance decision-making capabilities. Training programs should be tailored to develop skills in negotiation, contract management, and supplier relationship management, ensuring that staff are well-prepared to execute the strategy effectively.

Monitoring the implementation of purchasing strategies is essential to track progress, identify bottlenecks, and make timely adjustments as needed. This involves establishing key performance indicators (KPIs) aligned with the strategy's objectives, such as cost savings achieved, supplier performance metrics, or compliance with procurement policies. Regular reviews and checkpoints allow stakeholders to assess whether the strategy is on track to deliver expected outcomes and address any deviations or challenges promptly.

Identifying and addressing problems and issues that arise during implementation requires a proactive approach to problem-solving and decision-making. This may involve conducting root cause analyses, engaging cross-functional teams to brainstorm solutions, and implementing corrective actions swiftly. Communication channels should remain open to encourage feedback from frontline staff and stakeholders, enabling continuous improvement and adaptation of the strategy in response to evolving circumstances.

Providing reports on the implementation of purchasing strategies to relevant personnel and stakeholders is essential for transparency and accountability. These reports should highlight progress against established KPIs, achievements, challenges encountered, and lessons learned. They serve as a mechanism for sharing successes and areas for improvement, fostering continuous learning and refinement of procurement practices. Reports should be tailored to the needs of different stakeholders, presenting information in a clear and actionable format that supports informed decision-making and strategic alignment across the organization.

Evaluating Purchasing Strategies and Implementing Improvements

Reviewing the implementation of purchasing strategies involves conducting a comprehensive assessment of how well the strategies have been executed and their impact on organizational goals. This process begins by gathering data and feedback from various stakeholders involved in procurement processes. Key performance indicators (KPIs) established during the strategy development phase serve as benchmarks to evaluate performance against intended outcomes, such as cost savings, supplier performance, and operational efficiencies. Through this review, strengths and weaknesses in the current strategy become apparent, providing insights into areas needing improvement.

Identifying improvements to purchasing strategies from the review process requires a critical analysis of the findings and feedback gathered. This involves identifying recurring issues, bottlenecks, or missed opportunities that hindered the effectiveness of the strategy. Root cause analysis techniques, such as fishbone diagrams or brainstorming sessions with cross-functional teams, can help uncover underlying reasons for performance gaps. Additionally, benchmarking against industry best practices or competitor strategies can inspire innovative solutions to enhance procurement effectiveness and efficiency.

Gaining approval to implement improvements to purchasing strategies involves presenting a compelling business case to key decision-makers within the organization. This includes outlining the anticipated benefits of proposed improvements, such as enhanced cost savings, improved supplier relationships, or streamlined procurement processes. Decision-makers need to understand how these improvements align with strategic objectives and contribute to overall organizational success. Securing approval may involve formal presentations, stakeholder consultations, or obtaining financial backing to support implementation efforts.

Communicating improvements to relevant stakeholders is crucial to ensure alignment and engagement throughout the organization. Clear and transparent communication channels should be utilized to convey the rationale behind the proposed improvements, their expected impact, and how stakeholders can contribute to their success. This involves disseminating information through meetings, workshops, training sessions, or digital platforms to reach a diverse audience of procurement professionals, department heads, and executive leadership.

Monitoring and reviewing the implementation of improvements is essential to determine their effectiveness and identify any unforeseen challenges or unintended consequences. This process involves tracking performance metrics related to the improvements, comparing actual outcomes against projected targets, and soliciting ongoing feedback from stakeholders. Regular reviews allow for timely adjustments and course corrections as needed, ensuring that improvements achieve their intended objectives and deliver sustainable benefits to the organization. Evaluating the long-term impact of improvements ensures continuous learning and adaptation of purchasing strategies in response to changing market conditions, technological advancements, and organizational priorities.

Chapter 14

Implementing and Monitoring Environmental Protection Policies and Procedures

Climate change has increasingly become a critical issue influencing the logistics industry over the past decade. As global consumption rises and supply chains grow more complex, the demand for transportation services escalates. However, this growth also amplifies the industry's environmental footprint, leading to mounting pressures from governments, organizations, and consumers to foster more sustainable logistics practices. Addressing these challenges is crucial not only for mitigating environmental impact but also for gaining a competitive edge in the market [109].

Currently, the logistics sector accounts for approximately a quarter of global carbon dioxide emissions, a figure projected to potentially reach 40% by 2050 without significant intervention, as highlighted by the European Environment Agency [109]. These emissions primarily stem from road transport and aviation, contributing significantly to greenhouse gas accumulation and the resultant acceleration of global temperatures. Beyond climate impact, emissions from logistics operations also pose direct health risks, leading to respiratory and cardiovascular diseases and premature mortality.

In addition to air pollution, logistics activities pose threats to global water resources. Shipping, in particular, generates substantial volumes of wastewater and solid waste that are discharged into oceans, polluting marine ecosystems. Noise pollution from maritime transport disrupts underwater environments, affecting aquatic species that rely on sound for communication and navigation. Large marine mammals are particularly vulnerable to collisions with fast-moving vessels, further endangering their populations. Catastrophic events like oil spills further compound these environmental challenges, causing profound and long-lasting damage to ocean ecosystems and coastal habitats [109].

Non-renewable resource consumption, especially fuel, remains a significant environmental challenge within the logistics industry. Despite advancements in electric vehicles, the decarbonization of large-scale logistics operations involving cargo ships and airplanes remains a formidable task. Moreover, the industry's reliance on single-use packaging materials, pallets, and containers contributes to extensive waste generation and litter, exacerbating environmental degradation [109].

Despite these daunting environmental impacts, the logistics industry is exploring technological innovations to mitigate its footprint. Advancements in alternative fuels, including biofuels and hydrogen, hold promise for reducing emissions from transportation. Additionally, the adoption of electric and hybrid vehicles for urban deliveries and the development of sustainable packaging solutions are steps towards minimizing waste and resource consumption. Innovations in logistics management systems, such as route optimization software and real-time tracking technologies, are enhancing operational efficiency and reducing fuel consumption [109].

Environmental protection regulations related to transport and logistics vary significantly around the world due to differing environmental priorities, legislative frameworks, and economic conditions in each region. These regulations aim to mitigate the environmental impact of transport activities, including air pollution, greenhouse gas emissions, noise pollution, and habitat disruption. Here's an overview of how these regulations are structured and implemented globally:

In Europe, environmental regulations for transport and logistics are stringent and often lead global standards. The European Union (EU) has implemented various directives and regulations under the Clean Air Policy Package, which includes limits on vehicle emissions and requirements for cleaner fuels. The EU also promotes sustainable transport practices through incentives for electric vehicles (EVs), restrictions on diesel vehicles in urban areas, and initiatives to improve public transport infrastructure.

In North America, the United States and Canada have regulations that address emissions from vehicles and shipping activities. The Environmental Protection Agency (EPA) in the U.S. sets emission standards for vehicles and enforces regulations under the Clean Air Act. California, in particular, has adopted even stricter standards for vehicle emissions and mandates for zero-emission vehicles (ZEVs).

In Asia, countries like China and Japan are increasingly focusing on environmental regulations for transport and logistics. China has implemented policies to reduce air pollution, including stringent emission standards for vehicles and incentives for electric and hybrid vehicles. Japan promotes fuel efficiency standards for vehicles and has initiatives to reduce emissions from shipping and logistics operations.

In Australia, environmental regulations for transport and logistics are managed by federal and state governments. The Australian Government sets vehicle emission standards and promotes fuel efficiency through regulations and incentives. States like New South Wales and Victoria have additional measures to reduce transport-related emissions and promote sustainable freight practices.

In developing regions, such as parts of Africa and Latin America, environmental regulations for transport and logistics are emerging but may not be as comprehensive or strictly enforced compared to developed regions. These regions are increasingly recognizing the importance of environmental sustainability and are beginning to adopt measures to improve fuel efficiency, reduce emissions, and mitigate environmental impacts from transport activities.

Overall, the trend globally is towards stricter environmental regulations for transport and logistics, driven by concerns over climate change, air quality, and sustainable development. These regulations influence vehicle design, fuel standards, logistics planning, and operational practices in the transport sector, aiming to achieve a balance between economic growth and environmental protection. Compliance with these regulations is essential for businesses operating in the transport and logistics industry to mitigate risks, achieve regulatory compliance, and contribute to global environmental goals.

Implementing and monitoring environmental protection measures within any organization requires a range of equipment and resources to ensure compliance with regulations and minimize environmental impact. Key equipment includes pollution control devices such as scrubbers and filters for emissions control, monitoring equipment for air and water quality, and tools for waste management like recycling bins and hazardous material storage facilities. Resources include trained personnel for environmental monitoring and compliance, access to environmental databases and regulatory updates, and adequate funding for implementing sustainable practices and technologies.

The hierarchy of control principles for environmental risks is crucial for managing and mitigating environmental impacts effectively [110]. This hierarchy includes preferred models for risk elimination, which involves eliminating the source of environmental hazards whenever possible. Engineering controls focus on modifying equipment or processes to reduce emissions or waste generation, such as installing catalytic converters or using closed-loop systems. Administrative controls involve implementing policies, procedures, and training to minimize environmental risks, while specific environmental protection techniques include practices like spill containment procedures or noise abatement measures.

Administrative controls are also integral in managing environmental risks in the workplace. These controls involve implementing policies, procedures, and training programs to promote safe practices and behaviours among employees [111]. By establishing clear guidelines and protocols, organizations can ensure that environmental protection measures are consistently followed. Moreover, specific environmental protection techniques, such as waste management protocols and pollution control measures, are crucial for mitigating the impact of industrial activities on the environment [112].

Administrative controls complement engineering controls by focusing on organizational policies and practices to enhance environmental protection [111]. Through measures like training programs, signage, and work procedures, organizations can promote a culture of safety and environmental awareness among employees. By integrating administrative controls with engineering solutions, companies can establish comprehensive risk management strategies that address environmental concerns effectively.

Despite efforts to implement and monitor environmental protection procedures, several challenges and problems can arise. These may include insufficient resources or funding for adequate environmental monitoring and compliance, resistance to change within the organization, complexity in navigating regulatory requirements, and occasional technical failures or equipment malfunctions. Ensuring ongoing staff training and commitment to environmental goals can mitigate these challenges, along with regular audits and reviews of environmental management systems.

Effective environmental management systems and procedures are essential for ensuring compliance with relevant national, state/territory legislative and regulatory requirements, as well as codes of practice. These systems typically involve establishing environmental policies, conducting environmental risk assessments, setting objectives and targets for improvement, implementing operational controls, and conducting regular audits and reviews. They also include procedures for reporting incidents, monitoring environmental performance, and maintaining documentation to demonstrate compliance.

National and regional legislative and regulatory requirements vary widely but generally encompass laws related to air and water quality, waste management, hazardous materials handling, and environmental impact assessments. Codes of practice provide guidelines for industry-specific environmental management practices and standards, ensuring that organizations adopt best practices to minimize their environmental footprint.

Energy Efficient Opportunities (EEO) principles and practices are significant for environmental management as they promote the efficient use of energy resources to reduce greenhouse gas emissions and environmental impacts. EEO principles include measures such as energy audits, implementing energy-saving technologies and practices, optimizing energy use in operations, and promoting energy efficiency awareness among employees. By adopting EEO principles, organizations can not only reduce their operational costs but also contribute positively to environmental sustainability goals.

Workplace environmental hazards include risks such as exposure to hazardous chemicals, noise pollution, air and water contamination, and ergonomic hazards. Hazard control measures involve identifying hazards through risk assessments, implementing engineering controls like ventilation systems or noise barriers, administrative controls such as work practices and training, and personal protective equipment (PPE) where necessary. Regular monitoring and evaluation ensure that control measures remain effective and that new hazards are promptly addressed.

When implementing and monitoring environmental protection measures, a range of equipment and resources are essential to ensure compliance with relevant regulations and standards. Personal Protective Equipment (PPE) plays a crucial role in safeguarding employees from workplace hazards [113]. PPE includes items like gloves, masks, goggles, and protective clothing, designed to protect against various workplace risks such as chemical exposure, physical hazards, and infectious diseases. Additionally, engineering controls like ventilation systems and barriers are vital in reducing environmental risks [114]. These controls help in minimizing exposure to harmful substances and maintaining a safe work environment.

Operational risks related to workplace environmental impacts include incidents such as spills, emissions exceedances, waste mismanagement, and non-compliance with environmental regulations. Precautions to control these risks involve implementing emergency response plans, conducting regular inspections and audits, training employees in environmental procedures, and maintaining contingency plans for potential environmental incidents. Continuous improvement through lessons learned from incidents helps strengthen environmental protection standards and operational resilience.

Workplace environmental protection standards set clear guidelines for employees on how to implement and monitor environmental protection measures effectively. These standards include procedures for waste segregation and disposal, energy conservation practices, water and air quality monitoring, and sustainable procurement practices. Guidelines ensure consistency in environmental practices across the organization and promote a culture of environmental responsibility among employees.

Reporting and recording processes for workplace environmental protection involve documenting incidents, near misses, compliance issues, and environmental performance data. This includes maintaining records of emissions, waste disposal activities, energy consumption, and any environmental audits or inspections conducted. Timely reporting ensures transparency and accountability, facilitates regulatory compliance, and provides data for continuous improvement initiatives in environmental management.

Reducing the environmental impact of logistics has become increasingly crucial as the industry expands alongside global consumption. This environmental footprint is primarily driven by fuel usage and emissions from transportation modes such as road transport and aviation, which not only exacerbate climate change but also contribute to respiratory and cardiovascular health issues [109].

To address these challenges, several strategies have emerged within the logistics industry aimed at minimizing environmental impact while maintaining operational efficiency. Optimizing routes is a pivotal approach, leveraging advanced route optimization software that factors in variables like traffic conditions, weather, and vehicle availability. This technology enables logistics companies to select the shortest, most fuel-efficient routes in real-time, reducing both emissions and operational costs [109].

Another critical initiative involves tracking and minimizing empty miles, which occur when transport vehicles return empty after deliveries. Tools like fleet management systems and dedicated marketplace platforms facilitate tracking and coordination, optimizing logistics networks to minimize unnecessary trips and associated emissions. By utilizing these solutions, logistics operators can significantly reduce air and water pollution, aligning with sustainability goals [109].

Efforts to enhance transportation efficiency also extend to improving behaviours through telematics and AI-driven monitoring systems. These technologies monitor factors like idling and speeding, providing real-time feedback to drivers and fleet managers to optimize fuel consumption and reduce emissions. This approach not only contributes to environmental sustainability but also improves overall fleet safety and operational efficiency.

Choosing more sustainable transportation options is another key strategy. Compared to air and road transport, sea freight and rail transport generally have lower carbon footprints per ton-mile. Moreover, the adoption of electric and hybrid vehicles, though still in early stages for large-scale logistics, holds promise for further reducing emissions, especially when powered by renewable energy sources. These vehicles not only produce fewer emissions but also contribute to quieter and less polluting urban logistics solutions [109].

Warehouse management practices also play a vital role in reducing environmental impact within logistics. Innovations such as sensor networks and automated sorting systems help optimize operations, improve order accuracy, and enhance recycling processes for returned products. Some companies are pioneering sustainable practices by integrating energy-efficient technologies and eco-friendly materials into their warehouse operations, thereby reducing their overall environmental footprint [109].

Implementing green logistics practices involves reducing reliance on single-use plastics and maximizing packaging efficiency through practices like kitting and consolidated shipments. These approaches minimize waste and reduce packaging-related pollution, contributing to more sustainable supply chain operations. Collaborative efforts with suppliers and customers further enhance these practices, fostering transparency and efficiency across logistics networks and reducing inefficiencies such as empty miles [109].

Accessing Information about Environmental Protection Regulations and Procedures

Ensuring compliance with relevant environmental legislation and codes of practice is crucial for any organization aiming to operate responsibly and sustainably. This involves thorough understanding and implementation of laws governing environmental protection, waste management, emissions control, and resource conservation.

Organizations must maintain meticulous records and documentation to demonstrate adherence to these regulations. This includes keeping abreast of updates and amendments to environmental laws to ensure ongoing compliance.

Central to effective environmental management within the workplace is the accessibility and clarity of environmental policies, procedures, and programs. These documents should be stored in a readily accessible location that all employees can easily access. Clear communication and understanding among the workforce are essential, ensuring that all team members are informed about their roles and responsibilities in environmental protection. Regular updates and training sessions are necessary to align with any changes in workplace policies or environmental regulations, ensuring that everyone remains informed and compliant.

Transparent and accurate communication regarding the outcomes of environmental risk identification and control procedures is essential for maintaining a safe and sustainable work environment. This involves promptly sharing information about identified risks, control measures implemented, and the effectiveness of these measures with relevant personnel. By disseminating this information, organizations empower their workforce to contribute to ongoing improvement and compliance efforts, fostering a culture of environmental responsibility and accountability.

The concept of the 4 A's of Sustainable Logistics offers a structured approach for businesses aiming to integrate environmental sustainability into their transportation and logistics practices. Each "A" represents a crucial phase in this journey, emphasizing awareness, assessment, action, and achievement [115].

Firstly, awareness serves as the foundational step. In sustainable logistics, cultivating awareness involves educating stakeholders about the significant environmental impacts associated with logistics operations. This includes understanding how activities such as fuel consumption, packaging choices, and supply chain logistics contribute to carbon emissions and ecological footprints. By raising awareness among industry players, businesses can foster a collective understanding of the need for sustainable practices and lay the groundwork for informed decision-making [115].

Secondly, assessment is key to quantifying the environmental impact of logistics activities. This involves conducting comprehensive evaluations to gauge the carbon footprint and other ecological consequences of transportation and supply chain operations. Assessment methodologies range from lifecycle assessments to carbon footprint calculations, providing businesses with actionable insights into areas where environmental impacts are most pronounced. By systematically assessing their operations, companies can identify hotspots for improvement and prioritize areas where sustainability initiatives can yield the most significant benefits [115].

Next, action translates awareness and assessment into tangible strategies for emission reduction and waste management. This third "A" involves implementing practical measures to mitigate environmental impacts across the logistics chain. Strategies may include optimizing transportation routes to minimize fuel consumption, adopting alternative fuels or electric vehicles, improving packaging efficiency to reduce waste, and integrating sustainable practices into warehouse and distribution operations. By taking decisive action, businesses not only reduce their environmental footprint but also enhance operational efficiency and resilience in a changing regulatory and consumer landscape [115].

Finally, achievement signifies the culmination of efforts in sustainable logistics. It involves measuring the impact of implemented strategies using key performance indicators (KPIs) and metrics designed to assess environmental performance. These metrics allow businesses to track progress, monitor outcomes, and demonstrate the effectiveness of their sustainability initiatives. Achieving sustainability goals requires ongoing commitment and continuous improvement, as businesses strive to surpass benchmarks and set new standards for environmental stewardship in the logistics industry [115].

Implementing and Monitoring Environmental Hazard Procedures

Identifying and reporting existing and potential environmental hazards in the workplace is a critical aspect of maintaining a safe and sustainable work environment. This process begins with conducting comprehensive hazard assessments across all aspects of operations, from manufacturing processes to office environments. Hazards can range from chemical spills and emissions to improper waste disposal practices, ergonomic issues, and even energy inefficiencies that contribute to environmental impact.

The first step involves systematically assessing each area of the workplace to identify any hazards that could pose risks to the environment. This includes evaluating the handling, storage, and disposal of hazardous materials, as well as examining energy consumption patterns and potential sources of pollution. For example, in manufacturing settings, this might involve evaluating the use of chemicals and ensuring proper containment and disposal methods are in place. In an office environment, it could mean assessing energy use and implementing measures to reduce electricity consumption or improve recycling practices.

Once identified, these hazards must be reported promptly to designated personnel or environmental health and safety officers within the organization. Reporting mechanisms should be clear and accessible to all employees to encourage timely identification and communication of hazards. This ensures that corrective actions can be taken swiftly to mitigate risks before they escalate into incidents that could harm the environment or endanger employees.

Regular monitoring and auditing play a crucial role in maintaining vigilance over environmental hazards. This involves ongoing assessment of workplace practices and conditions to detect any new or evolving risks. Environmental audits can help verify compliance with regulatory requirements and identify areas for improvement in environmental management practices.

Effective communication is key throughout this process. Employees should be trained to recognize environmental hazards and encouraged to report any concerns they observe during their work. This fosters a proactive approach to hazard identification and helps cultivate a culture of environmental awareness and responsibility across the organization.

Assessing identified hazards in relation to relevant environmental protection policies is a crucial step in ensuring that organizations effectively manage and mitigate risks to the environment. This process involves evaluating each identified hazard against established policies, regulations, and standards that govern environmental protection. Here's a detailed look at how to approach this assessment:

Firstly, organizations need to refer to local, national, and international environmental protection policies that apply to their operations. These policies outline specific requirements, limits, and guidelines aimed at safeguarding natural resources, preventing pollution, and minimizing environmental impact. For example, policies may dictate permissible emission levels for air pollutants, standards for water quality, guidelines for waste disposal, and regulations on biodiversity conservation.

Once the relevant policies are identified, hazards within the workplace are assessed to determine their potential impact on compliance with these policies. Hazards can encompass various aspects such as chemical handling practices, emissions from industrial processes, waste management procedures, energy consumption patterns, and more. Each hazard is evaluated to understand how it aligns with or deviates from environmental protection policies and regulations.

Assessment criteria typically include evaluating the severity and likelihood of environmental harm posed by each hazard. This involves considering factors such as the volume and toxicity of materials involved, potential pathways of environmental contamination, and the sensitivity of local ecosystems or communities to the hazard's effects. For instance, a chemical spill near a water source may pose a higher risk than emissions within an industrial facility, depending on the volume and toxicity of the spill.

Furthermore, the assessment should take into account the organization's own environmental management objectives and commitments. This includes internal policies, procedures, and sustainability goals that go beyond regulatory requirements to promote proactive environmental stewardship. Aligning hazard assessments with these internal standards ensures comprehensive risk management and supports efforts to achieve broader environmental sustainability targets.

Throughout the assessment process, collaboration among multidisciplinary teams is essential. Environmental health and safety professionals, operations managers, compliance officers, and technical experts often collaborate to gather relevant data, conduct risk assessments, and develop mitigation strategies. This interdisciplinary approach ensures that assessments are thorough, informed by diverse perspectives, and grounded in both technical expertise and regulatory knowledge.

Finally, documentation and record-keeping are critical aspects of assessing hazards in relation to environmental protection policies. Clear documentation ensures transparency and accountability, facilitates regulatory compliance audits, and provides a basis for continuous improvement. This includes maintaining records of hazard assessments, mitigation plans, monitoring results, and any corrective actions taken to address identified risks.

Implementing workplace procedures for dealing with hazardous events is crucial to ensuring swift and effective response to emergencies or incidents that could pose risks to employees, the environment, and the surrounding community. These procedures are designed to mitigate the impact of hazardous events promptly and efficiently. Here's a detailed overview of how organizations can effectively implement these procedures:

Firstly, organizations need to establish clear and comprehensive procedures tailored to the specific hazards and risks present in their workplace. Hazardous events can vary widely, from chemical spills and fires to equipment malfunctions and natural disasters. Each type of event requires a specific response plan that outlines roles, responsibilities, and actions to be taken by employees and designated response teams.

The development of these procedures typically involves conducting a thorough hazard assessment and risk analysis. This process identifies potential scenarios and evaluates their likelihood and potential consequences. For instance, in a chemical manufacturing facility, procedures may include protocols for containing spills, evacuating affected areas, and notifying emergency services. In an office environment, procedures might focus on responding to fire alarms, conducting evacuations, and administering first aid.

Once procedures are established, they must be communicated clearly to all employees through training programs, drills, and regular updates. Training sessions ensure that employees understand their roles and responsibilities during hazardous events, know how to use emergency equipment (such as fire extinguishers or personal protective gear), and are familiar with evacuation routes and assembly points.

Furthermore, implementing workplace procedures involves integrating them into daily operations and ensuring they are easily accessible to employees. This includes posting emergency contact information, evacuation maps, and procedural documents in visible locations throughout the workplace. Clear signage and digital notifications can also help alert employees to hazards and emergency procedures in real-time.

Regular drills and exercises are essential to validate and improve the effectiveness of workplace procedures. Conducting simulated emergency scenarios allows employees to practice their roles, test communication systems, and identify areas for improvement. Feedback from drills helps refine procedures, update response protocols, and address any gaps in preparedness.

Collaboration with external stakeholders, such as local emergency responders and regulatory agencies, is another critical aspect of implementing effective workplace procedures. Organizations should establish partnerships and communication channels to coordinate responses, share information, and comply with regulatory requirements during hazardous events.

Lastly, continuous monitoring, evaluation, and review are essential components of maintaining effective workplace procedures. Organizations should regularly assess the adequacy of procedures based on changes in workplace conditions, new hazards, or lessons learned from real incidents. Updates should be made promptly to ensure procedures remain current, relevant, and aligned with best practices and regulatory standards.

Investigating hazardous events is a critical process aimed at understanding their root causes, identifying vulnerabilities in existing systems, and implementing effective control measures to prevent recurrence and minimize risks in the workplace. Here's a detailed explanation of how organizations can systematically approach this:

Firstly, when a hazardous event occurs, whether it's an accident, near miss, or environmental incident, it's essential to promptly initiate an investigation. The investigation team typically includes trained personnel with expertise relevant to the incident, such as safety officers, environmental specialists, and operational managers. Their primary goal is to gather factual information about the event and understand the sequence of events leading up to it.

During the investigation, gathering and preserving evidence is crucial. This includes documenting physical evidence, such as equipment involved, environmental conditions, and any relevant data logs or records. Eyewitness accounts and statements from personnel directly involved or affected by the event provide valuable insights into what happened and the conditions leading up to the incident.

A systematic approach to investigation involves using established protocols or methodologies, such as root cause analysis (RCA) or fault tree analysis (FTA). These methods help investigators trace back from the immediate cause of the event to identify underlying factors and systemic issues that contributed to its occurrence. For example, if a chemical spill occurs, investigators may analyse equipment failures, procedural lapses, human error, or inadequate training as contributing factors.

Once the root causes are identified, the next step is to develop and implement corrective and preventive actions (CAPAs). Corrective actions address immediate concerns to prevent recurrence of the specific event. This might include repairing equipment, revising procedures, or retraining employees. Preventive actions, on the other hand, aim to address underlying systemic issues to reduce the likelihood of similar events in the future. This could involve implementing new safety protocols, enhancing training programs, or upgrading equipment and infrastructure.

Implementation of CAPAs requires clear accountability and timelines. Assigning responsibilities to specific individuals or teams ensures that corrective and preventive measures are effectively implemented. Regular follow-up and monitoring are essential to track progress, address any barriers to implementation, and verify that control measures are effective in mitigating risks.

Communication is key throughout the investigation and implementation process. Providing timely updates to employees, stakeholders, and regulatory authorities fosters transparency and demonstrates commitment to improving safety and environmental practices. It also ensures that lessons learned from the investigation are shared across the organization to prevent similar incidents elsewhere.

Lastly, continuous improvement is integral to the investigation process. Organizations should conduct post-event reviews to evaluate the effectiveness of implemented CAPAs and identify opportunities for further enhancement. This may involve conducting periodic audits, reviewing incident trends, and updating risk assessments based on new information or changing conditions in the workplace.

Implementing and Monitoring Environmental Control Procedures

Implementing, monitoring, and reviewing existing environmental protection measures within an organization involves a systematic approach to ensure compliance with regulatory requirements and the continual improvement of environmental performance. This process begins with the implementation phase, where established environmental protection measures are put into practice across all relevant operations and activities. This may include adhering to waste management protocols, energy conservation practices, emissions control measures, and sustainable procurement policies tailored to minimize environmental impact.

Once implemented, these measures are subjected to rigorous monitoring to assess their effectiveness and identify any deviations from established environmental standards. Monitoring typically involves regular inspections, audits, and data collection to track key performance indicators (KPIs) related to environmental sustainability. For instance, monitoring may include measuring energy consumption levels, waste generation rates, emissions output, and adherence to environmental management systems (EMS) requirements.

Following monitoring, a critical aspect of the process is the review phase. Reviews are conducted to evaluate the outcomes of implemented measures against predefined environmental objectives and targets. This involves analysing monitoring data, identifying trends or areas of concern, and assessing whether the implemented measures are achieving the desired environmental outcomes. Reviews also provide an opportunity to solicit feedback from stakeholders, including employees, regulators, and community representatives, to ensure alignment with broader environmental goals and expectations.

Continuous improvement is central to the review phase, as it enables organizations to refine and enhance their environmental protection measures over time. This iterative process involves identifying opportunities for optimization, updating policies and procedures based on new regulatory requirements or technological advancements, and implementing corrective actions to address any identified deficiencies. By integrating feedback from stakeholders and leveraging best practices from industry peers, organizations can strengthen their environmental management frameworks and enhance overall environmental stewardship.

Throughout this entire cycle of implementation, monitoring, and review, effective communication and documentation play crucial roles. Clear communication ensures that all stakeholders understand their roles and responsibilities in upholding environmental protection measures, while robust documentation facilitates transparency, accountability, and compliance with regulatory reporting requirements. This comprehensive approach not only helps organizations meet legal obligations but also fosters a culture of environmental responsibility, innovation, and continuous improvement across all levels of the organization.

The following Environmental Control Procedure provides a framework for XYZ Transport Company to manage its environmental responsibilities systematically and effectively. It covers key areas such as risk assessment, environmental controls, compliance monitoring, training, emergency response, continuous improvement, and documentation, ensuring a comprehensive approach to environmental management within the organization.

Environmental Control Procedure for XYZ Transport Company

Objective: The objective of this Environmental Control Procedure is to ensure that XYZ Transport Company operates in compliance with environmental regulations, minimizes its environmental impact, and promotes sustainable practices across its operations.

Scope: This procedure applies to all activities, processes, and personnel within XYZ Transport Company that have the potential to impact the environment, including transportation operations, maintenance activities, and administrative functions.

Responsibilities:

- **Environmental Manager:** The Environmental Manager is responsible for overseeing the implementation of this procedure, monitoring environmental performance, and ensuring compliance with regulatory requirements.

- **Department Heads and Supervisors:** Department heads and supervisors are responsible for ensuring that their respective teams understand and adhere to environmental control measures relevant to their duties.

- **Employees:** All employees are responsible for following environmental procedures, reporting any environmental incidents or concerns promptly, and actively participating in environmental training and initiatives.

Procedure:

- **Environmental Risk Assessment:**

    - Conduct regular environmental risk assessments to identify potential environmental hazards associated with transportation operations, maintenance activities, and facilities.

- Assess risks in terms of air emissions, water discharges, waste generation, and hazardous materials handling.

- **Environmental Controls:**

  - Implement controls to minimize environmental impacts identified in the risk assessments.

  - Utilize best practices and technologies for pollution prevention, such as:

    - Regular maintenance of vehicles to reduce emissions.

    - Spill prevention and response procedures for fuelling stations and maintenance areas.

    - Waste segregation and recycling programs for materials such as oil, batteries, and tires.

- **Compliance Monitoring:**

  - Monitor compliance with environmental regulations, permits, and licenses applicable to XYZ Transport Company.

  - Conduct regular inspections and audits to verify adherence to environmental controls and identify opportunities for improvement.

  - Maintain records of compliance monitoring activities and corrective actions taken.

- **Training and Awareness:**

  - Provide environmental training to employees to ensure understanding of environmental policies, procedures, and regulatory requirements.

  - Foster environmental awareness and promote a culture of environmental responsibility among employees through regular communication and engagement initiatives.

- **Emergency Response:**

  - Develop and maintain an emergency response plan specific to environmental incidents, including spills, leaks, and accidents involving hazardous materials.

- Ensure all employees are trained on emergency response procedures and have access to appropriate spill containment and cleanup equipment.

- **Continuous Improvement:**

    - Periodically review and revise environmental objectives, targets, and performance indicators to drive continual improvement.

    - Implement corrective and preventive actions based on monitoring results, audits, and feedback to enhance environmental performance.

- **Documentation and Reporting:**

    - Maintain accurate and up-to-date records of environmental performance, including monitoring data, inspection reports, training records, and incident investigations.

    - Prepare and submit required environmental reports to regulatory authorities in accordance with applicable laws and regulations.

Review and Revision: This Environmental Control Procedure shall be reviewed annually by the Environmental Manager to ensure its effectiveness, relevance, and compliance with evolving environmental standards and company objectives. Amendments may be made as necessary based on regulatory changes, operational improvements, or feedback from stakeholders.

Approval: This Environmental Control Procedure is approved by the CEO of XYZ Transport Company and shall be communicated to all employees. Compliance with this procedure is mandatory for all personnel involved in the operations of XYZ Transport Company.

Implementing the Environmental Control Procedure for XYZ Transport Company involves a structured approach to ensure compliance, minimize environmental impact, and promote sustainable practices throughout the organization. Here's how each aspect of the procedure can be effectively implemented:

Environmental Risk Assessment:

- **Execution:** The Environmental Manager will initiate regular environmental risk assessments across all departments and facilities. This involves identifying potential hazards related to air emissions, water discharges, waste generation, and handling of hazardous materials.

- **Responsibility:** The Environmental Manager will coordinate with department heads and supervisors to conduct comprehensive assessments and document findings.

Environmental Controls:

- **Implementation:** Based on risk assessment outcomes, environmental controls will be implemented to mitigate identified risks. This includes adopting best practices and technologies for pollution prevention, such as vehicle maintenance schedules, spill prevention measures, and waste segregation programs.

- **Monitoring:** Department heads and supervisors will ensure that environmental controls are adhered to by their teams through regular inspections and audits.

Compliance Monitoring:

- **Execution:** The Environmental Manager will oversee compliance monitoring to ensure adherence to environmental regulations, permits, and licenses relevant to XYZ Transport Company.

- **Documentation:** Records of compliance activities, including inspections, audits, and corrective actions, will be maintained systematically to demonstrate regulatory compliance.

Training and Awareness:

- **Training Programs:** Environmental training sessions will be conducted to educate employees on environmental policies, procedures, and regulatory requirements. These sessions will be tailored to the specific roles and responsibilities of different teams within the company.

- **Awareness Campaigns:** The Environmental Manager will lead initiatives to promote environmental awareness and foster a culture of responsibility among employees through regular communication and engagement activities.

Emergency Response:

- **Plan Development:** A specific emergency response plan for environmental incidents, such as spills or leaks, will be developed and maintained. This plan will outline procedures for containment, cleanup, and reporting.

- **Training and Equipment:** All employees will undergo training on emergency response procedures, and necessary equipment for spill containment and cleanup will be made accessible and regularly maintained.

Continuous Improvement:

- **Review Process:** The Environmental Manager will conduct periodic reviews of environmental objectives, targets, and performance indicators to assess effectiveness and identify areas for improvement.

- **Action Plans:** Based on review outcomes, corrective and preventive actions will be implemented to enhance environmental performance and achieve sustainability goals.

Documentation and Reporting:

- **Record Keeping:** Accurate and up-to-date records of environmental performance, including monitoring data, inspection reports, training records, and incident investigations, will be maintained.

- **Regulatory Compliance:** Required environmental reports will be prepared and submitted to regulatory authorities in accordance with applicable laws and regulations.

Review and Revision:

- **Annual Review:** The Environmental Manager will lead an annual review of the Environmental Control Procedure to ensure its effectiveness, relevance, and alignment with evolving environmental standards and company objectives.

- **Feedback Incorporation:** Amendments to the procedure will be made as necessary based on regulatory changes, operational improvements, or feedback from stakeholders.

Approval and Communication:

- The Environmental Control Procedure, approved by the CEO, will be communicated to all employees to ensure understanding and compliance across the organization. Regular updates and training sessions will reinforce adherence to environmental policies and procedures.

By following this structured approach, XYZ Transport Company can effectively implement its Environmental Control Procedure, fostering a culture of environmental stewardship while ensuring regulatory compliance and operational efficiency.

Implementing environmental protection procedures and ensuring adherence by work groups involves a systematic approach focused on compliance, monitoring, and continuous improvement. Here's how this can be effectively carried out:

Implementation of Environmental Protection Procedures: To begin with, environmental protection procedures must be clearly defined and communicated throughout the organization. This involves translating policies into actionable steps that address specific environmental risks and promote sustainable practices. The Environmental Manager or designated personnel will play a crucial role in overseeing the implementation process. They will work closely with department heads and supervisors to ensure that procedures are integrated into daily operations across all work groups.

Implementation starts with training sessions and workshops aimed at familiarizing employees with the procedures. These sessions should emphasize the importance of environmental protection, highlight specific procedures relevant to each work group, and clarify roles and responsibilities. Practical demonstrations and case studies can help illustrate how adherence to these procedures contributes to reducing environmental impact and achieving organizational sustainability goals.

Monitoring Adherence to Environmental Procedures: Once procedures are in place, monitoring adherence becomes essential to ensure effectiveness and compliance. This involves regular inspections, audits, and performance reviews conducted by the Environmental Manager or assigned personnel. The monitoring process should be systematic and structured, focusing on key aspects such as:

- **Compliance Checks:** Assessing whether work groups are following prescribed environmental procedures and protocols. This includes verifying that proper waste management practices are observed, emissions are within permissible limits, and hazardous materials are handled safely.

- **Documentation Review:** Reviewing records and documentation to track compliance with environmental regulations and internal policies. This may include inspection reports, incident logs, training records, and corrective action plans.

- **Feedback Mechanisms:** Establishing mechanisms for gathering feedback from work groups regarding the practicality and effectiveness of implemented procedures. This feedback can provide insights into operational challenges, training needs, and areas for improvement.

Continuous Improvement: Achieving sustainable environmental practices requires a commitment to continuous improvement. Based on monitoring findings and feedback, the Environmental Manager should identify opportunities to enhance procedures and address any gaps or deficiencies. This may involve:

- **Training and Development:** Providing additional training sessions or refresher courses to reinforce adherence to procedures and ensure that employees remain informed about updates or changes.

- **Updating Procedures:** Revising procedures as necessary to incorporate best practices, reflect regulatory changes, or address emerging environmental risks. This ensures that the procedures remain relevant and effective over time.

- **Celebrating Successes:** Recognizing and celebrating achievements in environmental protection and sustainability can foster a positive organizational culture. This could include acknowledging teams or individuals who excel in adhering to procedures and contributing to environmental stewardship.

Implementing environmental protection procedures and monitoring adherence involves a coordinated effort to embed sustainable practices into the organizational culture. By focusing on clear communication, systematic monitoring, and continuous improvement, companies can effectively reduce their environmental footprint while complying with regulatory requirements and achieving long-term sustainability goals.

In the realm of sustainability, reducing the carbon footprint has become an imperative for both multinational corporations and independent freight forwarders alike. Embracing sustainability not only mitigates CO_2 emissions but also addresses concerns such as noise pollution and accidents, thereby fostering a more eco-friendly operational landscape. For independent freight forwarders specifically, implementing a series of practical sustainability tips can significantly contribute to minimizing environmental impact while maintaining operational efficiency [115, 116].

Alternative Fuels and Transportation Modes: One of the fundamental steps for independent freight forwarders is to transition towards alternative fuels and transportation modes that are more environmentally friendly. This includes investing in electric vehicles capable of long-haul journeys and leveraging rail freight whenever feasible. By replacing older, less efficient trucks with eco-friendly vehicles and adopting low-carbon fuels, freight forwarders can immediately reduce their carbon footprint and enhance operational sustainability.

Optimizing Freight Shipments: Choosing Less than Container Load (LCL) shipments over Full Container Load (FCL) shipments whenever possible is another strategy. LCL shipments optimize cargo space by consolidating shipments from multiple carriers into a single container, thereby reducing overall fuel consumption and emissions. This approach not only lowers costs but also aligns with ecological principles by maximizing the efficiency of transportation resources.

Sustainable Packaging Practices: Freight forwarders can make a significant impact on reducing environmental impact by adopting biodegradable and recyclable packaging materials. Participating in recycling programs and advocating for sustainable packaging practices across their supply chains can further mitigate the ecological footprint associated with packaging waste. By minimizing the use of non-biodegradable materials and promoting responsible recycling, forwarders contribute to a more sustainable logistics ecosystem.

Choosing Sustainable Transportation Modes: Avoiding air freight for non-time-sensitive shipments and opting for sea or rail freight can substantially reduce carbon emissions. Air freight is notorious for its high CO_2 emissions per ton-mile compared to sea and rail transport. By strategically selecting transportation modes based on urgency and environmental impact, freight forwarders can minimize their carbon footprint and support sustainable logistics practices.

Cross-Docking and Route Optimization: Implementing cross-docking practices helps streamline operations and reduce energy consumption within warehouse facilities. This method involves transferring goods directly from inbound trucks to outbound vehicles, minimizing storage time and optimizing delivery routes. Coupled with advanced route optimization software, which identifies the most fuel-efficient routes based on real-time data, forwarders can further reduce mileage and emissions while enhancing operational efficiency

Adopting Clean Energy and Digitization: Integrating renewable energy sources such as solar and wind power into warehouse and office operations reduces reliance on traditional energy sources and lowers carbon emissions. Additionally, transitioning to a paperless workplace through digital technologies and logistics management software not only improves operational efficiency but also eliminates paper waste, contributing to sustainability efforts.

Employee Engagement and Training: Training employees on sustainable practices and fostering a culture of environmental responsibility are essential components of reducing a freight forwarder's carbon footprint. By engaging staff in sustainability initiatives and encouraging proactive participation, forwarders can cultivate a workforce that champions eco-friendly operations and drives continuous improvement in environmental performance.

As such, by implementing these sustainable strategies—from adopting alternative fuels and optimizing freight shipments to embracing clean energy and engaging employees—independent freight forwarders can effectively reduce their carbon footprint. These initiatives not only align with global environmental goals but also position forwarders as leaders in sustainable logistics practices, contributing to a greener future for the transportation and logistics industry.

Identifying required improvements to existing control measures within any organization, particularly concerning environmental protection or safety protocols, involves a systematic approach to assessment, communication, and resource allocation. Initially, this process begins with a comprehensive review and evaluation of current control measures in place. This evaluation typically includes gathering feedback from frontline workers, conducting audits or inspections, and analysing incident reports or near-misses to identify areas where existing controls may be insufficient or ineffective.

Once potential improvements are identified, the next critical step is to determine the resources necessary for their implementation. This involves assessing both tangible resources (such as equipment, technologies, or materials) and intangible resources (such as additional training, personnel allocation, or procedural adjustments). The evaluation should consider not only the immediate costs but also the long-term benefits and impacts on operational efficiency and safety.

Communicating identified improvements to appropriate personnel is crucial for ensuring alignment and support across the organization. This typically involves engaging with key stakeholders, including department heads, safety officers, environmental managers, and operational teams. Clear and concise communication is essential to convey the rationale behind the proposed improvements, the expected outcomes, and any necessary adjustments in workflow or procedures.

Reporting these identified improvements to appropriate personnel often involves formal channels of communication within the organization. This may include submitting recommendations through established reporting mechanisms, such as safety committees, environmental management systems, or quality assurance processes. Providing detailed documentation that outlines the identified deficiencies, proposed improvements, resource requirements, and expected benefits helps streamline the approval process and ensures transparency throughout the organization.

Furthermore, it's important to ensure that the identified improvements align with organizational goals and objectives, regulatory requirements, and industry best practices. This alignment not only strengthens the case for implementation but also fosters a culture of continuous improvement and proactive risk management within the organization.

Chapter 15
Managing Work Area Safety

Safety management is a critical aspect of the transport and logistics industry due to the inherent risks and complexities involved. The sector faces numerous uncertainties and potential disruptions, highlighting the importance of risk and crisis management for effective operations [117]. This need is further underscored by the industry's operation within a highly regulated environment with strict safety and compliance standards [118]. Workplace safety practices are not only a legal requirement but also a corporate social responsibility for logistics and transportation companies [119].

Furthermore, safety management is essential for ensuring the well-being of employees. Research has shown that effective safety practices, such as management commitment to occupational health and safety, can reduce the likelihood of injuries among workers [120]. Protecting employees' health and comfort is a fundamental aspect of work health and safety in the logistics sector, especially during warehousing processes [121]. Implementing safety measures not only ensures the safety of employees but also fosters a positive safety culture within the organization [122].

In addition to human safety, safety management in the transport and logistics industry is crucial for preserving the integrity and quality of goods during transportation. For example, the efficient management of cold chain logistics is vital for maintaining the quality and safety of perishable products, minimizing waste, and preventing economic losses in industries such as fast-moving consumer goods [123]. Similarly, in the agricultural sector, safety monitoring systems utilizing technologies like the Internet of Things are employed to ensure the safety of agricultural products during transportation [124].

Moreover, safety management in logistics is closely intertwined with broader issues such as sustainability and environmental protection. Green logistics strategies focus on environmentally sustainable supply chains, highlighting the significance of managing logistics operations in an eco-friendly manner [10]. Sustainable leadership practices are also recognized as crucial in the logistics industry, with a need for enhancing leadership practices to improve sustainability and competitiveness [125]. Additionally, the interplay between sustainable logistics practices, environmental reputation, and financial performance emphasizes the importance of integrating safety management into overall sustainability efforts [23].

Safety management in the transport and logistics industry not only mitigates risks but also enhances overall performance and efficiency. Logistics performance benefits from safety management practices, with safety compliance playing a significant role in the sector's success [126]. Furthermore, safety management aids in building resilience in supply chains, particularly in industries like oil and gas where disruptions can have severe consequences [127]. By ensuring safety in operations, logistics companies can enhance their reputation, customer service, and financial performance [128].

Safety management in transport and logistics is critical to ensure the well-being of employees, protect assets, comply with regulations, and maintain operational efficiency. This includes:

- **Risk Assessment and Hazard Identification**: Conduct thorough risk assessments to identify potential hazards specific to transport and logistics operations. This includes evaluating risks related to vehicle operations, loading and unloading activities, maintenance tasks, and warehouse operations. Hazards such as slips, trips, falls, vehicle collisions, and hazardous material handling should be carefully assessed.

- **Safety Policies and Procedures**: Develop and implement comprehensive safety policies and procedures that address identified risks. These should cover areas such as vehicle operation, personal protective equipment (PPE) requirements, safe loading and unloading practices, emergency response protocols, and adherence to traffic laws and regulations. Ensure that policies are communicated effectively to all employees and contractors.

- **Training and Education**: Provide regular training programs to educate employees on safety policies, procedures, and best practices. Training should include defensive driving techniques, proper lifting and handling procedures, use of PPE, emergency response drills, and awareness of specific hazards related to their roles. Continuous education ensures that employees are aware of safety updates and maintain vigilance.

- **Equipment Maintenance and Inspection**: Implement a rigorous maintenance schedule for all vehicles, machinery, and equipment used in transport and logistics. Regular inspections should be conducted to identify and address potential mechanical issues that could compromise safety. This includes checking brakes, lights, tires, and ensuring compliance with safety standards for equipment operation.

- **Emergency Preparedness**: Develop and maintain emergency response plans tailored to transport and logistics operations. These plans should outline procedures for handling accidents, spills, fires, and other emergencies. Ensure that all employees are trained on emergency response protocols and have access to necessary emergency equipment, such as fire extinguishers and first aid kits.

- **Monitoring and Auditing**: Regularly monitor safety performance through inspections, audits, and incident investigations. Use key performance indicators (KPIs) to track safety metrics, such as accident rates, near misses, and compliance with safety procedures. Conduct regular safety audits to identify areas for improvement and ensure that corrective actions are implemented promptly.

- **Safety Culture and Engagement**: Foster a safety-first culture where all employees prioritize safety in their daily activities. Encourage open communication about safety concerns and provide avenues for employees to report hazards or suggest improvements. Recognize and reward safety-conscious behaviour to reinforce positive safety practices throughout the organization.

- **Compliance with Regulations**: Stay informed about relevant safety regulations, standards, and industry best practices. Ensure compliance with occupational health and safety laws, environmental regulations, and transportation regulations applicable to your operations. Regularly review and update safety policies and procedures to align with regulatory requirements and industry trends.

To effectively manage health and safety within an organization, it's crucial to follow a systematic approach that includes locating, adapting, adopting, and communicating health and safety policies. This process ensures that the organization not only complies with health and safety laws but also fosters a culture of safety among its workforce.

Locating, Adapting, Adopting, and Communicating Health and Safety Policies:

- Locating Policies: Begin by identifying existing health and safety policies that are relevant to the organization. This involves reviewing national, state/provincial, and local health and safety laws and regulations that apply to the industry in which the organization operates. Policies may also include industry best practices and guidelines recommended by health and safety authorities.

- Adapting and Adopting Policies: Once policies are located, they should be carefully reviewed and adapted to suit the specific needs and operations of the organization. This adaptation ensures that policies are practical, relevant, and effective in addressing the unique health and safety risks associated with the organization's activities. It may involve tailoring generic policies to include specific hazards and procedures relevant to the workplace.

- Communicating Policies: After adapting policies, it is essential to adopt them formally within the organization. This typically involves obtaining approval from senior management or the board of directors to ensure commitment and endorsement. Once approved, policies should be clearly communicated to all employees, contractors, and relevant stakeholders. Effective communication methods include staff meetings, training sessions, email notifications, and posting policies on intranet portals or notice boards.

Identifying Duty Holders and Defining Responsibilities:

- Identifying duty holders involves determining individuals or roles within the organization who have specific responsibilities for health and safety. This includes appointing a competent person or team to oversee health and safety management and ensuring that responsibilities are clearly defined for all personnel.

Defining Responsibilities:

- Responsibilities should be outlined in job descriptions, organizational charts, and health and safety manuals. Each employee should understand their role in implementing health and safety policies and procedures and how they contribute to maintaining a safe work environment. This clarity helps ensure accountability and promotes a proactive approach to health and safety management.

Identifying and Approving Resources:
- To effectively manage health and safety, organizations must allocate appropriate financial and human resources to support the health and safety management system.

Financial Resources:
- Identify the budget required for implementing health and safety initiatives, including training programs, equipment purchases, and maintenance costs. Financial resources should be approved through the organization's budgeting process to ensure adequate funding is available to address health and safety priorities.

Human Resources:
- Determine the staffing requirements for health and safety management, including the appointment of health and safety officers, first aiders, and emergency response teams. Ensure that personnel are adequately trained and competent to fulfill their roles in accordance with health and safety laws and organizational procedures.

Approval Process:
- The allocation of resources should be approved by senior management or the designated health and safety committee within the organization. This ensures that decisions are aligned with organizational goals and priorities and that resources are effectively utilized to mitigate health and safety risks.

Establishing and Maintaining Effective Consultative Arrangements for Managing Health and Safety in a Work Area

Setting up and maintaining consultative arrangements in compliance with Work Health and Safety (WHS) laws involves a structured approach to ensure effective communication and collaboration between management and employees. This process is essential for fostering a safe and healthy work environment where everyone's perspectives are considered.

The first step is to establish consultative arrangements as required by WHS laws. This typically involves identifying key personnel who will participate in the consultation process. In many jurisdictions, this includes setting up a Health and Safety Committee (HSC) or appointing Health and Safety Representatives (HSRs) who act as liaisons between workers and management.

Consultative arrangements should involve a cross-section of the workforce, including managers, supervisors, and frontline employees. Each stakeholder group brings valuable insights into workplace health and safety issues based on their roles and experiences. It's crucial to ensure representation from different departments or work areas to address diverse safety concerns effectively.

Once established, consultative arrangements need to be maintained and supported over time. This involves scheduling regular meetings or forums where health and safety matters can be discussed openly. These meetings should be inclusive and provide opportunities for all participants to raise concerns, suggest improvements, and discuss emerging issues related to workplace safety.

Consultation isn't just about discussing issues—it also requires a commitment to resolving them promptly and effectively. Issues raised through consultation should be taken seriously and addressed according to both WHS laws and organizational protocols. This may involve conducting risk assessments, implementing control measures, providing additional training, or making changes to policies and procedures as needed.

Throughout the consultation process, it's essential to adhere to WHS laws and regulations governing consultation requirements. This includes ensuring that all participants understand their rights and responsibilities regarding health and safety matters. Compliance with these laws helps to create a supportive and legally sound framework for addressing workplace safety concerns.

Communication is key to the success of consultation and participation arrangements. After discussions and decisions are made in consultation meetings, it's important to provide feedback and information about outcomes to all required personnel. This ensures transparency and accountability, demonstrating that their input is valued and that action is being taken to address identified issues.

Consultation outcomes should be documented and communicated according to organizational policies and procedures This may include distributing meeting minutes, action plans, and updates on implemented changes to relevant stakeholders. Clear communication ensures that everyone is informed about decisions affecting their health and safety and reinforces the organization's commitment to continuous improvement in workplace safety practices.

Establishing and Maintaining Procedures for Effectively Identifying Hazards, and Assessing and Controlling Risks in Work Area

Developing procedures for ongoing hazard identification, assessment, and control is fundamental to maintaining a safe work environment and complying with health and safety regulations. This process involves systematic steps to ensure that workplace hazards are continuously identified, assessed for risks they pose, and effectively controlled to minimize the potential for harm.

The first step is to establish procedures for ongoing hazard identification. This involves regular inspections, risk assessments, and incident investigations to identify both existing and new hazards that may arise from changes in the workplace or work processes. By systematically identifying hazards, organizations can prioritize risks and take appropriate actions to control them before they cause harm.

Hazard identification should be integrated into the planning, design, and evaluation stages of any workplace change. Whether it involves new equipment, processes, or organizational changes, conducting hazard assessments ensures that potential risks are identified early. This proactive approach helps prevent new hazards from being introduced and ensures that existing hazards are adequately controlled during the change process.

Developing procedures for selecting and implementing risk controls according to the hierarchy of control measures is crucial. This hierarchy prioritizes measures that eliminate or minimize hazards at the source, such as engineering controls, before considering administrative controls or personal protective equipment (PPE). Procedures should outline how controls are selected based on their effectiveness in reducing risks and complying with health and safety legislative requirements.

Regular reviews and assessments should identify inadequacies in existing risk controls. This involves evaluating whether current control measures are effective in reducing risks to an acceptable level. When inadequacies are identified, procedures should prompt organizations to promptly allocate resources and implement new measures. This ensures that risks are continually managed and that controls evolve with changes in the workplace environment or regulatory requirements.

Identifying requirements for expert health and safety advice is essential for addressing complex or specialized hazards. Organizations should establish procedures to request expert advice as needed, ensuring that decisions related to hazard control are informed by professional knowledge and experience. This may involve consulting with occupational health and safety specialists, engineers, or other technical experts who can provide specialized insights into risk mitigation strategies.

All procedures for hazard identification, risk assessment, and control should align with organizational policies and health and safety legislative requirements. Compliance ensures that the procedures are effective, legally sound, and contribute to a safer work environment. Documentation and record-keeping of hazard assessments, control measures, and expert advice requests are critical to demonstrating compliance and continuous improvement in workplace safety practices.

Evaluating and Maintaining a Work Area Health and Safety Management System

Developing and providing a comprehensive health and safety induction and training program for personnel is crucial to ensuring a safe work environment and compliance with health and safety regulations. This program should be integrated into the organization's broader training framework, focusing specifically on equipping new and existing personnel with the knowledge and skills necessary to identify hazards, understand safety protocols, and mitigate risks effectively.

The initial step is to develop a structured health and safety induction program tailored to the specific work area and organizational context. This program should cover essential topics such as workplace hazards, emergency procedures, use of personal protective equipment (PPE), safe work practices, and reporting procedures for incidents and hazards. Training sessions should be interactive and participatory, ensuring that personnel not only receive information but also have opportunities to ask questions and clarify doubts.

Implementing a robust system for health and safety recordkeeping is essential for tracking and analysing occupational injuries, illnesses, near misses, and safety decisions within the organization. This system allows for the identification of patterns or trends in incidents, enabling proactive measures to be taken to prevent future occurrences. Records should include details such as incident reports, risk assessments, training records, safety meeting minutes, and any actions taken to improve workplace safety based on incident analysis.

Measuring and Evaluating the Health and Safety Management System

To ensure continuous improvement, the health and safety management system should be measured and evaluated against the organization's quality systems framework. This involves setting measurable objectives and performance indicators related to health and safety, such as incident rates, compliance levels, and effectiveness of control measures. Regular audits, inspections, and reviews should be conducted to assess the system's performance and identify areas for enhancement.

Based on the evaluation outcomes and identified areas for improvement, organizations should develop and implement targeted improvements to their health and safety management system. This process involves analysing root causes of incidents, soliciting feedback from personnel, consulting with health and safety experts if necessary, and revising policies, procedures, and training programs accordingly. Continuous communication and engagement with employees are key to successfully implementing improvements and achieving health and safety objectives.

Compliance with health and safety legislative frameworks is a fundamental requirement to protect workers and minimize organizational risk. Organizations must stay informed about relevant health and safety laws, regulations, and standards applicable to their industry and location. Regular updates to policies and procedures should reflect changes in legislation, ensuring that the organization meets or exceeds minimum legal requirements for health and safety.

Maintaining Road Safety

In the bustling transport and logistics industry, a wide array of activities are conducted daily, ranging from the transportation of passengers and freight across various modes like road, rail, water, and air, to essential support services such as stevedoring, harbor operations, airport services, and customs agency duties. These operations also encompass postal services, pipeline transport, scenic transport, and the critical function of warehousing and storage of goods. However, amidst these vital functions lies a notable challenge: the industry experiences a disproportionately high rate of workplace health and safety incidents.

Truck accidents are a significant concern due to their potential for causing severe injuries and fatalities. Research has delved into various aspects of truck accidents to understand the contributing factors and patterns associated with these incidents. Studies have shown that multiple-trailer trucks have a higher likelihood of crash involvement compared to single-trailer trucks, especially under challenging driving conditions [129]. Factors such as driver characteristics, environmental conditions, and road infrastructure play crucial roles in the severity of truck accidents.

One study highlighted that young employed male truck drivers with less experience are at a higher risk of accidents, particularly when driving across sharp curves, down long steep grades, over bridges or through tunnels, during the midnight period, and on adverse weather days in rural areas [130]. Additionally, the analysis of European Heavy Goods Vehicle (HGV) crashes emphasized the importance of understanding crash statistics to gain insights into the prevalence and characteristics of accidents involving HGVs [131].

Factors such as icy and snowy road conditions, speeding, and improper lane usage have been identified as major contributors to truck-related crashes [132]. Moreover, the analysis of large truck rollover crashes revealed that drunk driving significantly contributes to the severity of injuries in such incidents [133]. Understanding these factors is crucial for developing effective safety measures and interventions to reduce the occurrence and impact of truck accidents.

Studies have also explored the injury severity of drivers in truck-related crashes, highlighting that occupants in other vehicles involved in collisions with trucks are at a greater risk of serious injuries or fatalities [134]. Furthermore, research on hazardous material (HAZMAT) truck crashes emphasized the substantial economic costs associated with such incidents, underlining the importance of mitigating risks in the transportation of hazardous materials [135].

In the United States, in 2022, there were 5,837 fatal crashes involving large trucks, marking a 1.8% increase from 2021 and a significant 49% increase over the past decade. The involvement rate per 100 million miles travelled by large trucks also rose by 3% compared to 2021 and by 24% over the last 10 years. Large trucks, defined as medium or heavy trucks exceeding a gross vehicle weight rating of 10,000 pounds, accounted for 6% of all vehicles involved in fatal crashes and represented 10% of total vehicle miles travelled [136].

Furthermore, in 2022, there were 120,200 large truck crashes resulting in injury, reflecting a 2.5% increase from 2021. Since 2016, the number of injury-involved trucks has risen by 18%, and the injury involvement rate per 100 million miles driven by large trucks has increased by 5.7% to 37 [136]. Starting in 2016, the National Highway Traffic Safety Administration (NHTSA) began using the Crash Report Sampling System (CRSS) to estimate nonfatal crashes, employing a different sampling approach that is not directly comparable to earlier data [136].

Tragically, a total of 5,936 fatalities occurred in large-truck crashes in 2022, representing a 2% increase from 2021 and a 49% increase over the past decade [136]. The majority of these fatalities—70%—were occupants of other vehicles involved in the crashes, while 19% were truck occupants, and 11% were non-occupants, primarily pedestrians and bicyclists [136].

Similarly, the number of injuries resulting from large-truck crashes increased by 3.9% in 2022, totalling 161,000 injuries. Like fatalities, most injuries (73%) affected occupants of other vehicles involved in the crashes, while 26% affected truck occupants, and 1% affected non-occupants [136].

In Australia, around 18% of road crash fatalities in 2019, totalling about 210 deaths, involved heavy vehicles. Despite heavy vehicles being involved in fewer crashes compared to other vehicles, these incidents are more likely to result in fatalities or serious injuries due to their mass and impact severity. While fatal crashes with articulated trucks have shown a gradual decline, crashes involving heavy rigid trucks and buses have not seen a reduction over the past decade [137, 138].

Each year, approximately 500 occupants of heavy trucks require hospitalization following road crashes. Among these cases, about 30% are classified as having high threat-to-life injuries. The sheer mass of heavy vehicles contributes significantly to the kinetic energy transferred during a crash, often resulting in severe impact on other vehicles or vulnerable road users involved in the collision [137, 138].

Evidence from Australia indicates that in roughly 80% of fatal multiple-vehicle crashes involving heavy trucks, fault is not assigned to the heavy vehicle. However, determining fault or key vehicle status can be complex and may not be feasible for all crashes [137, 138].

In 2021, crashes involving heavy trucks resulted in the deaths of 163 individuals, accounting for 15.4% of total road deaths for that year. Among the fatalities in these crashes, approximately half were occupants of light vehicles, a quarter were occupants of the heavy trucks themselves, and the remaining quarter were other road users such as pedestrians, motorcyclists, or cyclists [137, 138].

Looking specifically at bus-related crashes from 2012 to 2021, there were a total of 15 fatalities recorded. Recent trends show a consistent decline of 13.4% per year in fatalities involving buses. Of those killed in these crashes, approximately 11% were bus occupants, while the majority consisted of occupants of light vehicles (33%) and other road users (57%). Annually, around 254 bus occupants require hospitalization due to crashes [137, 138].

Figure 31: Trucking accident. Havang(nl), CC0, via Wikimedia Commons.

To enhance the safety of truck drivers, a multifaceted approach is essential, drawing on insights from various research studies. One critical aspect highlighted in the literature is the need to address the interaction between young drivers and trucks to reduce crash risks [139]. Initiatives aimed at increasing young driver awareness of trucks and safety should be evidence-based, rigorously evaluated, and focused on enhancing risk perception skills and reducing risky driving behaviours around trucks. Moreover, understanding the factors contributing to the severity of truck-involved crashes is crucial [140]. Research indicates that younger and middle-aged truck drivers are less likely to be involved in severe crashes, suggesting that age-related factors play a role in crash outcomes.

One of the most significant hazards faced in this sector is the management of fleet vehicles, which are essential yet inherently risky assets. The operation of fleets involves numerous risks, including accidents resulting from driver fatigue, distraction, substance impairment, and poor vehicle maintenance. These risks not only threaten the safety of employees but also pose substantial financial implications through increased insurance premiums, vehicle maintenance costs, fuel expenses, and potential penalties.

Key factors to consider in mitigating these risks include ensuring vehicles are safe and well-maintained, avoiding driving when fatigued or impaired, adhering to speed limits, and using the safest routes possible.

To address these challenges, Online Work Health and Safety Systems have emerged as invaluable tools for logistics companies. These systems assist in comprehensive compliance management by overseeing fleet servicing schedules, maintaining records of vehicle fitness and daily inspections, managing employee qualifications and training requirements, and more. They provide a structured framework for integrating safety protocols into daily operations, thereby reducing the likelihood of accidents and ensuring regulatory adherence.

Employers bear significant responsibilities in fostering a culture of road safety within their organizations. This begins with the development and implementation of a robust Road Safety Policy that outlines clear expectations, safety protocols, and procedures. It involves maintaining a fleet of safe and roadworthy vehicles equipped with modern safety features such as seatbelt reminders, airbags, electronic stability control, and autonomous emergency braking systems.

In vehicle purchasing or leasing within the transport and logistics industry, ensuring vehicles are equipped with the latest safety features is paramount to promoting driver and passenger safety, mitigating risks, and complying with regulatory standards. Modern vehicles come equipped with a range of advanced safety technologies designed to enhance overall vehicle safety and reduce the likelihood of accidents.

One of the foundational safety features is seatbelt reminders and pre-tension devices. These systems not only remind occupants to buckle up but also ensure that in the event of a crash, seatbelts are tightened to minimize movement and potential injuries. This feature is fundamental in preventing ejections and reducing the severity of injuries in collisions.

Driver, passenger, and side curtain airbags are essential components of vehicle safety systems. These airbags deploy upon impact to protect occupants from striking the interior of the vehicle or being ejected, significantly reducing the risk of severe injury or death in crashes.

Electronic Stability Control (ESC) is another critical safety feature that helps drivers maintain control of the vehicle during sudden manoeuvres or loss of traction. ESC sensors detect when a vehicle is skidding or losing steering control and automatically apply brakes to individual wheels or reduce engine power to stabilize the vehicle, thereby preventing loss of control and potential rollovers.

Brake Assist Systems (BAS) enhance braking performance in emergency situations. BAS detects when a driver applies the brakes suddenly and applies maximum braking force to reduce stopping distance, potentially averting collisions or minimizing their impact.

Autonomous Emergency Braking (AEB) is an advanced safety feature that detects potential collisions with vehicles or pedestrians ahead and automatically applies brakes if the driver fails to respond in time. AEB systems significantly reduce the incidence of rear-end collisions and mitigate their severity by either avoiding the collision altogether or reducing impact speed.

Lane support systems such as Blind Spot Monitoring, Lane Keeping Aid, and Lane Departure Warning are designed to prevent accidents caused by driver distraction or lane deviation. These systems use sensors and cameras to monitor vehicle position relative to lane markings and surrounding vehicles. They provide alerts or corrective actions, such as steering wheel vibration or gentle braking, to help the driver stay within the lane and avoid collisions.

Reverse collision systems, including reversing cameras, Rear Cross Traffic Alert (RCTA), or parking sensors, enhance safety during parking manoeuvres or reversing. These systems detect obstacles, pedestrians, or approaching vehicles behind the vehicle and provide visual or audible warnings to the driver, preventing collisions and ensuring safer manoeuvrability in tight spaces.

Regular maintenance and safety checks are crucial to ensuring the ongoing effectiveness of these safety features. It is essential for transport and logistics companies to implement rigorous maintenance schedules that include inspections of safety systems, ensuring they are functioning correctly and are up-to-date with the latest software updates and recalibrations.

Investing in vehicles equipped with these advanced safety features not only enhances the safety of drivers, passengers, and other road users but also aligns with regulatory requirements aimed at reducing road accidents and improving overall road safety standards. By prioritizing vehicle safety technology and maintenance, organizations in the transport and logistics industry can significantly mitigate risks, protect their workforce, and uphold their commitment to safety and operational excellence.

Work-related stress factors have been identified as significant contributors to truck crashes [141]. Ensuring appropriate compensation for truck drivers is crucial in predicting safety outcomes. Furthermore, addressing issues like driver fatigue is paramount in preventing accidents, particularly rear-end collisions [142]. Implementing measures that encourage rest and fatigue recovery based on physiological indicators can help mitigate the risks associated with driver fatigue.

Developing a Road Safety Policy is a critical step for any organization, particularly those in the transport and logistics sector where road-related risks are prevalent. This policy serves as a comprehensive framework that outlines the organization's commitment to ensuring the safety of employees, contractors, and the public during work-related travel.

The process begins with accessing a document designed specifically for developing a road safety policy. This resource is typically available for download, offering a structured approach to integrating road safety into the workplace. Such documents are crafted to be adaptable, recognizing the diverse needs and operational contexts of different organizations within the transport and logistics industry. This flexibility allows companies to tailor the policy to align closely with their specific operational requirements, existing health and safety protocols, and regulatory obligations.

The primary objective of developing a road safety policy is to establish clear guidelines and procedures that promote safe driving practices and mitigate road-related risks. These policies typically address a range of key areas, including vehicle safety standards, driver behaviour expectations, journey management protocols, and incident reporting procedures. By defining these aspects within a formal policy framework, organizations create a standardized approach to managing road safety across all levels of their operations.

Furthermore, a well-developed road safety policy not only outlines the responsibilities of drivers and management but also emphasizes the organization's commitment to continuous improvement in road safety practices. It sets measurable goals and targets for enhancing safety performance, such as reducing the frequency of road incidents, improving driver compliance with safety regulations, and implementing new technologies or training initiatives to bolster safety outcomes.

Effective communication and engagement are essential during the policy development process. Organizations should involve key stakeholders, including management, drivers, and safety personnel, to gather insights and ensure buy-in from all levels of the organization. This collaborative approach not only enhances the policy's relevance and practicality but also fosters a culture of safety where all employees feel empowered to contribute to and adhere to road safety guidelines.

Once developed, the road safety policy should be integrated seamlessly into existing health and safety frameworks within the organization. This integration ensures that road safety becomes a core component of the overall safety culture, reinforcing the organization's commitment to protecting its workforce and promoting responsible road behaviour.

Furthermore, engaging employees actively in promoting road safety is crucial. This can be achieved through various communication channels and engagement strategies, including one-on-one meetings, newsletters, training programs, presentations, and even incentivizing safe driving behaviours through rewards programs. By embedding road safety into the workplace culture, organizations not only enhance employee safety but also elevate their brand reputation as socially responsible entities.

Engaging workers effectively in promoting road safety within a transport and logistics organization is crucial for fostering a culture of safety and reducing risks associated with work-related travel. Employers can employ various engagement strategies to initiate meaningful conversations and emphasize the importance of safe practices on the road.

Figure 32: Truck driver ignored low clearance road signs. Kgbo, CC BY-SA 4.0, via Wikimedia Commons.

One-on-one meetings with workers provide a personalized approach to discuss road safety, allowing managers to address individual concerns and reinforce safety expectations directly. These meetings are an opportunity to listen to employees' feedback, clarify doubts, and highlight the organization's commitment to their well-being.

Company newsletters, blogs, emails, and intranet content serve as channels to regularly communicate road safety messages to a broader audience. These platforms can feature safety tips, success stories, updates on safety initiatives, and reminders about upcoming training sessions or policy changes. By keeping the message clear, concise, and accessible, organizations ensure that road safety remains a priority in employees' minds.

Educational materials such as fact sheets, FAQs, and top tips provide practical information that employees can easily reference to improve their understanding of road safety best practices. These resources can cover topics such as defensive driving techniques, managing fatigue, responding to emergencies, and vehicle maintenance tips.

Presentations delivered to large groups during company-wide staff days or meetings allow for comprehensive discussions on road safety. These sessions can feature guest speakers, including road safety ambassadors or experts, who share insights, real-life experiences, and effective strategies for mitigating road risks. Such events reinforce the organization's commitment to safety and encourage active participation from all employees.

Structured training programs and induction sessions specifically dedicated to road safety ensure that new hires and existing employees alike receive comprehensive education on safety protocols and expectations. These sessions cover essential topics such as policy updates, hazard identification, emergency procedures, and the use of safety equipment. Training also plays a vital role in equipping employees with the knowledge and skills needed to navigate potential road hazards confidently.

Utilizing multimedia formats such as videos to showcase road safety progress can be impactful in highlighting successful safety initiatives, sharing testimonials from employees, and reinforcing positive behaviours. These visual representations can effectively demonstrate the organization's dedication to improving road safety outcomes and inspire employees to maintain safe practices.

Introducing incentives such as a 'safe driver rewards program' recognizes and rewards employees who consistently adhere to safe driving practices. Incentives can include bonuses, gift cards, or other tangible rewards that motivate employees to prioritize safety while on the road. This approach not only fosters a competitive spirit among employees but also reinforces the organization's commitment to promoting a safe work environment.

Short toolbox talks, typically lasting between 10 to 20 minutes, are informal discussions focused on specific road safety topics. These talks can be integrated into regular team meetings, BBQ sessions, or other informal gatherings. They provide a platform for employees to share experiences, ask questions, and reinforce key safety messages in a relaxed setting.

Developing and implementing a robust Road Safety Policy is foundational to these engagement efforts. It serves as a blueprint for managing road-related risks systematically and ensures consistency in safety practices across the organization. By embedding road safety into organizational culture, companies motivate their workforce, minimize lost working days due to injuries, and enhance their reputation as a safe and socially responsible employer.

Monitoring and continuous improvement are integral to sustaining effective road safety practices. Regular review of crash data, safety performance metrics, and compliance records helps organizations track progress, identify areas for improvement, and adjust policies accordingly. This iterative approach ensures that road safety remains a top priority, safeguarding both employees and the broader community while optimizing operational efficiency and financial sustainability in the transport and logistics industry.

Strategic planning of truck service areas on expressways can also enhance truck driving safety [143]. By optimizing the layout and facilities of these areas, it is possible to improve overall safety for truck drivers. Moreover, investing in driver training programs has been recognized as a valuable strategy to enhance driving behaviour and reduce collisions [144]. Training initiatives can play a pivotal role in shaping safer interactions between truck drivers and other road users.

Violence in the workplace is another concern for truck drivers, prompting the adoption of personal safety strategies to mitigate risks [145]. Ensuring a safe work environment is essential for the well-being of truck drivers. Additionally, promoting the mandatory use of occupant safety restraints for both drivers and passengers in trucks can significantly reduce the risk of injuries in the event of accidents [146]. Safety policies within trucking companies should prioritize the use of safety restraints to safeguard individuals.

Managing truck loading weight is a critical aspect of ensuring road safety [147]. Educational programs that highlight the consequences of not adhering to traffic rules can play a pivotal role in promoting safe driving practices among truck drivers. Moreover, understanding the differences in injuries between short-haul and long-haul trucking can inform targeted injury prevention strategies tailored to specific contexts [148]. By addressing unique safety challenges in different trucking operations, tailored interventions can be developed to enhance driver safety.

The structural integrity of truck chassis is fundamental to driver safety, necessitating compliance with stringent standards [149]. Ensuring that truck components meet safety requirements is essential in minimizing risks for drivers. Furthermore, advancements in crashworthiness technologies can significantly enhance occupant protection in heavy-truck crashes [150]. By identifying opportunities to improve crashworthiness, fatalities and injuries among truck drivers can be reduced.

Driver drowsiness detection systems have been explored as a means to enhance safety for commercial vehicle drivers [151]. Given the heightened risks faced by truck drivers, implementing technologies that detect driver fatigue can prevent accidents. Financial and non-financial incentives have also been shown to influence the safety behaviour of heavy truck drivers [152]. By aligning incentives with safe driving practices, the frequency of accidents can be reduced.

Understanding truck drivers' attitudes toward safety regulations is crucial in shaping their behaviours on the road [153]. By considering the multifaceted influences on driver decisions, regulatory frameworks can be tailored to promote safer practices. Additionally, the classification of work and offenses of professional drivers underscores the importance of continual improvement in transportation safety [154]. Ongoing efforts to enhance safety standards are essential in mitigating risks for truck drivers.

Chapter 16

Managing People Performance

In transport and logistics, effective performance management involves balancing the dual responsibilities of nurturing employees while achieving departmental and organizational goals. Modern managers must adapt their strategies based on the specific contexts of performance management, assessing each situation individually and employing appropriate management styles.

For instance, when employees face challenges in their roles, such as adapting to new technologies or overcoming logistical hurdles, a compassionate approach is essential. Providing support, encouragement, and necessary training helps employees develop the skills needed to excel in their roles. Conversely, in matters concerning safety protocols, regulatory compliance, or critical operational processes, managers must emphasize accountability and responsibility to ensure adherence to standards and mitigate risks effectively.

Identifying and addressing low-performing employees is crucial for maintaining operational efficiency and achieving organizational goals. A low-performing employee in this context is characterized by their inability to meet established job requirements and expectations. This encompasses various facets essential to logistics operations, such as delivering consistent and accurate service, adhering to schedules and deadlines, adhering to operational procedures, effectively communicating with team members and stakeholders, collaborating effectively within teams, and adeptly solving logistical challenges as they arise [155].

The signs of a low-performing employee often manifest in several ways. It may include a lack of initiative, consistently missing targets or quality standards, displaying a disengaged attitude towards work tasks, or demonstrating a resistance to change or improvement efforts. Such behaviours not only hinder individual productivity but can also create ripple effects across the entire logistics chain. For instance, missed deadlines can lead to delayed shipments, resulting in customer dissatisfaction and potentially impacting business relationships. Errors in inventory management or order processing can further exacerbate operational inefficiencies and increase costs [155].

Behind the performance issues, there may be underlying reasons contributing to an employee's subpar performance. These can range from inadequate training or skill gaps to personal challenges affecting their ability to perform optimally. Addressing these issues requires a nuanced approach that combines performance management strategies with supportive interventions aimed at identifying root causes and providing necessary support [155].

From a managerial standpoint, dealing with low-performing employees in logistics management involves a structured approach. This includes setting clear performance expectations, providing ongoing feedback and coaching, offering training and development opportunities to enhance skills, and establishing a supportive work environment conducive to productivity. It may also involve conducting performance reviews to assess progress and adjust strategies as needed [155].

Moreover, the impact of low-performing employees extends beyond operational setbacks. It can affect team morale and cohesion, as high-performing employees may feel burdened by having to compensate for their colleagues' shortcomings. Addressing performance issues promptly and effectively not only mitigates immediate operational risks but also reinforces a culture of accountability and continuous improvement within the logistics team [155].

A cornerstone of effective performance management in transport and logistics is recognizing the inherent potential in every individual. Rather than attributing underperformance solely to personal deficiencies, managers should focus on identifying and addressing systemic issues within management practices or organizational structures. This approach fosters a culture of continuous improvement and empowerment, where employees are encouraged to contribute their best efforts.

Clear and transparent communication of performance expectations is pivotal in this industry. Managers should articulate both fundamental job requirements and broader responsibilities, ensuring alignment with organizational objectives. Proactive engagement with employees to understand their specific needs and challenges allows managers to offer tailored support and guidance, thereby enhancing overall performance and job satisfaction.

Addressing performance issues promptly and constructively is crucial. Instead of waiting for periodic performance reviews, managers should provide ongoing feedback and support. This continuous dialogue helps clarify expectations, identify obstacles early on, and implement corrective actions swiftly, promoting sustained improvement and operational efficiency.

Understanding the unique demands and resources within transport and logistics operations is essential for effective management. Engaging with internal stakeholders—such as drivers, warehouse staff, and logistics coordinators—to grasp operational nuances and challenges enables managers to optimize resource allocation and streamline workflows. By leveraging employees' diverse skill sets and interests, managers can strategically assign tasks and responsibilities, maximizing team effectiveness and fostering a collaborative work environment.

Responsibilities for performance are integral to effective management in the realm of transport and logistics. Each individual within our workplace plays a crucial role in driving organizational success through their high-quality contributions.

At the helm, Chief Executives bear the responsibility for overseeing their workforce. They are expected to wholeheartedly endorse the agency's performance management policies, procedures, and systems, actively demonstrating their commitment to achieving organizational goals.

Line Managers assume a pivotal role in guiding and supervising employee performance, both individually and collectively as a team. Their responsibilities encompass setting clear performance objectives, providing regular feedback, conducting comprehensive performance appraisals, fostering employee development, and ensuring that commendable performance is duly recognized and rewarded.

Employees, in turn, hold responsibility for their own performance and engagement in the performance management processes, whether through formal evaluations or ongoing informal feedback loops.

When crafting policies pertaining to performance management in transport and logistics, simplicity and adherence to fundamental principles are paramount. Policies should serve as clear, principle-based guidelines rather than cumbersome bureaucratic documents. This approach facilitates ease of application and minimizes complexities that could impede effective management practices. Specialist advice can supplement these policies as needed to address unique circumstances or challenges.

Performance management in this context involves continuously evaluating and guiding employee performance against predefined goals and behaviours. It operates on both formal levels, such as annual reviews, and informal levels, encompassing day-to-day interactions and feedback mechanisms.

Similar to a cohesive sports team, effective performance management ensures that each employee comprehends their role in achieving collective success and receives appropriate coaching to enhance their job performance.

Moreover, constructive performance management practices yield substantial benefits for both the organization and its employees. Recognizing and rewarding staff achievements fosters higher morale, promotes greater loyalty to the company, and reduces turnover rates. Additionally, providing constructive feedback and opportunities for skill development supports career growth, enhances job satisfaction, and improves overall employee retention.

Conversely, ineffective or poorly executed performance management strategies can lead to disputes, diminished morale, legal complications, and heightened turnover rates. Therefore, it is crucial for management in transport and logistics to approach performance management diligently, ensuring that practices are fair, transparent, and conducive to both individual growth and organizational success.

Performance management in transport and logistics encompasses a range of activities aimed at evaluating whether organizational goals are being met and fostering continuous improvement. It involves defining job roles, setting objectives, providing feedback, and nurturing professional development. Crucially, it hinges on shared responsibility and a clear understanding of roles, expectations, and performance standards among all team members.

Every day in the transport and logistics sector prompts essential questions:

- What tasks need to be accomplished?

- When should these tasks be prioritized?

- How can these tasks be executed to meet required standards?

These inquiries guide daily operations and strategic planning, ensuring alignment with immediate and long-term objectives.

Managers in transport and logistics play a pivotal role in assessing whether employees' achievements align with expectations. They are tasked not only with evaluating individual performance but also with connecting each employee's contributions to overarching organizational objectives, thereby providing clarity of roles.

While formal performance management systems may mandate annual appraisals, the crux of effective performance management lies in ongoing daily interactions and feedback loops. Neglecting regular feedback can leave employees unsure about their performance quality and value to the organization, potentially dampening motivation and job satisfaction. Moreover, failure to address underperformance promptly can adversely affect team morale and overall productivity.

Performance reviews within the organizational framework serve as structured sessions to assess past performance and plan future development. These reviews build upon continuous informal performance management processes, ensuring consistency across the organization and providing opportunities for constructive dialogue.

Effective performance management in transport and logistics entails:

- Clarifying performance expectations clearly and consistently.

- Providing timely and equitable informal feedback.

- Collaboratively addressing day-to-day challenges and opportunities for improvement.

Moreover, managers bear additional responsibilities:

- Ensuring a good fit between employees and their roles, optimizing job satisfaction and performance.

- Cultivating a positive relationship between employees and the organization through clear communication of vision, strategy, and support for innovation.

- Facilitating employees' understanding of their role in achieving organizational goals and demonstrating appreciation for their contributions.

- Fostering a performance-oriented culture through open communication, flexibility in problem-solving, and support for innovation.

- Facilitating networking among employees to share expertise and enhance collaboration.

- Committing to employee development by aligning current responsibilities with future career aspirations and providing opportunities for skill enhancement.

Ultimately, effective performance management in transport and logistics not only enhances operational efficiency and employee engagement but also strengthens organizational resilience and competitiveness. By embedding clear expectations, regular feedback, and proactive problem-solving into everyday practices, managers can foster a culture of continuous improvement and mutual success.

Allocating Work

Engaging staff in transport and logistics management involves soliciting their insights on effective workplace strategies and health initiatives, fostering a sense of ownership and enhancing participation rates.

Before commencing consultations with staff, it's essential to consider three key aspects: who to consult with, how to gather information, and what specific questions to ask.

Who to Consult With: It's critical to identify whether to consult the entire workforce or specific groups within it. Different segments of your organization may require tailored strategies to engage them effectively and promote healthy behaviour changes. For instance, approaches that resonate with office staff may not necessarily work for warehouse teams, and vice versa.

How to Gather Information: Choosing the right method to collect information from staff is paramount. The method should be well-suited to your workforce's characteristics and ensure comprehensive data collection. While online surveys are common, they may exclude workers without computer access, such as those on the road, and potentially only attract responses from employees already interested in health matters. To mitigate these challenges, consider diverse engagement strategies and incentives to improve response rates. Timely and transparent feedback is crucial to demonstrate that staff opinions are valued and action will be taken based on their input.

What to Ask Staff: Effective consultation should cover several key areas:

- Strategies employees would like to see implemented to enhance workplace health, such as policies, environmental changes, educational initiatives, and activities.

- Assessment of staff awareness levels, attitudes, and current behaviours regarding health-related practices.

- Identification of barriers hindering staff from engaging in healthy behaviours.

- Understanding factors motivating staff to participate in health initiatives.

By engaging employees early and involving them in decision-making processes, organizations can foster a culture of ownership and commitment, ultimately enhancing overall workplace health and performance in transport and logistics management.

In transport and logistics management, effective planning is hierarchical and essential for achieving organizational goals. Here's how the planning process unfolds [156]:

Strategic Planning: Strategic plans are formulated by the organization's board of directors. These plans set the overarching objectives and long-term direction for the company.

Operational Planning: Operational plans, created by upper management, translate strategic goals into actionable steps. For instance, if you're a manufacturing engineering manager, your operational plan would align with the strategic directives set by the board and your department's vice-president.

Work Planning: As a department manager, your role is to develop detailed work plans based on the operational objectives. These plans outline the scope, objectives, and purpose of what your department needs to accomplish to fulfill its responsibilities within the operational framework

At this stage, the focus is on defining departmental goals as a whole, rather than individual tasks or assignments.

It's crucial to stay aligned with the operational plan to avoid distractions and irrelevant tasks that can derail progress. Despite numerous potential distractions, your priority is to recognize and prioritize activities that directly contribute to departmental goals and operational success.

When developing your work plan, it's essential to establish realistic milestones and a feasible schedule. This ensures that your plan is achievable and considers variables such as workforce capabilities, resource availability, potential emergencies, and unforeseen challenges like staff absences [156].

A Performance Improvement Plan (PIP) in logistics management should include:

1. Specific areas of performance needing improvement, detailed with clarity.

2. Clear expectations for consistent work performance standards.

3. Support and resources provided to aid the employee in meeting expectations.

4. Regular feedback on progress, potentially including measurable metrics tied to performance standards.

Common issues in performance management include employees viewing it negatively and common complaints such as feeling set up for failure, issues with behaviour standards, personal circumstances affecting work, and perceived lack of seriousness in the process.

As a manager in transport and logistics:

1. Clearly define performance expectations and objectives.

2. Ensure employees understand and meet expected performance standards.

3. Provide necessary tools and resources for job completion.

4. Address poor performance promptly and effectively.

5. Understand reasons behind underperformance.

6. Set fair and achievable performance standards.

7. Provide regular and constructive feedback.

8. Maintain accurate documentation related to performance management processes.

By focusing efforts on developing and rewarding top performers rather than spending disproportionate time on underperformers, managers can significantly enhance team effectiveness and overall organizational success in transport and logistics operations.

In transport and logistics management, effective allocation of work is crucial for efficiency, cost-effectiveness, and achieving desired outcomes. This can be approached by:

Efficiency and Resource Management: When allocating tasks, your primary consideration should be efficiency. With limited resources—your workforce—it's essential to assess:

- Which team member can complete the task in the shortest time?

- Who can complete the task without unnecessary expenditure?

- Who possesses the most relevant knowledge and expertise for the task?

- What is the expected outcome of assigning this task?

- Are there additional benefits, such as skill development, from assigning this task to a specific individual?

While efficiency and cost-effectiveness are critical, the ultimate priority should be achieving the desired outcomes. Sometimes, circumstances necessitate prioritizing outcomes over efficiency or cost-effectiveness, such as meeting strict deadlines or satisfying key customers.

For example, in my experience in engineering, we faced a critical deadline for delivering customized transit buses. Despite it being inefficient and costly, we shipped the buses before completion and sent a team to finish them on-site at the customer's facility. This approach ensured we met our commitments and exceeded the customer's expectations, leading to additional business opportunities with that client.

However, such exceptional measures shouldn't become the norm. Typically, operations should strive for maximum efficiency and cost-effectiveness while achieving set objectives. Neglecting efficiency and cost-effectiveness can jeopardize financial sustainability, as income must always exceed expenditures.

Balancing Workload and Fairness: A common challenge in work allocation is overloading high-performing employees while underutilizing others. This imbalance not only undermines fairness but also risks burning out top performers. To address this, prioritize tasks that require high efficiency for your most capable team members. Simultaneously, distribute other tasks among the team to optimize overall performance and prevent burnout.

Communication and Motivation: To maximize team performance, always articulate the purpose behind each task assignment. While every task contributes to the company's goals, providing specific reasons helps employees connect their work directly to organizational success. This clarity enhances motivation and engagement, preventing disillusionment and fostering a sense of purpose among your team members.

Directing how tasks are executed hinges on the belief that correct procedures lead to high-quality results. Clearly defining the actions and behaviours necessary to fulfill job responsibilities is just as critical as outlining the desired outputs.

Performance expectations must be SPECIFIC and ACHIEVABLE, focusing on OBSERVABLE behaviours.

Being specific means being precise. For instance, it is more effective to specify, "I expect you to greet customers with a smile and a friendly 'hello'" rather than simply stating, "Provide good customer service." By emphasizing observable behaviours, managers can effectively communicate standards and expectations to employees. For example, "Kerry, I noticed you arrived 30 minutes after our team meeting started; is there a reason?" is more constructive and beneficial than a general reprimand like, "Kerry, you're late again."

Achievable means that employees can realistically meet expected outcomes within the constraints of their abilities, resources, and timeframes.

Observable means the behaviour can be objectively measured. For instance, describing specific actions such as "when you raised your voice…" clarifies the discussion compared to ambiguous terms like "aggressive," which can be open to interpretation and miscommunication.

Have you encountered individuals throughout their careers who remain unaware of personal work style traits that hinder their progress—while everyone else recognizes the need for improvement? This often results from insufficient constructive feedback. Don't withhold essential information that employees need to enhance their performance and advance in their careers.

Identifying reasons behind a decline in employee performance is crucial. Various factors, unknown to you, can contribute to diminished performance. Collaborate with employees to develop clear strategies they can implement to improve. Ensure they depart with a precise understanding of their improvement goals and your supportive role in achieving them.

When everyday communication includes effective feedback, managers need not dread delivering negative feedback during annual performance reviews, and employees need not fear unexpected criticisms. In effective organizations, formal meetings confirm information already shared during informal conversations. Feedback can then be used to further develop capabilities and devise plans for role and career advancement.

Certain performance expectations are fundamental standards integrated (or should be) into employment contracts or referenced in operational procedures. These standards and expectations constitute part of the 'psychological contract' between employer and employee. While other responsibilities and activities, such as optional developmental opportunities, also contribute to this contract, basic standards and job requirements are typically non-negotiable.

You must understand these expectations and secure a clear commitment from your team that they accept these as given, because managing these fundamental aspects should ideally be straightforward and self-regulating, allowing management to focus on higher-level responsibilities.

However, what if performance management is necessary in these fundamental areas?

If performance falls short in these critical areas, it may be necessary to revisit the 'psychological contract' and possibly the employment contract to promptly and clearly reaffirm basic, non-negotiable expectations.

Yet, approach this with compassion and consideration. Approach below-standard performance with creativity. Non-negotiable does not equate to ruthless or indifferent. Be empathetic, firm, and fair.

1. **Are the performance standards clearly defined and documented?** If not, ensure they are, and involve the HR department or relevant operational managers to reaffirm them. Without clear standards, any efforts to build upon them will be precarious.

2. **Are the standards and expectations well-understood?** Explain them thoroughly and confirm understanding and agreement. 'Understanding' extends beyond the literal description of standards—it involves ensuring that interpretations align practically and ethically with organizational expectations.

3. **Are the standards unequivocally agreed upon?** If not, this may necessitate disciplinary action, as disagreement here challenges the foundational 'contract' between employer and employee. Inform relevant senior personnel promptly about such discrepancies.

4. **Are the standards agreed upon, yet challenges persist?** Where clarity exists regarding expectations but performance still lags, engage in open dialogue with the employee to identify underlying issues hindering their adherence to standards. Exercise judgment with sensitivity, seeking advice from HR if needed for professional counselling or support options.

The more effectively you convey expectations—both personal and corporate—to your team, the better positioned you are to prevent misunderstandings and performance issues. Miscommunication often leads to unsatisfactory work results, interpersonal conflicts, and workplace disruptions.

Every job carries performance standards, whether explicit or implicit. Even when written, these standards may not always reflect current needs, risking misalignment between expectations and actual practice.

As a manager, your responsibility includes ensuring that team members grasp the performance standards to which they are held. These standards should clearly define the level of expected performance in both qualitative and quantitative terms. Failure to articulate both dimensions may lead one employee to prioritize flawless quality over quantity, while another focuses solely on quantity without maintaining quality standards.

Many companies display signs in work areas proclaiming goals like "Our Objective: 0% Defects!" While admirable, such statements may inadvertently prioritize quality improvements at the expense of production output. Instead, aim for messages like "Our Objective: 1000 units per day with 0% defects!" to emphasize both quantity and quality expectations.

Additionally, communicating the company's Code of Conduct to team members reinforces expectations regarding behaviour and interaction with colleagues and clients. This code, whether formalized in policies or ingrained in corporate culture, serves as a benchmark for assessing departmental performance.

Consistently monitor team performance in relation to established standards and the Code of Conduct using measurable criteria. This approach minimizes favouritism and ensures equitable treatment of all employees.

Maintain thorough records of employee performance to facilitate accurate performance reviews and inform future work assignments. When a team member falls short of standards, it's incumbent upon you, as manager, to diagnose the underlying cause—whether it's misunderstanding expectations, lacking resources, insufficient skills, or personal challenges—and implement corrective measures promptly.

Now, let's delve into the forward-looking aspects of performance:

The effectiveness of individual and team efforts, the quality of service that exceeds minimum expectations, and the response to challenges and opportunities are key indicators of outstanding performance. Achieving excellence in these areas involves actively engaging individuals and teams to contribute fully by:

- Defining the task, project, or opportunity.

- Choosing methods, or for larger projects, creating comprehensive project plans.

- Assigning responsibilities and ownership.

- Establishing objectives, metrics, and timelines.

- Developing and taking ownership of processes.

- Selecting tools and systems.

- Determining inter-departmental interfaces and communication requirements.

- Implementing and managing activities.

- Reporting progress, conducting checks, and ensuring completion.

- Conducting follow-ups, evaluations, and obtaining feedback.

- Identifying areas for future improvement and exploring related opportunities where feasible and appropriate.

The principles of delegation, meeting management, and motivation provide frameworks and methodologies for achieving these goals.

When collaborating with individuals or teams, consider the following factors (replace 'task' with 'project', 'opportunity', 'initiative', etc.):

- Evaluate the task's importance and criticality; first, make your assessment, then discuss, explain, and confirm understanding with all stakeholders involved.

- Assess the task's timeframe.

- Acknowledge individual specializations and strengths; utilize available indicators of individual strengths and encourage open communication.

- Consider people's preferred styles and natural inclinations; utilize personality indicators such as the VAK learning styles theory and encourage feedback.

- Take into account individuals' experience, maturity, confidence levels, workloads, and other priorities and demands; seek their input and adapt accordingly.

- Ensure alignment with the task's purpose and significance to individuals; encourage dialogue to foster commitment.

- Highlight the personal development and growth opportunities associated with the task or project; discuss how participation aligns with their aspirations and needs.

If uncertain about any of the above aspects—which often is the case—open communication is crucial. Seek clarification, gather evidence of competence, and provide the necessary support and autonomy.

Throughout, you must strike a balance—helping individuals and teams balance:

- The organization's imperative to complete tasks or projects on time, within budget, and to standard.

- Individuals' need for enjoyment, growth, learning, and taking responsibility.

Involving people and teams in defining this balance and determining your level of involvement—tailored to each task or project—enhances performance management effectiveness.

Central to this process is:

- Clearly defining and communicating (to all relevant parties) the task or project's purpose, criteria, outcomes, deliverables, parameters (including financials), and timelines.

- Developing a comprehensive plan outlining actions and their respective timelines.

- Assigning clear responsibilities and accountabilities, avoiding shared or ambiguous roles.

- Establishing metrics and implementing monitoring actions.

For recurring tasks, adopt standardized procedures or protocols instead of reinventing workflows. While operations manuals traditionally house such information, the rapid pace of change necessitates regular updates and adjustments.

Ownership fosters commitment. Encouraging a sense of ownership inspires individuals to go beyond expectations, achieving challenging goals within allotted timeframes and budgets. To cultivate this ownership, involve individuals in decision-making processes.

While it may be easier to impose performance criteria on employees, true achievement hinges on their sense of ownership in these benchmarks. Employees are more likely to embrace performance indicators they've had a hand in shaping.

Consider this scenario: as a manufacturing supervisor overseeing technicians conducting final tests and calibrations of electromechanical devices, quantity plays a significant role in performance evaluation due to production demands. However, what if a technician completes tasks quickly, but subsequent quality checks necessitate redoing their work? In this case, evaluating performance solely based on quantity would be misleading and unfair to other technicians who must correct errors.

In such instances, convening with all technicians to establish balanced performance indicators that incorporate quality and other relevant metrics would yield fairer evaluations. This approach promotes workforce satisfaction and acceptance of performance reviews.

Whether you determine performance indicators independently or in collaboration with staff, ensure they are agreed upon and communicated before work commences. Disseminate information directly to affected parties to prevent misunderstandings that could adversely impact performance.

Changes to performance indicators may initially provoke concerns about fairness among employees, even if intended to better recognize excellence. Approach changes with careful consideration, involving affected parties in decision-making processes. Provide advance notice and articulate the benefits of proposed changes to enhance acceptance.

In both life and business, risk is omnipresent. Regardless of the task at hand, there is always the potential for something to go awry. A critical team member might encounter a car accident on the way to a crucial presentation; ordered parts could arrive incorrectly manufactured; unexpected disruptions like extreme weather could halt facility operations.

While the chance of something as improbable as an alien spaceship landing on your desk is exceedingly low, the reality remains that all activities carry inherent risks. Many companies view "risk analysis" as a singular event, but in truth, it should be an ongoing process. Every project and task undertaken by a company involves some degree of risk, varying in magnitude and nature.

Risk assessment focuses on two fundamental aspects:

- Assessing the likelihood of negative events that could hinder the organization from achieving its goals.

- Evaluating the potential impact of such events on organizational performance.

For instance, while the likelihood of an alien spaceship event is minuscule, the probability of an employee falling ill and missing a deadline increases as deadlines approach.

Certain risks are regionally specific, such as weather conditions causing facility closures. In some areas, snowstorms pose a significant threat akin to an alien spaceship, whereas in others, seasonal shutdowns due to snow are a predictable occurrence. Other risks are industry-specific, like shortages of commonly used raw materials. Some risks are unique to individual businesses.

Typically, risk assessment employs a matrix where one axis considers likelihood and the other measures the severity of consequences. Each identified risk is positioned within the matrix according to its likelihood and potential impact.

The greater the likelihood and severity of a risk, the more crucial it becomes to develop contingency plans to mitigate its effects. Failing to prepare such plans could lead to catastrophic consequences for affected projects and, ultimately, jeopardize the entire company's stability.

Contingency plans outline strategies to address potential negative events. These plans can range from straightforward to complex, tailored to the specific needs of the situation. For example, mitigating the loss of a key designer could involve having a backup team member ready to step in. Safeguarding against catastrophic events, such as the destruction of a project by an alien spaceship, might involve storing duplicate copies in alternate locations.

To effectively evaluate workforce performance, a reliable assessment system is essential. While some companies rely on systems provided by Human Resources, many managers must develop or adapt their own systems. These systems must align with departmental goals, reflect the unique requirements of each role, and ensure assessments are objective and unbiased.

It is imperative to establish a fair and relevant performance evaluation system to uphold employee morale and initiative. When employees perceive that their efforts are recognized and rewarded based on clear and meaningful criteria, they are more likely to strive for excellence.

Assessing Performance

Regular formal performance reviews constitute a crucial element of effective performance management within transport and logistics operations. During these reviews, an employee meets with their manager to discuss their performance in relation to predefined objectives linked to their role description. These sessions also provide opportunities for employees to address any concerns they have about their responsibilities and to establish new objectives for the future. Investing time in developing and implementing a robust performance management strategy can yield significant benefits for your business.

Here are several outcomes that can be achieved through well-executed performance reviews:

- Managers and employees engage in constructive dialogues concerning the employee's role and performance.

- Feedback is provided based on agreed-upon goals and expectations.

- Objectives and expectations are reviewed and set for future performance.

- Recognition is given for achievements and effort, fostering motivation and morale.

- Identification of training needs and creation of development plans tailored to individual growth.

- Clear feedback is delivered on performance and behavioural issues.

- Employers gain insights into employees' career aspirations and future plans.

While it might be tempting to postpone performance reviews, especially during busy periods, making the effort to regularly meet with your team to discuss their progress can yield long-term benefits for your business and team cohesion.

Considerations When Planning Performance Reviews

Though performance reviews may appear straightforward, several considerations should be addressed before initiating the process. Timing is crucial:

- End of Financial Year: Often chosen for its alignment with budgeting and bonus cycles, but it may coincide with peak operational periods, necessitating alternative timing like late May.

- End of Calendar Year: Another viable option, but potential drawbacks include employees winding down for holidays, affecting their readiness to receive and act on feedback; late November might be more suitable in such cases.

Consistency across business units and managers is essential to ensure uniformity in evaluation processes. Some companies opt for 360-degree feedback, incorporating input from peers, clients, and other managers to provide a comprehensive view of performance, though this approach may require additional time for data collection and review.

The primary objective is to schedule reviews systematically, ensuring thoroughness and engagement from all parties involved.

Conducting Effective Performance Reviews

When delivering feedback, clarity and directness are paramount. Avoiding vague or circumstantial discussions enhances the effectiveness of feedback sessions. It's crucial to:

- Prepare thoroughly, ensuring all relevant data such as KPIs and sales figures are current.

- Notify external stakeholders in advance if their feedback is solicited.

- Adhere to a set schedule to maintain consistency and professionalism.

- Allocate sufficient time, typically at least one hour, for a comprehensive review session.

- Conduct reviews in a quiet, private setting like an office to minimize distractions and foster open communication.

- Encourage a two-way dialogue by allowing employees to share their perspectives and raise concerns.

- Provide balanced feedback, highlighting both strengths and areas for improvement.

- When addressing areas needing improvement, focus on factual observations rather than personal critiques.

Developing a Performance Management System

Creating a performance management system tailored to the specifics of transport and logistics requires careful consideration of organizational policies, departmental objectives, and industry norms. Key factors include:

- Defining the most critical performance metrics aligned with departmental goals.

- Establishing a review frequency that balances thorough assessment with operational needs.

- Ensuring data used for evaluation is relevant and reliable.

- Implementing a weighted evaluation system where criteria essential to job success carry more significant weight.

- Documenting the entire performance management process to ensure transparency and consistency, facilitating continuity and training efficiency.

Fear of the unknown is a common human trait. Many people would rather confront a known danger than face uncertainty. This fear can undermine productivity and morale within your team if your performance management and review process remains shrouded in secrecy.

Keeping your performance management system undisclosed breeds negative speculation among employees. Rather than motivating them to excel, it fosters unease and distraction, as they speculate about the implications of the "new system" instead of focusing on their tasks.

Once your performance management and review process is finalized, ensure comprehensive training for all involved parties—both reviewers and those being reviewed. Reviewers need a clear understanding of how the system operates, while employees must comprehend how they will be evaluated.

This transparency can work to your advantage. Clearly outlining the key evaluation criteria to your workforce directs their focus toward the most critical aspects of their roles. For example, in manufacturing, emphasizing quality and quantity sends a clear directive to production workers: prioritize producing high-quality work at a high volume.

When employees understand that their performance reviews and potential pay raises are tied to these metrics, they are incentivized to concentrate on delivering both quality and quantity consistently.

Conversely, a vague or misaligned performance management system can send conflicting messages. If, for instance, the system places undue emphasis on professional knowledge over production metrics, workers might prioritize gaining certifications rather than maximizing productivity. This could inadvertently lead to a decline in overall output.

To enhance engagement and effectiveness in performance management within transport and logistics:

- Regularize performance management as a positive routine, ideally conducted monthly, to maintain a proactive approach.

- Identify areas where employees wish to improve and provide targeted coaching to support their development.

- Acknowledge and praise achievements or improvements since the last coaching session to reinforce positive behaviours.

- Develop actionable plans collaboratively with employees to guide their focus until the next coaching session, fostering continuous improvement and goal alignment.

The performance assessment process should pinpoint an employee's work capabilities, highlighting areas for further development. Managers should consider the following:

- What existing strengths can the employee leverage to achieve their goals outlined in their individual performance plan?

- What skills and capabilities are essential for successfully meeting work objectives?

- Which capabilities will have the most significant impact on performance?

- What additional skills are necessary for the employee to advance in their career?

- Are there any barriers that could hinder career progression that need addressing?

The next step involves prioritizing and setting timelines for development.

Enhancing High Performance

Effective development aligns with both an individual's career aspirations and the organization's needs. Planning for development involves:

- Defining the responsibilities of the employee's current role.

- Assessing the potential for the employee to transition into different roles within the organization or broader public sector.

- Evaluating the readiness to take on new roles or career paths.

Simultaneously, developmental planning communicates management's dedication to employee success, fostering engagement and commitment to the organization.

Skills development, akin to feedback, is an ongoing process encompassing on-the-job training, mentoring, and formal education. Typically, development progress is reviewed during formal performance assessments. Ideally, these sessions facilitate forward-looking discussions between managers and employees about skill enhancement to improve current job performance and enable future career growth in desired directions.

Rewards and Recognition In the public sector, financial incentives are generally less applicable, with development opportunities and career growth highly valued. Non-monetary rewards, like acknowledgment and recognition, significantly impact employee performance and retention.

The most impactful form of recognition often involves informal verbal feedback on performance, especially when integrated into career planning discussions, thereby linking it with rewards.

Rewards play a crucial role in modern organizational strategies, particularly within logistics operations where employee motivation and retention are critical for sustained performance. Traditionally, rewards have encompassed both financial and non-monetary incentives aimed at encouraging desired behaviours and recognizing exemplary performance [157].

Financial rewards, such as profit-sharing schemes and performance bonuses, remain integral components of compensation packages. These incentives not only attract talent but also align employee efforts with organizational goals, fostering a culture of accountability and performance. In the competitive landscape of hiring, where prospective employees weigh multiple job offers, non-financial benefits are increasingly pivotal. Flexible work schedules, initiatives promoting work-life balance, and a supportive work environment are now pivotal factors that sway employment decisions [157].

Non-monetary rewards, however, are gaining prominence for their tangible impact on workplace engagement and productivity. Programs promoting health and well-being, such as subsidized gym memberships, onsite fitness classes, and health check-ups, not only enhance employee welfare but also reduce absenteeism and healthcare costs. Moreover, initiatives promoting environmental sustainability, like energy-saving practices, contribute directly to operational efficiencies and cost savings. For instance, rewarding employees for energy-efficient behaviours, such as closing doors to cooling chambers, conserves resources and lowers operational expenses, illustrating a clear win-win scenario for both employees and the company [157].

Effective reward programs are structured around well-defined performance criteria that are transparent and equitable. Key Performance Indicators (KPIs) must accurately measure performance while ensuring fairness in evaluation, thereby maintaining employee trust and commitment. Extrinsic rewards, such as financial incentives and career development opportunities, appeal to external motivators, while intrinsic rewards like challenging assignments and recognition for contributions foster a sense of personal fulfillment and engagement among employees [157].

Logistics operations have demonstrated significant success with varied reward systems tailored to their specific contexts. Beyond financial bonuses, initiatives like health-related programs, flexible work arrangements, and recognition for tenure have proven instrumental in boosting employee morale and operational efficiency. Companies that invest in comprehensive reward programs not only cultivate a motivated workforce but also enhance overall workplace satisfaction and organizational performance. Ultimately, integrating social sustainability through robust reward strategies yields long-term benefits, ensuring employee well-being and operational excellence in logistics operations [157].

Furthermore, besides acknowledging and encouraging good performance whenever feasible, managers should also recognize and support effort and improvement.

The frequency of formal performance evaluations varies among companies, typically occurring once or twice annually. It's crucial to be aware of your company's specific policies to ensure fairness and timeliness in conducting these reviews.

When initiating performance management evaluations, it's beneficial to revisit the established processes to ensure consistency and fairness. Remaining calm, friendly, and professional during these reviews is essential to maintaining a constructive atmosphere, even when addressing less favourable feedback.

Each employee has strengths and weaknesses, and how feedback is delivered significantly influences its reception. By balancing constructive criticism with positive reinforcement, managers can mitigate the potential negative impact of feedback sessions. Planning ahead, especially for discussions involving critical feedback, helps maintain a constructive tone.

Expectations and perceptions of performance may differ between managers and employees. It's essential to listen to employees' perspectives respectfully, acknowledging their viewpoints without necessarily altering evaluation priorities.

Ultimately, while employees are entitled to their opinions, managerial decisions are guided by organizational interests and responsibilities. Confidentiality during performance discussions is paramount to preserving employee morale and trust, ensuring that sensitive feedback remains private and respectful.

Effective performance evaluation serves as a crucial tool for employees to gain clarity on their manager's perspective regarding their work. It involves analysing work in terms of its timeliness and quality, using this insight to make adjustments for future tasks, ensuring alignment with organizational goals.

The primary responsibility of managers in performance assessment is to provide employees with transparent feedback on their effectiveness in fulfilling their duties and responsibilities.

Unlike ordinary feedback, formal appraisal involves measuring performance against predefined benchmarks. For instance, stating "You answer the phone promptly" is feedback, whereas "Your phone answering is competent because you consistently answer within six rings 50% of the time" is an example of formal assessment.

Implementing a structured approach to conduct performance-related discussions with employees enables managers to build better rapport and trust, fostering a culture where employees feel valued and recognized.

Typical topics covered in performance conversations include:

- Technical and professional skills: Assessing proficiency in specific roles such as administration, finance, or policy implementation.

- Leadership and management: Evaluating skills in guiding and overseeing the performance of others.

- Communication: Reviewing effectiveness in conveying information and ideas.

- Task and work output: Measuring productivity and quality of deliverables.

- Relationships: Evaluating collaborative efforts within the team and interactions with external stakeholders.

- Personal management and development: Assessing self-awareness, learning capability, stress management, and work-life balance.

Encouraging employees to conduct regular self-assessments provides managers with valuable insights for discussion, aligning their perceptions with employee perspectives.

To enhance the validity of performance appraisals, incorporating feedback from multiple sources is beneficial. Methods like 360-degree feedback gather input from supervisors, peers, and sometimes customers, providing a comprehensive view of performance.

Promoting a two-way dialogue where employees also rate their managers encourages collaborative discussions focused on actions and solutions. This approach nurtures an environment conducive to mutual growth and development.

Choosing the Right Performance Appraisal Method

Selecting an appropriate appraisal method is crucial for effective employee evaluation in transport and logistics:

- **Self-Assessment:** Employees evaluate their own strengths and weaknesses, serving as a foundation for discussions with managers.

- **Critical Incidents:** Focuses on specific critical behaviours that distinguish effective from ineffective performance.

- **Graphic Rating Scale:** Uses predefined performance indicators to rate employees across various dimensions.

- **Multi-person Comparison:** Compares an individual's performance with that of peers in similar roles.

- **Management by Objectives (MBO):** Popular for assessing managers and professionals, emphasizing goal-setting and measurable outcomes.

- **360-Degree Feedback:** Gathers feedback from multiple sources to evaluate performance comprehensively.

Regular performance evaluation throughout the year is essential. Waiting until formal review periods can lead to incomplete assessments. Consistent evaluation allows managers to track performance trends, address issues promptly, and support employees in overcoming challenges that may affect their work.

Recognizing the impact of personal factors on performance, such as health or interpersonal dynamics, ensures a holistic approach to assessment. This approach acknowledges that personal well-being influences job performance and supports employees in achieving their potential.

Ultimately, conducting fair and thorough performance evaluations ensures that feedback is objective and constructive, fostering a culture of continuous improvement and mutual trust within the organization.

Providing Feedback

Constructive feedback plays a crucial role in addressing areas where an employee's performance can be enhanced. It focuses on improvement without being negative or critical. Employing the same positive approach and criteria used for praising good performance, managers should:

- Provide feedback sensitively, ensuring it is delivered with empathy.
- Encourage employees to share their perspectives, allowing for open discussion.
- Clarify expectations and work together to reach mutual agreement.
- Set specific goals for behaviour change or improved work outcomes.
- Give employees a chance to openly discuss their own performance perceptions.

Combining constructive feedback with discussions about an employee's strengths is practical and enhances overall performance. By delivering feedback positively and offering specific advice on task improvement, managers can effectively foster growth and development.

Neglecting feedback for performance improvement may seem considerate, but it deprives employees of opportunities to progress. Waiting until formal evaluations, typically conducted annually, limits the potential for noticeable change or growth in employees. Regular, ongoing feedback is essential, tailored to individual needs based on expertise, work habits, and self-confidence levels. For many, this consistent feedback serves as crucial validation and support.

Additionally, informal feedback provides a valuable opportunity to collaborate with employees and encourage positive changes in their work habits. Whether it's offering suggestions, providing guidance, or acknowledging achievements, informal feedback helps steer employees in the desired direction.

It's imperative to deliver negative feedback privately to avoid undermining an employee's morale in front of their peers. Sarcastic remarks or jokes about performance issues should be avoided as they detract from the professionalism of feedback.

Conversely, positive feedback and recognition should be given publicly to celebrate achievements and boost team morale.

Maintaining open communication channels is key. Avoid formalizing feedback processes into scheduled meetings or monthly reviews. Instead, opt for personal, one-on-one interactions that demonstrate care and support for each employee's mission success.

Managers may find themselves providing more feedback to certain employees at different times, reflecting varying needs within the team. This natural adaptation ensures that individuals receive appropriate attention and support when required, promoting overall team effectiveness and morale.

Poor performance does not necessarily indicate a poor employee. There are various factors that could contribute to subpar performance, many of which may not be entirely within the employee's control. It's important not to dismiss the employee as irredeemable but rather to approach the situation with a positive outlook.

Every employee represents an investment for your company. It is often more financially advantageous to invest in improving the performance of a struggling employee than it is to replace them. Poor performance can stem from:

- Personal issues at home

- Knowledge gaps

- Health problems, including undisclosed issues

- Insufficient training

- Lack of necessary resources

- Distractions or interruptions

- Technical difficulties

- Being overwhelmed by responsibilities

- Lack of motivation

When addressing poor performance, it's crucial to investigate the root cause rather than accepting surface explanations. Employees may initially attribute their performance issues to external factors to alleviate immediate pressure. Adopt an investigative approach, systematically eliminating potential causes until the true issue is identified and addressed.

Think of yourself as a coach during this process, focusing on helping each employee achieve their best performance. Positive reinforcement tends to yield better results than negative criticism. Encouraging and supporting employees is more effective than resorting to punitive measures or threats of termination.

Considering the significant investment already made in each employee—through recruitment, training, and productivity during the learning phase—it makes strategic sense to invest further in developing their potential.

After completing a performance review, follow-up actions are crucial to maintain momentum and ensure agreed-upon actions are implemented effectively. Confidentiality must be maintained, and discussions from performance reviews should not be shared with peers.

It's advisable to schedule the next review meeting immediately, even if it's several months away, to ensure continuity and accountability. This also provides a clear timeline for employees to achieve their objectives.

Provide a summary of the review to the employee to document discussed points and agreed-upon actions. This summary helps maintain clarity and accountability, reducing the chances of misunderstandings or disputes.

If commitments were made during the review, such as arranging additional training, ensure these are fulfilled promptly. Following through on commitments demonstrates reliability and reinforces trust between managers and employees.

Employees whose managers provide solutions to work problems exhibit significantly higher levels of effort, commitment to the organization, and job satisfaction compared to those without managerial assistance [158]. This finding underscores the crucial role that effective employee involvement, facilitated by management commitment, plays in enhancing both customer perceptions of service performance and employees' job satisfaction [158]. Moreover, studies have shown that managers utilize various personal and contextual characteristics, such as impression management behaviours, job performance, and training investment, to form perceptions of employees' organizational commitment [159]. This highlights the intricate interplay between managerial perceptions and employee commitment within organizations.

Furthermore, research indicates that managers' assessments of employees' organizational career growth opportunities are influenced by factors like extra-role performance, work engagement, and perceived organizational commitment [160]. These commitment judgments serve as cues for managers to categorize employees, ultimately shaping their behaviour towards them [160]. Additionally, the literature emphasizes the significance of fostering commitment between managers and employees through initiatives like humanization programs and involving employees in decision-making processes [161]. Such practices are instrumental in promoting employee initiative and understanding of job requirements.

Transformational leadership has also been identified as a critical factor influencing employees' organizational commitment, particularly in public sector contexts [162]. Studies suggest that transformational leadership not only impacts employees' commitment but also influences how managers' commitment is conveyed to employees [162]. Moreover, the implementation of Total Quality Management (TQM) initiatives hinges on the commitment and professionalism of leaders and employees to ensure continuous participation in organizational training programs and a customer-centric focus [163]. This underscores the pivotal role of organizational commitment in driving quality management practices.

Employee job satisfaction has been found to mediate the relationship between retention management and organizational commitment, highlighting the importance of maintaining high job satisfaction levels to foster a strong sense of belonging among employees [164]. Additionally, internal marketing practices have been shown to influence both employee and manager commitment in various organizational settings, shedding light on the interconnectedness of commitment levels across different hierarchical levels [165]. This underscores the need for organizations to address factors that impact employee satisfaction and commitment to enhance overall organizational performance.

Ethical leadership and talent management have been linked to employee performance, with employee commitment playing a mediating role in this relationship [166]. This suggests that cultivating a culture of ethical leadership and effective talent management practices can positively influence employee commitment and, in turn, enhance performance outcomes [166]. Moreover, organizational justice, trust, and commitment have been identified as key factors in shaping management control systems and fostering employee commitment within organizations [167]. This highlights the intricate relationship between organizational dynamics and employee commitment levels.

Furthermore, the mediating role of organizational commitment has been explored in the context of career development and employee performance, indicating that commitment can positively influence the relationship between quality of work life, career development, and employee performance [168]. Similarly, the transactional leadership style of top managers has been found to impact employee commitment in state-owned enterprises, emphasizing the role of leadership in shaping organizational commitment levels [169]. This underscores the importance of leadership styles in fostering a committed workforce.

Performance in the transport and logistics sector can fluctuate due to various factors and circumstances. Improving performance is an integral part of effective performance management and should be viewed positively by both managers and employees. When informal feedback fails to yield improvements, a more structured approach may be necessary.

Identifying the Root Causes of Unsatisfactory Performance Addressing unsatisfactory performance begins with understanding its underlying causes. Managers should investigate key questions such as:

- What specific aspects of performance are lacking—is it related to technical duties or behavioural issues?

- Has the employee previously performed at the required standard, or are they still progressing towards it?

- Is there a misalignment between the employee's capabilities and the demands of their role?

- Is the performance issue temporary, possibly due to workload, health issues, or personal challenges?

Next Steps Both the manager and the employee should:

- Clearly define the expected level of performance or behaviour and outline what constitutes meeting these expectations.

- Establish realistic goals and timelines for improvement.

- Ensure adequate coaching, resources, and feedback mechanisms are in place to support the improvement process.

Support Resources Available Support for managing performance issues can be sourced from various avenues including:

- Human resources personnel within the organization.

- Employee assistance programs for personal support.

- External counsellors or specialists who can provide coaching or assist in problem resolution.

- Mediators or legal advisors for complex situations.

- Agency-specific resources such as industrial relations experts.

In complex cases, adopting a case management approach involving a multidisciplinary team—comprising managers, HR professionals, and specialists—can be beneficial. This collaborative effort allows for a holistic assessment and targeted interventions to address performance challenges effectively.

Avoiding Pitfalls in Giving Negative Feedback Providing constructive criticism during performance reviews is crucial for employee development and career progression. To minimize the risk of negative reactions or HR issues, avoid common pitfalls such as:

- Failing to conduct formal, documented performance reviews as per company policy.

- Ensuring reviews are comprehensive and align with both performance evaluation and salary discussions.

- Conducting additional counselling sessions when negative personnel actions are necessary, ensuring clarity on expectations and consequences.

- Safeguarding all personnel records securely and maintaining confidentiality.

Continuous Informal Feedback and Follow-Up Beyond formal reviews, ongoing informal feedback is essential for maintaining performance standards and fostering continuous improvement. This informal process involves:

- Regularly assessing and discussing performance to identify areas for growth or skills enhancement.

- Implementing action plans to support employee development or readiness for advancement opportunities within the company.

- Empowering team members through training and mentorship to build a capable and self-sufficient workforce.

Ultimately, effective management of performance improvement in transport and logistics requires a proactive and supportive approach that values employee development and aligns individual goals with organizational objectives. By investing in supportive resources and maintaining open communication, managers can foster a culture of continuous improvement and achievement.

Managing Follow Up

To effectively enhance professional skills, knowledge, and job performance among your team members in transport and logistics, having a structured plan is invaluable. While some companies integrate this into their performance review process and management systems, it's beneficial for all managers to consider implementing and agreeing upon such plans, regardless of formal procedures.

Often, managers reserve these plans for employees experiencing performance challenges. However, fostering a culture where all team members have personalized improvement plans can cultivate stars within your department. Each plan may differ based on individual goals and aspirations; for instance, preparing top performers for future managerial roles demonstrates proactive leadership.

Continuous improvement is key, regardless of current proficiency levels. In my own career experiences, whether in engineering or writing, ongoing learning has been essential for growth. Even with a doctoral degree, I prioritize learning and self-improvement.

Understanding your team members involves knowing their career aspirations. Incorporating discussions about their long-term goals into regular performance reviews can form the basis of their improvement plans. For example, supporting a technician aspiring to become an engineer by facilitating further education, or assisting a nurse aiming for a supervisory role, aligns job roles with career advancement opportunities.

By standardizing performance improvement plans for all team members, any stigma associated with plans designed to address performance issues is eliminated. This approach communicates a commitment to supporting each individual's development, irrespective of their current challenges. Additionally, including these plans in personnel files ensures transparency and accountability in performance management.

For employees requiring specific performance improvements, it's crucial to document these plans and share them with Human Resources. These documents serve as evidence of efforts to assist the individual, should disciplinary actions or termination discussions arise.

Each improvement plan should be signed by the employee, signifying their commitment to achieving outlined objectives. Refusal to sign may necessitate disciplinary actions, such as issuing a formal warning, to address performance concerns and maintain accountability.

In every team, there are diverse performers, from stars to those needing more support. It's crucial to recognize that each person holds potential, and as a manager, your role is to uncover and nurture that potential, thereby transforming their professional lives.

Poor performers require consistent monitoring and coaching to ensure they fulfill their job responsibilities effectively and avoid further decline. While lifting them up, managers must be vigilant against factors that could hinder progress.

Effective coaching extends beyond performance monitoring to guiding individuals through detailed performance improvement plans. These plans should be tailored to the individual, acknowledging that what motivates and improves one person may not apply universally.

Coaching emphasizes gradual improvement rather than immediate transformation. Just as elite athletes refine their skills incrementally, managers should focus on small, achievable milestones with underperforming employees. This approach prevents overwhelming them and fosters sustainable growth.

When managing underperformers, setting realistic goals is crucial. Expecting a significant leap in performance overnight can be daunting and counterproductive. Instead, focus on gradual progress—moving from 60% to 62%, then 64%, and so forth—eventually surpassing initial targets.

Celebrating every achievement, no matter how small, is essential. Recognizing progress from 60% to 62% should be as significant as applauding top performers. Such encouragement reinforces positive behaviour and motivates continued improvement.

Addressing unsatisfactory performance due to inability or health issues requires a sensitive approach. Temporary setbacks, such as personal problems or health challenges, should be managed with empathy and support. If issues persist, formal procedures may be necessary to ensure performance standards are met.

Ensuring procedural fairness in all performance management processes is critical. This includes adhering to legal standards and company policies, conducting thorough investigations, and documenting decisions based on factual evidence.

Human Resources (HR) specialists play a pivotal role in supporting managers dealing with performance issues. They provide expertise on legal matters, benefits, and training opportunities, ensuring fair and informed decisions in personnel management.

Consideration should also be given to reassigning employees who may be better suited to different roles within the company. This approach can often be more beneficial and cost-effective than termination, leveraging existing talent effectively.

Moreover, HR departments can facilitate training and development opportunities, including financial assistance for employees pursuing further education. In-house training programs offered by larger companies can also enhance job-related skills, preparing team members for advancement within the organization.

By leveraging HR support and implementing tailored coaching strategies, managers in transport and logistics can effectively develop their team members, maximize potential, and foster a culture of continuous improvement.

In management and supervision, some use the term "facilitator," which aptly describes the role. As a manager, your primary duty isn't to perform tasks but to empower your team to achieve their best work. This facilitative approach is pivotal in ensuring operational success.

Supporting your team's effectiveness involves various forms of assistance, including:

- Providing counselling during personal challenges.

- Allocating additional resources when necessary to meet job demands.

- Offering expert advice based on your experience.

- Securing extra personnel for project completion.

- Arranging training sessions to bridge skill gaps.

- Serving as a sounding board for brainstorming ideas.

- Managing conflicts with other departments on behalf of your team.

Regardless of the type of support needed, it's unreasonable to expect employees to meet performance expectations without adequate support.

Reflecting on my experience in engineering at a medical equipment plant years ago, I was tasked with a critical project to transition product connectors across our production line. Initially supported by other departments, their engagement waned as the project progressed, risking production disruptions. Addressing this in a departmental meeting prompted swift resolution from senior management, highlighting the importance of timely support.

In another instance, a team member faced personal hardship due to a spouse's severe illness. Despite exhausting sick leave, I arranged additional time off to support his family, demonstrating personalized support when needed.

Effective support can pre-empt excuses often made by underperformers. This phase of eliminating excuses is crucial before considering disciplinary actions, ensuring fairness in management practices.

Unfortunately, despite best efforts, some employees persist in underperformance due to indifference or entitlement. In such cases, escalating direct and private counselling sessions become necessary. Each session should be documented and signed by both parties, ensuring clarity and legal compliance.

When termination becomes the last resort for ongoing poor performance or serious misconduct—such as theft, endangerment, harassment, excessive absenteeism, misrepresentation, or physical altercations—adherence to company policies and legal procedures is crucial. Human Resources should be involved from the outset to navigate the process professionally and lawfully.

Termination should be handled with professionalism and sensitivity, avoiding emotional responses or justifications. Despite the difficulty, thorough documentation and adherence to established procedures help mitigate personal guilt and ensure procedural fairness.

Celebrating success is vital in management. If you have team members excelling, it's crucial to broadcast their achievements widely. This public acknowledgment not only boosts morale but also inspires individuals to live up to their potential.

Excellence thrives on encouragement. Many individuals who initially excel can falter without ongoing support and recognition. This is particularly evident in professions like teaching, where initial enthusiasm can wane due to lack of support or appreciation.

Everyone craves recognition, regardless of how small or informal it may seem. In my office, I cherish items received over the years as tokens of recognition—they symbolize acknowledgment from peers and leaders alike. Whether it's a simple certificate printed from a personal computer or a more elaborate award, every form of recognition encourages excellence.

Effective feedback is another cornerstone of management. Feedback should always remain focused on professional behaviours, devoid of personal bias, to foster continuous improvement. Timeliness is crucial—praise should be immediate to reinforce positive behaviours and correct any issues promptly.

Ultimately, as a manager in transport and logistics, your ability to recognize and nurture talent directly impacts team morale and performance. By actively listening, providing positive reinforcement, and consistently acknowledging achievements, you create an environment where excellence can thrive and individuals are motivated to continually improve.

References

1. Reyes, J., *Transport and Logistics: Definition, Importance, & Top Challenges*. 2024, SafetyCulture.
2. Placek, M., *Logistics industry worldwide - statistics & facts*. 2023, Statista.
3. Zähringer, M., et al., *Time vs. Capacity—The Potential of Optimal Charging Stop Strategies for Battery Electric Trucks*. Energies, 2022. **15**(19): p. 7137.
4. Lambrechts, W., et al., *Lean, Green and Clean? Sustainability Reporting in the Logistics Sector*. Logistics, 2019. **3**(1): p. 3.
5. Yekimov, S., *Improving the Efficiency of the Transport and Logistics Sector*. E3s Web of Conferences, 2023. **376**: p. 04004.
6. Klein, M., E. Gutowska, and P. Gutowski, *Innovations in the T&L (Transport and Logistics) Sector During the COVID-19 Pandemic in Sweden, Germany and Poland*. Sustainability, 2022. **14**(6): p. 3323.
7. Perkumienė, D., et al., *The Impact of COVID-19 on the Transportation and Logistics Industry*. Problems and Perspectives in Management, 2021. **19**(4): p. 458-469.
8. Herold, D.M. and K.H. Lee, *Carbon Management in the Logistics and Transportation Sector: An Overview and New Research Directions*. Carbon Management, 2017. **8**(1): p. 79-97.
9. Arshed, N., et al., *Moderating Effects of Logistics Infrastructure Development and Real Sector Productivity: A Case of Pakistan*. Global Business Review, 2019. **23**(3): p. 676-693.
10. Beškovnik, B. and E. Twrdy, *Green Logistics Strategy for South East Europe: To Improve Intermodality and Establish Green Transport Corridors*. Transport, 2012. **27**(1): p. 25-33.
11. Kajba, M., B. Jereb, and T.C. Ojsteršek, *Exploring Digital Twins in the Transport and Energy Fields: A Bibliometrics and Literature Review Approach*. Energies, 2023. **16**(9): p. 3922.

12. Shahraz, M., *Intelligent Transportation Systems: An Overview of Current Trends and Limitations.* Interantional Journal of Scientific Research in Engineering and Management, 2022. **06**(12).

13. McEwan, V., *8 logistics industry statistics you need to know.* 2024, SER.

14. Inbound Logistics, *Logistics Management: Definition, Functions, and Benefits.* 2023.

15. Cigu, E., et al., *Transport Infrastructure Development, Public Performance and Long-Run Economic Growth: A Case Study for the Eu-28 Countries.* Sustainability, 2018. **11**(1): p. 67.

16. Kenton, W., *Logistics: What It Means and How Businesses Use It.* 2024, Investopedia.

17. Jenkins, A., *What is Logistics? Importance, Benefits, and Examples.* 2024, Oracle NetSuite.

18. McClure, O., *Logistics Definition.* 2023, Built In.

19. Cin7, *Everything you Need to Know about Logistics Management.* 2024.

20. Wood, D.F., *logistics*, in *Encyclopedia Britannica.* 2024, Encyclopedia Britannica.

21. Song, C., *Understanding Logistics Information Systems.* 2024.

22. Lu, M., et al., *Green Transportation and Logistics Performance: An Improved Composite Index.* Sustainability, 2019. **11**(10): p. 2976.

23. Baah, C., et al., *Examining the Interconnections Between Sustainable Logistics Practices, Environmental Reputation and Financial Performance: A Mediation Approach.* Vision the Journal of Business Perspective, 2021. **25**(1): p. 47-64.

24. SafetyIQ, *The Top 5 Risks in the Transportation and Logistics Industry.* 2024.

25. Recovery Partners, *Transport Industry Risk Factors.* 2021.

26. Triple T Transport, *The Crucial Role of Due Diligence in the Transport Industry.* 2024.

27. Fleming, H., *Due Diligence Checklist for Logistics Companies.* 2022, Dropoff.

28. PLS Logistics, *What is International Shipping and How Does It Work?* 2024.

29. International Cargo Express Pty Ltd, *How the Shipping Process Works, Step-By-Step (+ Flow Chart).* 2022.

30. Sacks, G.S., S. Rough, and K.A. Kudsk, *Frequency and Severity of Harm of Medication Errors Related to the Parenteral Nutrition Process in a Large University Teaching Hospital.* Pharmacotherapy the Journal of Human Pharmacology and Drug Therapy, 2009. **29**(8): p. 966-974.

31. Masson, R., et al., *Managing Complexity in Agile Global Fashion Industry Supply Chains.* The International Journal of Logistics Management, 2007. **18**(2): p. 238-254.

32. Croxton, K.L., et al., *The Supply Chain Management Processes*. The International Journal of Logistics Management, 2001. **12**(2): p. 13-36.

33. Kot, S., *Sustainable Supply Chain Management in Small and Medium Enterprises*. Sustainability, 2018. **10**(4): p. 1143.

34. Betcheva, L., F. Erhun, and H. Jiang, *OM Forum—Supply Chain Thinking in Healthcare: Lessons and Outlooks*. Manufacturing & Service Operations Management, 2021. **23**(6): p. 1333-1353.

35. P.G.Yogindra and G.S. Vijaya, *A Systematic Literature Review of Strategic Partnership in Sustainable Supply Chain - Indian Aerospace Industries*. Ecs Transactions, 2022. **107**(1): p. 2315-2328.

36. Zhang, X.X., J. Huang, and L. Ling, *Study of China Green Supply Chain Management Policies and Standard*. Iop Conference Series Earth and Environmental Science, 2017. **94**: p. 012144.

37. Susanawati, S., et al., *Supply Chain Management of Red Chili Based on the Food Supply Chain Network in Yogyakarta Indonesia*. E3s Web of Conferences, 2021. **316**: p. 01010.

38. Du, Y., D. Zhang, and Y. Zou, *Sustainable Supplier Evaluation and Selection of Fresh Agricultural Products Based on IFAHP-TODIM Model*. Mathematical Problems in Engineering, 2020. **2020**: p. 1-15.

39. Sun, Z., *Research on the International Supply Chain Management of Chinese Bamboo Weaving and Cultural and Creative Products*. 2024.

40. Nagy-Bota, S. and L. Moldovan, *Key Differences and Common Aspects of Logistics and Supply Chain Management*. Acta Marisiensis Seria Technologica, 2022. **19**(1): p. 42-46.

41. Fahimnia, B., et al., *Decision Models for Sustainable Supply Chain Design and Management*. Annals of Operations Research, 2017. **250**(2): p. 277-278.

42. Marques-Perez, I., L.O.R.g. Mañay, and I. Guaita-Pradas, *Management Improvement of the Supply Chain of Perishable Agricultural Products by Combining the Scor Model and AHP Methodology. The Ecuadorian Flower Industry as a Case Study*. Revista De La Facultad De Ciencias Agrarias Uncuyo, 2022. **54**(2): p. 73-82.

43. Serve, M., et al., *B2B-enhanced Supply Chain Process: Toward Building Virtual Enterprises*. Business Process Management Journal, 2002. **8**(3): p. 245-253.

44. Wiśniewska-Sałek, A., *Managing a Sustainable Supply Chain – Statistical Analysis of Natural Resources in the Furniture Industry*. Management Systems in Production Engineering, 2021. **29**(3): p. 227-234.

45. Garoma, T. and D. Kitaw, *Application of Linear Programming Model for Industrial Supply Chain Network Design: A Case Study.* Science Technology and Arts Research Journal, 2013. **2**(2): p. 105.

46. Wu, Y., *The Design and Implementation of Regional Economic Application System Based on Supply Chain Management Model.* 2017.

47. Grzybowska, K. and G. Kovács, *Sustainable Supply Chain - Supporting Tools.* 2014.

48. Weerabahu, W.M.S.K. and L.D.J.F. Nanayakkara, *Linking Key Success Factors of Rice Supply Chain With the Operational Strategy in Sri Lanka: An Analytical Framework.* Sri Lanka Journal of Food and Agriculture, 2015. **1**(2): p. 49-56.

49. Schrödl, H., *Adoption of Cloud Computing in Supply Chain Management Solutions: A SCOR-Aligned Assessment.* 2012: p. 233-244.

50. Chen, W., *Research on Delivery Cost Management Method of Agricultural Enterprises Supply Chain Based on Heuristic Algorithms.* 2023.

51. Kaohua, Y., *Emergency Supply Chain Integration Based on Petri Net Thoery.* 2010.

52. Shao, N., *Riding on Waves and Filling the Cracks: Toward an Inclusive and Sustainable Sino-Thai Longan Supply Chain Management in Upper Thailand.* Asr Chiang Mai University Journal of Social Sciences and Humanities, 2022. **9**(2).

53. Mubiena, G.F. and A. Ma'ruf, *Development of an Assessment Model for Sustainable Supply Chain Management in Batik Industry.* Iop Conference Series Materials Science and Engineering, 2018. **319**: p. 012073.

54. Han, M. and J. Chen, *Managing Operational Risk in Supply Chain.* 2007.

55. Ruangkanjanases, A., et al., *Assessing Blockchain Adoption in Supply Chain Management, Antecedent of Technology Readiness, Knowledge Sharing and Trading Need.* Emerging Science Journal, 2022. **6**(5): p. 921-937.

56. Skiba, R., *Blockchain technology as a health and safety contributor in the transport and logistics industry–human resource requirements.* 2020.

57. Liu, L., C. Guo, and X. Niu, *Game Analysis of the Knowledge Sharing Mechanism for the Supply Chain Collaborative Innovation.* Journal of Industrial Engineering and Management, 2015. **8**(1).

58. Vaiana, D., *4 ways to strengthen your supply chain strategy (with examples).* 2022, Quickbooks.

59. Rennie, E., *What Is Supply Chain Strategy? An Overview of the Basics.* 2023, Association for Supply Chain Cahin Management.

60. DexNova Learning, *Maximizing the Flows: A Step-by-Step Guide to Successful Supply Chain Management.* 2023, LinkedIn.

61. MYOB, *Principles of supply chain management (SCM) for beginners.* 2024.

62. Angela, *Supplier Relationship Management: Strategies & Tools*. 2024, Simply Stakeholders.

63. Jenkins, A., *Supply Chain Efficiency: Definitions, Metrics and Steps to Improve*. 2022, Oracle NetSuite.

64. Wang, H., S. Chen, and Y. Xie, *An RFID-based Digital Warehouse Management System in the Tobacco Industry: A Case Study*. International Journal of Production Research, 2010. **48**(9): p. 2513-2548.

65. Mabotja, T., *Revitalizing Warehouse Management to Enhance Global Manufacturing Competitiveness: Insights From South Africa*. International Journal of Research in Business and Social Science (2147-4478), 2024. **13**(1): p. 108-120.

66. Enoch Oluwademilade Sodiya, N., et al., *AI-driven Warehouse Automation: A Comprehensive Review of Systems*. GSC Advanced Research and Reviews, 2024. **18**(2): p. 272-282.

67. Gils, T.v., et al., *Designing Efficient Order Picking Systems by Combining Planning Problems: State-of-the-Art Classification and Review*. European Journal of Operational Research, 2018. **267**(1): p. 1-15.

68. Lam, H.Y., K.L.T. Choy, and S.H. Chung, *Framework to Measure the Performance of Warehouse Operations Efficiency*. 2010.

69. Zhen, L. and H. Li, *A Literature Review of Smart Warehouse Operations Management*. Frontiers of Engineering Management, 2022. **9**(1): p. 31-55.

70. Wanjari, S.S., *Analyzing the Impact of Human and Technological Factors on Warehouse Productivity*. European Journal of Business Management and Research, 2020. **5**(5).

71. Ngaboyimbere, F., et al., *Development of RFID Based Automatic Warehouse Management System: a Case Study of ROK Industries Limited Kenya*. International Journal of Advances in Scientific Research and Engineering, 2021. **07**(08): p. 112-126.

72. Kusuma Dewi, I. and R. Nur Shofa, *Development of Warehouse Management System to Manage Warehouse Operations*. 2023. **1**(1).

73. Zou, X. and H. Jin, *A Study of Missing Collaborative Data Imputation Models Based on Same-City Delivery*. Journal of Advanced Transportation, 2022. **2022**: p. 1-11.

74. Arumsari, S.S. and A.M. Aamer, *Design and Application of Data Analytics in an Internet-of-Things Enabled Warehouse*. Journal of Science and Technology Policy Management, 2021. **13**(2): p. 485-504.

75. Jarašūnienė, A., K. Čižiūnienė, and A. Čereška, *Research on Impact of IoT on Warehouse Management*. Sensors, 2023. **23**(4): p. 2213.

76. Ng, S., et al., *SFlex-WMS: A Novel Multi-Expert System for Flexible Logistics and Warehouse Operation in the Context of Industry 4.0.* SHS Web of Conferences, 2021. **124**: p. 10002.

77. Muttaqin, P.S., W. Margareta, and A.D. Zahira, *Green Warehouse Performance Monitoring System Design Using Analytical Hierarchy Process and Supply Chain Operation Reference.* Applied Engineering and Technology, 2022. **1**(3): p. 146-153.

78. Binos, T., V. Bruno, and A. Adamopoulos, *Intelligent Agent Based Framework to Augment Warehouse Management Systems for Dynamic Demand Environments.* Australasian Journal of Information Systems, 2021. **25**.

79. Griffin, J., *How to Calculate Warehouse Space Needs.* 2022, Crown LPS Group.

80. Flora, M., *Calculate Warehouse Space Utilisation: Guide + Tips to Improve.* 2024, ShipBob.

81. Cadre Technologies, *The Ultimate Guide to Warehouse Safety: Best Practices and Regulations.* 2024.

82. Vector Solutions, *5 Essential Warehouse Safety Tips.* 2024.

83. Sunol, H., *Warehouse Safety: 10 Tips to Keep Your Employees Safe.* 2022, Cyzerg.

84. Smoteks, H., *Exploring the 5 Zones of a Warehouse.* 2024, Fulfyld.

85. Mecalux. *Warehouse areas: essential zones for efficient management.* 2023 [cited 2024 18/6/2024]; Available from: .

86. Seabeck, A., *How to Calculate Warehouse Space Utilization.* 2023, Camcode.

87. Singh, S.K. and M. Jenamani, *ProcessChain: A Blockchain-Based Framework for Privacy Preserving Cross-Organizational Business Process Mining From Distributed Event Logs.* Business Process Management Journal, 2023. **30**(1): p. 239-269.

88. Scholliers, J., et al., *Improving Security and Efficiency of Multimodal Supply Chains Using Monitoring Technology.* 2014: p. 38-52.

89. Roghani, M.A. and N. Naseer, *Enhancing Trade Between Pakistan and Afghanistan.* 2021. **1**(1): p. 15-28.

90. Čamaj, J., et al., *Digitisation of Rail Transport: The Application That Delivers Faster and More Efficient Services.* Transport Technic and Technology, 2023. **19**(2): p. 23-30.

91. Bhero, E. and A.J. Hoffman, *Using Information and Communication Technology to Improve the Efficiency of African Border Posts.* 2015.

92. Hoang, H.B., et al., *The Need for Improving Access to Emergency Care Through Community Involvement in Low- and Middle-income Countries: A Case Study of Cardiac Arrest in Hanoi, Vietnam.* Emergency Medicine Australasia, 2018. **30**(6): p. 867-869.

93. Razak, N.Y., et al., *Conceptualizing Food Bank Distribution Efficiency via Smart Mobility: A Systematic Literature Review.* International Journal of Academic Research in Business and Social Sciences, 2022. **12**(11).

94. Collins, T., et al., *Identifying Animal Welfare Impacts of Livestock Air Transport.* Australian Veterinary Journal, 2020. **98**(5): p. 197-199.

95. Schulman, M.L., et al., *The Effect of Consignment to Broodmare Sales on Physiological Stress Measured by Faecal Glucocorticoid Metabolites in Pregnant Thoroughbred Mares.* BMC Veterinary Research, 2014. **10**(1): p. 25.

96. Sung, H., et al., *Transport Management Characteristics of Urban Hazardous Material Handling Business Entities.* Sustainability, 2019. **11**(23): p. 6600.

97. Shrivastava, C., et al., *Digital Twins Enable the Quantification of the Trade-Offs in Maintaining Citrus Quality and Marketability in the Refrigerated Supply Chain.* Nature Food, 2022. **3**(6): p. 413-427.

98. Manders, T.N. and E.A.M. Klaassen, *Unpacking the Smart Mobility Concept in the Dutch Context Based on a Text Mining Approach.* Sustainability, 2019. **11**(23): p. 6583.

99. TVS Supply Chain Solutions, *Multimodal Transportation: What It Is And How It Can Benefit Your Businesses?* 2023.

100. FasterCapital, *Consignment tracking: Keeping Tabs: The Importance of Consignment Tracking.* 2024.

101. Kuehne+Nagel, *The 4 essential features of contingency planning for a resilient supply chain.* 2024, Kuehne+Nagel.

102. Ghangurde, A., *Export Logistics and its Process Explained with a Flowchart.* 2022, Drip Capital Inc.

103. Juan Andes Mantilla Mendoza, *How can you measure import/export logistics performance for shorter lead times?* 2024, LinkedIn.

104. FasterCapital, *International distribution: How to Choose and Manage Your International Distribution Channels and Partners.* 2024.

105. Reich, A., *Procurement Strategy vs Purchasing Strategy: Which is Better.* 2024.

106. PLS Logistics Services, *Best Practices for Your Procurement Strategy.* 2024.

107. Yeam Weporoc, *How do you analyse a company's purchasing and logistics processes?* 2023.

108. Abouzeid, E., *The Five Rights of Procurement.* 2018.

109. Applandeo, *The Environmental Impact of Logistics and How to Reduce It.* 2023.

110. Kolahi, H., et al., *Evaluation of respiratory protection program in petrochemical industries: application of analytic hierarchy process.* Safety and health at work, 2018. **9**(1): p. 95-100.

111. Gillespie, G.L., et al., *Workplace violence in healthcare settings: risk factors and protective strategies.* Rehabilitation Nursing Journal, 2010. **35**(5): p. 177-184.

112. Liu, Y. and Q. Zhu. *Research and Application of Environmental Protection Standardization System for Energy and Power Companies.* in E3S Web of Conferences. 2023. EDP Sciences.

113. Patil, B.K., M. Moinuddin, and P. Kengal, *Association of Personal Protective Equipments with Respiratory Morbidity among Puffed Rice Workers of Davanagere City.* Indian Journal of Public Health Research & Development, 2020. **11**(10).

114. Alcock, R., M. Wajrak, and J. Oosthuizen, *Assessment of the effectiveness of ventilation controls in managing airborne and surface lead levels at a newly commissioned indoor shooting range.* International Journal of Environmental Research and Public Health, 2022. **19**(18): p. 11711.

115. Onfleet Inc, *Transport and Logistics Management: How to Create Eco-Friendly Operations in 2024.* 2024.

116. Conqueror Freight Network, *World Environment Day 2021: How the transportation and logistics industry can play a role to protect the environment.* 2021.

117. Mızrak, F., *Managing Risks and Crises in the Logistics Sector: A Comprehensive Analysis of Strategies and Prioritization Using AHP Method.* 2023.

118. Damilola Emmanuel Ogedengbe, N., et al., *Strategic HRM in the Logistics and Shipping Sector: Challenges and Opportunities.* International Journal of Science and Research Archive, 2024. **11**(1): p. 2000-2011.

119. Cantor, D.E., *Workplace Safety in the Supply Chain: A Review of the Literature and Call for Research.* The International Journal of Logistics Management, 2008. **19**(1): p. 65-83.

120. Hon, C.K.H. and Y. Liu, *Exploring Typical and Atypical Safety Climate Perceptions of Practitioners in the Repair, Maintenance, Minor Alteration and Addition (RMAA) Sector in Hong Kong.* International Journal of Environmental Research and Public Health, 2016. **13**(10): p. 935.

121. Kirci, B.K., M.E. Özay, and R. Uçan, *A Case Study in Ergonomics by Using REBA, RULA and NIOSH Methods: Logistics Warehouse Sector in Turkey.* Hittite Journal of Science & Engineering, 2020. **7**(4): p. 257-264.

122. Silva, M.L.d., et al., *Safety Culture Maturity at Work in a Plastic Packaging Factory.* Revista De Administração Da Ufsm, 2023. **16**(1): p. e1.

123. Zego, S.I. and Z.J.B. Mohamad Husny, *Performance of Cold Chain Logistics Service Providers in the Fast-Moving Consumer Goods Industry in Nigeria: A Systematic Review.* Iop Conference Series Earth and Environmental Science, 2023. **1274**(1): p. 012021.

124. Zhang, M., J. Ren, and Q. Quan, *Design of Agricultural Product Cold Chain Logistics Safety Monitoring System Based on Internet of Things.* Inmateh Agricultural Engineering, 2022: p. 873-884.

125. Bulmer, E., M. Riera, and R.S. Rodríguez, *The Importance of Sustainable Leadership Amongst Female Managers in the Spanish Logistics Industry: A Cultural, Ethical and Legal Perspective.* Sustainability, 2021. **13**(12): p. 6841.

126. Mesjasz-Lech, A., *Logistics Performance and Management of Logistics System Safety.* System Safety Human - Technical Facility - Environment, 2019. **1**(1): p. 730-737.

127. Ekram, A., H.M. Elmesmary, and A.L. Sakr, *Developing a Framework to Achieve Resilience in the Oil and Gas Supply Chain During Logistics Disruptions: An Empirical Study.* International Journal of Energy Sector Management, 2023. **18**(4): p. 896-917.

128. Yorulmaz, M. and S. Birgün, *Maritime Transport Logistics Service Capabilities Impact on Customer Service and Financial Performance: An Application in the Turkish Maritime Sector.* Journal of Business Research - Turk, 2017. **3**(9): p. 468-486.

129. Lemp, J., K.M. Kockelman, and A. Unnikrishnan, *Analysis of Large Truck Crash Severity Using Heteroskedastic Ordered Probit Models.* Accident Analysis & Prevention, 2011. **43**(1): p. 370-380.

130. Chen, C. and J. Zhang, *Exploring Background Risk Factors for Fatigue Crashes Involving Truck Drivers on Regional Roadway Networks: A Case Control Study in Jiangxi and Shaanxi, China.* Springerplus, 2016. **5**(1).

131. Schindler, R., et al., *Exploring European Heavy Goods Vehicle Crashes Using a Three-Level Analysis of Crash Data.* International Journal of Environmental Research and Public Health, 2022. **19**(2): p. 663.

132. Haq, M.T., M. Zlatkovic, and K. Ksaibati, *Freeway Truck Traffic Safety in Wyoming: Crash Characteristics and Prediction Models.* Transportation Research Record Journal of the Transportation Research Board, 2019. **2673**(10): p. 333-342.

133. McKnight, A. and G. Bahouth, *Analysis of Large Truck Rollover Crashes.* Traffic Injury Prevention, 2009. **10**(5): p. 421-426.

134. Song, D., et al., *Bivariate Joint Analysis of Injury Severity of Drivers in Truck-Car Crashes Accommodating Multilayer Unobserved Heterogeneity.* Accident Analysis & Prevention, 2023. **190**: p. 107175.

135. Ahmed, I., S. Gaweesh, and M.M. Ahmed, *Exploration of Hazardous Material Truck Crashes on Wyoming's Interstate Roads Using a Novel Hamiltonian Monte Carlo Markov Chain Bayesian Inference.* Transportation Research Record Journal of the Transportation Research Board, 2020. **2674**(9): p. 661-675.

136. National Safety Council, *Large Trucks.* 2024.

137. The Department of Infrastructure, T., Regional Development, Communications and the Arts, , *Road Trauma Involving Heavy Vehicles—Annual Summaries.* 2023.

138. National Road Safety Strategy, *Fact sheet: Heavy vehicle safety.* 2024.

139. Freire, M.R., et al., *Identifying Interactive Factors That May Increase Crash Risk Between Young Drivers and Trucks: A Narrative Review*. International Journal of Environmental Research and Public Health, 2021. **18**(12): p. 6506.

140. Chen, S., et al., *Identifying the Factors Contributing to the Severity of Truck-Involved Crashes in Shanghai River-Crossing Tunnel*. International Journal of Environmental Research and Public Health, 2020. **17**(9): p. 3155.

141. Belzer, M.H., *Work-Stress Factors Associated With Truck Crashes: An Exploratory Analysis*. The Economic and Labour Relations Review, 2018. **29**(3): p. 289-307.

142. Mizuno, K., et al., *Relationship Between Truck Driver Fatigue and Rear-End Collision Risk*. Plos One, 2020. **15**(9): p. e0238738.

143. Ding, W., et al., *Safety-Oriented Planning of Expressway Truck Service Areas Based on Driver Demand*. Frontiers in Public Health, 2022. **10**.

144. Galal, A., B. Donmez, and M.J. Roorda, *Improving Truck Driver and Vulnerable Road User Interactions Through Driver Training: An Interview Study With Canadian Subject Matter Experts*. Transportation Research Record Journal of the Transportation Research Board, 2023. **2677**(12): p. 398-408.

145. Gray, G.C. and K. Lindsay, *Workplace Violence: Examining Interpersonal and Impersonal Violence Among Truck Drivers*. Law & Policy, 2019. **41**(3): p. 271-285.

146. Bunn, T.L., S. Slavova, and M. Robertson, *Motor Vehicle Injuries Among Semi Truck Drivers and Sleeper Berth Passengers*. Journal of Safety Research, 2013. **44**: p. 51-55.

147. Aliakbari, M. and S. Moridpoure *Management of Truck Loading Weight: A Critical Review of the Literature and Recommended Remedies*. Matec Web of Conferences, 2016. **81**: p. 03007.

148. Chandler, M., T.L. Bunn, and S. Slavova, *Narrative and Quantitative Analyses of Workers' Compensation-Covered Injuries in Short-Haul vs. Long-Haul Trucking*. International Journal of Injury Control and Safety Promotion, 2016. **24**(1): p. 120-130.

149. Tin, C.T. and H.M. Tun, *Buckling Analysis on Various Material Profiles for Truck Chassis of Ladder Frame Type*. Journal of Engineering Researcher and Lecturer, 2022. **1**(1): p. 25-29.

150. Dobrovolny, C.S., N. Schulz, and D.F. Blower, *Finite Element Approach to Identify the Potential of Improved Heavy-Truck Crashworthiness and Occupant Protection in Frontal Impacts*. Transportation Research Record Journal of the Transportation Research Board, 2016. **2584**(1): p. 77-87.

151. Eskandarian, A. and A. Mortazavi, *Evaluation of a Smart Algorithm for Commercial Vehicle Driver Drowsiness Detection*. 2007.

152. Škerlič, S. and V. Erčulj, *The Impact of Financial and Non-Financial Work Incentives on the Safety Behavior of Heavy Truck Drivers*. International Journal of Environmental Research and Public Health, 2021. **18**(5): p. 2759.

153. Douglas, M.A. and S.M. Swartz, *A Multi-dimensional Construct of Commercial Motor Vehicle Operators' Attitudes Toward Safety Regulations*. The International Journal of Logistics Management, 2009. **20**(2): p. 278-293.

154. Poliak, M., et al., *The Classification of Work and Offenses of Professional Drivers From Slovakia and the Czech Republic*. Applied Sciences, 2024. **14**(7): p. 3000.

155. Logistics Management, *How can you identify low-performing employees in Logistics Management through performance evaluations?* 2024, LinkedIn.

156. Jaksch, E., *Managing Poor Performance—What is Wrong And Right?* 2016, HR Gurus.

157. RedPilot, *Reward Systems That Drive Performance in Logistics Operations*. 2023.

158. Cheung, M.F.Y. and W.M. To, *Management Commitment to Service Quality and Organizational Outcomes*. Managing Service Quality, 2010. **20**(3): p. 259-272.

159. Shore, T.H., W.H. Bommer, and L.M. Shore, *An Integrative Model of Managerial Perceptions of Employee Commitment: Antecedents and Influences on Employee Treatment*. Journal of Organizational Behavior, 2008. **29**(5): p. 635-655.

160. Weer, C.H. and J.H. Greenhaus, *Managers' Assessments of Employees' Organizational Career Growth Opportunities: The Role of Extra-Role Performance, Work Engagement, and Perceived Organizational Commitment*. Journal of Career Development, 2017. **47**(3): p. 280-295.

161. Brewer, A.M., *Developing Commitment Between Managers and Employees*. Journal of Managerial Psychology, 1996. **11**(4): p. 24-34.

162. Jacobsen, C.B. and C.D. Staniok, *Sharing the Fire? The Moderating Role of Transformational Leadership Congruence on the Relationship Between Managers' and Employees' Organizational Commitment*. International Public Management Journal, 2018. **23**(4): p. 564-588.

163. Krajcsák, Z., *Implementing Open Innovation Using Quality Management Systems: The Role of Organizational Commitment and Customer Loyalty*. Journal of Open Innovation Technology Market and Complexity, 2019. **5**(4): p. 90.

164. Pudjiono, B. and P.R. Sihombing, *Effect of Retention Management on Organizational Commitment With Employee Satisfaction as a Mediation Variable*. Jurnal Manajemen Dan Supervisi Pendidikan, 2021. **5**(3): p. 144-153.

165. Bermúdez-González, G., I. Sasaki, and D. Tous-Zamora, *Understanding the Impact of Internal Marketing Practices on Both Employees ' and Managers ' Organizational*

Commitment in Elderly Care Homes. Journal of Service Theory and Practice, 2016. **26**(1): p. 28-49.

166. Hamid, M., N.F.A. Rahim, and Y. Salamzadeh, *Influence of Ethical Leadership and Talent Management on Employee Performance: Does Employee Commitment Matter in Malaysian Hotel Industry?* International Journal of Human Resource Studies, 2020. **10**(3): p. 77.

167. Latan, H. and N.A. Ramli, *The Role of Organizational Justice, Trust and Commitment in a Management Control System (MCS)- Gain Sharing.* International Journal of Accounting and Financial Reporting, 2014. **1**(1): p. 186.

168. Yuesti, A. and I.D. Adnyana, *The Role of Organizational Commitment Mediation on Career Development and Employee Performance.* Nexo Revista Científica, 2022. **35**(01): p. 306-315.

169. Mabasa, T. and C.E. Eresia-Eke, *Facets of the Transactional Leadership Style of Black Top-Managers and Employee Commitment in State-Owned Enterprises.* Journal of Contemporary Management, 2022. **19**(1): p. 412-431.

Index

A

Air Freight, 11, 22, 74, 222, 224, 245, 255, 408–409

B

Bill of Lading, 226, 256–257, 259

Brokerage, 35, 248

Buyer, 56, 63–64, 213, 225, 227, 248–260, 284, 337, 379, 457

C

Carbon management, 555

Cargo, 9, 11, 22–23, 28, 30–31, 34, 37, 43, 45, 48, 50, 53, 74, 88, 103–105, 114–115, 125–130, 157, 165, 169, 172, 174, 177–178, 196–198, 200–201, 205–206, 208–209, 213, 215, 217, 219–221, 225, 227–228, 244, 255, 257–258, 260, 262, 271, 273, 281, 284–286, 383, 398, 400, 407–409, 430, 478, 498, 556

Carrier, 11–12, 24, 52, 59, 76–77, 82–83, 85, 90, 100, 102–103, 126, 129, 152, 185, 210, 212–213, 221, 225, 228, 230–233, 235–241, 243, 245–246, 249, 255–257, 262–263, 268, 366–367, 371, 379, 403, 413, 460, 467, 498

Chain of Responsibility, 184, 216–217

Cold Chain, 45, 501

Commodity Manager, 67

Consolidation, 59, 230, 312, 343, 384, 398, 401, 421, 455

Container, 11, 23, 30, 52–53, 78, 84, 93, 103–104, 205, 209, 224–225, 230, 232, 255, 257–258, 260, 271, 273, 287, 360, 372, 377, 381–382, 384–385, 398, 408–410, 412, 478, 498

Contract Administrator, 63

Courier, 24, 39–41, 213

Cross-Border Logistics, 266

Cross-Docking, 38, 222, 498

Customs, 21, 24, 34–35, 37, 44, 48, 50, 74, 76–77, 84, 90, 115, 126, 128–130, 152–153, 157, 219–223, 225–227, 229–230, 232–240, 242–254, 257–259, 261, 263–266, 268, 270–271, 273–275, 281, 283–286, 314, 325, 378, 385, 398–400, 402–409, 411, 413–419, 422, 424–426, 442, 509

Customs Broker, 35, 223, 248, 254, 259, 263, 425–426

D

Delivery Schedule, 57, 100, 114, 160, 162, 164, 232, 246, 311, 317, 381–382, 387, 390, 392, 395, 409

Demand Forecasting, 36, 59, 302–303, 308, 311–312, 315, 318–319, 322, 326, 391, 417, 424, 466

Dispatch, 53, 162–163, 178, 240, 366, 398, 410

Dispatching, 38, 100, 326, 372

Distribution, 22–25, 34–35, 37–39, 41, 43, 45, 47–50, 52, 55, 57–58, 60–62, 68, 96, 174, 197–198, 208, 240, 258, 268, 282, 290–291, 294–296, 298, 301–302, 314, 316, 319, 322, 324, 336, 380, 385, 387, 390, 392, 418–449, 467

Distribution Center, 390

Distribution Centre Manager, 61

Documentation, 37, 53, 112, 116, 118, 121, 126, 130–131, 139–140, 143, 150, 152, 154, 168, 171, 177–178, 182, 184, 193, 198, 200, 203, 207, 210, 219, 222–223, 225–226, 230–232, 237, 239–240, 242, 244–251, 253–257, 259, 261–263, 265–268, 270–274, 276–277, 281–284, 286, 320, 366, 378, 385, 394–395, 401–404, 406–407, 411, 413, 415–417, 422, 425–426, 434, 439, 448, 471, 493–496, 527

E

Electronic data interchange, 222, 225, 262, 417

Export, 398–404, 407, 409, 412–417

F

Facilities Manager, 60

Fleet Manager, 59

Freight, 11–13, 17, 22–26, 28–29, 31, 33–34, 37, 43–44, 48, 50, 73–74, 79, 82, 90, 93, 103, 152, 206, 219–226, 228–233, 236, 241–251, 253–256, 260–265, 267–270, 272–277, 279–286, 295, 325, 379–380, 398–399, 408–409, 413, 418, 421–423, 432, 460, 498, 509

Freight Forwarder, 37, 228, 230–232, 246, 248–251, 253–256, 260, 263, 275, 284, 418, 422–423, 432

Freight Forwarding, 247–248, 256, 274–277, 279

Freight Rate, 221, 245, 283

G

Global Trade, 22–23, 30, 37, 41, 44, 49, 220, 226, 234–235, 237–238, 241, 251, 285

GPS Tracking, 169

H

Hazardous Materials, 510

I

Import, 35, 50, 84, 152, 219, 222, 225–226, 234–235, 239, 247–248, 250, 254, 258–259, 400, 416–417, 425

Incoterms, 242, 248, 250–253, 256, 258–260, 264, 271, 274, 415

Intermodal, 23, 104, 378, 383–384, 412

Intermodal Transport, 104, 412

Intermodality, 17

Inventory, 22, 24, 33–36, 38, 44–45, 47, 49–59, 62, 66–68, 100–102, 106, 110, 123, 132, 134–137, 142, 145, 155–157, 159, 162, 221–222, 225, 264–265, 267–269, 273, 291–292, 294–295, 298–301, 303–304, 307, 309–326, 328, 336–337, 343–353, 359, 366–376, 378, 381–382, 384, 386–387, 389–391, 393, 395, 398, 406, 411–412, 417, 419, 421, 423–424, 428, 430, 441–442, 444, 446–447, 521

Inventory Control, 36, 49–50, 58, 100, 222, 311, 323, 326, 345, 384, 389–390

Inventory Management, 36, 38, 45, 47, 49–50, 52–53, 59, 62, 66–68, 100, 102, 110, 123, 132, 155, 157, 159, 221, 267–268, 273, 291, 294–295, 299–301, 309–312, 314, 317–318, 321–322, 325–326, 343–344, 346–347, 371, 374, 384, 386–387, 389–391, 398, 406, 417, 419, 421, 423–424, 428, 430, 442, 444, 446–447, 521

L

Load Planning, 196, 208, 346

Logistics, 9–25, 27–29, 31–35, 37, 39–41, 43–59, 61–63, 65–99, 101–103, 105–107, 109–111, 113–133, 135, 137–143, 145, 147–149, 151–165, 167, 169, 171–177, 179, 181–185, 187, 189, 191–201, 203–205, 207, 209–213, 215, 217, 219–225, 227–231, 233–237, 239–241, 243–251, 253–257, 259–277, 279–287, 289, 291–297, 299–301, 303, 305, 307, 309–315, 317, 319, 321–327, 329, 331, 333, 335–337, 339, 341, 343–347, 349, 351, 353, 355, 357, 359,

361, 363, 365, 367, 369, 371–373, 375, 377–385, 387–423, 425, 427–435, 437, 439–443, 445, 447, 449, 451, 453, 455–463, 465–467, 469, 471–473, 475, 477–479, 481–485, 487, 489, 491, 493, 495, 497–499, 501–503, 505, 507, 509, 511, 513–527, 529, 531, 533, 535, 537, 539–541, 543, 545, 547–553, 555–557, 559–563, 565

Logistics Analyst, 58

Logistics coordinator, 50, 54–55, 107, 109, 111, 119–120, 124, 132, 138, 192, 243, 266, 282, 377, 381, 385, 399, 414, 522

Logistics Manager, 19–20, 47–48, 55, 57–58, 72, 88–89, 91, 102, 165, 171, 221, 325, 378, 381–382, 388, 395, 402

M

Maritime, 11, 23, 30–32, 84, 105, 129, 187, 205, 219–220, 244, 407, 478

Maritime Transport, 30–32, 220

Material Handling, 21, 105, 224, 348, 350, 354, 371, 373, 502

O

Operations Analyst, 65

Order Picking, 222

P

Packaging, 39, 70–71, 73, 77–78, 85, 96, 219, 223–226, 228–229, 231–232, 243–245, 263, 270–271, 273–274, 286–287, 289, 309, 313, 344, 398, 400–401, 408, 410–411, 414–415, 417, 498

Packaging Materials, 78, 224, 243, 414

Pallet, 38, 78–79, 103, 224, 345, 348–349, 351–352, 369–370, 408, 410, 414

Port, 11, 15, 19, 23, 30–31, 50, 74, 84, 87, 103, 114–115, 126, 128, 140, 149, 156–157, 220–221, 223, 226, 230, 249–250, 255–257, 259–260, 284–286, 379, 394, 399, 403, 409, 413–414, 458, 463, 475, 551, 561

Procurement, 15, 47–50, 54–58, 62–68, 71, 82, 86, 90, 93, 98, 243, 266–268, 291, 297, 299–302, 307, 310, 312, 314, 317–322, 324–326, 331–333, 337, 341, 343, 428, 450–476

Procurement Manager, 66, 243

Production Manager, 57, 62

Purchasing Manager, 64

R

Rail, 22–23, 28–29, 43, 47–48, 50, 71, 74, 80, 105, 114–115, 160, 211, 213–214, 219–221, 223, 227, 229, 231–232, 241, 243, 245, 271, 273, 283–284, 288, 291, 295, 378–379, 383–384, 394, 400, 404–405, 407–408, 421, 483, 498, 509

Rail Transport, 23, 28–29, 43, 213, 221, 229, 273, 284, 379, 383–384

Reverse Logistics, 160, 311, 314

Route Optimization, 309, 312, 498

S

Shipment Tracking, 89–91, 248, 268, 277, 416, 428

Shipping, 11–12, 18, 21, 23–24, 36–37, 39–41, 43, 45, 53, 55, 58, 71, 74, 77, 80, 93, 121, 129, 157, 219–222, 224, 228, 230–231, 233–248, 250–260, 262, 265–266, 268–270, 272, 274, 291, 344, 347, 366, 369, 371–372, 385, 398–399, 404, 408–409, 411–413, 420–421, 466

Supplier relationship management, 19, 24, 56, 66, 291, 319, 321–322, 338, 341, 459, 470, 474

Supply Chain, 9–15, 18–24, 30, 32–39, 43–58, 65, 67–69, 99, 102–103, 105, 114–115, 122, 125, 128, 152, 156–160, 184–185, 210–214, 217, 219, 221–228, 235, 240, 255, 259, 264, 269, 274, 283, 285–286, 289–290, 292–329, 331–344, 351, 372, 378–380, 383–384, 386–388, 390–394, 396–398, 400, 403–404, 406, 410–412, 416, 419–426, 428–430, 434, 442–443, 446, 451–454, 456–460, 465–466, 468–469, 471–473, 502, 558, 561

Supply Chain Management, 24, 34–36, 44, 48–51, 54, 56–58, 65, 219, 221, 228, 286, 290, 292–294, 296, 298, 302, 304, 308–310, 312–317, 319–320, 322–325, 329, 334, 339, 341–343, 391, 419–420, 423–426, 442, 446, 451, 471

Supply Chain Manager, 44, 47, 50, 68, 307, 325

Supply Chain Network, 290, 293–296, 301, 314–315, 323

Supply Chain Visibility, 44, 52, 269, 285, 292, 295, 300, 318, 343, 390

Supply Manager, 55

T

Tariff, 126, 128, 157, 222–223, 225, 229, 237, 247, 258, 263, 271, 273, 284, 304, 400, 403, 406–407, 409, 417, 422, 424–425

Terminal, 23, 220–221, 383–384

Third-Party Logistics, 24, 34–35, 44, 432

TMS, 230, 262, 268–269, 283

Trade Compliance, 426

Transport Infrastructure, 42

Transportation, 9–17, 19–34, 36–37, 39, 41–45, 47–52, 55, 57–60, 62, 68, 70–74, 77–78, 80–85, 89–93, 96–102, 104, 106–107, 109, 114–118, 121, 125, 128–129, 156, 163, 185–186, 191, 198, 204, 210–212, 217, 221–224, 227, 229–233, 236, 239, 243–244, 246, 248–249, 251–255, 257, 259–260, 262–263, 268, 270–273, 281–286, 290–291, 293, 295, 299–300, 303–304, 309–310, 312, 314–315, 318, 324, 326, 336, 343, 345–346, 377–384, 387, 391, 394, 396, 398–399, 402–410, 412–418, 420–423, 430, 433–434, 441–442, 461, 466–467, 473, 497–498, 501, 503, 509–510, 519, 555–556, 559, 561, 563–564

Transportation Management System, 20, 36, 44, 102, 230, 262, 283

Trucking, 186, 201, 219–220, 260, 291, 512, 518–519

V

Vehicle Maintenance, 60, 127, 130, 154, 164–166, 169, 171–172, 177, 184–186, 188, 193, 203, 215–216, 380, 512–513, 517

Vendor Management, 54, 343

W

Warehouse, 36, 38–39, 44, 222, 256, 268, 282, 291, 295, 303, 312, 325, 344–376, 434, 441–442, 502, 522, 525

Warehouse Automation, 346

Warehouse Management System, 36, 44, 222, 347, 350, 370

www.ingramcontent.com/pod-product-compliance
Lightning Source LLC
Chambersburg PA
CBHW072141070526
44585CB00015B/979